D1474076

THE BEST (AND WORST) OF BASEBALL'S MODERN ERA

THE BEST (AND WORST) OF BASEBALL'S MODERN ERA

THE TOP (AND BOTTOM) TEAMS AND PLAYERS FROM 1961 THROUGH 2016

G. SCOTT THOMAS

 NIAWANDA BOOKS

The Best (and Worst) of Baseball's Modern Era: The Top (and Bottom) Teams and Players From 1961 Through 2016

Copyright © 2016 by G. Scott Thomas

Niawanda Books
949 Delaware Road
Buffalo, NY 14223
www.bestworstbaseball.com

Printed in the United States of America

First Edition
10 9 8 7 6 5 4 3 2 1

"You can't win the game without moving the pieces on the board. It's all about capturing bases."

— Doug Melvin

CONTENTS

THE BEST
(AND WORST)
OF BASEBALL'S
MODERN ERA

HEARTFELT THANKS

Three Key Sources

This would typically be called the "acknowledgments" section of the book, but that title would be insufficient.

I have never met any of the following people, yet I owe them a great debt. Their pioneering work greatly eased my workload (as it has for thousands upon thousands of baseball researchers). I send my heartfelt thanks to all:

• David Smith and his army of volunteers at Retrosheet collected the play-by-play accounts of more than 100,000 major-league games, entered the resulting statistics into massive databases, and posted everything on the internet.

That would be amazing enough, but Retrosheet has gone even further by making all of its information available without charge. Its databases supplied much of the raw material necessary for my calculations.

The only request Retrosheet makes of any author is the publication of two sentences, which I do gladly:

The information used here was obtained free of charge from and is copyrighted by Retrosheet. Interested parties may contact Retrosheet at 20 Sunset Road, Newark, DE 19711.

• Sean Forman was a college math professor who was fascinated by baseball's numerical heritage. He fused his passions in 2000 by founding Baseball-Reference.com, which has evolved into the sport's ultimate statistical source.

Michael Weinreb recently paid tribute to the site in, of all places, *Rolling Stone*. "It's a measure of how indispensable Forman's website has become," he wrote, "that everyone with even a passing interest in baseball uses it at some point, from casual fans to sabermetric seamheads."

I'm a member of that wide-ranging group. Baseball-Reference.com answered 1,001 important questions as I assembled this book. It also lured me into hours of counterproductive clicking as new subjects of interest popped onto my screen in rapid succession. Anybody who has visited the site knows what I mean.

• *Total Baseball* may seem to be a dinosaur — a print encyclopedia that runs more than 2,500 pages — but it remains incredibly useful in our digital age. I own the 1999 edition that was complied by John Thorn, Pete Palmer, Michael Gershman, David Pietrusza, Matthew Silverman, and Sean Lahman, all of whom are giants in the fields of sabermetrics and baseball research.

The essays in *Total Baseball* pointed me in productive directions as I planned this book, and its careful explication of park factors was invaluable as I began my statistical work. The eighth edition of *Total Baseball* was published in 2004, and it seems unlikely there will be a ninth. Yet its place in the game's history — and in the hearts of true fans — is secure.

INTRODUCTION

One Era Ends, Another Begins

Oddsmakers had no doubts about the 1960 World Series. They installed the New York Yankees as heavy favorites over the Pirates on the eve of Game One at Pittsburgh's Forbes Field. The ancient stadium had treated the Yanks kindly in the past. It was there that New York commenced a four-game sweep of the Pirates in the World Series 33 years earlier. And it was there that Babe Ruth, the ultimate Yankees icon, launched the final home run of his historic career (albeit as a member of the Boston Braves) in 1935. History was not on Pittsburgh's side.

Nor were the numbers. The Yankees had just won the American League pennant for the 11th time in 14 years, while the Pirates were making their first postseason appearance since the ill-fated matchup with New York in 1927. The Yanks set an American League record by blasting 193 homers in 1960, and they led the league in runs scored per game (4.81), slugging percentage (.426), and shutouts pitched (16). The National League Pirates were deficient on all counts, with 120 homers, 4.74 runs per game, a slugging average of .407, and 11 shutouts.

New York manifested its superiority in three lopsided victories. The Yankees buried the Pirates by scores of 16-3, 10-0, and 12-0. "Pour it on. Don't let 'em up," rasped Casey Stengel, the Yanks' 70-year-old manager, as he stomped up and down the dugout. His sluggers rapped out 52 hits in those three games, while his pitchers yielded only 24. "When we won, we destroyed them," said infielder Joe DeMaestri.

But the Pirates were nothing if not tenacious. They had battled back to win 22 regular-season games in which they trailed or were tied as late as the eighth inning. "Every game we were in, we got the big hit when we needed it," said Dick Groat, the scrappy shortstop who would win the National League's Most Valuable Player Award for 1960. His team lived up to its billing in the World Series, interspersing stomach-churning 6-4, 3-2, and 5-2 victories among the overwhelming defeats.

That set the stage for Game Seven on October 13, a winner-take-all finale that the experts had doubted would be necessary.

The smart money was still on the Yankees, who had statistically dominated the series. New York had outhit Pittsburgh by precisely 100 points (.341 to .241) during the first six games. Mickey Mantle had pounded three homers, Roger Maris had contributed two more, and the Yanks had knocked eight in all. The Pirates had managed just one home run, a shot by the usually light-hitting Bill Mazeroski in Game One. The gap between the earned run averages for the two pitching staffs was equally stark through six games: a streamlined 2.38 for New York, a bloated 6.79 for Pittsburgh.

The morning papers on October 13 quoted Mantle and Maris as saying that the Yankees were clearly the better team. They spoke not boastfully, but matter-of-factly. The Pirates registered dissent by breaking to a 4-0 lead in Game Seven, but the American League champs began chipping away in the fifth inning. Yogi Berra drove a pitch over the right-field fence in the sixth, reclaiming the lead for the Yanks, 5-4, and they tacked on two insurance runs in the top of the eighth. The world title — their ninth since 1947 — was within sight.

It was at this point that luck intervened, coupled with a healthy dose of Pittsburgh's famed persistence. A double-play ball took a surprisingly high skip in the bottom of the eighth, striking New York shortstop Tony Kubek in the throat and sending him to the hospital. The Pirates, who had expected two outs, were blessed with a pair of baserunners instead. "The bad hop," announcer Mel Allen told the national TV audience, "gives the Pirates a new lease on life." And indeed it did. Backup catcher Hal Smith would soon cap a five-run inning by popping a three-run homer over the left-field wall. Bedlam ensued. The Pirates were now up, 9-7. They needed just three outs to lock down the championship.

But they couldn't finish the job. The Yankees, seemingly indestructible, responded with two runs in the top of the ninth, tying the game. Forbes Field grew quiet as Pittsburgh's fans envisioned their triumph slipping away. The pervasive gloom affected their heroes. Mazeroski, who watched the latest New York rally from his post at second base, could never forget the feeling of despair. "When I took the field," he recalled, "running out there in the… ninth inning, with a two-run lead, I said, 'All we have to do is get three outs and it's over,' but gee whiz…."

A teammate broke through Mazeroski's haze, reminding him that he was the first Pirates batter due up in the bottom of the ninth. He stepped in against New York reliever Ralph Terry, a hard-throwing righthander whose first pitch soared high. Catcher Johnny Blanchard impatiently snapped the ball back to the mound. "Fire it in there," he yelled to Terry.

The next pitch was destined for immortality. Terry did indeed fire it down the middle, and Mazeroski whipped his bat in a tight arc. "Here's a high fly ball going deep to left," shouted announcer Chuck Thompson on the national radio broadcast. "This may do it. Back to the wall goes Berra. It is over the fence. Home run! The Pirates win!" The glory of that moment has been captured in a classic photograph, with Mazeroski rounding third base, his right arm high in triumph, his left hand clutching his cap. He is frozen in time, frantically scrambling to reach home plate ahead of an onrushing mob of fans.

The term had not yet been coined, but Bill Mazeroski's blast was the first walk-off home run to win Game Seven of a World Series. More than half a century has passed, but it remains the only one.

Reaching a Turning Point

Tens of thousands of fans jammed downtown Pittsburgh to celebrate the Pirates' improbable championship, their first world title since 1925. Church bells rang, sirens wailed, confetti drifted everywhere. Traffic ground to a dead halt. "People parked cars wherever they stopped, often right in the middle of the street," recalled pitcher Tom Cheney. "The police couldn't do anything about it, so they just joined the people who went into bars to celebrate." Shortstop Dick Schofield was more succinct. "The town," he said, "went nuts."

Pittsburgh's ecstatic fans couldn't have known — and probably wouldn't have cared — that Mazeroski's home run marked a turning point for Major League Baseball. One era was ending, and another was soon to begin.

The majors had changed remarkably little since the beginning of the 20th century. The American and National Leagues contained eight teams apiece in 1960, just as they had in 1901. Each squad still played a 154-game regular-season schedule, a tradition that dated back to 1904. Only the two league champions advanced to the single round of postseason play — the World Series itself — which had first been staged in 1903.

This 60-year period of stability was commonly known as baseball's Modern Era, differentiating it from the rougher, loosely structured game of the late 1800s. The distinction was reinforced by the official record book, the collection of the best and worst statistical performances of all time. Dozens of its entries were accompanied by the same parenthetical restriction — "(since 1900)" — a clear sign that the numbers from the 19th century were considered to be unrepresentative and unreliable. Only the Modern Era truly mattered.

But change was in the air in October 1960, change that would permanently disrupt a sport that had been bound to tradition for so long.

It was the Yankees who launched the new era, making a decision of symbolic importance just five days after the World Series. They fired Stengel, one of the greatest managers in the history of the game, and replaced him with Ralph Houk, who was 29 years younger. Out with the old, in with the new.

Team officials spoke respectfully of a living legend's well-deserved retirement, but Stengel refused to play along. "Casey, tell us the truth," a sportswriter demanded at the press conference. "Were you fired?"

"You're goddamn right I was fired," Stengel shot back. He was the victim of a youth movement, and he wanted everybody to know it. "I'll never make the mistake of being 70 again," he said bitterly.

There was even bigger news to come. A ragtag group of young heirs and middle-aged financiers had been struggling since 1958 to establish a third major league, the Continental League. They had yet to play a single game, but their intentions threatened the very structure of Major League Baseball. The leaders of the two established leagues met behind closed doors and decided to rid themselves of the upstarts.

Their strategy unfolded rapidly that October. The National League announced that it would add teams in New York and Houston in 1962, deftly swiping two of the Continental League's prime territories. The American League shifted the Washington Senators to Minneapolis-Saint Paul (a third member of the proposed league), replaced them with a brand-new version of the Senators, and granted an expansion franchise to Los Angeles, all to begin play in April 1961, just six months away. Both leagues lengthened their schedules to 162 games. The Continental League had no choice but to disband.

"The future was upon them all," declared Michael Shapiro, the author of the definitive history of the Continental League. Expansion had opened the floodgates, and the resulting stream would rise toward flood stage in the decades to come. Ten more expansion teams before the end of the century. Divisional play and a second round of playoffs in 1969. Two wild cards and a third postseason round in 1995. Two more wild cards in 2012. And a dizzying array of other innovations — designated hitters, free agency, multimillion-dollar contracts, interleague play, and ubiquitous coverage on cable television.

This amazing metamorphosis — baseball's journey from the somnolence of the 1950s to the brave new world of the 21st century — began at precisely 3:37 on the chaotic afternoon of October 13, 1960. That was the moment when Bill Mazeroski's home run landed among the trees outside of Forbes Field, and everything began to change.

Redefining the Modern Era

Major League Baseball's record-keepers like to pretend that the post-Mazeroski revolution never occurred. They still define the Modern Era as the period from 1901 to the present day.

It's an improper use of the adjective, of course. Few aspects of American life in 1901 could be considered modern. Hardly anybody owned an automobile back then. The airplane hadn't been invented, nor had commercial radio or television. Most families were without indoor plumbing. The average female died at 48, the average male at 46. Women weren't allowed to vote.

The 1901 version of baseball was equally lacking in modernity. There were no night games. No black or Latin American players. No teams west of Saint Louis or south of Washington. No power hitters: Sam Crawford led the majors that year with 16 home runs. No closers: Starting pitchers went the distance 86 percent of the time. The spitball was still legal, foul balls didn't count as strikes in the American League, and scorekeepers didn't keep track of earned runs or runs batted in.

It's clearly time to redefine the Modern Era. It's also clear that 1961, not 1901, should be the starting point. Here are six reasons why:

• The first expansion teams in the history of baseball took the field in 1961. The new-look Washington Senators debuted on April 10, predictably losing to the Chicago White Sox. The Los Angeles Angels opened a day later, pounding the Baltimore Orioles, 7-2. (It was not, however, a sign of things to come. The Angels lost their next eight games.)

• Both leagues stretched from coast to coast for the first time in 1961, finally acknowledging the nation's westward growth. The National League had taken the leap three years earlier, when the Brooklyn Dodgers and New York Giants relocated respectively to Los Angeles and San Francisco. But the American League didn't extend beyond Kansas City until the Angels came into being.

• The 162-game schedule, a commonly accepted feature of present-day baseball, was adopted by the American League in 1961. The National League would follow suit a year later when the New York Mets and Houston Colt .45s began play.

• Power became a more prominent component of the game in 1961. Batters launched 0.95 home runs per game that year, the highest ratio for any season up to then and a considerable increase from 1960's average of 0.86. (The ratio would peak at 1.17 in 2000.) Roger Maris hit 61 homers in 1961, establishing a new single-season record. His Yankees set a new mark for any team with 240.

• Speed also grew in importance. Runners stole an average of 0.37 bases per game in 1961, the highest ratio since World War II. The following season saw a jump to 0.42 per game, thanks in part to the unprecedented daring of Maury Wills, who stole a record total of 104 bases. (The ratio has remained above 0.50 since 1973.)

• Relief pitchers also reached a key milestone in 1961, foreshadowing the heightened role they would assume. Saves were not granted official status until 1969, but researchers would later calculate them retroactively. They determined that the annual total of saves first topped 500 in 1961. That year's sum of 501 was 16 percent higher than the mark for any previous season.

Oh, and one more thing.

Modern, as defined by the *Merriam-Webster Dictionary*, means "of, relating to, or characteristic of the present or the immediate past." So it's logical that the Modern Era should encompass teams and players of recent vintage, those we have seen in person or on television.

Honus Wagner, Christy Mathewson, and Babe Ruth don't fit that bill. Nor do the 1908 Chicago Cubs, the 1927 New York Yankees, or the 1955 Brooklyn Dodgers. They're essential components of baseball's rich history, to be sure, but they don't belong to our era.

If we assume that a boy or girl forges the first strong attachment to baseball at roughly eight or nine years of age, it's evident that nobody born after 1952 will retain any memories of the game prior to 1961. This demographic group encompasses 88 percent of all Americans alive today — and absolutely everybody who has not yet reached retirement age.

The solution is obvious, isn't it? There can be no doubt that baseball's parenthetical limitation must be adjusted from "(since 1900)" to "(since 1961)." The record book must be rewritten to fit baseball's real Modern Era.

Let's get to work.

EXPLANATION

Not a New Stat, But a Better Stat

It came as a giddy flash of inspiration.

Statisticians keep tabs on almost every activity on a baseball field — at bats, runs, hits, innings pitched, strikeouts, errors, and on and on. But, for whatever reason, they don't add up the bases that a batter reaches. It occurred to me that singles, doubles, triples, home runs, walks, hit batters, stolen bases, and other productive outcomes could be blended into a convenient, easily understood stat. Surely this was a fresh idea!

My excitement lingered for a few seconds before clarity returned. I knew deep down that the concept couldn't be original. An army of sabermetricians pores through baseball's records on a daily basis. Dozens of researchers, if not hundreds, must already have experienced the same thought. A quick search of the internet confirmed my suspicions.

Yet the idea retained its appeal. The object of the game, of course, is to score more runs than your opponent, but the name of the sport is *base*ball, not *run*ball. We're blessed with a plethora of run-related statistics — runs scored, runs allowed, runs batted in, earned runs, earned run averages — but virtually nothing for bases. (An exception is total bases, the collective stat for bases reached through singles, doubles, triples, and homers. TB is accurate as far as it goes, though the term itself is misleading. It reflects not "total" bases, but only those attained by hits.)

The omission is mystifying. Insiders know the importance of reaching as many bases as possible, even if the impact hasn't been quantified. The epigraph of this book comes from Doug Melvin, former general manager of the Milwaukee Brewers and Texas Rangers. "You can't win the game without moving the pieces on the board," he said. "It's all about capturing bases."

Writers in recent decades have proposed several formulas for the tabulation of bases, but I haven't found evidence of comprehensive follow-through. None of these statistical innovators seems to have taken the next logical step by calculating base totals and averages for prior seasons. (I'm not saying it never happened, just that I didn't uncover any results.) I decided to try to fill this apparent void, so here is my formula for bases:

$$B = TB + BB + HBP + SB + SH + SF$$

I start with total bases, of course, but my aim is to go further, encompassing the other ways that a player can get on base or achieve an extra base for his team. That's why I've added walks, hit batters, stolen bases, sacrifice hits, and sacrifice flies. Every proposed formula that I've seen includes TB and BB. The remaining components vary in popularity, but I consider them all to be sensible and essential.

Let's put the formula into action, comparing two of the National League's outstanding batters in 2013, Joey Votto of the Cincinnati Reds and Andrew McCutchen of the Pittsburgh Pirates:

$$B = TB + BB + HBP + SB + SH + SF$$

$$Votto = 285 + 135 + 4 + 6 + 0 + 6 = 436$$

$$McCutchen = 296 + 78 + 9 + 27 + 0 + 4 = 414$$

McCutchen outpaced Votto in batting average (.317 to .305) and slugging percentage (.508 to .491), so his edge in TB comes as no surprise. The Pirates center fielder also proved to be far better at stealing bases and slightly more likely to be hit by a pitch. But Votto's great weapon was his batting eye. The Reds first baseman drew 57 more walks than McCutchen, resulting in an overall victory in bases, 436 to 414.

That's interesting as far as it goes, though it doesn't tell the whole story. Votto played five more games and went to the plate 52 times more than McCutchen in 2013. There are two ways to statistically eliminate this disparity in playing time. We could divide bases by plate appearances, much as we divide hits by at bats to determine a batting average. The other method — the one I've chosen — is to calculate a ratio between bases and outs.

That poses the obvious need to add up a batter's outs:

$$O = AB - H + CS + GDP + SH + SF$$

I begin by subtracting hits from at bats, yielding the total number of outs the batter made while swinging away. (This figure will most likely include a few occasions when he reached base because of a fielder's error. He ideally would have been out in those instances, so that's how he'll be credited. It's the very same principle that applies to batting averages.) I add the times the player was caught stealing, created an additional out by hitting into a double play, laid down a sacrifice bunt, or rapped a sacrifice fly. The latter two are included in both formulas above, since they involve the trade of an out for a base.

Let's go back to our examples from 2013:

$$O = AB - H + CS + GDP + SH + SF$$

$$Votto = 581 - 177 + 3 + 15 + 0 + 6 = 428$$

$$McCutchen = 583 - 185 + 10 + 13 + 0 + 4 = 425$$

The two players were virtually even in this category, with Votto creating 428 outs and McCutchen 425. We're now able to determine each player's ratio of bases per out (BPO), using simple division:

$$BPO = B / O$$

$$Votto = 436 / 428 = 1.019$$

$$McCutchen = 414 / 425 = .974$$

Joey Votto reached 1.019 bases for every out that he made in 2013, putting him slightly ahead of Andrew McCutchen's ratio of .974 bases per out. Both men enjoyed outstanding seasons, but our BPO matchup shows Votto to be a bit more effective at the plate. That's the same conclusion yielded by the pet statistic of the sabermetric crowd, on-base-plus-slugging percentage (OPS). Votto posted an OPS of .926 in 2013, compared to McCutchen's .911.

You may be curious, by the way, as to what constitutes a good or bad BPO. I gathered the statistics for everybody who made at least 250 plate appearances in 2013 and two other seasons, and then I ranked their batting averages and BPOs from top to bottom. Here are the breakdowns for both stats, showing the relevant numbers at various steps on the ladder:

Percentiles	1968 BA	1999 BA	2013 BA	1968 BPO	1999 BPO	2013 BPO
100%	.335	.379	.348	1.015	1.350	1.183
90%	.287	.317	.300	.790	1.009	.846
80%	.274	.303	.285	.725	.910	.784
75%	.269	.300	.283	.694	.894	.762
70%	.263	.294	.278	.676	.867	.747
60%	.253	.285	.268	.638	.814	.711
50%	.248	.279	.260	.603	.770	.681
40%	.240	.272	.251	.567	.732	.654
30%	.232	.262	.243	.539	.700	.631
25%	.228	.255	.238	.526	.680	.616
20%	.223	.252	.234	.511	.650	.601
10%	.208	.239	.222	.461	.598	.545
0%	.171	.192	.179	.314	.433	.442

A BPO at the median (50%) tends to be roughly two-and-a-half times bigger than the BA for the same year. This ratio widens a bit as we go up the ladder, and shrinks slightly as we drop toward the bottom. That's true even in the Modern Era's very worst season for batting (which was 1968) or its very best year (1999).

Leveling the Statistical Field

The Votto/McCutchen case may seem to be closed, but it isn't.

If a comparison of two players is to be completely fair, the statistical field must be truly level. That means each batter's numbers must be adjusted to neutralize the positive or negative impact of his home stadium, an especially important consideration in this instance. Votto played in Cincinnati's Great American Ball Park, renowned as a hitter-friendly facility, while McCutchen's home was Pittsburgh's PNC Park, a haven for pitchers.

Several variables determine whether batters or pitchers are more comfortable in a given park — among them, the distance and height of the outfield fences, the size of foul territory, the quality of the background in center field, the length of the grass, the existence or lack of a dome, and the persistence of the prevailing winds. Sabermetricians have devised an algebraic formula that reduces these intangibles to a set of numbers for each stadium, known as park factors. Each factor corresponds to an individual stat. One indicates the relative ease or difficulty of scoring runs in a particular ballpark, another does the same for homers, and so on.

I have calculated the park factors for every stadium in every season of the Modern Era. If you're a fan of complex denominators, you'll want to sneak a peek at *Total Baseball*, where the step-by-step process is explained with painstaking precision. But if advanced algebra isn't your thing, don't bother. All you need to know is that each park factor indicates the likelihood that a specific outcome will occur on a specific field, based on a three-year running average of relevant statistics.

The disparity between the stadiums in Cincinnati and Pittsburgh is dramatized by their park factors for bases. Great American Ball Park's 1.027 was the third-highest factor in the National League in 2013, trailing only Colorado's Coors Field and Milwaukee's Miller Park. Cincinnati's factor was 2.7 percent above the league average of 1.000, which means it was 2.7 percent easier to reach base in Cincinnati than in the typical NL stadium. PNC Park, on the other hand, had a reading of 0.959, which was the second-smallest in the league, 4.1 percent below the norm. (The only stadium with a lower mark was San Diego's Petco Park.)

Park factors make it possible to adjust Votto's and McCutchen's statistics. We begin by dividing the player's BPO by a corresponding leaguewide number, thereby determining whether the individual was better or worse than the overall level of competition. We want a reasonably strong benchmark, so we'll eliminate pitchers and fringe players before calculating the league's BPO. Our figure (LgBPO) is confined to batters who averaged at least 1.55 plate appearances per game, the equivalent of 251 appearances in a 162-game season. (What's the reason for such a strange threshold? It's precisely half of the official qualification standard for the batting championship, 3.10 PA per game or 502 PA in a full season.)

The next step is to divide the BPO/LgBPO quotient by the relevant batting park factor for bases, which is abbreviated as BPF[B]. Then we multiply the answer by 100, yielding BPO+, the player's adjusted BPO. Any figure above 100 is superior to the performance of a typical batter who played regularly in the same league during the same season. A mark below 100 is below average.

Here are the calculations for our two players, using the National League's LgBPO of .703 for 2013:

$$BPO+ = 100 \cdot (BPO / LgBPO) / BPF[B]$$
$$Votto = 100 \cdot (1.019 / .703) / 1.027 = 141.1$$
$$McCutchen = 100 \cdot (.974 / .703) / 0.959 = 144.5$$

Votto posted a better BPO in 2013, as we've already seen, but BPO+ favors McCutchen. The Pittsburgh star eclipsed the output of the typical National League batter by 44.5 percent, surpassing his Cincinnati rival's margin of 41.1 percent. Both performances were impressive, though McCutchen's was slightly more so, given that he played in a more difficult environment.

BPO+ is a valuable tool, yet it's not the only adjusted stat at our disposal. Base value (BV) offers a second perspective, showing the difference between the number of bases a player might have been expected to reach and the number he actually attained.

The former element — the expected total of bases — is calculated by multiplying three figures: LgBPO, the outs a batter made, and the park factor for bases. The product is the number of bases that an average player would attain with the same amount of playing time in a neutral ballpark. This total is then subtracted from the given player's real number of bases:

$$BV = B - (LgBPO \cdot O \cdot BPF[B])$$
$$Votto = 436 - (.703 \cdot 428 \cdot 1.027) = 127.1$$
$$McCutchen = 414 - (.703 \cdot 425 \cdot 0.959) = 127.6$$

We end up with a dead heat. Our formula expected McCutchen to generate 286.4 bases, but he actually reached 414, giving him a BV of 127.6. Votto finished just half a base behind with a BV of 127.1. (If you did the math, you probably came up with BV results that were off by a tenth of a base for each player. That's because the calculations for this book have actually been carried to six decimal places. LgBPO, for example, was really .702974, not .703, and the park factor for Cincinnati was 1.026744, not 1.027. But you don't really want to get that deep into decimals, do you? I didn't think so.)

I can sense your confusion. I have now introduced one system that pronounced Votto to be the better batter (BPO), one that gave the edge to McCutchen (BPO+), and one that showed the two stars in a deadlock (BV). Which of these indicators is the accurate one?

They all are.

BPO's aim is identical to the principle behind batting average, slugging percentage, and a myriad of baseball statistics. It quantifies a player's actual output without making any adjustments whatsoever. BPO+ and BV, on the other hand, are designed to neutralize the impacts of a given ballpark and a given season. The former is an average; the latter is a count. Both allow us to accurately compare performances throughout the Modern Era. Take a look at these examples:

Batter	Year	Team	G	HR	BA	B	O	BPO	BPO+
Roger Maris	1961	Yankees	161	61	.269	474	454	1.044	144.5
Joe Morgan	1977	Reds	153	22	.288	422	391	1.079	144.5
Andrew McCutchen	2013	Pirates	157	21	.317	414	425	.974	144.5

You undoubtedly know the names, and you're certainly familiar with their accomplishments. Maris broke Babe Ruth's iconic single-season home-run record in 1961, and Morgan was the best player on one of the greatest squads in baseball history, the Big Red Machine of the mid-1970s. Both posted BPOs that were considerably better than McCutchen's .974 in 2013. Yet both also played under easier conditions:

Batter	Year	Team	Lg	LgBPO	Ballpark	BPF[B]
Roger Maris	1961	Yankees	AL	.737	Yankee Stadium	0.981
Joe Morgan	1977	Reds	NL	.739	Riverfront Stadium	1.011
Andrew McCutchen	2013	Pirates	NL	.703	PNC Park	0.959

The LgBPOs for Maris's and Morgan's seasons were more than 30 points higher than the National League's average for 2013, proving that McCutchen played in a tougher year for hitters. And in a tougher park, too, as shown by

OPS's defenders insist that it just seems to work, so we should ignore its weak mathematical foundation. But the same could be said about adding Fahrenheit and Celsius temperatures — different denominators again — to determine the hottest city in Florida:

City	Average high in January (F°)	Average high in January (C°)	Sum
Miami	76	24	100
Key West	74	23	97
Tampa	70	21	91
Jacksonville	65	18	83

The four cities are in the correct order, so hey, our seemingly crazy formula must actually make sense. That, in a nutshell, is the rationale behind OPS.

2. They measure all aspects of a batter's performance.

Scouts refer to the perfect prospect as a five-tool player. This ideal athlete is somebody who can hit for average, hit for power, run the bases with skill and speed, throw accurately, and field his position well.

Most baseball statistics are confined to one of these characteristics. Among the obvious examples are hits, batting average, home runs, slugging percentage, and stolen bases. But BPO, BPO+, and BV encompass all three batting tools. Every hit or stolen base increases a batter's number of bases, with homers and other extra-base hits providing the biggest boost.

I understand the importance of the latter two skills. Throwing and fielding aren't always given the emphasis they deserve, an oversight that might be rectified as sabermetricians continue to devise better ways to quantify their impact. But it's a simple fact that we judge non-pitchers primarily by their ability at the plate. Ty Cobb, Babe Ruth, and Ted Williams aren't in the Hall of Fame because of their ability to hit the cutoff man. Harmon Killebrew and Frank Thomas didn't join them in Cooperstown because they were dazzling infielders. The dominant skills of these all-time greats are best expressed by BPO and its relatives.

3. They apply equally to batters and pitchers.

I didn't make this point previously because I wanted to keep my explanation of base-related statistics as simple as possible. But now is the time to stress a key strength of BPO, BPO+, and BV: The very same formulas that we use for batters can also be used for pitchers. (There are just two small changes. Pitchers have their own LgBPO, which varies slightly from the corresponding average for batters. The same is true for the pitching park factor (PPF), which is a bit different from its BPF counterpart. You'll find more details in the definitions of abbreviations at the end of this chapter.)

It's important to remember that the scale of excellence is reversed. A batter wants to drive his BPO+ above 100, the higher the better. A pitcher wants to head in the opposite direction, pushing as far below 100 as possible. That makes sense. A pitcher's job, after all, is to keep runners off the basepaths. The lower his BPO, the better his performance.

Seven pitchers started at least 12 games for the world champion San Francisco Giants in 2014. Let's look at their total numbers (encompassing starts and relief appearances) for a better idea of the way that BPO's statistical family works for pitchers:

Pitcher	G	IP	ERA	BA	B	O	BPO	BV	BPO+
Jake Peavy	12	78.2	2.17	.231	129	240	.538	-16.5	88.6
Madison Bumgarner	33	217.1	2.98	.240	371	658	.564	-28.0	93.0
Yusmeiro Petit	39	117.0	3.69	.223	204	352	.580	-9.4	95.6
Tim Hudson	31	189.1	3.57	.270	366	570	.642	20.4	105.9
Matt Cain	15	90.1	4.18	.242	186	273	.681	20.5	112.4
Ryan Vogelsong	32	184.2	4.00	.254	380	556	.683	42.8	112.7
Tim Lincecum	33	155.2	4.74	.258	361	468	.771	77.2	127.2

Note how nicely BPO+ tracks with ERA. Jake Peavy was the best pitcher in both categories, and Tim Lincecum was the worst. Peavy didn't arrive from the Red Sox until a late July trade, so Madison Bumgarner carried the load for San Francisco for most of the season. He yielded 28.0 fewer bases than would have been expected, which was the best BV for any Giant starter.

We're accustomed to single-duty stats — BA for batters, ERA for pitchers — so the switch-hitting role for the BPO family is a bit unusual. But it's also remarkably convenient to be able to measure all players against the same benchmark. I use BPO, BPO+, and BV for batters and pitchers throughout this book.

4. They're closely linked to the odds of victory.

Perhaps the greatest strength of these base-related stats is their tight correlation with winning. And winning, need we say, is what baseball is all about.

I crunched the numbers for all 112,821 major-league games between 1961 and 2014, searching for the best predictors of team success. My first subjects were 11 counting statistics — eight for batting, two for pitching, and one for fielding. I compared the better team in each category with the team that won the game. ("Better" means exactly what you think it does — more bases and hits by batters, fewer walks by pitchers, fewer errors in the field, and so on.)

Prepare yourself for a big surprise. The best predictor was runs. The team that scored the most runs won every single game. Quite the coincidence, no?

Bases finished second on the list. The winning team accumulated more bases than the losing squad in 81.8 percent of all games. No other counting stat topped 77 percent as a predictor, and most had accuracy rates below 65 percent:

Counting statistic	Winning team was better (W)	Losing team was better (L)	Both teams were same (S)	W%	L%	S%
R (bat)	112,821	0	0	100.0%	0.0%	0.0%
B (bat)	92,249	16,020	4,552	81.8%	14.2%	4.0%
TB (bat)	86,630	20,217	5,974	76.8%	17.9%	5.3%
H (bat)	80,244	22,168	10,409	71.1%	19.6%	9.2%
EXH (bat)	71,171	21,803	19,847	63.1%	19.3%	17.6%
BB (pitch)	63,236	33,271	16,314	56.0%	29.5%	14.5%
SO (pitch)	57,107	43,014	12,700	50.6%	38.1%	11.3%
HR (bat)	53,775	19,668	39,378	47.7%	17.4%	34.9%
E (field)	45,526	25,744	41,551	40.4%	22.8%	36.8%
LOB (bat)	44,840	55,344	12,637	39.7%	49.1%	11.2%
SB (bat)	41,487	23,108	48,226	36.8%	20.5%	42.7%

My next move was to compute averages for both teams in each game, once again comparing the statistical results with the final outcome. (I need to add a note of clarification: Every average was solely for the game in question. If a team rapped 11 hits in 37 at bats, for example, its BA for the game was .297.) There were eight sets of averages in all — five for batters, two for pitchers, one for fielders.

Earned run average topped the rankings. The team with the lowest ERA won 93.7 percent of the 112,821 games. No big shock there.

A base-related stat again took the runner-up slot, as the team with the better BPO emerged victorious 86.1 percent of the time. All other averages trailed in importance, even the venerated OPS, which connected with 84.9 percent of the winners:

Average	Winning team was better (W)	Losing team was better (L)	Both teams were same (S)	W%	L%	S%
ERA (pitch)	105,726	3,609	3,486	93.7%	3.2%	3.1%
BPO (bat)	97,152	14,715	954	86.1%	13.0%	0.8%
OPS (bat)	95,789	17,014	18	84.9%	15.1%	0.0%
SLG (bat)	91,888	20,072	861	81.4%	17.8%	0.8%
WHIP (pitch)	91,480	17,593	3,748	81.1%	15.6%	3.3%
OBP (bat)	91,350	20,183	1,288	81.0%	17.9%	1.1%
BA (bat)	89,091	22,229	1,501	79.0%	19.7%	1.3%
FLD% (field)	54,149	30,307	28,365	48.0%	26.9%	25.1%

We have always lacked a simple all-purpose stat that simultaneously measures the run-generating ability of batters and run-prevention skills of pitchers. It is true that sabermetricians have devised complex systems to serve this purpose, such as linear weights and wRC+. These advanced metrics are logically and cleverly constructed, and they yield plausible results. But they fall short of the first strength I mentioned a few pages ago. They are not easy to calculate and understand. So, despite their many attributes, they are unlikely to gain wide circulation.

I nominate BPO, BPO+, and BV as the logical candidates to fill this void. They're the tools that make it possible for me to identify the best and worst teams and players of the Modern Era. I don't have the seasoned eye of a front-office executive or a scout or an ex-player or a beat writer or a play-by-play broadcaster, but I do have plenty of experience with statistics. That's what I bring to the discussion.

The rankings in this book are based on objective numbers. Barry Bonds and Mark McGwire aren't members of the Hall of Fame, but their BV totals suggest that they should be. (No, I haven't made any statistical adjustments for steroid use, either real or alleged. I understand the outrage voiced by millions of fans, but my job is simply to bring the numbers. It's up to you to supply the anger.) I may not have seen Don Schwall pitch for the Red Sox or Ken Hubbs play second base for the Cubs, but their BPO+ readings suggest that they were poor choices for Rookie of the Year. You might believe that the 1998 Yankees were the greatest team of the Modern Era, but the stats give that honor to the 1984 Tigers.

Thousands of judgments like these are scattered throughout the following chapters. If you want to disagree, please be my guest. That, of course, is the fun of it.

A Few Final Notes

There are a handful of housekeeping details that require our attention — specifically, a few points to be clarified and a whole bunch of abbreviations to be explained.

This book employs two formats. Chapters 1 to 29 contain lists of the best and worst teams and players in 221 categories, with each list preceded by explanatory text. But the concluding chapter is formatted differently. It's essentially a statistical appendix, summarizing team records and top individual performances in each season of the Modern Era.

All of the charts in this book follow the same format. The lefthand column shows the rank of a given team or player. The extreme righthand column displays the statistic on which the rankings are based. (A few charts use a second indicator to break ties. Those cases are noted in the text.)

All stats are confined to the Modern Era (1961 to the present), with the exception of six charts that focus on the Hall of Fame (Lists #187 to #192). Hank Aaron, Mickey Mantle, and Willie Mays were superstars in the 1950s, and they retained their brilliance as the new era dawned. Their full body of work, of course, must be considered when we discuss their qualifications for Cooperstown. But their rankings on other lists are based solely on their stats from 1961 until retirement. (That includes all lists of multiyear achievements. If you see "career" in a chart's heading, be aware that the accompanying statistics do not extend beyond the Modern Era.)

Each list shows the 10 best or worst performances in a particular category. There are two exceptions. If 10th place is deadlocked, you'll see every player who is entangled in the tie, no matter how long the list grows. And if a heading applies equally to batters and pitchers, such as a list of No. 1 draft choices or Most Valuable Players or Rookies of the Year, I'll show the top seven batters and top three pitchers.

Rankings for a single season are confined to players who met the qualification standards for that year — at least 3.1 plate appearances or one inning pitched per game. The minimum requirements are 502 appearances or 162 innings in a normal season, slightly fewer in a strike-shortened year. I have relaxed the standards for a few lists, especially those involving relief pitchers. These rare exceptions have been flagged.

Chapters 14 through 16 offer position-by-position rankings of the best and worst players. Each man is assigned to the position he played most frequently during his career or a given season. Harmon Killebrew, for instance, was a first baseman, third baseman, left fielder, and designated hitter. His career is rated as the seventh-best in the Modern Era for a first baseman, since that was his most common position. (All of his statistics, regardless of position, are counted toward his career totals.) But Killebrew primarily played third base in 1969, when he was named the American League's Most Valuable Player. His performance that year is rated as the fifth-best season for a third baseman.

Baseball insiders typically use team and organization as interchangeable nouns. I'm a bit pickier. I define a team as a particular squad in a particular season, such as the 2011 Milwaukee Brewers. Organization refers to a team and its lineal predecessors and descendants. The Brewers organization, for example, dates back to the 1969 debut of the Seattle Pilots, who decamped to Wisconsin the following year.

You're a baseball fan, so I know you're familiar with the game's standard abbreviations. I've included them in the following list anyway, largely out of a compulsion for thoroughness. You'll also see citations for new statistics that are introduced in this book, as well as a few terms that require elaboration.

2B: Doubles.

3B: Triples.

AB: At bats.

AFSI: Average fan support index for a given team over a defined span. It's the average of the team's year-by-year FSI scores. (See FSI.)

Age: A player's age on June 30 of a given year. I could have chosen a different date — January 1, opening day, the end of the World Series — but June 30 is the benchmark favored by Baseball-Reference.com, and that's good enough for me. The listed age applies to the whole season. Mike Trout turned 24 on August 7, 2015, but what really matters is that he was 23 on June 30. That's why 2015 is labeled as his age-23 season.

Attend: Home attendance for a season.

Att/G: Attendance per home date.

Att/W: Attendance-win ratio. It's the quotient of a team's attendance per home date (Att/G) divided by its seasonal total of wins.

Average TS: Average team score for a given team over a defined span. It's the average of the team's year-by-year TS scores. (See TS.)

B: Bases. It's the sum of total bases (bases reached by hits), walks, hit batters, stolen bases, sacrifice hits, and sacrifice flies.

B2: Joint total of bases for both teams in a game.

BA: Batting average.

BA2: Joint batting average for both teams in a game.

BB: Walks.

BBV: Walk value. It's the difference between the number of walks a batter might have been expected to obtain (or a pitcher might have been expected to yield) and the actual number. (See BV.)

BPF: Batting park factor. It indicates the likelihood that a specific batting outcome will occur. A different factor exists for each statistic in a given ballpark in a given season. The relevant stat is denoted in brackets, as in BPF[B] for bases or BPF[HR] for home runs.

BPO: Bases per out. It's the quotient of bases divided by outs.

BPO2: Joint bases per out for both teams in a game.

BPO+: Adjusted bases per out. The formula, described at length on previous pages, neutralizes the positive or negative effects of a given ballpark and season. The resulting number is tied to a benchmark of 100. Similar stats in this book, all carrying titles that end with a + sign, are calculated in the same manner.

BPOA: Bases per out allowed.

BV: Base value. The formula, also described earlier in this chapter, determines the difference between the number of bases a batter might have been expected to reach (or a pitcher might have been expected to yield) and the actual number. Similar stats in this book, all carrying titles that end with the word value, are calculated in the same way.

Change: Difference between the same statistical measure in successive years, such as BPO in 2014 and 2015.

CS: Times caught stealing.

CT: Contact rate. It's calculated in two steps: (1) subtracting strikeouts from at bats, (2) dividing that number by at bats.

CT+: Adjusted contact rate. It neutralizes the positive or negative effects of a given ballpark and season, and is tied to a benchmark of 100. (See BPO+.)

E: Errors.

Edge: Difference between two statistics in the same year, such as home BPO and road BPO.

ER: Earned runs.

ERA: Earned run average.

ERA2: Joint earned run average for both teams in a game.

ERA+: Adjusted earned run average. It neutralizes the positive or negative effects of a given ballpark and season, and is tied to a benchmark of 100. (See BPO+.) There are other versions of ERA+ out there. But they tend to award triple-digit scores to the best performances, which doesn't make sense to me.

A pitcher strives for the lowest possible ERA, so his corresponding ERA+ should also be low. ERA+ readings below 100 are the best ones in this book.

ERV: Earned run value. It's the difference between the number of earned runs a pitcher might have been expected to yield and the actual number. (See BV.)

EXH: Extra-base hits. It's the sum of doubles, triples, and home runs. Not the bases reached, just the number of those hits.

EXV: Extra-base value. It's the difference between the number of extra bases a batter might have been expected to reach (or a pitcher might have been expected to yield) and the actual number. Extra bases are those beyond first base. A double is worth one extra base, a triple two, and a home run three. (See BV.)

EY: Batting eye rate. It's calculated in three steps: (1) subtracting intentional walks from total walks, (2) subtracting intentional walks from plate appearances, (3) dividing the number from Step 1 by the number from Step 2.

EY+: Adjusted batting eye rate. It neutralizes the positive or negative effects of a given ballpark and season, and is tied to a benchmark of 100. (See BPO+.)

FLD%: Fielding percentage. It's calculated in three steps: (1) adding putouts and assists, (2) adding putouts, assists, and errors, (3) dividing the number from Step 1 by the number from Step 2.

FSI: Fan support index. It's calculated in two steps: (1) dividing a team's attendance-win ratio (Att/W) by the average ratio for all major-league teams in the same season, (2) multiplying the result by 100.

G: Games.

GB: Games behind.

GDP: Times grounded into double plays.

H: Hits.

H2: Joint total of hits for both teams in a game.

HBP: Times hit by a pitch, also known as hit batters or hit batsmen.

HR: Home runs.

HR2: Joint total of home runs for both teams in a game.

IBB: Intentional walks.

IP: Innings pitched.

ISO: Isolated power average. It's calculated in two steps: (1) adding a batter's extra bases, with one for each double, two for each triple, and three for each home run, (2) dividing that number by his at bats. The same stat can be calculated for the extra bases yielded by pitchers.

ISO+: Adjusted isolated power average. It neutralizes the positive or negative effects of a given ballpark and season, and is tied to a benchmark of 100. (See BPO+.)

L: Losses.

League titles: Number of league championships.

Lg: League.

LgBPO: Average BPO for a league in a given season, though it isn't quite that simple. LgBPO for batters is confined to those who averaged at least 1.55 plate appearances per game. This eliminates pitchers and fringe players from consideration, leaving us with the average BPO for regulars and key substitutes. LgBPO for pitchers is confined to those who averaged at least 0.5 innings per game or appeared in at least 25 percent of their team's games. This eliminates seldom-used pitchers from consideration, leaving us with the average BPO for starters and key relievers. A season's LgBPOs for batters and pitchers will differ because of these exclusions. (Which version of LgBPO is used to calculate BPO+ or BV depends on whether the stat is for batters or pitchers.) The same principles apply to other league averages, such as LgCT and LgEY, that are used in related adjustments.

LOB: Runners left on base.

Next: The heading for any statistic for the following season.

O: Outs. It's calculated in two steps: (1) subtracting hits from at bats, (2) adding the number from Step 1 to the sum of double plays, caught stealings, sacrifice hits, and sacrifice flies.

O2: Joint total of outs for both teams in a game.

OBP: On-base percentage. It's calculated in three steps: (1) adding hits, walks, and hit batters, (2) adding at bats, walks, hit batters, and sacrifice flies, (3) dividing the number from Step 1 by the number from Step 2.

OPS: On-base-plus-slugging percentage. It's the sum of on-base percentage and slugging percentage.

Overall: Win-loss record for the season (with postseason results in parentheses).

PA: Plate appearances.

Pct.: Winning percentage.

Playoffs: Number of years qualifying for the playoffs.

Pos: Position.

Post: Postseason results, with P for any team that reached the playoffs, LP for any team that won its league title, and WLP for any team that won the World Series.

PPF: Pitching park factor. It indicates the likelihood that a specific pitching outcome will occur. A different factor exists for each statistic in a given ballpark in a given season. The principle is the same as for BPF, and the relevant stat is once again denoted in brackets, as in PPF[R] for runs or PPF[B] for bases.

Prev: The heading for any statistic for the previous season.

R: Runs scored, sometimes presented as an average per game.

RA: Runs allowed, sometimes presented as an average per game.

RBI: Runs batted in.

S: Saves.

SB: Stolen bases.

SC: Scoring. It's calculated in two steps: (1) adding runs and runs batted in, (2) subtracting home runs from that number. Sabermetricians will hate this stat. They will say — correctly — that it doesn't give credit to everybody who helps to produce a run. Consider this example involving the 1961 Yankees: Tony Kubek gets hit by a pitch, Roger Maris doubles him to third base, and Mickey Mantle drives in the run with an uncharacteristically weak infield squib. Both Kubek and Mantle get credit in the SC column, while Maris, the man who made the key hit, gets nothing. That's unfortunate, but there are parallels in most sports. Football, basketball, and hockey statisticians tally touchdowns, baskets, and goals respectively, without concern for the lineman who makes a key block, the forward who zips an effective outlet pass, or the goalie who triggers a breakaway.

SCV: Scoring value. It's the difference between the scoring total (SC) a batter might have been expected to attain and the actual number. (See BV.)

SE: Scoring efficiency rate. It's the quotient of scoring (SC) divided by plate appearances.

SE+: Adjusted scoring efficiency. It neutralizes the positive or negative effects of a given ballpark and season, and is tied to a benchmark of 100. (See BPO+.)

SF: Sacrifice flies.

SH: Sacrifice hits.

SLG: Slugging percentage. It's the quotient of total bases divided at bats. (See TB.)

SO: Strikeouts.

SOV: Strikeout value. It's the difference between the number of strikeouts a batter might have been expected to make (or a pitcher might have been expected to deliver) and the actual number. (See BV.)

Span: The first and last years of a period, accounting for a player's tenure with a team or during a decade. It may also cover an entire career, or the portion of a career within the Modern Era (for players who reached the majors before 1961). The two years listed are the first and last of the span. Gaps because of trades, trips to the minors, or temporary retirement are not indicated.

TB: Total bases. It's the confusing name for a stat that counts only the bases reached by hits.

TS: Team score. It's the measure of the relative excellence of a given team in a given season, as expressed on a 100-point scale. The formula gives equal weight to four factors: winning percentage, the differential between runs scored and allowed per game, the differential between BPO and BPOA, and postseason success. The score for each of the first three factors is based on a comparison of the team's number and the respective category's leaguewide average and standard deviation for that year. The result (known as a z-score) is added to 2.75, multiplied by 25, and divided by 5.5. These calculations yield a score between 0 and 25 for each of the three factors. The fourth category gives 25 points to any World Series champion and 20 points to any league champion that lost the World Series. Any other team receives a bonus from 0 to 15 points after .250 is subtracted from its winning percentage and the resulting number is multiplied by 32.2. The four category scores are added to yield the team score, which I consider to be an excellent indicator of a team's relative strength. There are good reasons for all of the numerical machinations that I described in this paragraph, but I see no reason to go into greater detail. This entry is already long enough.

UBB: Unintentional walks. It's the difference between walks and intentional walks.

W: Wins.

WHIP: Walks and hits per inning pitched.

World titles: Number of World Series championships.

1. TEAMS

List #1: Best Organization in the Modern Era

Who else but the Yankees?

New York won the first two World Series of the Modern Era — crushing the Cincinnati Reds in 1961 and squeaking past the San Francisco Giants the following year. That pair of titles exceeds the totals for 14 other organizations in the entire era, including such long-established franchises as the Braves, Cubs, and White Sox (one world championship apiece) and the Astros, Indians, and Rangers (none at all).

But the Yankees didn't stop in 1962. They went on to win two more World Series in the 1970s, three in the 1990s, and an additional pair during the first decade of the 21st century. Their nine world titles between 1961 and 2015 are nearly twice the next best total, five for the Saint Louis Cardinals.

The Yanks also set the pace for the Modern Era in league championships (15), playoff appearances (27), and regular-season winning percentage (.558). So it comes as no surprise that they have the era's best average team score, 60.194, roughly three-and-a-half points ahead of the runner-up Dodgers. Los Angeles did about half as well in the Yanks in two key categories, earning eight National League titles and four world championships. The Cardinals hold third place in the TS rankings.

The 10 best organizations triumphed in two-thirds of the Modern Era's World Series — 37 of 55. This list includes all eight franchises that won at least three world titles after 1960.

The Best 10

Rank	Organization	Years	W	L	Pct.	Play-offs	League titles	World titles	Average TS
1	Yankees	56	4,979	3,946	.558	27	15	9	60.194
2	Dodgers	56	4,807	4,130	.538	20	8	4	56.646
3	Cardinals	56	4,731	4,194	.530	19	10	5	54.681
4	Red Sox	56	4,736	4,199	.530	16	6	3	53.405
5	Giants	56	4,642	4,297	.519	12	6	3	50.545
6	Reds	56	4,652	4,279	.521	12	6	3	50.298
7	Orioles	56	4,637	4,282	.520	13	6	3	50.218
8	Braves	56	4,601	4,319	.516	19	5	1	50.189
9	Blue Jays	40	3,167	3,188	.498	7	2	2	47.620
10	Athletics	56	4,502	4,435	.504	18	6	4	47.596

List #2: Worst Organization in the Modern Era

San Diego's fans became familiar with defeat at the very start. The Padres, who were admitted to the National League as an expansion team in 1969, posted the worst record in the majors during their inaugural season: 52 wins and 110 losses.

The organization's winning percentage was mired below .400 for the first six years, resulting in six straight last-place finishes in the NL West. It wasn't until 1978 — their 10th season of play — that the Padres finally poked their heads above the .500 mark.

Success came sporadically in the years that followed. San Diego made five playoff appearances, including two visits to the World Series. But the latter proved to be quick disappointments, with the Padres winning only a single game from the Tigers in 1984 and none at all from the Yankees in 1998.

The typical outcome in San Diego, despite occasional flashes of prosperity, has been defeat. Two-thirds of the Padres' seasons (32 of 48) ended below .500 — including 10 years lower than .400 — resulting in an average team score of 37.521, the worst in the Modern Era. Three other organizations have scores below 40 points: the Mariners, Rays, and Rockies.

The list of baseball's 10 worst organizations is littered with expansion teams, including the four previously mentioned. The Chicago Cubs and Texas Rangers (who began as the Washington Senators) are the only entries that took the field throughout the era.

The Worst 10

Rank	Organization	Years	W	L	Pct.	Play-offs	League titles	World titles	Average TS
1	Padres	48	3,540	4,110	.463	5	2	0	37.521
2	Mariners	40	2,984	3,371	.470	4	0	0	38.535
3	Rays	19	1,420	1,656	.462	4	1	0	38.658
4	Rockies	24	1,784	2,042	.466	3	1	0	39.887
5	Marlins	24	1,793	2,026	.469	2	2	2	40.308
6	Rangers (Senators)	56	4,277	4,649	.479	8	2	0	40.927
7	Cubs	56	4,287	4,633	.481	8	1	1	41.321
8	Brewers (Pilots)	48	3,642	4,001	.477	4	1	0	41.530
9	Royals	48	3,704	3,933	.485	9	4	2	42.873
10	Mets	55	4,215	4,555	.481	9	5	2	43.278

List #3: Best Team in a Season

Sparky Anderson always said that his recipe for managerial success was simple. "I got good players," he said, "stayed out of the way, let 'em win a lot, and then just hung around for 26 years."

Anderson was certainly blessed with great players in the 1970s in Cincinnati, where his Reds won two World Series. But he never managed a better team than the 1984 Tigers, who posted the highest team score (97.109) in the Modern Era. Detroit won its first nine games that year, soared to a 37-9 record by the end of May, and never let up. The Tigers finished the regular season with 104 wins, then lost only one postseason game in breezing to the world title.

Kirk Gibson (27 HR, 137.8 BPO+) and Alan Trammell (.314 BA, 123.8 BPO+) paced a Detroit attack that led the majors in home runs and runs scored. Reliever Willie Hernandez (1.92 ERA, 66.2 BPO+) won the American League's Most Valuable Player Award, and Jack Morris (19 W, 93.1 BPO+) anchored a solid starting rotation.

The 1998 New York Yankees are second on this list, even though they had 10 more wins and better offensive stats than the Tigers. But the TS formula rewarded Detroit for excelling in a more competitive climate. The Tigers played 88 games against teams that ended the 1984 season with records of .500 or better; the 1998 Yanks faced just 64 opponents of that caliber.

The Best 10

Rank	Team	Year	Post	W	L	Pct.	R	RA	BPO	BPOA	TS
1	Detroit Tigers	1984	WLP	104	58	.642	5.12	3.97	.747	.606	97.109
2	New York Yankees	1998	WLP	114	48	.704	5.96	4.05	.823	.649	96.123
3	New York Mets	1986	WLP	108	54	.667	4.83	3.57	.714	.600	94.962
4	Chicago Cubs	2016	WLP	103	58	.640	4.99	3.43	.755	.594	92.166
5	Cincinnati Reds	1975	WLP	108	54	.667	5.19	3.62	.748	.625	90.713
6	Oakland Athletics	1990	LP	103	59	.636	4.52	3.52	.708	.602	89.366
7	Baltimore Orioles	1966	WLP	97	63	.606	4.72	3.76	.682	.595	88.282
8	Baltimore Orioles	1970	WLP	108	54	.667	4.89	3.54	.726	.600	87.901
9	New York Yankees	2009	WLP	103	59	.636	5.65	4.65	.838	.708	87.433
10	Cincinnati Reds	1976	WLP	102	60	.630	5.29	3.91	.789	.629	87.331

List #4: Worst Team in a Season

Fair is fair. Detroit fans enjoyed watching the best team in the Modern Era, the 1984 Tigers, so it was only right that they also endured the worst squad of all in 1996.

Alan Trammell was the only big name from the 1980s who was still around in 1996, though he played just 66 games in what would be his final season. Manager Sparky Anderson had retired the previous fall. He said he was leaving because the game seemed to have changed, and not for the better. Skeptics insisted that the Tigers' top brass had pushed him out.

If so, they did him a favor. A 12-game losing streak in May set the stage for a dismal season for new manager Buddy Bell. Another 12-game skid in September wrapped things up. The Tigers lost games in bunches all year, suffering nine losing streaks of five games or longer. The final dispiriting numbers: 109 defeats, 6.81 runs allowed per game (the worst mark for any pitching staff since 1961), and a team score of just 5.197.

The Modern Era's second-worst team also called Detroit home. The Tigers slowly improved after their 1996 debacle, but then they stumbled again. They lost 119 games in 2003, 10 more than in 1996, though their other statistics were a bit more presentable. Their TS of 7.040 was also slightly better, yet a long, long way from the 97.109 mark set by the hallowed 1984 Tigers.

The Worst 10

Rank	Team	Year	Post	W	L	Pct.	R	RA	BPO	BPOA	TS
1	Detroit Tigers	1996	—	53	109	.327	4.83	6.81	.701	.902	5.197
2	Detroit Tigers	2003	—	43	119	.265	3.65	5.73	.619	.791	7.040
3	Pittsburgh Pirates	2010	—	57	105	.352	3.62	5.35	.620	.787	7.550
4	New York Mets	1963	—	51	111	.315	3.09	4.78	.524	.690	8.162
5	Detroit Tigers	1989	—	59	103	.364	3.81	5.04	.619	.748	8.859
6	Philadelphia Phillies	1961	—	47	107	.305	3.77	5.14	.606	.724	8.887
7	New York Mets	1965	—	50	112	.309	3.02	4.59	.520	.680	9.282
8	Baltimore Orioles	1988	—	54	107	.335	3.42	4.90	.601	.725	9.850
9	Cleveland Indians	1991	—	57	105	.352	3.56	4.69	.592	.674	9.976
10	New York Mets	1962	—	40	120	.250	3.83	5.89	.628	.771	10.038

List #5: Worst Team to Win a World Series

The Minnesota Twins surrendered 806 runs in 1987, 20 more than they scored. They finished 10th in the American League in both batting average and earned run average. Their .525 winning percentage would have consigned them to fifth place in the AL East, 13 games behind the division-leading Detroit Tigers.

And, oh yes, the Twins were the world champions that year. Their team score of 59.810 was easily the worst for any World Series winner in the Modern Era.

It was Minnesota's great fortune to play in the weak AL West in 1987. The Twins' record of 85-77 was barely sufficient to edge the Kansas City Royals (83-79) for the divisional crown. They entered the American League Championship Series as heavy underdogs, but their bats suddenly sprang alive. Minnesota's relentless attack — eight homers and 34 runs — subdued the Tigers in five games.

Most observers expected the Twins' magic to run out in the World Series, where they faced the imposing Saint Louis Cardinals (95-67). But Minnesota battered the Cards in the first two contests, 10-1 and 8-4, survived three straight defeats, and rallied with two final victories for a totally unexpected world title.

Saint Louis turned the tables 19 years later. The Cardinals stumbled into the playoffs in 2006, losing 35 of their final 60 regular-season games. But they swiftly switched gears in the postseason — winning 11 of 16 games — to take the world championship, as well as second place on this list.

The Worst 10

Rank	Team	Year	Post	W	L	Pct.	R	RA	BPO	BPOA	TS
1	Minnesota Twins	1987	WLP	85	77	.525	4.85	4.98	.721	.764	59.810
2	Saint Louis Cardinals	2006	WLP	83	78	.516	4.85	4.73	.729	.739	67.156
3	Kansas City Royals	1985	WLP	91	71	.562	4.24	3.94	.669	.625	71.710
4	New York Yankees	2000	WLP	87	74	.540	5.41	5.06	.787	.730	71.883
5	San Francisco Giants	2014	WLP	88	74	.543	4.10	3.79	.635	.619	72.008
6	Florida Marlins	2003	WLP	91	71	.562	4.64	4.27	.727	.674	72.426
7	San Francisco Giants	2012	WLP	94	68	.580	4.43	4.01	.682	.666	72.475
8	Saint Louis Cardinals	1964	WLP	93	69	.574	4.41	4.02	.652	.616	72.585
9	New York Mets	1969	WLP	100	62	.617	3.90	3.34	.604	.583	72.856
10	Florida Marlins	1997	WLP	92	70	.568	4.57	4.13	.720	.685	73.229

List #6: Best Team Not to Win a World Series

The 1990 Oakland Athletics had it all. Rickey Henderson (.325 BA, 65 SB) was a dominant leadoff man, and Mark McGwire (39 HR) and Jose Canseco (37 HR) were an imposing pair of sluggers. Henderson led the American League with a BPO+ of 190.1. Canseco (145.7) and McGwire (136.3) also finished in the top five.

The pitching staff was equally solid. Bob Welch won 27 games, and Dave Stewart (22 W) topped the league in shutouts and complete games. Closer Dennis Eckersley racked up 48 saves.

This superior firepower propelled the A's to a 103-59 record and a TS of 89.366, the fifth-best score in the Modern Era. Oakland demolished Boston in the American League Championship Series — outscoring the Red Sox 20-4 — and turned its sights to Cincinnati. The Reds had won only 91 games in the regular season, and oddsmakers anticipated a World Series sweep.

That's what they got, though they were wrong about the champion. Cincinnati's Jose Rijo shut down Oakland's sluggers, 7-0, in the opening game. He returned four days later to clinch the title with a 2-1 nail-biter, stamping the A's as the best team ever to fall short of a world title.

Nine of the 10 squads on this list made it to the World Series before self-destructing. The 2001 Seattle Mariners didn't even do that. They won 116 games in the regular season — the most by any Modern Era team — before submitting to the Yankees in a five-game ALCS.

The Best 10

Rank	Team	Year	Post	W	L	Pct.	R	RA	BPO	BPOA	TS
1	Oakland Athletics	1990	LP	103	59	.636	4.52	3.52	.708	.602	89.366
2	Cleveland Indians	1995	LP	100	44	.694	5.83	4.22	.835	.677	87.220
3	Baltimore Orioles	1969	LP	109	53	.673	4.81	3.19	.726	.547	86.161
4	Atlanta Braves	1996	LP	96	66	.593	4.77	4.00	.723	.618	83.372
5	Baltimore Orioles	1971	LP	101	57	.639	4.70	3.35	.717	.572	83.333
6	Saint Louis Cardinals	1968	LP	97	65	.599	3.60	2.91	.577	.518	83.157
7	Los Angeles Dodgers	1978	LP	95	67	.586	4.49	3.54	.722	.598	82.060
8	Seattle Mariners	2001	P	116	46	.716	5.72	3.87	.811	.624	81.959
9	Los Angeles Dodgers	1974	LP	102	60	.630	4.93	3.46	.718	.568	81.722
10	New York Yankees	1976	LP	97	62	.610	4.59	3.62	.678	.582	81.368

List #7: Worst Team to Win a League Title

The National League's East Division was the embodiment of mediocrity in 1973. All six teams hovered around the .500 mark as August came to a close. Saint Louis held the lead with a 68-66 record, followed by Pittsburgh at 65-65. Nobody seemed worthy of the divisional title.

The Cardinals went into a tailspin in September, as did three other participants in the slow-motion pennant race. Only Montreal (16-13) and New York (20-8) came to life during the final month. The Mets, who had been 12 games below .500 as recently as August 26, emerged as the NL East champions with the unimpressive record of 82-79.

New York's prospects in the National League Championship Series were bleak. The Mets were facing the powerful Cincinnati Reds (99-63), soon to gain everlasting fame as the Big Red Machine. But stellar pitching by Jon Matlack, Jerry Koosman, and Tom Seaver quieted the bats of the mighty Reds, who scored just eight runs in five games. The Mets, with a TS of 57.307, became the most unlikely winner of a league title in the Modern Era.

New York fought valiantly in the World Series, extending Oakland to seven games before losing. That was a common fate for teams on this list. Only the 1987 Twins and 2006 Cardinals went on to win world championships, but the 1973 Mets and three others (the 2014 Royals, 1997 Indians, and 2001 Yankees) battled all the way to a seventh game.

The Worst 10

Rank	Team	Year	Post	W	L	Pct.	R	RA	BPO	BPOA	TS
1	New York Mets	1973	LP	82	79	.509	3.78	3.65	.583	.607	57.307
2	Minnesota Twins	1987	WLP	85	77	.525	4.85	4.98	.721	.764	59.810
3	Kansas City Royals	2014	LP	89	73	.549	4.02	3.85	.634	.625	62.588
4	Detroit Tigers	2012	LP	88	74	.543	4.48	4.14	.707	.669	64.777
5	Saint Louis Cardinals	2006	WLP	83	78	.516	4.85	4.73	.729	.739	67.156
6	Cleveland Indians	1997	LP	86	75	.534	5.39	5.06	.810	.758	67.467
7	Texas Rangers	2010	LP	90	72	.556	4.86	4.24	.721	.674	67.736
8	San Diego Padres	1984	LP	92	70	.568	4.23	3.91	.639	.632	67.737
9	Cincinnati Reds	1961	LP	93	61	.604	4.61	4.24	.694	.662	68.297
10	New York Yankees	2001	LP	95	65	.594	4.99	4.43	.748	.679	68.361

List #8: Best Team Not to Win a League Title

No team has started a season more emphatically than the 2001 Mariners. Seattle streaked to a 32-12 record by May 22 and then shifted into overdrive, winning its next 15 games. The Mariners woke on June 9 with 47 wins against 12 losses (.797 winning percentage), 17 games ahead of runner-up Anaheim in the AL West.

Did the Mariners ease off the throttle? Not at all. They played 69-34 ball the rest of the way, finishing with 116 wins, the most for any team since 1906. Their TS of 81.959 was the 31st-highest in the Modern Era — and the best for any squad that failed to win a league title.

The Mariners were heavily favored over the Yankees (95-65) in the American League Championship Series. Five of their batters had outperformed the leaguewide average by at least 19 percent: Edgar Martinez (BPO+ of 145.2), Bret Boone (130.4), Mike Cameron (122.8), John Olerud (120.6), and Ichiro Suzuki (119.8). Their pitchers had posted the lowest ERA in the majors. Seattle seemed to have everything.

Except momentum. The Yankees rattled the Mariners by taking the first two games at Safeco Field, 4-2 and 3-2. Seattle exploded with 14 runs in the third game, but went silent for the rest of the ALCS. New York won in five games.

Eight other teams on this list also flamed out in the postseason. The Expos were denied the chance after a players' strike forced cancellation of the 1994 playoffs.

The Best 10

Rank	Team	Year	Post	W	L	Pct.	R	RA	BPO	BPOA	TS
1	Seattle Mariners	2001	P	116	46	.716	5.72	3.87	.811	.624	81.959
2	Atlanta Braves	1997	P	101	61	.623	4.88	3.59	.742	.600	78.525
3	Toronto Blue Jays	2015	P	93	69	.574	5.50	4.14	.776	.642	77.296
4	Atlanta Braves	1998	P	106	56	.654	5.10	3.59	.777	.594	77.144
5	Saint Louis Cardinals	2005	P	100	62	.617	4.97	3.91	.726	.643	76.624
6	Montreal Expos	1994	—	74	40	.649	5.13	3.98	.772	.636	75.628
7	Philadelphia Phillies	2011	P	102	60	.630	4.40	3.27	.680	.598	75.484
8	Washington Nationals	2014	P	96	66	.593	4.23	3.43	.675	.572	75.183
9	New York Mets	1988	P	100	60	.625	4.39	3.33	.695	.577	74.761
10	New York Mets	2006	P	97	65	.599	5.15	4.51	.769	.699	74.757

List #9: Worst Team to Qualify for the Playoffs

The 1981 season was an embarrassment, and the postseason surpassed it in absurdity. The complicating factor in both cases was a players' strike that forced the cancellation of more than 700 games between mid-June and early August.

The owners crafted a ridiculous playoff system when action resumed on August 10. They split the season into halves and tacked on an additional set of postseason games, thereby reclaiming revenue lost during the idle summer. Each division's pair of first-place teams would meet in a preliminary round — first half vs. second half — prior to the league championship series.

It was inevitable that an undeserving team would slip through, and Kansas City filled the bill. A modest five-game winning streak in late September and early October was sufficient to capture the second-half American League West crown, making the Royals the only team ever to qualify for the playoffs with a losing record (50-53 for the whole season). Their TS of 44.815 was also the worst for any postseason squad.

Need additional proof of the idiocy of 1981's system? Sixteen franchises posted better team scores than the Royals that year. Yet nine of them missed the playoffs, including the Cardinals (60.148), Reds (59.552), and Rangers (56.719).

The 2005 Padres were nearly as bad as the 1981 Royals, as evidenced by their team score of 45.745, but at least they secured their playoff berth the old-fashioned way. They earned it — sort of — by taking the NL West title with an 82-80 mark.

The Worst 10

Rank	Team	Year	Post	W	L	Pct.	R	RA	BPO	BPOA	TS
1	Kansas City Royals	1981	P	50	53	.485	3.85	3.93	.656	.639	44.815
2	San Diego Padres	2005	P	82	80	.506	4.22	4.48	.691	.689	45.745
3	Kansas City Royals	1984	P	84	78	.519	4.15	4.23	.653	.639	47.973
4	Texas Rangers	2015	P	88	74	.543	4.64	4.52	.706	.703	50.348
5	Minnesota Twins	2009	P	87	76	.534	5.01	4.69	.741	.726	51.137
6	Chicago Cubs	1998	P	90	73	.552	5.10	4.86	.736	.740	51.311
7	Baltimore Orioles	2016	P	89	73	.549	4.59	4.41	.706	.703	51.407
8	Philadelphia Phillies	1981	P	59	48	.551	4.59	4.41	.698	.700	51.460
9	Colorado Rockies	1995	P	77	67	.535	5.45	5.44	.807	.783	51.516
10	Arizona Diamondbacks	2007	P	90	72	.556	4.40	4.52	.706	.715	52.105

List #10: Best Team Not to Qualify for the Playoffs

Montreal and success were mutually exclusive, at least as far as baseball was concerned. The Expos made the playoffs only once in their history, and that was under the two-half system cobbled together after the 1981 players' strike.

But 1994 — the Expos' 26th season — promised to be different. The team was loaded with young talent. Larry Walker (.322 BA, 136.7 BPO+), Moises Alou (.339 BA, 133.0 BPO+), and Marquis Grissom (36 SB) formed the best outfield in the National League. A 22-year-old phenom, Pedro Martinez, was the rising star of the pitching staff.

The Expos caught fire after June 1, winning 46 of 64 games, including four victories over their closest pursuer in the NL East, the Braves. "I remember leaving Atlanta, and we were just laughing," Walker would recall. "Like, 'This is our competition?'"

But Montreal's dream season ended abruptly on August 12. The players' union called another strike, and a stalemate ensued. Commissioner Bud Selig called off the season on September 14. The Expos boasted a record of 74-40 and an impressive team score of 75.628, but they would not play again in 1994. They had the unhappy distinction of being the best team in the Modern Era to miss the playoffs.

Three other strike-haunted franchises from 1994 can be found on the list below. The best non-playoff team to play a full schedule was the 1987 New York Mets (92-70), who finished three games behind the Cardinals in the NL East.

The Best 10

Rank	Team	Year	Post	W	L	Pct.	R	RA	BPO	BPOA	TS
1	Montreal Expos	1994	—	74	40	.649	5.13	3.98	.772	.636	75.628
2	New York Yankees	1994	—	70	43	.619	5.93	4.73	.828	.717	71.457
3	New York Mets	1987	—	92	70	.568	5.08	4.31	.763	.667	71.263
4	New York Yankees	1985	—	97	64	.602	5.21	4.10	.760	.654	70.868
5	Toronto Blue Jays	1987	—	96	66	.593	5.22	4.04	.754	.674	70.746
6	Chicago White Sox	1994	—	67	46	.593	5.60	4.41	.807	.669	70.266
7	San Francisco Giants	1993	—	103	59	.636	4.99	3.93	.735	.638	69.504
8	Detroit Tigers	1961	—	101	61	.623	5.16	4.12	.749	.640	68.177
9	Cleveland Indians	1994	—	66	47	.584	6.01	4.97	.834	.714	67.331
10	Milwaukee Brewers	1992	—	92	70	.568	4.57	3.73	.685	.613	67.284

2. BATTING CAREERS

List #11: Best Batting in a Career

I trust that you read the explanatory section in the front of the book, especially the part about steroids. If you skipped it, please allow me the rare thrill of quoting myself: "My job is simply to bring the numbers. It's up to you to supply the anger."

That's known in the legal business as a disclaimer, a necessary preface to our first discussion of Barry Bonds. You'll see his name with great frequency in these pages, like it or not (and many of you won't). But it remains a fact that, no matter how he did it, Bonds was the most consistently productive batter in the Modern Era.

Only four players posted a BPO+ higher than 200 in any year after 1960. All four were Bonds. Ten batters ran up a BV higher than 230 in a given season. Seven of them were Bonds. He accumulated 9,249 bases during his 22-year career — 870 more than runner-up Rickey Henderson — and he surpassed expectations by 3,847.2 bases. That last figure, Bonds's career BV, is almost 1,500 ahead of the next guy (Henderson again).

That's dominance. There's nothing else to call it.

This list offers an interesting mix of mighty sluggers and speedy line-drive hitters. And then there is Hank Aaron, who was both in one. The pre-Modern Era phase of his career (1954-1960) is not counted below. If it were, Aaron would vault past Henderson with a BV of 2,366.6.

The Best 10

Rank	Batter	Span	G	BA	B	O	BPO	BPO+	BV
1	Barry Bonds	1986-2007	2,986	.298	9,249	7,313	1.265	170.7	3,847.2
2	Rickey Henderson	1979-2003	3,081	.279	8,379	8,510	.985	140.0	2,350.9
3	Frank Thomas	1990-2008	2,322	.301	6,457	6,101	1.058	140.6	1,854.9
4	Albert Pujols	2001-2016	2,426	.309	6,753	6,790	.995	135.5	1,801.4
5	Joe Morgan	1963-1984	2,649	.271	6,703	7,174	.934	136.0	1,775.7
6	Alex Rodriguez	1994-2016	2,784	.295	7,783	7,915	.983	128.5	1,733.9
7	Manny Ramirez	1993-2011	2,302	.312	6,394	6,038	1.059	136.3	1,707.8
8	Jim Thome	1991-2012	2,543	.276	6,577	6,354	1.035	134.3	1,679.8
9	Hank Aaron	1961-1976	2,259	.298	5,915	6,140	.963	139.4	1,674.3
10	Mark McGwire	1986-2001	1,874	.263	5,124	4,797	1.068	146.2	1,648.3

List #12: Worst Batting in a Career

This is a touchy one. We're dealing with players who were good enough to stay in the major leagues for 15 years or more, and yet we're hanging the "worst" tag on them. Not very nice.

It's true that all of the guys on this list were durable. It's also true that their career batting averages were respectable — well, except for Ed Brinkman's — and yet they were somehow lacking at the plate. Don't misunderstand. I'm not equating them with a batter who strikes out four times in his only game in the majors — not at all — but I am saying that they fell far short of expectations.

Take Larry Bowa. He was a fiery presence and a proven winner who batted .260 during his 16 years with the Phillies and Cubs (and a very brief tour with the Mets). But he had absolutely no power at all (just 15 lifetime homers), and he didn't walk very much. A typical batter would have reached 4,778.2 bases under the conditions in which Bowa played, but he fell short by 1.079.2. That's the worst career BV in the Modern Era.

A couple of interesting things about the men on this list: All 10 were shortstops, some of them extremely gifted in the field. And three went on to become managers: Bowa, Ozzie Guillen (the runner-up with a BV of minus-1,036.7), and Don Kessinger. Make of that what you will.

The Worst 10

Rank	Batter	Span	G	BA	B	O	BPO	BPO+	BV
1	Larry Bowa	1970-1985	2,247	.260	3,699	6,647	.556	77.4	-1,079.2
2	Ozzie Guillen	1985-2000	1,993	.264	2,877	5,345	.538	73.7	-1,036.7
3	Neifi Perez	1996-2007	1,403	.267	2,362	4,040	.585	69.7	-1,016.6
4	Tim Foli	1970-1985	1,696	.251	2,478	4,932	.502	71.2	-999.2
5	Alfredo Griffin	1976-1993	1,962	.249	2,903	5,498	.528	74.5	-998.8
6	Don Kessinger	1964-1979	2,078	.252	3,365	6,109	.551	77.2	-990.9
7	Ed Brinkman	1961-1975	1,845	.224	2,437	4,998	.488	72.6	-918.6
8	Royce Clayton	1991-2007	2,108	.258	3,723	5,968	.624	80.9	-876.1
9	Rey Sanchez	1991-2005	1,490	.272	2,070	3,828	.541	70.3	-875.7
10	Omar Vizquel	1989-2012	2,968	.272	5,558	8,433	.659	86.4	-855.5

List #13: Best Run Production in a Career

The other major sports keep track of scoring. Football tallies up the points each player accumulates, ranging from touchdowns to safeties. Basketball does the same with field goals and free throws, as does hockey with goals and assists.

But not baseball. Separate counts are maintained of runs and runs batted in, yet there is no combined measure of scoring.

Until now. This list begins with a stat I call SC, which is calculated by adding R and RBI, then subtracting HR. (A batter who hits a solo home run is credited with both a run scored and a run driven in, even though his team gets the benefit of just a single run on the scoreboard. That's the reason for the subtraction.) Sabermetricians will dismiss SC as a simplistic concept, but I think it's kind of fun, and that's sufficient for me to add it here.

Barry Bonds, as you would expect, is again atop the standings. It's the natural spot for the sport's all-time leader in home runs and the Modern Era's runner-up in both R and RBI. Bonds was directly involved in 3,461 runs, which was 827.4 more than the average player would have generated under similar conditions.

The gap between first and second place is 100.5 runs in scoring value. But the still-active Albert Pujols has surpassed 30 SCV in 12 different seasons, giving him an outside chance of catching Bonds before retirement.

The Best 10

Rank	Batter	Span	G	R	HR	RBI	SC	SE	SE+	SCV
1	Barry Bonds	1986-2007	2,986	2,227	762	1,996	3,461	.275	131.4	827.4
2	Albert Pujols	2001-2016	2,426	1,670	591	1,817	2,896	.274	133.2	726.9
3	Alex Rodriguez	1994-2016	2,784	2,021	696	2,086	3,411	.279	123.0	643.8
4	Hank Aaron	1961-1976	2,259	1,460	536	1,554	2,478	.263	130.7	583.2
5	Frank Robinson	1961-1976	2,073	1,328	421	1,363	2,270	.264	134.2	581.5
6	Dave Winfield	1973-1995	2,973	1,669	465	1,833	3,037	.246	123.0	555.0
7	Jeff Bagwell	1991-2005	2,150	1,517	449	1,529	2,597	.275	126.9	548.6
8	Manny Ramirez	1993-2011	2,302	1,544	555	1,831	2,820	.289	124.0	547.8
9	Miguel Cabrera	2003-2016	2,096	1,321	446	1,553	2,428	.270	127.6	522.3
10	Willie Stargell	1962-1982	2,360	1,194	475	1,540	2,259	.250	126.9	475.3

List #14: Best Power Hitting in a Career

Yes, Barry Bonds again. Who could possibly outrank him on a list of power hitters?

The case for Bonds is ironclad. Start with his 762 home runs, seven more than Hank Aaron's lifetime total and 48 more than Babe Ruth's. (Take a deep breath, and reread my disclaimer about steroids.) Then consider his 1,440 extra-base hits, 5,976 total bases, and .607 slugging percentage, the Modern Era's best performances in all three categories.

If any doubt remains, look at EXV, a comparison of the extra bases that a batter might have been expected to reach and the number he actually attained. (A quick note: Extra bases are not the same as extra-base hits. The former are all bases beyond first base — one for a double, two for a triple, three for a home run.)

Bonds spent his entire 22-year career in ballparks that weren't easy on power hitters: Three Rivers Stadium in Pittsburgh, Candlestick Park and the newer facility with a thousand different names in San Francisco. Yet he accumulated an EXV surplus of 1,536.3, which is nothing short of amazing.

Mark McGwire was called up to the majors in 1986, the same year as Bonds, and actually held the edge in career homers after 16 seasons, 583 to 567. But McGwire retired in 2001, and Bonds kept blasting away for another six years. Hence the latter's lead of almost 435 EXV.

The Best 10

Rank	Batter	Span	G	2B	3B	HR	ISO	ISO+	EXV
1	Barry Bonds	1986-2007	2,986	601	77	762	.309	200.4	1,536.3
2	Mark McGwire	1986-2001	1,874	252	6	583	.325	218.7	1,101.9
3	Mike Schmidt	1972-1989	2,404	408	59	548	.260	188.1	1,009.3
4	Hank Aaron	1961-1976	2,259	399	41	536	.253	189.0	986.2
5	Reggie Jackson	1967-1987	2,820	463	49	563	.228	178.9	978.5
6	Albert Pujols	2001-2016	2,426	602	16	591	.263	165.7	956.7
7	Jim Thome	1991-2012	2,543	451	26	612	.278	165.1	922.4
8	Willie Stargell	1962-1982	2,360	423	55	475	.247	188.0	916.2
9	Alex Rodriguez	1994-2016	2,784	548	31	696	.255	151.0	910.8
10	Sammy Sosa	1989-2007	2,354	379	45	609	.261	160.9	886.4

List #15: Best Contact Hitting in a Career

Tony Gwynn's skill was evident from the start. He lined a pair of hits for the Padres in his 1982 big-league debut. The opposing first baseman was Pete Rose of the Phillies. "I thought, boy, wouldn't it be great to have a career like his, to be able to do some of the things that he was able to do," Gwynn recalled.

That, of course, is exactly what he did. Gwynn couldn't match Rose's 4,256 hits — nobody ever has — but he did qualify for the elite 3,000-hit club (with 141 to spare) while batting .338, the best career BA in the Modern Era. "There isn't a pitcher in the league who wants Tony Gwynn up with a runner on third base," said one of his hitting coaches, Deacon Jones. "You know he'll make contact."

He was right about that. Gwynn whiffed just 434 times in 20 years. His worst single-season strikeout total was 40 in 1988. That's a normal month for some present-day sluggers.

My calculations suggest that a typical San Diego player would have struck out 1,538.7 times between 1982 and 2001. Gwynn, the era's greatest contact hitter, did dramatically better than that, as confirmed by his negative strikeout value (SOV) of 1,104.7.

The 10 men on this list registered nearly four times as many hits (28,108) as strikeouts (7,455). They batted .298 as a group, striking out just once every 12.7 at bats.

The Best 10

Rank	Batter	Span	G	AB	H	SO	CT	CT+	SOV
1	Tony Gwynn	1982-2001	2,440	9,288	3,141	434	.953	385.7	-1,104.7
2	Juan Pierre	2000-2013	1,994	7,525	2,217	479	.936	303.3	-928.8
3	Bill Buckner	1969-1990	2,517	9,397	2,715	453	.952	313.8	-875.7
4	Pete Rose	1963-1986	3,562	14,053	4,256	1,143	.919	188.9	-850.4
5	Ichiro Suzuki	2001-2016	2,500	9,689	3,030	1,037	.893	184.3	-827.4
6	Placido Polanco	1998-2013	1,927	7,214	2,142	538	.925	255.4	-795.7
7	Ozzie Smith	1978-1996	2,573	9,396	2,460	589	.937	248.0	-782.5
8	Omar Vizquel	1989-2012	2,968	10,586	2,877	1,087	.897	172.6	-749.7
9	Albert Pujols	2001-2016	2,426	9,138	2,825	1,053	.885	170.2	-715.0
10	Mark Grace	1988-2003	2,245	8,065	2,445	642	.920	219.2	-713.4

List #16: Best Batting Eye in a Career

Rickey Henderson was able to drive almost any pitch that passed over the plate. That's why he finished his career with 3,055 hits. But he was equally able to lay off anything just a touch too high or a couple of inches outside. That's why he was such an effective leadoff hitter for more than two decades.

Superior discipline and a keen batting eye enabled Henderson to draw more than 100 walks in seven seasons, leading the American League in that category four times. His mantra was simple. "Learn the strike zone," he told anybody who asked. "What is your strike zone? Stay inside your strike zone."

It was easier said than done. Barry Bonds is the only batter in baseball history to be credited with a greater number of bases on balls than Henderson, but that's only if intentional walks are included. Here are the lifetime totals for unintentional walks only: Henderson 2,129, Bonds 1,870.

Henderson's career could best be described as peripatetic. He played for nine different franchises, including four stretches in Oakland alone. If an average player had followed this nomadic path from 1979 to 2003, he would have drawn 1,084.3 unintentional walks. Henderson nearly doubled that total, giving him an astronomical BBV of 1,044.7.

Runner-up Joe Morgan finished slightly more than 120 BBV behind the leader. Morgan coaxed more walks than strikeouts in every season but the first two of his 22-year career. He drew at least 100 walks eight different times.

The Best 10

Rank	Batter	Span	G	AB	H	UBB	EY	EY+	BBV
1	Rickey Henderson	1979-2003	3,081	10,961	3,055	2,129	.160	197.0	1,044.7
2	Joe Morgan	1963-1984	2,649	9,277	2,517	1,789	.159	206.9	923.1
3	Barry Bonds	1986-2007	2,986	9,847	2,935	1,870	.157	190.5	887.2
4	Jim Thome	1991-2012	2,543	8,422	2,328	1,574	.155	179.6	697.9
5	Frank Thomas	1990-2008	2,322	8,199	2,468	1,499	.151	179.0	658.6
6	Darrell Evans	1969-1989	2,687	8,973	2,223	1,464	.138	172.9	618.9
7	Jim Wynn	1963-1977	1,920	6,653	1,665	1,140	.144	189.9	545.2
8	Jason Giambi	1995-2014	2,260	7,267	2,010	1,269	.144	175.5	540.2
9	Harmon Killebrew	1961-1975	2,045	6,905	1,775	1,219	.148	177.3	530.4
10	Mark McGwire	1986-2001	1,874	6,187	1,626	1,167	.155	181.4	526.2

3. PITCHING CAREERS

List #17: Best Pitching in a Career

Who could have doubted that Roger Clemens was destined for stardom? He earned All-American honors as a pitcher at the University of Texas, was snapped up in the first round of the 1983 amateur draft, and vaulted through the minor leagues in less than a year. He made it all look easy.

But things changed when Clemens was called up to Boston. The Red Sox lost nine of his first 13 starts in 1984, while his ERA hovered in the vicinity of 6.00. A trip back to the minors seemed imminent as he took the mound against the White Sox on July 26.

It proved to be his turning point. Clemens struck out 11 Chicago batters that night and coasted to a 7-0 complete-game victory. The Red Sox went on to win his next eight starts, launching a glorious 24-year career that brought him seven Cy Young Awards (the most for any pitcher ever) and the 1986 American League Most Valuable Player trophy. Clemens established himself as the best pitcher of the Modern Era, yielding 1,782.8 fewer bases than an average pitcher would have allowed under identical circumstances. His BV total is more than 300 bases better than anybody else's.

Clemens, of course, was dogged in his later years by allegations of steroid abuse, which have effectively prevented his elevation to the Hall of Fame. The three runners-up on this list — Greg Maddux, Pedro Martinez, and Randy Johnson — have already been enshrined in Cooperstown.

The Best 10

Rank	Pitcher	Span	G	ERA	B	O	BPO	BPO+	BV
1	Roger Clemens	1984-2007	709	3.12	8,645	14,856	.582	82.9	-1,782.8
2	Greg Maddux	1986-2008	744	3.16	8,846	15,149	.584	85.7	-1,481.1
3	Pedro Martinez	1992-2009	476	2.93	4,737	8,489	.558	79.6	-1,234.6
4	Randy Johnson	1988-2009	618	3.29	7,718	12,509	.617	87.7	-1,133.5
5	Curt Schilling	1988-2007	569	3.46	5,838	9,792	.596	85.4	-1,012.2
6	Kevin Brown	1986-2005	486	3.28	5,681	9,864	.576	85.1	-993.9
7	John Smoltz	1988-2009	723	3.33	6,152	10,475	.587	86.4	-979.7
8	Gaylord Perry	1962-1983	777	3.11	9,178	16,192	.567	90.6	-938.9
9	Tom Seaver	1967-1986	656	2.86	8,199	14,410	.569	89.8	-917.3
10	Mariano Rivera	1995-2013	1,115	2.21	1,835	3,881	.473	67.7	-877.8

List #18: Worst Pitching in a Career

Bobby Witt could bring the heat, that's for sure. His fastball could intimidate the hardiest of big-league hitters, often zipping close to 100 miles per hour. He rang up 174 strikeouts in just 158 innings during his rookie season with the Rangers in 1986.

The problem was that Witt didn't always know where the ball was headed. He dished out 143 walks that same year, the worst total in the American League, and he compounded his difficulties with 22 wild pitches, also a league-leading sum. "I wasn't going to finesse you," he laughed years later. "My thought process was to go out there and let it go."

Witt improved his control as the years rolled along — he would play 16 seasons with seven different teams — but he never attained precision. He averaged 5.0 walks per nine innings during his career, topping the AL three times in walks and twice in wild pitches. He surrendered 5,717 bases in all, exceeding the expected total by 573.8. That's the worst lifetime BV for any pitcher in the Modern Era.

Nine men on this list amassed career BVs of 400 or more. It took more than 360 games for eight of them to reach that level. The exception was Kevin Jarvis, who rang up a BV of 400.8 in just 187 appearances for 10 teams. His career BPO+ of 124.5 was 24.5 percent worse than average.

The Worst 10

Rank	Pitcher	Span	G	ERA	B	O	BPO	BPO+	BV
1	Bobby Witt	1986-2001	430	4.83	5,717	7,414	.771	111.0	573.8
2	Livan Hernandez	1996-2012	519	4.44	7,013	9,546	.735	107.4	473.7
3	Jim Slaton	1971-1986	496	4.03	5,603	8,068	.694	108.8	446.7
4	Jeff Suppan	1995-2012	448	4.70	5,864	7,661	.765	108.2	432.4
5	Steve Trachsel	1993-2008	420	4.39	5,676	7,512	.756	108.2	428.9
6	Tom Griffin	1969-1982	401	4.07	3,229	4,521	.714	115.2	427.2
7	Edwin Jackson	2003-2016	361	4.65	3,879	5,171	.750	112.3	417.7
8	Kevin Gross	1983-1997	474	4.11	5,328	7,485	.712	108.4	413.9
9	Kevin Jarvis	1994-2006	187	6.03	2,052	2,351	.873	124.5	400.8
10	Jose Lima	1994-2006	348	5.26	3,699	4,708	.786	111.8	392.4

List #19: Best Run Prevention in a Career

Roger Clemens won 354 games during his career, the ninth-best total for any pitcher throughout the 140 years that big-league ball has been played. He threw hard for 24 years, and he proved to be uncannily consistent at preventing the other team from scoring.

Clemens posted the best earned run average in his league seven times — six years in the AL, one in the NL. He was a youthful 23 on the first occasion, spinning a 2.48 ERA for the Red Sox in 1986. And he was an ancient (yet indestructible) 42 the final time he led the pack, dealing an amazing 1.87 ERA for the Astros in 2005.

The Rocket posted 12 sub-3.00 ERAs during his 24 seasons. It's an impressive number, though not the ideal measure of success. ERA+ and ERV offer a more precise indication of a pitcher's performance under varying conditions, and Clemens excelled in both. He kept his ERA+ below 100 — hence superior to the leaguewide norm — in 20 seasons. And his career ERV was minus-605, which means he allowed 605 fewer earned runs than a typical pitcher would have.

Greg Maddux, a contemporary of Clemens, is the runner-up on this list with an ERV of minus-442.3. The stats for these two aces were remarkably similar, though their styles were not. Maddux was four inches shorter and at least 30 pounds lighter than Clemens, and he relied on subtlety and control, not power and ferocity.

The Best 10

Rank	Pitcher	Span	G	IP	SO	BB	ERA	ERA+	ERV
1	Roger Clemens	1984-2007	709	4,916.2	4,672	1,580	3.12	73.6	-605.0
2	Greg Maddux	1986-2008	744	5,008.1	3,371	999	3.16	80.0	-442.3
3	Randy Johnson	1988-2009	618	4,135.1	4,875	1,497	3.29	79.0	-423.1
4	Pedro Martinez	1992-2009	476	2,827.1	3,154	760	2.93	69.7	-415.5
5	Tom Seaver	1967-1986	656	4,783.0	3,640	1,390	2.86	81.1	-346.8
6	Bob Gibson	1961-1975	488	3,722.0	3,000	1,249	2.84	79.4	-296.8
7	Mariano Rivera	1995-2013	1,115	1,283.2	1,173	286	2.21	51.6	-292.9
8	Jim Palmer	1965-1984	558	3,948.0	2,212	1,311	2.86	82.3	-265.1
9	Curt Schilling	1988-2007	569	3,261.0	3,116	711	3.46	83.7	-250.2
10	Bert Blyleven	1970-1992	692	4,970.0	3,701	1,322	3.31	88.1	-244.3

List #20: Best Power Prevention in a Career

A different list, yet a familiar outcome.

We've already seen Roger Clemens and Greg Maddux occupying the top two positions in the rankings for best pitching and best run prevention. Here they hold first and second place respectively in power prevention.

How difficult was it to hit for extra bases against this dynamic duo? They faced virtually the same number of batters — 20,240 for Clemens, 20,421 for Maddux — and were similarly stingy with the long ball. Clemens allowed just 363 home runs, Maddux 353. Those totals compare favorably with the sums for several recent Hall of Famers, including Fergie Jenkins (484 homers allowed), Phil Niekro (482), Don Sutton (472), Bert Blyleven (430), Steve Carlton (414), and Randy Johnson (411).

This list is based on EXV, the difference between the extra bases yielded by a pitcher and the number a typical pitcher would have been expected to allow. (Extra bases are those beyond first base. A double is worth one extra base, a triple two, and a home run three.) Clemens gave up 2,053 extra bases in 24 years, which was 696.3 below the norm for those seasons. Maddux was a strong runner-up with an EXV of minus-606.8.

Nine of the men on this list were starters. Mariano Rivera was the exception. The Yankee reliever faced just 5,103 batters — 514th in the Modern Era in that category — yet he was so dominant that he was able to finish ninth in EXV.

The Best 10

Rank	Pitcher	Span	G	2B	3B	HR	ISO	ISO+	EXV
1	Roger Clemens	1984-2007	709	796	84	363	.112	74.7	-696.3
2	Greg Maddux	1986-2008	744	817	84	353	.108	76.8	-606.8
3	Kevin Brown	1986-2005	486	493	53	208	.099	71.8	-470.7
4	Roy Halladay	1998-2013	416	471	45	236	.121	78.7	-347.0
5	Tommy John	1963-1989	760	699	117	302	.102	84.7	-336.8
6	Nolan Ryan	1966-1993	807	649	106	321	.095	84.9	-335.9
7	Bob Gibson	1961-1975	488	424	81	246	.096	79.8	-334.4
8	Tom Glavine	1987-2008	682	786	76	356	.120	85.9	-332.5
9	Mariano Rivera	1995-2013	1,115	141	15	71	.081	54.1	-328.7
10	Tim Hudson	1999-2015	482	503	71	248	.118	81.6	-324.6

List #21: Best Power Pitching in a Career

Nolan Ryan is the logical candidate to top this list. He is, after all, the major-league leader with 5,714 strikeouts in 27 seasons with the Mets, Angels, Astros, and Rangers — 839 more than the runner-up, Randy Johnson. Ryan also holds the Modern Era's single-season record with 383 whiffs in 1973. He led the American League in strikeouts nine times and the National League twice.

So much for his resumé. What most players and fans remember about Nolan Ryan was his frightening velocity. "He's faster than instant coffee," said Reggie Jackson, who suffered 22 Ryan strikeouts in his career. Mickey Stanley once returned to the dugout after enduring the same fate. "Those were the best pitches I ever heard," he said.

Something called a "coherent infrared radar" tracked one of Ryan's pitches in 1974 at 100.8 miles per hour, unusually fast for any era. But the radar took its reading 10 feet in front of home plate. Experts estimated that the peak speed for the same delivery was closer to 108 mph, which would make it the fastest pitch ever recorded.

A typical pitcher, playing in the same ballparks and seasons as Ryan, would have registered 3,070.2 strikeouts. He surpassed that figure by 2,643.8, shown below as his SOV. It's fitting that the number-two man in the all-time strikeout standings also holds second place here. Randy Johnson, a/k/a the Big Unit, posted an SOV of 2,024.4.

The Best 10

Rank	Pitcher	Span	G	IP	H	SO	CT	CT+	SOV
1	Nolan Ryan	1966-1993	807	5,386.0	3,923	5,714	.703	54.7	2,643.8
2	Randy Johnson	1988-2009	618	4,135.1	3,346	4,875	.678	60.6	2,024.4
3	Roger Clemens	1984-2007	709	4,916.2	4,185	4,672	.744	70.2	1,428.5
4	Pedro Martinez	1992-2009	476	2,827.1	2,221	3,154	.695	64.4	1,189.6
5	Steve Carlton	1965-1988	741	5,217.2	4,672	4,136	.787	79.3	963.7
6	Sam McDowell	1961-1975	425	2,492.1	1,948	2,453	.729	64.7	892.3
7	Bert Blyleven	1970-1992	692	4,970.0	4,632	3,701	.802	80.3	801.0
8	Tom Seaver	1967-1986	656	4,783.0	3,971	3,640	.793	82.1	792.0
9	David Cone	1986-2003	450	2,898.2	2,504	2,668	.753	73.2	759.7
10	Bob Gibson	1961-1975	488	3,722.0	3,105	3,000	.782	77.2	722.3

List #22: Best Control Pitching in a Career

Greg Maddux wasn't imposing on the mound. He didn't loom above hitters like six-foot-10 Randy Johnson or come after them with the blazing speed of Nolan Ryan. The six-foot, 170-pound, bespectacled Maddux subdued them with the best control exhibited by any pitcher in the Modern Era.

"He can hit a target like no pitcher I've ever seen," said Leo Mazzone, who was Maddux's pitching coach for 11 seasons in Atlanta, where an additional pair of Hall of Famers, Tom Glavine and John Smoltz, worked at the same time. Maddux was the acknowledged ace of that staff, known as "The Professor" for his cerebral approach to pitching and his ability to put the ball precisely where he wanted.

The bottom line for Maddux's 23-year career shows 822 unintentional walks in 740 starts and four relief appearances, which equaled a paltry 1.48 bases on balls per nine innings. The typical pitcher would have walked 1,530.9 batters under the same circumstances, 708.9 more than Maddux did. That disparity is reflected as a BBV of minus-708.9, the best for anybody who has pitched in the majors since 1961.

Jim Kaat and David Wells are second and third on this list, more than 200 bases behind Maddux in the BBV column. Both men pitched for a couple of decades, and both were known for efficiency and control, allowing fewer than 1.90 unintentional walks per nine innings over their careers.

The Best 10

Rank	Pitcher	Span	G	IP	H	UBB	EY	EY+	BBV
1	Greg Maddux	1986-2008	744	5,008.1	4,726	822	.041	54.5	-708.9
2	Jim Kaat	1961-1983	882	4,475.1	4,565	934	.050	65.0	-491.8
3	David Wells	1987-2007	660	3,439.0	3,635	654	.046	57.9	-472.3
4	Fergie Jenkins	1965-1983	664	4,500.2	4,142	881	.048	67.2	-450.1
5	Dennis Eckersley	1975-1998	1,071	3,285.2	3,076	647	.048	61.4	-405.3
6	Brad Radke	1995-2006	378	2,451.0	2,643	433	.042	52.8	-376.9
7	Mike Mussina	1991-2008	537	3,562.2	3,460	756	.052	67.6	-366.2
8	Curt Schilling	1988-2007	569	3,261.0	2,998	668	.050	65.6	-356.5
9	Bret Saberhagen	1984-2001	399	2,562.2	2,452	437	.042	55.2	-355.6
10	Jon Lieber	1994-2008	401	2,198.0	2,388	370	.040	51.1	-350.9

4. BATTING SEASONS

List #23: Best Batting in a Season

Barry Bonds went on an unprecedented tear as the 21st century began, posting a BPO+ above 200 each year from 2001 to 2004. No other batter in the Modern Era has enjoyed a single season above 199.

Here are the collective stats for Bonds's four-year reign of terror for the San Francisco Giants: 209 homers, 438 RBIs, 2,164 bases, a BA of .349, a BPO of 1.958, and four Most Valuable Player Awards. It is difficult to imagine any batter achieving such exalted numbers over such an extensive period in the future.

Bonds had long been an outstanding player. He was named MVP three times in the early 1990s — twice with Pittsburgh, once with San Francisco — but reporters wondered about his sudden shift into overdrive. "Some things I can't understand right now," Bonds told them. "The balls I used to line off the wall, I'm lining out (of the park). I can't tell you why. Call God. Ask Him." Cynics suggested that a call to his pharmacist would have been more appropriate.

Bonds blasted a career-high 73 home runs in 2001, followed by his ultimate batting average (.370) a year later. But his best season — indeed, the best for anybody in the Modern Era — came in 2004, the summer he turned 40. Bonds reached base 376 times in 617 appearances that year. His OBP of .609 was the highest in baseball history, and his BPO+ of 284.5 climbed to the top of this list.

The Best 10

Rank	Batter	Year	Team	G	BA	B	O	BPO	BV	BPO+
1	Barry Bonds	2004	Giants	147	.362	553	247	2.239	358.6	284.5
2	Barry Bonds	2002	Giants	143	.370	540	262	2.061	348.6	282.2
3	Barry Bonds	2001	Giants	153	.328	612	330	1.855	365.5	248.3
4	Barry Bonds	2003	Giants	130	.341	459	266	1.726	255.7	225.8
5	Mark McGwire	1998	Cardinals	155	.299	556	369	1.507	276.5	199.0
6	Barry Bonds	1992	Pirates	140	.311	473	350	1.351	230.5	195.1
7	Mickey Mantle	1962	Yankees	123	.321	362	262	1.382	175.0	193.6
8	Joe Morgan	1976	Reds	141	.320	459	344	1.334	221.8	193.5
9	Jeff Bagwell	1994	Astros	110	.368	394	279	1.412	187.9	191.2
10	Mickey Mantle	1961	Yankees	153	.317	497	360	1.381	236.8	191.0

List #24: Worst Batting in a Season

Scouting reports predicted that Matt Walbeck would be a dependable big-league hitter, and his record in the minors buttressed the point. Walbeck batted .301 at the AA level in 1992 and a solid .281 when he climbed to AAA a year later. The Minnesota Twins had high expectations when they named him their regular catcher in 1994.

They were quickly disappointed. Walbeck batted just .198 in April, struggled to boost his average to .232 by June 10, then entered a two-month slump that lasted until a players' strike ended the season in August. Walbeck got only 27 hits in his final 157 at bats (.172), dropping his overall BA to .204.

His ineffectiveness at the plate was compounded by the fact that he rarely drew walks (just 17 all year) and was slow on the basepaths. His resulting BPO+ of 54.4 is the lowest single-season mark for any batter who met qualification standards during the Modern Era.

Walbeck stuck around the majors for another nine years. He improved a bit at the plate, posting a BPO+ as high as 81.4, though he didn't become the solid hitter the scouts had envisioned. Hal Lanier, on the other hand, never really got better. He played the infield for 10 years, mostly for the Giants, and registered a BPO+ below 70 in nine of those seasons. Three can be found on this list.

The Worst 10

Rank	Batter	Year	Team	G	BA	B	O	BPO	BV	BPO+
1	Matt Walbeck	1994	Twins	97	.204	118	279	.423	-98.8	54.4
2	Tommy Helms	1970	Reds	150	.237	194	468	.415	-154.0	55.8
3	Hal Lanier	1967	Giants	151	.213	168	446	.377	-126.0	57.1
4	Hal Lanier	1968	Giants	151	.206	150	425	.353	-108.0	58.1
5	Neifi Perez	2002	Royals	145	.236	207	454	.456	-147.7	58.4
5	Hal Lanier	1969	Giants	150	.228	166	416	.399	-118.2	58.4
7	Marty Perez	1972	Braves	141	.228	166	400	.415	-116.4	58.8
8	Mike Caruso	1999	White Sox	136	.250	204	429	.476	-139.2	59.4
9	Alfredo Griffin	1990	Dodgers	141	.210	164	382	.429	-108.1	60.3
10	Rey Ordonez	1996	Mets	151	.257	181	393	.461	-114.2	61.3

List #25: Best Run Production in a Season

Most batters are overjoyed when a hot streak lasts for a month or two, perhaps an entire year if they're especially fortunate. Jeff Bagwell's hot streak with the Houston Astros persisted for a dozen seasons. He posted a BPO+ above 120 every year from 1991 to 2002.

But one season always stood above the rest — 1994. "Crazy stuff happened that year," he recalled. "Every pitch that I was looking for, I got. And when I got it, I didn't miss it. It was ridiculous." Bagwell hit 39 homers, scored 104 runs, drove in 116 more, and batted .368 in 110 games during that strike-shortened season. His BPO+ of 191.2 was the ninth-best in the Modern Era — and the fourth-best for anybody not named Barry Bonds.

Bagwell was directly responsible for 181 runs in 1994, based on the SC formula of R + RBI - HR. That was 79 percent better than a typical batter's output under the same circumstances. Bagwell's 179.0 still ranks as the best single-season SE+ during the Modern Era.

Runner-up Tommy Davis was not a slugger of Bagwell's caliber — he would hit only 153 homers in 18 seasons — but he was nearly as reliable at run production. Davis drove in 153 runs for the Dodgers in 1962, an astounding total for a man who was largely a singles hitter. He finished that year with an SE+ of 170.7.

The Best 10

Rank	Batter	Year	Team	G	R	HR	RBI	SC	SE	SCV	SE+
1	Jeff Bagwell	1994	Astros	110	104	39	116	181	.378	79.9	179.0
2	Tommy Davis	1962	Dodgers	163	120	27	153	246	.346	101.9	170.7
3	George Brett	1980	Royals	117	87	24	118	181	.351	72.7	167.1
4	Joe Morgan	1976	Reds	141	113	27	111	197	.329	76.4	163.4
5	Sammy Sosa	2001	Cubs	160	146	64	160	242	.340	90.5	159.8
6	Manny Ramirez	1999	Indians	147	131	44	165	252	.394	94.0	159.5
7	Roberto Clemente	1967	Pirates	147	103	23	110	190	.301	68.6	156.5
8	Mike Schmidt	1981	Phillies	102	78	31	91	138	.318	49.6	156.0
9	Reggie Jackson	1973	Athletics	151	99	32	117	184	.293	66.0	155.9
10	Mickey Mantle	1961	Yankees	153	131	54	128	205	.317	73.1	155.9

List #26: Worst Run Production in a Season

Marty Perez generally batted eighth for the Braves in 1972, so he clearly wasn't a key component of Atlanta's attack. Minimal expectations were placed on Perez, a career .225 hitter to that point. Manager Lum Harris wanted him to get aboard when possible, steal an occasional base, move runners along with timely bunts, and generally stay out of trouble.

Perez couldn't do any of it. His on-base percentage of .276 was the worst in the National League. He didn't steal a base all year, he laid down only three sacrifices, and he led the league by grounding into 21 double plays. The latter nearly equaled his 28 RBIs, indicating that he was almost as effective at wiping out his team's runners as in batting them home.

An average hitter who played 141 games for Atlanta in 1972 would have been directly involved in 108.1 runs, either by crossing the plate or driving in a teammate. Perez's total of 60 in the SC column fell 44.5 percent below that benchmark, leaving him with an adjusted scoring efficiency rate (SE+) of 55.5, the worst mark in the Modern Era.

Skill with the glove kept Perez in the majors for 10 years, and he gradually boosted his career batting average to .246. Another middle infielder who enjoyed a long career, Walt Weiss, is second on this list. He drove in only 25 runs in 1995, pushing his SE+ down to 58.4.

The Worst 10

Rank	Batter	Year	Team	G	R	HR	RBI	SC	SE	SCV	SE+
1	Marty Perez	1972	Braves	141	33	1	28	60	.116	-48.1	55.5
2	Walt Weiss	1995	Rockies	137	65	1	25	89	.166	-63.5	58.4
3	Jim Piersall	1962	Senators	135	38	4	31	65	.126	-42.7	60.3
4	Manny Trillo	1985	Giants	125	36	3	25	58	.115	-38.0	60.4
5	Alfredo Griffin	1981	Blue Jays	101	30	0	21	51	.123	-33.3	60.5
6	Adeiny Hechavarria	2013	Marlins	148	30	3	42	69	.119	-44.2	60.9
7	Denny Doyle	1972	Phillies	123	33	1	26	58	.120	-37.1	61.0
8	Mario Guerrero	1978	Athletics	143	27	3	38	62	.114	-39.5	61.1
9	Leo Cardenas	1972	Angels	150	25	6	42	61	.101	-38.0	61.6
10	Felix Fermin	1989	Indians	156	50	0	21	71	.126	-43.8	61.8

List #27: Best Power Hitting in a Season

Barry Bonds launched 73 home runs in 2001, setting a record that millions of fans refuse to acknowledge. Some of today's players are among the naysayers. Among them is Baltimore's Chris Davis, who confessed in 2013 that he harbored his own dreams of becoming the home-run king.

Do you really believe, reporters asked, that you can hit more than 73 homers in a season? No, said Davis, he was aiming for 61, the mark set by Roger Maris in 1961. It didn't matter that Mark McGwire had blasted 70 home runs in 1998, or that Bonds had followed with 73 three years later. Davis insisted that Maris remained the true record-holder. "The reason being," the Orioles slugger said, "he was the last guy to do it clean."

Davis's attention was subsequently diverted by his own suspension for amphetamine abuse. And Bonds, like it or not, is still atop the single-season home-run rankings, just as he holds first place on this list. His adjusted isolated power average (ISO+) in 2001 was a breathtaking 314.6, which means he was 214.6 percent better than the typical player at piling up extra bases with his hits.

Here's a second way to look at this unprecedented display of power: Bonds garnered 255 extra bases in 2001, counting one per double, two per triple, and three per homer. How many would an average batter have reached under the same circumstances? Less than one-third of Bonds's output — just 81.1 extra bases, all told.

The Best 10

Rank	Batter	Year	Team	G	2B	3B	HR	ISO	EXV	ISO+
1	Barry Bonds	2001	Giants	153	32	2	73	.536	173.9	314.6
2	Mark McGwire	1998	Cardinals	155	21	0	70	.454	149.0	281.9
3	Barry Bonds	2002	Giants	143	31	2	46	.429	110.4	276.5
4	Kevin Mitchell	1989	Giants	154	34	6	47	.344	117.0	267.2
5	Hank Aaron	1971	Braves	139	22	3	47	.341	105.2	264.8
6	Reggie Jackson	1969	Athletics	152	36	3	47	.333	113.1	261.9
7	Mike Schmidt	1981	Phillies	102	19	2	31	.328	71.3	259.5
8	Barry Bonds	2004	Giants	147	27	3	45	.450	102.5	256.3
9	Willie McCovey	1969	Giants	149	26	2	45	.336	100.6	256.0
10	Mickey Mantle	1961	Yankees	153	16	6	54	.370	115.8	255.9

List #28: Worst Power Hitting in a Season

Hal Lanier was an aggressive manager for the Houston Astros in the late 1980s. He believed in bunting, stealing, and taking the extra base whenever possible. "I like to put people in motion and make the defense come up with a lot of mistakes," he once said.

It was precisely the approach that Lanier's old teammates with the Giants and Yankees would have expected. If he had chosen to rely on the long ball instead, they would have been flabbergasted.

That's because Lanier was the very antithesis of a power hitter. He appeared at the plate 3,940 times during his 10-year career, yet he managed to hit only eight home runs. His career slugging percentage was .275 — a respectable number for a batting average, but truly abysmal for SLG.

Lanier reached the pinnacle of powerlessness with the Giants in 1969, posting the worst ISO+ (16.9) of the Modern Era. A typical batter who played 150 games for San Francisco would have reached 65 extra bases that season. Lanier's grand total was 11 — a pair with his sole triple of the year, the other nine on as many doubles.

This list is dominated by weak-hitting infielders whose glove skills kept them in the majors. The runner-up, Sandy Alomar, is best known not for his own career, but as the father of a second baseman who lined 210 home runs and batted exactly .300 over 17 seasons, Hall of Famer Roberto Alomar.

The Worst 10

Rank	Batter	Year	Team	G	2B	3B	HR	ISO	EXV	ISO+
1	Hal Lanier	1969	Giants	150	9	1	0	.022	-54.0	16.9
2	Sandy Alomar	1973	Angels	136	7	1	0	.019	-43.8	17.1
3	Felix Fermin	1989	Indians	156	9	1	0	.023	-47.7	18.7
4	Don Kessinger	1966	Cubs	150	8	2	1	.028	-62.3	19.4
5	Horace Clarke	1968	Yankees	148	6	1	2	.024	-55.8	20.1
6	Elvis Andrus	2010	Rangers	148	15	3	0	.036	-78.0	21.2
7	Curt Wilkerson	1984	Rangers	153	12	0	1	.031	-52.9	22.1
8	Otis Nixon	1996	Blue Jays	125	15	1	1	.040	-68.7	22.5
9	Enzo Hernandez	1971	Padres	143	9	3	0	.027	-51.1	22.7
9	Jerry Remy	1981	Red Sox	88	9	1	0	.031	-37.5	22.7

List #29: Best Contact Hitting in a Season

Dave Cash would play a key role in the Phillies' transformation from losers to winners in the mid-1970s, but he initially had his doubts. The Pirates traded Cash to Philadelphia in October 1973. His new club had been mired below .500 for six straight seasons. "It was tough going from a first-place team, a team that was in the race every year, to a last-place team," he said.

But Cash evolved into the Phillies' emotional spark plug. "Yes, we can!" he shouted after a doubleheader sweep of the Expos in May 1974. The team adopted his impromptu exclamation as its rallying cry, climbing to third place that year, second place the next, and its first National League East title in 1976.

Cash was the Phillies' leadoff man. It was the ideal slot for his blend of speed and an uncanny ability to make contact. An average batter would have suffered 88.3 strikeouts in Cash's circumstances in 1976, but he was 6.8 times better than that, tallying just 13 whiffs in 666 at bats. His adjusted contact rate was an astronomical 679.4, the best mark in the Modern Era.

Nellie Fox was a renowned contact hitter who had reached the tail-end of his career by 1961, but he still produced three of the 10 performances on this list. Fox struck out 216 times in his entire 19-year career — seven times fewer than Mark Reynolds's single-season record of 223 strikeouts in 2009.

The Best 10

Rank	Batter	Year	Team	G	AB	H	SO	CT	SOV	CT+
1	Dave Cash	1976	Phillies	160	666	189	13	.980	-75.3	679.4
2	Nellie Fox	1962	White Sox	157	621	166	12	.981	-67.6	663.2
3	Nellie Fox	1961	White Sox	159	606	152	12	.980	-66.9	657.2
4	Tony Gwynn	1995	Padres	135	535	197	15	.972	-78.4	622.5
5	Matty Alou	1970	Pirates	155	677	201	18	.973	-85.7	576.1
6	Felix Fermin	1993	Indians	140	480	126	14	.971	-62.9	549.6
7	Tony Gwynn	1992	Padres	128	520	165	16	.969	-64.7	504.3
8	Nellie Fox	1964	Colt .45s	133	442	117	13	.971	-51.6	496.5
9	Tim Foli	1979	Mets-Pirates	136	532	153	14	.974	-54.9	492.0
10	Ozzie Smith	1993	Cardinals	141	545	157	18	.967	-68.7	481.6

List #30: Worst Contact Hitting in a Season

Nellie Fox and Dave Nicholson wore the same uniform in 1963, but that was one of the few characteristics they shared.

The 35-year-old Fox was a legend in Chicago, where he was playing his 14th (and final) season as a second baseman for the White Sox. He was a magician at the plate, choking up on his distinctive bottle bat and deftly putting the ball in play. The future Hall of Famer struck out only 17 times all year.

Nicholson, a 23-year-old left fielder, was incredibly strong — the longest home run of his career would soar an estimated 573 feet — but he was also a wild, undisciplined swinger. He set a big-league record in 1963 with 175 strikeouts, shattering the previous mark of 142. His CT+ of 36.1 was 63.9 percent below normal, the worst adjusted contact rate of the Modern Era.

And one more set of contrasts: Fox played an entire month in 1963 — late June to late July — without a single strikeout, and he didn't whiff more than once in any game the entire year. Nicholson rang up four strikeouts in three different games, and three strikeouts another 15 times.

The name that occurs most frequently on this list is that of Rob Deer, an outfielder for the Brewers and Tigers in the 1980s and 1990s. He turned in three of the 10 worst seasons for contact hitting. Deer ended his 11-year career with 230 home runs — and 1,409 strikeouts.

The Worst 10

Rank	Batter	Year	Team	G	AB	H	SO	CT	SOV	CT+
1	Dave Nicholson	1963	White Sox	126	449	103	175	.610	111.9	36.1
2	Gary Alexander	1978	Indians-Athletics	148	498	112	166	.667	102.6	38.6
3	Mike Schmidt	1975	Phillies	158	562	140	180	.680	107.5	40.3
4	Jack Cust	2007	Athletics	124	395	101	164	.585	95.9	41.5
5	Gorman Thomas	1979	Brewers	156	557	136	175	.686	100.9	42.3
5	Dave Kingman	1975	Mets	134	502	116	153	.695	88.3	42.3
7	Rob Deer	1987	Brewers	134	474	113	186	.608	106.9	42.5
8	Rob Deer	1991	Tigers	134	448	80	175	.609	100.5	42.6
9	Bo Jackson	1989	Royals	135	515	132	172	.666	98.2	42.9
10	Jack Cust	2008	Athletics	148	481	111	197	.590	111.8	43.3
10	Rob Deer	1986	Brewers	134	466	108	179	.616	101.6	43.3

List #31: Best Batting Eye in a Season

Pitchers worked very carefully when facing Barry Bonds, and it was easy to understand why. Two powerful impulses — fear and logic — suggested it was wiser to hand a free pass to the Modern Era's greatest slugger, rather than allow him to swing away.

Diamondbacks manager Buck Showalter offered the ultimate compliment in 1998, ordering pitcher Gregg Olson to walk Bonds intentionally with the bases loaded. "It might not have been good," Showalter said, "but it was better than the option we had." Bonds received 688 intentional walks over his career, nearly 400 more than anybody else since 1961.

This list, however, is concerned with unintentional walks, the type a pitcher yields while ostensibly trying to retire a batter. Bonds drew more than 100 UBB six times, peaking at 142 in 2001 and 130 a year later. It was the latter season, 2002, when his batting eye was sharpest. He received unintentional walks in 23.9 percent of his competitive plate appearances (those when he was not being walked intentionally), yet another post-1961 record.

A typical batter would have drawn 45 UBB for the Giants in 2002, but Bonds received an additional 85. His adjusted batting eye rate (EY+) of 288.6 was the best in the Modern Era.

Bonds occupies three slots on this list. The only other player with multiple entries is Jim Wynn, a squat, yet powerful outfielder who played primarily for the Astros. Wynn twice led the National League in walks.

The Best 10

Rank	Batter	Year	Team	G	AB	H	UBB	EY	BBV	EY+
1	Barry Bonds	2002	Giants	143	403	149	130	.239	85.0	288.6
2	Barry Bonds	2001	Giants	153	476	156	142	.226	92.4	286.3
3	Jack Clark	1987	Cardinals	131	419	120	123	.225	78.6	277.2
4	Toby Harrah	1985	Rangers	126	396	107	111	.214	70.7	275.8
5	Jim Wynn	1976	Braves	148	449	93	126	.216	79.9	273.1
6	Barry Bonds	2004	Giants	147	373	135	112	.225	70.7	271.1
7	Jim Wynn	1969	Astros	149	495	133	134	.210	83.7	266.2
8	Rickey Henderson	1996	Padres	148	465	112	123	.205	76.6	265.1
9	Gene Tenace	1977	Padres	147	437	102	115	.201	71.2	262.4
10	Jason Giambi	2005	Yankees	139	417	113	103	.191	63.4	260.0

List #32: Worst Batting Eye in a Season

Doug Flynn stuck around the big leagues for 11 years because he was amazingly smooth as a second baseman, even winning a Gold Glove in 1980. His bat was not a factor in his longevity. Flynn amassed a lifetime total of seven home runs, a career batting average of .238, and an overall BPO+ of 63.9. He wasn't what you would call a clutch hitter.

Some good-field, no-hit players supplement their meager offensive abilities by stealing bases, bunting runners along, and working pitchers for walks. Not Flynn. He averaged fewer than two stolen bases and six sacrifice bunts per year, and he hardly ever drew a base on balls.

The latter was especially true during the strike-shortened season of 1981, when Flynn made 343 plate appearances for the Mets. The typical batter would have received 25.1 unintentional walks in the same amount of playing time. How many UBB did Flynn get? Exactly three. His adjusted batting eye rate was a stunningly tiny 11.9, which was 88.1 percent below the National League norm. Nobody in the Modern Era has done worse.

Manny Sanguillen and Shawon Dunston each made this list three times. Both loved to swing at pitches outside the strike zone, and neither was apologetic. "When I started, nobody told me what a strike was. They gave me a bat, and I swung at the ball," Sanguillen insisted. Dunston was more succinct: "You want to see a walk? Then go watch the mailman."

The Worst 10

Rank	Batter	Year	Team	G	AB	H	UBB	EY	BBV	EY+
1	Doug Flynn	1981	Mets	105	325	72	3	.009	-22.1	11.9
2	Manny Sanguillen	1971	Pirates	138	533	170	6	.011	-37.6	13.7
3	Shawon Dunston	1995	Cubs	127	477	141	7	.014	-33.6	17.2
4	Andres Thomas	1988	Braves	153	606	153	8	.013	-38.1	17.4
5	Manny Sanguillen	1973	Pirates	149	589	166	9	.015	-41.0	18.0
5	Shawon Dunston	1997	Pirates-Cubs	132	490	147	8	.016	-36.6	18.0
7	Tommy Helms	1968	Reds	127	507	146	6	.012	-26.1	18.7
8	Deivi Cruz	2000	Tigers	156	583	176	11	.018	-47.6	18.8
8	Manny Sanguillen	1970	Pirates	128	486	158	8	.016	-34.6	18.8
10	Shawon Dunston	1988	Cubs	155	575	143	8	.014	-34.3	18.9

5. PITCHING SEASONS

List #33: Best Pitching in a Season

Pedro Martinez was the only realistic candidate for the American League's Cy Young Award in 2000. The Red Sox righthander led the league in several categories, including most shutouts (four), strikeouts (284), strikeouts per walk (8.9), fewest hits per nine innings (5.3), and lowest earned run average (1.74). He was so dominant that all 28 voters listed him at the top of their ballots. They really had no choice.

Two stats offered definitive proof of Martinez's superiority in 2000. The first was his ERA, which was almost two runs ahead of the AL's runner-up, Roger Clemens at 3.70. The second was his microscopic BPO+ of 53.0, which was nearly 23 points better than the scores for anybody else in either league. It was, in fact, the best single-season BPO+ for any member of a starting rotation in the Modern Era.

This list is bound to offend fans with fond memories of the durable, tenacious pitchers of the 1960s and 1970s. You won't find any of those icons here. Bob Gibson was truly remarkable in 1968, as evidenced by an astonishing ERA of 1.12, but his BPO+ of 70.3 just missed the top 10.

It's an unfortunate fact that Gibson set his mark during the Modern Era's worst year for hitters, while Martinez starred when sluggers were at their peak. The latter performance was definitely more impressive on an adjusted statistical scale.

The Best 10

Rank	Pitcher	Year	Team	G	ERA	B	O	BPO	BV	BPO+
1	Pedro Martinez	2000	Red Sox	29	1.74	258	657	.393	-228.8	53.0
2	Greg Maddux	1995	Braves	28	1.63	256	633	.404	-181.0	58.6
3	Greg Maddux	1994	Braves	25	1.56	258	614	.420	-167.3	60.7
4	Pedro Martinez	1999	Red Sox	31	2.07	301	650	.463	-182.9	62.2
5	Kevin Brown	1996	Marlins	32	1.89	314	705	.445	-161.5	66.0
6	Roger Clemens	1997	Blue Jays	34	2.05	375	796	.471	-191.8	66.2
7	Zack Greinke	2015	Dodgers	32	1.66	278	671	.414	-138.5	66.7
8	Randy Johnson	2004	Diamondbacks	35	2.60	366	747	.490	-176.9	67.4
9	Roger Clemens	2005	Astros	32	1.87	301	642	.469	-144.8	67.5
10	Greg Maddux	1997	Braves	33	2.20	328	698	.470	-153.7	68.1

List #34: Worst Pitching in a Season

The 2013 season begin on a promising note for Edinson Volquez. Manager Bud Black chose him as the opening-day starter for the San Diego Padres, a reward for his staff-leading 174 strikeouts the previous year. Volquez still seemed to have the stuff to be a big winner — as he had once been with the Reds — and this was his chance to prove it.

Opening day didn't go well. The Mets shelled Volquez for six runs in three innings. His following three starts also ended in defeat. The big righthander improved the next few times out, but then the Rockies blasted him for nine runs in two-and-a-third innings in early June. Volquez's ERA was 6.01 in late August when Black's patience ran out. The Padres released him, and the Dodgers swooped in.

Things went a bit better in Los Angeles, but the Dodgers still lost four of Volquez's six appearances. He ended the season with a 9-12 record and a 5.71 ERA. His BPO+ of 138.5 was the worst for any starter in the Modern Era. The typical pitcher would have yielded 306.4 bases under similar circumstances. Volquez gave up 424.

Jim Deshaies, who tied for second place on this list, was the only starting pitcher in any season since 1961 to attain fewer outs (388) than the number of bases he surrendered (393). His raw BPO of 1.013 for the Twins in 1994 translated to a BPO+ of 137.2.

The Worst 10

Rank	Pitcher	Year	Team	G	ERA	B	O	BPO	BV	BPO+
1	Edinson Volquez	2013	Padres-Dodgers	33	5.71	424	513	.827	117.6	138.5
2	Jose Lima	2005	Royals	32	6.99	472	505	.935	128.0	137.2
2	Jim Deshaies	1994	Twins	25	7.39	393	388	1.013	106.5	137.2
4	Phil Ortega	1965	Senators	35	5.11	446	530	.842	118.4	136.1
5	Jack Lamabe	1964	Red Sox	39	5.89	458	532	.861	119.3	135.2
6	Joe Saunders	2013	Mariners	32	5.26	468	554	.845	120.5	134.7
7	Matt Keough	1982	Athletics	34	5.72	537	626	.858	133.9	133.2
8	Ubaldo Jimenez	2012	Indians	31	5.40	455	528	.862	110.9	132.2
9	Brandon Backe	2008	Astros	31	6.05	455	496	.917	110.0	131.9
10	Colby Lewis	2014	Rangers	29	5.18	425	510	.833	102.3	131.7

List #35: Best Run Prevention in a Season

Pedro Martinez was deceptively wiry — five-feet-11, 170 pounds — and always seemed to be smiling off the field. If you saw him in civilian clothes, you might have guessed that he was a journeyman who was simply happy to be hanging around the majors.

But Martinez was entirely different on the mound. "I saw everybody as an enemy," the Hall of Famer said. "I saw everybody like in the jungle. You just kill to survive." He mixed an unexpectedly strong fastball with a sharp curve and the best changeup of his times. His repertoire rendered him virtually unhittable — a description that was especially true in 2000.

Martinez made 29 starts for the Red Sox that year, giving up fewer than six hits in 21 games. He allowed just 0.74 hits and walks per inning, the lowest WHIP in baseball's entire history, a particularly impressive accomplishment during a boom year for hitters.

The Boston star was even stingier on the scoreboard, surrendering more than three earned runs in just two starts. His ERA+ of 36.5 was 63.5 percent better than the American League norm for 2000. No starter did a better job of run prevention in any season in the Modern Era.

Martinez qualified twice for this list, as did Greg Maddux and Roger Clemens. All but two of the top 10 performances occurred after 1993. The exceptions were Bob Gibson in 1968 and Dwight Gooden in 1985.

The Best 10

Rank	Pitcher	Year	Team	G	IP	SO	BB	ERA	ERV	ERA+
1	Pedro Martinez	2000	Red Sox	29	217.0	284	32	1.74	-73.1	36.5
2	Greg Maddux	1994	Braves	25	202.0	156	31	1.56	-55.2	38.8
3	Greg Maddux	1995	Braves	28	209.2	181	23	1.63	-56.8	40.1
4	Bob Gibson	1968	Cardinals	34	304.2	268	62	1.12	-56.4	40.2
5	Pedro Martinez	1999	Red Sox	31	213.1	313	37	2.07	-63.8	43.5
6	Dwight Gooden	1985	Mets	35	276.2	268	69	1.53	-54.7	46.2
7	Roger Clemens	2005	Astros	32	211.1	185	62	1.87	-50.5	46.6
8	Roger Clemens	1997	Blue Jays	34	264.0	292	68	2.05	-65.3	47.9
9	Zack Greinke	2015	Dodgers	32	222.2	200	40	1.66	-44.3	48.1
10	Kevin Brown	1996	Marlins	32	233.0	159	33	1.89	-52.8	48.2

List #36: Worst Run Prevention in a Season

San Diego's Petco Park, which opened in April 2004, quickly became known as a haven for pitchers, a reputation that still held true nine years later. Petco's pitching park factor for bases in 2013 was 0.955, tying it with Pittsburgh's PNC Park for the National League's lowest PPF[B]. Dodger Stadium in Los Angeles (0.973) was nearly as favorable for pitchers.

All of which makes Edinson Volquez's disastrous 2013 season even more mysterious. Volquez spent the first five months with the San Diego Padres and the final few weeks with the Dodgers. But his agreeable surroundings couldn't prevent him from yielding at least six runs in six different starts. He posted an ERA of 5.71, the highest for any starter who reached qualification levels in either league that year.

The typical pitcher who split 170 innings between San Diego and Los Angeles would have allowed 60.6 earned runs in 2013. Volquez exceeded that total by 47.4 ER, giving up a total of 108. His resulting ERA+ of 178.6 — 78.6 percent worse than the leaguewide norm — established an unfortunate record for the Modern Era.

Jim Deshaies (7.39 for the Twins in 1994) and Jose Lima (6.99 for the Royals in 2005) registered the worst single-year ERAs among all qualified pitchers since 1961. Adjustment for seasonal and ballpark factors pushed Lima into second place on this list with an ERA+ of 169.5. Deshaies settled into third at 159.8.

The Worst 10

Rank	Pitcher	Year	Team	G	IP	SO	BB	ERA	ERV	ERA+
1	Edinson Volquez	2013	Padres-Dodgers	33	170.1	142	77	5.71	47.4	178.6
2	Jose Lima	2005	Royals	32	168.2	80	61	6.99	53.7	169.5
3	Jim Deshaies	1994	Twins	25	130.1	78	54	7.39	40.1	159.8
4	Jack Lamabe	1964	Red Sox	39	177.1	109	57	5.89	43.2	159.4
5	Eric Milton	2005	Reds	34	186.1	123	52	6.47	49.8	159.1
6	Mark Davis	1984	Giants	46	174.2	124	54	5.36	37.9	157.3
6	Bob Knepper	1989	Astros-Giants	35	165.0	64	75	5.13	34.3	157.3
8	Rick Wise	1968	Phillies	30	182.1	97	37	4.54	33.0	155.8
9	Warren Spahn	1964	Braves	38	173.2	78	52	5.29	36.0	154.4
10	Steve Arlin	1973	Padres	34	180.0	98	72	5.10	35.6	153.7

List #37: Best Power Prevention in a Season

It's a baseball truism that the faster a pitch comes in, the faster it goes out. The idea seems reasonable. If a pitcher supplies a few extra miles per hour, wouldn't a batter have a better chance of launching the ball toward the fences?

But there are two problems with this rule. The first is that scientists can't find any proof of its accuracy. "You're either able to hit the ball harder or you're not, and it really doesn't depend on the speed of the pitch," says John Olshan, a pioneer in the technological analysis of baseball.

The second problem is that a batter must be able to hit a ball before he can propel it anywhere. That was especially difficult when the man on the hill was Nolan Ryan, who brought the greatest velocity in the Modern Era.

The extent of this challenge was quantified by Ryan's statistics for the Astros in 1981. A total of 605 batters stepped in against him. Nearly a quarter (140) struck out. Only 99 got hits, and just 10 were for extra bases. The isolated power average against Ryan in 1981 was .028, the lowest ISO versus any starter since 1961. Ryan's ISO+ of 28.3 remains the era's best example of power prevention.

This list contains other fireballers, such as Bob Veale and Sam McDowell. But crafty pitchers like Greg Maddux and Bruce Dal Canton proved there was more than one way to keep the ball inside the fences.

The Best 10

Rank	Pitcher	Year	Team	G	2B	3B	HR	ISO	EXV	ISO+
1	Nolan Ryan	1981	Astros	21	7	1	2	.028	-38.0	28.3
2	Greg Maddux	1994	Braves	25	22	2	4	.052	-64.8	37.0
3	Dean Chance	1964	Angels	46	20	4	7	.049	-66.1	42.6
4	Greg Maddux	1995	Braves	28	22	0	8	.061	-59.0	43.8
5	Kevin Brown	1998	Padres	36	32	0	8	.059	-71.2	44.0
6	Bob Veale	1965	Pirates	39	27	5	5	.053	-63.8	44.9
7	Bruce Dal Canton	1974	Royals	31	17	2	5	.056	-42.9	45.6
8	Dennis Lamp	1981	White Sox	27	9	1	4	.049	-27.1	45.9
9	Sam McDowell	1965	Indians	42	30	0	9	.059	-62.9	47.5
10	Dock Ellis	1973	Pirates	28	12	4	7	.056	-45.0	47.7

List #38: Worst Power Prevention in a Season

Ian Kennedy is a fly-ball pitcher, seemingly an ideal match for San Diego's spacious Petco Park. But that didn't prove to be the case in 2015.

The year started badly for Kennedy, who strained a hamstring in the third inning of his first start for the Padres, sending him to the disabled list. He returned against the Dodgers in late April, but was unable to find his rhythm. Los Angeles shelled him for three home runs, and Colorado added a pair six days later. Both games were at Petco.

Kennedy had a 2-5 record by the end of May. His ERA was an atrocious 7.15, and he had already dished out 12 home runs. "After June came, I felt normal again," he said, and that was true in some respects. His ERA for the final four months of 2015 was a respectable 3.41.

But the home runs kept flying. Kennedy allowed 31 in all, 19 at home. The typical pitcher in his circumstances would have yielded 87.7 extra bases (one per double, two per triple, three per homer). He gave up 154. Kennedy's ISO+ of 174.4 was 74.4 percent worse than the leaguewide average, making it the poorest case of power prevention in the Modern Era.

The runner-up on this list, Bronson Arroyo, surrendered 46 home runs for the Reds in 2011. Opponents blasted at least three homers in six of his 32 starts.

The Worst 10

Rank	Pitcher	Year	Team	G	2B	3B	HR	ISO	EXV	ISO+
1	Ian Kennedy	2015	Padres	30	39	11	31	.239	65.7	174.4
2	Bronson Arroyo	2011	Reds	32	47	3	46	.241	80.8	173.3
3	Willie Fraser	1988	Angels	34	47	7	33	.210	65.5	169.3
4	Mark Davis	1984	Giants	46	38	5	25	.179	49.6	167.6
5	Larry McWilliams	1980	Braves	30	34	6	27	.193	51.1	167.3
6	Matt Keough	1982	Athletics	34	43	4	38	.201	65.1	165.2
7	Phil Ortega	1965	Senators	35	22	9	33	.207	54.2	163.9
8	Brandon Backe	2008	Astros	31	46	4	36	.242	63.0	163.6
9	Dave Johnson	1990	Orioles	30	43	2	30	.196	53.0	163.1
10	Sid Fernandez	1994	Orioles	19	25	4	27	.260	44.1	163.0

List #39: Best Power Pitching in a Season

Welcome to Nolan Ryan's list.

Ryan produced eight of the 10 best seasons of power pitching in the Modern Era, and all but one occurred in the 1970s. His streak began after the Mets committed a truly horrendous trade in December 1971, acquiring shortstop Jim Fregosi from the California Angels in exchange for Ryan and three other players.

Fregosi would stay with the Mets for a season and a half, batting just .233 and hitting only five home runs. Ryan went on to spin four no-hitters for the Angels by the end of the decade, while winning 138 games and delivering 2,416 strikeouts. Fregosi, who was noted for his sense of humor, always called the trade "my biggest contribution in Anaheim."

Ryan's first season in California can be found in ninth place on this list. He improved the next two seasons — moving up to sixth and then fifth — before an elbow injury temporarily derailed him in 1975. But he bounced back in 1976 with the greatest demonstration of power pitching in the Modern Era.

An average pitcher in Anaheim would have registered 134.8 strikeouts in 284 innings that year. Ryan blew past that expected total by 192.2, whiffing 327 batters. The adjusted contact rate against him was a miserly 41.2, the lowest CT+ recorded since 1961.

The men who kept this from being a unanimous list were Pedro Martinez in 1999 and Frank Tanana in 1975. The latter was Ryan's teammate at the time.

The Best 10

Rank	Pitcher	Year	Team	G	IP	H	SO	CT	SOV	CT+
1	Nolan Ryan	1976	Angels	39	284.1	193	327	.670	192.2	41.2
2	Nolan Ryan	1978	Angels	31	234.2	183	260	.688	145.0	44.2
3	Nolan Ryan	1977	Angels	37	299.0	198	341	.668	186.4	45.3
4	Pedro Martinez	1999	Red Sox	31	213.1	160	313	.599	170.6	45.5
5	Nolan Ryan	1974	Angels	42	332.2	221	367	.685	196.9	46.3
6	Nolan Ryan	1973	Angels	41	326.0	238	383	.673	204.0	46.7
7	Nolan Ryan	1989	Rangers	32	239.1	162	301	.653	160.2	46.8
8	Nolan Ryan	1979	Angels	34	222.2	169	223	.721	114.1	48.8
9	Nolan Ryan	1972	Angels	39	284.0	166	329	.662	167.7	49.0
9	Frank Tanana	1975	Angels	34	257.1	211	269	.711	137.1	49.0

List #40: Worst Power Pitching in a Season

Nate Cornejo looked like a power pitcher. He towered over hitters on the mound, standing six-feet-five and weighing 200 to 220 pounds. Scouts raved about the blazing fastball and sharp curve that had made him a high-school star in Kansas. It seemed he couldn't miss.

Except that he did. His fastball slowed and his curve somehow vanished by the time the Tigers called him up. Cornejo proved to be shockingly hittable in the big leagues, especially in 2003, his one full year as a starter for Detroit.

The season, to be sure, began promisingly. Cornejo won three of his first 10 starts, maintaining an ERA of 3.00. The only sign of danger was his inability to register third strikes. He notched just 11 strikeouts in his first 60 innings. Yet Cornejo was outperforming the other members of the Tigers' young, ineffective rotation. Demoting him or sending him to the bullpen was out of the question.

The wheels began to come off with three straight losses in June. Cornejo went 3-14 with a 5.59 ERA in his final 20 starts, largely because of his inability to shut down the opposition with strikeouts. He ended the year with a total of 46 whiffs, which was 83.4 below expectations. His CT+ of 281.2 was the worst single-season adjusted contact rate in the Modern Era.

The runner-up, Kirk Rueter, made 33 starts for the Giants in 2004. He didn't record more than five strikeouts in any of them.

The Worst 10

Rank	Pitcher	Year	Team	G	IP	H	SO	CT	SOV	CT+
1	Nate Cornejo	2003	Tigers	32	194.2	236	46	.940	-83.4	281.2
2	Kirk Rueter	2004	Giants	33	190.1	225	56	.926	-93.5	266.9
3	Ed Lynch	1983	Mets	30	174.2	208	44	.936	-73.3	266.7
4	Steve Kline	1972	Yankees	32	236.1	210	58	.935	-89.2	253.8
5	Joe Niekro	1969	Cubs-Padres	41	221.1	237	62	.928	-88.0	243.1
6	Clyde Wright	1973	Angels	37	257.0	273	65	.935	-87.9	235.2
7	Bill Swift	1988	Mariners	38	174.2	199	47	.930	-63.0	234.1
8	Jim Barr	1978	Giants	32	163.0	180	44	.931	-57.8	231.3
9	Ross Grimsley	1977	Orioles	34	218.1	230	53	.936	-68.9	229.9
10	Jeff Ballard	1989	Orioles	35	215.1	240	62	.926	-78.4	226.4
10	Bill Lee	1979	Expos	33	222.0	230	59	.932	-74.6	226.4

List #41: Best Control Pitching in a Season

Carlos Silva displayed amazing accuracy during his nine years in the big leagues, consistently slipping his pitches into the strike zone or just off the margin. Such a rare degree of control was bound to be impressive, though it wasn't necessarily good for his career. Batters eventually figured out that he always left them something good to hit.

That problem was still in the future in 2004, Silva's third year in the majors and first in the American League. The Twins acquired the 25-year-old reliever from the Phillies and converted him into a starter. Silva thrived in his new league and new role. He went 14-8, issuing just 1.55 walks per nine innings, the fourth-lowest rate in the AL.

He was even sharper in 2005, yielding only nine bases on balls (seven unintentional) in 27 starts. His rate of 0.43 walks per nine innings was the best for any pitcher since 1880. Silva's control was 86 percent better than the leaguewide average, translating to an EY+ of 14.0, the lowest adjusted batting eye rate against any Modern Era pitcher.

Silva would lead the league again the following year — not for the fewest walks, but for the most home runs allowed (38). He vanished from big-league ball within a half-decade.

The two runner-up slots on this list — and three of the top five — belong to Greg Maddux. The Hall of Famer issued only 822 UBB in 23 seasons, an average of 35.7 per year.

The Best 10

Rank	Pitcher	Year	Team	G	IP	H	UBB	EY	BBV	EY+
1	Carlos Silva	2005	Twins	27	188.1	212	7	.009	-42.9	14.0
2	Greg Maddux	1997	Braves	33	232.2	200	14	.016	-58.0	19.4
3	Greg Maddux	1996	Braves	35	245.0	225	17	.018	-54.9	23.6
4	Cliff Lee	2010	Mariners-Rangers	28	212.1	195	16	.019	-49.7	24.4
5	Greg Maddux	2001	Braves	34	233.0	220	17	.019	-51.4	24.9
6	Bret Saberhagen	1994	Mets	24	177.1	169	13	.019	-36.7	26.2
7	Phil Hughes	2014	Twins	32	209.2	221	15	.018	-41.9	26.4
8	Dennis Eckersley	1985	Cubs	25	169.1	145	15	.023	-36.7	29.0
9	LaMarr Hoyt	1985	Padres	31	210.1	210	18	.022	-43.6	29.2
10	Bob Tewksbury	1993	Cardinals	32	213.2	258	19	.021	-45.0	29.7

List #42: Worst Control Pitching in a Season

Previous pages have reinforced the well-known fact that Nolan Ryan was blazingly fast. But another facet of his Hall of Fame career deserves equal time: He often was stunningly wild, especially during his early years.

Tom Grieve, an outfielder for the Texas Rangers in the 1970s, recalled that Ryan's effectiveness was enhanced by his combination of speed and inaccuracy. "He was throwing so hard, and he was wild, and you knew he was mean," Grieve said. "He'd knock you down, and you never knew whether it was on purpose or not."

Ryan led his league 11 times in strikeouts and eight times in walks. He topped the categories simultaneously in six seasons, including 1976, a year when his lack of precision was especially pronounced. He passed out 181 unintentional walks, exceeding the expectations for a typical pitcher by 98.3 bases on balls. His EY+ of 218.8 was inferior to the leaguewide average by 118.8 percent. No pitcher in the Modern Era ever suffered a worse lack of control.

This list is dominated by fireballers who didn't always get as close to the strike zone as they would have liked. Ryan occupies four slots. The other pitcher with multiple entries is Randy Johnson, who attributed his youthful wildness to his six-foot-10-inch height. "For someone who is 6-1, 6-2, he has less body to keep under control, so it's a lot easier," Johnson said. "For me, it was difficult because I was so tall."

The Worst 10

Rank	Pitcher	Year	Team	G	IP	H	UBB	EY	BBV	EY+
1	Nolan Ryan	1976	Angels	39	284.1	193	181	.152	98.3	218.8
2	Randy Johnson	1991	Mariners	33	201.1	151	152	.171	81.7	216.1
3	Nolan Ryan	1977	Angels	37	299.0	198	197	.156	103.6	211.0
4	Nolan Ryan	1974	Angels	42	332.2	221	199	.143	103.3	208.0
5	Jose de Jesus	1991	Phillies	31	181.2	147	124	.156	63.8	206.1
6	Bob Veale	1967	Pirates	33	203.0	184	109	.124	55.6	203.9
7	Nolan Ryan	1975	Angels	28	198.0	152	132	.153	67.2	203.6
8	Randy Johnson	1992	Mariners	31	210.1	154	143	.155	71.1	198.9
9	Todd Van Poppel	1994	Athletics	23	116.2	108	87	.164	42.9	197.4
10	J.R. Richard	1975	Astros	33	203.0	178	138	.152	67.7	196.4

6. BATTING GAMES

List #43: Best Team Batting in a Game

The Red Sox broke quickly from the gate in 2003, winning 31 of their first 50 games. They held a two-and-a-half-game lead in the American League East on May 26. Their fans began to believe that Boston might finally earn its first world title since 1918.

Those dreams were swiftly punctured. The Sox lost their next five games and eventually slipped to third place before their fortunes suddenly revived on June 23. Boston went on a five-game tear that culminated in an amazing display of hitting prowess against the Florida Marlins on June 27.

Johnny Damon led off the bottom of the first by doubling against Florida pitcher Carl Pavano. Todd Walker quickly singled Damon home, Nomar Garciaparra doubled, and Manny Ramirez smashed a three-run homer. Two more hits chased Pavano to the showers. Reliever Michael Tejera gave up four hits and a walk, and he too was done. Boston set a big-league record by scoring 10 runs before making its first out.

The Sox piled up 28 hits and 58 bases on their way to a 25-8 victory. Their single-game BPO of 2.636 was the highest in the Modern Era, securing one of Boston's two entries on this list. The Yankees were the other team to make it twice. (Any ties in the BPO rankings were broken by batting averages.) And no, the mighty Red Sox did not go on to win the pennant in 2003. That honor went to the briefly hapless Marlins.

The Best 10

Rank	Team	Opp	Date	Score	H	HR	SO	B	BA	BPO
1	Red Sox	Marlins	June 27, 2003	25-8	28	3	7	58	.609	2.636
2	Yankees	Devil Rays	July 22, 2007	21-4	25	6	8	60	.521	2.500
3	Expos	Braves	July 30, 1978	19-0	28	8	6	64	.549	2.462
4	Rangers	Orioles	April 19, 1996	26-7	19	5	2	59	.500	2.458
5	Yankees	Athletics	Aug. 25, 2011	22-9	21	5	9	55	.488	2.391
6	Blue Jays	Orioles	Sept. 14, 1987	18-3	21	10	4	57	.477	2.375
7	Diamondbacks	Dodgers	May 17, 2014	18-7	21	5	9	56	.488	2.333
8	Reds	Rockies	May 19, 1999	24-12	28	6	8	67	.528	2.310
9	Phillies	Cubs	June 23, 1986	19-1	20	4	7	55	.476	2.292
10	Red Sox	Tigers	Sept. 4, 2013	20-4	19	8	10	55	.463	2.292

List #44: Worst Team Batting in a Game

The team at the top of this list, of course, would inevitably be the victim of a no-hitter. Nothing is more indicative of "worst team batting" than the inability to eke out a single hit — not even a Texas Leaguer or infield bleeder.

But that doesn't sufficiently narrow the list. Pitchers have tossed 153 no-hitters during the Modern Era, including 17 perfect games, which gives us a plethora of candidates. BPO and BA were all we needed to rank the best examples of team batting, but an additional stat is required to break the massive tie among the worst cases.

My choice is strikeouts, on the theory that the most dismal performance involves not only the lack of hits, but a failure to hit the ball at all.

That factor propels the New York Mets to the top of this list. They had already clinched a divisional title when they took the field against Max Scherzer and the Washington Nationals on the final weekend of the 2015 regular season. Scherzer whiffed 17 New York batters as he cruised to his second no-hitter of the year. Only two Mets managed to get the ball out of the infield. The sole baserunner reached on an error.

Second place belongs to the Rockies, who were no-hit by Clayton Kershaw of the Dodgers in June 2014. Kershaw needed just 107 pitches to strike out 15 Colorado batters. The Rockies, too, got their only runner through an error.

The Worst 10

Rank	Team	Opp	Date	Score	H	HR	SO	B	BA	BPO
1	Mets	Nationals	Oct. 3, 2015	0-2	0	0	17	0	.000	.000
2	Rockies	Dodgers	June 18, 2014	0-8	0	0	15	0	.000	.000
3	Cubs	Dodgers	Sept. 9, 1965	0-1	0	0	14	0	.000	.000
3	Astros	Giants	June 13, 2012	0-10	0	0	14	0	.000	.000
5	Braves	Diamondbacks	May 18, 2004	0-2	0	0	13	0	.000	.000
6	Rays	Mariners	Aug. 15, 2012	0-1	0	0	12	0	.000	.000
7	Twins	Athletics	May 8, 1968	0-4	0	0	11	0	.000	.000
7	Blue Jays	Indians	May 15, 1981	0-3	0	0	11	0	.000	.000
7	Twins	Yankees	May 17, 1998	0-4	0	0	11	0	.000	.000
7	Padres	Giants	July 10, 2009	0-8	0	0	11	0	.000	.000
7	Marlins	Phillies	May 29, 2010	0-1	0	0	11	0	.000	.000

List #45: Best Batting in a Game for Both Teams

Chicago's Wrigley Field is an especially cozy park for hitters when the wind is right, and the 20-mile-per-hour breeze on May 17, 1979, was absolutely perfect. It streamed toward the bleachers all afternoon.

The visiting Phillies took immediate advantage, with Mike Schmidt and Bob Boone launching a pair of three-run homers in the top of the first. Cubs left fielder Dave Kingman answered with his own three-run shot in the bottom of the inning, but the Phillies retaliated with eight runs in the third, seemingly putting the game out of reach. The score by the middle of the fifth was Philadelphia 21, Chicago 9.

But Larry Bowa still didn't feel comfortable. "Every time we came up to hit," the Phillies shortstop recalled, "I kept saying, 'It's not enough.'" And it wasn't. The Cubs struck back with seven runs in the bottom of the fifth, and eventually tied the game at 22. It took another mighty blast by Schmidt in the 10th inning to seal a 23-22 win for Philadelphia.

The Phillies and Cubs combined for 11 home runs (three by Kingman, two by Schmidt), 50 hits, 117 bases, and a joint BPO of 1.857. It was the greatest offensive show by two teams in the Modern Era.

All 10 games on this list featured a minimum of 26 runs, 30 hits, and 85 bases. Four of these contests took place in Denver, where the Colorado Rockies (and their opponents) enjoy the most hitter-friendly park in the majors.

The Best 10

Rank	Winner	Loser	Date	Score	H2	HR2	B2	O2	BA2	BPO2
1	Phillies	Cubs	May 17, 1979	23-22	50	11	117	63	.459	1.857
2	Reds	Rockies	May 19, 1999	24-12	43	9	100	55	.462	1.818
3	Rockies	Marlins	July 4, 2008	18-17	43	8	94	52	.462	1.808
4	Expos	Cubs	May 14, 2000	16-15	37	7	88	49	.446	1.796
5	Rockies	Dodgers	June 30, 1996	16-15	38	10	100	56	.413	1.786
6	White Sox	Tigers	May 28, 1995	14-12	31	12	101	57	.373	1.772
7	Rockies	Giants	June 28, 2000	17-13	30	8	90	51	.370	1.765
8	Yankees	Athletics	Aug. 25, 2011	22-9	36	7	88	50	.434	1.760
9	Athletics	Twins	July 20, 2009	14-13	39	8	85	49	.459	1.735
10	Yankees	Devil Rays	June 21, 2005	20-11	41	9	90	52	.456	1.731

List #46: Worst Batting in a Game for Both Teams

The game between the Los Angeles Dodgers and Chicago Cubs on September 9, 1965, was almost completely devoid of hitting, but it would go down in baseball history as a classic.

It seemed a mismatch on paper. The Dodgers ace, Sandy Koufax, was gunning for his 22nd win of the season. The Cubs starter, Bob Hendley, had a 2-2 record. But both pitchers were virtually unhittable that night in Los Angeles.

The Dodgers wangled a run in the fifth inning on a walk, sacrifice, stolen base, and Cubs error, yet they didn't get their first hit until Lou Johnson blooped a double into short right field in the seventh. That would be their final line score — one run, one hit — but it would be enough. The Cubs were shut out in both categories, the victims of Koufax's fourth no-hitter and first perfect game.

The two teams combined for an .020 batting average (one hit in 51 at bats), a total of five bases, and a joint BPO of .098. Those were the worst batting statistics for any of the 117,760 big-league games between 1961 and 2016. "I'm glad we got the run," said Koufax, "or we might have been here all night."

The Dodgers also played in the two games that come next on this list. (Any ties in BPO were broken by BA.) Los Angeles split a pair of 1-0 contests in which the combined offensive output was eight hits and 12 bases.

The Worst 10

Rk	Winner	Loser	Date	Score	H2	HR2	B2	O2	BA2	BPO2
1	Dodgers	Cubs	Sept. 9, 1965	1-0	1	0	5	51	.020	.098
2	Reds	Dodgers	Sept. 16, 1988	1-0	3	0	5	50	.057	.100
3	Dodgers	Athletics	June 10, 1998	1-0	5	0	7	53	.089	.132
4	Cubs	Reds	June 30, 1964	1-0	3	0	7	52	.056	.135
5	Angels	Twins	May 7, 1963	2-0	6	0	7	52	.105	.135
6	Expos	Dodgers	July 28, 1991	2-0	4	0	8	56	.069	.143
7	Padres	Giants	May 13, 2010	1-0	6	0	8	56	.100	.143
8	Marlins	Braves	April 22, 2014	1-0	7	0	8	55	.115	.145
9	Diamondbacks	Dodgers	April 10, 2001	2-0	5	1	8	52	.091	.154
10	Royals	White Sox	April 14, 1973	3-0	5	0	9	58	.083	.155

List #47: Best Batting in a Game

Shawn Green was mired in a terrible slump when his Dodgers arrived in Milwaukee on May 21, 2002. He had enjoyed a banner year in 2001 — 49 home runs and a .297 batting average. But his numbers for the first 42 games of 2002 were miserable: just three homers and a BA of .231.

The first two games in Miller Park gave Green cause for hope. He swatted a pair of home runs on Tuesday and tripled on Wednesday. But what happened on Thursday, May 23, was of an entirely different dimension.

Green doubled in the first inning, homered in the second, launched another home run in the fourth, yet another in the fifth, singled in the eighth, and homered for a fourth time in the ninth. The final blast soared 450 feet. "It gave me chills," said Los Angeles third-base coach Glenn Hoffman. "To see a ball go out like that, it's history, man."

Green had reached 19 bases, the greatest one-game total in the Modern Era. "The ball had been looking like a ping-pong ball," he said of his slump. "Today, it probably looked like a softball."

This list is ranked by bases. If we stopped there, all sorts of ties would result. The logjam is broken by highest SC, lowest PA, highest HR, and highest H. Five other batters in these standings hit four home runs, joining Green among the 16 co-holders of that big-league record for a single game.

The Best 10

Rank	Batter	Date	Team	Opp	PA	H	HR	SC	B
1	Shawn Green	May 23, 2002	Dodgers	Brewers	6	6	4	9	19
2	Josh Hamilton	May 8, 2012	Rangers	Orioles	5	5	4	8	18
3	Mike Schmidt	April 17, 1976	Phillies	Cubs	6	5	4	8	17
4	Mike Cameron	May 2, 2002	Mariners	White Sox	6	4	4	4	17
5	Mark Whiten	Sept. 7, 1993	Cardinals	Reds	5	4	4	12	16
6	Fred Lynn	June 18, 1975	Red Sox	Tigers	6	5	3	11	16
7	Yoenis Cespedes	Aug. 21, 2015	Mets	Rockies	6	5	3	9	16
8	Willie Mays	April 30, 1961	Giants	Braves	5	4	4	8	16
9	Willie Stargell	May 22, 1968	Pirates	Cubs	5	5	3	8	16
10	Edgardo Alfonzo	Aug. 30, 1999	Mets	Astros	6	6	3	8	16

List #48: Worst Batting in a Game

Ron Swoboda endured a couple of shaky years after being called up to the big leagues, but his third season, 1967, was indisputably successful. The Mets right fielder batted a solid .281, and his BPO+ fit nicely above the leaguewide norm at 106.5.

Swoboda entered 1968 with high hopes, which were instantly confirmed by a five-for-13 hitting streak in New York's first four outings. But the fifth game was rough enough to shake anybody's confidence.

Two young fireballers took the mound on April 15 — Tom Seaver for the Mets, Don Wilson for the Astros. Neither team scored before the game reached extra innings, and the zeros kept rolling for more than six hours. Houston finally tallied the game's lone run on a Mets error in the bottom of the 24th.

Nobody had a good day at the plate, but Swoboda's was the worst of all. It was the worst, in fact, of the entire Modern Era, based on this list of the most outs, with ties broken by the fewest bases and the most strikeouts.

Swoboda went 0 for 10 with five strikeouts on April 15. His BA for the young season was .385 when the day began, .217 when it ended. He would finish 1968 at .242, almost 40 points below 1967.

Bobby Darwin matched Swoboda by going hitless while making 10 outs for the Twins in 1972. But Darwin did manage to draw a walk, dropping him to second place in these rankings.

The Worst 10

Rank	Batter	Date	Team	Opp	PA	H	SO	B	O
1	Ron Swoboda	April 15, 1968	Mets	Astros	10	0	5	0	10
2	Bobby Darwin	May 12, 1972	Twins	Brewers	10	0	5	1	10
3	Jim Thome	July 2, 2004	Phillies	Orioles	8	0	5	0	9
3	Chris Davis	May 6, 2012	Orioles	Red Sox	8	0	5	0	9
5	Rick Reichardt	May 31, 1966	Angels	Indians	8	0	6	0	8
5	Billy Cowan	July 9, 1971	Angels	Athletics	8	0	6	0	8
5	Cecil Cooper	June 14, 1974	Red Sox	Angels	8	0	6	0	8
8	Byron Browne	July 19, 1966	Cubs	Reds	8	0	5	0	8
8	Tony Conigliaro	July 9, 1971	Angels	Athletics	8	0	5	0	8
8	Brandon Belt	July 8, 2013	Giants	Mets	8	0	5	0	8

7. PITCHING GAMES

List #49: Best Team Pitching in a Game

Most pundits believed the Washington Nationals pitching staff would be the best in the majors in 2015. It made sense. The Nats had posted the lowest ERA in either league the previous year (3.03), and they had acquired high-powered righthander Max Scherzer in free agency. The World Series seemed inevitable.

But Washington's pitchers couldn't live up to the hype. Their ERA of 3.62 was only sixth-best in the National League in 2015. Scherzer, their new ace, was unexpectedly erratic, winning only 14 games and losing 12. The Nats didn't even make the playoffs, let alone the World Series.

Yet there were flashes of brilliance. Scherzer gave up two earned runs or less in 21 of his 33 starts, including three complete-game shutouts. Two of the latter were no-hitters, making him just the sixth pitcher in big-league history to toss a pair of hitless gems in the same season.

The second of Scherzer's no-hitters qualified for first place on this list. This category technically is for the best team pitching in a game, but each of the 11 performances was the work of a single man. None of them surrendered any runs or bases, so the standings were determined by strikeouts.

Scherzer's — okay, the Nationals' — 17 strikeouts against the Mets constituted the most dominant game of the Modern Era. If you're interested in matching pitchers to teams, the five runners up were Clayton Kershaw, Sandy Koufax, Matt Cain, Randy Johnson, and Felix Hernandez.

The Best 10

Rank	Team	Opp	Date	Score	H	HR	SO	B	ERA	BPO
1	Nationals	Mets	Oct. 3, 2015	2-0	0	0	17	0	0.00	.000
2	Dodgers	Rockies	June 18, 2014	8-0	0	0	15	0	0.00	.000
3	Dodgers	Cubs	Sept. 9, 1965	1-0	0	0	14	0	0.00	.000
3	Giants	Astros	June 13, 2012	10-0	0	0	14	0	0.00	.000
5	Diamondbacks	Braves	May 18, 2004	2-0	0	0	13	0	0.00	.000
6	Mariners	Rays	Aug. 15, 2012	1-0	0	0	12	0	0.00	.000
7	Athletics	Twins	May 8, 1968	4-0	0	0	11	0	0.00	.000
7	Indians	Blue Jays	May 15, 1981	3-0	0	0	11	0	0.00	.000
7	Yankees	Twins	May 17, 1998	4-0	0	0	11	0	0.00	.000
7	Giants	Padres	July 10, 2009	8-0	0	0	11	0	0.00	.000
7	Phillies	Marlins	May 29, 2010	1-0	0	0	11	0	0.00	.000

List #50: Worst Team Pitching in a Game

Ninety-one pitches can be a very good outing. Greg Maddux tossed four complete games that required no more than 91 pitches in 1995, when he won his fourth consecutive Cy Young Award. He needed only 82 in his most efficient start.

But 91 pitches can also spell disaster, as they did for the Florida Marlins in a 25-8 shellacking by the Boston Red Sox on June 27, 2003. The Marlins threw 91 pitches in the first inning alone, giving up 14 runs on 13 hits and four walks. Starter Carl Pavano and reliever Michael Tejera surrendered 10 runs without an out. Allen Levrault brought the 50-minute inning to a merciful close after three more Boston runners crossed the plate.

Pavano remained upbeat. "I've got another start in five or six days," he said, "so I'm looking forward to that." But Florida third baseman Mike Lowell was closer to reality. "It was miserable," he said. "It was embarrassing."

Five Marlins pitchers yielded 58 bases in all. Boston's BPO against Florida was 2.636, marking the worst single-game performance by a pitching staff since 1961. (These rankings were based on BPO, with ties broken by highest ERA and highest BB.)

Another Florida team, the Tampa Bay Devil Rays, was second-worst in this category. The Yankees battered starter James Shields for 10 runs in 3.1 innings on July 22, 2007. Four relievers gave up another 11 runs. New York attained 60 bases for a BPO of 2.500.

The Worst 10

Rank	Team	Opp	Date	Score	H	HR	BB	B	ERA	BPO
1	Marlins	Red Sox	June 27, 2003	8-25	28	3	7	58	28.13	2.636
2	Devil Rays	Yankees	July 22, 2007	4-21	25	6	7	60	23.63	2.500
3	Braves	Expos	July 30, 1978	0-19	28	8	3	64	19.00	2.462
4	Orioles	Rangers	April 19, 1996	7-26	19	5	13	59	29.25	2.458
5	Athletics	Yankees	Aug. 25, 2011	9-22	21	5	13	55	24.75	2.391
6	Orioles	Blue Jays	Sept. 14, 1987	3-18	21	10	4	57	20.25	2.375
7	Dodgers	Diamondbacks	May 17, 2014	7-18	21	5	6	56	20.25	2.333
8	Rockies	Reds	May 19, 1999	12-24	28	6	9	67	22.00	2.310
9	Cubs	Phillies	June 23, 1986	1-19	20	4	7	55	21.38	2.292
10	Tigers	Red Sox	Sept. 4, 2013	4-20	19	8	4	55	21.38	2.292

List #51: Best Pitching in a Game for Both Teams

This page, for obvious reasons, is identical to List #46. Games that featured the worst batting by both teams inevitably lined up in the same order here. That means the September 9, 1965, duel between the Dodgers' Sandy Koufax and the Cubs' Bob Hendley holds first place.

The Cubs were under no illusions about Koufax. They had already faced him twice in 1965, eking out a lone run and 10 hits against 21 strikeouts. But Hendley didn't inspire the same fear in the Dodgers. He had won only 37 games in five seasons with three teams. His record for 1965 was 2-2.

Koufax, as expected, was dazzling. Chicago batters chased his incomparable fastball all night, never catching up to it. Fourteen Cubs struck out. None reached base. Yet Hendley was nearly as effective, yielding one hit — a bloop at that — and one walk. He lost on an unearned run. The combined BPO for the two pitchers was .098, the lowest for any game in the Modern Era.

Koufax, though ecstatic about his perfect game, was gracious in victory. "It's a shame Hendley had to get beaten that way," he told reporters. Hendley was philosophical. "This game is the most recognizable thing I've ever done in baseball," he said. "And I came out a loser."

These rankings are sorted by BPO, then by ERA. Second place goes to a 1988 contest between the Reds and Dodgers that had three hits and a .100 BPO.

The Best 10

Rank	Winner	Loser	Date	Score	H2	HR2	BB2	B2	ERA2	BPO2
1	Dodgers	Cubs	Sept. 9, 1965	1-0	1	0	1	5	0.00	.098
2	Reds	Dodgers	Sept. 16, 1988	1-0	3	0	1	5	0.00	.100
3	Dodgers	Athletics	June 10, 1998	1-0	5	0	1	7	0.00	.132
4	Cubs	Reds	June 30, 1964	1-0	3	0	2	7	0.53	.135
5	Angels	Twins	May 7, 1963	2-0	6	0	1	7	1.06	.135
6	Expos	Dodgers	July 28, 1991	2-0	4	0	1	8	0.00	.143
7	Padres	Giants	May 13, 2010	1-0	6	0	1	8	0.50	.143
8	Marlins	Braves	April 22, 2014	1-0	7	0	0	8	0.50	.145
9	Diamondbacks	Dodgers	April 10, 2001	2-0	5	1	0	8	0.53	.154
10	Royals	White Sox	April 14, 1973	3-0	5	0	4	9	0.00	.155

List #52: Worst Pitching in a Game for Both Teams

It figured that Randy Lerch would be the Phillies starter on May 17, 1979. He had been pitching well that season, though his luck had been poor. Lerch gave up three or fewer runs in seven of his first eight starts, but his record was only 2-2 because of weak run support. And now he had to face the Cubs on a blustery day in Wrigley Field.

His teammates took care of that problem with seven runs in the first. "Whenever Lerch pitched, we never scored any runs for him," recalled shortstop Larry Bowa. "We got those early ones and said to him, 'Okay, there's your runs.'"

But Lerch couldn't take advantage. He gave up three consecutive singles in the bottom of the first, followed by a monstrous home run by Dave Kingman and a double by Jerry Martin. He was lifted with one out and a 7-4 lead. Philadelphia's relievers surrendered another 18 runs the rest of the afternoon.

And yet the Phillies were 23-22 winners on the worst day for pitching in the Modern Era. Eleven pitchers for Chicago and Philadelphia yielded 11 homers, 50 hits, and 117 bases. Their joint BPO was a horrifying 1.857.

The 10 games on this list featured a total of 953 bases. (Any ties in BPO were broken by ERA.) The runner-up was a Reds-Rockies game in May 1999, with the two teams combining for 100 bases. Cincinnati won, 24-12.

The Worst 10

Rank	Winner	Loser	Date	Score	H2	HR2	BB2	B2	ERA2	BPO2
1	Phillies	Cubs	May 17, 1979	23-22	50	11	15	117	18.00	1.857
2	Reds	Rockies	May 19, 1999	24-12	43	9	15	100	17.00	1.818
3	Rockies	Marlins	July 4, 2008	18-17	43	8	11	94	18.00	1.808
4	Expos	Cubs	May 14, 2000	16-15	37	7	16	88	16.10	1.796
5	Rockies	Dodgers	June 30, 1996	16-15	38	10	11	100	11.72	1.786
6	White Sox	Tigers	May 28, 1995	14-12	31	12	14	101	12.00	1.772
7	Rockies	Giants	June 28, 2000	17-13	30	8	19	90	14.82	1.765
8	Yankees	Athletics	Aug. 25, 2011	22-9	36	7	15	88	16.41	1.760
9	Athletics	Twins	July 20, 2009	14-13	39	8	11	85	13.76	1.735
10	Yankees	Devil Rays	June 21, 2005	20-11	41	9	8	90	15.35	1.731

List #53: Best Pitching in a Game

Eight perfect games are included on this list of the Modern Era's greatest individual pitching performances. The man on top, ironically enough, did not pitch one of them.

These rankings were based on a series of comparisons. The initial filter was the lowest number of bases allowed, then lowest ER, highest IP, and highest SO. The top 11 entries were tied in the first three categories — no bases or earned runs in nine innings — so strikeouts became the determining factor.

Max Scherzer of the Nationals nailed down first place by whiffing 17 Mets on October 3, 2015. Scherzer didn't yield a base that day, but an error by third baseman Yunel Escobar ended his flirtation with perfection in the sixth inning. It was Scherzer's second no-hitter of the year — a rare feat — and also his second near-perfect game. A hit batsman (with two outs in the ninth, no less) was the only blemish in his whitewashing of the Pirates on June 20. That game did not qualify for this list, since Scherzer surrendered a base with the HBP.

The runner-up in these standings, Clayton Kershaw, also lost a perfect game to an error, as did Jonathan Sanchez, who is tangled in a five-way tie for seventh place. Everybody else sailed through nine innings without a baserunner of any kind. Two of these perfect pitchers, Sandy Koufax and Matt Cain, are tied for third place with 14 strikeouts apiece.

The Best 10

Rk	Pitcher	Date	Team	Opp	IP	H	SO	ER	B
1	Max Scherzer	Oct. 3, 2015	Nationals	Mets	9.0	0	17	0	0
2	Clayton Kershaw	June 18, 2014	Dodgers	Rockies	9.0	0	15	0	0
3	Sandy Koufax	Sept. 9, 1965	Dodgers	Cubs	9.0	0	14	0	0
3	Matt Cain	June 13, 2012	Giants	Astros	9.0	0	14	0	0
5	Randy Johnson	May 18, 2004	Diamondbacks	Braves	9.0	0	13	0	0
6	Felix Hernandez	Aug. 15, 2012	Mariners	Rays	9.0	0	12	0	0
7	Catfish Hunter	May 8, 1968	Athletics	Twins	9.0	0	11	0	0
7	Len Barker	May 15, 1981	Indians	Blue Jays	9.0	0	11	0	0
7	David Wells	May 17, 1998	Yankees	Twins	9.0	0	11	0	0
7	Jonathan Sanchez	July 10, 2009	Giants	Padres	9.0	0	11	0	0
7	Roy Halladay	May 29, 2010	Phillies	Marlins	9.0	0	11	0	0

List #54: Worst Pitching in a Game

The Texas Rangers selected pitcher Rick Helling in the first round of the 1992 amateur draft, projecting him to be a future ace. Not the next Nolan Ryan, but a solid, consistent winner. And that's what they got when Helling reached the majors in 1994. He won three of his first six starts.

The sixth appearance was the most impressive, a 7-0 shutout of the Twins on May 6. Helling was primed for his next start against the Angels on the 11th. "Before the game, in the bullpen, [pitching coach] Claude Osteen said I looked the best I had all season," he recalled. "But in the game, I threw the worst I have in my life."

California batted around in the first inning, pounding two homers, two triples, a double, and two singles. Helling somehow survived, so manager Kevin Kennedy sent him back out for the second. The Angels greeted him with a single and two more homers. His day was over.

Helling eventually fulfilled his promise, notching 20 wins for the Rangers in 1998. But his start on May 11, 1994, remains the Modern Era's worst individual pitching performance. He surrendered nine earned runs and 27 bases in one inning pitched. His BPO was an astronomical 9.000.

These rankings are based on averages (BPO, then ERA) instead of raw counts because the number of innings varied. Nobody on this list lasted more than 3.2 IP. Everybody gave up at least 25 bases.

The Worst 10

Rk	Pitcher	Date	Team	Opp	IP	H	ER	B	ERA	BPO
1	Rick Helling	May 11, 1994	Rangers	Angels	1.0	10	9	27	81.00	9.000
2	Zack Greinke	July 20, 2004	Royals	Orioles	2.0	9	8	25	36.00	4.167
3	Denny Stark	April 16, 2004	Rockies	Cardinals	2.1	10	8	33	30.86	4.125
4	Casey Daigle	April 9, 2004	Diamondbacks	Cardinals	2.2	10	8	27	27.00	3.857
5	Craig Skok	July 30, 1978	Braves	Expos	2.2	9	8	26	27.00	3.250
6	Josh Fogg	Aug. 22, 2007	Rockies	Pirates	3.0	11	8	26	24.00	3.250
7	Pedro Astacio	July 22, 2001	Rockies	Dodgers	3.2	12	8	32	19.64	3.200
8	Jack Fisher	July 30, 1967	Mets	Astros	3.0	13	9	25	27.00	3.125
9	R.A. Dickey	April 6, 2006	Rangers	Tigers	3.1	8	7	27	18.90	3.000
10	Ben Sheets	May 2, 2010	Athletics	Blue Jays	3.1	10	9	29	24.30	2.900

8. 1960s

List #55: Best Organization in the 1960s

The Yankees won American League and world championships in 1961 and 1962, the first two years of the Modern Era. They took another pair of league crowns in the two seasons that followed, though they came up short in the World Series both times.

No big-league club surpassed New York's two world and four league titles during the 1960s. (This "decade," don't forget, ran for only nine years, since 1960 itself was excluded.) The natural assumption is that the Yankees were the outstanding organization between 1961 and 1969.

But they weren't. They didn't even come close.

The Orioles took top honors for the 1960s by winning the World Series in 1966, taking another Anerican League title three years later, and accumulating more than 90 victories in six of nine seasons. Baltimore's average team score of 61.616 was the best of the decade.

The Giants played in only one World Series during the 1960s — and failed to win it — yet they finished second on this list. San Francisco's winning percentage was .543 or better in every season of the nine-year span.

And what of the Yankees? They disintegrated after the 1964 World Series, plummeting to sixth place in the AL in 1965, then 10th (and last) a year later. The Yanks finished at least 20 games out of first place every season from 1965 to 1969, driving them down to seventh place in the decade's overall standings.

The Best 10

Rank	Organization	Years	W	L	Pct.	Play-offs	League titles	World titles	Average TS
1	Orioles	9	822	633	.565	2	2	1	61.616
2	Giants	9	823	629	.567	1	1	0	60.906
3	Cardinals	9	798	650	.551	3	3	2	60.682
4	Tigers	9	811	646	.557	1	1	1	59.329
5	Twins	9	789	666	.542	2	1	0	59.108
6	Dodgers	9	796	657	.548	3	3	2	57.802
7	Yankees	9	790	663	.544	4	4	2	57.692
8	Reds	9	793	655	.548	1	1	0	54.458
9	White Sox	9	765	693	.525	0	0	0	51.697
10	Braves	9	763	687	.526	1	0	0	51.567

List #56: Worst Organization in the 1960s

Only six teams won a world title between 1961 and 1969. The New York Mets were a member of that elite group, yet they still ranked as the very worst organization of the 1960s.

What made such a dichotomy possible? Years of stunning ineptitude countered the single glorious season of 1969, leaving the Mets with an average team score of 22.242, the lowest for the decade. New York's newest franchise debuted in April 1962 and went on to lose 799 games during its first eight seasons, a hair short of 100 defeats per year. Its winning percentage over that span was a miserable .382.

"You see, the Mets are losers, just like nearly everybody else in life," author Jimmy Breslin wrote in 1963. "This is a team for the cab driver who gets held up and the guy who loses out on a promotion because he didn't maneuver himself to lunch with the boss enough."

Another expansion team, the reincarnation of the Washington Senators, was nearly as incompetent, taking second place on this list. Washington finished at least 32 games out of first place in six of nine seasons. A move to Texas awaited in the decade to come.

Organizations had to play five seasons during the 1960s to qualify for these rankings. The Expos and Padres were equally terrible upon their birth in 1969 (posting identical 52-110 records), but a single year was insufficient for a valid assessment.

The Worst 10

Rank	Organization	Years	W	L	Pct.	Play-offs	League titles	World titles	Average TS
1	Mets	8	494	799	.382	1	1	1	22.242
2	Senators	9	607	844	.418	0	0	0	26.933
3	Athletics	9	628	826	.432	0	0	0	29.800
4	Astros (Colt .45s)	8	555	739	.429	0	0	0	30.940
5	Angels	9	685	770	.471	0	0	0	38.974
6	Cubs	9	675	774	.466	0	0	0	39.626
7	Phillies	9	700	748	.483	0	0	0	40.786
8	Red Sox	9	699	756	.480	1	1	0	41.829
9	Indians	9	707	748	.486	0	0	0	42.298
10	Pirates	9	753	696	.520	0	0	0	50.828

List #57: Best Team in the 1960s

The Baltimore Orioles won 97 games in 1964, then another 94 in 1965, yet they had nothing to show for their high level of play. No world championships. No league titles. Just a pair of third-place finishes.

But 1966 was the year they got even. The Orioles took 12 of their first 13 games, briefly stumbled in May, then roared back to life with a 44-18 record in June and July. Baltimore led the American League by 13 games on August 1 and coasted to the title from there. The World Series was almost as easy, a four-game sweep of the Dodgers.

How did the Orioles finally get over the hump in 1966? The key was their acquisition of right fielder Frank Robinson from the Reds. Cincinnati owner Bill DeWitt famously contended that the future Hall of Famer was "not a young 30," but a rejuvenated Robinson won the Triple Crown in Baltimore, posting a stratospheric BPO+ of 166.9.

Two other players ticketed for Cooperstown, third baseman Brooks Robinson and shortstop Luis Aparicio, anchored the Orioles infield. First baseman Boog Powell (136.4 BPO+) and left fielder Curt Blefary (129.1) thrived at the plate. And 20-year-old Jim Palmer paced the pitching staff with 15 wins.

Baltimore had fewer victories than the three runners-up on this list. But those 97 wins came against a tougher level of competition (according to the TS formula) than the 1968 Tigers, 1969 Orioles, or 1961 Yankees confronted.

The Best 10

Rk	Team	Year	Post	W	L	Pct.	R	RA	BPO	BPOA	TS
1	Baltimore Orioles	1966	WLP	97	63	.606	4.72	3.76	.682	.595	88.282
2	Detroit Tigers	1968	WLP	103	59	.636	4.09	3.00	.634	.550	87.102
3	Baltimore Orioles	1969	LP	109	53	.673	4.81	3.19	.726	.547	86.161
4	New York Yankees	1961	WLP	109	53	.673	5.07	3.75	.729	.617	85.319
5	New York Yankees	1962	WLP	96	66	.593	5.04	4.20	.723	.631	85.088
6	Saint Louis Cardinals	1967	WLP	101	60	.627	4.32	3.46	.642	.563	84.556
7	Saint Louis Cardinals	1968	LP	97	65	.599	3.60	2.91	.577	.518	83.157
8	Minnesota Twins	1965	LP	102	60	.630	4.78	3.70	.690	.610	78.002
9	New York Yankees	1963	LP	104	57	.646	4.43	3.40	.651	.578	77.023
10	Los Angeles Dodgers	1963	WLP	99	63	.611	3.93	3.37	.609	.559	75.294

List #58: Worst Team in the 1960s

The New York Mets were destined to occupy first place on this list. Eighteen big-league teams lost at least 100 games between 1961 and 1969. Nearly a third of those squads — five in all — wore Mets uniforms. The numbers were definitely in their favor.

Yet this abundance of ineptitude poses a quandary: Which New York team was truly the lousiest of the 1960s? The obvious choice might seem to be the 1962 Mets, who still hold the Modern Era record for most defeats in a season (120). But the following year's squad was actually worse, earning the lowest team score of the decade, 8.162.

The 1963 Mets posted a better record (51-111) than their predecessors, yet they plumbed new depths of offensive incompetence, suffering 30 shutouts. No other team since 1961 has been blanked more than 27 times. The 1962 Mets had just six shutouts.

There was no doubt that the 1961 Phillies were a bad team, but they didn't seem to be historically terrible until sinking into a 23-game losing streak from July 29 to August 20. It remains the longest skid in big-league history. Philadelphia finally broke through with a 7-4 win in Milwaukee, yet the celebration was muted. "We were so embarrassed by then that we had no elation," recalled Gene Mauch, the team's manager. The Phillies ended up with a 47-107 record and second place on this list.

The Worst 10

Rk	Team	Year	Post	W	L	Pct.	R	RA	BPO	BPOA	TS
1	New York Mets	1963	—	51	111	.315	3.09	4.78	.524	.690	8.162
2	Philadelphia Phillies	1961	—	47	107	.305	3.77	5.14	.606	.724	8.887
3	New York Mets	1965	—	50	112	.309	3.02	4.59	.520	.680	9.282
4	New York Mets	1962	—	40	120	.250	3.83	5.89	.628	.771	10.038
5	New York Mets	1964	—	53	109	.327	3.49	4.76	.551	.683	10.277
6	San Diego Padres	1969	—	52	110	.321	2.89	4.60	.533	.691	10.456
7	New York Mets	1967	—	61	101	.377	3.07	4.15	.530	.645	14.743
8	Washington Senators	1963	—	56	106	.346	3.57	5.01	.586	.707	14.790
9	Montreal Expos	1969	—	52	110	.321	3.59	4.88	.603	.722	15.677
10	Kansas City Athletics	1964	—	57	105	.352	3.81	5.13	.628	.767	16.031

List #59: Best Batting in the 1960s

Frank Robinson's adaptability during the 1960s has not been matched by any player in any decade.

Robinson began the Modern Era as Cincinnati's right fielder, leading the Reds to the National League pennant in 1961. (They would lose the World Series to the Yankees.) He topped the NL in BPO+ (151.3) and was named its Most Valuable Player.

Four outstanding seasons followed, including another league-best BPO+ in 1962, but the Reds suspected that Robinson was nearing the end of his prime. They traded him in December 1965 to Baltimore, where he quickly adjusted to a leadership role with the Orioles. "When you see a guy who could play at his level and could play with the vigor and intensity that he did," said pitcher Jim Palmer, "I can't see how it could not have affected all of us."

The results in 1966 were even better than in 1961. Robinson won the Triple Crown (49 HR, 122 RBI, .316 BA), posted the best BPO+ in the American League (166.9) and again earned Most Valuable Player honors. He remains the only player in baseball history to be MVP of both leagues. The Orioles capped the year by sweeping the World Series.

Robinson reached 3,650 bases between 1961 and 1969, exceeding the output of a typical player by 1,201.9. It was the decade's best performance at the plate, though just barely. Another great right fielder, the Braves' Hank Aaron, finished 3.6 bases behind with a base value of 1,198.3.

The Best 10

Rank	Batter	Span	G	BA	B	O	BPO	BPO+	BV
1	Frank Robinson	1961-1969	1,329	.305	3,650	3,554	1.027	149.1	1,201.9
2	Hank Aaron	1961-1969	1,387	.309	3,872	3,919	.988	144.9	1,198.3
3	Willie Mays	1961-1969	1,345	.297	3,501	3,609	.970	142.9	1,052.4
4	Harmon Killebrew	1961-1969	1,305	.266	3,475	3,514	.989	141.2	1,016.0
5	Mickey Mantle	1961-1968	1,002	.284	2,469	2,313	1.067	157.7	915.0
6	Willie McCovey	1961-1969	1,221	.282	2,913	3,008	.968	144.3	890.3
7	Dick Allen	1963-1969	866	.300	2,317	2,380	.974	145.3	722.9
8	Norm Cash	1961-1969	1,321	.274	3,069	3,411	.900	129.1	702.8
9	Al Kaline	1961-1969	1,175	.298	2,822	3,112	.907	130.7	656.6
10	Carl Yastrzemski	1961-1969	1,383	.293	3,398	3,899	.872	123.1	620.4

List #60: Best Batting in a Season in the 1960s

It's true that Mickey Mantle's best seasons occurred prior to the Modern Era — a Triple Crown in 1956, the highest BPO+ of his career in 1957 (an astronomical 217.0), and Most Valuable Player Awards for both of those years.

It's also true that Mantle's final seasons with the Yankees were not easy. Physical woes and an alcohol-fueled lifestyle took their toll in the 1960s. "With all of the injuries, coupled with the deteriorating legs," he later wrote, "no doubt I could have called in sick and stayed away from the ballpark." But he stuck around until 1968, no longer performing at the level of a star. He batted a weak .237 in his final season.

But it would be incorrect to assume that Mantle was merely an average player for a prolonged period. No batter enjoyed better seasons in the 1960s. Mantle's BPO+ of 193.6 in 1962 brought a third MVP trophy, as well as first place on this list. It topped his 191.0 from the preceding year. Nobody else between 1961 and 1969 exceeded 189.0 in a single season.

The first and last years of the period are represented by three players in the top 10 — Mantle, Norm Cash, and Jim Gentile from 1961, and Willie McCovey, Reggie Jackson, and Jim Wynn from 1969. The irony is that only McCovey won a league MVP Award, and he barely edged a pitcher, Tom Seaver.

The Best 10

Rank	Batter	Year	Team	G	BA	B	O	BPO	BV	BPO+
1	Mickey Mantle	1962	Yankees	123	.321	362	262	1.382	175.0	193.6
2	Mickey Mantle	1961	Yankees	153	.317	497	360	1.381	236.8	191.0
3	Willie McCovey	1969	Giants	149	.320	454	352	1.290	213.6	188.8
4	Norm Cash	1961	Tigers	159	.361	502	367	1.368	226.6	182.3
5	Reggie Jackson	1969	Athletics	152	.275	475	413	1.150	193.7	168.9
6	Carl Yastrzemski	1967	Red Sox	161	.326	471	409	1.152	191.8	168.7
7	Frank Robinson	1966	Orioles	155	.316	479	430	1.114	192.0	166.9
8	Jim Wynn	1969	Astros	149	.269	432	381	1.134	172.5	166.5
9	Jim Gentile	1961	Orioles	148	.302	430	360	1.194	170.7	165.9
10	Hank Aaron	1963	Braves	161	.319	484	451	1.073	190.2	164.8

List #61: Best Batting in a Game in the 1960s

Willie Mays was at the peak of his considerable powers in 1961. His rare blend of strength and speed had enabled him to lead the National League in slugging percentage three times and stolen bases four times since 1954. These divergent skills, coupled with his excellence in center field, made him an unquestioned superstar.

There was no reason to expect any deviation from greatness in this new season, even though Mays had started a bit slowly. He was batting a quiet .291 with just two home runs in 15 games when the Giants took the field in Milwaukee on April 30.

What happened on that Sunday was anything but quiet. Mays homered off Braves starter Lew Burdette in the first inning, a towering shot over the center-field fence. He took Burdette deep again in the third, flied out in the fifth against a Milwaukee reliever, then wrapped up his day with another pair of homers in the sixth and eighth.

Mays reached 16 bases in five appearances, the greatest game enjoyed by any batter in the 1960s. "All I know is, I was hitting behind him," said teammate Willie McCovey, "and I kept shaking his hand when he crossed home plate."

Willie Stargell finished as the runner-up on this list. He also attained 16 bases on May 22, 1968, but his three home runs left him one short of Mays. (See List #47 for an explanation of the tiebreakers used in this category.)

The Best 10

Rank	Batter	Date	Team	Opp	PA	H	HR	SC	B
1	Willie Mays	April 30, 1961	Giants	Braves	5	4	4	8	16
2	Willie Stargell	May 22, 1968	Pirates	Cubs	5	5	3	8	16
3	Carl Yastrzemski	May 14, 1965	Red Sox	Tigers	6	5	2	5	15
4	Bill White	July 5, 1961	Cardinals	Dodgers	6	4	3	4	15
5	Don Demeter	Sept. 12, 1961	Phillies	Dodgers	6	4	3	9	14
6	Gene Oliver	July 30, 1966	Braves	Giants	5	4	3	8	14
7	Roberto Clemente	May 15, 1967	Pirates	Reds	5	4	3	7	14
8	Willie Stargell	June 24, 1965	Pirates	Dodgers	5	4	3	6	14
9	Joe Morgan	July 8, 1965	Astros	Braves	6	6	2	5	14
10	Ernie Banks	May 29, 1962	Cubs	Braves	5	4	3	4	14

List #62: Best Pitching in the 1960s

Sandy Koufax was frustrated when the 1960 season drew to a close, so terribly frustrated that he thought about quitting baseball. He went 8-13 for the Dodgers that year, giving him a mediocre career record of 36-40 with a 4.10 ERA. Why continue? He tossed his glove and spikes into the trash after the final game and stalked out of the clubhouse.

Koufax returned in 1961, of course. He had decided during the long winter that he needed to get serious. "I didn't work hard enough," he said of his former self. "I didn't do what I should have done."

His newfound focus paid off immediately. Koufax won 18 games for Los Angeles in 1961, finally emerging as the star the Dodgers had been awaiting since 1955. His dynamic fastball and sweeping curve earned him a 129-47 record with a 2.19 ERA during the first six years of the Modern Era, a span that ended when the strain on his fabled left arm forced him to retire at age 30. He yielded 678.4 fewer bases than a typical pitcher would have given up between 1961 and 1966, the best base value for any pitcher throughout the 1960s.

The two runners-up on this list, Bob Gibson and Juan Marichal, were Koufax's greatest contemporaries, surely the outstanding righthanders of the decade. Gibson was fiercely intimidating, while Marichal was the master of a vast repertoire. Both came within 31 bases of Koufax's BV.

The Best 10

Rank	Pitcher	Span	G	ERA	B	O	BPO	BPO+	BV
1	Sandy Koufax	1961-1966	223	2.19	2,307	4,955	.466	77.1	-678.4
2	Bob Gibson	1961-1969	309	2.64	3,794	7,133	.532	84.9	-656.0
3	Juan Marichal	1961-1969	317	2.57	3,825	7,475	.512	85.5	-648.0
4	Larry Jackson	1961-1968	297	3.26	3,530	6,236	.566	90.2	-386.3
5	Hoyt Wilhelm	1961-1969	516	1.99	1,391	2,911	.478	79.5	-358.7
6	Dean Chance	1961-1969	327	2.77	3,108	5,765	.539	90.0	-340.5
7	Don Drysdale	1961-1969	330	2.83	3,900	7,118	.548	92.7	-303.9
8	Whitey Ford	1961-1967	220	2.80	2,373	4,275	.555	89.4	-283.3
9	Sam McDowell	1961-1969	262	2.95	2,671	4,831	.553	90.8	-271.2
10	Fergie Jenkins	1965-1969	189	2.95	1,851	3,351	.552	88.4	-246.1

List #63: Best Pitching in a Season in the 1960s

Joe Horlen is a forgotten man, and unfairly so. He was an excellent starting pitcher for the highly competitive (albeit weak-hitting) Chicago White Sox during the 1960s. Horlen notched 99 victories for the Sox between 1961 and 1969, four times posting an ERA below 2.50.

Yet Chicago never made it to the World Series — despite seasons with 89, 94, 95, and 98 wins — and Horlen faded into obscurity. He is rarely mentioned when the top pitchers of his decade are discussed.

Knowledgeable fans recall Horlen's brilliance in 1967, which is usually cited as his best season. He went 19-7, led the American League with a 2.06 ERA, and finished second for the Cy Young Award. But he was even better in 1964, when the Sox made an unexpected bid for the pennant, finishing a single game behind the AL champion Yankees.

Horlen's ERA of 1.88 was second-best to Dean Chance's 1.65 that year, but their positions were reversed in another key category. The White Sox ace yielded only 273 bases in 210.2 innings, despite the vastness of Chicago's Comiskey Park. His resulting BPO+ of 70.0 edged out Chance's 70.1. It ranked as the preeminent single-season performance by a pitcher in the 1960s.

Chance won the Cy Young Award with the Angels in 1964. He also took second place on this list, while Bob Gibson registered the decade's best BPO+ in any season other than 1964 (70.3 in 1968).

The Best 10

Rank	Pitcher	Year	Team	G	ERA	B	O	BPO	BV	BPO+
1	Joe Horlen	1964	White Sox	32	1.88	273	642	.425	-117.2	70.0
2	Dean Chance	1964	Angels	46	1.65	350	846	.414	-148.9	70.1
3	Bob Gibson	1968	Cardinals	34	1.12	346	917	.377	-146.5	70.3
4	Luis Tiant	1968	Indians	34	1.60	319	777	.411	-120.4	72.6
5	Hank Aguirre	1962	Tigers	42	2.21	318	660	.482	-117.5	73.0
6	Dick Ellsworth	1963	Cubs	37	2.11	401	890	.451	-145.2	73.4
7	Mike Cuellar	1969	Orioles	39	2.38	399	878	.454	-141.5	73.8
8	Sandy Koufax	1963	Dodgers	40	1.88	394	945	.417	-139.4	73.9
9	Juan Marichal	1966	Giants	37	2.23	424	934	.454	-149.1	74.0
10	Sandy Koufax	1965	Dodgers	43	2.04	445	1,022	.435	-155.6	74.1

List #64: Best Pitching in a Game in the 1960s

Outstanding performances were not unusual for Sandy Koufax. The lefthander tossed 40 shutouts for the Dodgers between 1955 and 1966. He pitched 53 complete games in which he surrendered no more than four hits, including eight two-hitters, a pair of one-hitters, and four no-hitters.

But only one of those outings was a perfect game.

It took Koufax just 113 pitches to retire 27 Cubs in order on September 9, 1965. Fourteen Chicago batters struck out. Only seven managed to get the ball out of the infield. Future Hall of Famer Ernie Banks whiffed all three times he came to the plate that night. "Most of the time we knew what was coming, because he held his hands closer to his head when he threw a curveball, but it didn't matter," Banks once said of Koufax. "Even though he was tipping off his pitches, you still couldn't hit him."

Three pitchers delivered perfect games in the 1960s. Koufax earned first place on this list because of his 14 strikeouts. The runners-up, Catfish Hunter and Jim Bunning, were equally flawless, though they recorded fewer outs on strikes. (See List #53 for an explanation of the tiebreakers for this category.)

Seven of the decade's 10 best showings were no-hitters. The other three pitchers allowed one harmless single apiece. Koufax was the only man to make the list more than once, both times without giving up a hit.

The Best 10

Rank	Pitcher	Date	Team	Opp	IP	H	SO	ER	B
1	Sandy Koufax	Sept. 9, 1965	Dodgers	Cubs	9.0	0	14	0	0
2	Catfish Hunter	May 8, 1968	Athletics	Twins	9.0	0	11	0	0
3	Jim Bunning	June 21, 1964	Phillies	Mets	9.0	0	10	0	0
4	Gary Peters	July 15, 1963	White Sox	Orioles	9.0	1	13	0	1
5	Sandy Koufax	June 4, 1964	Dodgers	Phillies	9.0	0	12	0	1
6	Tom Seaver	July 9, 1969	Mets	Cubs	9.0	1	11	0	1
7	Dave Morehead	Sept. 16, 1965	Red Sox	Indians	9.0	0	8	0	1
8	Woodie Fryman	July 1, 1966	Pirates	Mets	9.0	1	8	0	1
9	Bill Monbouquette	Aug. 1, 1962	Red Sox	White Sox	9.0	0	7	0	1
9	Sonny Siebert	June 10, 1966	Indians	Senators	9.0	0	7	0	1

9. 1970s

List #65: Best Organization in the 1970s

The Athletics seemed destined to be the outstanding organization of the 1970s. Oakland won three straight World Series from 1972 to 1974, the first team to accomplish that feat in the Modern Era. The A's were outrageously colorful — literally so in their gold and kelly green uniforms — and justifiably arrogant. "It's mind-boggling winning three straight," boasted pitcher Vida Blue. "What we did is one of the great accomplishments in sports."

But the Athletics' dynasty could not withstand the onslaught of free agency, which decimated their roster and dropped them to last place by 1977. Oakland was supplanted atop the baseball pyramid by the powerful Cincinnati Reds, better known as the Big Red Machine. Cincinnati seized a pair of world titles (1975 and 1976), won more games than any other franchise during the 1970s (953), and finished with the decade's best average team score (68.473).

The Reds' attack was paced by four stars who outperformed the National League norm by at least 400 bases between 1970 and 1979. Second baseman Joe Morgan led the majors with a 10-year base value of 1,247.7. He was backed by Johnny Bench (540.0 BV for the decade), Pete Rose (480.9), and Tony Perez (421.7). All but Rose are now in the Hall of Fame.

The best organization of the 1960s, the Orioles, remained strong in the 1970s, taking second place on this list. But the Athletics, once seen as Baltimore's heir apparent, plummeted to sixth by the end of the decade.

The Best 10

Rank	Organization	Years	W	L	Pct.	Play-offs	League titles	World titles	Average TS
1	Reds	10	953	657	.592	6	4	2	68.473
2	Orioles	10	944	656	.590	5	3	1	66.764
3	Dodgers	10	910	701	.565	3	3	0	64.517
4	Pirates	10	916	695	.569	6	2	2	63.496
5	Yankees	10	892	715	.555	3	3	2	60.869
6	Athletics	10	838	772	.520	5	3	3	57.717
7	Red Sox	10	895	714	.556	1	1	0	57.435
8	Royals	10	851	760	.528	3	0	0	52.269
9	Twins	10	812	794	.506	1	0	0	48.123
10	Cardinals	10	800	813	.496	0	0	0	45.263

List #66: Worst Organization in the 1970s

The Padres debuted inauspiciously in the expansion year of 1969, losing 110 games and posting a pitifully small team score, 10.456. They would improve in the 1970s, though not all that much.

San Diego's first full decade in the National League began with eight consecutive losing seasons. A shocking detour to the positive side of the ledger in 1978 — 84 victories against 78 defeats — was quickly reversed to a more familiar 68-93 the following year. The Padres lost more than 90 games in eight different seasons between 1970 and 1979. Their average team score of 25.729 was far and away the worst for any organization over that span.

San Diego's ineptitude was remarkably balanced. The 1971 team eked out 3.02 runs per game, the weakest offensive performance by any NL club in the decade. The 1977 pitching staff, not to be outdone, allowed 5.15 runs per game, a miserable showing that was eclipsed only once in 10 years — 5.52 per contest by the Braves, also in 1977. It was little wonder that the Padres finished 275 games below .500 during the 1970s.

Their aforementioned pitching woes doomed the Braves to second place on this list, which was confined to organizations in existence for at least five years. The average team scores for 1977's expansion teams, the Blue Jays and Mariners, were actually worse than San Diego's. But both franchises mercifully fell two seasons short of eligibility.

The Worst 10

Rank	Organization	Years	W	L	Pct.	Play-offs	League titles	World titles	Average TS
1	Padres	10	667	942	.415	0	0	0	25.729
2	Braves	10	725	883	.451	0	0	0	33.818
3	Indians	10	737	866	.460	0	0	0	35.606
4	Expos	10	748	862	.465	0	0	0	37.571
5	Brewers	10	738	873	.458	0	0	0	37.753
6	Rangers (Senators)	10	747	860	.465	0	0	0	38.090
7	White Sox	10	752	853	.469	0	0	0	38.824
8	Tigers	10	789	820	.490	1	0	0	39.776
9	Angels	10	781	831	.484	1	0	0	40.201
10	Mets	10	763	850	.473	1	1	0	41.967

List #67: Best Team in the 1970s

The batting order for the Cincinnati Reds was imposing and remarkably consistent in the mid-1970s. Manager Sparky Anderson penciled in the same position players — the so-called Great Eight — night after night. Five of these stalwarts outperformed the National League norm by at least 12 percent in 1975, led by Joe Morgan's MVP-worthy 182.6 BPO+ and Johnny Bench's 126.6. The Great Eight reached 2,595 bases that year, exceeding expectations by 391.8.

But this firepower was slow to mesh. The Reds were a pedestrian 28-21 in April and May, lingering behind the Dodgers in the NL West. A double-header sweep of the Cubs pushed them into first place on June 8, and they shifted into overdrive. Cincinnati won 80 of its final 113 contests — waltzing away with the division by 20 games, then edging the Red Sox in a classic World Series.

The 1975 Reds generated a team score of 90.713, the best in the 1970s. The 1976 version won 102 regular-season games — six fewer than the year before — yet was more impressive in the postseason. The Big Red Machine swept the NL Championship Series from the Phillies, then the World Series from the Yankees. Many fans consider the 1976 Reds to be superior, but their TS of 87.331 is third on this list.

Tucked between Cincinnati's two entries are the 1970 Orioles, who won 108 games, the World Series over (who else?) the Reds, and second place for the decade.

The Best 10

Rk	Team	Year	Post	W	L	Pct.	R	RA	BPO	BPOA	TS
1	Cincinnati Reds	1975	WLP	108	54	.667	5.19	3.62	.748	.625	90.713
2	Baltimore Orioles	1970	WLP	108	54	.667	4.89	3.54	.726	.600	87.901
3	Cincinnati Reds	1976	WLP	102	60	.630	5.29	3.91	.789	.629	87.331
4	Pittsburgh Pirates	1971	WLP	97	65	.599	4.86	3.70	.693	.597	87.094
5	Oakland Athletics	1974	WLP	90	72	.556	4.25	3.40	.663	.575	86.731
6	Oakland Athletics	1972	WLP	93	62	.600	3.90	2.95	.621	.535	84.430
7	Baltimore Orioles	1971	LP	101	57	.639	4.70	3.35	.717	.572	83.333
8	Pittsburgh Pirates	1979	WLP	98	64	.605	4.75	3.94	.719	.642	83.113
9	Los Angeles Dodgers	1978	LP	95	67	.586	4.49	3.54	.722	.598	82.060
10	Los Angeles Dodgers	1974	LP	102	60	.630	4.93	3.46	.718	.568	81.722

List #68: Worst Team in the 1970s

The Padres entered the 1973 season with no illusions. They had averaged 101 losses per year since 1969, and an upswing seemed unlikely. The people of San Diego registered their disgust by avoiding the ballpark. Home attendance would amount to just 611,826, the lowest in the majors that year.

The situation was so dire that the Padres began negotiating a move to the nation's capital. Press accounts in late May said that everything was in order. "Baseball's Back," shrieked a headline in the *Washington Post*. It proved to be premature (and inaccurate). City officials in San Diego threatened a lawsuit, and the team meekly agreed to abide by its lease.

This off-field drama obscured a stream of on-field disasters. The Padres plummeted 10 games off the pace in the National League West before the end of April and just kept dropping. They finished with a 60-102 record, 39 games behind the division-leading Reds. Their TS of 10.185 was the decade's worst.

The Padres were so weak that their first-round choice in June's amateur draft bypassed the minors and vaulted directly to the majors. It was perhaps the only positive development of the year. Dave Winfield started his drive to the Hall of Fame against the Astros on June 19 with the first of 3,110 hits.

The strongest team at the beginning of the decade, the Athletics, deteriorated badly by the end. Second place on this list went to the 1979 Oakland squad, which absorbed 108 defeats.

The Worst 10

Rk	Team	Year	Post	W	L	Pct.	R	RA	BPO	BPOA	TS
1	San Diego Padres	1973	—	60	102	.370	3.38	4.75	.578	.696	10.185
2	Oakland Athletics	1979	—	54	108	.333	3.54	5.31	.587	.771	11.385
3	Texas Rangers	1972	—	54	100	.351	2.99	4.08	.529	.644	11.812
4	Texas Rangers	1973	—	57	105	.352	3.82	5.21	.617	.739	12.786
5	Detroit Tigers	1975	—	57	102	.358	3.58	4.94	.587	.713	13.022
6	Toronto Blue Jays	1979	—	53	109	.327	3.78	5.32	.604	.762	13.628
7	San Diego Padres	1974	—	60	102	.370	3.34	5.12	.579	.758	13.763
8	Atlanta Braves	1977	—	61	101	.377	4.19	5.52	.639	.804	16.259
9	Cleveland Indians	1971	—	60	102	.370	3.35	4.61	.570	.715	16.585
10	Montreal Expos	1976	—	55	107	.340	3.28	4.53	.565	.689	16.785

List #69: Best Batting in the 1970s

Joe Morgan was not a big man — five-feet-seven, 160 pounds — but he was a dominant player in his time. Morgan demonstrated great patience at the plate, made consistent contact when he swung, and flashed tremendous speed on the basepaths. Mix in his five Gold Gloves at second base, and he was the epitome of a five-tool star.

Morgan reached his peak in the mid-1970s, winning back-to-back National League Most Valuable Player Awards. "I have never seen anyone, and I mean anyone, play better than Joe has played this year," raved Cincinnati manager Sparky Anderson in 1975, the first of the MVP seasons. Morgan batted .327 that year, stole 67 bases, and posted a 182.6 BPO+. Nobody else in the league did better than 133.3. He turned on the power the following year, leading the NL in slugging percentage and pushing his BPO+ up to 193.5. Next came Mike Schmidt at 139.0.

Morgan couldn't maintain that exalted level of play — who could? — but he remained strong throughout the decade. He kept his BPO+ above 110.0 for 10 straight seasons, two with the Astros and eight with the Reds. And he accumulated 4,008 bases, surpassing expectations by 1,247.7, easily the top base value of the 1970s.

The runner-up on this list, Reggie Jackson, trailed Morgan by 324.1 in the BV column. Jackson blasted 292 home runs during the decade for the Athletics, Orioles, and Yankees.

The Best 10

Rank	Batter	Span	G	BA	B	O	BPO	BPO+	BV
1	Joe Morgan	1970-1979	1,458	.282	4,008	3,942	1.017	145.4	1,247.7
2	Reggie Jackson	1970-1979	1,440	.275	3,570	3,954	.903	135.0	923.6
3	Bobby Bonds	1970-1979	1,479	.274	3,983	4,457	.894	128.5	885.0
4	Willie Stargell	1970-1979	1,255	.287	3,130	3,269	.957	136.5	832.0
5	Rod Carew	1970-1979	1,358	.343	3,326	3,762	.884	128.7	744.2
6	Mike Schmidt	1972-1979	1,084	.255	2,807	2,932	.957	131.7	676.8
7	Reggie Smith	1970-1979	1,286	.292	3,141	3,495	.899	126.7	660.7
8	Ken Singleton	1970-1979	1,405	.289	3,140	3,658	.858	125.8	640.7
9	Cesar Cedeno	1970-1979	1,293	.289	3,234	3,813	.848	124.4	631.3
10	Gene Tenace	1970-1979	1,229	.245	2,571	2,962	.868	130.2	599.0

List #70: Best Batting in a Season in the 1970s

Joe Morgan reached base by any means possible. Consider his exemplary versatility for the Reds in 1976, which brought him a second consecutive Most Valuable Player Award. Morgan displayed a keen eye at the plate (114 BB, second in the National League), hit for a strong average (.320 BA, fifth), showed considerable power (27 HR, also fifth), and posed a constant threat on the bases (60 SB, second).

His grand total for 1976 was 459 bases, which topped both leagues. Only three other batters finished above 400 that year — Mike Schmidt (441), Rod Carew (411), Pete Rose (402) — and each of them played 15 to 21 more games than Morgan. The gap was considerably wider in BPO+, with Morgan posting the highest mark of the decade, 193.5. Everybody else in the majors remained below 140.0.

The previous season had been virtually the same. Morgan's batting average and stolen bases were slightly higher in 1975 (.327 and 67), while his home run total was lower at 17. His BPO+ was also a bit smaller (182.6), though it was still the second-highest of the 1970s.

Dick Allen reached third place on this list with the greatest season of his colorful career. The White Sox first baseman registered a 177.2 BPO+ in 1972, fueled by his American League-leading 37 homers. His performance moved famed sportswriter Jerome Holtzman to proclaim Allen to be "as gifted a ballplayer as there ever was in the major leagues."

The Best 10

Rank	Batter	Year	Team	G	BA	B	O	BPO	BV	BPO+
1	Joe Morgan	1976	Reds	141	.320	459	344	1.334	221.8	193.5
2	Joe Morgan	1975	Reds	146	.327	461	354	1.302	208.6	182.6
3	Dick Allen	1972	White Sox	148	.308	427	374	1.142	186.0	177.2
4	Hank Aaron	1971	Braves	139	.327	410	348	1.178	169.6	170.6
5	Willie McCovey	1970	Giants	152	.289	446	368	1.212	173.8	163.9
6	Willie Stargell	1971	Pirates	141	.295	416	373	1.115	160.8	163.0
7	Joe Morgan	1974	Reds	149	.293	440	387	1.137	169.9	162.9
8	Willie Stargell	1973	Pirates	148	.299	424	376	1.128	162.6	162.2
9	Carl Yastrzemski	1970	Red Sox	161	.329	489	407	1.201	184.5	160.6
10	Bobby Murcer	1971	Yankees	146	.331	396	375	1.056	148.9	160.3

List #71: Best Batting in a Game in the 1970s

Mike Schmidt had led the National League in home runs the previous two years, but his power was nowhere to be seen in mid-April 1976. The Phillies third baseman had eked out a homer against the Pirates in the season's second game, but he was having trouble making contact. His bottom line for the first four games: that lone homer, a pair of singles, and nine strikeouts.

But then came the fifth game in Chicago's Wrigley Field on a breezy April 17. Philadelphia fell behind the Cubs by 12-1 after three innings, but Schmidt felt good. He singled in the fourth, then blasted a home run an inning later. The Phillies kept clawing back, and Schmidt more than did his part. He launched three more homers in the seventh, eighth and 10th. The latter shot clinched an 18-16 Philadelphia victory.

Schmidt modestly credited the wind. "I didn't have to catch all of the ball that day," he recalled. "In a uniform ballpark, some of those balls wouldn't have been home runs." But 26 other men went to the plate that day, hitting just five homers between them. Schmidt had performed at a higher level, amassing 17 bases, the best single-game total in the 1970s.

Fred Lynn was a rookie when he took second place on this list. The Red Sox center fielder had played only 69 big-league games when he went five-for-six against the Tigers on June 18, 1975, with three homers, a triple, and a single.

The Best 10

Rank	Batter	Date	Team	Opp	PA	H	HR	SC	B
1	Mike Schmidt	April 17, 1976	Phillies	Cubs	6	5	4	8	17
2	Fred Lynn	June 18, 1975	Red Sox	Tigers	6	5	3	11	16
3	George Mitterwald	April 17, 1974	Cubs	Pirates	5	4	3	8	15
4	George Brett	May 28, 1979	Royals	Orioles	8	5	2	5	15
5	Davey Lopes	Aug. 20, 1974	Dodgers	Cubs	6	5	3	4	15
6	Willie Stargell	Aug. 1, 1970	Pirates	Braves	6	5	2	9	14
7	Steve Garvey	Aug. 28, 1977	Dodgers	Cardinals	5	5	2	8	14
8	Dave Kingman	May 14, 1978	Cubs	Dodgers	8	4	3	8	14
9	Larry Parrish	May 29, 1977	Expos	Cardinals	5	5	3	7	14
10	Rico Carty	May 31, 1970	Braves	Phillies	5	4	3	7	14

List #72: Best Pitching in the 1970s

Tom Seaver is frozen in the popular mind as a pitcher of the 1960s. Fans still remember his dramatic arrival in 1967, posting 16 victories for the hapless Mets and being named Rookie of the Year. And who could forget the dreamlike season of 1969? Seaver morphed into Tom Terrific that year. He went 25-7, won the Cy Young Award, and led the Mets to the most improbable of world titles.

But Seaver was only 25 when the 1970s began, and he had plenty of baseball left. He won 178 games for the Mets and Reds during the decade, topping the National League in strikeouts five times. He was rewarded with Cy Youngs in 1973 and 1975.

The typical pitcher would have yielded 5,034.1 bases under Seaver's circumstances between 1970 and 1979, but he allowed only 4,242. His resulting base value of minus-792.1 was the best of the decade.

Gaylord Perry couldn't match the zip on Seaver's fastball, but his wide array of pitches earned him the runner-up slot on this list. Perry had a BV of minus-695.9 for four teams during the 1970s, the Giants, Indians, Rangers, and Padres.

The future Hall of Famer was frequently accused of throwing a spitball, a charge he always denied with a grin. A TV reporter once jokingly pursued the issue with Perry's five-year-old daughter. "Does your daddy throw a grease ball?" he asked. She already knew the expected response. "It's a hard slider," she said.

The Best 10

Rank	Pitcher	Span	G	ERA	B	O	BPO	BPO+	BV
1	Tom Seaver	1970-1979	348	2.61	4,242	7,996	.531	84.3	-792.1
2	Gaylord Perry	1970-1979	369	2.92	4,853	8,767	.554	87.4	-695.9
3	Jim Palmer	1970-1979	355	2.58	4,502	8,243	.546	88.7	-579.0
4	Bert Blyleven	1970-1979	353	2.88	4,531	7,910	.573	89.2	-549.1
5	Fergie Jenkins	1970-1979	360	3.38	4,893	8,189	.598	90.6	-506.8
6	Don Sutton	1970-1979	352	3.07	4,361	7,733	.564	91.0	-422.3
7	Phil Niekro	1970-1979	406	3.26	5,369	8,723	.615	92.7	-418.4
8	Tommy John	1970-1979	294	3.09	3,389	6,007	.564	89.5	-405.2
9	Vida Blue	1970-1979	330	3.07	4,086	7,250	.564	91.5	-369.9
10	Steve Rogers	1973-1979	230	3.13	2,840	4,930	.576	89.1	-346.4

List #73: Best Pitching in a Season in the 1970s

Ron Guidry fashioned an impressive 14-year career with the Yankees. He won 170 games, a total surpassed by only four pitchers in the history of that fabled franchise. The lefty wasn't Cooperstown material, but his place in Yankees lore is secure. The organization retired his number in 2003.

Yet Guidry didn't earn lasting fame for his career statistics. He is best remembered for a single season in which he dominated the American League.

Guidry notched 13 victories before suffering 1978's first defeat in early July. He tossed nine shutouts — the most by any AL lefthander since Babe Ruth in 1916 — and capped the regular season for the Yanks by defeating the Red Sox in a one-game playoff for the AL East title. His final line featured a 25-3 record, 1.74 ERA, and 69.0 BPO+. The latter was the best for any starter in the 1970s.

Guidry would pitch another decade in pinstripes. He would win at least 20 games twice more, but never as many as 25. He would post a sub-100 BPO+ in seven seasons, but never as low as 69.0. "Of course, I never expected another year like 1978," he admitted. "You're just not likely to put it all together that way in any one season."

Second place on this list went to Don Sutton. The best year of his 23-season Hall of Fame career was 1972, when he went 19-9 with a 71.5 BPO+.

The Best 10

Rank	Pitcher	Year	Team	G	ERA	B	O	BPO	BV	BPO+
1	Ron Guidry	1978	Yankees	35	1.74	367	826	.444	-164.6	69.0
2	Don Sutton	1972	Dodgers	33	2.08	358	829	.432	-143.0	71.5
3	Mike Caldwell	1978	Brewers	37	2.36	421	889	.474	-154.3	73.2
4	Vida Blue	1971	Athletics	39	1.82	411	936	.439	-144.3	74.0
5	Steve Carlton	1972	Phillies	41	1.97	490	1,040	.471	-169.1	74.3
6	Mark Fidrych	1976	Tigers	31	2.34	364	764	.476	-120.7	75.1
7	Tom Seaver	1971	Mets	36	1.76	392	855	.458	-128.1	75.4
8	Catfish Hunter	1975	Yankees	39	2.58	489	989	.494	-154.4	76.0
9	Tom Seaver	1973	Mets	36	2.08	421	880	.478	-129.8	76.4
10	Dennis Leonard	1977	Royals	38	3.04	469	886	.529	-137.5	77.3
10	Rick Reuschel	1977	Cubs	39	2.79	417	758	.550	-122.6	77.3

List #74: Best Pitching in a Game in the 1970s

Dick Bosman was a journeyman pitcher. He was good enough to stick around the big leagues for 11 years, but his career record of 82-85 was nothing special. He spent most of his time pitching for the Senators, Rangers, and Indians, mediocre teams that never played deep into October. His grand total of post-season experience was one-third of an inning for Oakland in 1975.

But Bosman was the greatest pitcher on the planet for one night, tossing a near-perfect game in Cleveland on July 19, 1974. His opponent was no patsy. The Athletics were two-time defending world champions who would add a third title that fall.

Bosman was amazingly efficient that night. He needed just 79 pitches to no-hit Oakland, inducing 15 of 27 outs on ground balls. A lone mistake kept him from perfection. Slow-footed Sal Bando dropped a bunt for the A's in the fourth inning. Bosman grabbed it cleanly, but his throw pulled first baseman Tommy McCraw off the bag. "If I had set myself a little bit, I certainly would have had the play," Bosman said. "That's why it was an error, because I had plenty of time, but I hurried the throw."

Yet his performance was still the best of the decade, the only game in which a starter worked nine innings without yielding a base. Another Indian, Dennis Eckersley, took second place with a 12-strikeout no-hitter in 1977. A lone walk marred that outing.

The Best 10

Rank	Pitcher	Date	Team	Opp	IP	H	SO	ER	B
1	Dick Bosman	July 19, 1974	Indians	Athletics	9.0	0	4	0	0
2	Dennis Eckersley	May 30, 1977	Indians	Angels	9.0	0	12	0	1
3	Bill Singer	July 20, 1970	Dodgers	Phillies	9.0	0	10	0	1
4	Vida Blue	Sept. 21, 1970	Athletics	Twins	9.0	0	9	0	1
5	John Candelaria	Aug. 9, 1976	Pirates	Dodgers	9.0	0	7	0	1
5	Bert Blyleven	Sept. 22, 1977	Rangers	Angels	9.0	0	7	0	1
7	Silvio Martinez	June 27, 1979	Cardinals	Expos	9.0	1	7	0	1
8	Milt Pappas	Sept. 2, 1972	Cubs	Padres	9.0	0	6	0	1
9	Nelson Briles	Aug. 22, 1972	Pirates	Giants	9.0	1	6	0	1
10	John Montefusco	Sept. 29, 1976	Giants	Braves	9.0	0	4	0	1

10. 1980s

List #75: Best Organization in the 1980s

There was something monotonous about the way the Yankees dominated baseball between the early 1920s and the mid-1960s. New York won 29 American League pennants and 20 world championships in a 44-year span. The great sports columnist Jim Murray couldn't imagine how any fan could derive joy from supporting such an overdog. "Rooting for the Yankees," he wrote, "is like rooting for U.S. Steel."

And then, poof, it all went away. The Yanks plummeted to sixth place in 1965, then to 10th (and last) place a year later. So began a 32-year drought — broken only by a pair of world titles in the late 1970s — that endured until the Yankees finally re-emerged as a consistent contender in 1996.

The irony is that the organization enjoyed several strong seasons in the midst of that dry spell, including five years with 89 to 103 wins during the 1980s. The Yankees' winning percentage of .547 was the best for that decade, as was their average team score of 57.373, despite a lone league championship in 1981 and an absence of world titles.

The Yanks ascended to first place on this list because of the decade's lack of an overpowering team. Nine organizations won world championships in the 1980s, with only Los Angeles taking more than one. Yet the Dodgers also suffered four sub-.500 seasons between 1980 and 1989, dropping them to second place overall.

The Best 10

Rank	Organization	Years	W	L	Pct.	Play-offs	League titles	World titles	Average TS
1	Yankees	10	854	708	.547	2	1	0	57.373
2	Dodgers	10	825	741	.527	4	2	2	56.905
3	Tigers	10	839	727	.536	2	1	1	56.459
4	Cardinals	10	825	734	.529	3	3	1	55.927
5	Royals	10	826	734	.529	4	2	1	53.716
6	Red Sox	10	821	742	.525	2	1	0	52.953
7	Expos	10	811	752	.519	1	0	0	51.619
8	Blue Jays	10	817	746	.523	2	0	0	50.955
9	Athletics	10	803	764	.512	3	2	1	50.573
10	Mets	10	816	743	.523	2	1	1	50.384

List #76: Worst Organization in the 1980s

The Mariners were destined to struggle throughout the 1980s. Their goal was simply to play .500 ball for the first time since their creation in 1977. They never succeeded.

Seattle made some progress, to be sure. Its worst record of the 10-year span came at the very start (59-103 in 1980), while its best performance occurred near the end (78-84 in 1987). But all 10 seasons ended with more defeats than victories. The Mariners posted the decade's lowest winning percentage (.430) and weakest average team score (29.488).

Sports fans in the Pacific Northwest reacted with predictable lethargy. Empty seats usually outnumbered customers at the cavernous Kingdome. Home attendance fell short of 1.3 million every year during the 1980s, failing to reach 900,000 in four of those seasons. "I remember a game against Cleveland when somebody hit a foul ball into the stands down the left-field line," said Lee Pelekoudas, who worked in the Mariners' front office. "Nobody went down to get it. Everybody was sitting behind the plate between the dugouts."

The next two teams on this list were much better than the Mariners — more than six points superior in average TS — yet they endured tough times in the 1980s. The Indians balanced a pair of winning seasons against two years with more than 100 defeats. The Braves won as many as 89 games in a single season, though they also lost as many as 106.

The Worst 10

Rank	Organization	Years	W	L	Pct.	Play-offs	League titles	World titles	Average TS
1	Mariners	10	673	893	.430	0	0	0	29.488
2	Indians	10	710	849	.455	0	0	0	35.660
3	Braves	10	712	845	.457	1	0	0	35.933
4	Twins	10	733	833	.468	1	1	1	36.814
5	Cubs	10	735	821	.472	2	0	0	37.668
6	Rangers	10	720	839	.462	0	0	0	38.401
7	Padres	10	762	805	.486	1	1	0	41.573
8	Pirates	10	732	825	.470	0	0	0	41.716
9	Reds	10	781	783	.499	0	0	0	42.322
10	White Sox	10	758	802	.486	1	0	0	42.672

List #77: Best Team in the 1980s

The Detroit Tigers were a bit of a surprise in 1984. Everybody knew they were good — any team blessed with Kirk Gibson, Alan Trammell, Lou Whitaker, Lance Parrish, and Jack Morris was bound to be competitive — but nobody expected them to be dominant. Detroit, after all, had finished six games behind Baltimore in the American League East the year before.

But the Tigers quickly squelched any doubts. They roared through their first 40 games, outscoring their opponents 236-120 en route to a supernatural 35-5 record. It was an unsustainable pace, of course, but Detroit still led the division from wire to wire, wrapping up 104 regular-season victories and a World Series title.

Whitaker would insist 30 years later that the 1984 Tigers were "probably the best team that ever walked on a baseball field," and the stats make a plausible case. Detroit outscored its opponents by more than a run per game (5.12 to 3.97) and posted a BPO 141 points greater than the BPO it allowed (.747 to .606). Only two world champions in the Modern Era could match that feat — the 1976 Reds and 1998 Yankees — but their team scores were inferior to the Tigers' 97.109.

The 1984 Detroit squad obviously was the best of the decade, just as the 1986 Mets (108 wins, 94.962 TS) clearly deserved runner-up honors. Nobody else in the 1980s topped 86 points on the team-score scale.

The Best 10

Rk	Team	Year	Post	W	L	Pct.	R	RA	BPO	BPOA	TS
1	Detroit Tigers	1984	WLP	104	58	.642	5.12	3.97	.747	.606	97.109
2	New York Mets	1986	WLP	108	54	.667	4.83	3.57	.714	.600	94.962
3	Oakland Athletics	1989	WLP	99	63	.611	4.40	3.56	.675	.593	85.486
4	Baltimore Orioles	1983	WLP	98	64	.605	4.93	4.02	.720	.638	81.677
5	Saint Louis Cardinals	1985	LP	101	61	.623	4.61	3.53	.718	.594	80.680
6	Oakland Athletics	1988	LP	104	58	.642	4.94	3.83	.704	.622	80.527
7	Los Angeles Dodgers	1981	WLP	63	47	.573	4.09	3.24	.641	.574	78.333
8	San Francisco Giants	1989	LP	92	70	.568	4.31	3.70	.662	.612	76.226
9	Philadelphia Phillies	1980	WLP	91	71	.562	4.49	3.94	.684	.653	75.971
10	Saint Louis Cardinals	1982	WLP	92	70	.568	4.23	3.76	.671	.646	75.018

List #78: Worst Team in the 1980s

The Tigers may have been the most fearsome team in baseball in 1984, but their mystique dissipated quickly. Detroit made only one subsequent play-off appearance — losing the American League Championship Series to the Twins in 1987 — before the wheels fell off in 1989.

Hall of Fame manager Sparky Anderson was still at the helm, but his lineup had changed dramatically in five years. Only three regulars from 1984's batting order remained prominent in 1989. Lou Whitaker (126.6 BPO+) was still in his prime, but Chet Lemon (89.6) and Alan Trammell (89.4) were decidedly subpar. Jack Morris, the ace of the 1984 staff, struggled to a 6-14 mark with a 4.86 ERA.

Their new teammates were unable to pick up the slack. Detroit finished last in the league in both batting average (.242) and ERA (4.53). The bleakest part of the season was the heart of summer, with the Tigers posting a miserable 17-43 record in July and August. They wound up with 103 losses and a team score of 8.859, the lowest for any team in the 1980s.

The 1988 Orioles seemed destined for first place on this list. They suffered a 12-0 whipping at the hands of the Brewers on opening day, then dropped their next 20 games for good measure. They didn't break into the win column until April 29. Baltimore finished with a 54-107 record, but its 9.850 TS wasn't quite bad enough to pass the Tigers.

The Worst 10

Rk	Team	Year	Post	W	L	Pct.	R	RA	BPO	BPOA	TS
1	Detroit Tigers	1989	—	59	103	.364	3.81	5.04	.619	.748	8.859
2	Baltimore Orioles	1988	—	54	107	.335	3.42	4.90	.601	.725	9.850
3	Atlanta Braves	1988	—	54	106	.338	3.47	4.63	.576	.681	12.913
4	Toronto Blue Jays	1981	—	37	69	.349	3.10	4.40	.547	.654	13.370
5	Cleveland Indians	1987	—	61	101	.377	4.58	5.91	.711	.795	15.631
6	Minnesota Twins	1981	—	41	68	.376	3.44	4.42	.547	.680	16.267
7	New York Mets	1983	—	68	94	.420	3.55	4.20	.586	.677	17.063
8	Seattle Mariners	1983	—	60	102	.370	3.44	4.57	.608	.717	17.114
9	Minnesota Twins	1982	—	60	102	.370	4.06	5.06	.641	.766	17.191
10	San Francisco Giants	1984	—	66	96	.407	4.21	4.98	.646	.721	17.387

List #79: Best Batting in the 1980s

The primary objective of a leadoff man is to get on base. And nobody in the 1980s handled that assignment more skillfully than Rickey Henderson.

The future Hall of Famer entered the decade with only 89 games of big-league experience, yet he took charge at the top of the Athletics' batting order. Henderson rapped 179 hits, drew 117 walks, and stole 100 bases in 1980. The 21-year-old left fielder reached 467 bases in all, 51 more than anybody else in the American League that year. His BPO+ of 153.8 was second only to George Brett's 180.0.

That set the tone for the decade. It seemed that Henderson was always on base, and always itching to steal another. He was constantly on the move. "If my uniform doesn't get dirty," he liked to say, "I haven't done anything in the baseball game." He led the American League in stolen bases nine times during the 10-year span, while setting the pace for walks in three seasons and hits once.

An average batter who mirrored Henderson's playing time with the Athletics and Yankees would have reached 2,717.7 bases in the 1980s, but he surpassed those expectations by 52 percent. Henderson attained a total of 4,125 bases, yielding the decade's highest base value, 1,407.3.

Another speedy leadoff man, the Expos' Tim Raines, took second place on this list. His BV of 954.5 was slightly better than the 936.7 for slugger Mike Schmidt of the Phillies.

The Best 10

Rank	Batter	Span	G	BA	B	O	BPO	BPO+	BV
1	Rickey Henderson	1980-1989	1,383	.291	4,125	3,976	1.037	152.0	1,407.3
2	Tim Raines	1980-1989	1,269	.303	3,498	3,589	.975	137.5	954.5
3	Mike Schmidt	1980-1989	1,320	.277	3,481	3,558	.978	136.8	936.7
4	George Brett	1980-1989	1,252	.311	3,229	3,410	.947	134.1	822.2
5	Eddie Murray	1980-1989	1,500	.293	3,668	4,184	.877	126.2	757.8
6	Dwight Evans	1980-1989	1,466	.280	3,715	4,075	.912	124.9	739.0
7	Wade Boggs	1982-1989	1,183	.352	3,026	3,148	.961	131.3	723.8
8	Jack Clark	1980-1989	1,189	.268	2,918	3,208	.910	130.6	690.1
9	Pedro Guerrero	1980-1989	1,212	.308	2,844	3,135	.907	131.4	679.7
10	Darryl Strawberry	1983-1989	957	.260	2,490	2,628	.947	136.8	672.5

List #80: Best Batting in a Season in the 1980s

George Brett missed more than 40 games in 1980 — fully a quarter of the season — because of thumb, ankle, and wrist injuries. Yet he still won the American League's Most Valuable Player Award with ease.

It was an unimaginable outcome early in the season. Brett's batting average was .301 on June 1 — respectable, though short of the .329 he had hit in 1979. Reggie Jackson, Eddie Murray, and Rickey Henderson appeared to be better MVP candidates for 1980.

But Brett got hot as the summer progressed. He rapped two hits against the Tigers on July 10, three more the next day, then another six in a three-game series in Baltimore. It was the start of an incredible 40-game stretch in which Brett shelled opposing pitchers for 77 hits in 161 at bats.

Sportswriters descended on Kansas City, anxious to report on the first .400 hitter since Ted Williams. "You're a bunch of idiots," Brett told them. "I'm not going to hit .400." But his average soared to .407 by August 26, and the nation was riveted. "When I got to September," he recalled, "I decided it was within reach."

But it wasn't to be. Brett batted .324 in the final month, excellent by most standards, but insufficient for his goal. He finished with a BA of .390 and a BPO+ of 180.0, topping the 1980s in both categories.

Runner-up Mike Schmidt launched 31 homers in the strike-shortened 1981 season, helping him to a 176.7 BPO+.

The Best 10

Rank	Batter	Year	Team	G	BA	B	O	BPO	BV	BPO+
1	George Brett	1980	Royals	117	.390	379	298	1.272	168.5	180.0
2	Mike Schmidt	1981	Phillies	102	.316	320	258	1.240	138.9	176.7
3	Rickey Henderson	1985	Yankees	143	.314	469	398	1.178	187.8	166.8
4	Rickey Henderson	1983	Athletics	145	.292	433	395	1.096	168.8	163.9
5	Jack Clark	1987	Cardinals	131	.286	390	309	1.262	151.6	163.6
6	Kevin Mitchell	1989	Giants	154	.291	445	402	1.107	172.7	163.4
7	Pedro Guerrero	1985	Dodgers	137	.320	387	353	1.096	147.8	161.8
8	George Brett	1985	Royals	155	.335	446	388	1.149	167.0	159.8
9	Howard Johnson	1989	Mets	153	.287	444	425	1.045	162.9	157.9
10	Paul Molitor	1987	Brewers	118	.353	385	321	1.199	140.2	157.3

List #81: Best Batting in a Game in the 1980s

Bob Horner was an ideal cleanup man for the Braves in 1986, a nine-year veteran with an intense swing. His career highlights included three years with more than 30 home runs and four seasons with at least 89 runs batted in.

But Horner was suffering a power shortage on July 6. He hadn't homered in half a month. A pair of doubles were his only extra-base hits since June 21.

His dry spell came to a dramatic end against the Expos that day. Horner blasted a homer off Montreal's Andy McGaffigan in the second inning. He took McGaffigan deep again in the fourth and fifth, popped up in the seventh, and came to the plate one last time in the bottom of the ninth. The Braves were well behind, so often the case in what would be a 72-89 season. Horner stepped in against one of the National League's top relievers, Jeff Reardon, and smashed the ball over the left-field fence.

It was the best day enjoyed by any batter in the 1980s — 16 bases in five appearances — yet the Braves still lost 11-8. Sixteen big-league batters have hit four homers in one game. Only Horner and Ed Delahanty of the 1896 Phillies ended up on the losing side.

Behind Horner are nine batters with 14 bases. Eddie Murray took second place on tiebreakers. (See List #47 for details.) He homered three times, singled, and walked for the Orioles on August 26, 1985.

The Best 10

Rk	Batter	Date	Team	Opp	PA	H	HR	SC	B
1	Bob Horner	July 6, 1986	Braves	Expos	5	4	4	6	16
2	Eddie Murray	Aug. 26, 1985	Orioles	Angels	6	4	3	9	14
3	Freddie Patek	June 20, 1980	Angels	Red Sox	6	4	3	8	14
4	Eric Davis	May 3, 1987	Reds	Phillies	5	4	3	7	14
5	Mickey Brantley	Sept. 14, 1987	Mariners	Indians	6	5	3	7	14
6	Darryl Strawberry	Aug. 5, 1985	Mets	Cubs	5	4	3	6	14
6	Eric Davis	Sept. 10, 1986	Reds	Giants	5	4	3	6	14
6	Darnell Coles	Sept. 30, 1987	Pirates	Cubs	5	4	3	6	14
9	Kirby Puckett	Aug. 30, 1987	Twins	Brewers	6	6	2	6	14
10	Claudell Washington	June 22, 1980	Mets	Dodgers	5	4	3	5	14

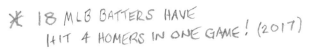

* 18 MLB BATTERS HAVE HIT 4 HOMERS IN ONE GAME! (2017)

List #82: Best Pitching in the 1980s

There was no shortage of star pitchers during the 1980s, but many either left or arrived in the middle of the decade. Out the door were Fergie Jenkins and Gaylord Perry (both retired in 1983), Jim Palmer (1984), Rollie Fingers (1985), and Tom Seaver (1986). In to replace them were Orel Hershiser (called up in 1983) and Roger Clemens, Bret Saberhagen, and Dwight Gooden (all in 1984).

These comings and goings yielded a surprise winner on this list, Dave Stieb of the Blue Jays. Other top-flight pitchers may have had only five or six years to make their mark, but Stieb was a key member of Toronto's staff throughout the 1980s, scoring 140 wins and being named to six All-Star teams.

Stieb's consistent excellence is largely forgotten these days. He twice posted the best BPO+ in the American League, 79.5 in 1982 and 80.4 in 1985, and he ranked among the league's 10 BPO+ leaders eight times. Sportswriter Joe Posnanski suggested that Stieb might even have qualified for Cooperstown under better circumstances. "He had the Hall of Fame misfortune of wasting some of those years on terrible teams," Posnanski wrote, "and the Hall of Fame misfortune of spending just about his entire career in Canada where he often went unnoticed."

Stieb's base value of minus-577.8 was the best for any pitcher during the 1980s. The runner-up was Clemens, who pitched only six seasons in the decade, yet picked up two Cy Young Awards along the way.

The Best 10

Rank	Pitcher	Span	G	ERA	B	O	BPO	BPO+	BV
1	Dave Stieb	1980-1989	339	3.32	4,204	6,999	.601	87.9	-577.8
2	Roger Clemens	1984-1989	175	3.06	2,163	3,876	.558	81.5	-490.7
3	Orel Hershiser	1983-1989	231	2.69	2,359	4,436	.532	85.9	-387.2
4	Bret Saberhagen	1984-1989	204	3.23	2,287	3,987	.574	85.6	-383.7
5	Dan Quisenberry	1980-1989	637	2.67	1,670	3,024	.552	83.7	-331.1
6	Teddy Higuera	1985-1989	154	3.28	1,925	3,272	.588	87.1	-284.6
7	Dwight Gooden	1984-1989	177	2.64	2,134	3,887	.549	88.8	-274.1
8	John Tudor	1980-1989	250	3.13	2,947	4,879	.604	91.5	-262.8
9	Bert Blyleven	1980-1989	291	3.64	3,957	6,254	.633	93.8	-254.0
10	Nolan Ryan	1980-1989	314	3.14	3,730	6,349	.587	94.3	-232.1

List #83: Best Pitching in a Season in the 1980s

John Tudor was the perfect third or fourth guy for a starting rotation. The lefty almost always won more games than he lost, reaching double digits in victories eight times during his 12-year career. Yet he never seemed good enough to be a staff's ace. He never topped 13 wins.

Except in 1985, which would be a magical year for the Cardinals. Tudor, newly arrived from the Pirates in a trade, would be a major contributor to Saint Louis's first 100-win season in nearly two decades.

Both of those outcomes were impossible to imagine during the first couple of months. The Cardinals were mired in fourth place in the National League East at the end of May, and Tudor was struggling with a 1-7 record and a 3.74 ERA.

The turnaround began in early June, when Tudor altered the way he released his pitches. "Since that time," he told reporters, "everything has just fallen into place." He won nine straight starts, lost to the Dodgers in late July, then racked up another 11 wins as the Cards breezed to the NL pennant. Tudor tossed 10 shutouts in the final four months of the season, finishing with a 21-8 record. His BPO+ of 69.3 was the lowest for any pitcher in the 1980s.

Tudor squeaked past Roger Clemens on this list by a tenth of a point. Clemens went 24-4 with a 69.4 BPO+ in 1986, as he led the Red Sox to a pennant of their own.

The Best 10

Rank	Pitcher	Year	Team	G	ERA	B	O	BPO	BV	BPO+
1	John Tudor	1985	Cardinals	36	1.93	358	826	.433	-158.9	69.3
2	Roger Clemens	1986	Red Sox	33	2.48	369	776	.476	-162.7	69.4
3	Dwight Gooden	1985	Mets	35	1.53	367	827	.444	-142.6	72.0
4	Jimmy Key	1987	Blue Jays	36	2.76	413	790	.523	-147.6	73.7
5	Bret Saberhagen	1989	Royals	36	2.16	370	789	.469	-131.4	73.8
6	Jerry Reuss	1980	Dodgers	37	2.51	333	705	.472	-114.1	74.5
7	Rick Reuschel	1985	Pirates	31	2.27	281	591	.475	-94.7	74.8
8	Teddy Higuera	1988	Brewers	31	2.45	335	682	.491	-108.4	75.5
9	Nolan Ryan	1981	Astros	21	1.69	212	454	.467	-65.8	76.3
10	Mike Witt	1986	Angels	34	2.84	420	815	.515	-128.5	76.6

List #84: Best Pitching in a Game in the 1980s

It took several years, but Len Barker finally broke through. The six-foot-five righthander was tabbed as a future star when the Rangers drafted him in 1973, but he fell short of expectations. Texas gave up after the 1978 season and dealt him to the Indians. His first year in Cleveland also went poorly.

Everything finally came together in 1980. Barker won 19 games — not easily done on a team with a 79-81 record — and he led the American League in strikeouts. He remained hot at the beginning of 1981, surrendering only six earned runs in his first four starts.

The Blue Jays knew they were in for a tough time when Barker took the mound on May 15. It was a damp, cold night in Cleveland Stadium, and only 7,290 fans were in attendance. Latecomers wandered in as the Indians pitcher briskly induced three Toronto groundouts in the top of the first.

It was that way all night. Barker demonstrated the best control of his life, mixing a lively fastball and an elusive hard curve. Eleven Jays went down on strikes, and nine others were retired on grounders. Barker never faced a three-ball count as he pitched the 10th perfect game in big-league history. It was the outstanding performance of the 1980s.

Mike Witt and Tom Browning also pitched perfect games during the decade, but they generated fewer strikeouts, respectively consigning them to second and third place on this list.

The Best 10

Rank	Pitcher	Date	Team	Opp	IP	H	SO	ER	B
1	Len Barker	May 15, 1981	Indians	Blue Jays	9.0	0	11	0	0
2	Mike Witt	Sept. 30, 1984	Angels	Rangers	9.0	0	10	0	0
3	Tom Browning	Sept. 16, 1988	Reds	Dodgers	9.0	0	7	0	0
4	Jerry Reuss	June 27, 1980	Dodgers	Giants	9.0	0	2	0	0
5	Jose DeLeon	Aug. 30, 1989	Cardinals	Reds	11.0	1	8	0	1
6	Floyd Bannister	Sept. 13, 1987	White Sox	Mariners	9.0	1	10	0	1
7	Milt Wilcox	April 15, 1983	Tigers	White Sox	9.0	1	8	0	1
7	LaMarr Hoyt	May 2, 1984	White Sox	Yankees	9.0	1	8	0	1
7	Mike Scott	June 12, 1988	Astros	Braves	9.0	1	8	0	1
10	Bob Welch	May 29, 1980	Dodgers	Braves	9.0	1	7	0	1

11. 1990s

List #85: Best Organization in the 1990s

The Braves were awful throughout the latter half of the 1980s. They finished last in the National League West three times between 1985 and 1989, next to last the other two seasons. Their five-year record was 324-480.

The new decade started in familiar fashion, with a 65-97 mark bringing another last-place visit in 1990. General manager Bobby Cox was so disgusted that he fired manager Russ Nixon in late June and took the job himself. It appeared to be a stopgap move, but actually proved to be the pivotal moment for a dramatic turnaround.

The Braves were blessed with outstanding young arms — Tom Glavine was 23 and John Smoltz 22 at the start of the decade — and Cox quickly harnessed their skills, leading the Braves to an unexpected NL pennant in 1991. Greg Maddux arrived in Atlanta as a free agent two years later, solidifying the best pitching staff in baseball. The Braves would win five league titles and one world championship in the 1990s. Their 925 regular-season wins were 74 more than any other organization produced, and their average team score of 71.790 was 12-and-a-half points better than anybody else's.

Atlanta's lone weakness was its inability to come through in the World Series, where it lost four of five matchups with American League champions. Two organizations actually won multiple world titles during the decade — three for the Yankees and two for the Blue Jays. They're the runners-up on this list.

The Best 10

Rank	Organization	Years	W	L	Pct.	Play-offs	League titles	World titles	Average TS
1	Braves	10	925	629	.595	8	5	1	71.790
2	Yankees	10	851	702	.548	5	3	3	59.249
3	Blue Jays	10	801	754	.515	3	2	2	53.844
4	Reds	10	809	746	.520	2	1	1	53.640
5	Indians	10	823	728	.531	5	2	0	53.387
6	White Sox	10	816	735	.526	1	0	0	52.980
7	Astros	10	813	742	.523	3	0	0	50.719
8	Red Sox	10	814	741	.523	4	0	0	50.508
9	Orioles	10	794	757	.512	2	0	0	50.019
10	Dodgers	10	797	757	.513	2	0	0	49.655

List #86: Worst Organization in the 1990s

Florida joined the National League as an expansion team in 1993. Everybody knew what to expect. The Marlins would be terrible for at least five years, perhaps as many as 10. They might become competitive around the turn of the century.

The first three seasons went according to form, with Florida losing nearly 57 percent of its games. But the Marlins suddenly accelerated the timetable, closing in on .500 in 1996 (80-82) and jumping to 92 wins in 1997. They shocked the baseball world by grabbing a wild-card berth the latter year, then edging the Indians for one of the most unlikely World Series titles in history.

Their success was shortlived. Owner Wayne Huizenga claimed that the Marlins had hemorrhaged $34 million in 1997 despite their success on the field. He initiated a massive fire sale, dealing away veteran stars Gary Sheffield (132.7 BPO+ in 1997), Moises Alou (116.7), and Bobby Bonilla (110.9), as well as pitching ace Kevin Brown (2.69 ERA, 81.6 BPO+). Florida plummeted to a 54-108 mark in 1998, becoming the only world titlist to lose at least 100 games the following year.

The Marlins wrapped up the decade with a .442 winning percentage, the worst for any franchise in existence for at least five seasons. Their average team score of 35.729 edged the Tigers (35.772) for first place on this list. Detroit enjoyed two winning seasons during the 1990s, but also endured three years with more than 90 defeats.

The Worst 10

Rank	Organization	Years	W	L	Pct.	Play-offs	League titles	World titles	Average TS
1	Marlins	7	472	596	.442	1	1	1	35.729
2	Tigers	10	702	852	.452	0	0	0	35.772
3	Twins	10	718	833	.463	1	1	1	37.152
4	Angels	10	738	817	.475	0	0	0	37.268
5	Cubs	10	739	813	.476	1	0	0	37.838
6	Phillies	10	732	823	.471	1	1	0	38.025
7	Rockies	7	512	559	.478	1	0	0	38.870
8	Royals	10	725	825	.468	0	0	0	39.674
9	Brewers	10	742	811	.478	0	0	0	40.793
10	Cardinals	10	758	794	.488	1	0	0	42.992

List #87: Best Team in the 1990s

Many experts believe the 1998 Yankees were the best — not just of the Modern Era, but of all time. ESPN's Buster Olney contends that they put together "the greatest season in the history of baseball." *Sports Illustrated's* Tom Verducci hails them as "the greatest team in the history of integrated baseball."

The players themselves agreed. Their 1998 World Series rings carried an immodest two-word engraving: "Best Ever." It was a bold declaration, given that 23 Yankee squads had won world championships before them.

This book disagrees with the consensus, ranking the 1984 Tigers ahead of the 1998 Yankees for the Modern Era. But there is no doubt that New York fielded the greatest team of the 1990s. The Yanks posted 114 wins in 1998, outscoring their opponents by 1.91 runs per game. (Nobody else in the decade did better than 1.62.) Their average team score of 96.123 was easily the best on this list.

The 1998 Yankees possessed a remarkable array of weapons. Bernie Williams (.339 BA, 139.6 BPO+), Derek Jeter (.324, 118.1), and Paul O'Neill (116.8) powered the attack. David Wells (18-4 W-L, 81.2 BPO+) and David Cone (20-7, 90.6) anchored the rotation. Closer Mariano Rivera locked down 36 saves.

The 1990 Athletics rank second in this category despite being swept by the Reds in the World Series. Oakland earned extra credit for winning 103 games in an unusually competitive American League. Only one AL team suffered more than 88 losses in 1990.

The Best 10

Rk	Team	Year	Post	W	L	Pct.	R	RA	BPO	BPOA	TS
1	New York Yankees	1998	WLP	114	48	.704	5.96	4.05	.823	.649	96.123
2	Oakland Athletics	1990	LP	103	59	.636	4.52	3.52	.708	.602	89.366
3	Cleveland Indians	1995	LP	100	44	.694	5.83	4.22	.835	.677	87.220
4	Atlanta Braves	1995	WLP	90	54	.625	4.48	3.75	.699	.632	84.662
5	New York Yankees	1999	WLP	98	64	.605	5.56	4.51	.814	.705	83.564
6	Atlanta Braves	1996	LP	96	66	.593	4.77	4.00	.723	.618	83.372
7	Toronto Blue Jays	1993	WLP	95	67	.586	5.23	4.58	.776	.695	82.767
8	Minnesota Twins	1991	WLP	95	67	.586	4.79	4.02	.717	.662	82.261
9	Toronto Blue Jays	1992	WLP	96	66	.593	4.81	4.21	.720	.655	81.049
10	Atlanta Braves	1992	LP	98	64	.605	4.21	3.51	.666	.600	80.453

List #88: Worst Team in the 1990s

Nobody expected much out of the Tigers in 1996. They had gone 60-84 in the abbreviated 1995 season, and a housecleaning was underway.

Franchise icon Kirk Gibson and Hall of Fame manager Sparky Anderson retired as soon as the final game of 1995 was played. The lone Detroit starter with a winning record, David Wells (10-3), moved on to Baltimore. And both Tigers who exceeded leaguewide norms at the plate, Cecil Fielder (103.1 BPO+ in 1995) and Chad Curtis (101.9), would be traded away by July of 1996.

That left Detroit with the youngest lineup in the majors. The senior starting pitcher was 28. Not a single position player was older than 27. The bottom line inevitably suffered. The Tigers stumbled to a 13-41 record by the end of May, rallied briefly in midsummer, then disintegrated during a 4-22 September.

Pitching was Detroit's greatest weakness. The staff's earned run average of 6.38 was 0.79 higher than the ERA for any other big-league team in 1996, and its BPOA of .902 was 85 points higher. The Tigers finished with 109 losses and a team score of 5.197, marking them as the worst team of the 1990s.

The 1991 Indians were nearly as bad, racking up 105 defeats and a 9.976 TS. They were especially inept with the bat. Cleveland was shut out 18 times that year and scored a single run apiece in 24 games.

The Worst 10

Rk	Team	Year	Post	W	L	Pct.	R	RA	BPO	BPOA	TS
1	Detroit Tigers	1996	—	53	109	.327	4.83	6.81	.701	.902	5.197
2	Cleveland Indians	1991	—	57	105	.352	3.56	4.69	.592	.674	9.976
3	Florida Marlins	1998	—	54	108	.333	4.12	5.70	.641	.823	12.978
4	Oakland Athletics	1997	—	65	97	.401	4.72	5.84	.731	.852	16.589
5	New York Yankees	1990	—	67	95	.414	3.72	4.62	.610	.703	17.305
6	Atlanta Braves	1990	—	65	97	.401	4.21	5.07	.653	.730	20.029
7	Philadelphia Phillies	1997	—	68	94	.420	4.12	5.19	.662	.766	20.921
8	Pittsburgh Pirates	1995	—	58	86	.403	4.37	5.11	.670	.755	20.970
9	Houston Astros	1991	—	65	97	.401	3.73	4.43	.605	.681	21.015
10	Minnesota Twins	1995	—	56	88	.389	4.88	6.17	.719	.836	21.344

List #89: Best Batting in the 1990s

Barry Bonds evolved greatly during the 1990s. He grew from 185 pounds at the decade's start to 210 pounds by its end. (Some observers gave the credit to training, others to pharmaceuticals.) He gradually amped up his power, while relying a bit less on speed. And he moved as a free agent from Pittsburgh to San Francisco after the 1992 season.

The one constant was his magnificent level of play. Bonds posted a BPO+ between 145.4 and 195.1 every season in the decade, meaning he was 45 to 95 percent better than the typical batter, an enormous advantage. He won three Most Valuable Player Awards between 1990 and 1999 and undoubtedly deserved more. Why? Because he led the National League in BPO+ an amazing seven times and was the runner-up in two of the remaining three years.

An average player who made the same number of appearances in the same ballparks would have amassed 2,700.6 bases during the 1990s. But Bonds obliterated that total. He reached 4,539 bases, giving him an astronomical BV of 1,838.4 for the 10-year span.

If Frank Thomas had accumulated a base value of 1,370.1 during the 1960s or 1970s, he would have been hailed as the decade's outstanding batter. The same figure in the 1980s would have put him just 37.2 bases behind frontrunner Rickey Henderson. But it was a much different story in the 1990s. The White Sox slugger trailed Bonds by almost 470 in the BV column.

The Best 10

Rank	Batter	Span	G	BA	B	O	BPO	BPO+	BV
1	Barry Bonds	1990-1999	1,434	.302	4,539	3,667	1.238	168.3	1,838.4
2	Frank Thomas	1990-1999	1,371	.320	4,031	3,580	1.126	151.8	1,370.1
3	Mark McGwire	1990-1999	1,221	.268	3,521	3,076	1.145	155.4	1,271.9
4	Jeff Bagwell	1991-1999	1,317	.304	3,791	3,571	1.062	144.0	1,169.0
5	Ken Griffey Jr.	1990-1999	1,408	.302	4,081	3,970	1.028	135.9	1,082.8
6	Rickey Henderson	1990-1999	1,261	.276	3,398	3,390	1.002	139.1	935.7
7	Edgar Martinez	1990-1999	1,295	.322	3,457	3,336	1.036	136.4	931.6
8	Albert Belle	1990-1999	1,336	.299	3,776	3,835	.985	130.7	900.4
9	Gary Sheffield	1990-1999	1,189	.294	3,170	3,189	.994	133.7	806.4
10	Larry Walker	1990-1999	1,278	.313	3,440	3,325	1.035	128.8	787.1

List #90: Best Batting in a Season in the 1990s

No player attracted more media attention during the 1990s than Mark McGwire in 1998. His assault on Roger Maris's single-season home-run record was chronicled by an army of reporters and photographers. The demand for news about the Cardinals first baseman was insatiable. "America is a Baseball Nation again," gushed *Sports Illustrated*, "and McGwire is its head of state."

That was true on September 8, when his 62nd homer erased Maris from the books. And it was doubly true in the final week of the season, as McGwire dueled Sammy Sosa to establish the new home-run mark. The contest ended in McGwire's favor, 70 to 66.

The gap was even wider in base production. McGwire accumulated 556 bases, the highest annual total of the decade. His BPO+ of 199.0 also reigned supreme, stamping his performance in 1998 as the best by any batter between 1990 and 1999. Sosa finished well behind with 513 bases and a 136.5 BPO+, yet he received a nifty consolation prize, the National League's Most Valuable Player Award. (Steroid allegations, of course, eventually tarnished the legacies of both men.)

Barry Bonds occupied four of the 10 slots on this list, including the runner-up position. He posted a BPO+ of 195.1 in 1992, his final year with the Pirates and his finest season of the decade. Bonds finished 3.9 points behind McGwire, yet he accomplished something the Saint Louis slugger was unable to do. He was named that year's NL MVP.

The Best 10

Rank	Batter	Year	Team	G	BA	B	O	BPO	BV	BPO+
1	Mark McGwire	1998	Cardinals	155	.299	556	369	1.507	276.5	199.0
2	Barry Bonds	1992	Pirates	140	.311	473	350	1.351	230.5	195.1
3	Jeff Bagwell	1994	Astros	110	.368	394	279	1.412	187.9	191.2
4	Rickey Henderson	1990	Athletics	136	.325	452	357	1.266	214.2	190.1
5	Frank Thomas	1994	White Sox	113	.353	411	283	1.452	192.2	187.8
6	Barry Bonds	1993	Giants	159	.336	529	388	1.363	244.3	185.8
7	Mark McGwire	1996	Athletics	130	.312	434	306	1.418	194.3	181.1
8	Barry Bonds	1996	Giants	158	.308	516	382	1.351	230.4	180.7
9	Barry Bonds	1994	Giants	112	.312	365	284	1.285	154.2	173.1
10	Gary Sheffield	1996	Marlins	161	.314	498	387	1.287	203.9	169.3

List #91: Best Batting in a Game in the 1990s

Mark Whiten guaranteed himself a nice day with one swing on September 7, 1993. The Saint Louis center fielder blasted a grand slam in the top of the first inning, supplying all the runs the Cardinals would need in an eventual 15-2 shellacking of the Reds.

But Whiten wasn't through. He homered in the sixth and again in the seventh, a pair of three-run shots. That set the stage for his final appearance in the ninth. He was one home run and two RBIs short of the respective big-league records for a single game.

Whiten dug in against flamethrowing Reds reliever Rob Dibble with a runner on first. He doubted he would get an opportunity to go deep. "I thought he was going to pitch around me," Whiten said. But Dibble was determined to attack — "I knew it was history" — and he let loose with his best fastball. Whiten muscled the pitch over the center-field fence.

That made him the 12th batter to hit four homers in a game, as well as the second to drive in 12 runs. The latter tied a mark set by fellow Cardinal Jim Bottomley in 1924. Whiten's 16 bases in five appearances went in the books as the best performance by a batter in the 1990s.

The runner-up on this list, Edgardo Alfonzo of the Mets, also amassed 16 bases, but with fewer homers in more appearances than Whiten. (See List #47 to learn about this category's tiebreakers.)

The Best 10

Rank	Batter	Date	Team	Opp	PA	H	HR	SC	B
1	Mark Whiten	Sept. 7, 1993	Cardinals	Reds	5	4	4	12	16
2	Edgardo Alfonzo	Aug. 30, 1999	Mets	Astros	6	6	3	8	16
3	Harold Baines	May 7, 1991	Athletics	Orioles	5	4	3	8	15
4	Dave Winfield	April 13, 1991	Angels	Twins	6	5	3	7	15
5	Jeffrey Hammonds	May 19, 1999	Reds	Rockies	7	4	3	7	15
6	Albert Belle	July 25, 1999	Orioles	Angels	6	4	3	6	15
7	John Valentin	June 2, 1995	Red Sox	Mariners	5	5	3	4	15
8	Tino Martinez	April 2, 1997	Yankees	Mariners	7	4	3	9	14
9	Ken Griffey Jr.	May 24, 1996	Mariners	Yankees	5	4	3	8	14
10	Jose Canseco	June 13, 1994	Rangers	Mariners	6	5	3	8	14

List #92: Best Pitching in the 1990s

The National League gave out 10 Cy Young Awards during the 1990s. Four were presented to Greg Maddux. The remaining six were divvied up by five other pitchers. (Tom Glavine, Maddux's teammate in Atlanta, was the lone double winner.)

His collection of prestigious trophies confirmed that Maddux was one of the decade's elite pitchers, and his stats reinforced the point. The bespectacled righty worked the most innings in the NL five times between 1990 and 1999, posted the lowest ERA four times, and registered the most victories in three seasons. Maddux's ERA of 2.54 was the best for any big-league pitcher who tossed at least 1,000 innings in the 1990s. Nobody else did better than Jose Rijo's 2.74.

Pinpoint control was the key ingredient in Maddux's recipe for success. He always kept the ball around the plate, thanks to an unparalleled ability to change speeds and locate pitches. Batters coaxed only 443 walks from him in 331 starts in the 1990s, working out to just 1.66 walks per nine innings.

Maddux divided the decade between the Cubs (three years) and Braves (seven). A typical pitcher would have surrendered 4,933.1 bases under his circumstances, but he finished 1,198.1 below that figure. It was easily the best BV on this list.

Roger Clemens was more imposing on the mound — he topped Maddux by 337 strikeouts during the decade — but his base value wasn't quite as impressive. He settled for second place with a BV of minus-929.5.

The Best 10

Rank	Pitcher	Span	G	ERA	B	O	BPO	BPO+	BV
1	Greg Maddux	1990-1999	331	2.54	3,735	7,256	.515	75.8	-1,198.1
2	Roger Clemens	1990-1999	305	3.02	3,779	6,594	.573	80.1	-929.5
3	Kevin Brown	1990-1999	316	3.25	3,802	6,690	.568	84.2	-714.3
4	Pedro Martinez	1992-1999	249	2.83	2,263	4,082	.554	79.0	-609.5
5	John Smoltz	1990-1999	315	3.32	3,782	6,463	.585	86.4	-604.5
6	Randy Johnson	1990-1999	298	3.14	3,797	6,245	.608	87.0	-590.2
7	Tom Glavine	1990-1999	327	3.21	4,030	6,716	.600	88.2	-538.2
8	Kevin Appier	1990-1999	287	3.47	3,425	5,636	.608	86.6	-529.6
9	Mike Mussina	1991-1999	254	3.50	3,216	5,314	.605	85.9	-525.0
10	Curt Schilling	1990-1999	317	3.31	2,906	5,024	.578	85.1	-510.9

List #93: Best Pitching in a Season in the 1990s

Only one pitcher during the 1990s enjoyed a better year than Greg Maddux in 1994. It was Greg Maddux in 1995.

The Braves ace delivered a pair of astounding seasons as the decade reached its midpoint. He was at his very best in 1995, confounding batters with his uncanny accuracy and deceptive off-speed stuff. "Radar guns get a giggle out of his 85-mph fastball," *Sports Illustrated's* Tom Verducci joked that year. He wrote in praise, not ridicule.

The biggest laugh belonged to Maddux, who finished with 19 wins against two losses, leading the Braves to a world championship. He paced the majors with a 1.63 ERA. Nobody else in either league was below 2.48.

Consistency was the hallmark of Maddux's entire career, but especially 1995. He yielded more than two runs in only four of his 28 starts. His BPO+ of 58.6 was the second-lowest of the whole Modern Era — and the very lowest of the 1990s.

The previous season, 1994, had been remarkably similar in many ways — only five games with more than two runs allowed, a 1.56 ERA, and a BPO+ of 60.7. The latter ranked second for the 1990s. You'll also find a third Maddux entry below, sixth place in 1997.

Pedro Martinez is the only other pitcher whose name appears more than once on this list. He peaked with the Red Sox in 1999, going 23-4 with a 62.2 BPO+. It was the best non-Maddux season of the decade.

The Best 10

Rank	Pitcher	Year	Team	G	ERA	B	O	BPO	BV	BPO+
1	Greg Maddux	1995	Braves	28	1.63	256	633	.404	-181.0	58.6
2	Greg Maddux	1994	Braves	25	1.56	258	614	.420	-167.3	60.7
3	Pedro Martinez	1999	Red Sox	31	2.07	301	650	.463	-182.9	62.2
4	Kevin Brown	1996	Marlins	32	1.89	314	705	.445	-161.5	66.0
5	Roger Clemens	1997	Blue Jays	34	2.05	375	796	.471	-191.8	66.2
6	Greg Maddux	1997	Braves	33	2.20	328	698	.470	-153.7	68.1
7	Steve Ontiveros	1994	Athletics	27	2.65	168	349	.481	-77.3	68.5
8	Pedro Martinez	1997	Expos	31	1.90	344	733	.469	-157.6	68.6
9	Randy Johnson	1995	Mariners	30	2.48	332	650	.511	-141.9	70.1
10	Kevin Appier	1993	Royals	34	2.56	353	714	.494	-149.3	70.3

List #94: Best Pitching in a Game in the 1990s

David Wells didn't feel particularly good on May 17, 1998. He would later write that he took the mound in Yankee Stadium that day "half-drunk, with bloodshot eyes, monster breath, and a raging, skull-rattling hangover." He had stayed up until 5 a.m., not the ideal bedtime before a Sunday afternoon game.

Yet Wells was surprisingly effective in the early going. He needed only nine pitches to retire the Twins in the first inning, then 13 in the second. But it was the third inning that offered the first hint of something special, as he struck out the side.

Minnesota would hit only seven pitches out of the infield, all of which were snared by New York outfielders. Wells chipped in with 11 strikeouts to clinch the 15th perfect game in big-league history — and the best single-game pitching performance of the 1990s.

The decade featured four perfect games in all, the most for any 10-year span up to then. David Cone and Kenny Rogers respectively finished second and third on this list, while Dennis Martinez took fifth place. Their positions were determined by strikeouts. (See List #53 to learn more about tiebreakers.)

Terry Mulholland also pitched a no-hit game while facing only 27 batters, but his outing on August 15, 1990, was marred by a throwing error by third baseman Charlie Hayes. Mulholland erased the runner by inducing the next batter to ground into a double play. He tied for third place.

The Best 10

Rank	Pitcher	Date	Team	Opp	IP	H	SO	ER	B
1	David Wells	May 17, 1998	Yankees	Twins	9.0	0	11	0	0
2	David Cone	July 18, 1999	Yankees	Expos	9.0	0	10	0	0
3	Terry Mulholland	Aug. 15, 1990	Phillies	Giants	9.0	0	8	0	0
3	Kenny Rogers	July 28, 1994	Rangers	Angels	9.0	0	8	0	0
5	Dennis Martinez	July 28, 1991	Expos	Dodgers	9.0	0	5	0	0
6	Bobby Witt	June 23, 1994	Athletics	Royals	9.0	1	14	0	1
7	Mike Mussina	May 30, 1997	Orioles	Indians	9.0	1	10	0	1
8	Darryl Kile	Sept. 8, 1993	Astros	Mets	9.0	0	9	0	1
9	Trevor Wilson	June 13, 1990	Giants	Padres	9.0	1	9	0	1
10	Ramon Martinez	July 14, 1995	Dodgers	Marlins	9.0	0	8	0	1

12. 2000s

List #95: Best Organization in the 2000s

The first decade of the 21st century belonged to the New York Yankees.

The Yanks qualified for the playoffs in nine of the 10 seasons, falling short only in 2008, when they still managed to win 89 games. No other team went to the playoffs more than seven times during the 2000s. Seven of the 30 organizations didn't even go once.

The Yankees also boasted four American League titles — doubling the next best total in either league — and they tied the Red Sox with a pair of world championships. The other six World Series between 2000 and 2009 were won by six different organizations.

The New York squads of this period were known for their firepower. Only six batters in the decade amassed base values above 1,000, and two of them spent considerable time with the Yankees. Alex Rodriguez, who came to New York in 2004, posted a BV of 1,324.1 for the 2000s. Jason Giambi, who played with the Yanks from 2002 to 2008, piled up 1,025.1.

The Yankees scored the most runs (8,834) and reached the most bases (34,245) of any organization during this 10-year span. It's no surprise that they also registered the best average team score (68.902).

The Red Sox finished second in all three of those categories, but they still had reason to be greatly pleased. Their world title in 2004 broke an 86-year drought, bringing unrestrained joy to New England.

The Best 10

Rank	Organization	Years	W	L	Pct.	Play-offs	League titles	World titles	Average TS
1	Yankees	10	965	651	.597	9	4	2	68.902
2	Red Sox	10	920	699	.568	6	2	2	63.528
3	Cardinals	10	913	706	.564	7	2	1	62.279
4	Braves	10	892	726	.551	6	0	0	59.128
5	Phillies	10	850	769	.525	3	2	1	56.129
6	Angels	10	900	720	.556	6	1	1	56.058
7	Dodgers	10	862	758	.532	4	0	0	54.045
8	Athletics	10	890	728	.550	5	0	0	53.846
9	Giants	10	855	762	.529	3	1	0	52.424
10	White Sox	10	857	764	.529	3	1	1	52.284

List #96: Worst Organization in the 2000s

The Royals had once been a model franchise. They excelled in the 1970s and 1980s, finishing eighth and then fifth in the organizational rankings for those decades. They reached the American League Championship Series six times between 1976 and 1985, capping that wondrous 10-year span with a world title in the final season.

But those halcyon days were distant memories by the turn of the century. Kansas City faded to eighth-worst in the organizational standings for the 1990s. The most dismal year of that period came at the very end — 64-97 in 1999 — setting the stage for a miserable decade to come.

And, make no mistake, the 2000s truly were miserable. The Royals did win 83 games in 2003, but that brief flash of success was surrounded by nine sub-.500 seasons, with four in the frigid depths below .400. They reached their nadir in 2005, losing 19 games in a row and 106 in total.

Kansas City suffered the most defeats in the decade (948), reached the fewest bases (29,602), and registered the lowest average team score (25.240). It was, by any measure, the worst organization of the 2000s.

But Pittsburgh, another franchise with a proud past, came close. The Pirates went the Royals one better — or worse — by racking up 10 consecutive losing seasons. But they won nine more games during the 2000s, and their average team score of 26.693 was nearly one-and-a-half points better.

The Worst 10

Rank	Organization	Years	W	L	Pct.	Play-offs	League titles	World titles	Average TS
1	Royals	10	672	948	.415	0	0	0	25.240
2	Pirates	10	681	936	.421	0	0	0	26.693
3	Nationals (Expos)	10	711	908	.439	0	0	0	30.263
4	Orioles	10	698	920	.431	0	0	0	30.669
5	Rays (Devil Rays)	10	694	923	.429	1	1	0	31.809
6	Reds	10	751	869	.464	0	0	0	35.521
7	Brewers	10	741	878	.458	1	0	0	37.269
8	Tigers	10	729	891	.450	1	1	0	37.854
9	Padres	10	769	852	.474	2	0	0	40.429
10	Rangers	10	776	844	.479	0	0	0	40.706

List #97: Best Team in the 2000s

The Yankees faced the 2009 season with an aging lineup. Four everyday players and two key pitchers were at least 35 years old. Prominent among the gray-beards were closer Mariano Rivera (39), starter Andy Pettitte and catcher Jorge Posada (both 37), and left fielder Johnny Damon and shortstop Derek Jeter (both 35).

Skeptics doubted that a team so long in the tooth could have the necessary staying power to win a championship. They noted that New York's victory total had spiraled from 97 to 94 to 89 over the previous three-year span, a decidedly downward trend. But the Yanks defied expectations by gaining strength as the 2009 season dragged on. They set a blistering 59-27 pace after July 1, then won 11 of 15 playoff games en route to a world title. "Geezers Win! Geezers Win!" exclaimed the headline in *Slate*.

Relative youngsters Alex Rodriguez (30 HR, 129.7 BPO+) and Mark Teixeira (39 HR, 126.0 BPO+) paced New York's attack, but Jeter (115.3), Damon (111.8), and Posada (111.7) also made major contributions. The ace of the staff was 28-year-old CC Sabathia (19-8 W-L, 82.4 BPO+), but Pettitte added 14 wins and Rivera locked down 44 saves. The resulting team score of 87.433 was the best of the decade.

The next two slots on this list belong to a pair of world champions from Boston. The 2007 team had better pitching, giving it a slight edge over its 2004 Red Sox compatriots.

The Best 10

Rk	Team	Year	Post	W	L	Pct.	R	RA	BPO	BPOA	TS
1	New York Yankees	2009	WLP	103	59	.636	5.65	4.65	.838	.708	87.433
2	Boston Red Sox	2007	WLP	96	66	.593	5.35	4.06	.797	.660	85.711
3	Boston Red Sox	2004	WLP	98	64	.605	5.86	4.74	.824	.691	84.936
4	Seattle Mariners	2001	P	116	46	.716	5.72	3.87	.811	.624	81.959
5	Saint Louis Cardinals	2004	LP	105	57	.648	5.28	4.07	.788	.658	81.249
6	Arizona Diamondbacks	2001	WLP	92	70	.568	5.05	4.18	.757	.669	81.168
7	Philadelphia Phillies	2008	WLP	92	70	.568	4.93	4.20	.762	.701	78.344
8	San Francisco Giants	2002	LP	95	66	.590	4.83	3.80	.767	.639	77.832
9	Anaheim Angels	2002	WLP	99	63	.611	5.25	3.98	.742	.654	77.467
10	Saint Louis Cardinals	2005	P	100	62	.617	4.97	3.91	.726	.643	76.624

List #98: Worst Team in the 2000s

The Tigers came dangerously close to a pair of unhappy Modern Era records in 2003. They lost 119 games, second only to the 120 defeats suffered by the immortal 1962 Mets. And they posted a team score of 7.040, worse than every TS except the 5.197 endured by another Detroit squad in 1996.

But the 2003 Tigers weren't doomed to runner-up status in every category. They took first place on this list, emerging as the worst team in the majors between 2000 and 2009.

Detroit's ineptitude in 2003 was incontrovertible. The Tigers piled up eight more defeats than any other team in the decade. They lost by an average margin of 2.08 runs per game, the worst disparity in the 10-year span. The chasm between their BPOA and BPO was 172 points, 16 points bigger than the next-largest gap in the 2000s.

The Tigers' season degenerated into a series of demoralizing slumps, sometimes lasting a month at a time: 3-20 in April, 5-22 in June, 6-23 in August. Their pitching rotation showed the scars. Each starter lost more than twice as many games as he won, and each finished with an anemic BPO+ between 108 and 128.

The 2004 Diamondbacks took second place with 111 losses and a team score of 10.445. They never recovered from a 14-game losing streak in July, limping to a 20-53 record after the All-Star break.

The Worst 10

Rk	Team	Year	Post	W	L	Pct.	R	RA	BPO	BPOA	TS
1	Detroit Tigers	2003	—	43	119	.265	3.65	5.73	.619	.791	7.040
2	Arizona Diamondbacks	2004	—	51	111	.315	3.80	5.55	.635	.779	10.445
3	Kansas City Royals	2005	—	56	106	.346	4.33	5.77	.651	.801	10.715
4	Kansas City Royals	2006	—	62	100	.383	4.67	5.99	.691	.827	14.785
5	Seattle Mariners	2008	—	61	101	.377	4.14	5.01	.642	.762	14.853
6	Kansas City Royals	2004	—	58	104	.358	4.44	5.59	.661	.803	14.882
7	Milwaukee Brewers	2002	—	56	106	.346	3.87	5.07	.660	.786	15.584
8	Pittsburgh Pirates	2001	—	62	100	.383	4.06	5.30	.654	.750	16.421
9	Washington Nationals	2008	—	59	102	.366	3.98	5.12	.642	.761	17.664
10	Detroit Tigers	2002	—	55	106	.342	3.57	5.37	.609	.762	17.911

List #99: Best Batting in the 2000s

Eight of the 10 batters who amassed the biggest base values during the 2000s were active from the beginning of the decade until the end. That makes sense. BV is a counting stat, so the ideal way to run up an impressive total is to play at a very high level for a very long time.

A ninth member of the top 10 debuted in 2001, giving him nine years to pump up his BV, still a decent period. But the 10th guy essentially played only seven seasons. An injury wiped out all but 14 games in 2005, and he left baseball after 2007. How could be possibly compete with his fellow stars?

Barry Bonds did just fine. He played 319 fewer games than anybody noted above, yet he dominated this list. His BV of 1,785.7 put him 367.6 bases in front of runner-up Albert Pujols, the nine-year man mentioned earlier. No 10-year batter exceeded Alex Rodriguez's 1,324.1.

Bonds was light-years ahead of the pack during the first years of the 21st century. His slugging percentage for the 2000s was .724, nearly 100 points better than Pujols, his closest rival. And his BPO+ for the decade was an astounding 216.0. Pujols again was the hardiest challenger, albeit a distant one at 150.5.

Rodriguez finished third in the BV rankings, but he stood out in a couple of ways. He hit more homers (435) and reached more bases (4,577) than anybody else between 2000 and 2009.

The Best 10

Rank	Batter	Span	G	BA	B	O	BPO	BPO+	BV
1	Barry Bonds	2000-2007	986	.322	3,333	2,024	1.647	216.0	1,785.7
2	Albert Pujols	2001-2009	1,399	.334	4,227	3,695	1.144	150.5	1,418.1
3	Alex Rodriguez	2000-2009	1,524	.304	4,577	4,239	1.080	140.8	1,324.1
4	Manny Ramirez	2000-2009	1,358	.317	3,909	3,572	1.094	141.9	1,155.4
5	Lance Berkman	2000-2009	1,473	.300	4,040	3,815	1.059	135.4	1,056.4
6	Jason Giambi	2000-2009	1,305	.275	3,457	3,229	1.071	142.0	1,025.1
7	Todd Helton	2000-2009	1,466	.331	4,151	3,760	1.104	131.3	999.1
8	Jim Thome	2000-2009	1,368	.271	3,661	3,506	1.044	135.5	952.5
9	Bobby Abreu	2000-2009	1,574	.297	4,278	4,351	.983	127.9	937.8
10	Chipper Jones	2000-2009	1,387	.311	3,711	3,617	1.026	132.1	901.4

List #100: Best Batting in a Season in the 2000s

There was only one question in this category: Which of Barry Bonds's seasons would rank as the best of the decade?

Bonds massively outperformed all rivals during the first half of the 2000s. He blasted 258 homers, drove in 544 runs, and batted .339 between 2000 and 2004. His BPO+ for that five-year span was a superhuman 238.1. It was inconceivable that anybody but Bonds would occupy first place on this list.

There were subtle variations in his yearly output. Bonds posted his best scoring efficiency rate (.306) in 2000, launched the most home runs (73) in 2001, produced his highest batting average (.370) in 2002, accumulated the most HBPs (10) in 2003, and drew the most walks (232) in 2004.

Yet these stats, impressive though they undoubtedly are, can't render the final judgment on Bonds's performance. That assignment goes to BPO+, which opts for the final season of the half-decade. Bonds amassed 553 bases while making only 247 outs in 2004, generating a BPO+ of 284.5, the highest of the entire Modern Era. The next-best batter in the National League that year, Jim Edmonds, boasted a 156.0 BPO+, normally a very impressive figure, but 128.5 points behind the leader in this instance.

Bonds secured five of the top 10 positions on this list, including the four highest. The best non-Bonds year belonged to Jim Thome, who rang up a 181.0 BPO+ for the Indians in 2002.

The Best 10

Rank	Batter	Year	Team	G	BA	B	O	BPO	BV	BPO+
1	Barry Bonds	2004	Giants	147	.362	553	247	2.239	358.6	284.5
2	Barry Bonds	2002	Giants	143	.370	540	262	2.061	348.6	282.2
3	Barry Bonds	2001	Giants	153	.328	612	330	1.855	365.5	248.3
4	Barry Bonds	2003	Giants	130	.341	459	266	1.726	255.7	225.8
5	Jim Thome	2002	Indians	147	.304	459	347	1.323	205.3	181.0
6	Sammy Sosa	2001	Cubs	160	.328	559	408	1.370	249.3	180.5
7	Jason Giambi	2001	Athletics	154	.342	496	368	1.348	216.9	177.7
8	Jason Giambi	2000	Athletics	152	.333	486	357	1.361	206.0	173.6
9	Barry Bonds	2000	Giants	143	.306	468	349	1.341	195.7	171.9
10	Albert Pujols	2008	Cardinals	148	.357	466	364	1.280	192.4	170.3

List #101: Best Batting in a Game in the 2000s

Shawn Green said goodbye in 2007 after 15 seasons with the Blue Jays, Dodgers, Diamondbacks, and Mets. Nobody thought of him as Cooperstown material, even though he played in a couple of All-Star Games and once led the American League in doubles. His was the type of career that draws accolades from contemporaries, but fades swiftly into obscurity after retirement.

Yet Green avoided anonymity solely because of what happened on May 23, 2002. He drilled four balls over the fence in Milwaukee's Miller Park, tying a big-league record, and posted the highest single-game base total for any batter in the 2000s — indeed, in the entire Modern Era.

His performance is remembered to this day. "A friend of mine texted me, saying it must be nice every time somebody has three home runs in a game to be remembered," Green told a reporter in 2015. "It's true. It's nice to be thought of a couple of times a year."

It took Green just six at bats to reach 19 bases on that Thursday afternoon in Milwaukee, with a single and double supplementing his four homers. No other batter since 1961 has accumulated more than 18 bases in a game, and nobody in the 2000s topped 17.

Second place went to Mike Cameron, who lined four home runs (and was hit by a pitch) for the Mariners on May 2, 2002, just three weeks before Green's date with destiny. (See List #47 to learn how these rankings were determined.)

The Best 10

Rk	Batter	Date	Team	Opp	PA	H	HR	SC	B
1	Shawn Green	May 23, 2002	Dodgers	Brewers	6	6	4	9	19
2	Mike Cameron	May 2, 2002	Mariners	White Sox	6	4	4	4	17
3	Carlos Delgado	Sept. 25, 2003	Blue Jays	Devil Rays	4	4	4	6	16
4	Larry Walker	June 25, 2004	Rockies	Indians	6	4	3	6	16
5	Shea Hillenbrand	July 7, 2003	Diamondbacks	Rockies	5	5	3	8	15
6	Jeff Cirillo	June 28, 2000	Rockies	Giants	6	4	3	8	15
7	Victor Martinez	July 16, 2004	Indians	Mariners	6	5	3	7	15
8	Albert Pujols	July 20, 2004	Cardinals	Cubs	5	5	3	6	15
9	Dmitri Young	May 6, 2003	Tigers	Orioles	5	5	2	5	15
10	Kelly Shoppach	July 30, 2008	Indians	Tigers	7	5	2	5	15

List #102: Best Pitching in the 2000s

It was Roy Halladay's misfortune to pitch for the Blue Jays throughout the first decade of the 21st century. Halladay was one of the outstanding pitchers in the major leagues, but Toronto's mediocrity severely limited his exposure. The Jays struggled to a 805-814 record between 2000 and 2009, missing the playoffs all 10 seasons.

Yet Halladay always pitched as if his team were locked in a pennant race. The tall righthander won 139 games and lost only 69 in the 2000s, exhibiting exceptional durability in the process. He led the American League in complete games five times in the decade, and pitched the most innings three times. He was rewarded with a Cy Young Award in 2003 and six All-Star Game appearances.

The average pitcher who worked 1,883 innings for the Blue Jays during the 2000s would have yielded 4,005.3 bases. Halladay kept his total down to 3,334, giving him a base value of minus-671.3. No pitcher in the decade did better.

A pair of Hall of Famers came close. Pedro Martinez surrendered 625.1 fewer bases than normal, and Randy Johnson was 598.9 bases to the good. But both men were considerably older than Halladay, and they were unable to match his consistency. BPO+ told the tale, with Halladay dipping below 85.0 in seven of the 10 years. His two challengers reached that level of excellence in only five seasons apiece.

The Best 10

Rank	Pitcher	Span	G	ERA	B	O	BPO	BPO+	BV
1	Roy Halladay	2000-2009	275	3.40	3,334	5,678	.587	83.1	-671.3
2	Pedro Martinez	2000-2009	227	3.01	2,474	4,407	.561	80.2	-625.1
3	Randy Johnson	2000-2009	287	3.34	3,499	5,700	.614	85.6	-598.9
4	Johan Santana	2000-2009	310	3.12	2,960	5,141	.576	83.8	-569.0
5	Curt Schilling	2000-2007	243	3.54	2,855	4,697	.608	84.5	-533.0
6	Mariano Rivera	2000-2009	651	2.08	975	2,165	.450	64.8	-529.2
7	Roy Oswalt	2001-2009	283	3.23	3,299	5,416	.609	86.8	-502.7
8	Tim Hudson	2000-2009	290	3.50	3,582	5,801	.617	88.4	-470.9
9	Brandon Webb	2003-2009	199	3.27	2,462	4,016	.613	84.2	-466.1
10	Mark Buehrle	2000-2009	326	3.80	4,006	6,192	.647	90.9	-401.7

List #103: Best Pitching in a Season in the 2000s

Pedro Martinez wrapped up the 1990s in grand style, going 23-4 for the Red Sox in 1999. His stingy ERA of 2.07 was coupled with a breathtaking BPO+ of 62.2. The latter was the fourth-best score in the Modern Era.

Martinez considered 1999 to be the pinnacle of his career — "I would have to say that's the highlight" — and few observers expected to see its like again. But the Boston ace picked up in April 2000 where he had left off the previous September. He surrendered no more than five hits in any of his five starts that first month, then followed with a two-hitter and a three-hitter in May. His earned run average after 11 starts was a ridiculously microscopic 0.95.

Martinez's ERA climbed a bit in the second half, though only to 1.74. He started 29 games for the Red Sox in 2000, holding opponents to three or fewer runs in all but two of them. His base value of minus-228.8 for the single season would have ranked as the 26th-best total for the full decade. And his BPO+ of 53.0 took first place not only for any of the 10 seasons in the 2000s (by 14.4 points over runner-up Randy Johnson), but also for the whole era after 1960.

Martinez was overpowering in 2000, as evidenced by his 284 strikeouts, but Johnson went him six better with 290 whiffs for the Diamondbacks in 2004. What made Johnson's 67.4 BPO+ truly amazing was his age. He turned 41 that September.

The Best 10

Rk	Pitcher	Year	Team	G	ERA	B	O	BPO	BV	BPO+
1	Pedro Martinez	2000	Red Sox	29	1.74	258	657	.393	-228.8	53.0
2	Randy Johnson	2004	Diamondbacks	35	2.60	366	747	.490	-176.9	67.4
3	Roger Clemens	2005	Astros	32	1.87	301	642	.469	-144.8	67.5
4	Johan Santana	2004	Twins	34	2.61	331	684	.484	-153.6	68.3
5	Pedro Martinez	2002	Red Sox	30	2.26	293	603	.486	-124.0	70.3
6	Derek Lowe	2002	Red Sox	32	2.58	324	663	.489	-134.4	70.7
7	Chris Carpenter	2009	Cardinals	28	2.24	275	576	.477	-112.5	71.0
8	Tim Hudson	2003	Athletics	34	2.70	363	728	.499	-146.9	71.2
9	Curt Schilling	2002	Diamondbacks	36	3.23	405	780	.519	-160.5	71.6
9	Pedro Martinez	2003	Red Sox	29	2.22	284	558	.509	-112.5	71.6

List #104: Best Pitching in a Game in the 2000s

Randy Johnson possessed a fearsome arsenal of pitches — a blazing fastball and a sweeping slider — and he threw large numbers of them.

Johnson struck out 10.6 batters per nine innings in his 22-year career. His emphasis on power required him to expend extra effort, often working deep in the count, bearing down to get that third strike. It was a tiring way to pitch, especially for a man who turned 40 before the 2004 season began.

The Cardinals tagged the Arizona lefty for five runs in his second start of the year, then the Brewers shelled him for six. Skeptics wondered if he was finally feeling the strain. But Johnson rounded into form, and on May 18, 2004, he proved the critics wrong. He became the oldest pitcher to toss a perfect game.

And he did it his way. Johnson threw 117 pitches and struck out 13 Braves. "A lot of guys came back to the dugout shaking their heads," said Atlanta third baseman Chipper Jones. "It was a situation where a dominant pitcher caught a struggling team." Johnson's final pitch was clocked at 98 miles per hour, wrapping up the greatest pitching gem of the 2000s.

Jonathan Sanchez and Mark Buehrle had the decade's only other zero-base complete games. An error marred the former performance, but the latter was perfect. Their strikeout totals put Sanchez in second place and Buehrle in third. (See List #53 for details.)

The Best 10

Rk	Pitcher	Date	Team	Opp	IP	H	SO	ER	B
1	Randy Johnson	May 18, 2004	Diamondbacks	Braves	9.0	0	13	0	0
2	Jonathan Sanchez	July 10, 2009	Giants	Padres	9.0	0	11	0	0
3	Mark Buehrle	July 23, 2009	White Sox	Rays	9.0	0	6	0	0
4	Mike Mussina	Sept. 2, 2001	Yankees	Red Sox	9.0	1	13	0	1
5	Mark Mulder	July 6, 2001	Athletics	Diamondbacks	9.0	1	9	0	1
6	Mark Buehrle	April 18, 2007	White Sox	Rangers	9.0	0	8	0	1
7	Derek Lowe	April 27, 2002	Red Sox	Devil Rays	9.0	0	6	0	1
8	Odalis Perez	April 26, 2002	Dodgers	Cubs	9.0	1	6	0	1
9	Billy Traber	July 8, 2003	Indians	Yankees	9.0	1	5	0	1
9	Ben Sheets	June 8, 2004	Brewers	Angels	9.0	1	5	0	1

13. 2010s

List #105: Best Organization in the 2010s

The Giants clearly have been the dominant team of the 2010s, haven't they? San Francisco famously adopted a two-year cycle, winning the World Series in 2010, 2012, and 2014 — three championships in the decade's first five seasons. Who possibly could have topped that?

The Cardinals, that's who. Their consistently strong play has been unsurpassed — even by the Giants — during the portion of the 2010s that is already in the books. Saint Louis has qualified for the playoffs five times, won at least 90 games in four seasons, and posted a winning percentage above .530 all seven years. The Giants can't make any of those claims. Their breakdown includes four appearances in the playoffs and only two years above 90 wins, balanced by two seasons below .530.

There is, of course, the matter of those three world titles. No Modern Era organization has been able to exceed that total in any decade. Only the Athletics of the 1970s and Yankees of the 1990s matched it. And the Giants still have three seasons left to set a new mark.

But the Cardinals have enjoyed their own shining moments. They won a world championship in 2011 and a National League pennant in 2013. And their average team score for the 2010s (64.480) is five points better than San Francisco's 59.437. That's an enormous margin, which is why the Cardinals rank as the best organization of the decade — so far.

The Best 10

Rank	Organization	Years	W	L	Pct.	Play-offs	League titles	World titles	Average TS
1	Cardinals	7	637	497	.562	5	2	1	64.480
2	Giants	7	607	527	.535	4	3	3	59.437
3	Dodgers	7	617	516	.545	4	0	0	57.250
4	Nationals	7	607	526	.536	3	0	0	56.807
5	Rangers	7	620	515	.546	5	2	0	55.515
6	Yankees	7	627	507	.553	4	0	0	55.390
7	Tigers	7	607	525	.536	4	1	0	53.139
8	Red Sox	7	587	547	.518	2	1	1	52.851
9	Rays	7	594	541	.523	3	0	0	51.920
10	Blue Jays	7	578	556	.510	2	0	0	50.075

List #106: Worst Organization in the 2010s

Nobody begrudged Jim Crane's strong sense of satisfaction in October 2015. The plan had worked. The team he owned, the Astros, had qualified for the playoffs for the first time in 10 years.

The Houston franchise that Crane purchased in 2011 was mired in mediocrity, having posted a 76-86 record the year before. He gave the go-ahead for a youth movement. High-priced veterans were shown the door, replaced by a locker room of raw youngsters.

"I think we went under a lot of scrutiny when we took over and really kind of stripped the team down," Crane said. "We made a lot of changes in the front office, too. I don't know if it's ever been done with that magnitude, but hopefully we got a couple of believers now."

Progress was painful. The Astros suffered 106 losses in 2011, 107 in 2012, and 111 in 2013. The 2014 season (70-92) finally offered a hint of success, and 2015 brought a wild-card berth and a brief run in the playoffs. Optimism reigned in Houston.

But this list takes the entire decade (or at least its first seven seasons) into account, and the sad truth is that the Astros have been the worst organization. They've piled up 23 more losses than anybody else, and their average team score of 29.681 is the lowest among all 30 teams.

The Twins occupy second place, the result of five sub-.435 seasons and four dead-last finishes in the American League Central.

The Worst 10

Rank	Organization	Years	W	L	Pct.	Play-offs	League titles	World titles	Average TS
1	Astros	7	478	656	.422	1	0	0	29.681
2	Twins	7	501	633	.442	1	0	0	30.682
3	Marlins	7	510	623	.450	0	0	0	35.917
4	Rockies	7	503	631	.444	0	0	0	36.207
5	Mariners	7	523	611	.461	0	0	0	36.724
6	White Sox	7	542	592	.478	0	0	0	38.469
7	Padres	7	532	602	.469	0	0	0	39.004
8	Diamondbacks	7	533	601	.470	1	0	0	39.841
9	Phillies	7	560	574	.494	2	0	0	42.359
10	Cubs	7	546	587	.482	2	1	1	43.370

List #107: Best Team in the 2010s

Teams that rely on young players are destined to lose. It's a baseball truism.

Confirmation was supplied by 2016's four youngest rosters. The Astros, Diamondbacks, Phillies, and Twins struggled to a combined record of 283-365, finishing a collective 92-and-a-half games out of first place.

But the fifth-youngest team defied the odds. The Chicago Cubs rolled to 103 victories and a world championship, the franchise's first since 1908. The Cubs fielded the most youthful lineup in World Series history, starting six players under the age of 25 in Game Two and five in Game Seven.

Chicago's attack was paced by two of the National League's six best batters: Kris Bryant (133.7 BPO+) and Anthony Rizzo (127.2). The starting rotation featured the league's top-rated pitcher, Kyle Hendricks (77.3 BPO+). Bryant was 24 years old; his fellow stars were 26.

Joe Maddon, who had been a big-league manager since 2006, marveled at the precocity of his 2016 Cubs. "It is the most complete group and the young-est group I've had," he said. "That's the part that really blows me away. If you take a moment to look out there, there's a lot of young, inexperienced players."

And yet the Cubs exhibited a level of skill unmatched in the 2010s. Their team score of 92.166 was easily the best of the decade (to this point) — and the fourth-best of the entire Modern Era.

The Red Sox took second place on this list, rising from last place in 2012 to a world championship in 2013.

The Best 10

Rk	Team	Year	Post	W	L	Pct.	R	RA	BPO	BPOA	TS
1	Chicago Cubs	2016	WLP	103	58	.640	4.99	3.43	.755	.594	92.166
2	Boston Red Sox	2013	WLP	97	65	.599	5.27	4.05	.781	.672	81.732
3	Saint Louis Cardinals	2013	LP	97	65	.599	4.83	3.68	.673	.606	78.949
4	Texas Rangers	2011	LP	96	66	.593	5.28	4.18	.774	.639	78.226
5	Toronto Blue Jays	2015	P	93	69	.574	5.50	4.14	.776	.642	77.296
6	Kansas City Royals	2015	WLP	95	67	.586	4.47	3.96	.680	.659	75.761
7	Saint Louis Cardinals	2011	WLP	90	72	.556	4.70	4.27	.717	.656	75.595
8	Philadelphia Phillies	2011	P	102	60	.630	4.40	3.27	.680	.598	75.484
9	Washington Nationals	2014	P	96	66	.593	4.23	3.43	.675	.572	75.183
10	Cleveland Indians	2016	LP	94	67	.584	4.83	4.20	.734	.652	74.722

List #108: Worst Team in the 2010s

The Brewers fielded an unimpressive team in 2010 — as noted by their 77-85 record — but they definitely had the Pirates' number.

Milwaukee won 13 of 18 games against Pittsburgh that year. Several of the Brewers' victories were routs, with scores like 8-0, 8-1, 17-3, and 20-0. "At some point, it's got to turn around," moaned Pittsburgh manager John Russell. "It's a young team, and they need to decide when they want to do that. It's not just Milwaukee. Everyone's kicking us right now."

The 2010 Pirates went 23-57 between June 1 and August 31, a three-month span that featured consecutive streaks of 12, six, seven, five, seven, and five defeats. They scored no more than two runs in 67 games during the full season. And they lost 105 games in all, including 39 by at least five runs.

Two young position players, center fielder Andrew McCutchen (33 SB, 120.1 BPO+) and second baseman Neil Walker (107.6), looked to be building blocks for a future winner. But the pitching staff offered no immediate reason for hope. The Pirates were outscored by 1.73 runs per game, the largest negative margin in the decade.

A TS of 7.550 ticketed the 2010 Pirates as the worst team of the 2010s (and third-worst of the Modern Era). Three versions of the Astros took runner-up slots in the decade rankings, with the 2013 Houston team a bit worse than the other two.

The Worst 10

Rk	Team	Year	Post	W	L	Pct.	R	RA	BPO	BPOA	TS
1	Pittsburgh Pirates	2010	—	57	105	.352	3.62	5.35	.620	.787	7.550
2	Houston Astros	2013	—	51	111	.315	3.77	5.23	.618	.769	10.531
3	Houston Astros	2011	—	56	106	.346	3.80	4.91	.627	.752	11.311
4	Houston Astros	2012	—	55	107	.340	3.60	4.90	.621	.743	13.628
5	Minnesota Twins	2016	—	59	103	.364	4.46	5.49	.700	.767	15.628
6	Minnesota Twins	2011	—	63	99	.389	3.82	4.96	.599	.737	18.200
7	Texas Rangers	2014	—	67	95	.414	3.93	4.77	.624	.724	18.535
8	Arizona Diamondbacks	2014	—	64	98	.395	3.80	4.58	.613	.692	19.252
9	Chicago Cubs	2012	—	61	101	.377	3.78	4.69	.620	.741	19.962
10	Miami Marlins	2013	—	62	100	.383	3.17	3.99	.557	.657	20.020

List #109: Best Batting in the 2010s

If there were such a thing as a Triple Crown for a full decade, Miguel Cabrera would be the frontrunner for the 2010s.

The Detroit infielder posted a .330 batting average (1,299 hits in 3,932 at bats) from 2010 through 2016. Joey Votto's .314 was a distant second among all batters with more than 2,500 appearances. Cabrera drove in 800 runs during the same span, giving him a substantial lead over runner-up Adrian Gonzalez's 722.

Only in home runs has he taken a back seat. His seven-year total of 237 is second to Jose Bautista's 249. But don't forget that Cabrera is two-and-a-half years younger than Bautista, potentially an important factor as the decade nears its conclusion.

Another indicator of Cabrera's superiority is his base value of 898.1, the highest total for any batter in the 2010s. Cabrera's BPO+ has exceeded the American League norm by at least 27 percent every year since 2010, peaking at 164.4 in 2013. That was the year after he won the single-season Triple Crown with 44 homers, 139 RBI, and a .330 BA.

But Cabrera is far from a lock for the base-value crown in the 2010s. The Angels' Mike Trout didn't reach the majors until July 2011, yet he has already pulled within 15.7 bases on the BV list. Trout's youth might give him an edge. He will be only 28 years old when the decade ends — a prime age for a ballplayer — while Cabrera will be a relatively old 36.

The Best 10

Rank	Batter	Span	G	BA	B	O	BPO	BPO+	BV
1	Miguel Cabrera	2010-2016	1,056	.330	2,932	2,833	1.035	144.1	898.1
2	Mike Trout	2011-2016	811	.306	2,374	2,183	1.087	159.0	882.4
3	Joey Votto	2010-2016	962	.314	2,679	2,486	1.078	146.6	852.3
4	Jose Bautista	2010-2016	944	.264	2,617	2,644	.990	136.4	696.8
5	Andrew McCutchen	2010-2016	1,082	.293	2,765	3,018	.916	131.0	647.2
6	David Ortiz	2010-2016	957	.292	2,523	2,612	.966	131.4	603.7
7	Paul Goldschmidt	2011-2016	779	.299	2,105	2,114	.996	135.3	547.3
8	Giancarlo Stanton	2010-2016	827	.266	2,087	2,276	.917	129.7	475.1
9	Ryan Braun	2010-2016	932	.302	2,415	2,637	.916	123.8	468.2
10	Edwin Encarnacion	2010-2016	957	.269	2,410	2,703	.892	122.5	442.0

List #110: Best Batting in a Season in the 2010s

Bryce Harper entered 2015 with a simple goal. He wanted to stay in the lineup.

The Nationals outfielder, still only 22 years old, had suffered the worst season of his three-year career in 2014. A thumb injury shunted him to the disabled list for 57 games and diminished his power once he returned. His bottom line had been disappointingly weak: 13 home runs and 32 RBIs. "I'm just trying to go in there, stay healthy and be on the field, and play the way I need to play," Harper said when reporters pressed him about the season ahead.

The early results were mixed at best, with Harper batting just .245 through the first week of May. But then he caught fire, pounding pitchers at a .349 pace the rest of the way. He topped the National League with 42 home runs, finished second with a .330 BA, ranked fifth with 99 RBIs, and achieved his goal by playing in 153 games. He was a logical (and unanimous) choice as the NL's Most Valuable Player.

Harper reached 477 bases in 2015, surpassing an average player's production by 213.0. It was the largest single-season BV of the 2010s, just as his BPO+ of 180.7 was the highest. His performance clearly was the best by any batter in the decade.

Another young superstar, Mike Trout of the Angels, is second on this list with the 170.5 BPO+ that he racked up at the age of 21.

The Best 10

Rk	Batter	Year	Team	G	BA	B	O	BPO	BV	BPO+
1	Bryce Harper	2015	Nationals	153	.330	477	372	1.282	213.0	180.7
2	Mike Trout	2013	Angels	157	.323	488	422	1.156	201.8	170.5
3	Jose Bautista	2011	Blue Jays	149	.302	463	375	1.235	188.0	168.4
4	Mike Trout	2016	Angels	159	.315	464	393	1.181	187.1	167.5
5	Miguel Cabrera	2013	Tigers	148	.348	453	383	1.183	177.5	164.4
6	Joey Votto	2015	Reds	158	.314	456	390	1.169	177.7	163.9
7	Mike Trout	2012	Angels	139	.326	444	396	1.121	167.7	160.7
8	Mike Trout	2015	Angels	159	.299	457	426	1.073	168.6	158.4
9	Paul Goldschmidt	2015	Diamondbacks	159	.321	471	413	1.140	169.2	156.1
10	Miguel Cabrera	2011	Tigers	161	.344	453	405	1.119	161.3	155.3

List #111: Best Batting in a Game in the 2010s

Batters often approach a game's final at bat with desperation, willing to do almost anything to avoid an oh-for-four collar. But Josh Hamilton didn't have that problem on May 8, 2012.

"I just went up like it was any other at bat," he said. "Because if I don't hit one, I've still had a really good night." Indeed he had. The Rangers center fielder had already shelled Baltimore pitchers for three home runs and a double when he stepped in against Darren O'Day in the eighth inning.

O'Day ran the count to 0-2 with a swinging strike and a foul ball. But his third pitch was redirected over the center-field fence in Camden Yards. Hamilton rounded the bases as the 16th player to launch four homers in a single game. "It reminds you of when you're in Little League and a little kid, and just the excitement and why we play the game," he told reporters.

Hamilton's final line looked as if it came from a Little League scorecard: five-for-five, eight RBIs, 18 bases. The latter is the highest total achieved by any batter in the 2010s, falling short of Shawn Green's Modern Era record by a single base.

The midseason acquisition of Yoenis Cespedes ignited the Mets' drive to the National League pennant in 2015. His best game — and second-best for anybody in the decade — was a three-homer, 16-base performance against the Rockies. (See List #47 to learn how ties were broken on this list.)

The Best 10

Rank	Batter	Date	Team	Opp	PA	H	HR	SC	B
1	Josh Hamilton	May 8, 2012	Rangers	Orioles	5	5	4	8	18
2	Yoenis Cespedes	Aug. 21, 2015	Mets	Rockies	6	5	3	9	16
3	Kris Bryant	June 27, 2016	Cubs	Reds	5	5	3	7	16
4	Dustin Pedroia	June 24, 2010	Red Sox	Rockies	6	5	3	6	16
5	Kendrys Morales	Sept. 20, 2015	Royals	Tigers	5	4	3	5	16
6	Lonnie Chisenhall	June 9, 2014	Indians	Rangers	5	5	3	9	15
7	Ryan Braun	April 30, 2012	Brewers	Padres	5	4	3	6	15
8	Jackie Bradley	Aug. 15, 2015	Red Sox	Mariners	6	5	2	10	14
9	Joey Votto	May 13, 2012	Reds	Nationals	5	4	3	7	14
10	Yasmani Grandal	July 8, 2016	Dodgers	Padres	5	5	3	6	14

List #112: Best Pitching in the 2010s

Several outstanding pitchers have taken the mound during the current decade — Johnny Cueto, Zack Greinke, Felix Hernandez, David Price, and Justin Verlander, to name a few. But none can compare with Clayton Kershaw.

"He's the best pitcher on the planet," Dodgers catcher A.J. Ellis said of Kershaw in 2015. His bias was obvious — the two men were batterymates in Los Angeles — yet the facts and figures bear him out.

Kershaw earned three Cy Young Awards during the first five years of the 2010s. No other pitcher received more than one. The Dodgers lefthander registered the lowest earned run average in the majors in four consecutive seasons (2011-2014). And his cumulative ERA for the decade (2.18) is easily the best for any starter. Nobody else who tossed at least 800 innings has done better than 2.86.

But the best indicator of Kershaw's dominance is his BV of minus-759.7. The typical Los Angeles starter would have yielded 2,811.7 bases between 2010 and 2016, yet he restricted opponents to 2,052. No other pitcher was even half as stingy during the seven-year period. The two runners-up on this list, Cueto and Verlander, have respective base values of minus-378.6 and minus-370.5.

Kershaw has been remarkably consistent in his pursuit of excellence. The decade's pitchers have posted 16 single-season BVs lower than minus-100. Five of those 16 gems were Kershaw's work. Verlander, with two, is the only other starter to do it more than once.

The Best 10

Rank	Pitcher	Span	G	ERA	B	O	BPO	BPO+	BV
1	Clayton Kershaw	2010-2016	212	2.18	2,052	4,460	.460	72.9	-759.7
2	Johnny Cueto	2010-2016	197	2.86	2,176	3,875	.562	85.1	-378.6
3	Justin Verlander	2010-2016	220	3.22	2,606	4,496	.580	87.7	-370.5
4	Chris Sale	2010-2016	228	3.00	1,852	3,333	.556	83.7	-359.9
5	David Price	2010-2016	225	3.12	2,629	4,605	.571	88.0	-359.8
6	Cliff Lee	2010-2014	134	2.95	1,585	2,892	.548	84.1	-302.2
7	Felix Hernandez	2010-2016	221	2.98	2,574	4,545	.566	89.5	-301.8
8	Zack Greinke	2010-2016	213	3.22	2,368	4,113	.576	88.7	-296.6
9	Madison Bumgarner	2010-2016	213	3.00	2,383	4,201	.567	90.1	-261.2
10	Craig Kimbrel	2010-2016	412	1.86	533	1,220	.437	67.5	-256.4

List #113: Best Pitching in a Season in the 2010s

No team in the Modern Era possessed a one-two punch like the Dodgers in 2015.

The two stars of Los Angeles's rotation, Zack Greinke and Clayton Kershaw, produced the two best single-season performances of the 2010s. Their joint record was 35-10, including back-to-back victories on nine occasions. Their dominance was a key factor as the Dodgers breezed to first place in the National League West.

"These guys are filthy," Dodgers shortstop Jimmy Rollins said of his team's dynamic duo. "You go out there, and you just smile. I'll watch the first inning and talk to our catcher, and I'll tell him, '[Opposing hitters] have no shot today.'"

Kershaw had posted the lowest ERA in the big leagues in the previous four seasons, but Greinke outdid him in ERA (1.66) and BPO+ (66.7) in 2015. Both figures were the best for any starter during the decade's first seven years. Kershaw wasn't far behind. His ERA of 2.13 was actually the fourth-lowest of his nine-year career, and his BPO+ of 68.4 was the second-best for anybody in the 2010s.

Their excellence was historic. The Modern Era has seen only 18 instances of a qualified pitcher registering a BPO+ below 70.0. This was the lone time that the feat was accomplished by two men on the same team.

The irony is that neither won the NL Cy Young Award for 2015. That honor went to the Cubs' Jake Arrieta, fourth on this list at 70.0.

The Best 10

Rk	Pitcher	Year	Team	G	ERA	B	O	BPO	BV	BPO+
1	Zack Greinke	2015	Dodgers	32	1.66	278	671	.414	-138.5	66.7
2	Clayton Kershaw	2015	Dodgers	33	2.13	296	697	.425	-136.7	68.4
3	Clayton Kershaw	2014	Dodgers	27	1.77	250	596	.419	-110.9	69.3
4	Jake Arrieta	2015	Cubs	33	1.77	306	687	.445	-131.4	70.0
5	Matt Harvey	2013	Mets	26	2.27	228	535	.426	-95.8	70.4
6	Clayton Kershaw	2013	Dodgers	33	1.83	304	711	.428	-127.2	70.5
7	Justin Verlander	2011	Tigers	34	2.40	358	752	.476	-139.2	72.0
8	Clayton Kershaw	2011	Dodgers	33	2.28	335	704	.476	-118.4	73.9
9	Jose Fernandez	2013	Marlins	28	2.19	238	520	.458	-83.1	74.1
10	Cliff Lee	2010	Mariners-Rangers	28	3.18	328	642	.511	-109.3	74.7

List #114: Best Pitching in a Game in the 2010s

The 2015 season didn't go as Max Scherzer planned. The righthander had signed a seven-year, $210 million contract with the Nationals over the winter, pushing expectations sky-high in Washington. "This organization is capable of winning — and winning a lot," Scherzer declared at his introductory press conference.

The Nats stumbled out of the gate, losing 14 of their first 25 games, before clawing their way to first place in the National League East. But a disastrous 25-34 stretch in July and August doomed their title hopes. Scherzer's inconsistency was a key factor. His record during those two dark months was 2-6.

There were bright spots in 2015 — notably a no-hitter against the Pirates on June 20 — but Scherzer took the mound for his final start on October 3 with a disappointing 13-12 record. He proceeded to rekindle Washington's hopes for the year ahead, striking out 17 Mets en route to his second no-hitter of the season.

An error by his third baseman ruined Scherzer's chances for a perfect game, but he didn't yield any bases on his own. He was credited with the best pitching performance of the decade, and indeed of the entire Modern Era, based on a series of tiebreakers. (See List #53 for details.)

There have been five perfect games in the 2010s — the highest total for any decade — but neither of this list's two leaders was among them. Clayton Kershaw's spotless outing on June 18, 2014, was also marred by an infield error.

The Best 10

Rank	Pitcher	Date	Team	Opp	IP	H	SO	ER	B
1	Max Scherzer	Oct. 3, 2015	Nationals	Mets	9.0	0	17	0	0
2	Clayton Kershaw	June 18, 2014	Dodgers	Rockies	9.0	0	15	0	0
3	Matt Cain	June 13, 2012	Giants	Astros	9.0	0	14	0	0
4	Felix Hernandez	Aug. 15, 2012	Mariners	Rays	9.0	0	12	0	0
5	Roy Halladay	May 29, 2010	Phillies	Marlins	9.0	0	11	0	0
6	Philip Humber	April 21, 2012	White Sox	Mariners	9.0	0	9	0	0
7	Dallas Braden	May 9, 2010	Athletics	Rays	9.0	0	6	0	0
8	R.A. Dickey	June 13, 2012	Mets	Rays	9.0	1	12	0	1
8	Matt Harvey	May 7, 2013	Mets	White Sox	9.0	1	12	0	1
10	Matt Cain	April 13, 2012	Giants	Pirates	9.0	1	11	0	1
10	Josh Tomlin	June 28, 2014	Indians	Mariners	9.0	1	11	0	1

14. INFIELDERS

List #115: Best First Baseman in a Career

Albert Pujols didn't fit into the Cardinals' plans for 2001. The muscular infielder had played only one year of minor-league ball, and the team's scouts agreed that he needed seasoning. The Cards decided to tantalize him with a non-roster invitation to spring training. He would be treated to a few weeks with the big club, then shipped out for another year or two in the minors.

But Pujols didn't follow the script. He played his way onto the squad that spring and stayed hot all summer. He drove in 130 runs, posted a BPO+ of 133.5, and was unanimously selected as the National League's Rookie of the Year. It was the start of a 10-year span in which his BPO+ hovered in an exalted range between 130.5 and 170.3.

Pujols was named the NL's Most Valuable Player three times during this decade-long hot streak, establishing him as the outstanding first baseman in the game. His production began to decline in 2011 — a year before he departed the Cardinals for the Angels — yet his annual BV totals have never slipped into negative territory.

Pujols's cumulative base value of 1,801.4 is the best for anybody categorized as a first baseman in the Modern Era. (Pujols also dabbled at third base, designated hitter, and the outfield, but I have applied all of his stats to his primary position.) Three runners-up came within 220 BV of first place on this list: Jim Thome, Mark McGwire, and Jeff Bagwell.

The Best 10

Rank	Batter	Span	G	BA	B	O	BPO	BPO+	BV
1	Albert Pujols	2001-2016	2,426	.309	6,753	6,790	.995	135.5	1,801.4
2	Jim Thome	1991-2012	2,543	.276	6,577	6,354	1.035	134.3	1,679.8
3	Mark McGwire	1986-2001	1,874	.263	5,124	4,797	1.068	146.2	1,648.3
4	Jeff Bagwell	1991-2005	2,150	.297	6,049	5,887	1.028	135.5	1,584.7
5	Miguel Cabrera	2003-2016	2,096	.321	5,600	5,713	.980	133.0	1,381.4
6	Willie McCovey	1961-1980	2,435	.269	5,409	5,923	.913	133.7	1,363.9
7	Harmon Killebrew	1961-1975	2,045	.257	5,026	5,429	.926	133.0	1,252.6
8	Dick Allen	1963-1977	1,749	.292	4,494	4,772	.942	139.1	1,252.3
9	Jason Giambi	1995-2014	2,260	.277	5,414	5,530	.979	129.4	1,235.6
10	Lance Berkman	1999-2013	1,879	.293	4,893	4,836	1.012	131.2	1,168.7

List #116: Best First Baseman in a Season

Mark McGwire's monumental performance in 1998 inspired a succession of intense emotions.

Excitement came first. Tens of millions of fans were enthralled by the duel between the Cardinals first baseman and Cubs right fielder Sammy Sosa to establish a new single-season home-run record. McGwire, of course, came out on top. He blasted 70 homers, obliterating Roger Maris's mark of 61, and the nation rewarded him with veneration. "He made us remember how and why we came to love baseball in the first place," wrote columnist Mike Lupica.

But euphoria eventually gave way to disappointment. McGwire would finally admit, after years of evasion, that he had taken steroids in 1998. He denied that the drugs had enhanced his power, yet he expressed deep regret. "I wish I had never played during the steroid era," he said.

McGwire's home-run record endured for only three years, but his BPO+ of 199.0 remains the best single-year figure for a first baseman in the Modern Era. He reached 556 bases in 1998, the highest total for any player between 1960 and 2000. An average batter would have fared only half as well (279.5 bases) under the same circumstances.

Jeff Bagwell didn't possess McGwire's power — he never hit more than 47 homers in a season — but he was much more consistent at the plate. His .368 batting average in 1994 yielded a BPO+ of 191.2, putting him second on this list.

The Best 10

Rank	Batter	Year	Team	G	BA	B	O	BPO	BV	BPO+
1	Mark McGwire	1998	Cardinals	155	.299	556	369	1.507	276.5	199.0
2	Jeff Bagwell	1994	Astros	110	.368	394	279	1.412	187.9	191.2
3	Willie McCovey	1969	Giants	149	.320	454	352	1.290	213.6	188.8
4	Frank Thomas	1994	White Sox	113	.353	411	283	1.452	192.2	187.8
5	Norm Cash	1961	Tigers	159	.361	502	367	1.368	226.6	182.3
6	Mark McGwire	1996	Athletics	130	.312	434	306	1.418	194.3	181.1
7	Jim Thome	2002	Indians	147	.304	459	347	1.323	205.3	181.0
8	Jason Giambi	2001	Athletics	154	.342	496	368	1.348	216.9	177.7
9	Dick Allen	1972	White Sox	148	.308	427	374	1.142	186.0	177.2
10	Jason Giambi	2000	Athletics	152	.333	486	357	1.361	206.0	173.6

List #117: Worst First Baseman in a Season

Enos Cabell posted some respectable numbers during his 15-year career. Like the two seasons with batting averages north of .300 — .311 in 1983, .310 a year later. Or his 42 stolen bases in 1977. Or his National League-leading 660 at bats in 1978, proof of his durability.

But 1981 doesn't enter the discussion. The Astros traded the 31-year-old infielder to the Giants prior to that season, and he had difficulty getting untracked. His batting average slipped from .276 in 1980 to .255. Speed suddenly disappeared from his arsenal, as indicated by his anemic total of six stolen bases. Cabell's BPO+ consequently plummeted to 73.1, roughly 10 points below the worst of his six seasons in Houston. It was, in fact, the smallest BPO+ for any regular first baseman in the Modern Era.

First base is considered to be a power position, but Cabell never fit that mold. His high-water mark was 16 homers in 1977, and he hit only two in 1981. The Giants had seen enough, and they dealt Cabell to Detroit during the offseason. Reggie Smith arrived in San Francisco to replace him, launching 18 home runs in the last of his 17 years in the majors.

Pete Rose is commonly remembered as a second or third baseman or an outfielder, but he played first base in 1983. His batting average that year was .245, the second-worst of his career. His BPO+ of 74.2 takes second place on this list.

The Worst 10

Rank	Batter	Year	Team	G	BA	B	O	BPO	BV	BPO+
1	Enos Cabell	1981	Giants	96	.255	152	314	.484	-55.8	73.1
2	Pete Rose	1983	Phillies	151	.245	210	398	.528	-73.2	74.2
3	Darin Erstad	1999	Angels	142	.253	285	465	.613	-85.8	76.9
4	Danny Cater	1969	Athletics	152	.262	248	466	.532	-69.4	78.1
5	Dave Stapleton	1983	Red Sox	151	.247	254	442	.575	-70.9	78.2
6	Ron Coomer	2000	Twins	140	.270	273	427	.639	-75.4	78.4
7	Kevin Young	1993	Pirates	141	.236	215	369	.583	-58.9	78.5
8	J.T. Snow	1996	Angels	155	.257	288	457	.630	-78.2	78.6
9	Keith Moreland	1988	Padres	143	.256	222	411	.540	-59.5	78.9
10	Ron Coomer	1999	Twins	127	.263	234	364	.643	-62.1	79.0

List #118: Best Second Baseman in a Career

Joe Morgan finished fifth in the career rankings of 10,070 Modern Era batters, stamping him as one of the very greatest hitters of the past half-century. (See List #11.) The four men who topped him, as you would expect, all played the power positions of first base or the outfield. He stood alone at second base.

Morgan was a prototypical middle infielder in some respects. He was swift, stealing at least 40 bases in nine different years. And he possessed an excellent batting eye, drawing walks (1,865) almost twice as frequently as he struck out (1,015). But the pop in his bat was unusual for somebody who played second. He posted double-digit home-run totals in 13 of his 22 seasons.

Morgan's blend of speed, consistency, and power produced outstanding BPO+ scores. His best marks were generated during his two-year reign as the National League's Most Valuable Player: 182.6 in 1975 and 193.5 the following season.

But career ratings are determined by base value, not BPO+, and no second baseman came remotely close to Morgan in that stat. He reached 6,703 bases overall, exceeding expectations by 1,775.7 bases. Bobby Grich, who starred for the Orioles and Angels, is a very distant runner-up with a BV of 670.6.

Sharp-eyed readers may have noticed the omission of Rod Carew from this list. His 875.7 BV would have earned second place, but Carew actually played 54 more games at first base than at second, rendering him ineligible here.

The Best 10

Rank	Batter	Span	G	BA	B	O	BPO	BPO+	BV
1	Joe Morgan	1963-1984	2,649	.271	6,703	7,174	.934	136.0	1,775.7
2	Bobby Grich	1970-1986	2,008	.266	4,353	5,454	.798	118.5	670.6
3	Roberto Alomar	1988-2004	2,379	.300	5,819	6,914	.842	111.2	599.0
4	Craig Biggio	1988-2007	2,850	.281	6,752	8,272	.816	108.7	526.4
5	Chase Utley	2003-2016	1,723	.278	4,098	4,788	.856	114.2	521.1
6	Lou Whitaker	1977-1995	2,390	.276	5,191	6,599	.787	111.1	517.5
7	Davey Lopes	1972-1987	1,812	.263	4,011	5,045	.795	114.5	512.9
8	Jeff Kent	1992-2008	2,298	.290	5,379	6,434	.836	109.9	488.1
9	Robinson Cano	2005-2016	1,848	.307	4,274	5,335	.801	109.8	376.1
10	Ryne Sandberg	1981-1997	2,164	.285	5,028	6,347	.792	108.2	373.9

List #119: Best Second Baseman in a Season

Young Joe Morgan idolized Nellie Fox for obvious reasons. Fox starred for the White Sox in the 1950s as a second baseman, the same position Morgan dreamed of playing in the majors. Fox performed at a Hall of Fame level despite weighing 160 pounds. Morgan was even smaller, only 140 pounds when he entered the minors.

Fate brought the two men together in 1964. The 36-year-old Fox had been traded to the Colt .45s, while the 20-year-old Morgan had been invited to Houston's spring camp for the first time. The veteran took the rookie under his wing. "He taught me in one year what it takes most players five years to learn," Morgan recalled. "He told me I had twice as much ability as he had."

That seemed a stretch, though it proved to be true. Fox had won the American League's Most Valuable Player Award in 1959. Morgan would earn a pair of NL MVP trophies. Fox's BPO+ peaked at 115.2 in 1957. Morgan would top 150 on five occasions, the best seasons enjoyed by any second baseman in the Modern Era.

Morgan attained his zenith in 1976, pounding 27 homers, stealing 60 bases, and posting a BPO+ of 193.5. He was named the MVP that year, duplicating the previous season's feat, when he had reached 182.6.

Morgan appears on this list six times. The best performance at second base by anybody else was Rod Carew's 145.5 for the Twins in 1975.

The Best 10

Rank	Batter	Year	Team	G	BA	B	O	BPO	BV	BPO+
1	Joe Morgan	1976	Reds	141	.320	459	344	1.334	221.8	193.5
2	Joe Morgan	1975	Reds	146	.327	461	354	1.302	208.6	182.6
3	Joe Morgan	1974	Reds	149	.293	440	387	1.137	169.9	162.9
4	Joe Morgan	1973	Reds	157	.290	473	443	1.068	171.2	156.7
5	Joe Morgan	1972	Reds	149	.292	426	420	1.014	150.6	154.7
6	Rod Carew	1975	Twins	143	.359	383	379	1.011	119.7	145.5
7	Joe Morgan	1977	Reds	153	.288	422	391	1.079	129.9	144.5
8	Craig Biggio	1997	Astros	162	.309	482	445	1.083	146.4	143.6
9	Bobby Grich	1981	Angels	100	.304	245	262	.935	73.5	142.9
10	Jeff Kent	2000	Giants	159	.334	470	426	1.103	137.6	141.4

List #120: Worst Second Baseman in a Season

The Reds anticipated that Tommy Helms would be their second baseman for at least a decade, a natural assumption after his breakout season in 1966. Helms batted .284, played a respectable third base, and won the National League's Rookie of the Year Award. Manager Dave Bristol shifted him to second the following year, and he adjusted easily to his new position, eventually winning a pair of Gold Gloves.

But Helms began to struggle at the plate. His BPO+ had always been below 100 — even during that promising rookie season — though it plummeted to a new depth in 1970. Helms batted just .237, coaxed only 21 walks, and stole a grand total of two bases. The resulting BPO+ of 55.8 was the worst for any second baseman who played regularly in the Modern Era.

The Reds gave him one more chance. Helms inched his batting average up to .258 in 1971, but it wasn't good enough. He was shipped off to Houston in an eight-man trade. Cincinnati's front office hoped that one of the players acquired from the Astros, Joe Morgan, might play an adequate second base. That wish was fulfilled.

The runner-up on this list is the Giants' Hal Lanier, who batted .226 in 1965, scattering only 24 extra-base hits through 159 games. His BPO+ was 61.7. San Francisco moved Lanier to shortstop a couple of years later, and you'll also find him (three times) on that position's list of worst seasons.

The Worst 10

Rank	Batter	Year	Team	G	BA	B	O	BPO	BV	BPO+
1	Tommy Helms	1970	Reds	150	.237	194	468	.415	-154.0	55.8
2	Hal Lanier	1965	Giants	159	.226	187	439	.426	-116.2	61.7
3	Doug Flynn	1981	Mets	105	.222	114	274	.416	-69.8	62.0
4	Jose Lind	1992	Pirates	135	.235	167	384	.435	-99.0	62.8
5	Billy Ripken	1988	Orioles	150	.207	187	431	.434	-107.4	63.5
6	Doug Flynn	1979	Mets	157	.243	201	446	.451	-109.1	64.8
6	Mike Champion	1977	Padres	150	.229	187	412	.454	-101.5	64.8
8	Julian Javier	1970	Cardinals	139	.251	201	415	.484	-108.1	65.0
9	Glenn Beckert	1965	Cubs	154	.239	228	497	.459	-122.2	65.1
10	Denny Doyle	1977	Red Sox	137	.240	187	370	.505	-96.4	66.0

List #121: Best Shortstop in a Career

Young fans will be puzzled by the name at the top of this list. They think of Alex Rodriguez as a third baseman/designated hitter — and for good reason. Those are the only positions he has played in the past decade (with the exception of a two-game trial at first base).

But the standings in this book are based on the spot each player fielded most frequently. Rodriguez joined the Mariners in 1994 as an 18-year-old shortstop, and he went on to make seven All-Star teams at that position. His career totals still include more games at short (1,272) than at third (1,194) or as a DH (298).

So Rodriguez's lifetime numbers apply to this list, where they are far superior to everybody else's. He has piled up 7,783 bases for the Mariners, Rangers, and Yankees. That's 1,097 more than the next-highest total for a shortstop (6,686 by fellow Yankee Derek Jeter). Rodriguez's career BPO+ of 128.5 and BV of 1,733.9 also stand unchallenged by anybody at short.

Rodriguez was a better hitter as a shortstop (.308 BA from 1994 to 2003) than after shifting to third (.283 BA since 2004). The same trend is evident for the runner-up in these rankings, Hanley Ramirez, who has a career BV of 625.7.

Ramirez batted .306 in six years as the Marlins shortstop. He began roaming in 2012 — third base, then left field, then first base — and his hitting suffered. His BA has been .279 since those moves began.

The Best 10

Rank	Batter	Span	G	BA	B	O	BPO	BPO+	BV
1	Alex Rodriguez	1994-2016	2,784	.295	7,783	7,915	.983	128.5	1,733.9
2	Hanley Ramirez	2005-2016	1,475	.295	3,758	4,212	.892	119.9	625.7
3	Barry Larkin	1986-2004	2,180	.295	5,026	5,978	.841	110.1	454.7
4	Robin Yount	1974-1993	2,856	.285	6,242	8,415	.742	107.7	448.1
5	Derek Jeter	1995-2014	2,747	.310	6,686	8,269	.809	106.5	427.1
6	Nomar Garciaparra	1996-2009	1,434	.313	3,533	4,067	.869	111.1	358.0
7	Jose Reyes	2003-2016	1,622	.289	4,035	5,123	.788	107.2	266.0
8	Troy Tulowitzki	2006-2016	1,220	.292	2,928	3,441	.851	108.7	231.4
9	Alan Trammell	1977-1996	2,293	.285	4,765	6,388	.746	105.3	226.5
10	Jim Fregosi	1961-1978	1,902	.265	3,554	5,094	.698	106.6	217.4

List #122: Best Shortstop in a Season

Everything came together for Alex Rodriguez at the perfect time. He launched 41 homers, drove in 132 runs, and batted .316 for the Mariners in 2000. His BPO+ of 148.3 would have been exceptional for a first baseman or outfielder, but it was especially dazzling for a shortstop. And it carried extra significance because Rodriguez was about to become a free agent.

Other teams bid eagerly for his services. They were awed by Rodriguez's excellence at the plate in 2000 — it remains the best season for any shortstop in the Modern Era — and they were equally impressed by his consistency. He batted over .300 in every month but the last, when he compensated with a burst of power. His nine home runs in September were his most in any month that year.

Rangers owner Tom Hicks stepped forward with a jaw-dropping contract: 10 years, $252 million. "Alex is the player we believe will allow this franchise to fulfill its dream of becoming a World Series champion," Hicks said confidently. But the deal proved to be so onerous that the Rangers bailed out after three last-place finishes in the AL West. They traded Rodriguez to the Yankees.

The outcome was different for the second shortstop on this list. Robin Yount's 145.4 BPO+ secured the American League's Most Valuable Player Award in 1982. (Rodriguez finished third in 2000's MVP election.) Yount led the Brewers to the World Series, where they fell to the Cardinals in seven games.

The Best 10

Rank	Batter	Year	Team	G	BA	B	O	BPO	BV	BPO+
1	Alex Rodriguez	2000	Mariners	148	.316	469	404	1.161	152.8	148.3
2	Robin Yount	1982	Brewers	156	.331	450	461	.976	140.5	145.4
3	Rico Petrocelli	1969	Red Sox	154	.297	426	402	1.060	128.4	143.1
4	Alex Rodriguez	2001	Rangers	162	.318	511	460	1.111	151.2	142.0
5	Alex Rodriguez	2002	Rangers	162	.300	499	459	1.087	146.9	141.7
6	Barry Larkin	1996	Reds	152	.298	439	400	1.098	126.5	140.5
7	Alan Trammell	1987	Tigers	151	.343	421	413	1.019	119.4	139.6
8	Nomar Garciaparra	2000	Red Sox	140	.372	392	349	1.123	110.0	139.0
8	Toby Harrah	1975	Rangers	151	.293	371	395	.939	104.0	139.0
10	Cal Ripken Jr.	1991	Orioles	162	.323	441	469	.940	122.5	138.5

List #123: Worst Shortstop in a Season

Everybody knew why the Giants and Yankees employed Hal Lanier between 1964 and 1973. He played all four infield positions, and he handled them cleanly.

"Hal was a smart guy, fun to be around," recalled Fritz Peterson, who pitched in New York when Lanier was there. "He was a good fielder, which helped because you didn't keep him on the team for his bat."

Lanier played at a time when pitchers held the upper hand, but his stats were weak even by the standards of that period. The Modern Era's two worst seasons for batters were 1967 (when the cumulative BA was .242) and 1968 (when it dropped to .237). Lanier fell far below those anemic benchmarks, posting respective batting averages of .213 and .206.

Nor did he possess complementary skills that might have been offensively useful. He didn't have power, his batting eye wasn't especially keen, and he wasn't a threat on the bases. These were the numbers he accumulated in a 1,196-game career: eight homers, 136 walks, and 11 stolen bases.

The result was a series of atrocious BPO+ scores, including three of the four worst for a shortstop. (You'll also find Lanier in second place on List #120, the corresponding rankings for second basemen.) He reached his nadir in 1967 with a BPO+ of 57.1.

Neifi Perez was the only shortstop to interrupt Lanier's dominance of this category. Perez tied for third place with a 58.4 season for the Royals in 2002.

The Worst 10

Rank	Batter	Year	Team	G	BA	B	O	BPO	BV	BPO+
1	Hal Lanier	1967	Giants	151	.213	168	446	.377	-126.0	57.1
2	Hal Lanier	1968	Giants	151	.206	150	425	.353	-108.0	58.1
3	Neifi Perez	2002	Royals	145	.236	207	454	.456	-147.7	58.4
3	Hal Lanier	1969	Giants	150	.228	166	416	.399	-118.2	58.4
5	Marty Perez	1972	Braves	141	.228	166	400	.415	-116.4	58.8
6	Mike Caruso	1999	White Sox	136	.250	204	429	.476	-139.2	59.4
7	Alfredo Griffin	1990	Dodgers	141	.210	164	382	.429	-108.1	60.3
8	Andres Thomas	1989	Braves	141	.213	195	461	.423	-123.0	61.3
8	Rey Ordonez	1996	Mets	151	.257	181	393	.461	-114.2	61.3
10	Tom Veryzer	1979	Indians	149	.220	168	379	.443	-105.3	61.5

List #124: Best Third Baseman in a Career

Philadelphia fans made up their minds in 1973. They could see that Mike Schmidt was a bust. The rookie third baseman batted a pathetic .196 that season, striking out in more than 30 percent of his plate appearances. They booed him mercilessly.

Their snap judgment, of course, proved to be outrageously inaccurate. Schmidt righted himself the following year by batting .282 and pacing the National League with 36 home runs. He went on to blast 548 homers in 18 seasons (all with the Phillies), win three Most Valuable Player Awards, and enter the Hall of Fame in his first year of eligibility.

Schmidt was not only a powerful hitter, but also a fluid fielder and strong leader. Many observers consider him the greatest to ever play his position. "No other third baseman ever did what he did with both his bat and his glove. Not Brooks Robinson, not Eddie Mathews, not Pie Traynor," insisted *New York Times* columnist Dave Anderson.

There can be no doubt about Schmidt's supremacy in the Modern Era. His career BPO+ of 134.5 is nearly eight points higher than the score for any other third baseman who played at least 1,000 games. And Schmidt's base value of 1,613.5 is easily the best on this list.

Two other third basemen exceeded 1,000 on the BV scale. And they, like Schmidt, were one-team players. Chipper Jones spent 19 seasons with the Braves, and George Brett donned a Royals uniform for 21 years.

The Best 10

Rank	Batter	Span	G	BA	B	O	BPO	BPO+	BV
1	Mike Schmidt	1972-1989	2,404	.267	6,288	6,490	.969	134.5	1,613.5
2	Chipper Jones	1993-2012	2,499	.303	6,535	6,657	.982	126.6	1,380.4
3	George Brett	1973-1993	2,707	.305	6,520	7,673	.850	120.6	1,117.1
4	Darrell Evans	1969-1989	2,687	.248	5,728	7,075	.810	115.7	781.6
5	Wade Boggs	1982-1999	2,440	.328	5,648	6,566	.860	116.1	775.0
6	David Wright	2004-2016	1,583	.296	4,012	4,501	.891	122.3	736.1
7	Ron Santo	1961-1974	2,148	.278	4,890	6,017	.813	114.0	591.8
8	Scott Rolen	1996-2012	2,038	.281	4,866	5,614	.867	112.9	560.1
9	Toby Harrah	1969-1986	2,155	.264	4,528	5,845	.775	113.0	531.3
10	Sal Bando	1966-1981	2,019	.254	4,184	5,587	.749	112.7	466.2

List #125: Best Third Baseman in a Season

George Brett won the American League batting title in 1976 and excelled in three AL Championship Series from 1976 to 1978. He played in tiny Kansas City, yet he was one of baseball's hottest stars. He was a big deal, and everybody knew it.

But Brett's fame expanded to unexpected dimensions in 1980. He entered August with a batting average of .390, attracting a swarm of reporters who peppered him with the same questions day after day. Could he stay hot for two more months? Could he become the first .400 hitter since Ted Williams in 1941?

The hoopla was impossible to ignore. "My batting average is in the papers every day," Brett said, "and every time I go up to hit in Royals Stadium, it's up there out in center field on the scoreboard that's as high as a six-story building." The numbers seemed massive after he went four-for-four against the Blue Jays on August 17. "George Brett is hitting .401," the scoreboard declared. The crowd roared.

Brett gave it his best shot, keeping his average above .400 until September 20, but a late slump dropped him to .390. "No regrets," he said. "I had a good run." His BPO+ of 180.0 marked it as the best season for any third baseman in the Modern Era.

Mike Schmidt came close in 1981, reaching 176.7 on the BPO+ scale. He batted a solid .316 during that strike-shortened season and paced the major leagues with 31 home runs.

The Best 10

Rank	Batter	Year	Team	G	BA	B	O	BPO	BV	BPO+
1	George Brett	1980	Royals	117	.390	379	298	1.272	168.5	180.0
2	Mike Schmidt	1981	Phillies	102	.316	320	258	1.240	138.9	176.7
3	Miguel Cabrera	2013	Tigers	148	.348	453	383	1.183	177.5	164.4
4	Alex Rodriguez	2007	Yankees	158	.314	525	428	1.227	201.8	162.4
5	Harmon Killebrew	1969	Twins	162	.276	486	424	1.146	183.0	160.4
6	George Brett	1985	Royals	155	.335	446	388	1.149	167.0	159.8
7	Dick Allen	1966	Phillies	141	.317	416	377	1.103	153.7	158.6
8	Dick Allen	1967	Phillies	122	.307	359	336	1.068	132.5	158.5
9	Alex Rodriguez	2005	Yankees	162	.321	500	428	1.168	184.4	158.4
10	Howard Johnson	1989	Mets	153	.287	444	425	1.045	162.9	157.9

List #126: Worst Third Baseman in a Season

Vinny Castilla was a reliable power source for the Rockies, blasting at least 32 homers each season from 1995 to 1999. Denver's thin air clearly deserved some of the credit. (How else to explain the fact that Castilla's BPO+ was lower than 100 three times in that five-year span?) But his teammates happily sang his praises. Larry Walker, the National League's reigning Most Valuable Player, declared in 1998 that Castilla was "probably the most underrated guy in baseball."

Those laudatory words were distant memories by 2002. Castilla had bounced from the Rockies to the Devil Rays, Astros, and Braves in the intervening years. His home-run stroke had weakened, as had the consistency that once kept his batting average above .300 for five consecutive seasons in Colorado.

Castilla began 2002 in a terrible slump. He eked out only 35 hits in his first 40 games, barely outnumbering his 27 strikeouts. His batting average was a sickly .215 on May 20. He improved after that, yet he finished with just 12 home runs and a .232 BA. Castilla's BPO+ of 67.7 was the worst for any regular third baseman in the Modern Era.

Managers wrote Castilla into the lineup for 16 years because of his solid reputation as a hitter. But the second man on this list, Aurelio Rodriguez, made his mark in the field, winning a Gold Glove with the Tigers in 1976. He wasn't nearly as proficient at the plate, settling for a 68.5 BPO+ in 1974.

The Worst 10

Rk	Batter	Year	Team	G	BA	B	O	BPO	BV	BPO+
1	Vinny Castilla	2002	Braves	143	.232	228	446	.511	-108.9	67.7
2	Aurelio Rodriguez	1974	Tigers	159	.222	214	470	.455	-98.6	68.5
3	Jose Hernandez	2003	Rockies-Cubs-Pirates	150	.225	234	424	.552	-105.1	68.9
3	Scott Brosius	1997	Athletics	129	.203	208	404	.515	-94.1	68.9
5	Jose Lopez	2010	Mariners	150	.239	233	476	.489	-101.6	69.6
6	Manny Castillo	1982	Mariners	138	.257	207	406	.510	-89.2	69.9
7	Terry Pendleton	1996	Marlins-Braves	153	.238	248	460	.539	-106.2	70.1
7	Clete Boyer	1964	Yankees	147	.218	205	419	.489	-87.4	70.1
9	Matt Dominguez	2014	Astros	157	.215	229	476	.481	-95.2	70.6
10	Hubie Brooks	1983	Mets	150	.251	232	467	.497	-94.0	71.2

15. OUTFIELDERS

List #127: Best Left Fielder in a Career

Four of the top seven players on this list have been enshrined in the Hall of Fame, yet all of them are overshadowed by a slugger who may never be admitted to Cooperstown.

Barry Bonds is the dominant figure among the Modern Era's left fielders. He swatted 762 home runs during his 22-year career, the greatest display of power in baseball history. His 2,558 walks and seven Most Valuable Player Awards also outrank everybody else. And his collection of 12 Silver Slugger Awards and eight Gold Gloves testify to his exceptional ability in all facets of the game.

Yet Bonds has never received more than 45 percent of the votes in a Hall of Fame election, well short of the necessary 75 percent. His alleged use of performance-enhancing drugs has convinced a majority of voters to bar the door, though Bonds predicts that they will eventually punch his ticket to Cooperstown. "I deserve to be there," he says.

Bonds's rank among left fielders is more clear-cut than his murky Hall of Fame status. He reached 9,249 bases — itself a career record for the Modern Era — and exceeded expectations by the enormous total of 3,847.2. That's far and away the highest base value on this list.

Hall of Famer Rickey Henderson is the unfortunate runner-up. His BV of 2,350.9 would take first place in the rankings for any other position on the diamond. But it's almost 1,500 behind the leader here.

The Best 10

Rank	Batter	Span	G	BA	B	O	BPO	BPO+	BV
1	Barry Bonds	1986-2007	2,986	.298	9,249	7,313	1.265	170.7	3,847.2
2	Rickey Henderson	1979-2003	3,081	.279	8,379	8,510	.985	140.0	2,350.9
3	Manny Ramirez	1993-2011	2,302	.312	6,394	6,038	1.059	136.3	1,707.8
4	Tim Raines	1979-2002	2,502	.294	6,066	6,670	.909	126.3	1,252.1
5	Willie Stargell	1962-1982	2,360	.282	5,306	5,938	.894	129.7	1,215.6
6	Carl Yastrzemski	1961-1983	3,308	.285	7,710	9,126	.845	117.6	1,134.8
7	Billy Williams	1961-1976	2,458	.291	5,822	6,904	.843	118.7	917.9
8	Albert Belle	1989-2000	1,539	.295	4,208	4,443	.947	125.7	875.4
9	Frank Howard	1961-1973	1,761	.274	3,839	4,610	.833	125.8	785.1
10	Adam Dunn	2001-2014	2,001	.237	4,879	5,419	.900	118.9	780.2

List #128: Best Left Fielder in a Season

The Modern Era has seen four instances of a batter posting a BPO+ higher than 200. All four were left fielders — the very same left fielder, in fact.

Barry Bonds became the first player to cross the 200 threshold when he pounded 73 home runs in 2001. His BPO+ of 248.3 signified that he was 148.3 percent better than an average batter, a truly astounding gap.

The Giants star broke two records that year. Bonds surpassed the 70 homers hit by Cardinals first baseman Mark McGwire in 1998. And he deposed McGwire's BPO+ of 199.0 as the era's best. "We have never seen a season like this in our lifetime," said Ned Colletti, the Giants assistant general manager, "and we probably never will again."

He was wrong. Bonds hit a relatively meager 46 home runs in 2002, though he amped his batting average to .370, topping the majors. His BPO+ soared to a new record of 282.2. The following season brought a slump (a technically correct noun that nonetheless sounds absurd) to 225.8, which briefly ranked as the era's third-best performance.

But Bonds was soon to reach his zenith. He drew 232 walks in 2004, while launching 45 homers and batting .362. It was the recipe for the highest BPO+ of the Modern Era, 284.5, and the best of his nine scores on this list. Rickey Henderson is the only other left fielder to make the top 10, based on his 190.1 for the Athletics in 1990.

The Best 10

Rank	Batter	Year	Team	G	BA	B	O	BPO	BV	BPO+
1	Barry Bonds	2004	Giants	147	.362	553	247	2.239	358.6	284.5
2	Barry Bonds	2002	Giants	143	.370	540	262	2.061	348.6	282.2
3	Barry Bonds	2001	Giants	153	.328	612	330	1.855	365.5	248.3
4	Barry Bonds	2003	Giants	130	.341	459	266	1.726	255.7	225.8
5	Barry Bonds	1992	Pirates	140	.311	473	350	1.351	230.5	195.1
6	Rickey Henderson	1990	Athletics	136	.325	452	357	1.266	214.2	190.1
7	Barry Bonds	1993	Giants	159	.336	529	388	1.363	244.3	185.8
8	Barry Bonds	1996	Giants	158	.308	516	382	1.351	230.4	180.7
9	Barry Bonds	1994	Giants	112	.312	365	284	1.285	154.2	173.1
10	Barry Bonds	2000	Giants	143	.306	468	349	1.341	195.7	171.9

List #129: Worst Left Fielder in a Season

Brian Hunter's blazing speed was his ticket to the major leagues. He stole 74 bases for Detroit in 1997, the highest total for any player that season (or the nine seasons to come). The 26-year-old center fielder, recently acquired in a trade with Houston, looked to be a potential star for the rebuilding Tigers.

But there were a few warning signs. Hunter struck out an awful lot (121 times in 1997) without generating any power (four home runs). His batting average of .269 was far from ideal for a leadoff man. And his 1997 BPO+ was a subpar 96.5.

Hunter slipped to a miserable 77.7 the year after that, inspiring the Tigers to ship him to Seattle 18 games into the 1999 season. The Mariners already had a serviceable center fielder — a young guy named Griffey — so they moved Hunter to left.

The trade initially seemed to be a good one. Hunter went 18-for-51 (.353) and swiped four bases in his first two weeks in Seattle. But he couldn't maintain the momentum. He batted .171 during the final two months of the season, finishing with a BPO+ of 73.9, the worst for any Modern Era left fielder. The Mariners released him in the offseason.

The runner-up on this list also had Detroit and Seattle connections. Dan Meyer posted a 74.9 BPO+ in 1975, his second season with the Tigers. The Mariners snatched him up in the expansion draft a year later.

The Worst 10

Rank	Batter	Year	Team	G	BA	B	O	BPO	BV	BPO+
1	Brian Hunter	1999	Tigers-Mariners	139	.232	256	441	.580	-90.1	73.9
2	Dan Meyer	1975	Tigers	122	.236	199	383	.520	-66.6	74.9
3	Garret Anderson	1996	Angels	150	.285	288	473	.609	-91.0	76.0
4	Reed Johnson	2004	Blue Jays	141	.270	255	417	.612	-74.9	77.3
5	Lou Piniella	1973	Royals	144	.250	230	422	.545	-66.4	77.6
6	Billy Sample	1984	Rangers	130	.247	217	393	.552	-59.9	78.4
7	Terrence Long	2003	Athletics	140	.245	227	379	.599	-61.3	78.7
8	Gary Ward	1987	Yankees	146	.248	252	425	.593	-66.0	79.2
9	Chris James	1989	Phillies-Padres	132	.243	216	394	.548	-55.1	79.6
10	Billy Hatcher	1989	Astros-Pirates	135	.231	211	388	.544	-50.3	80.7

List #130: Best Center Fielder in a Career

Everybody agreed that Ken Griffey Jr. was an outstanding ballplayer. He possessed all of the essential qualities — power, speed, grace, and consistency.

So it came as no surprise when Griffey was admitted to Cooperstown in 2016, his first year of eligibility. His box was checked on 99.3 percent of the 440 Hall of Fame ballots, surpassing the previous record of 98.8 percent for Tom Seaver. "It's truly an honor to be elected," Griffey said, "and to have the highest percentage is definitely a shock."

The election stamped Griffey as the greatest center fielder of the Modern Era. Voters were swayed by his excellence in the field (10 Gold Gloves) and at the plate (630 home runs). He generated a BPO+ higher than 130.0 in seven seasons, peaking at 151.5 in 1993. The typical batter who played 22 years for the Mariners, Reds, and White Sox would have reached 5,645.4 bases, but Griffey exceeded that total by 1,312.6, the strongest BV on this list.

Yet Griffey's supremacy comes with an asterisk. The two runners-up, Willie Mays and Mickey Mantle, reached the majors a decade before the Modern Era began. These rankings cover only the latter portions of their careers.

Mays nonetheless took second place with a BV of 1,268.2 in 13 seasons, while Mantle was third with 915.0 in eight years. Both men finished far ahead of Griffey in lifetime base value — Mantle (1951-1968) at 2,418.0 and Mays (1951-1973) at 2,374.1.

The Best 10

Rank	Batter	Span	G	BA	B	O	BPO	BPO+	BV
1	Ken Griffey Jr.	1989-2010	2,671	.284	6,958	7,398	.941	123.2	1,312.6
2	Willie Mays	1961-1973	1,774	.290	4,450	4,656	.956	139.9	1,268.2
3	Mickey Mantle	1961-1968	1,002	.284	2,469	2,313	1.067	157.7	915.0
4	Jim Wynn	1963-1977	1,920	.250	4,483	5,312	.844	125.7	914.3
5	Mike Trout	2011-2016	811	.306	2,374	2,183	1.087	159.0	882.4
6	Jim Edmonds	1993-2010	2,011	.284	4,804	5,156	.932	120.7	828.4
7	Carlos Beltran	1998-2016	2,457	.281	6,105	7,049	.866	115.1	799.0
8	Cesar Cedeno	1970-1986	2,006	.285	4,613	5,672	.813	118.4	708.5
9	Andrew McCutchen	2009-2016	1,190	.292	3,051	3,339	.914	130.0	695.6
10	Eric Davis	1984-2001	1,626	.269	3,742	4,122	.908	121.6	664.3

List #131: Best Center Fielder in a Season

Sportswriters didn't fully understand what they were seeing in 1961. They knew that an outfielder for the Yankees was putting together a dominant season, but they incorrectly thought it was Roger Maris.

The media (then known as the press) focused on the duel between right fielder Maris and center fielder Mickey Mantle to break Babe Ruth's record of 60 home runs. Maris swatted his 61st in the final game of the season, thereby earning a place in history, as well as the American League's Most Valuable Player Award.

But the writers should have chosen Mantle as MVP. His 54 homers and .317 batting average translated to a league-leading BPO+ of 191.0. Maris, who batted .269, was far behind at 144.5.

The voters got a second chance in 1962. Injuries restricted Mantle to 123 games, yet he still hit 30 homers, led the majors in on-base percentage (.486), and upped his BA to .321. His BPO+ rose to 193.6 — 38 points better than anybody else in the majors. It remains the best performance by any center fielder in the Modern Era.

The writers conceded that Mantle was 1962's MVP, though they were not unanimous. Five of the 20 voters inexplicably opted for Yankees second baseman Bobby Richardson, whose unimpressive BPO+ was 93.8.

The next two places on this list belong to Mike Trout, who posted a score of 170.5 for the Angels in 2013, then followed it up with a BPO+ of 167.5 in 2016.

The Best 10

Rank	Batter	Year	Team	G	BA	B	O	BPO	BV	BPO+
1	Mickey Mantle	1962	Yankees	123	.321	362	262	1.382	175.0	193.6
2	Mickey Mantle	1961	Yankees	153	.317	497	360	1.381	236.8	191.0
3	Mike Trout	2013	Angels	157	.323	488	422	1.156	201.8	170.5
4	Mike Trout	2016	Angels	159	.315	464	393	1.181	187.1	167.5
5	Rickey Henderson	1985	Yankees	143	.314	469	398	1.178	187.8	166.8
6	Jim Wynn	1969	Astros	149	.269	432	381	1.134	172.5	166.5
7	Willie Mays	1965	Giants	157	.317	449	400	1.123	172.8	162.5
8	Mickey Mantle	1964	Yankees	143	.303	383	339	1.130	146.4	161.9
9	Mike Trout	2012	Angels	139	.326	444	396	1.121	167.7	160.7
10	Bobby Murcer	1971	Yankees	146	.331	396	375	1.056	148.9	160.3

List #132: Worst Center Fielder in a Season

Alex Rios seemed to be a star in the making. The young right fielder blossomed during his six years in Toronto, occasionally flashing an impressive ability to hit for average (.302 in 2006), pound home runs (24 in 2007), and steal bases (32 in 2008). He was rewarded with a seven-year, $69.8 million contract in April 2008.

But Rios's inconsistency baffled the Blue Jays, who began to doubt that he would ever combine his various skills in the same season. He was batting a pedestrian .264 when Toronto waived him (and his hefty paycheck) in August 2009.

The White Sox, just three games out of first place in the American League Central, eagerly scooped him up. Manager Ozzie Guillen put Rios in center field for the stretch run, but the move didn't pay off. He batted .199 the rest of the way, and the Sox missed the playoffs.

Rios followed his up-and-down pattern in coming seasons, pumping his BPO+ to 102.9 in 2010, then dive-bombing to 69.1 the following year. Everything about 2011 was miserable. Rios went hitless in 63 of his 145 games, finishing with a .227 BA, 13 homers, and 11 steals. His BPO+ was the worst for a regular center fielder since 1961.

Bill Virdon once won a Gold Glove, but never earned trophies as a hitter. His two seasons below 72.0 for the Pirates — 70.2 in 1964 and 71.1 in 1962 — are ranked right behind Rios on this list.

The Worst 10

Rank	Batter	Year	Team	G	BA	B	O	BPO	BV	BPO+
1	Alex Rios	2011	White Sox	145	.227	231	445	.519	-103.4	69.1
2	Bill Virdon	1964	Pirates	145	.243	180	383	.470	-76.3	70.2
3	Bill Virdon	1962	Pirates	156	.247	276	527	.524	-112.1	71.1
4	Darren Lewis	1999	Red Sox	135	.240	229	390	.587	-85.4	72.8
5	Marquis Grissom	2000	Brewers	146	.244	274	475	.577	-102.0	72.9
6	Rick Bosetti	1979	Blue Jays	162	.260	275	500	.550	-88.1	75.7
7	Peter Bergeron	2000	Expos	148	.245	266	424	.627	-83.4	76.1
8	Endy Chavez	2003	Expos	141	.251	232	388	.598	-72.3	76.2
9	Kirby Puckett	1984	Twins	128	.296	227	416	.546	-69.6	76.5
10	Darren Lewis	1995	Giants-Reds	132	.250	227	394	.576	-69.6	76.6

List #133: Best Right Fielder in a Career

Hank Aaron may not have been the best right fielder of all time — Babe Ruth played the same position — but he was clearly preeminent during the 70-season span following World War II.

The 20-year-old Aaron joined the Braves in 1954, establishing himself as the regular left fielder and producing a decent BPO+ of 98.4. He wouldn't spend another season below 110.0 until he was 41. The intervening period, played mostly as a right fielder, included six years with a BPO+ above 150.0, peaking at a breathtaking 170.6 in 1971.

Aaron is best remembered as the man who broke Ruth's hallowed career home-run record, but he did much more than swing for the fences. He remains the all-time leader in extra-base hits (1,477) and runs batted in (2,297). And only Pete Rose and Ty Cobb generated more hits than his 3,771.

Aaron's lifetime BV was a massive 2,366.6, but this book ranks only the final 16 of his 23 seasons, the portion of his career that began in 1961. He surmounted this statistical handicap, taking first place among the Modern Era's right fielders with a base value of 1,674.3, a tribute to his continuing excellence throughout his 30s and into his early 40s.

Frank Robinson faced a similar predicament. The initial five seasons of his 21 year career predated the Modern Era, yet he was strong enough between 1961 and 1976 to take second place here with a base value of 1,612.8.

The Best 10

Rank	Batter	Span	G	BA	B	O	BPO	BPO+	BV
1	Hank Aaron	1961-1976	2,259	.298	5,915	6,140	.963	139.4	1,674.3
2	Frank Robinson	1961-1976	2,073	.292	5,328	5,473	.974	143.3	1,612.8
3	Gary Sheffield	1988-2009	2,576	.292	6,720	6,987	.962	128.4	1,503.9
4	Reggie Jackson	1967-1987	2,820	.262	6,614	7,659	.864	127.7	1,425.5
5	Bobby Abreu	1996-2014	2,425	.291	6,027	6,395	.942	123.8	1,175.3
6	Larry Walker	1989-2005	1,988	.313	5,257	5,048	1.041	127.6	1,158.4
7	Bobby Bonds	1968-1981	1,849	.268	4,824	5,513	.875	126.7	1,014.7
8	Vladimir Guerrero	1996-2011	2,147	.318	5,591	6,000	.932	121.1	980.9
9	Brian Giles	1995-2009	1,847	.291	4,696	4,909	.957	125.9	978.2
10	Jack Clark	1975-1992	1,994	.267	4,711	5,348	.881	125.7	967.3

List #134: Best Right Fielder in a Season

Bryce Harper and Sammy Sosa both played right field, though they had little else in common. The disparity was especially evident during their greatest seasons, the best years enjoyed by any right fielder in the Modern Era.

The 22-year-old Harper, renowned for his brash self-confidence, rang up a BPO+ of 180.7 for the Nationals in 2015, earning first place on this list. He topped the National League with 42 home runs, though power wasn't his chief attribute. His true skills were his consistent ability to make solid contact (.330 batting average) and his discipline at the plate (124 walks).

Harper earned the National League's Most Valuable Player Award, making him the youngest winner to be elected unanimously. He was predictably unsurprised. "All I wanted to do was stay healthy and stay on the field every single day I could," Harper said. "I knew if I could do that, I'd be winning this award at the end of the year."

Sosa was a 32-year-old veteran when he peaked in 2001 with a BPO+ of 180.5, two-tenths of a point behind Harper. Fans revered Sosa, who was always smiling, always modest. "He was lovable, just a fun guy," said *Chicago Sun-Times* columnist Jay Mariotti. He also possessed an impressive dimension of power, blasting 64 homers and driving in 160 runs.

Rumors of steroid abuse would eventually tarnish Sosa's legacy. "My numbers don't lie," he insisted on several occasions, but he always refused to address the topic of performance-enhancing drugs.

The Best 10

Rank	Batter	Year	Team	G	BA	B	O	BPO	BV	BPO+
1	Bryce Harper	2015	Nationals	153	.330	477	372	1.282	213.0	180.7
2	Sammy Sosa	2001	Cubs	160	.328	559	408	1.370	249.3	180.5
3	Gary Sheffield	1996	Marlins	161	.314	498	387	1.287	203.9	169.3
4	Reggie Jackson	1969	Athletics	152	.275	475	413	1.150	193.7	168.9
5	Jose Bautista	2011	Blue Jays	149	.302	463	375	1.235	188.0	168.4
6	Frank Robinson	1966	Orioles	155	.316	479	430	1.114	192.0	166.9
7	Hank Aaron	1963	Braves	161	.319	484	451	1.073	190.2	164.8
8	Manny Ramirez	2000	Indians	118	.351	400	299	1.338	154.5	162.9
9	Larry Walker	1997	Rockies	153	.366	538	387	1.390	206.6	162.3
10	Frank Robinson	1967	Orioles	129	.311	362	349	1.037	137.0	160.9

List #135: Worst Right Fielder in a Season

Few phenoms have faced as much pressure as Jeff Francoeur, and even fewer have handled it so well — at first.

The Braves called up the 21-year-old Atlanta native in July 2005, installing him in right field. The hometown fans greeted him with high expectations, which Francoeur promptly exceeded. He blasted a three-run homer in his debut and maintained a .400 batting average through his first 25 games. *Sports Illustrated* featured him on its cover, hailing him as "The Natural."

Francoeur inevitably drifted back to earth, though he finished his 70-game rookie season with a .300 BA and a BPO+ of 112.9. The sky seemed the limit. But the rest of his 12-year career failed to deliver on its early promise. He did win a Gold Glove and twice drove in more than 100 runs, yet he never batted .300 again.

Francoeur's struggles became evident in his fourth season. He spiraled into a three-month slump in 2008, registering more strikeouts (64) than hits (58) between May 15 and August 15. He finished the season with a 73.4 BPO+, the lowest for any regular right fielder in the Modern Era.

The Braves shipped Francoeur to the Mets the following year, and he subsequently played for six other teams. He finished below 97 on the BPO+ scale every season but one between 2006 and 2016.

Glenn Wilson of the 1987 Phillies and Mike Hershberger of the 1965 Athletics are tied for second place. Both men posted BPO+ scores of 75.9.

The Worst 10

Rank	Batter	Year	Team	G	BA	B	O	BPO	BV	BPO+
1	Jeff Francoeur	2008	Braves	155	.239	268	479	.559	-97.0	73.4
2	Glenn Wilson	1987	Phillies	154	.264	265	449	.590	-84.0	75.9
2	Mike Hershberger	1965	Athletics	150	.231	208	407	.511	-66.2	75.9
4	Derek Bell	1999	Astros	128	.236	255	420	.607	-80.6	76.0
5	Jason Heyward	2016	Cubs	142	.230	245	427	.574	-74.4	76.7
5	Cory Snyder	1989	Indians	132	.215	211	404	.522	-64.2	76.7
7	Brennan Boesch	2012	Tigers	132	.240	214	373	.574	-64.4	76.9
8	Mike Hershberger	1964	White Sox	141	.230	197	370	.532	-57.1	77.5
9	Dave May	1974	Brewers	135	.226	197	389	.506	-56.5	77.7
10	Jose Guillen	1997	Pirates	143	.267	234	386	.606	-66.8	77.8

List #136: Best Designated Hitter in a Career

Designated hitters aren't outfielders, yet many outfielders become designated hitters. That's a lame rationale for the inclusion of DHs in this chapter, though it will need to suffice. They do have to be categorized somewhere.

The pool of players is smaller than for any other position, given that the DH wasn't adopted until 1973 and then only by the American League. Teams in the National League weren't introduced to the designated hitter until the advent of interleague play in 1997.

All 10 men on this list played most or all of their careers in the AL. Frank Thomas's journey was typical, even if his results were decidedly superior. The White Sox called him up in 1990 to play first base. He was a revelation at the plate — blasting 257 home runs and batting .330 in his first eight seasons — though he was far from a Gold Glove contender in the field.

The Sox named Thomas their fulltime designated hitter in 1998. He would spend 1,310 games at DH, surpassing the 971 at first base. Thomas wrapped up his Hall of Fame career with 521 homers, a .301 BA, and a BV of 1,854.9. The latter total exceeds the runner-up DH, David Ortiz, by 557.9 bases.

Ortiz, like Thomas, arrived in the majors as a first baseman, though the Twins converted him to a DH in his fourth season. He achieved fame — and second place on this list — as a slugger for the Red Sox between 2003 and 2016.

The Best 10

Rank	Batter	Span	G	BA	B	O	BPO	BPO+	BV
1	Frank Thomas	1990-2008	2,322	.301	6,457	6,101	1.058	140.6	1,854.9
2	David Ortiz	1997-2016	2,408	.286	6,233	6,507	.958	126.4	1,297.0
3	Edgar Martinez	1987-2004	2,055	.312	5,226	5,273	.991	131.3	1,259.6
4	Paul Molitor	1978-1998	2,683	.306	6,683	8,040	.831	116.2	917.3
5	Jose Canseco	1985-2001	1,887	.266	4,903	5,528	.887	122.2	873.7
6	Don Baylor	1970-1988	2,292	.260	5,059	6,510	.777	114.1	613.7
7	Brian Downing	1973-1992	2,344	.267	4,846	6,125	.791	114.1	607.5
8	Chili Davis	1981-1999	2,436	.274	5,379	6,737	.798	110.5	521.5
9	Travis Hafner	2002-2013	1,183	.273	2,750	3,073	.895	122.0	499.8
10	Andre Thornton	1973-1987	1,565	.254	3,439	4,200	.819	116.3	480.4

List #137: Best Designated Hitter in a Season

Edgar Martinez was one of the Mariners' most valuable players in 1995, even though he rarely picked up a fielder's mitt. He spent 56 innings on the diamond that year — four games at third base, another three at first — but his natural habitat was the Seattle dugout.

Martinez made his mark as a designated hitter, stepping off the bench four or five times a night to power the Mariners' offense. Manager Lou Piniella penciled him into the DH slot for 138 of 145 games during that strike-shortened season. He responded with 29 homers, 113 runs batted in, and an American League-leading .356 batting average.

The typical Seattle hitter would have reached 273.9 bases in 1995. Martinez exceeded that total by 65.4 percent, translating to a BPO+ of 165.4, the best single-season score ever for a designated hitter. His base value of 179.1 also remains the standard for DHs.

Martinez was especially dangerous because he was so consistent. He rapped two or three hits in 54 games — more than one-third of the Mariners' 1995 schedule — and he drew at least two walks in 29 contests. Downsides were few: He struck out twice or more in only 17 games.

Martinez is one of four designated hitters to appear twice on this list. The others are Travis Hafner, Frank Thomas, and David Ortiz. Hafner earned second place with his performance for the Indians in 2006, when he smashed 42 home runs and led the AL with a 163.5 BPO+.

The Best 10

Rank	Batter	Year	Team	G	BA	B	O	BPO	BV	BPO+
1	Edgar Martinez	1995	Mariners	145	.356	453	347	1.305	179.1	165.4
2	Travis Hafner	2006	Indians	129	.308	408	326	1.252	158.5	163.5
3	Frank Thomas	1991	White Sox	158	.318	451	405	1.114	168.8	159.8
4	Paul Molitor	1987	Brewers	118	.353	385	321	1.199	140.2	157.3
5	David Ortiz	2007	Red Sox	149	.332	462	387	1.194	161.2	153.6
6	Travis Hafner	2005	Indians	137	.305	381	351	1.085	127.3	150.2
7	David Ortiz	2006	Red Sox	151	.287	484	415	1.166	160.5	149.6
8	Edgar Martinez	1996	Mariners	139	.327	435	358	1.215	143.3	149.1
9	Victor Martinez	2014	Tigers	151	.335	400	398	1.005	126.8	146.4
10	Frank Thomas	2000	White Sox	159	.328	490	415	1.181	154.3	146.0

List #138: Worst Designated Hitter in a Season

Ted Simmons was one of baseball's preeminent catchers throughout the 1970s. He rapped 1,550 hits and batted .297 for the Cardinals between 1970 and 1979, qualifying for six National League All-Star teams during that stretch. His 10-year BPO+ of 110.2 compared favorably to the gold standard for contemporary catchers, Johnny Bench's 118.9.

But those halcyon days were merely a memory by 1984. The 34-year-old Simmons had grown too creaky to spend his nights crouching behind the plate, though he seemed to have retained his skills with a bat. The Brewers made the obvious decision and tapped him as their designated hitter.

The move didn't pan out. Simmons had batted a robust .308 the year before, but he couldn't get untracked in 1984. His BA floundered below .210 until mid-June and improved only marginally to .221 by the end of September. His BPO+ followed the same arc, plummeting from 108.2 in 1983 to 67.2 in 1984. The latter remains the worst score ever posted by a designated hitter.

There was a silver lining of sorts. Simmons may have been the worst DH in the American League in 1984, but he still outproduced the pitchers who went to the plate in the National League that season. Their cumulative BPO+ was a miserable 48.1.

Only three other designated hitters have finished a season below 80.0 on the BPO+ scale. The runner-up to Simmons on this list is Michael Young of the 2012 Rangers at 73.8.

The Worst 10

Rank	Batter	Year	Team	G	BA	B	O	BPO	BV	BPO+
1	Ted Simmons	1984	Brewers	132	.221	187	412	.454	-91.2	67.2
2	Michael Young	2012	Rangers	156	.277	268	476	.563	-95.4	73.8
3	Scott Hatteberg	2005	Athletics	134	.256	218	372	.586	-55.8	79.6
4	Ruben Sierra	1996	Yankees-Tigers	142	.247	267	415	.643	-67.5	79.8
5	Delmon Young	2012	Tigers	151	.267	270	450	.600	-65.9	80.4
6	Joe Carter	1997	Blue Jays	157	.234	308	492	.626	-70.0	81.5
7	Dave Parker	1991	Angels-Blue Jays	132	.239	225	397	.567	-49.8	81.8
8	Alvin Davis	1991	Mariners	145	.221	221	381	.580	-48.5	82.0
9	Larry Sheets	1988	Orioles	136	.230	208	369	.564	-44.0	82.5
10	Vladimir Guerrero	2011	Orioles	145	.290	264	428	.617	-50.8	83.9

16. BATTERIES

List #139: Best Catcher in a Career

Tommy Lasorda had a distant cousin in Pennsylvania whose son was a decent ballplayer. The Dodgers manager thought the kid might get a kick out of being drafted by a big-league team. Perhaps the small jolt of publicity would attract the attention of college recruiters. The kid really wanted a scholarship.

The Dodgers' scouts didn't see the point. "They said this guy couldn't hit, couldn't throw," Lasorda recalled. But he persevered, and Los Angeles selected Mike Piazza in the 62nd round of the 1988 draft. A total of 1,389 players had been picked before him. "I got a mailgram from the Dodgers," Piazza said. "They didn't even call me. It was more or less their way of saying good luck."

Piazza defied the odds by becoming the lowest draft choice enshrined in the Hall of Fame. Los Angeles called him up in 1992, and he remained in the big leagues until 2007, mostly with the Dodgers and Mets. He batted .300 or better in nine of those years — peaking at .362 in 1997 — and he swatted at least 20 home runs in 12 seasons. His career base value of 837.5 was the highest for any catcher in the Modern Era.

The runner-up on this list might come as a surprise. Gene Tenace didn't hit for a high average — his BA never topped .263 in a full season — but he had respectable power and a fantastic batting eye. The result was a 15-year BV of 704.9.

The Best 10

Rank	Batter	Span	G	BA	B	O	BPO	BPO+	BV
1	Mike Piazza	1992-2007	1,912	.308	4,619	5,078	.910	122.3	837.5
2	Gene Tenace	1969-1983	1,555	.241	3,053	3,509	.870	129.9	704.9
3	Johnny Bench	1967-1983	2,158	.267	4,723	5,955	.793	113.5	561.7
4	Joe Torre	1961-1977	2,207	.297	4,509	5,907	.763	111.3	462.3
5	Mickey Tettleton	1984-1997	1,485	.241	3,179	3,749	.848	117.2	461.5
6	Joe Mauer	2004-2016	1,590	.308	3,588	4,351	.825	113.9	446.4
7	Jorge Posada	1995-2011	1,829	.273	3,966	4,683	.847	111.3	404.2
8	Carlton Fisk	1969-1993	2,499	.269	5,224	6,767	.772	108.1	384.0
9	Darrell Porter	1971-1987	1,782	.247	3,336	4,390	.760	109.1	286.4
10	Buster Posey	2009-2016	899	.307	1,987	2,423	.820	117.0	286.1

List #140: Best Catcher in a Season

Mike Piazza arrived in the Dodgers clubhouse as an unheralded September callup in 1992, though his anonymity did not long endure. He earned a national reputation the following season by smashing 12 home runs and batting .344 in his first 60 games. His final line for 1993 included 35 homers, a .318 BA, a BPO+ of 128.7, and a unanimous selection as the National League's Rookie of the Year.

Piazza kept getting better, pushing his BPO+ to 145.8 by 1995. Had he reached his ceiling, or was there room for further growth? He supplied the answer in 1997: 40 home runs, 124 runs batted in, and a .362 batting average. "That was probably the best season he had and arguably the greatest season any catcher has had," said ESPN analyst Tim Kurkjian.

A typical batter who played 152 games for the Dodgers in 1997 would have reached 276.3 bases. Piazza exceeded that standard by 58.2 percent, piling up a total of 437 bases. His BPO+ of 158.2 established the benchmark for Modern Era catchers, confirming Kurkjian's assessment.

Piazza qualified for this list three times, supplementing his first-place finish with the fifth and seventh slots. The other seven places were filled by seven different catchers, with Joe Mauer of the 2009 Twins as the runner-up. Mauer's batting average of .365 topped the majors that year, and his 149.1 BPO+ was the best in the American League.

The Best 10

Rank	Batter	Year	Team	G	BA	B	O	BPO	BV	BPO+
1	Mike Piazza	1997	Dodgers	152	.362	437	380	1.150	160.7	158.2
2	Joe Mauer	2009	Twins	138	.365	394	351	1.123	129.7	149.1
3	Johnny Bench	1972	Reds	147	.270	411	429	.958	129.7	146.1
4	Chris Hoiles	1993	Orioles	126	.310	330	306	1.078	103.9	145.9
5	Mike Piazza	1995	Dodgers	112	.346	305	295	1.034	95.8	145.8
6	Darren Daulton	1992	Phillies	145	.270	365	365	1.000	110.7	143.5
7	Mike Piazza	1996	Dodgers	148	.336	392	389	1.008	109.6	138.8
8	Buster Posey	2012	Giants	148	.336	372	381	.976	103.3	138.4
9	Gene Tenace	1975	Athletics	158	.255	363	390	.931	100.4	138.2
10	Dick Dietz	1970	Giants	148	.300	373	369	1.011	100.1	136.7

List #141: Worst Catcher in a Season

There were flashes of excellence during Matt Walbeck's rookie season with the Twins.

The April 25, 1994, game against the Indians offered an early taste. Walbeck singled his first time up, drove in a run with a groundout in the sixth inning, added two more RBIs with a double in the seventh, and finished with a single in the ninth. He was a key player in Minnesota's 9-7 victory.

Walbeck produced a second three-hit game on May 20, another sign that he might become a solid big-league catcher. But the intervening span provided evidence to the contrary. Walbeck went just 10-for-55 (.182) in the 17 games between April 26 and May 19. Only three of his hits went for extra bases.

That stretch of futility became the template for Walbeck's year. He struggled to a .198 batting average during the month of June, then fell to .171 for July. A players' strike mercifully brought the 1994 season to a close on August 12. Walbeck finished with a .204 BA and a BPO+ of 54.4. The latter was the lowest not only for any catcher in the Modern Era, but for any regular player at any position. (See List #24.)

Joe Girardi batted .262 for the Rockies in 1995 — nearly 60 points better than Walbeck the year before — but the friendly confines of Coors Field inflated his numbers. Statistical adjustment left Girardi with a BPO+ of 64.4, which is second-worst on this list.

The Worst 10

Rank	Batter	Year	Team	G	BA	B	O	BPO	BV	BPO+
1	Matt Walbeck	1994	Twins	97	.204	118	279	.423	-98.8	54.4
2	Joe Girardi	1995	Rockies	125	.262	213	372	.573	-117.9	64.4
3	Brad Ausmus	2006	Astros	139	.230	191	372	.513	-102.5	65.1
4	Brad Ausmus	2003	Astros	143	.229	195	367	.531	-90.6	68.3
5	Jim Sundberg	1975	Rangers	155	.199	192	408	.471	-83.7	69.6
6	Michael Barrett	2001	Expos	132	.250	209	376	.556	-88.0	70.4
7	Tony Pena	1991	Red Sox	141	.231	205	390	.526	-80.5	71.8
8	Wilson Ramos	2015	Nationals	128	.229	199	390	.510	-77.8	71.9
9	Bob Boone	1986	Angels	144	.222	197	377	.523	-72.6	73.1
10	Bob Boone	1974	Phillies	146	.242	213	401	.531	-77.5	73.3

List #142: Best Starting Pitcher in a Career

Roger Clemens and Greg Maddux were different types of pitchers, though both were stunningly effective.

Clemens (six-feet-four, 205 pounds) seemed tall and beefy, especially when compared to the six-foot, 170-pound Maddux. His nickname, the "Rocket," perfectly matched Clemens's repertoire of a blazing fastball and a sharp-breaking splitter. Maddux, known as the "Professor," wielded an array of deceptive pitches, including a cutter, a sinker, and one of the best changeups ever.

Their divergent styles yielded similar results. Clemens compiled nine seasons with a BPO+ lower than 80.0, an astounding level of excellence. Maddux was right behind him with eight. No other pitcher since 1961 has spent more than seven seasons in that elite range.

So it's fitting that Clemens and Maddux occupy the top two spots on this list. Clemens accumulated a slight edge in subsidiary stats — ERA (3.12 to Maddux's 3.16) and BPO+ (82.9 to 85.7) — and a bigger lead in the most important column. His base value of minus-1,782.8 surpassed Maddux by roughly 300 bases, the best career performance by a starting pitcher in the Modern Era. (This list is confined to pitchers who started more than half of the games in which they appeared. All of their performances — starting and relieving — are included.)

The two starters who posted seven seasons below the BPO+ threshold of 80.0 were Pedro Martinez and Randy Johnson. They respectively rank third and fourth in the career BV standings.

The Best 10

Rank	Pitcher	Span	G	ERA	B	O	BPO	BPO+	BV
1	Roger Clemens	1984-2007	709	3.12	8,645	14,856	.582	82.9	-1,782.8
2	Greg Maddux	1986-2008	744	3.16	8,846	15,149	.584	85.7	-1,481.1
3	Pedro Martinez	1992-2009	476	2.93	4,737	8,489	.558	79.6	-1,234.6
4	Randy Johnson	1988-2009	618	3.29	7,718	12,509	.617	87.7	-1,133.5
5	Curt Schilling	1988-2007	569	3.46	5,838	9,792	.596	85.4	-1,012.2
6	Kevin Brown	1986-2005	486	3.28	5,681	9,864	.576	85.1	-993.9
7	John Smoltz	1988-2009	723	3.33	6,152	10,475	.587	86.4	-979.7
8	Gaylord Perry	1962-1983	777	3.11	9,178	16,192	.567	90.6	-938.9
9	Tom Seaver	1967-1986	656	2.86	8,199	14,410	.569	89.8	-917.3
10	Mike Mussina	1991-2008	537	3.68	6,612	10,696	.618	88.7	-849.4

List #143: Best Starting Pitcher in a Season

Take a good look at this list. Seems familiar, doesn't it?

It should. It's identical to List #33, which chronicled the best pitching in a season. That version was restricted to those who met the qualification level of one inning per game, essentially limiting it to starters.

We therefore get another opportunity to look back to 2000, which was magical from beginning to end for Pedro Martinez of the Red Sox. He tossed a seven-inning two-hitter against the Mariners on opening day, commencing a streak of five straight victories in April. Subsequent months brought additional highlights: a pair of complete-game shutouts in May, eight innings of one-hit ball against the Indians in June, 15 strikeouts in a July shutout of the White Sox, another one-hitter against the Devil Rays in August, three concluding wins in September.

Martinez's performance was especially impressive because hitters were operating at peak efficiency in 2000. The collective BPO for American League batters was .768 that year, the second-highest percentage for either league since 1961, exceeded only by the AL's .775 in 1996. Yet the BPO against Martinez was a measly .393, translating to a BPO+ of 53.0. The latter was the best score for any starter in the Modern Era.

Martinez appears twice on this list, as does Roger Clemens. But Greg Maddux is the name that occurs most frequently. The Braves righthander took second, third, and 10th places for three of his four seasons between 1994 and 1997.

The Best 10

Rank	Pitcher	Year	Team	G	ERA	B	O	BPO	BV	BPO+
1	Pedro Martinez	2000	Red Sox	29	1.74	258	657	.393	-228.8	53.0
2	Greg Maddux	1995	Braves	28	1.63	256	633	.404	-181.0	58.6
3	Greg Maddux	1994	Braves	25	1.56	258	614	.420	-167.3	60.7
4	Pedro Martinez	1999	Red Sox	31	2.07	301	650	.463	-182.9	62.2
5	Kevin Brown	1996	Marlins	32	1.89	314	705	.445	-161.5	66.0
6	Roger Clemens	1997	Blue Jays	34	2.05	375	796	.471	-191.8	66.2
7	Zack Greinke	2015	Dodgers	32	1.66	278	671	.414	-138.5	66.7
8	Randy Johnson	2004	Diamondbacks	35	2.60	366	747	.490	-176.9	67.4
9	Roger Clemens	2005	Astros	32	1.87	301	642	.469	-144.8	67.5
10	Greg Maddux	1997	Braves	33	2.20	328	698	.470	-153.7	68.1

List #144: Worst Starting Pitcher in a Season

This list extends from the Modern Era's dawn (Jack Lamabe in 1964) to its recent years (Colby Lewis in 2014). It's usually inadvisable to combine statistics from such disparate seasons, but let's make an exception just this once.

Here's a joint look at the 10 worst years endured by starting pitchers. They notched 91 victories, but were saddled with 147 defeats. They surrendered a massive number of bases, yielding 10.7 hits and 3.8 walks per nine innings. Their collective ERA was 5.82, which would have been considered miserable at any point during the past half-century.

Edinson Volquez suffered the worst season in the bunch. He pitched 33 games in 2013 — 27 for the Padres and six for the Dodgers — and gave up at least five runs in nine of them. His lowlights included a nine-run, 11-hit outing in Colorado that lasted just two-and-a-third innings, eight runs apiece in starts against the Giants and Rockies (again), and seven walks to Dodgers batters while still with the Padres.

A typical pitcher would have yielded 306.4 bases under Volquez's circumstances. But he soared 38.5 percent past that benchmark with a total of 424. His BPO+ of 138.5 remains the highest for any starting pitcher since 1961.

Two starters are tied for second place at 137.2 on the BPO+ scale: Jose Lima of the 2005 Royals and Jim Deshaies of the 1994 Twins. Lima's 128.0 BV was worse, while Deshaies's 7.39 ERA was higher.

The Worst 10

Rank	Pitcher	Year	Team	G	ERA	B	O	BPO	BV	BPO+
1	Edinson Volquez	2013	Padres-Dodgers	33	5.71	424	513	.827	117.6	138.5
2	Jose Lima	2005	Royals	32	6.99	472	505	.935	128.0	137.2
2	Jim Deshaies	1994	Twins	25	7.39	393	388	1.013	106.5	137.2
4	Phil Ortega	1965	Senators	35	5.11	446	530	.842	118.4	136.1
5	Jack Lamabe	1964	Red Sox	39	5.89	458	532	.861	119.3	135.2
6	Joe Saunders	2013	Mariners	32	5.26	468	554	.845	120.5	134.7
7	Matt Keough	1982	Athletics	34	5.72	537	626	.858	133.9	133.2
8	Ubaldo Jimenez	2012	Indians	31	5.40	455	528	.862	110.9	132.2
9	Brandon Backe	2008	Astros	31	6.05	455	496	.917	110.0	131.9
10	Colby Lewis	2014	Rangers	29	5.18	425	510	.833	102.3	131.7

List #145: Best Relief Pitcher in a Career

The Yankees envisioned Mariano Rivera as a starting pitcher. His fastball clocked at only 90 miles per hour, but he was successful as a starter in the minor leagues. So the Yanks called him up in May 1995 and sent him out against the Angels.

It didn't go well. Rivera surrendered eight hits and three walks in three-and-a-third innings, and New York lost 10-0. Subsequent starts weren't any better. Rivera's ERA was a stratospheric 10.20 when he was shipped back to the minors.

General manager Gene Michael was leaning toward trading the young pitcher when he learned that Rivera — always a diligent worker — had boosted his speed to 95 on the radar gun. Michael decided to give him another shot, this time as a reliever.

It proved to be the right move, especially after Rivera added a devastating cutter to his repertoire in 1997. "When he throws it, you think it's straight," said Tony Womack, a 13-year big-league infielder, "and the next thing you know, it's on your thumbs."

Rivera spent 19 seasons with the Yankees, piling up 652 saves, 51 more than anybody else in the game's history. His base value of minus-877.8 also ranks as the best for any reliever in the Modern Era. (This list encompasses all pitchers who relieved in more than half of their appearances.)

Billy Wagner is the distant runner-up in this category. The 16-year veteran amassed a BV of minus-502.3, falling 375.5 short of Rivera's total.

The Best 10

Rank	Pitcher	Span	G	ERA	B	O	BPO	BPO+	BV
1	Mariano Rivera	1995-2013	1,115	2.21	1,835	3,881	.473	67.7	-877.8
2	Billy Wagner	1995-2010	853	2.31	1,387	2,735	.507	73.4	-502.3
3	Dennis Eckersley	1975-1998	1,071	3.50	6,225	9,868	.631	93.4	-420.8
4	Trevor Hoffman	1993-2010	1,035	2.87	1,798	3,298	.545	81.3	-414.4
5	Hoyt Wilhelm	1961-1972	597	2.17	1,638	3,295	.497	81.7	-361.6
6	Dan Quisenberry	1979-1990	674	2.76	1,772	3,169	.559	84.6	-328.7
7	Bob Stanley	1977-1989	637	3.64	3,298	5,184	.636	91.3	-316.4
8	Jonathan Papelbon	2005-2016	689	2.44	1,175	2,186	.538	80.0	-298.1
9	Joe Nathan	1999-2016	787	2.87	1,598	2,778	.575	84.4	-296.0
10	Kent Tekulve	1974-1989	1,050	2.85	2,571	4,394	.585	89.9	-295.2

List #146: Best Relief Pitcher in a Season

Dennis Eckersley had two careers. He made 359 starts for the Indians, Red Sox, and Cubs between 1975 and 1986, winning 151 games. But his role changed upon his arrival in Oakland in 1987. Manager Tony La Russa converted him into a reliever, the title he would carry until retiring in 1998.

Eckersley excelled as a closer, not that he was initially excited by the assignment. "Tony said [in 1988], 'Do you still want to close or start?' I said I wanted to start," Eckersley recalled. "Meanwhile, I didn't. Thank God. That's how it all went down. Everybody did their job."

No reliever ever did the job better than Eckersley in 1990. He posted 48 saves for the Athletics, who won the American League title. His ERA was a microscopic 0.61, and his BPO+ of 46.2 was the lowest for any Modern Era reliever who appeared in at least one-quarter of his team's games.

Eckersley finished fifth in the balloting for the AL's Cy Young Award that year, but the man in second place on this list, Eric Gagne, did receive a Cy in 2003, a rare honor for a reliever. Gagne saved 55 wins for the Dodgers with a BPO+ of 47.1.

But don't despair for Eckersley. He would win the Cy Young and the AL's Most Valuable Player Award in 1992, even though his BPO+ of 75.6 was higher than in 1990. Election to the Hall of Fame would follow in 2004.

The Best 10

Rank	Pitcher	Year	Team	G	ERA	B	O	BPO	BV	BPO+
1	Dennis Eckersley	1990	Athletics	63	0.61	64	222	.288	-74.4	46.2
2	Eric Gagne	2003	Dodgers	77	1.20	78	247	.316	-87.5	47.1
3	Koji Uehara	2013	Red Sox	73	1.09	73	224	.326	-78.5	48.2
3	Craig Kimbrel	2012	Braves	63	1.01	61	192	.318	-65.6	48.2
5	Zach Britton	2016	Orioles	69	0.54	69	202	.342	-68.1	50.3
6	Joey Devine	2008	Athletics	42	0.59	46	136	.338	-44.5	50.8
7	Mariano Rivera	2008	Yankees	64	1.40	74	213	.347	-71.5	50.9
8	Takashi Saito	2007	Dodgers	63	1.40	70	192	.365	-65.2	51.8
9	B.J. Ryan	2006	Blue Jays	65	1.37	82	219	.374	-73.9	52.6
10	Fernando Rodney	2012	Rays	76	0.60	77	227	.339	-68.9	52.8

List #147: Worst Relief Pitcher in a Season

Steve Colyer had reason to be optimistic as the 2004 season began.

The hard-throwing lefty had spent half a decade clawing his way through the minor leagues, finally reaching the majors the previous year. He made 13 relief appearances for the Dodgers in 2003, rang up 16 strikeouts, and finished with a respectable 2.75 ERA.

The Dodgers rattled Colyer at the end of spring training in 2004, suddenly trading him to Detroit. But the Tigers, who were coming off a disastrous 43-119 season, desperately needed relievers. It was a great opportunity.

Yet Colyer bungled it with several rocky appearances in April. The worst came in a lopsided loss to the Blue Jays. The Tigers were already down 8-0 when Colyer walked the first batter in the ninth inning. A home run and a pair of doubles came in quick succession. Detroit lost 11-0.

The following months weren't much better. Colyer's ERA stood at 7.01 on July 8. He had almost as many walks (22) as strikeouts (24), earning a two-month trip to the minors. He returned to the Tigers in September, wrapping up the Modern Era's worst season for a reliever. A typical Detroit pitcher would have surrendered 64.4 bases under his circumstances, but Colyer yielded 104 for a BPO+ of 161.5. The Tigers soon traded him to the Mets.

Gene Nelson posted an excellent BPO+ of 76.0 for the Athletics in 1990. But he ballooned to a horrendous 160.8 in 1991, taking the runner-up slot here.

The Worst 10

Rank	Pitcher	Year	Team	G	ERA	B	O	BPO	BV	BPO+
1	Steve Colyer	2004	Tigers	41	6.47	104	93	1.118	39.6	161.5
2	Gene Nelson	1991	Athletics	44	6.84	150	147	1.020	56.7	160.8
3	Tommie Sisk	1964	Pirates	42	6.16	174	185	.941	63.1	156.9
4	Steve Peters	1988	Cardinals	44	6.40	128	135	.948	45.6	155.4
5	Mike Perez	1994	Cardinals	36	8.71	101	95	1.063	35.9	155.2
6	Jaret Wright	2003	Padres-Braves	50	7.35	170	166	1.024	59.9	154.8
7	Jim Johnson	2014	Athletics-Tigers	54	7.09	153	160	.956	53.6	154.0
8	Claude Raymond	1963	Braves	45	5.40	141	159	.887	48.8	152.9
9	Jim Todd	1979	Athletics	51	6.56	243	242	1.004	83.4	152.2
10	Rob Murphy	1990	Red Sox	68	6.32	179	175	1.023	60.7	151.3

17. BALLPARKS

List #148: Best Ballpark in the Era for Batters

The blueprints show Coors Field to be a great ballpark for pitchers. The dimensions are enormous: 350 feet down both foul lines, 390 feet along the left-center power alley, and 415 feet to straightaway center. It's easy to imagine sluggers swinging mightily, yet failing to reach those distant fences in Denver. Or to envision swift outfielders easily tracking down a succession of fly balls.

But the blueprints omit one key number — 5,211 feet. That's the elevation of Coors Field above sea level. (No other big-league park is higher than 1,100 feet.) Curveballs and sliders don't break as sharply in Denver's thin air, but batted balls soar farther. "It's always going to be the toughest park to pitch in because there are so many unique issues," said Marcel Lachemann, who spent two seasons as the Rockies pitching coach.

He's right. The average BPF[B] — batting park factor for bases — is 1.094 at Coors Field, indicating that it's 9.4 percent easier for batters to reach base in Denver than in a typical big-league stadium. The runner-up, the version of Saint Louis's Busch Stadium that closed in 1966, finished well back at 1.060.

Each park's BPF[B], of course, varies from year to year. This category is based on an average of those annual factors. (The rankings are confined to parks in use for at least five years.) Coors Field peaked at 1.169 in 1996, its second year of operation, and dropped as low as 1.033 in 2008.

The Best 10

Rk	Ballpark	Market	Home team	Seasons	Span	Average BPF[B]
1	Coors Field	Denver	Rockies	22	1995-2016	1.094
2	Busch Stadium 1	Saint Louis	Cardinals	6	1961-1966	1.060
3	Fenway Park	Boston	Red Sox	56	1961-2016	1.038
4	Chase Field	Phoenix	Diamondbacks	19	1998-2016	1.033
5	Globe Life Park	Dallas	Rangers	23	1994-2016	1.028
6	Crosley Field	Cincinnati	Reds	10	1961-1970	1.025
6	Exhibition Stadium	Toronto	Blue Jays	13	1977-1989	1.025
8	Atlanta-Fulton County Stadium	Atlanta	Braves	31	1966-1996	1.024
9	Wrigley Field	Chicago	Cubs	56	1961-2016	1.023
10	Yankee Stadium 2	New York	Yankees	8	2009-2016	1.022

List #149: Best Ballpark in the Era for Pitchers

Pitchers loved San Diego's Petco Park from the moment it opened in 2004. "It's a truly fair ballpark. No cheap runs seem to get scored there," insisted Jake Peavy, who enjoyed several outstanding seasons with the Padres, even winning the National League's Cy Young Award in 2007.

Peavy and his fellow pitchers had good reason to be fond of Petco. The outfield was enormous, especially the right-center power alley that originally extended 411 feet from home plate. It was nicknamed Death Valley, a place where long fly balls perished. Padres batters quickly learned the park's limitations. They swatted only 111 homers in Petco during its first two seasons, falling 29.7 percent below their road output of 158.

"Petco plays a little bigger than what we originally thought it would," conceded former Padres general manager Kevin Towers. He was guilty of understatement. The stadium's pitching park factor for bases, PPF[B], has averaged 0.958 since 2004, the most favorable tilt toward pitchers in the Modern Era.

But the balance is shifting in San Diego. The Padres have tinkered with the dimensions over the years, gradually boosting Petco's annual PPF[B] from its nadir of 0.919 in 2009 to an equitable 0.995 by 2016. "When a hitter gets hold of a ball," said former Padres CEO Tom Garfinkel, "it should go out."

Dodger Stadium ranks second in favorability for pitchers. Its PPF[B] has averaged 0.969 in 55 seasons for the Dodgers and four years for the Angels.

The Best 10

Rk	Ballpark	Market	Home team	Seasons	Span	Average PPF[B]
1	Petco Park	San Diego	Padres	13	2004-2016	0.958
2	Dodger Stadium	Los Angeles	Dodgers, Angels	59	1962-2016	0.969
3	Oakland Alameda Coliseum	Oakland	Athletics	49	1968-2016	0.970
3	Astrodome	Houston	Astros	35	1965-1999	0.970
5	Safeco Field	Seattle	Mariners	18	1999-2016	0.972
6	Citi Field	New York	Mets	8	2009-2016	0.975
7	Qualcomm Stadium	San Diego	Padres	35	1969-2003	0.978
8	Memorial Stadium	Baltimore	Orioles	31	1961-1991	0.980
9	Marlins Park	Miami	Marlins	5	2012-2016	0.981
9	AT&T Park	San Francisco	Giants	17	2000-2016	0.981
9	Busch Stadium 3	Saint Louis	Cardinals	11	2006-2016	0.981

List #150: Best Ballpark in the Era for Home Runs

Expansion teams are usually saddled with inept pitching staffs, composed of castoffs from other clubs and prospects who should still be toiling in the minors. Such was the case for the Rockies, whose ace, Armando Reynoso, had made a grand total of six big-league starts prior to 1993.

Colorado's staff was predictably miserable in that initial season. Rockies pitchers surrendered 181 homers — 13 more than any other National League squad — and finished with a horrendous ERA of 5.41. Expansion was a factor, of course, but so was elevation. Colorado played in Mile High Stadium, roughly 4,000 feet above any other big-league park.

Altitude was expected to be less of a problem when the Rockies' permanent home, Coors Field, opened in 1995. Architects tried to counter power with distance, giving the new park the deepest fences in the majors. They didn't succeed. Four Rockies batters launched at least 30 home runs in Coors' inaugural year. Dante Bichette, who never hit more than 15 homers in a season for the Angels or Brewers, blasted a league-leading 40 for Colorado.

So it has gone. Coors Field's batting park factor for home runs, BPF[HR], has averaged 1.178 since 1995. That means it's 17.8 percent easier to hit a homer in Denver than in the typical ballpark.

The runner-up on this list is a former home of the Braves, Atlanta-Fulton County Stadium, whose favorability for sluggers earned it the nickname of "The Launching Pad." Its average BPF[HR] was 1.159.

The Best 10

Rk	Ballpark	Market	Home team	Seasons	Span	Average BPF[HR]
1	Coors Field	Denver	Rockies	22	1995-2016	1.178
2	Atlanta-Fulton County Stadium	Atlanta	Braves	31	1966-1996	1.159
3	Busch Stadium 1	Saint Louis	Cardinals	6	1961-1966	1.135
4	Yankee Stadium 2	New York	Yankees	8	2009-2016	1.134
5	Kingdome	Seattle	Mariners	23	1977-1999	1.112
6	Wrigley Field	Chicago	Cubs	56	1961-2016	1.109
7	Great American Ball Park	Cincinnati	Reds	14	2003-2016	1.100
8	Tiger Stadium	Detroit	Tigers	39	1961-1999	1.096
9	Jarry Park	Montreal	Expos	8	1969-1976	1.077
10	U.S. Cellular Field	Chicago	White Sox	26	1991-2016	1.070

List #151: Worst Ballpark in the Era for Home Runs

Jim Wynn was a powerful man. He stood five-feet-10 and weighed 160 pounds, but his muscular physique and forceful swing earned him the nickname of the "Toy Cannon." It didn't seem that any ballpark could contain the fly balls rocketing off his bat.

Except the Astrodome. It was Wynn's misfortune to become the regular center fielder for the Colt .45s in late 1964, on the eve of their rechristening as the Astros. They moved to baseball's first indoor stadium the following April and quickly learned of its unfriendliness to power hitters. Wynn and other sluggers were thwarted by the distant fences, high walls, and stagnant air. "They built that ballpark for defense and speed," Wynn said. "For me to hit a home run in the dome, it was a godsend."

Yet he somehow came close to winning the 1967 National League crown with 37 homers — 15 in the dome, 22 on the road — topped only by Hank Aaron's 39 for the Braves. Aaron always said that he considered Wynn the real champ that year, given the disparity in their playing conditions. The batting park factor for home runs, BPF[HR], was a beneficial 1.160 in Atlanta in 1967, but a detrimental 0.800 in Houston.

The longterm numbers weren't much better for the Astrodome. The average BPF[HR] during its 35-year history was 0.844, the worst disadvantage for sluggers in the Modern Era. It's followed on this list by Forbes Field, home of the Pirates until June 1970.

The Worst 10

Rank	Ballpark	Market	Home team	Seasons	Span	Average BPF[HR]
1	Astrodome	Houston	Astros	35	1965-1999	0.844
2	Forbes Field	Pittsburgh	Pirates	10	1961-1970	0.870
3	Marlins Park	Miami	Marlins	5	2012-2016	0.883
4	AT&T Park	San Francisco	Giants	17	2000-2016	0.896
5	Municipal Stadium	Kansas City	Athletics, Royals	11	1961-1972	0.904
6	Petco Park	San Diego	Padres	13	2004-2016	0.912
7	PNC Park	Pittsburgh	Pirates	16	2001-2016	0.924
8	Kauffman Stadium	Kansas City	Royals	44	1973-2016	0.925
9	Busch Stadium 3	Saint Louis	Cardinals	11	2006-2016	0.933
10	Busch Stadium 2	Saint Louis	Cardinals	40	1966-2005	0.940

List #152: Best Home Advantage for a Team in a Season

The Twins wrapped up a homestand in June 1987 with four consecutive wins, giving them a four-and-a-half game lead in the American League West. But the comfortable cushion quickly vanished. Minnesota lost seven of eight road games to the Rangers and Royals, slipping into a first-place tie with the latter.

This bipolar behavior continued the rest of the year. The Twins returned to the Metrodome in early July and began to win. But they went 4-9 on a subsequent West Coast swing. Minnesota again found itself in a first-place tie, only to surge back on top with five straight victories at home.

Four road trips remained on the schedule, and all went badly. The Twins lost 16 of their final 21 games away from Minneapolis, yet hung on to win the division. They finished 56-25 (.691) at home and 29-52 (.358) on the road, an imbalance of .333 in winning percentage. It was the biggest home-field advantage for any team in the Modern Era.

Former Twins star Jim Kaat credited Minnesota's fans and the Metrodome itself. "It was loud, the sightlines were difficult, the roof made it easy to lose fly balls," he said. "In short, the Twins usually had the advantage there." Minnesota stayed true to form in the 1987 World Series, winning all four home games to take the championship.

The 1996 Rockies also enjoyed a home-field edge of .333, but their story wasn't nearly as compelling. They went 83-79, well out of playoff contention. (Ties on this list were broken by home winning percentage.)

The Best 10

Rk	Team	Year	Overall	Home W	Home L	Home pct.	Road W	Road L	Road pct.	Home edge
1	Twins	1987	85-77 (WLP)	56	25	.691	29	52	.358	.333
2	Rockies	1996	83-79 (—)	55	26	.679	28	53	.346	.333
3	Astros	1978	74-88 (—)	50	31	.617	24	57	.296	.321
4	Rockies	2014	66-96 (—)	45	36	.556	21	60	.259	.297
5	Marlins	1996	80-82 (—)	52	29	.642	28	53	.346	.296
6	Red Sox	1961	76-86 (—)	50	31	.617	26	55	.321	.296
7	Rockies	2003	74-88 (—)	49	32	.605	25	56	.309	.296
8	White Sox	1972	87-67 (—)	55	23	.705	32	44	.421	.284
9	Astros	1969	81-81 (—)	52	29	.642	29	52	.358	.284
9	Tigers	2010	81-81 (—)	52	29	.642	29	52	.358	.284

List #153: Worst Home Disadvantage for a Team in a Season

The Cubs flashed their competitive zeal during the strike-truncated 1994 season. They traveled to Montreal, whose team had the National League's best record, and won two of three games. They showed similar spunk against the NL's other division leaders, taking a series in Los Angeles and splitting a four-game set in Cincinnati.

But it was a different story when the Cubs returned to Wrigley Field. The Expos, Dodgers, and Reds won eight of 12 games in Chicago. The collective score: Other Guys 52, Cubs 34.

The whole season was like that. The Cubs went absolutely cold in Wrigley Field in 1994, a trend they established by losing all nine home games in April. Manager Tom Trebelhorn waded into a crowd of 200 angry fans outside the stadium after the ninth defeat, inviting questions for half an hour. The mob heckled him at first, but was cheering by the end. "They root hard, but they root fair," said a smiling Trebelhorn. "You gotta love it."

But things didn't get much better. The Cubs lost 39 of the 59 games in Chicago before the August 12 walkout. Their home winning percentage of .339 was .198 below their road figure of .537. No other team in the Modern Era has done so badly in its own ballpark while playing winning ball everywhere else.

The 1998 Royals came closest to that standard. Kansas City finished five games above .500 on the road, but 22 games under at home.

The Worst 10

Rank	Team	Year	Overall	Home W	Home L	Home pct.	Road W	Road L	Road pct.	Road edge
1	Cubs	1994	49-64 (—)	20	39	.339	29	25	.537	.198
2	Royals	1998	72-89 (—)	29	51	.363	43	38	.531	.168
3	Red Sox	1980	83-77 (—)	36	45	.444	47	32	.595	.151
4	Royals	1981	50-53 (P)	19	28	.404	31	25	.554	.150
5	Reds	2001	66-96 (—)	27	54	.333	39	42	.481	.148
6	Reds	1972	95-59 (LP)	42	34	.553	53	25	.679	.126
7	Cardinals	2016	86-76 (—)	38	43	.469	48	33	.593	.124
8	Athletics	1971	101-60 (P)	46	35	.568	55	25	.688	.120
9	Dodgers	1970	87-74 (—)	39	42	.481	48	32	.600	.119
9	Brewers	1999	74-87 (—)	32	48	.400	42	39	.519	.119

List #154: Best Home Advantage for a Batter in a Career

List #148 proved Coors Field to be the best ballpark for hitters in the Modern Era. So it's unsurprising that the first man on this list — the batter who has enjoyed the strongest home-field advantage during his career — is a player for the Colorado Rockies (Carlos Gonzalez).

The same with the second man (Larry Walker). And the third (Todd Helton). And the fourth, fifth, and sixth (D.J. LeMahieu, Dante Bichette, and Charlie Blackmon).

Gonzalez was called up by the Athletics in 2008. Oakland Alameda Coliseum is a notoriously bad ballpark for hitters, and the rookie struggled there, as shown by his weak BPO+ of 74.5. Oakland dealt him to the Rockies in the offseason.

Gonzalez quickly blossomed in Denver's thin air, posting a BPO+ of 115.0 or better in each of his first five seasons there. His home-field BPO for his entire career (Athletics and Rockies) has been a robust 1.037, compared to a much more sedate .718 on the road. The difference of .319 is the biggest gap for any batter making at least 2,000 plate appearances.

Walker and Helton both played for 17 seasons. The former spent 10 of those years in Denver, while the latter remained throughout his career. Sixty-two percent of Helton's 369 home runs occurred at Coors Field, as did 61 percent of his 1,406 runs batted in.

Gordy Coleman is the top-rated non-Rockie on this list. He enjoyed a home BPO edge of .246 with the Reds between 1961 and 1967.

The Best 10

Rank	Batter	Span	G	Home BA	Road BA	Home BPO	Road BPO	Home BPO edge
1	Carlos Gonzalez	2008-2016	1,064	.323	.258	1.037	.718	.319
2	Larry Walker	1989-2005	1,988	.348	.278	1.200	.898	.302
3	Todd Helton	1997-2013	2,247	.345	.287	1.163	.865	.298
4	D.J. LeMahieu	2011-2016	672	.334	.263	.833	.556	.277
5	Dante Bichette	1988-2001	1,704	.328	.269	.934	.661	.273
6	Charlie Blackmon	2011-2016	605	.334	.261	.962	.691	.271
7	Gordy Coleman	1961-1967	701	.302	.242	.852	.606	.246
8	Bob Horner	1978-1988	1,020	.295	.260	.926	.683	.243
9	Albie Pearson	1961-1966	689	.301	.249	.876	.645	.231
10	Rico Petrocelli	1963-1976	1,553	.272	.230	.834	.604	.230

List #155: Worst Home Disadvantage for a Batter in a Career

The Cubs considered Rick Wilkins to be a promising young catcher, and he fulfilled their expectations in 1993, his first year as a regular. Wilkins smashed 30 home runs, batted .303, and posted a BPO+ of 129.7. The Cubs enjoyed their first winning season in four years, and Wilkins was a big reason why.

But there was something strange about his stats. Wrigley Field is a very good park for hitters, yet Wilkins fared better on the road. He finished with 10 homers and a .256 BA at Wrigley in 1993, compared to 20 and .356 everywhere else.

This unusual pattern held for the rest of his 11-year career. Wilkins never duplicated his breakout season, and the Cubs dealt him to the Astros in 1995. The baseball merry-go-round would spin him to six other teams before retirement in 2001. The one constant was his relative strength on the road (49 lifetime homers, .272 BA) and weakness at his various home parks (32 HR, .216 BA).

The gap between Wilkins's career BPO on the road (.851) and at home (.593) was .258, the biggest home-field disadvantage for any batter who went to the plate at least 2,000 times in the Modern Era.

Runner-up Khalil Greene also enjoyed an outstanding debut. The Padres shortstop batted .273 in 2004, finishing second in balloting for the National League's Rookie of the Year. But he never played as well again during his seven-year career, and he always seemed to struggle at home.

The Worst 10

Rank	Batter	Span	G	Home BA	Road BA	Home BPO	Road BPO	Road BPO edge
1	Rick Wilkins	1991-2001	720	.216	.272	.593	.851	.258
2	Khalil Greene	2003-2009	736	.225	.264	.601	.745	.144
3	Tomas Perez	1995-2008	789	.214	.267	.481	.612	.131
4	Ron Karkovice	1986-1997	939	.212	.229	.569	.691	.122
5	Ben Grieve	1997-2005	976	.253	.285	.738	.857	.119
6	Kevin Kouzmanoff	2006-2014	685	.244	.270	.587	.702	.115
7	Brady Anderson	1988-2002	1,834	.241	.269	.785	.898	.113
7	Jim Ray Hart	1963-1974	1,125	.258	.296	.709	.822	.113
9	Mike Piazza	1992-2007	1,912	.294	.320	.852	.964	.112
10	Desmond Jennings	2010-2016	567	.228	.261	.660	.771	.111

List #156: Best Home Advantage for a Pitcher in a Career

Barry Latman had impeccable taste in ballparks. The tall righthander bounced around the majors for 11 seasons, always landing in a facility that favored pitchers.

Latman launched his big-league career in 1957 with the White Sox. The foul poles in cavernous Comiskey Park were 352 feet distant from home plate, and the fence in straightaway center was a deep 415. He pitched there until a 1960 trade took him to the Indians, whose home park, Cleveland Stadium, was nearly as vast as Comiskey. Subsequent trades deposited Latman in two of the all-time great parks for pitchers — Dodger Stadium (with the Angels) and the Astrodome.

These venues had a substantial impact on the Modern Era portion of Latman's career, the 1961-1967 span with the Indians, Angels, and Astros. His ERA for those seven seasons was a tidy 3.13 at home, but an unkempt 5.15 on the road. A BPO comparison reveals the same pattern: .571 at home, .816 away. The gap of .245 indicates that Latman enjoyed the biggest home-field advantage of any of the era's regular pitchers. (This list is limited to those who worked at least 640 innings.)

Gary Ross certainly didn't catch a break at his first stop in the majors, cozy (and windy) Wrigley Field. But the Cubs dealt him to San Diego in his second season, and he spent the rest of his career there and with the Angels. Their parks strongly favored pitchers, boosting Ross to second place here.

The Best 10

Rank	Pitcher	Span	G	Home ERA	Road ERA	Home BPO	Road BPO	Home BPO edge
1	Barry Latman	1961-1967	256	3.13	5.15	.571	.816	-.245
2	Gary Ross	1968-1977	283	3.10	4.91	.615	.823	-.208
3	Chris Codiroli	1982-1990	144	3.95	5.77	.618	.821	-.203
4	Scott Downs	2000-2014	619	2.94	4.25	.556	.748	-.192
5	Andrew Cashner	2010-2016	202	2.87	4.93	.592	.779	-.187
6	Ismael Valdez	1994-2005	325	3.31	4.92	.607	.787	-.180
7	Don Stanhouse	1972-1982	294	3.21	4.46	.625	.801	-.176
8	Gary Lucas	1980-1987	409	2.13	3.97	.525	.699	-.174
9	Mark Petkovsek	1991-2001	390	3.69	5.94	.659	.830	-.171
9	Clayton Richard	2008-2016	206	3.38	4.98	.607	.778	-.171

List #157: Worst Home Disadvantage for a Pitcher in a Career

Brian Bohanon played for six big-league teams, though he donned the uniforms of the Rangers or Rockies for the bulk of his 12-year career. He pitched 742 innings for Texas and Colorado, nearly twice the 374 innings for his other four employers.

Bohanon's career was shaped indelibly by the ballparks where he spent the most time. Arlington Stadium, the Rangers' home for four of his five years on their roster, was a relatively neutral park. It wasn't harmful to pitchers, though it wasn't any help either. The Rockies' stadium, Coors Field, was considerably worse — far and away the most hazardous venue for pitchers in the Modern Era.

If Arlington and Coors are removed from the calculations, Bohanon's earned run average for all remaining parks (including the other facilities where he was temporarily based) drops to a passable 4.42. But he fared much more poorly at the dangerous duo — 5.20 in Arlington Stadium, 7.54 in Coors Field — causing his career ERA to balloon to a precarious 5.19.

No other pitcher since 1961 has found home to be so inhospitable. Bohanon ran up a BPO of .874 in his teams' ballparks, dwarfing his .707 on the road. The resulting gap of .167 marked the biggest home disadvantage for any Modern Era pitcher with at least 640 innings under his belt.

Steve Reed could certainly sympathize. Reed spent seven of his 14 seasons with the Rockies, a key reason for the .143 road edge that earned second place on this list.

The Worst 10

Rank	Pitcher	Span	G	Home ERA	Road ERA	Home BPO	Road BPO	Road BPO edge
1	Brian Bohanon	1990-2001	304	6.05	4.31	.874	.707	-.167
2	Steve Reed	1992-2005	833	4.17	3.07	.737	.594	-.143
3	George Culver	1966-1974	335	4.68	2.65	.739	.604	-.135
4	Claudio Vargas	2003-2010	217	5.44	4.24	.852	.726	-.126
4	Rolando Arrojo	1998-2002	158	5.19	3.89	.806	.680	-.126
6	Carlos Carrasco	2009-2016	143	4.58	3.27	.699	.587	-.112
7	Danny Graves	1996-2006	518	4.49	3.62	.773	.664	-.109
8	John Wyatt	1961-1969	435	3.81	3.12	.761	.662	-.099
8	Jason Jennings	2001-2009	225	5.36	4.59	.845	.746	-.099
10	Homer Bailey	2007-2016	174	4.56	3.92	.741	.643	-.098

18. FANS

List #158: Best Fan Support in the Era

Walter O'Malley moved the Dodgers to Los Angeles in 1958, infuriating the fans left behind in Brooklyn. They consoled themselves with gallows humor. A favorite joke involved a Dodgers supporter who found himself in the same room with Adolf Hitler, Joseph Stalin, and O'Malley. He had a gun, but only two bullets. Which of the notorious villains should he shoot?

Every true blue Brooklynite knew the answer: O'Malley. Twice.

But the last laugh would belong to the Dodgers owner. Attendance had been on the wane in Brooklyn — never reaching 1.3 million after 1949 — and O'Malley hoped for an upswing on the West Coast. His dreams were fulfilled. The Dodgers have attracted more than 3 million fans in 29 of 56 seasons since 1961.

The franchise's box-office success is reflected by the best fan support index in the big leagues, averaging 151.6 points during the Modern Era. FSI tracks the annual relationship between a team's attendance and its victory total. A score of 100 indicates support commensurate with the team's quality on the field. The Dodgers have exceeded that benchmark every year in Los Angeles, showing a superior level of fan devotion. They peaked at 212.8 in 1964, leading the majors at the gate (2.23 million) despite a losing record (80-82).

The Rockies have enjoyed only seven winning seasons since their creation in 1993, but their attendance has topped 3 million nine times. Their average FSI of 135.7 puts them in second place.

The Best 10

Rk	Team	Years	Span	Attend	Att/G	W	L	AFSI
1	Los Angeles Dodgers	56	1961-2016	163,817,930	36,665	4,807	4,130	151.6
2	Colorado Rockies	24	1993-2016	70,789,304	37,024	1,784	2,042	135.7
3	New York Mets	55	1962-2016	116,745,421	26,612	4,215	4,555	123.1
4	Saint Louis Cardinals	56	1961-2016	133,032,854	29,721	4,731	4,194	118.9
5	New York Yankees	56	1961-2016	133,821,858	29,998	4,979	3,946	112.6
6	Toronto Blue Jays	40	1977-2016	93,739,758	29,506	3,167	3,188	111.7
7	Philadelphia Phillies	56	1961-2016	114,345,261	25,546	4,437	4,495	109.3
8	Boston Red Sox	56	1961-2016	120,349,097	26,900	4,736	4,199	108.5
9	Chicago Cubs	56	1961-2016	112,608,237	25,119	4,287	4,633	108.4
10	Los Angeles-California-Anaheim Angels	56	1961-2016	117,214,597	26,141	4,477	4,465	108.1

List #159: Worst Fan Support in the Era

It was taken as gospel by the mid-1980s that the Tampa-Saint Petersburg area would be ideal for big-league baseball. The region seemed to have all of the necessary ingredients — rapid population growth, warm weather, a new stadium. It couldn't miss.

The White Sox nearly moved to Tampa Bay in 1989. "It's the greatest opportunity in baseball since Walter O'Malley took the Dodgers west," exclaimed Mike McClure, a Sox marketing executive. But a last-minute deal for a new ballpark kept the Sox in Chicago.

The Giants were the next to express interest, revving up the moving vans for a cross-country trip in 1992. But the National League's owners, unwilling to abandon San Francisco, refused to grant permission.

The expansion Devil Rays finally brought big-league ball to Tampa Bay in 1998, almost immediately proving to be a box-office dud. Attendance was a respectable 2.5 million in the inaugural season, but plummeted to 1.07 million within four years. The Rays haven't reached 1.9 million since then, not even in the World Series season of 2008.

Tampa Bay's fan support index has averaged 67.2 points — 32.8 percent below normal. It's the worst FSI for any franchise in the Modern Era. "What else do you have to do to draw fans in this place?" Rays star Evan Longoria asked plaintively in 2010. Nobody has found an answer.

The reincarnated Washington Senators, with an average FSI of 71.1, are next on this list. The Senators survived for 11 seasons before morphing into the Texas Rangers.

The Worst 10

Rk	Team	Years	Span	Attend	Att/G	W	L	AFSI
1	Tampa Bay Rays-Devil Rays	19	1998-2016	28,285,525	18,367	1,420	1,656	67.2
2	Washington Senators	11	1961-1971	7,314,695	8,284	740	1,032	71.1
3	Oakland Athletics	49	1968-2016	73,797,869	18,889	4,044	3,763	72.7
4	Milwaukee Braves	5	1961-1965	4,107,875	10,219	427	375	73.6
5	Kansas City Athletics	7	1961-1967	4,753,246	8,398	458	672	75.6
6	Miami-Florida Marlins	24	1993-2016	39,467,324	20,685	1,793	2,026	76.5
7	Cleveland Indians	56	1961-2016	83,115,540	18,648	4,362	4,558	77.4
8	Pittsburgh Pirates	56	1961-2016	81,128,253	18,154	4,422	4,498	79.9
9	Montreal Expos	36	1969-2004	48,749,549	17,232	2,755	2,943	82.7
10	Chicago White Sox	56	1961-2016	89,577,910	20,058	4,490	4,439	85.6

List #160: Best Fan Support in a Season

The Mets were absolutely terrible in their early years, losing at least 101 games five times between 1962 and 1967. "This was a group effort," manager Casey Stengel said as one of those disastrous seasons came to an end. "No one player could have done all this." A reporter, looking for a silver lining, asked if Stengel had at least enjoyed himself. "I would have to say no to that one," Casey replied.

And yet the Mets were a marketing phenomenon in the 1960s. Stengel's colorful personality rubbed off on his team, which was idealized by New York fans as a collection of lovable losers. Shea Stadium added to the Mets' appeal. Shea would quickly become outdated, but it seemed wonderfully modern when it opened in 1964. Everybody wanted to see it. "Isn't it marvelous, simply marvelous?" asked team owner Joan Payson. "Isn't this the most beautiful stadium in the world?"

Fans kept streaming into Shea, even as the losses piled up. The Mets attracted nearly 1.8 million in 1965 — third-best in the majors — despite a horrendous 50-112 record. That translated to a fan support index of 252.5, surpassing the big-league average by 152.5 percent. It remains the best single-season FSI in the Modern Era.

The 1964 Mets finished second on this list at 246.7, followed by another team that benefited from a new stadium. Houston christened the Astrodome in 1965, drawing more than 2.1 million fans and posting an FSI of 239.2.

The Best 10

Rank	Team	Year	Attend	Att/G	W	L	Att/W	FSI
1	New York Mets	1965	1,768,389	21,566	50	112	431	252.5
2	New York Mets	1964	1,732,597	21,129	53	109	399	246.7
3	Houston Astros	1965	2,151,470	26,561	65	97	409	239.2
4	New York Mets	1970	2,697,479	32,896	83	79	396	216.9
5	Colorado Rockies	1993	4,483,350	55,350	67	95	826	216.1
6	Los Angeles Dodgers	1964	2,228,751	27,515	80	82	344	212.8
7	Los Angeles Dodgers	1963	2,538,602	31,341	99	63	317	202.6
8	Toronto Blue Jays	1995	2,826,483	39,257	56	88	701	201.7
9	Los Angeles Dodgers	1962	2,755,184	33,195	102	63	325	199.6
10	Colorado Rockies	1994	3,281,511	57,570	53	64	1,086	198.5

List #161: Worst Fan Support in a Season

It quickly became apparent that 1979 would be a dismal year for the Athletics. They lost their first five games — and nine of their first 10. Oakland had already fallen six games behind the AL West leaders, the Rangers, by April 17.

Oakland-Alameda County Coliseum was virtually empty when the A's took the field against the Mariners on that chilly evening. It came as no surprise to pitcher Dave Heaverlo, who would work in relief for Oakland. "I think we were mathematically eliminated coming out of spring training," he said. "We just didn't have the horses."

It didn't help that most fans had grown disenchanted with penurious owner Charlie Finley. Or that the stadium was in disrepair. Or that the concessions were terrible. Fans registered their disgust by staying away from the Coliseum, which the players jokingly renamed the Oakland Mausoleum.

The attendance on April 17 was announced as 653, the smallest turnout for any big-league game during the 44-year span that began in 1972. It was the first of 21 home dates that would attract fewer than 2,000 people to the Coliseum in 1979.

The A's finished the season with a record of 54-108 and attendance of 306,763. The latter figure was the lowest for any team in the Modern Era. Oakland's pathetic FSI of 27.2 holds the same distinction.

The Expos appear five times on this list. Their worst year was 2001, when their home attendance in Montreal totaled 642,745 and their FSI was 31.6.

The Worst 10

Rank	Team	Year	Attend	Att/G	W	L	Att/W	FSI
1	Oakland Athletics	1979	306,763	3,787	54	108	70	27.2
2	Montreal Expos	2001	642,745	7,935	68	94	117	31.6
3	Montreal Expos	2002	812,045	10,025	83	79	121	34.9
4	Florida Marlins	2002	813,118	10,038	79	83	127	36.7
5	Montreal Expos	2004	749,550	9,369	67	95	140	37.6
6	Montreal Expos	1999	773,277	9,547	68	94	140	39.3
7	Oakland Athletics	1978	526,999	6,587	69	93	96	39.9
8	San Francisco Giants	1975	522,919	6,456	80	81	81	42.2
9	Oakland Athletics	1977	495,599	6,119	63	98	97	42.7
10	Montreal Expos	2003	1,025,639	12,662	83	79	153	44.4

19. DRAFTS

List #162: Best No. 1 Draft Pick

Baseball came late to the idea of an amateur draft. Football, basketball, and hockey were drafting young players long before the first big-league session in 1965. Football's version dated all the way back to 1936.

The Athletics held the first pick in 1965. They selected Rick Monday, an outfielder with Arizona State University. It was an auspicious choice. Monday would play 19 seasons with the A's, Cubs, and Dodgers, accumulating a solid career BPO+ of 117.1 and a base value of 556.3.

But the No. 1 pick came with no guarantee of future stardom. The Mets led off the 1966 draft by selecting Steve Chilcott, a high-school catcher from California. A spate of injuries in the minor leagues kept Chilcott from ever reaching the majors. He and 1991's Brien Taylor were the only No. 1 selections prior to 2013 who would never play in a big-league game.

Alex Rodriguez ranks as the best No. 1 choice ever, running up a BV of 1,733.9 after being selected by the Mariners at the start of the 1993 draft. Two other top picks attained four-figure base values: Chipper Jones at 1,380.4 and Ken Griffey Jr. at 1,312.6.

Seventeen No. 1 selections were pitchers, who have their own section on this bifurcated list. The Devil Rays drafted David Price from Vanderbilt University with the first choice in 2007. His BV of minus-371.1 for four clubs is the best for any pitcher who was a top pick.

The Best 10

Rk	Batter	Year (pick)	Team	Span	G	BPO	BPO+	BV
1	Alex Rodriguez	1993 (#1)	Mariners	1994-2016	2,784	.983	128.5	1,733.9
2	Chipper Jones	1990 (#1)	Braves	1993-2012	2,499	.982	126.6	1,380.4
3	Ken Griffey Jr.	1987 (#1)	Mariners	1989-2010	2,671	.941	123.2	1,312.6
4	Darryl Strawberry	1980 (#1)	Mets	1983-1999	1,583	.913	129.3	873.1
5	Adrian Gonzalez	2000 (#1)	Marlins	2004-2016	1,804	.828	115.8	567.8
6	Rick Monday	1965 (#1)	Athletics	1966-1984	1,986	.808	117.1	556.3
7	Joe Mauer	2001 (#1)	Twins	2004-2016	1,590	.825	113.9	446.4
Rk	Pitcher	Year (pick)	Team	Span	G	BPO	BPO+	BV
1	David Price	2007 (#1)	Devil Rays	2008-2016	253	.579	88.7	-371.1
2	Stephen Strasburg	2009 (#1)	Nationals	2010-2016	156	.561	87.3	-229.7
3	Ben McDonald	1989 (#1)	Orioles	1989-1997	211	.648	93.2	-192.8

List #163: Best First-Round Draft Pick from No. 2 to No. 10

The player chosen first in baseball's annual draft might become a star or a flop. Nobody knows on draft day. A later selection may well become the greatest success.

That point was driven home in 1966. The Mets led off by drafting high-school catcher Steve Chilcott, leaving the Athletics free to choose Arizona State University outfielder Reggie Jackson with the No. 2 pick. Chilcott never reached the majors, while Jackson is immortalized in Cooperstown.

Barry Bonds is the best example of a later selection who outperformed prior picks. B.J. Surhoff, Will Clark, Bobby Witt, Barry Larkin, and Kurt Brown were the first five choices in 1985. The initial four would have solid careers; Larkin would even make the Hall of Fame. But Bonds, taken by the Pirates with the No. 6 pick, would put them all in the shade. He posted a BV of 3,847.2, the highest of the Modern Era.

This list shows the best players drafted with picks No. 2 to No. 10. The runner-up to Bonds is Frank Thomas, taken No. 7 by the White Sox in 1989, who went on to accumulate a base value of 1,854.9. Two players drafted prior to Thomas never made the majors. Two others played fewer than 100 games.

Kevin Brown ranks as the best pitcher to be chosen in the range between No. 2 and No. 10. He was a No. 4 pick for the Rangers in 1986 and went on to post a BV of minus-993.9.

The Best 10

Rk	Batter	Year (pick)	Team	Span	G	BPO	BPO+	BV
1	Barry Bonds	1985 (#6)	Pirates	1986-2007	2,986	1.265	170.7	3,847.2
2	Frank Thomas	1989 (#7)	White Sox	1990-2008	2,322	1.058	140.6	1,854.9
3	Mark McGwire	1984 (#10)	Athletics	1986-2001	1,874	1.068	146.2	1,648.3
4	Gary Sheffield	1986 (#6)	Brewers	1988-2009	2,576	.962	128.4	1,503.9
5	Reggie Jackson	1966 (#2)	Athletics	1967-1987	2,820	.864	127.7	1,425.5
6	Todd Helton	1995 (#8)	Rockies	1997-2013	2,247	1.011	120.7	1,018.6
7	Dave Winfield	1973 (#4)	Padres	1973-1995	2,973	.807	116.4	939.8
Rk	Pitcher	Year (pick)	Team	Span	G	BPO	BPO+	BV
1	Kevin Brown	1986 (#4)	Rangers	1986-2005	486	.576	85.1	-993.9
2	Clayton Kershaw	2006 (#7)	Dodgers	2008-2016	265	.484	76.0	-801.6
3	Justin Verlander	2004 (#2)	Tigers	2005-2016	352	.599	89.0	-524.5

List #164: Best First-Round Draft Pick After No. 10

The original concept of the amateur draft was straightforward. Each team would make one pick in each round, progressing in reverse order of the previous season's standings. There were 20 big-league teams in 1965, so 20 selections were made in the first round that inaugural year.

Simplicity rarely lasts, and that was true for the amateur draft. Complicated layers of compensatory picks inflated the first round, which encompassed 42 selections by 2015. This list covers all choices from No. 11 to the end of each year's first round, regardless of length.

Manny Ramirez stayed on the board until the 13th pick in 1991. The Indians selected him after other organizations had judged Brien Taylor, Mike Kelly, Ken Henderson, John Burke, and Joe Vitiello to be superior players. Ramirez would spend 19 seasons with five franchises, making 12 All-Star teams and running up a career BV of 1,707.8, the highest for any batter on the list.

Roger Clemens deserves equal time. His base value of minus-1,782.8 was even larger than Ramirez's, albeit in reverse, and was easily the best for any pitcher selected later than No. 10 in the first round.

The Red Sox drafted Clemens in 1983, when he was the 19th player (and 11th pitcher) taken. Only five of that year's previously selected pitchers would ever wear a big-league uniform. The most successful was the overall No. 1 pick, Tim Belcher, who finished his 14-year career with a 146-140 record and a BV of minus-46.2.

The Best 10

Rk	Batter	Year (pick)	Team	Span	G	BPO	BPO+	BV
1	Manny Ramirez	1991 (#13)	Indians	1993-2011	2,302	1.059	136.3	1,707.8
2	Lance Berkman	1997 (#16)	Astros	1999-2013	1,879	1.012	131.2	1,168.7
3	Rafael Palmeiro	1985 (#22)	Cubs	1986-2005	2,831	.898	119.2	1,153.0
4	Mike Trout	2009 (#25)	Angels	2011-2016	811	1.087	159.0	882.4
5	David Wright	2001 (#38)	Mets	2004-2016	1,583	.891	122.3	736.1
6	Andrew McCutchen	2005 (#11)	Pirates	2009-2016	1,190	.914	130.0	695.6
7	Bobby Grich	1967 (#19)	Orioles	1970-1986	2,008	.798	118.5	670.6
Rk	Pitcher	Year (pick)	Team	Span	G	BPO	BPO+	BV
1	Roger Clemens	1983 (#19)	Red Sox	1984-2007	709	.582	82.9	-1,782.8
2	Mike Mussina	1990 (#20)	Orioles	1991-2008	537	.618	88.7	-849.4
3	Roy Halladay	1995 (#17)	Blue Jays	1998-2013	416	.596	85.8	-811.2

20. AGE GROUPS

List #165: Best Career for a Batter Through Age 23

Mike Trout was two months short of his 18th birthday when the Angels drafted him in 2009. They shipped him directly from Millville Senior High School in New Jersey to the lowest classification in the minors.

He didn't stay there long. Trout raced up the minor-league ladder, shining at every level. He was promoted to the majors in July 2011, a month before turning 20. Angels fans had heard all about his batting prowess, blazing speed, and high baseball IQ. They anticipated immediate stardom, only to be disappointed. The phenom batted a weak .220 in 40 games.

Trout's stats would never again be preceded by negative adjectives. His BPO+ soared above 150 the next four seasons, propelling him to the American League's Rookie of the Year Award in 2012 and Most Valuable Player Award in 2014. (Both selections were unanimous.) He accumulated a base value of 695.3 through his age-23 season, the best performance by any young batter in the Modern Era.

A quick note: Baseball-Reference.com has decreed that a player's age on June 30 is his age for the whole year, which seems as good a rule as any. Trout was 23 at 2015's midpoint, so the entire season counts for this list, even though he turned 24 in August.

Trout outperformed every other young star by at least 260 bases. The race for second place was a tight contest between Rickey Henderson (432.6 BV through age 23), Ken Griffey Jr. (422.6), and Albert Pujols (402.1).

The Best 10

Rank	Batter	Span	G	BA	B	O	BPO	BPO+	BV
1	Mike Trout	2011-2015	652	.304	1,910	1,790	1.067	157.2	695.3
2	Rickey Henderson	1979-1982	504	.291	1,431	1,497	.956	143.7	432.6
3	Ken Griffey Jr.	1989-1993	734	.303	1,871	2,040	.917	128.9	422.6
4	Albert Pujols	2001-2003	475	.334	1,358	1,259	1.079	142.1	402.1
5	Bryce Harper	2012-2016	657	.279	1,662	1,786	.931	128.8	369.1
6	Cesar Cedeno	1970-1974	689	.294	1,726	2,033	.849	123.8	331.5
7	Alex Rodriguez	1994-1999	642	.308	1,806	1,903	.949	120.4	307.4
8	Tim Raines	1979-1983	421	.287	1,133	1,220	.929	130.3	262.8
9	Giancarlo Stanton	2010-2013	489	.265	1,206	1,336	.903	126.0	248.5
10	Miguel Cabrera	2003-2006	563	.311	1,428	1,555	.918	120.9	248.1

List #166: Best Career for a Batter Through Age 29

Albert Pujols was supposed to spend the 2001 season playing AAA ball. He was a third baseman back then, and the Cardinals were counting on veteran Bobby Bonilla to handle that position. The 21-year-old Pujols had only 133 minor-league games under his belt. He definitely needed more seasoning.

That, at least, was the original plan. But manager Tony La Russa was forced to improvise after Bonilla suffered a hamstring injury in spring training. Pujols proved to be a surprisingly effective replacement. He blistered big-league pitching from the start — 16 homers and a .357 BA in his first 50 games — and went on to win the National League's Rookie of the Year Award. Bonilla retired at the end of the season.

Pujols sustained his white-hot pace throughout his 20s. He blasted 366 homers and drove in 1,112 runs for the Cardinals between 2001 and 2009. (The latter was his age-29 year.) His batting average ranged between .314 and .359 during those nine seasons, and his BPO+ always remained above 130. Pujols's cumulative base value of 1.418.1 was the highest for any Modern Era player prior to his 30th birthday.

Rickey Henderson (1,266.1 BV through age 29) and Frank Thomas (1,253.7) dueled for second place on this list. Henderson flashed exceptional speed for the Athletics and Yankees, stealing 794 bases before turning 30. Thomas unleashed raw power for the White Sox, launching 257 home runs in his 20s. Both men ended up in Cooperstown.

The Best 10

Rank	Batter	Span	G	BA	B	O	BPO	BPO+	BV
1	Albert Pujols	2001-2009	1,399	.334	4,227	3,695	1.144	150.5	1,418.1
2	Rickey Henderson	1979-1988	1,322	.292	3,897	3,838	1.015	148.3	1,266.1
3	Frank Thomas	1990-1997	1,076	.330	3,280	2,761	1.188	161.7	1,253.7
4	Barry Bonds	1986-1994	1,281	.285	3,620	3,429	1.056	147.9	1,171.5
5	Alex Rodriguez	1994-2005	1,592	.307	4,707	4,563	1.032	132.8	1,160.2
6	Ken Griffey Jr.	1989-1999	1,535	.299	4,339	4,321	1.004	133.4	1,093.9
7	Tim Raines	1979-1989	1,275	.303	3,500	3,589	.975	137.5	954.5
8	Miguel Cabrera	2003-2012	1,512	.318	4,021	4,133	.973	129.8	918.5
9	Dick Allen	1963-1971	1,143	.297	3,018	3,142	.961	142.1	892.7
10	Mike Trout	2011-2016	811	.306	2,374	2,183	1.087	159.0	882.4

List #167: Best Career for a Batter From Age 30

Barry Bonds achieved greatness while still in his 20s. His cumulative BPO+ for seven seasons with the Pirates and two years with the Giants was a stratospheric 147.9. He led the National League three times each in slugging and on-base percentage, twice in walks, and once apiece in homers and runs batted in. Three Most Valuable Player trophies came his way before he turned 30.

But it was the latter portion of Bonds's 22-year career that stamped him as one of the all-time greats. He kicked into overdrive when a typical player would have begun the descent toward retirement. His BPO+ zoomed to an otherworldly 190.8 for his final 13 seasons, and he racked up a BV of 2,675.7. No other player in that stage of life came close.

What inspired this new level of excellence? You know all of the various theories — steroids, exercise, maturity. Bonds was noncommittal. "Call God," he told reporters. "Ask Him."

What we know for certain is that Bonds led the National League seven times in OBP and four times in slugging after his 30th birthday. He picked up another four MVPs, giving him a total of seven, the most for anybody in baseball history.

The next two men on this list debuted in the 1950s, yet played a majority of their games in the Modern Era. Willie Mays accumulated a base value of 1,268.2 after turning 30 in 1961, while Hank Aaron had a 1,196.2 BV for the same age span.

The Best 10

Rank	Batter	Span	G	BA	B	O	BPO	BPO+	BV
1	Barry Bonds	1995-2007	1,705	.309	5,629	3,884	1.449	190.8	2,675.7
2	Willie Mays	1961-1973	1,774	.290	4,450	4,656	.956	139.9	1,268.2
3	Hank Aaron	1964-1976	1,787	.292	4,528	4,820	.939	135.8	1,196.2
4	Mark McGwire	1994-2001	931	.277	2,860	2,253	1.269	163.8	1,114.1
5	Rickey Henderson	1989-2003	1,759	.268	4,482	4,672	.959	133.2	1,084.8
6	Edgar Martinez	1993-2004	1,534	.312	4,096	3,944	1.039	134.8	1,064.8
7	Joe Morgan	1974-1984	1,452	.272	3,662	3,761	.974	139.0	1,030.4
8	Jim Thome	2001-2012	1,469	.270	3,748	3,635	1.031	136.1	990.1
9	David Ortiz	2006-2016	1,516	.288	4,092	4,165	.982	130.9	968.1
10	Frank Robinson	1966-1976	1,306	.284	3,208	3,416	.939	141.8	945.6

List #168: Best Career for a Batter From Age 36

The most common age for a big-league player is 26. A total of 2,089 batters in the Modern Era made at least 100 plate appearances during their age-26 seasons. That's the strongest representation for any cohort, edging out the 2,056 qualifiers who were 27 years old and the 1,960 who were 28.

But relatively few youngsters endure into the latter half of their 30s. Only 454 batters went to the plate a minimum of 100 times during their age-36 seasons. That was roughly one-fifth the number of players who were 26.

Barry Bonds was clearly the best of the era's longtime survivors. He was 36 years old on opening day in 2001, the season he set the current record by blasting 73 home runs. His reward was being named the National League's Most Valuable Player, a distinction he also earned the three subsequent years.

An average batter in San Francisco would have reached 1,275 bases between 2001 and 2007, but Bonds accumulated 2,865. How amazing was this accomplishment? Bonds posted a BV of 1,590.0 from age 36 to retirement, surpassing the lifetime base values for all but 11 other players in the Modern Era.

Hank Aaron also knew how to maintain a powerful stroke in his later years. He launched 38 homers in 1970 (the year he turned 36) and followed with 47, 34, and 40 in the next three seasons. Aaron finished a distant second on this list with a BV of 476.0.

The Best 10

Rank	Batter	Span	G	BA	B	O	BPO	BPO+	BV
1	Barry Bonds	2001-2007	843	.325	2,865	1,675	1.710	225.2	1,590.0
2	Hank Aaron	1970-1976	872	.278	2,043	2,221	.920	129.9	476.0
3	Edgar Martinez	1999-2004	810	.302	2,034	2,096	.970	128.7	455.9
4	David Ortiz	2012-2016	666	.294	1,789	1,828	.979	133.5	450.4
5	Willie Mays	1967-1973	835	.272	1,801	2,104	.856	127.4	383.5
6	Rickey Henderson	1995-2003	1,001	.254	2,286	2,628	.870	115.0	297.3
7	Darrell Evans	1983-1989	976	.242	2,037	2,480	.821	116.8	296.1
8	Jim Thome	2007-2012	662	.259	1,457	1,560	.934	125.1	290.8
9	Brian Downing	1987-1992	758	.270	1,701	2,028	.839	120.4	290.2
10	Rafael Palmeiro	2001-2005	733	.266	1,827	2,012	.908	118.0	280.3

List #169: Best Career for a Pitcher Through Age 23

Nobody envisioned Bert Blyleven as a future Hall of Famer. The Twins didn't take him until the 55th pick of the 1969 amateur draft. Sixteen other pitchers had already been selected.

But Blyleven proved to be precocious. He made just 18 minor-league starts before Minnesota called him up in June 1970. The very first batter he faced, Lee Maye, walloped a home run, causing Twins manager Bill Rigney to head to the mound. Blyleven expected a quick hook: "I'm thinking on the back of my bubble-gum card, it's going to say Bert Blyleven 0-1, an ERA of infinity."

But Rigney merely wanted to calm his 19-year-old starter. Blyleven didn't allow another run the rest of the night, defeating the Senators for the first of 10 victories that season. He had taken his initial step down the path toward Cooperstown.

Blyleven won 80 games before he turned 24. The best season in the first phase of his 22-year career was 1973, when he notched 20 wins and posted a league-leading BPO+ of 82.6. His base value of minus-298.0 between 1970 and 1974 was the best for any Modern Era pitcher through the age of 23.

Dwight Gooden surpassed Blyleven on two counts. His fastball was clocked as high as 100 miles per hour, and he won a Cy Young Award at age 20. But Gooden's youthful BV of minus-281.4 wasn't quite as low. Nor could he sustain the consistency needed for a Hall of Fame career.

The Best 10

Rank	Pitcher	Span	G	ERA	B	O	BPO	BPO+	BV
1	Bert Blyleven	1970-1974	181	2.74	2,228	4,023	.554	88.4	-298.0
2	Dwight Gooden	1984-1988	158	2.62	1,910	3,521	.542	87.2	-281.4
3	Bret Saberhagen	1984-1987	133	3.39	1,422	2,420	.588	85.5	-240.8
4	Clayton Kershaw	2008-2011	118	2.88	1,193	2,152	.554	84.8	-211.3
5	Roger Clemens	1984-1986	69	3.15	807	1,469	.549	80.1	-200.6
6	Jose Fernandez	2013-2016	76	2.58	712	1,421	.501	79.4	-183.3
7	Frank Tanana	1973-1977	142	2.69	1,829	3,275	.558	91.1	-180.9
8	Dean Chance	1961-1964	146	2.65	1,201	2,282	.526	86.7	-179.2
9	Mark Fidrych	1976-1978	45	2.47	522	1,076	.485	74.8	-175.2
10	Vida Blue	1969-1973	119	2.74	1,290	2,432	.530	89.0	-158.3

List #170: Best Career for a Pitcher Through Age 29

Pedro Martinez worked out of the bullpen for the Dodgers in 1993, and he was incredibly effective. He wrapped up his rookie year with a 10-5 record, a 2.61 ERA, and 119 strikeouts in 107 innings. "Even if we'd had five strikes against him, we couldn't have hit him," said Rich Donnelly, a coach for the Pirates.

So what did the Dodgers do? They sent Martinez to the Expos in a controversial swap for Delino DeShields, a swift second baseman who had stolen 187 bases the previous four seasons. "It was safer not to make the trade," Los Angeles general manager Fred Claire said at the time. "But it made all the sense in the world."

DeShields would spend three seasons in Los Angeles, never batting above .256. Martinez, who was converted into a starter in Montreal, would evolve into a Hall of Famer. He posted the National League's second-best BPO+ in 1997, his final year with the cash-starved Expos. They dealt him to Boston, where he finished second, first, and first in the American League in BPO+ the next three seasons.

And he was still only 29 years old. Martinez would accumulate a base value of minus-926.4 before his 30th birthday, the best performance by any pitcher in that age group during the Modern Era.

Roger Clemens came close. He debuted with the Red Sox in 1984 and went on to win three Cy Young Awards before turning 30. His BV through his age-29 season was minus-873.0.

The Best 10

Rank	Pitcher	Span	G	ERA	B	O	BPO	BPO+	BV
1	Pedro Martinez	1992-2001	296	2.66	2,679	5,088	.527	74.6	-926.4
2	Roger Clemens	1984-1992	273	2.80	3,326	6,143	.541	79.2	-873.0
3	Clayton Kershaw	2008-2016	265	2.37	2,563	5,291	.484	76.0	-801.6
4	Greg Maddux	1986-1995	301	2.88	3,554	6,413	.554	83.9	-688.3
5	Tom Seaver	1967-1974	283	2.47	3,434	6,526	.526	86.0	-566.5
6	Bert Blyleven	1970-1980	387	2.96	4,947	8,559	.578	90.0	-554.5
7	Johan Santana	2000-2008	285	3.11	2,646	4,636	.571	82.9	-542.6
8	Fergie Jenkins	1965-1972	304	3.02	3,425	6,162	.556	86.6	-539.8
9	Kevin Appier	1989-1997	256	3.30	2,954	5,023	.588	84.8	-539.0
10	Bret Saberhagen	1984-1993	288	3.24	3,240	5,691	.569	86.0	-527.0

List #171: Best Career for a Pitcher From Age 30

Randy Johnson was a late bloomer. The Braves drafted him as an 18-year-old, yet he opted to attend the University of Southern California. He jumped back into the draft pool at 21, signed with the Expos, and trekked off to the minors.

That first summer in Class A was rocky. Johnson went 0-3 with a 5.93 ERA. Control problems limited him to an average of three-and-a-third innings per start. He improved in subsequent seasons, though the big leagues didn't beckon until he turned 25. His famous contemporaries, Greg Maddux and Pedro Martinez, debuted when they were 20.

Johnson's height was both a drawback and an asset. "I'm 6-10, so you're dealing with more arms and more legs," he said. "To keep them under control is a job in and of itself." But his enormous wingspan generated tremendous power, especially after he fine-tuned his delivery. He led his league in strike-outs nine times — the first at the age of 28, the last at 40.

Johnson won only 68 games before his age-30 season, then accelerated to another 235 victories. Other stats were equally stark. Johnson's BPO+ was a middling 102.0 during his 20s, but a sterling 82.6 thereafter. His respective base values were plus-36.0 and minus-1,169.5. The latter was the best for any Modern Era pitcher from age 30 onward.

Roger Clemens won four of his seven Cy Young Awards after entering his 30s. He is the runner-up on this list with a BV of minus-909.8.

The Best 10

Rank	Pitcher	Span	G	ERA	B	O	BPO	BPO+	BV
1	Randy Johnson	1994-2009	453	3.12	5,518	9,263	.596	82.6	-1,169.5
2	Roger Clemens	1993-2007	436	3.36	5,319	8,713	.610	85.5	-909.8
3	Kevin Brown	1995-2005	299	2.93	3,263	5,981	.546	79.8	-826.1
4	Curt Schilling	1997-2007	337	3.45	4,091	6,809	.601	83.9	-794.1
5	Greg Maddux	1996-2008	443	3.36	5,292	8,736	.606	87.1	-792.8
6	Gaylord Perry	1969-1983	528	3.12	6,956	12,055	.577	90.3	-732.4
7	Mariano Rivera	2000-2013	849	2.05	1,246	2,743	.454	65.8	-648.4
8	John Smoltz	1997-2009	457	3.19	2,894	5,023	.576	82.3	-617.2
9	Bob Gibson	1966-1975	307	2.70	3,929	7,343	.535	87.7	-532.9
10	Tom Glavine	1996-2008	420	3.55	5,228	8,111	.645	92.7	-414.7

List #172: Best Career for a Pitcher From Age 36

The Braves sent up 27 batters against Diamondbacks pitcher Randy Johnson on May 18, 2004. All 27 quickly returned to the dugout. Thirteen were strikeout victims. Only seven hit the ball out of the infield, all for easy outs.

Johnson breezed to the 17th perfect game in big-league history. Just 30 of the tall lefthander's 117 pitches passed outside the strike zone. "Not bad for being 40 years old," he laughed.

His age was the most unusual aspect of Johnson's gem. It's rare enough to stick around the majors after turning 40, a feat accomplished by only 2.1 percent of the Modern Era's pitchers. But nobody past the age of 37 had ever fashioned a perfect game until Johnson came along.

He capped his magical 2004 season by topping the major leagues with 290 strikeouts and finishing second in the National League's Cy Young Award balloting. Not bad for 40, indeed.

Johnson pitched for 10 seasons after his 36th birthday. He notched 143 victories during that span, considerably better than the 124 wins in his initial decade. He earned three Cy Youngs from age 36 onward, while amassing a cumulative base value of minus-598.9. Nobody else on this list came within 230 bases of his total.

The runners-up took different routes to second and third place. Roger Clemens made 258 starts (and a lone relief stint) from age 36 until retirement, while Mariano Rivera's 458 appearances all came out of the bullpen.

The Best 10

Rank	Pitcher	Span	G	ERA	B	O	BPO	BPO+	BV
1	Randy Johnson	2000-2009	287	3.34	3,499	5,700	.614	85.6	-598.9
2	Roger Clemens	1999-2007	259	3.48	3,113	4,950	.629	89.6	-363.4
3	Mariano Rivera	2006-2013	458	2.00	655	1,436	.456	66.5	-331.0
4	John Smoltz	2003-2009	256	3.28	1,639	2,765	.593	84.6	-294.6
5	Dennis Martinez	1990-1998	264	3.37	2,786	4,576	.609	90.3	-288.6
6	Gaylord Perry	1975-1983	291	3.51	3,744	6,186	.605	93.1	-272.2
7	Nolan Ryan	1983-1993	320	3.33	3,728	6,238	.598	94.3	-236.9
8	Koji Uehara	2011-2016	332	2.17	453	984	.460	68.2	-212.9
9	Rick Reuschel	1985-1991	187	3.17	2,109	3,597	.586	92.0	-187.1
10	Curt Schilling	2003-2007	143	3.75	1,607	2,513	.639	90.2	-180.5

21. STARTS AND FINISHES

List #173: Best First Month in a Season

Pundits expected the Indians to wallow in the American League standings in 1966. Rocky Colavito, Leon Wagner, and Fred Whitfield brought decent power to Cleveland's lineup, having combined for 80 homers the year before. Pitcher Sam McDowell was blazingly fast, as proved by his league-leading 325 strikeouts in 1965. But the rest of the squad was nothing special. A .500 season seemed in store.

Yet the Indians shocked everybody by taking their first 10 games in 1966, coasting to a .909 winning percentage by the end of April. It was the second-best opening month for any team in the Modern Era.

There was just one problem. Baltimore chose the same season to enjoy the best April of all. The Orioles' incredibly deep roster was led by future Hall of Famers Luis Aparicio, Jim Palmer, Brooks Robinson, and Frank Robinson. They scored 5.9 runs per game in April, amassing an 11-1 record for a .917 winning percentage.

The two teams followed divergent paths as the season progressed. The Orioles breezed to the AL title, then swept the Dodgers in the 1966 World Series. The Indians stumbled badly, winning only 38 of their final 90 games. They finished exactly where predicted, fifth in a 10-team league at 81-81.

This list is based on records at the end of April, regardless of when a given season began. (A team had to play at least 10 games to qualify.) Ties in winning percentage were broken by the number of wins.

The Best 10

Rank	Team	Year	League	Overall	W	L	Pct.
1	Orioles	1966	AL	97-63 (WLP)	11	1	.917
2	Indians	1966	AL	81-81 (—)	10	1	.909
3	Tigers	1984	AL	104-58 (WLP)	18	2	.900
4	Athletics	1981	AL	64-45 (P)	18	3	.857
4	Brewers	1987	AL	91-71 (—)	18	3	.857
6	Dodgers	1977	NL	98-64 (LP)	17	3	.850
7	Phillies	1964	NL	92-70 (—)	9	2	.818
8	Mets	1986	NL	108-54 (WLP)	13	3	.813
8	Reds	1990	NL	91-71 (WLP)	13	3	.813
10	Mariners	2001	AL	116-46 (P)	20	5	.800

List #174: Worst First Month in a Season

Presidents typically place phone calls to winners. They congratulate coaches for championships, superstars for milestones, Olympic athletes for gold medals.

But Ronald Reagan was motivated by a different impulse on April 25, 1988. He called Frank Robinson, the Hall of Fame outfielder who had signed on as Baltimore's manager earlier in the month. The Orioles had sputtered to an 0-6 start before Robinson's arrival, and they couldn't stop losing. Their record was 0-18 when the phone rang.

"Frank, I know what you're going through," Reagan began.

Robinson was compelled to interrupt. "With all due respect," he said, "no you don't, Mr. President."

The Orioles would suffer three more defeats before finally securing their first victory on April 29. They finished the month with a 1-22 record, having been outscored by 3.4 runs per game. Their April winning percentage of .043 was easily the worst for any team in the Modern Era.

The Orioles improved as the 1988 season went on, though they finished 53 games below .500. Their record was a miserable 54-107, which was 14 games worse than anybody else in the American League.

The irony is that the same franchises with the best Aprils (List #173) also suffered the worst opening months. The Orioles top both rankings, with the Indians as runners-up. Cleveland lost its first five games in 1969, squeaked past the Tigers in extra innings, and then suffered 10 straight defeats en route to a 2-15 mark.

The Worst 10

Rank	Team	Year	League	Overall	W	L	Pct.
1	Orioles	1988	AL	54-107 (—)	1	22	.043
2	Indians	1969	AL	62-99 (—)	2	15	.118
3	Tigers	2003	AL	43-119 (—)	3	21	.125
4	Senators	1962	AL	60-101 (—)	2	13	.133
4	Cubs	1981	NL	38-65 (—)	2	13	.133
6	White Sox	1968	AL	67-95 (—)	2	12	.143
7	Royals	1992	AL	72-90 (—)	3	17	.150
8	Braves	1988	NL	54-106 (—)	3	16	.158
9	Astros	1969	NL	81-81 (—)	4	20	.167
10	Cardinals	1973	NL	81-81 (—)	3	15	.167

List #175: Best First Half in a Season

The 1998 Yankees possessed two remarkable attributes, as they eagerly confirmed to anybody who would listen.

The first was their unalloyed brilliance. New York went 114-48 (.704) to become one of two Modern Era teams with a winning percentage greater than .700. Their TS of 96.123 stamped them as the second-best squad to take the diamond since 1961.

"They are as great as any team there has ever been," bragged owner George Steinbrenner after his Yanks swept the Padres in the World Series.

Their incredible consistency was equally notable. The Yankees broke from the gate with 17 wins in 23 games (.739) in April. Their records in subsequent months were virtually identical: .741 in May, .731 in June, .741 in July. They eased off the accelerator in August (.688) and September (.593), though even the latter pace would have been sufficient to win either of the American League's other two divisional crowns that year.

"When you play as well as we have for six months," asserted first baseman Tino Martinez, "we have to be considered among the best."

The first half of their 1998 season, in fact, was the very best in the Modern Era. The Yankees went 56-20 for a .737 winning percentage through June 30, defined here as the annual midpoint. Next on this list are the 2001 Mariners, the other team to finish a year above .700. They went 58-21 (.734) in the first half, leaving them just three percentage points behind the 1998 Yanks.

The Best 10

Rank	Team	Year	League	Overall	W	L	Pct.
1	Yankees	1998	AL	114-48 (WLP)	56	20	.737
2	Mariners	2001	AL	116-46 (P)	58	21	.734
3	Orioles	1969	AL	109-53 (LP)	55	21	.724
3	Tigers	1984	AL	104-58 (WLP)	55	21	.724
5	Phillies	1976	NL	101-61 (P)	50	20	.714
6	Indians	1995	AL	100-44 (LP)	41	17	.707
7	Mets	1986	NL	108-54 (WLP)	50	21	.704
8	Reds	1970	NL	102-60 (LP)	52	22	.703
9	Red Sox	1978	AL	99-64 (—)	52	23	.693
10	Orioles	1979	AL	102-57 (LP)	53	24	.688
10	White Sox	2005	AL	99-63 (WLP)	53	24	.688

List #176: Worst First Half in a Season

Nobody was foolish enough to envision Detroit making the 2003 World Series. The Tigers hadn't posted a winning percentage above .488 since 1993. They staggered to a cumulative record of 579-812 (.416) during the intervening nine years, punctuated by 106 losses in 2002.

Yet there was reason for optimism in Comerica Park. Franchise icon Alan Trammell, a Tigers shortstop for two decades, took the reins as manager in 2003. He inherited one of the youngest teams in the majors, with six everyday players and all five starting pitchers under the age of 27. Perhaps a winning tradition could be restored in Detroit.

Those hopes were quickly crushed. The Tigers lost their first nine games under Trammell's tutelage, eked out a lone victory over the White Sox, then dropped the next eight. Additional losing streaks lay ahead — six straight defeats in late April and early May, seven in mid-May, eight in early June, and nine late in that month.

The Tigers reached the midway point, the end of June, with a 19-61 record, precisely matching the number of losses the Yankees would suffer all season. Detroit's winning percentage of .238 was the worst first-half performance by any team in the Modern Era, setting the stage for a final mark of 43-119.

The Twins started the 1982 season poorly — dropping 27 of their first 39 games — and were completely doomed by a subsequent 14-game losing streak. Their first-half record of 20-56 earned second place on this list.

The Worst 10

Rank	Team	Year	League	Overall	W	L	Pct.
1	Tigers	2003	AL	43-119 (—)	19	61	.238
2	Twins	1982	AL	60-102 (—)	20	56	.263
3	Mets	1962	NL	40-120 (—)	20	53	.274
4	Blue Jays	1981	AL	37-69 (—)	16	42	.276
5	Athletics	1979	AL	54-108 (—)	22	57	.278
6	Tigers	1996	AL	53-109 (—)	23	58	.284
7	Orioles	1988	AL	54-107 (—)	22	55	.286
8	Expos	1969	NL	52-110 (—)	21	52	.288
9	Twins	1995	AL	56-88 (—)	17	42	.288
10	Cubs	1981	NL	38-65 (—)	15	37	.288

List #177: Best Second Half in a Season

The Athletics entered 2001 with a lofty goal. They had won the American League West the previous year — their first divisional championship in eight seasons — and they expected nothing less than a world title this time around.

And why not? Oakland's attack had ranked second in the AL in home runs and third in runs scored in 2000. It was anchored by the reigning Most Valuable Player, first baseman Jason Giambi (43 HR, 173.6 BPO+ in 2000), and fellow infielders Miguel Tejada (30 HR) and Eric Chavez (26 HR). The starting rotation featured a trio of budding stars: Tim Hudson, Mark Mulder, and Barry Zito.

Yet the Athletics, despite all of this firepower, struggled mightily during the first half of the 2001 season. The AL West standings at the end of June seemed to foreclose any playoff hopes. Seattle held first place with a sizzling 58-21 record, while Oakland sat 20 games back at 38-41.

But the Athletics refused to surrender. They belatedly shifted into overdrive, igniting an amazing 64-19 run during the latter three months. It propelled them to an overall mark of 102-60 and a wild-card berth. Their second-half winning percentage of .771 was the Modern Era's best (though it did not lead to the desired championship).

The runner up on this list comes with an asterisk. The 1994 Expos played .730 ball after June 30, though they were limited to 37 games. A players' strike brought the second half to a premature close on August 12.

The Best 10

Rank	Team	Year	League	Overall	W	L	Pct.
1	Athletics	2001	AL	102-60 (P)	64	19	.771
2	Expos	1994	NL	74-40 (—)	27	10	.730
3	Royals	1977	AL	102-60 (P)	64	25	.719
4	Braves	1993	NL	104-58 (P)	60	24	.714
5	Yankees	1961	AL	109-53 (WLP)	64	26	.711
6	Athletics	2002	AL	103-59 (P)	57	24	.704
7	Cardinals	2004	NL	105-57 (LP)	59	25	.702
8	Orioles	1970	AL	108-54 (WLP)	61	26	.701
9	Mariners	2001	AL	116-46 (P)	58	25	.699
10	Reds	1973	NL	99-63 (P)	60	26	.698

List #178: Worst Second Half in a Season

The 1962 Mets displayed few positive qualities, though they could at least be credited with consistency.

New York slogged to a 20-53 record during the first three months of its expansion season. The resulting winning percentage of .274 was the third-worst performance during any first half in the Modern Era.

Pitcher Jay Hook remained unaccountably optimistic, even though the Mets sat 28 games behind the National League-leading Giants on June 30. "I never thought we were as bad as we turned out to be," Hook said. "I thought every time we went out, we had a shot at winning."

He was wrong. The Mets duplicated their first-half total of 20 wins during the final three months of the 1962 season. They plodded along at a .230 pace between July 1 (a 5-1 loss to the Dodgers) and September 30 (another 5-1 loss to the Cubs). No team since 1961 has suffered a worse second half.

The Mets finished with a breathtakingly bad 40-120 record. Their TS of 10.038 marked them as the 10th-worst team of the Modern Era. Hook, despite his upbeat nature, came dangerously close to a 20-loss season, finishing 8-19.

The 1963 Mets were even more inept than their predecessors. They notched 11 more victories, to be sure, though their TS dropped to 8.162, fourth-lowest in the Modern Era. But the relevant fact here is that the Mets went 22-63 (.259) in the second half of 1963, earning the runner-up slot on this list.

The Worst 10

Rank	Team	Year	League	Overall	W	L	Pct.
1	Mets	1962	NL	40-120 (—)	20	67	.230
2	Mets	1963	NL	51-111 (—)	22	63	.259
3	Astros	2013	AL	51-111 (—)	21	59	.263
4	Diamondbacks	2004	NL	51-111 (—)	23	61	.274
4	Astros	2012	NL	55-107 (—)	23	61	.274
6	Mets	1965	NL	50-112 (—)	24	62	.279
7	Indians	1971	AL	60-102 (—)	24	61	.282
8	Phillies	1961	NL	47-107 (—)	25	62	.287
9	Tigers	2003	AL	43-119 (—)	24	58	.293
10	Blue Jays	1977	AL	54-107 (—)	26	62	.295

List #179: Best Surge in the Final Month

The Red Sox seemed to have everything under control as August 1974 drew to a close. Boston led the American League East by three games over New York, with Baltimore six games back in third. The Red Sox intended to winnow the field by eradicating the Orioles in a three-game series beginning on Labor Day.

But things didn't go as planned. Orioles starter Ross Grimsley blanked the Sox, then colleagues Mike Cuellar and Jim Palmer tossed shutouts of their own. The three Baltimore pitchers limited the Sox to eight hits in 27 innings. Boston had been the stronger team in August — with 17 victories to Baltimore's 14 — but momentum had shifted with the calendar.

"What took us through the division race that year was our pitching," Orioles catcher Elrod Hendricks asserted, and nobody could disagree. Baltimore's starters delivered eight shutouts in September and surrendered one run apiece in five contests. Their dominance ignited a 25-6 stretch drive, capped by a season-ending nine-game winning streak. The Orioles clinched the division by two games over the Yankees and seven over the bewildered Red Sox.

Baltimore's .806 winning percentage ranks as the Modern Era's greatest surge — the best final month for a team that would not have qualified for the postseason on August 31, yet went on to make it.

The Yankees earned second place by going 22-6 at the tail-end of 1995, rising from a sub-.500 record at the start of September to a wild-card berth a month later.

The Best 10

Rank	Team	Year	League	Overall	W	L	Pct.
1	Orioles	1974	AL	91-71 (P)	25	6	.806
2	Yankees	1995	AL	79-65 (P)	22	6	.786
3	Indians	2013	AL	92-70 (P)	21	6	.778
4	Astros	2004	NL	92-70 (P)	23	7	.767
5	Athletics	2000	AL	91-70 (P)	22	7	.759
6	Mets	1969	NL	100-62 (WLP)	24	8	.750
7	Phillies	1983	NL	90-72 (LP)	23	8	.742
8	Braves	1969	NL	93-69 (P)	20	7	.741
9	Braves	1993	NL	104-58 (P)	22	8	.733
10	Twins	2003	AL	90-72 (P)	19	7	.731

List #180: Worst Collapse in the Final Month

If the regular season had concluded on August 31, 2011, Boston would have secured the top seed in the American League playoffs. The Red Sox sat atop the AL East with an 83-52 record. The league's only other team with more than 77 victories was New York with 81.

Yet the Red Sox staggered through September. The division's other four teams played .500 ball or better during the month. Not the Sox. They suffered separate losing streaks of five, three, and four games, while failing to win even two in a row. Their 7-20 record (.259) ranks as the Modern Era's worst collapse, defined as a final-month decline resulting in unexpected elimination from the postseason.

The Sox could have avoided that dismal fate to the very end. They would have limped into the playoffs if they had won and the Rays had lost on the season's final night. But Boston closer Jonathan Papelbon blew a ninth-inning lead against the Orioles, and Evan Longoria smashed a homer a few minutes later to cap a Tampa Bay victory over the Yankees. The Rays advanced.

Theo Epstein, soon to depart as the Red Sox general manager, struggled for words that dreary night. "This is one for the ages, isn't it?" he finally said. No one dissented.

The 1996 Astros suffered the second-worst collapse, winning just eight of 25 games in September. They began with a divisional lead of two-and-a-half games over the Cardinals, but finished six games behind.

The Worst 10

Rank	Team	Year	League	Overall	W	L	Pct.
1	Red Sox	2011	AL	90-72 (—)	7	20	.259
2	Astros	1996	NL	82-80 (—)	8	17	.320
3	Cubs	1969	NL	92-70 (—)	9	18	.333
3	Braves	2011	NL	89-73 (—)	9	18	.333
5	Brewers	2014	NL	82-80 (—)	9	17	.346
6	Angels	1998	AL	85-77 (—)	9	15	.375
7	Red Sox	1974	AL	84-78 (—)	12	19	.387
8	Angels	1995	AL	78-67 (—)	11	17	.393
9	Royals	1995	AL	70-74 (—)	12	18	.400
10	White Sox	2006	AL	90-72 (—)	12	17	.414

22. RISES AND FALLS

List #181: Best Season-To-Season Gain by a Team

Nobody else could be blamed for Bobby Cox's predicament. The Braves general manager had grown so frustrated with his team's losing ways that he fired manager Russ Nixon in June 1990. So who did he pick for the job? Himself.

Cox's squad was one of the worst in the majors. The Braves had bumbled to a 469-659 record between 1984 and 1990, and the preseason magazines predicted another miserable year in 1991. The new skipper ignored them. "We'll be all right," he told his players.

Two of his young pitchers, both destined for the Hall of Fame, found Cox's calm demeanor to be precisely what the Braves needed. Tom Glavine called him "a fatherly figure," and John Smoltz concluded that "a small part of Bobby Cox changes you as a baseball player."

The changes weren't immediately evident. The Braves floundered below .500 into July, but everything suddenly clicked during an amazing 45-22 stretch drive. Atlanta surged into first place in the final week, winning the National League West by one game over the Dodgers.

The 1991 Braves posted a TS of 76.629, a gain of 56.600 points from 1990, the best year-to-year improvement by any team in the Modern Era. They made it all the way to the seventh game of the World Series, which they lost 1-0 to the Twins.

The Red Sox rank second on this list. They finished last in their division in 2012, then rebounded to win the 2013 World Series.

The Best 10

Rk	Team	Year	W	L	Pct.	TS	Prev W	Prev L	Prev pct.	Prev TS	TS change
1	Braves	1991	94	68	.580	76.629	65	97	.401	20.029	56.600
2	Red Sox	2013	97	65	.599	81.732	69	93	.426	29.636	52.096
3	Twins	1991	95	67	.586	82.261	74	88	.457	32.363	49.898
4	Rays	2008	97	65	.599	73.410	66	96	.407	24.089	49.321
5	Red Sox	1967	92	70	.568	73.514	72	90	.444	29.204	44.310
6	Reds	1990	91	71	.562	76.558	75	87	.463	32.947	43.611
7	Diamondbacks	1999	100	62	.617	71.067	65	97	.401	28.902	42.165
8	Dodgers	1988	94	67	.584	74.718	73	89	.451	33.288	41.430
9	Athletics	1980	83	79	.512	51.673	54	108	.333	11.385	40.288
10	Mets	1969	100	62	.617	72.856	73	89	.451	32.901	39.955

List #182: Worst Season-To-Season Decline by a Team

The Marlins should have exuded optimism in 1998. They had won the World Series the previous October — an improbable accomplishment for a five-year-old expansion team — and their future should have been astonishingly bright.

But the outlook actually was bleak. Owner Wayne Huizenga claimed the Marlins had lost $34 million during their championship season, which inspired him to order an immediate fire sale. Among the players shown the door were Florida's three best batters — Gary Sheffield (132.7 BPO+ in 2007), Moises Alou (116.7), and Bobby Bonilla (110.9) — as well as ace pitcher Kevin Brown, whose BPO+ of 81.6 was fifth-best among National League starters.

Manager Jim Leyland was left with the most inexperienced roster in the majors. His oldest everyday player was left fielder Cliff Floyd, who had turned 25 the previous winter. His starting pitchers were all 24 or younger.

Defeats came rapidly. The Marlins lost 11 of their first 12 contests and plummeted 20 games out of first place before the end of May. They finished 54-108 with a team score of 12.978. Their decline of 60.251 points represented the Modern Era's worst year-to-year drop in TS. Leyland quit after the final game, and Huizenga then sold the franchise.

The Red Sox enjoyed the second-best upswing in team score in 2013 — see List #181 — but they followed it with the second-worst reversal in 2014. They plummeted from a world title to last place in the American League East, a drop of 53.145 points.

The Worst 10

Rk	Team	Year	W	L	Pct.	TS	Prev W	Prev L	Prev pct.	Prev TS	TS change
1	Marlins	1998	54	108	.333	12.978	92	70	.568	73.229	-60.251
2	Red Sox	2014	71	91	.438	28.587	97	65	.599	81.732	-53.145
3	Athletics	1991	84	78	.519	43.721	103	59	.636	89.366	-45.645
4	Tigers	1989	59	103	.364	8.859	88	74	.543	52.643	-43.784
5	Tigers	1985	84	77	.522	54.409	104	58	.642	97.109	-42.700
6	Twins	2011	63	99	.389	18.200	94	68	.580	60.262	-42.062
7	Blue Jays	1994	55	60	.478	40.913	95	67	.586	82.767	-41.854
8	Reds	1982	61	101	.377	18.446	66	42	.611	59.552	-41.106
9	Dodgers	1992	63	99	.389	23.311	93	69	.574	64.006	-40.695
10	Athletics	1993	68	94	.420	22.975	96	66	.593	63.655	-40.680

List #183: Best Season-To-Season Gain by a Batter

Barry Bonds enjoyed a wonderful season in 2000, launching 49 home runs and posting a BPO+ of 171.9, the National League's best score. But he earned first place on this list by zipping into an entirely new dimension the following year.

Bonds entered the record books in 2001 by blasting 73 homers, still the all-time mark. He led the majors in several other categories, including walks (177), on-base percentage (.515), slugging percentage (.863), and BPO+ (248.3). He became the first batter in the Modern Era to exceed 200 on the BPO+ scale, a feat he would duplicate in each of the three seasons to follow, but that nobody else would accomplish.

Bonds's BPO+ soared by 76.4 points between 2000 and 2001, the biggest year-to-year improvement by any batter since 1961. (This list and the next three are limited to consecutive qualified seasons, ignoring years with per-game averages below 3.1 plate appearances or one inning pitched.)

You might assume that Bonds's fellow Giants applauded his shift into over-drive in 2001, but they almost universally detested his me-first attitude. "On the field, we're fine," said second baseman Jeff Kent. "But off the field, I don't care about Barry, and Barry doesn't care about me. Or anybody else." *Sports Illustrated* suggested that Bonds's funeral could be held in a fitting room.

Congenial Jeff Bagwell was considerably more popular with the Astros, especially after boosting his BPO+ by 65.8 points to 191.2 in 1994. That gain ranks second here.

The Best 10

Rank	Batter	Year	BPO	BV	BPO+	Prev BPO	Prev BV	Prev BPO+	BPO+ change
1	Barry Bonds	2001	1.855	365.5	248.3	1.341	195.7	171.9	76.4
2	Jeff Bagwell	1994	1.412	187.9	191.2	.914	73.6	125.4	65.8
3	Carl Yastrzemski	1967	1.152	191.8	168.7	.768	27.1	108.4	60.3
4	Barry Bonds	2004	2.239	358.6	284.5	1.726	255.7	225.8	58.7
5	Cesar Cedeno	1972	1.010	140.7	150.2	.630	-18.3	94.3	55.9
6	Kevin Mitchell	1989	1.107	172.7	163.4	.723	22.0	108.3	55.1
7	John Olerud	1993	1.231	181.5	165.6	.815	31.1	112.2	53.4
8	Willie Stargell	1971	1.115	160.8	163.0	.803	28.7	110.7	52.3
9	Jose Canseco	1988	1.046	172.9	155.9	.750	13.9	103.9	52.0
10	Matt Kemp	2011	1.088	166.4	153.1	.727	4.3	101.2	51.9

List #184: Worst Season-To-Season Decline by a Batter

It's a simple rule first propounded by Isaac Newton or Casey Stengel or some other savant: What goes up must come down.

Bryce Harper learned its impact in 2016. Harper's previous season had been glorious. He was named 2015's Most Valuable Player after leading the National League in home runs (42), runs scored (118), slugging percentage (.649), on-base percentage (.460), and BPO+ (180.7). The latter was 77.7 points better than 2014's mark, an improvement that would have topped List #183 if Harper hadn't fallen short of the qualification standard in the initial year.

That was the going-up part. The downside soon followed. Harper launched nine homers in his first 18 games in 2016 before falling into a protracted slump. His batting average over the next 90 games was an un-MVP-like .221, featuring more strikeouts (70) than hits (67).

What had gone wrong? Reporters suggested that Harper had a stiff neck (confirmed) and a shoulder injury (denied), he was too selective at the plate, and his swing didn't follow the same smooth arc as in 2015. Nobody knew for sure.

The final two months of 2016 brought modest improvement. Harper finished with a BPO+ of 118.6, which was 14th-best in the league. But it was 62.1 points lower than his 2015 score, the biggest year-to-year decline in the Modern Era.

Jeff Bagwell had a similar story. He also won an MVP Award for a tremendous season (191.2 BPO+ in 1994), only to fall back to earth a year later.

The Worst 10

Rank	Batter	Year	BPO	BV	BPO+	Prev BPO	Prev BV	Prev BPO+	BPO+ change
1	Bryce Harper	2016	.882	57.3	118.6	1.282	213.0	180.7	-62.1
2	Jeff Bagwell	1995	.962	77.6	131.4	1.412	187.9	191.2	-59.8
3	John Mayberry	1976	.627	-20.1	93.7	1.066	150.8	152.7	-59.0
4	Don Buford	1972	.577	-21.6	90.0	.991	106.5	147.9	-57.9
5	Barry Bonds	2003	1.726	255.7	225.8	2.061	348.6	282.2	-56.4
6	John Olerud	1994	.878	26.3	111.6	1.231	181.5	165.6	-54.0
7	Norm Cash	1962	.958	90.9	130.6	1.368	226.6	182.3	-51.7
8	Carl Yastrzemski	1971	.788	26.5	109.1	1.201	184.5	160.6	-51.5
8	Willie McGee	1986	.616	-39.1	86.2	.960	110.5	137.7	-51.5
10	George Brett	1981	.839	48.4	129.2	1.272	168.5	180.0	-50.8

List #185: Best Season-To-Season Gain by a Pitcher

Rick Honeycutt improved so rapidly for the Rangers in 1983 that they had no choice but to trade him.

Their predicament would have been unimaginable a few months earlier. Honeycutt had registered five wins against 17 losses for Texas in 1982, running up a BPO+ of 118.0, third-worst in the American League. He was entering his free-agent year, though nobody expected serious competition for his services.

The outlook changed in the very first month of the new season. Honeycutt won three of his five starts in April 1983, surrendering a grand total of three earned runs. He bumped up his record to 10-4 with a 1.61 ERA by the end of June, and the Rangers swooped in with a contract offer. It was rebuffed.

"Once we got into the marketplace with Rick," said general manager Joe Klein, "we felt we would not be able to sign him." So Texas dealt its new ace to the Dodgers in August, even though Honeycutt's ERA (2.42) and BPO+ (80.5) were the league's best. He had stripped 37.5 points off his BPO+, the best year-to-year improvement by any Modern Era pitcher. (The two leagues don't combine annual statistics, so Honeycutt's 1982 numbers are compared below with his 1983 AL stats.)

Edinson Volquez's 2013 season was the worst suffered by any starting pitcher — see List #34 — but he bounced back nicely. He trimmed 35.9 points from his BPO+ in 2014 for second place on this list.

The Best 10

Rank	Pitcher	Year	BPO	BV	BPO+	Prev BPO	Prev BV	Prev BPO+	BPO+ change
1	Rick Honeycutt	1983	.532	-67.5	80.5	.766	58.3	118.0	-37.5
2	Edinson Volquez	2014	.628	9.2	102.6	.827	117.6	138.5	-35.9
3	Frank Viola	1984	.582	-78.1	85.2	.832	87.8	120.4	-35.2
4	James Shields	2011	.541	-69.3	85.2	.787	81.1	120.2	-35.0
5	Dennis Lamp	1981	.500	-43.5	81.6	.782	68.3	116.5	-34.9
6	Dick Ellsworth	1963	.451	-145.2	73.4	.721	32.8	107.8	-34.4
6	Gary Peters	1966	.474	-62.3	82.5	.685	52.5	116.9	-34.4
8	Larry Dierker	1969	.483	-119.4	79.0	.617	50.2	113.2	-34.2
9	Phil Ortega	1966	.620	8.8	102.5	.842	118.4	136.1	-33.6
10	Rick Porcello	2016	.544	-106.9	77.3	.738	32.7	109.3	-32.0

List #186: Worst Season-To-Season Decline by a Pitcher

Denny McLain emerged as a superstar in 1968. He won 31 games for the world champion Tigers, becoming the last pitcher to cross the 30-victory threshold. He was the logical (and unanimous) choice for the American League's Cy Young Award.

Yet it was McLain himself who nominated another candidate, Luis Tiant of the mediocre Indians. "Luis and I would each be fighting for 30 wins," said McLain, "if he had our kind of hitting to go with his kind of pitching."

It was a valid point. McLain's stats were dazzling (1.96 ERA, 84.3 BPO+), but Tiant's were better. They were, in fact, the best in the league (1.60 ERA, 72.6 BPO+). The acrobatic Cleveland righthander, known for a jerky motion that propelled a blazing fastball, tossed four straight shutouts in April and May — and a league-leading nine the entire season.

But the following year was much different. The Indians plummeted to a 62-99 record in 1969 — their worst mark in 54 years — and Tiant dropped with them. He suffered 20 losses as his BPO+ skyrocketed by 44.3 points to 116.9, the worst seasonal decline for any starter since 1961.

Tiant would enjoy better times again, notching at least 15 wins for the Red Sox every year from 1972 through 1976. The runner-up on this list, Bob Knepper, was nearly as resilient. His BPO+ soared by 40.9 points in 1979, though he rebounded to reach the 15-win mark three consecutive seasons in the mid-1980s.

The Worst 10

Rank	Pitcher	Year	BPO	BV	BPO+	Prev BPO	Prev BV	Prev BPO+	BPO+ change
1	Luis Tiant	1969	.749	81.4	116.9	.411	-120.4	72.6	44.3
2	Bob Knepper	1979	.795	107.8	127.6	.533	-63.9	86.7	40.9
3	Dave Stieb	1986	.833	88.6	121.0	.548	-107.2	80.4	40.6
4	Jose Lima	2000	.966	126.5	128.5	.653	-47.4	91.0	37.5
4	Esteban Loaiza	2004	.830	58.3	115.1	.557	-109.9	77.6	37.5
6	Matt Keough	1982	.858	133.9	133.2	.581	-8.6	96.6	36.6
7	Ken Forsch	1972	.724	56.9	120.2	.507	-54.3	84.3	35.9
8	Darrell May	2004	.902	108.2	127.1	.664	-37.9	91.7	35.4
9	Dave Stewart	1991	.782	100.7	123.2	.548	-60.7	87.9	35.3
10	Jim Perry	1971	.726	90.1	118.1	.533	-91.1	83.1	35.0

23. HALL OF FAMERS

List #187: Best Batter Chosen for Hall of Fame

Chapter 23 is the sole exception to this book's calendar restrictions. The six lists within this chapter are limited to players from the Modern Era, of course, but the statistics encompass their entire careers, even seasons prior to 1961.

There really is no other way to proceed. Admission to Cooperstown is based on an individual's complete record from rookie year to retirement, so it would be senseless to ignore part of that span when discussing a player's qualifications. (Yet I did find it necessary to establish a separate rule to guarantee that a Hall of Famer cast a significant shadow during the Modern Era: If more than two-thirds of his outs were registered before 1961, as was true for Richie Ashburn or Yogi Berra or Duke Snider, he is not covered here.)

The top three batters straddled both eras, with Mickey Mantle emerging from a tight race as the preeminent batter. A typical member of the Yankees would have reached 4,053 bases between 1951 and 1968, but Mantle piled up 6,471, exceeding expectations by almost 60 percent. He posted a base value greater than 200 in three seasons (1956, 1957, and 1961). No other modern Hall of Famer did it more than twice.

Willie Mays and Hank Aaron both came within 52 bases of Mantle's lifetime BV, respectively taking second and third place. Rickey Henderson, who finished fourth overall, is the top Hall of Famer whose entire career fit within the Modern Era.

The Best 10

Rank	Batter	Span	G	BA	B	O	BPO	BPO+	BV
1	Mickey Mantle	1951-1968	2,401	.298	6,471	5,899	1.097	158.9	2,418.0
2	Willie Mays	1951-1973	2,992	.302	8,016	8,056	.995	142.0	2,374.1
3	Hank Aaron	1954-1976	3,298	.305	8,672	9,136	.949	137.6	2,366.6
4	Rickey Henderson	1979-2003	3,081	.279	8,379	8,510	.985	140.0	2,350.9
5	Frank Robinson	1956-1976	2,808	.294	7,314	7,529	.971	139.5	2,064.4
6	Frank Thomas	1990-2008	2,322	.301	6,457	6,101	1.058	140.6	1,854.9
7	Joe Morgan	1963-1984	2,649	.271	6,703	7,174	.934	136.0	1,775.7
8	Mike Schmidt	1972-1989	2,404	.267	6,288	6,490	.969	134.5	1,613.5
9	Eddie Mathews	1952-1968	2,391	.271	5,981	6,478	.923	134.3	1,533.4
10	Willie McCovey	1959-1980	2,588	.270	5,734	6,259	.916	133.9	1,453.7

List #188: Worst Batter Chosen for Hall of Fame

"Worst" is a terribly inappropriate adjective for a Hall of Famer, don't you think? Yet this is a book of bests and worsts, and we need to stick to the theme. Just keep in mind that we're talking about the least favorable performances by exceptional athletes.

Forty-eight everyday players from the Modern Era have been elected to Cooperstown — see the definition preceding List #187 — and 44 ended their careers with positive base values. The four exceptions were hailed universally for their expertise as fielders, with Luis Aparicio earning extra credit for his baserunning skills.

Bill Mazeroski may have blasted the most famous homer in Pittsburgh history, yet he was no threat at the plate. He never posted a BPO+ better than 92.0 during his 17 years with the Pirates, which means he finished every season with a negative base value, bottoming out at minus-86.9 in 1959. His career BV of minus-762.4 is the worst for any of the era's Hall of Fame batters.

Fielding was an entirely different matter. Mazeroski won eight Gold Gloves as a second baseman, including five straight in the mid-1960s. "The impressive thing about Maz was that he did everything perfectly," said center fielder Bill Virdon. "I backed him up for 10 years and never got a ball."

Aparicio led the American League in stolen bases for nine consecutive years, and he also earned nine Gold Gloves at shortstop. Much less impressive was his career BV of minus-643.3 for 18 seasons.

The Worst 10

Rank	Batter	Span	G	BA	B	O	BPO	BPO+	BV
1	Bill Mazeroski	1956-1972	2,163	.260	3,499	6,113	.572	82.1	-762.4
2	Luis Aparicio	1956-1973	2,599	.262	5,010	8,110	.618	88.6	-643.3
3	Ozzie Smith	1978-1996	2,573	.262	5,046	7,528	.670	95.0	-265.2
4	Brooks Robinson	1955-1977	2,896	.267	5,426	8,340	.651	96.3	-204.4
5	Cal Ripken Jr.	1981-2001	3,001	.276	6,536	8,893	.735	102.1	102.5
6	Gary Carter	1974-1992	2,296	.262	4,584	6,233	.735	104.4	196.4
7	Kirby Puckett	1984-1995	1,783	.318	4,174	5,285	.790	107.5	291.9
8	Ryne Sandberg	1981-1997	2,164	.285	5,028	6,347	.792	108.2	373.9
9	Carlton Fisk	1969-1993	2,499	.269	5,224	6,767	.772	108.1	384.0
10	Tony Perez	1964-1986	2,777	.279	5,664	7,462	.759	108.2	422.9

List #189: Best Pitcher Chosen for Hall of Fame

Everybody knew that Greg Maddux would be elected to the Hall of Fame in 2014, his first year of eligibility. Maddux's resumé was impeccable — four Cy Young Awards, eight All-Star berths, 18 Gold Gloves, and 355 wins, the eighth-highest victory total in baseball history. He was a shoo-in.

Maddux's longtime manager, Bobby Cox, unleashed a torrent of rhetorical questions in support of his former ace. "Was he the best pitcher I ever saw? Was he the smartest pitcher I ever saw? Was he the best competitor I ever saw?" asked Cox. "The answer is yes to all of the above."

He could have added this question: Was Maddux better than any other Hall of Fame pitcher in the Modern Era? The response again would have been affirmative.

Thirty big leaguers who pitched after 1960 are immortalized in Cooperstown. Satchel Paige, Robin Roberts, Warren Spahn, and Early Wynn registered more than two-thirds of their career outs prior to the Modern Era, making them ineligible for this list. But Maddux was clearly the best of the remaining 26, amassing a base value of minus-1,481.1 in 23 seasons with the Braves, Cubs, Dodgers, and Padres.

The only other Hall of Fame pitchers to reach four figures in BV were Pedro Martinez and Randy Johnson. Martinez actually posted a lower BPO+ than Maddux (79.6 to 85.7), but the latter proved to be much more durable. Maddux pitched 2,181 innings more than Martinez, cementing his overall lead in base value.

The Best 10

Rank	Pitcher	Span	G	ERA	B	O	BPO	BPO+	BV
1	Greg Maddux	1986-2008	744	3.16	8,846	15,149	.584	85.7	-1,481.1
2	Pedro Martinez	1992-2009	476	2.93	4,737	8,489	.558	79.6	-1,234.6
3	Randy Johnson	1988-2009	618	3.29	7,718	12,509	.617	87.7	-1,133.5
4	John Smoltz	1988-2009	723	3.33	6,152	10,475	.587	86.4	-979.7
5	Gaylord Perry	1962-1983	777	3.11	9,178	16,192	.567	90.6	-938.9
6	Tom Seaver	1967-1986	656	2.86	8,199	14,410	.569	89.8	-917.3
7	Bob Gibson	1959-1975	528	2.91	6,572	11,728	.560	89.1	-777.5
8	Bert Blyleven	1970-1992	692	3.31	9,064	14,965	.606	92.4	-741.1
9	Juan Marichal	1960-1975	471	2.89	5,764	10,622	.543	89.2	-686.5
10	Fergie Jenkins	1965-1983	664	3.34	8,189	13,625	.601	92.7	-651.1

List #190: Worst Pitcher Chosen for Hall of Fame

A substantial number of voters had doubts about Catfish Hunter. Did his 15-year career with the Athletics and Yankees truly measure up to the Hall of Fame? Only 54 percent answered yes in 1985, his initial year of eligibility. Seventy-five percent is the threshold for Cooperstown, so Hunter returned to the pool. He improved to 68 percent a year later, then rode the momentum to induction in 1987.

But the doubts persist. Columnists and analysts frequently cite Hunter as a marginal Hall of Famer, despite his 224 victories and five World Series rings. A typical objection was voiced by CBS's Matt Snyder in 2013: "You can argue Hunter was a Hall-of-Fame caliber pitcher for five seasons — and I'd agree — but other than that, he was either average or below average."

It's a valid point. Hunter's BPO+ rose above 100 in seven seasons, which means he was worse than the American League's typical pitcher. He hovered between 96.2 and 99.3 in four other years — slightly better than average, but hardly exceptional. That leaves only four seasons when Hunter outperformed the norm by more than 5 percent, capped by a brilliant 76.0 BPO+ for the Yanks in 1975.

This up-and-down career yielded a base value of minus-143.4, barely better than dead-even, the worst BV for any Hall of Fame pitcher in the Modern Era. Right behind Hunter is his comrade from those great Oakland teams in the early 1970s, reliever Rollie Fingers, at minus-221.4.

The Worst 10

Rank	Pitcher	Span	G	ERA	B	O	BPO	BPO+	BV
1	Catfish Hunter	1965-1979	500	3.26	6,175	10,385	.595	97.7	-143.4
2	Rollie Fingers	1968-1985	944	2.90	2,924	5,117	.571	92.9	-221.4
3	Jim Bunning	1955-1971	591	3.27	6,918	11,350	.610	96.7	-243.7
4	Rich Gossage	1972-1994	1,002	3.01	3,265	5,437	.601	93.1	-248.1
5	Bruce Sutter	1976-1988	661	2.83	1,821	3,170	.574	87.4	-271.6
6	Nolan Ryan	1966-1993	807	3.19	9,808	16,259	.603	97.3	-295.7
7	Dennis Eckersley	1975-1998	1,071	3.50	6,225	9,868	.631	93.4	-420.8
8	Phil Niekro	1964-1987	864	3.35	10,171	16,335	.623	95.3	-477.4
9	Don Drysdale	1956-1969	518	2.95	5,829	10,356	.563	91.8	-523.1
10	Hoyt Wilhelm	1952-1972	1,070	2.52	3,716	6,819	.545	87.2	-529.9

List #191: Best Batter Not in the Hall of Fame

Barry Bonds won't predict the exact year, but he is adamant about his induction to the Hall of Fame. "I don't have any doubts that I'll get there in time," he once said.

Bonds is the ideal candidate for Cooperstown — on paper. Nobody in the history of big-league ball has blasted more homers (762), drawn more walks (2,558), or earned more Most Valuable Player Awards (seven). And nobody else in the Modern Era has posted a single-season BPO+ higher than 200, the stratospheric level Bonds reached each year from 2001 to 2004.

His career base value of 3,847.2 is more than 2,000 bases ahead of any other Modern Era batter outside the Hall as of late 2016. (This book was published before the Hall announced its 2017 class.) But Bonds, who has been eligible since 2013, is unlikely to be elected in the near future. Too many voters believe he used performance-enhancing drugs, despite his contention that he never failed a drug test.

"Do the best players in the game deserve to be in the Hall of Fame? Yes," Bonds said. "Everything that everyone has accomplished in baseball is in [the record] book. Correct? So if that's correct, then [I] need to be in there. End of story."

The next two batters on this list have not yet faced the voters. Albert Pujols and Alex Rodriguez boast Hall-worthy numbers, but they were active players in 2016. Neither will become eligible until five years after retirement. Pujols appears to be a shoo-in, but Rodriguez will be hampered by his own PED history.

The Best 10

Rank	Batter	Span	G	BA	B	O	BPO	BPO+	BV
1	Barry Bonds	1986-2007	2,986	.298	9,249	7,313	1.265	170.7	3,847.2
2	Albert Pujols	2001-2016	2,426	.309	6,753	6,790	.995	135.5	1,801.4
3	Alex Rodriguez	1994-2016	2,784	.295	7,783	7,915	.983	128.5	1,733.9
4	Manny Ramirez	1993-2011	2,302	.312	6,394	6,038	1.059	136.3	1,707.8
5	Jim Thome	1991-2012	2,543	.276	6,577	6,354	1.035	134.3	1,679.8
6	Mark McGwire	1986-2001	1,874	.263	5,124	4,797	1.068	146.2	1,648.3
7	Jeff Bagwell	1991-2005	2,150	.297	6,049	5,887	1.028	135.5	1,584.7
8	Gary Sheffield	1988-2009	2,576	.292	6,720	6,987	.962	128.4	1,503.9
9	Miguel Cabrera	2003-2016	2,096	.321	5,600	5,713	.980	133.0	1,381.4
10	Chipper Jones	1993-2012	2,499	.303	6,535	6,657	.982	126.6	1,380.4

List #192: Best Pitcher Not in the Hall of Fame

There are striking parallels between the careers of Barry Bonds and Roger Clemens. Both stars were statistical trailblazers. Bonds led Modern Era batters in career base value, and Clemens did the same for pitchers. Both were accused of steroid use, indicted for perjury, and eventually acquitted. And both have been barred from the Hall of Fame by an unforgiving electorate.

They have diverged only in their reactions. Bonds, as noted in the introduction to List #191, insists that he belongs in Cooperstown. But Clemens has donned a mask of indifference. "I have distanced myself from the subject and have moved on," he said after being named on only 45 percent of the Hall's ballots in 2016. The threshold for induction is 75 percent.

Twenty-four pitchers won at least 300 games during their big-league careers. Twenty-three have been immortalized in the Hall of Fame. The exception is Clemens, who ranks ninth with 354 victories for the Red Sox, Blue Jays, Yankees, and Astros. His BV of minus-1,782.8 stamps him as the preeminent Modern Era pitcher still outside the Hall. The only contender to do better than minus-1,000, Curt Schilling, is a distant second.

Schilling doesn't have any PED skeletons in his closet — he has long been an outspoken critic of steroids — but he once suggested that his conservative views were hurting his chances. "I know, as a Republican, that there's some people that really don't like that," he said. He subsequently insisted that he was joking.

The Best 10

Rank	Pitcher	Span	G	ERA	B	O	BPO	BPO+	BV
1	Roger Clemens	1984-2007	709	3.12	8,645	14,856	.582	82.9	-1,782.8
2	Curt Schilling	1988-2007	569	3.46	5,838	9,792	.596	85.4	-1,012.2
3	Kevin Brown	1986-2005	486	3.28	5,681	9,864	.576	85.1	-993.9
4	Mariano Rivera	1995-2013	1,115	2.21	1,835	3,881	.473	67.7	-877.8
5	Mike Mussina	1991-2008	537	3.68	6,612	10,696	.618	88.7	-849.4
6	Roy Halladay	1998-2013	416	3.38	4,939	8,280	.596	85.8	-811.2
7	Clayton Kershaw	2008-2016	265	2.37	2,563	5,291	.484	76.0	-801.6
8	Bret Saberhagen	1984-2001	399	3.34	4,523	7,692	.588	87.0	-671.0
9	Tim Hudson	1999-2015	482	3.49	5,749	9,427	.610	89.9	-655.1
10	Dave Stieb	1979-1998	443	3.44	5,301	8,696	.610	89.2	-636.1

24. ALL-STARS

List #193: Best Choice for All-Star Starting Position Player

Baseball fans got it right in 2001. They cast 2.14 million votes for Barry Bonds in the All-Star balloting, the highest total for any National League player that year. It was an appropriate honor, given that Bonds had outperformed everybody else during the first half.

His numbers at the All-Star break were astounding. Bonds led the majors with 39 home runs as of July 10, a figure that only 11 other batters would surpass by October. He also set a brisk midseason pace for walks (88) and bases (317), leaving all challengers far behind.

The concept behind the All-Star Game is admittedly strange. Selection of the very best players is based not on the results of an entire season, but solely on April, May, and June. It's not uncommon for a three-month wonder to make the squad, only to flame out in the second half.

This chapter's six lists take a broader view. They use a complete year of stats to rate each All-Star choice. You might expect BPO+ to be the ideal indicator, but BV is better suited. Some All-Stars don't reach the qualifying thresholds for at bats or innings over an entire season, so we need an indicator that reflects both excellence and durability.

Bonds displayed both attributes in 2001, piling up the Modern Era's highest BV (365.5), making him the most deserving position player to start an All-Star Game. His 2004 and 2002 seasons took the next two slots.

The Best 10

Rk	Batter	Year	Team	Lg	Pos	G	BA	BPO	BPO+	BV
1	Barry Bonds	2001	Giants	NL	LF	153	.328	1.855	248.3	365.5
2	Barry Bonds	2004	Giants	NL	LF	147	.362	2.239	284.5	358.6
3	Barry Bonds	2002	Giants	NL	LF	143	.370	2.061	282.2	348.6
4	Mark McGwire	1998	Cardinals	NL	1B	155	.299	1.507	199.0	276.5
5	Barry Bonds	2003	Giants	NL	DH	130	.341	1.726	225.8	255.7
6	Sammy Sosa	2001	Cubs	NL	RF	160	.328	1.370	180.5	249.3
7	Barry Bonds	1993	Giants	NL	LF	159	.336	1.363	185.8	244.3
8	Mickey Mantle	1961	Yankees	AL	CF	153	.317	1.381	191.0	236.8
9	Barry Bonds	1992	Pirates	NL	LF	140	.311	1.351	195.1	230.5
10	Barry Bonds	1996	Giants	NL	LF	158	.308	1.351	180.7	230.4

List #194: Best Choice for All-Star Starting Pitcher

Manager Joe Torre weighed several options for the American League's starting pitcher in the 1999 All-Star Game. He considered Mike Mussina, already an 11-game winner for the Orioles. And Charles Nagy of the Indians, who also had 11 victories. And David Cone, with nine wins and a sterling 2.86 ERA for Torre's Yankees.

But one contender stood head and shoulders above the others. Pedro Martinez of the Red Sox had spun a dazzling first-half record of 15-3 with an earned run average of 2.10. His three-month total of 184 strikeouts would exceed the full-season counts for all but two AL pitchers.

There was bad blood between Martinez and the Yankees. "Pedro wasn't anybody's favorite, obviously," Torre once said. But the manager put passion aside and made the obvious move. He gave the ball to Martinez, which ranks as the best choice of an All-Star starting pitcher in the Modern Era.

That's because the second half of 1999 went nearly as well for Martinez as the first. His final line featured 23 victories, a 2.07 ERA, 313 strikeouts, and the Cy Young Award (which he won unanimously). His base value of minus-182.9 was the best full-year total for any All-Star starter. (This chapter's rankings are based on stats from entire seasons, as explained in the intro to List #193.)

The three runners-up posted base values slightly better than minus-160 during their seasons as All-Star starting pitchers: Greg Maddux, Roger Clemens, and Curt Schilling.

The Best 10

Rank	Pitcher	Year	Team	Lg	G	ERA	BPO	BPO+	BV
1	Pedro Martinez	1999	Red Sox	AL	31	2.07	.463	62.2	-182.9
2	Greg Maddux	1994	Braves	NL	25	1.56	.420	60.7	-167.3
3	Roger Clemens	1986	Red Sox	AL	33	2.48	.476	69.4	-162.7
4	Curt Schilling	2002	Diamondbacks	NL	36	3.23	.519	71.6	-160.5
5	Randy Johnson	2001	Diamondbacks	NL	35	2.49	.526	71.7	-156.8
6	Greg Maddux	1997	Braves	NL	33	2.20	.470	68.1	-153.7
7	Dean Chance	1964	Angels	AL	46	1.65	.414	70.1	-148.9
8	Greg Maddux	1998	Braves	NL	34	2.22	.488	71.8	-146.8
8	John Smoltz	1996	Braves	NL	35	2.94	.507	72.5	-146.8
10	Vida Blue	1971	Athletics	AL	39	1.82	.439	74.0	-144.3

List #195: Worst Choice for All-Star Starting Position Player

The public was stripped of its All-Star voting rights after Cincinnati fans indulged in ballot-stuffing in 1957. Players and managers picked the honorees the next 12 years, until Commissioner Bowie Kuhn brought the nation's fans back into the process in 1970.

The results were mixed. Public interest was stimulated by the distribution of 26 million ballots, but some of the selections were strange. That was especially true at second base for the National League, where the Cubs' Glenn Beckert was voted the starter.

Beckert was solid in the field — he had earned a Gold Glove in 1968 — and his BA was a passable .261 at the All-Star break. Yet he could not be called a productive batter. He rapped only 10 extra-base hits during the first half of 1970, while drawing 19 walks. He would end the season with a base value of minus-101.2, the worst output by any position player who started an All-Star Game since 1961.

Well, you say, perhaps Beckert was the best the league had to offer. Not so. Joe Morgan was emerging as a star with the Astros. His midseason numbers (.279 BA, 25 EXH, 66 BB) easily trumped Beckert's. And Morgan would finish the year with a positive BV of 53.1, tops among second basemen in both leagues.

It's interesting that every player on this list started at second base or shortstop. Many were fielding whizzes, to be sure, but all finished on the minus side in BV.

The Worst 10

Rk	Batter	Year	Team	Lg	Pos	G	BA	BPO	BPO+	BV
1	Glenn Beckert	1970	Cubs	NL	2B	143	.288	.565	71.3	-101.2
2	Don Kessinger	1968	Cubs	NL	SS	160	.240	.473	73.4	-90.2
3	Bobby Richardson	1964	Yankees	AL	2B	159	.267	.534	76.4	-88.1
4	Luis Aparicio	1971	Red Sox	AL	SS	125	.232	.511	70.8	-84.6
5	Alcides Escobar	2015	Royals	AL	SS	148	.257	.541	76.3	-81.5
6	Dick Groat	1962	Pirates	NL	SS	161	.294	.578	78.5	-79.9
7	Cal Ripken Jr.	2001	Orioles	AL	SS	128	.239	.540	72.7	-79.1
7	Don Kessinger	1970	Cubs	NL	SS	154	.266	.633	79.8	-79.1
9	Manny Trillo	1982	Phillies	NL	2B	149	.271	.528	74.6	-77.8
10	Nellie Fox	1963	White Sox	AL	2B	137	.260	.492	72.9	-77.5

List #196: Worst Choice for All-Star Starting Pitcher

Denny McLain's first couple of seasons with the Tigers were rocky. The hard-throwing righthander struggled with his control in 1963 and 1964, walking seven batters in a single game and averaging 3.9 walks per nine innings. "I think the first year or two you're in the big leagues you're intimidated," he later explained. "The intimidation factor is overwhelming."

He got over it.

McLain eventually became renowned for his cockiness — *Time* magazine would liken him to a "high-school wise guy" — and his relentless ability to throw strikes. He notched 16 wins in 1965 at the tender age of 21, and he took direct aim at 20 victories the following year.

The goal seemed easily attainable. McLain reached 1966's midseason break with a record of 13-4, which was dazzling enough to earn the American League's starting assignment for the All-Star Game. Few observers noted the link between his success and Detroit's powerful attack. The Tigers had scored between five and 16 runs in 10 of his first-half victories.

McLain finished 1966 with the desired 20 wins, though they were offset by a bloated 3.92 ERA, 14 percent higher than the AL average of 3.44. His base value of plus-18.2 was the worst for any Modern Era pitcher during a season in which he started an All-Star Game.

Second on this list is Dave Stewart, who posted a BV of 17.7 for the Athletics in 1989. That was his only All-Star appearance during a 16-year career.

The Worst 10

Rank	Pitcher	Year	Team	Lg	G	ERA	BPO	BPO+	BV
1	Denny McLain	1966	Tigers	AL	38	3.92	.634	103.8	18.2
2	Dave Stewart	1989	Athletics	AL	36	3.32	.640	103.7	17.7
3	Dwight Gooden	1988	Mets	NL	34	3.19	.602	101.8	8.1
4	Johnny Podres	1962	Dodgers	NL	40	3.81	.629	101.4	6.6
5	Bob Welch	1990	Athletics	AL	35	2.95	.628	100.7	3.2
6	Dave Stenhouse	1962	Senators	AL	34	3.65	.657	100.3	1.1
7	Brad Penny	2006	Dodgers	NL	34	4.33	.719	99.4	-2.3
8	Rick Reuschel	1989	Giants	NL	32	2.94	.605	99.2	-3.1
9	Catfish Hunter	1973	Athletics	AL	36	3.34	.611	99.3	-3.4
10	Jim Bunning	1962	Tigers	AL	41	3.59	.655	99.3	-3.7

List #197: Worst Choice for All-Star Bench Player

Nobody who rides the bench is named an All-Star. Honorees are supposed to be superior position players, accomplished starting pitchers, or devastating relievers.

But there are only so many positions. Each league starts nine players (including a designated hitter) chosen by the fans, along with a pitcher tapped by the All-Star manager. Everybody else is relegated to the dugout or bullpen.

This list uses "bench player" to refer to any non-pitching All-Star not in the starting lineup. These backups were once chosen exclusively by each league's manager, but all players, managers, and coaches have been involved in the process since 2003. They operate under one constraint, a requirement that every franchise has an All-Star representative every year.

The Red Sox didn't need such help in 1978. Boston boasted the best record in the majors (57-26) at the midseason break, and seven of its players were designated as All-Stars. Among them was shortstop Rick Burleson, despite a prolonged slump that had depressed his batting average below .230 until mid-June.

Burleson pushed his BA up to .248 by the end of 1978, but his 74.5 BPO+ fell 25.5 percent below the American League's norm. His anemic base value of minus-95.7 ranks as the worst for any Modern Era batter who served as an All-Star bench player.

Nellie Fox was near the end of his Hall of Fame career when he was named to the AL squad in 1961. His BV of minus-92.4 was only 3.3 better than Burleson's.

The Worst 10

Rank	Batter	Year	Team	Lg	G	BA	BPO	BPO+	BV
1	Rick Burleson	1978	Red Sox	AL	145	.248	.547	74.5	-95.7
2	Nellie Fox	1961	White Sox	AL	159	.251	.546	74.6	-92.4
3	Sandy Alomar	1998	Indians	AL	117	.235	.510	65.2	-92.1
4	Alfredo Griffin	1984	Blue Jays	AL	140	.241	.461	64.2	-88.1
5	Rafael Ramirez	1984	Braves	NL	145	.266	.520	73.7	-87.6
6	Bobby Richardson	1965	Yankees	AL	160	.247	.512	76.0	-85.1
7	Larry Bowa	1976	Phillies	NL	156	.248	.528	76.0	-84.0
8	Cesar Izturis	2005	Dodgers	NL	106	.257	.523	69.3	-81.8
9	Don Wert	1968	Tigers	AL	150	.200	.468	72.3	-81.5
9	Ed Brinkman	1973	Tigers	AL	162	.237	.505	72.8	-81.5

List #198: Worst Choice for All-Star Bullpen Pitcher

Jim Perry wasn't a reliever. The brother of Hall of Famer Gaylord Perry was a durable pitcher in his own right. He twice led the American League in games started, wrapping up his 17-year career with 215 victories and 109 complete games.

Yet Perry was dispatched to the bullpen for all three of his All-Star Games, including a surprising selection in 1971. The Twins ace had won the AL's Cy Young Award in 1970, probably inspiring All-Star manager Earl Weaver to add him to the following year's staff. It's unlikely that Weaver was impressed by Perry's unflashy midseason 1971 record (12-8 W-L, 4.10 ERA) or his rocky four starts before the break (38 hits and 10 walks in 29 innings).

Perry would finish 1971 with a 17-17 mark, hampered by a sudden proclivity for gopher balls. He had allowed 38 homers in the previous two seasons combined, but he coughed up 39 in 1971 alone, the highest total in the majors. The result was a 90.1 BV that remains the worst for any Modern Era pitcher who worked out of an All-Star bullpen.

Runner-up Esteban Loaiza's BPO+ in 2004 was only marginally better than Perry's 1971 figure (115.1 to 118.1), but the disparity in base value was much wider because of their respective workloads. Perry tossed 270 innings, greatly increasing his opportunities to surrender bases. Loaiza worked just 183 innings for the White Sox and Yankees, who acquired him after the All-Star Game.

The Worst 10

Rank	Pitcher	Year	Team	Lg	G	ERA	BPO	BPO+	BV
1	Jim Perry	1971	Twins	AL	40	4.23	.726	118.1	90.1
2	Esteban Loaiza	2004	White Sox	AL	31	5.70	.830	115.1	58.3
3	Doyle Alexander	1988	Tigers	AL	34	4.32	.716	112.1	53.5
4	Livan Hernandez	2005	Nationals	NL	35	3.98	.732	110.9	52.9
5	Hector Santiago	2015	Angels	AL	33	3.59	.713	114.3	49.0
6	Milt Pappas	1962	Orioles	AL	35	4.03	.709	112.2	47.6
7	Dick Ruthven	1981	Phillies	NL	23	5.15	.751	116.5	47.0
8	Ken Schrom	1986	Indians	AL	34	4.54	.749	111.1	46.8
9	Mark Buehrle	2006	White Sox	AL	32	4.99	.793	110.6	45.9
10	Kevin Correia	2011	Pirates	NL	27	4.79	.726	115.3	44.7

25. MOST VALUABLE PLAYERS

List #199: Best Choice for Most Valuable Player

Fourteen of the Modern Era's Most Valuable Players have been unanimous selections, named first on every ballot. What's strange is that only one of these uncontested MVPs is on the list below: Barry Bonds with an impressive BPO+ of 282.2 in 2002.

Bonds was actually a touch better in 2004, when he won his fourth straight National League MVP trophy, the seventh of his career. His 284.5 was the highest single-season BPO+ for any batter since 1961, distinguishing him as the best choice for Most Valuable Player honors in the Modern Era.

Not everybody agreed. Eight of the 32 voters opted for somebody else in 2004. Perhaps they were tired of Bonds's infamous ego and his MVP monopoly. Or maybe they truly believed another player had a greater impact, a conclusion not supported by the stats. Six voters chose the Dodgers' Adrian Beltre (137.5 BPO+), and the other two preferred a pair of Cardinals, Albert Pujols (146.8) and Scott Rolen (140.1). All were at least 137 points behind Bonds, an enormous disparity in BPO+.

This list is divided among seven batters and three pitchers, a split I make in cases where all players are eligible for a particular distinction. Batters aim for the highest BPO+, while pitchers seek the lowest, making direct comparisons difficult. Willie Hernandez's 66.2 in 1984 was the best for any pitcher named an MVP. His BPO+ may not have been Bonds-like, but it was outstanding nonetheless.

The Best 10

Rk	Batter	Year	Team	Lg	G	BA	B	O	BPO	BV	BPO+
1	Barry Bonds	2004	Giants	NL	147	.362	553	247	2.239	358.6	284.5
2	Barry Bonds	2002	Giants	NL	143	.370	540	262	2.061	348.6	282.2
3	Barry Bonds	2001	Giants	NL	153	.328	612	330	1.855	365.5	248.3
4	Barry Bonds	2003	Giants	NL	130	.341	459	266	1.726	255.7	225.8
5	Barry Bonds	1992	Pirates	NL	140	.311	473	350	1.351	230.5	195.1
6	Mickey Mantle	1962	Yankees	AL	123	.321	362	262	1.382	175.0	193.6
7	Joe Morgan	1976	Reds	NL	141	.320	459	344	1.334	221.8	193.5
Rk	Pitcher	Year	Team	Lg	G	ERA	B	O	BPO	BV	BPO+
1	Willie Hernandez	1984	Tigers	AL	80	1.92	182	423	.430	-92.9	66.2
2	Clayton Kershaw	2014	Dodgers	NL	27	1.77	250	596	.419	-110.9	69.3
3	Roger Clemens	1986	Red Sox	AL	33	2.48	369	776	.476	-162.7	69.4

List #200: Worst Choice for Most Valuable Player

Ivan Rodriguez put up impressive numbers in 1999. The Rangers catcher blasted 35 homers, drove in 113 runs, and batted .332. Seems like he would be a solid candidate for Most Valuable Player, right? That's what the voters thought, and they awarded him the American League's trophy.

It proved to be the worst MVP choice of the Modern Era. Rodriguez's BPO+ was a fairly routine 105.7, only 5.7 percent better than the leaguewide average. He reached just 21 bases more than a typical player would have attained under the same conditions. The only category in which he led the league was grounding into double plays (31).

Voters were confronted with a broad array of MVP candidates in 1999. Manny Ramirez posted the American League's best BPO+ (151.8), buttressed by 44 homers and 165 RBIs. He was followed by Edgar Martinez at 142.7, Rafael Palmeiro at 139.3, and Derek Jeter at 137.8. A total of 34 AL batters outperformed Rodriguez's 105.7. And then there was Pedro Martinez, the league's best pitcher with a 23-4 record, 2.07 ERA, and 62.2 BPO+. The latter was 37.8 percent better than average.

Four batters on this list became MVPs despite BPO+ readings within 10 percent of their leaguewide norms. The three pitchers below were all excellent — just check their ERAs — but Denny McLain fared the worst with a BPO+ of 84.3, even though he was credited with 31 wins in 1968.

The Worst 10

Rk	Batter	Year	Team	Lg	G	BA	B	O	BPO	BV	BPO+
1	Ivan Rodriguez	1999	Rangers	AL	144	.332	390	449	.869	21.0	105.7
2	Thurman Munson	1976	Yankees	AL	152	.302	329	469	.701	21.1	106.9
3	Steve Garvey	1974	Dodgers	NL	156	.312	349	463	.754	29.4	109.2
4	Miguel Tejada	2002	Athletics	AL	162	.308	396	485	.816	35.2	109.8
5	Andre Dawson	1987	Cubs	NL	153	.287	405	463	.875	44.2	112.3
6	Zoilo Versalles	1965	Twins	AL	160	.273	397	510	.778	44.1	112.5
7	Dustin Pedroia	2008	Red Sox	AL	157	.326	415	474	.876	51.1	114.0
Rk	Pitcher	Year	Team	Lg	G	ERA	B	O	BPO	BV	BPO+
1	Denny McLain	1968	Tigers	AL	41	1.96	483	1,002	.482	-89.8	84.3
2	Dennis Eckersley	1992	Athletics	AL	69	1.91	114	239	.477	-36.8	75.6
3	Vida Blue	1971	Athletics	AL	39	1.82	411	936	.439	-144.3	74.0

List #201: Best Player Who Didn't Win Most Valuable Player

There were two frontrunners for the National League's Most Valuable Player Award in 1998.

Mark McGwire of the Cardinals and Sammy Sosa of the Cubs electrified the nation with their battle for home-run supremacy. Columnists hailed the two sluggers for "saving" baseball in the wake of 1994's contentious players' strike. Both men shattered Roger Maris's single-season HR record. McGwire set the new mark with 70 homers. Sosa finished with 66.

Yet the baseball writers picked Sosa by an overwhelming margin, giving him 30 first-place votes, leaving just two for McGwire. It was a strange choice. McGwire clearly posted the better numbers — the best for any Modern Era player who was spurned for the MVP Award. He outperformed Sosa not only in home runs, but also in walks, on-base percentage, slugging percentage, and BPO+ by a wide margin (199.0 to 136.5).

The two runner-up batters on this list were also involved in a famous home-run chase. Mickey Mantle and Norm Cash lost the American League's 1961 MVP Award to Maris and his 61 homers, even though their BPO+ scores were far superior: Mantle 191.0, Cash 182.3, Maris 144.5.

The pitcher with the best non-MVP season was reliever Dennis Eckersley, who finished sixth in the American League's balloting in 1990. His BPO+ was a microscopic 46.2. The three runners-up also worked out of the bullpen. They all received MVP support, but not enough votes to win the award.

The Best 10

Rk	Batter	Year	Team	Lg	G	BA	B	O	BPO	BV	BPO+
1	Mark McGwire	1998	Cardinals	NL	155	.299	556	369	1.507	276.5	199.0
2	Mickey Mantle	1961	Yankees	AL	153	.317	497	360	1.381	236.8	191.0
3	Norm Cash	1961	Tigers	AL	159	.361	502	367	1.368	226.6	182.3
4	Mark McGwire	1996	Athletics	AL	130	.312	434	306	1.418	194.3	181.1
5	Jim Thome	2002	Indians	AL	147	.304	459	347	1.323	205.3	181.0
6	Barry Bonds	1996	Giants	NL	158	.308	516	382	1.351	230.4	180.7
7	Sammy Sosa	2001	Cubs	NL	160	.328	559	408	1.370	249.3	180.5

Rk	Pitcher	Year	Team	Lg	G	ERA	B	O	BPO	BV	BPO+
1	Dennis Eckersley	1990	Athletics	AL	63	0.61	64	222	.288	-74.4	46.2
2	Eric Gagne	2003	Dodgers	NL	77	1.20	78	247	.316	-87.5	47.1
3	Koji Uehara	2013	Red Sox	AL	73	1.09	73	224	.326	-78.5	48.2
3	Craig Kimbrel	2012	Braves	NL	63	1.01	61	192	.318	-65.6	48.2

List #202: Best Improvement to Win Most Valuable Player

It was impossible to think of Bryce Harper as a Most Valuable Player in 2014. The same was true of Denny McLain in 1967.

Harper debuted as the National League's Rookie of the Year in 2012. But a thumb injury sidelined him for two months in his third season. He hit just 13 home runs, batted .273, and posted a middling BPO+ of 103.0. He was serviceable, but definitely not great.

McLain won 20 games in 1966, his second full year in the majors. But his ERA of 3.92 was unusually high at a time when pitchers had the upper hand. McLain slipped in 1967 to a BPO+ of 112.7, which was 12.7 percent worse than the American League average.

The fourth season proved to be the charm for both. Harper exploded to 42 HR, a .330 BA, and a 180.1 BPO+ in 2015. McLain sizzled to 31 wins, a 1.96 ERA, and an 84.3 BPO+ in 1968. They were chosen unanimously as MVPs.

Harper made the greatest improvement of any MVP batter in the Modern Era, boosting his BV from a paltry 5.7 in 2014 to 212.2 in 2015, a jump of 206.5 bases. McLain did the best of any MVP pitcher, trimming his BV by 142.5.

This list does not include the two rookies who were named MVPs: Fred Lynn (1975) and Ichiro Suzuki (2001). There is simply no way to measure how much they improved during their magical seasons.

The Best 10

Rk	Batter	MVP year	Team	Lg	G	BPO+	BV	Prev BPO+	Prev BV	BV change
1	Bryce Harper	2015	Nationals	NL	153	180.1	212.2	103.0	5.7	206.5
2	Larry Walker	1997	Rockies	NL	153	162.3	206.6	111.9	21.9	184.7
3	Barry Bonds	2001	Giants	NL	153	248.3	365.5	171.9	195.7	169.8
4	Carl Yastrzemski	1967	Red Sox	AL	161	168.7	191.8	108.4	27.1	164.7
5	Jose Canseco	1988	Athletics	AL	158	155.9	172.9	103.9	13.9	159.0
6	Sammy Sosa	1998	Cubs	NL	159	136.5	137.1	95.8	-16.9	154.0
7	Kevin Mitchell	1989	Giants	NL	154	163.4	172.9	108.3	22.0	150.7
Rk	Pitcher	MVP year	Team	Lg	G	BPO+	BV	Prev BPO+	Prev BV	BV change
1	Denny McLain	1968	Tigers	AL	41	84.3	-89.8	112.7	53.1	-142.9
2	Roger Clemens	1986	Red Sox	AL	33	69.4	-162.7	84.2	-31.8	-130.9
3	Vida Blue	1971	Athletics	AL	39	74.0	-144.3	64.7	-25.7	-118.6

List #203: Worst Decline After Winning Most Valuable Player

Barry Bonds was on top of the baseball world in 2004. He posted the best BPO+ in the Modern Era (284.5) and won his fourth consecutive Most Valuable Player Award. His 703 career home runs put him within striking distance of Hank Aaron's all-time mark of 755.

Sure, Bonds was 40 years old. And sure, the rumors about possible steroid abuse were getting louder. But there were no reasons to anticipate a sizable drop in production.

No reasons, that is, except for a serious injury and mental fatigue. Bonds recovered slowly from two knee operations during the offseason. His progress was hampered, he said, by the rumbling about steroids. "You finally brought me and my family down," he snapped at a group of reporters during spring training. "So now go pick a different person."

Bonds didn't regain his mobility and equanimity until September, when he played in 14 games. His BV of 14.8 for the 2005 season was 343.8 below his total for the previous year, easily the worst decline for any MVP winner in the Modern Era. Bonds was left off all of the MVP ballots that fall, the first time since 1989 that he didn't receive any votes.

Vida Blue experienced the worst deterioration of any MVP pitcher, as his BV total soared by 129.0 between 1971 and 1972. A salary holdout contributed to his decline from a 24-8 record to a mark of 6-10.

The Worst 10

Rk	Batter	MVP year	Team	Lg	G	BPO+	BV	Next BPO+	Next BV	BV change
1	Barry Bonds	2004	Giants	NL	147	284.5	358.6	163.6	14.8	-343.8
2	Cal Ripken Jr.	1991	Orioles	AL	162	138.5	122.5	90.0	-34.9	-157.4
3	Bryce Harper	2015	Nationals	NL	153	180.7	213.0	118.6	57.3	-155.7
4	Willie McGee	1985	Cardinals	NL	152	137.7	110.5	86.2	-39.1	-149.6
5	Don Baylor	1979	Angels	AL	162	134.0	114.0	85.6	-27.2	-141.2
6	Jose Canseco	1988	Athletics	AL	158	155.9	172.9	134.7	41.2	-131.7
7	George Brett	1980	Royals	AL	117	180.0	168.5	129.2	48.4	-120.1
Rk	Pitcher	MVP year	Team	Lg	G	BPO+	BV	Next BPO+	Next BV	BV change
1	Vida Blue	1971	Athletics	AL	39	74.0	-144.3	94.0	-15.3	129.0
2	Roger Clemens	1986	Red Sox	AL	33	69.4	-162.7	82.2	-107.0	55.7
3	Bob Gibson	1968	Cardinals	NL	34	70.3	-146.5	82.5	-99.6	46.9

26. CY YOUNG AWARDS

List #204: Best Choice for Cy Young Award

A strong case could be made that Jason Schmidt was the National League's best pitcher in 2003. The Giants righthander posted a 2.34 ERA and a base value of minus-108.7. Both stats led the league, as did his .773 winning percentage on a 17-5 record.

But the Cy Young Award electorate disagreed. All but four voters opted for Dodgers closer Eric Gagne, even though his workload was 60 percent smaller than Schmidt's (82.1 innings vs. 207.2). Gagne's conversion rate was the determining factor. He made good on all 55 save opportunities he faced.

Several columnists were annoyed that a reliever would be honored above a starter. "The point that needs to be made: He doesn't pitch nine innings at a time. He pitches one inning at a time," sniped the *Chicago Tribune*'s Rick Morrissey. His candidate for the NL's top pitcher was the Cubs' Mark Prior (18-6 W-L, 79.6 BPO+).

But Gagne had another strong point in his favor. His BPO+ of 47.1 was the best for any Cy Young winner in the Modern Era. Even his competitors said he deserved the trophy. "To do what he did and to not blow a save, especially in the situations he was put in, one-run games a lot of times, and to rattle off 50-some odd straight saves, is unbelievable," said Prior.

Second on this list is Pedro Martinez. His brilliant 2000 performance for the Red Sox was highlighted by a 1.74 ERA and a 53.0 BPO+.

The Best 10

Rk	Pitcher	Year	Team	Lg	G	ERA	B	O	BPO	BV	BPO+
1	Eric Gagne	2003	Dodgers	NL	77	1.20	78	247	.316	-87.5	47.1
2	Pedro Martinez	2000	Red Sox	AL	29	1.74	258	657	.393	-228.8	53.0
3	Greg Maddux	1995	Braves	NL	28	1.63	256	633	.404	-181.0	58.6
4	Greg Maddux	1994	Braves	NL	25	1.56	258	614	.420	-167.3	60.7
5	Pedro Martinez	1999	Red Sox	AL	31	2.07	301	650	.463	-182.9	62.2
6	Bruce Sutter	1979	Cubs	NL	62	2.22	138	311	.444	-76.5	64.3
7	Roger Clemens	1997	Blue Jays	AL	34	2.05	375	796	.471	-191.8	66.2
7	Willie Hernandez	1984	Tigers	AL	80	1.92	182	423	.430	-92.9	66.2
9	Johan Santana	2004	Twins	AL	34	2.61	331	684	.484	-153.6	68.3
10	Pedro Martinez	1997	Expos	NL	31	1.90	344	733	.469	-157.6	68.6

List #205: Worst Choice for Cy Young Award

The Brewers enjoyed a miraculous season in 1982. They won the American League championship — still the only league title in franchise history — and came within a single victory of taking the World Series.

Major awards inevitably followed. Milwaukee shortstop Robin Yount was named the league's MVP, and starter Pete Vuckovich won the Cy Young. "I can't take full credit," Vuckovich said modestly. "I just happen to be lucky enough to be out there on the days when the team's playing well enough for me to be a winner."

It was true. The Brewers gave him tremendous support, scoring at least six runs in half of his 30 starts. Vuckovich's 18 victories included six in which he surrendered at least six walks or 10 hits. He yielded an average of 1.50 walks and hits per inning, the sixth-highest WHIP in the league. And his BPO+ of 112.9 was the worst for any Cy Young honoree in the Modern Era.

So who should have won in 1982? Two solid choices would have been the runner-up in the balloting, the Orioles' Jim Palmer (15-5 W-L, 3.13 ERA), or the league's BPO+ leader, the Blue Jays' Dave Stieb (79.5). Or the voters could have cast a wider net, since 43 AL starters had better BPO+ scores than Vuckovich.

It might seem amazing that Bob Welch is second on this list, given that he won 27 games for the Athletics in 1990. But his BPO+ of 100.7 was — surprisingly — no better than average.

The Worst 10

Rk	Pitcher	Year	Team	Lg	G	ERA	B	O	BPO	BV	BPO+
1	Pete Vuckovich	1982	Brewers	AL	30	3.34	480	669	.717	54.8	112.9
2	Bob Welch	1990	Athletics	AL	35	2.95	449	715	.628	3.2	100.7
3	Mike McCormick	1967	Giants	NL	40	2.85	445	793	.561	-13.5	97.1
4	Steve Stone	1980	Orioles	AL	37	3.23	473	751	.630	-14.4	97.0
5	Jim Lonborg	1967	Red Sox	AL	39	3.16	475	825	.576	-39.0	92.4
6	Roger Clemens	2001	Yankees	AL	33	3.51	431	663	.650	-37.1	92.1
7	Jim Palmer	1976	Orioles	AL	40	2.51	515	944	.546	-50.2	91.1
8	Jack McDowell	1993	White Sox	AL	34	3.37	468	768	.609	-50.4	90.3
9	Bartolo Colon	2005	Angels	AL	33	3.48	406	670	.606	-44.6	90.1
10	Gaylord Perry	1978	Padres	NL	37	2.73	431	786	.548	-48.8	89.8

List #206: Best Pitcher Who Didn't Win the Cy Young

The Athletics relied heavily on Dennis Eckersley for nine years. The sidearming righty was a lights-out closer, saving 320 regular-season victories between 1987 and 1995, plus 11 more in the playoffs.

Eckersley's hallmark was his pinpoint control. He struck out 9.3 batters for every unintentional walk during his Oakland years, itself an impressive ratio. But he dialed it up in 1990, registering 73 strikeouts while issuing just three UBB. Fellow pitchers marveled at his 24.3-to-1 ratio. "Eck's numbers are unbelievable," said Jesse Orosco, himself a prolific reliever. "I don't know how, but he doesn't walk anybody."

Nor did he often allow opponents to score. Eckersley surrendered five earned runs in 1990, giving him a microscopic ERA of 0.61. His 48 saves were a key factor in Oakland's American League championship, though the Reds swept the A's in the World Series.

Award winners for 1990 were announced after the playoffs, with Eckersley a contender for the Cy Young. He hadn't reached the qualification standard of 162 innings — few relievers do — but his 46.2 BPO+ was almost 28 points better than the score for any AL starter that season.

The voters didn't care. They gave the trophy to Bob Welch, another member of Oakland's staff. Eckersley finished fifth, though he is noted here for posting the Modern Era's best BPO+ that was not rewarded with a Cy.

This list is limited to pitchers who received votes in Cy Young balloting, yet fell short. Nine of them — all but Clayton Kershaw — were relievers.

The Best 10

Rk	Pitcher	Year	Team	Lg	G	ERA	B	O	BPO	BV	BPO+
1	Dennis Eckersley	1990	Athletics	AL	63	0.61	64	222	.288	-74.4	46.2
2	Koji Uehara	2013	Red Sox	AL	73	1.09	73	224	.326	-78.5	48.2
2	Craig Kimbrel	2012	Braves	NL	63	1.01	61	192	.318	-65.6	48.2
4	Zach Britton	2016	Orioles	AL	69	0.54	69	202	.342	-68.1	50.3
5	Mariano Rivera	2008	Yankees	AL	64	1.40	74	213	.347	-71.5	50.9
6	Fernando Rodney	2012	Rays	AL	76	0.60	77	227	.339	-68.9	52.8
7	Billy Wagner	1999	Astros	NL	66	1.57	88	227	.388	-74.8	54.0
8	Mariano Rivera	1996	Yankees	AL	61	2.09	130	323	.402	-109.6	54.2
9	Wade Davis	2014	Royals	AL	71	1.00	76	219	.347	-62.9	54.7
10	Clayton Kershaw	2016	Dodgers	NL	21	1.69	160	444	.360	-127.7	55.6

List #207: Best Improvement to Win the Cy Young

Steve Carlton was a workhorse for the Cardinals in 1971. He pitched 273.1 innings, notched 20 wins, and was named to the National League's All-Star team. His reward was to be traded.

The problem was money. Carlton asked for $65,000, a salary that now sounds quaint. But the outraged Cards dealt him straight-up to the Phillies for pitcher Rick Wise, a fellow All-Star whose 2.88 ERA had outshone Carlton's 3.56.

The deal's punitive element was clearly understood. The Cardinals had barely missed the playoffs in 1971, while the Phillies had blundered into last place in the NL East. Saint Louis executives undoubtedly chuckled about the mess awaiting their former star in Philadelphia.

And yes, the Phillies were as terrible as predicted in 1972. They won only 30 of 115 games not started by Carlton — for a so-called winning percentage of .261 — but their mark with him on the mound was an astounding 29-12 (.707).

If Carlton intended to prove the Cardinals wrong, he succeeded. He posted a personal record of 27-10, drove his ERA down to 1.97, and was unanimously selected for the NL's Cy Young Award. This list uses BV to measure year-to-year swings, with Carlton's 187.3-base reduction the greatest improvement by any Cy Young honoree.

Runner-up Pat Hentgen wasn't traded, but he did step up his game for the Blue Jays. He improved by 156.9 bases to be named the American League's top pitcher in 1996.

The Best 10

Rk	Pitcher	Cy year	Team	Lg	G	BPO+	BV	Prev BPO+	Prev BV	BV change
1	Steve Carlton	1972	Phillies	NL	41	74.3	-169.1	103.6	18.2	-187.3
2	Pat Hentgen	1996	Blue Jays	AL	35	79.0	-124.8	107.3	32.1	-156.9
3	Cliff Lee	2008	Indians	AL	31	75.7	-110.0	120.0	40.8	-150.8
4	Denny McLain	1968	Tigers	AL	41	84.3	-89.8	112.7	53.1	-142.9
5	Rick Porcello	2016	Red Sox	AL	33	77.3	-106.9	109.3	32.7	-139.6
6	Dean Chance	1964	Angels	AL	46	70.1	-148.9	97.4	-11.8	-137.1
7	Jim Palmer	1975	Orioles	AL	39	81.3	-114.2	105.9	19.2	-133.4
8	Roger Clemens	1986	Red Sox	AL	33	69.4	-162.7	84.2	-31.8	-130.9
9	Mike Cuellar	1969	Orioles	AL	39	73.8	-141.5	95.4	-13.1	-128.4
10	Randy Johnson	1999	Diamondbacks	NL	35	75.9	-146.0	93.5	-23.4	-122.6

List #208: Worst Decline After Winning the Cy Young

Steve Carlton's meteoric rise with the Phillies in 1972 was followed by a quick and precipitous decline. He endured surprising spells of ineffectiveness a year after winning the National League's Cy Young Award.

Carlton's pinpoint control vanished at times. He had fashioned 14 starts in 1972 that blended endurance (at least nine innings) and precision (no more than one walk). But he managed only four of those pristine appearances in 1973, outnumbered by six occasions on which he issued at least five walks. The nadir came on June 17, when Carlton walked eight Giants, gave up eight hits, and was yanked in the seventh inning.

Philadelphia's so-called attack, to be fair, deserved a share of the blame. The Phils had provided Carlton with weak support in 1972, just 3.8 runs per start, yet he somehow posted 27 victories. A further drop to 3.6 runs per game enhanced the degree of difficulty in 1973. Carlton wound up with 20 losses, the most for any NL pitcher.

The symmetry of his rise and fall was striking. Carlton had reduced his BV by 187.3 bases in 1972, only to see it balloon by 187.6 in 1973. His deterioration — the worst in a season directly after a Cy Young Award — essentially put him back where he had been in 1971.

Jim Perry, who won a Cy in 1970, suffered a subsequent decline nearly as deep (181.2 bases). His BV in 1971 was an unimpressive plus-90.1.

The Worst 10

Rk	Pitcher	Cy year	Team	Lg	G	BPO+	BV	Next BPO+	Next BV	BV change
1	Steve Carlton	1972	Phillies	NL	41	74.3	-169.1	103.2	18.5	187.6
2	Jim Perry	1970	Twins	AL	40	83.1	-91.1	118.1	90.1	181.2
3	Dean Chance	1964	Angels	AL	46	70.1	-148.9	102.7	10.7	159.6
4	Randy Johnson	2002	Diamondbacks	NL	35	76.3	-135.3	104.3	10.8	146.1
5	Pedro Martinez	2000	Red Sox	AL	29	53.0	-228.8	64.2	-88.1	140.7
6	Randy Jones	1976	Padres	NL	40	80.7	-109.9	106.7	19.4	129.3
7	Vida Blue	1971	Athletics	AL	39	74.0	-144.3	94.0	-15.3	129.0
8	Roger Clemens	1998	Blue Jays	AL	33	75.0	-128.4	99.8	-0.8	127.6
9	Randy Johnson	1995	Mariners	AL	30	70.1	-141.9	85.3	-20.4	121.5
10	Tim Lincecum	2009	Giants	NL	32	73.8	-123.1	99.4	-2.7	120.4

27. ROOKIES OF THE YEAR

List #209: Best Choice for Rookie of the Year

There was no suspense in 2012. Everybody knew by July that the Angels' Mike Trout would be named the American League's Rookie of the Year at season's end.

Trout arrived at the midsummer break with 12 home runs, 26 stolen bases, and a .341 batting average. The 20-year-old center fielder won a spot on the AL All-Star team, becoming the seventh-youngest position player to do so. He came to the plate twice in the All-Star Game and (naturally) reached base both times with a single and a walk.

So there was no doubt about Trout becoming Rookie of the Year. The only question was whether he would be picked unanimously.

He was. No other result was conceivable after Trout finished 2012 with 30 homers, a league-leading 49 steals, a .326 BA, and the highest BPO+ in the majors, 160.7. The latter score was the highest for any non-pitcher honored as either league's best rookie, precisely 15 points better than the 145.7 for runner-up Jose Abreu of the 2014 White Sox.

Pitchers are also eligible for the Rookie of the Year Award, which is why they have their own section on this list.

Andrew Bailey scuffled to a 5-9 record with a 4.32 ERA in AA ball in 2008, only to emerge as Oakland's closer in 2009. His 26 saves and 1.84 ERA capped his improbable rise with an ROY trophy — and his 59.9 BPO+ marked him as the best pitcher to earn that distinction in the Modern Era.

The Best 10

Rk	Batter	Year	Team	Lg	G	BA	B	O	BPO	BV	BPO+
1	Mike Trout	2012	Angels	AL	139	.326	444	396	1.121	167.7	160.7
2	Jose Abreu	2014	White Sox	AL	145	.317	392	399	.982	122.9	145.7
3	Mark McGwire	1987	Athletics	AL	151	.289	429	411	1.044	132.3	144.6
4	Al Bumbry	1973	Orioles	AL	110	.337	240	253	.949	71.0	142.0
5	Dick Allen	1964	Phillies	NL	162	.318	431	452	.954	127.1	141.8
6	Fred Lynn	1975	Red Sox	AL	145	.331	386	381	1.013	108.8	139.2
7	Ryan Braun	2007	Brewers	NL	113	.324	342	328	1.043	90.1	135.8
Rk	Pitcher	Year	Team	Lg	G	ERA	B	O	BPO	BV	BPO+
1	Andrew Bailey	2009	Athletics	AL	68	1.84	103	253	.407	-69.0	59.9
2	Neftali Feliz	2010	Rangers	AL	70	2.73	90	208	.433	-57.2	61.2
3	Craig Kimbrel	2011	Braves	NL	79	2.10	100	232	.431	-51.5	66.0

List #210: Worst Choice for Rookie of the Year

Ken Hubbs was precocious in the field. The Cubs second baseman won a Gold Glove in 1962, the first rookie to receive the award. He was revered by Chicago fans for his outgoing personality — and respected by teammates for his self-effacing approach. "He was a great human being," said third baseman Ron Santo.

But Hubbs was no prodigy at the plate. His 1962 BA of .260 was decent enough, though he had scant power (five homers) and an unimpressive batting eye (35 walks). He struck out 129 times and grounded into 20 double plays, leading the National League in both of those unhappy categories.

These deficiences had no impact on the nation's sportswriters, who chose Hubbs as the NL's Rookie of the Year. His selection imbued him with a golden aura that would never fade, especially after his death in a February 1964 plane crash. "There isn't a man in Chicago who wouldn't have been proud to have him as a son," said no less an eminence than Richard Daley, the city's mayor.

Yet Hubbs's BPO+ of 72.4 still ranks as the worst for any position player named Rookie of the Year during the Modern Era. Next is another Chicago honoree, Ozzie Guillen, who posted a 74.9 BPO+ with the 1985 White Sox.

The weakest ROY performance by a pitcher belonged to Carl Morton, who fashioned a respectable 18-11 record with the Expos in 1970, despite a bloated BPO+ of 105.9.

The Worst 10

Rk	Batter	Year	Team	Lg	G	BA	B	O	BPO	BV	BPO+
1	Ken Hubbs	1962	Cubs	NL	160	.260	286	532	.538	-109.2	72.4
2	Ozzie Guillen	1985	White Sox	AL	150	.273	205	375	.547	-68.6	74.9
3	Tommy Helms	1966	Reds	NL	138	.284	245	418	.586	-61.3	80.0
4	Walt Weiss	1988	Athletics	AL	147	.250	208	367	.567	-38.1	84.5
5	Alfredo Griffin	1979	Blue Jays	AL	153	.287	313	491	.637	-43.6	87.8
6	Ted Sizemore	1969	Dodgers	NL	159	.271	267	456	.586	-34.3	88.6
7	John Castino	1979	Twins	AL	148	.285	213	316	.674	-19.2	91.7

Rk	Pitcher	Year	Team	Lg	G	ERA	B	O	BPO	BV	BPO+
1	Carl Morton	1970	Expos	NL	43	3.60	594	847	.701	33.0	105.9
2	Butch Metzger	1976	Padres	NL	77	2.92	230	371	.620	10.5	104.8
3	Don Schwall	1961	Red Sox	AL	25	3.22	367	539	.681	-1.4	99.6

List #211: Best Player Who Didn't Win Rookie of the Year

The Reds' new manager in 1970, Sparky Anderson, had never run a big-league team. Many neophytes would have played it safe, yet Anderson penciled a pair of rookies into his opening-day lineup, left fielder Bernie Carbo and shortstop Dave Concepcion.

Both moves paid off. Concepcion would be superior over the long haul (2,326 hits, five Gold Gloves), but Carbo was a short-term smash. He homered in that initial game and never stopped hitting, finishing with 21 homers, a .310 BA, and a BPO+ of 158.3. The latter would have been second-best in the National League if Carbo hadn't fallen 35 PA short of the qualification standard.

His consolation prize, you might assume, was the NL's Rookie of the Year Award. Eighty-two non-pitchers have earned ROY trophies in the Modern Era, with only Mike Trout surpassing Carbo's 158.3. Yet Expos pitcher Carl Morton prevailed in a close vote, despite vastly inferior stats. (See List #210.) Carbo ranks as the best first-year position player to be spurned for Rookie of the Year.

His pitching counterpart was Joey Devine, who made 42 relief appearances for the 2008 Athletics, yielding only three earned runs. Devine's BPO+ was a microscopic 50.8, yet he finished sixth in the American League balloting.

This list encompasses all players who received Rookie of the Year votes, even if they didn't play often, like Gregg Jefferies (29 games). But take note of Jefferies's 27.8 BV. Thirty-seven ROY position players since 1961 have posted base values worse than that.

The Best 10

Rk	Batter	Year	Team	Lg	G	BA	B	O	BPO	BV	BPO+
1	Bernie Carbo	1970	Reds	NL	125	.310	313	266	1.177	115.2	158.3
2	Phil Plantier	1991	Red Sox	AL	53	.331	118	103	1.146	42.6	156.5
3	Tim Raines	1981	Expos	NL	88	.304	258	239	1.079	91.6	155.1
4	Mitchell Page	1977	Athletics	AL	145	.307	394	366	1.077	138.9	154.5
5	Gregg Jefferies	1988	Mets	NL	29	.321	79	77	1.026	27.8	154.3
6	Gary Sanchez	2016	Yankees	AL	53	.299	161	148	1.088	52.1	147.9
7	Trea Turner	2016	Nationals	NL	73	.342	224	211	1.062	67.2	142.8
Rk	Pitcher	Year	Team	Lg	G	ERA	B	O	BPO	BV	BPO+
1	Joey Devine	2008	Athletics	AL	42	0.59	46	136	.338	-44.5	50.8
2	Jonathan Papelbon	2006	Red Sox	AL	59	0.92	82	205	.400	-62.8	56.6
3	Ken Giles	2014	Phillies	NL	44	1.18	49	136	.360	-36.4	57.4

List #212: Worst Decline After Winning Rookie of the Year

The American League's 1994 Rookie of the Year Award was a mixed blessing for Bob Hamelin.

It was nice to receive recognition for a job well done — 24 homers, 65 runs batted in, and a .282 batting average in 101 games for the Royals. The unfortunate side effect was an increase in pressure. "Nothing is ever for good," Hamelin said. "That was a great season in 1994. But the next year, there were expectations, mostly that I put on myself."

He couldn't get untracked in 1995. His BA at the start of Memorial Day weekend was a sickly .155, accompanied by 23 strikeouts and a lone home run. The Royals ran out of patience by the middle of June, shipping Hamelin to the minors. He would return to Kansas City later that summer, though his confidence never did. "It was becoming a bit of a frustrating situation," he admitted.

Hamelin's BPO+ was a robust 133.9 in his ROY season, followed by a feeble 69.0 in 1995. His base value declined from plus-64.0 to minus-44.1. This 108.1-base dive was the worst by any Modern Era position player after being named Rookie of the Year.

Pat Zachry's sparkling 14-7 record for the Reds brought him the National League's rookie award in 1976. But Zachry struggled to a 3-7 mark in 1977 before being packaged in a midseason trade to the Mets for Tom Seaver. Zachry's BV soared by 92.0 in his sophomore year.

The Worst 10

Rk	Batter	ROY year	Team	Lg	G	BPO+	BV	Next BPO+	Next BV	BV change
1	Bob Hamelin	1994	Royals	AL	101	133.9	64.0	69.0	-44.1	-108.1
2	Al Bumbry	1973	Orioles	AL	110	142.0	71.0	86.4	-19.1	-90.1
3	Carlton Fisk	1972	Red Sox	AL	131	135.2	80.1	98.6	-4.0	-84.1
4	Jose Abreu	2014	White Sox	AL	145	145.7	122.9	115.5	48.7	-74.2
5	Mark McGwire	1987	Athletics	AL	151	144.6	132.3	121.6	61.7	-70.6
6	Fred Lynn	1975	Red Sox	AL	145	139.2	108.8	116.9	44.7	-64.1
7	Alvin Davis	1984	Mariners	AL	152	134.5	102.2	112.4	39.1	-63.1

Rk	Pitcher	ROY year	Team	Lg	G	BPO+	BV	Next BPO+	Next BV	BV change
1	Pat Zachry	1976	Reds	NL	38	88.9	-42.0	113.1	50.0	92.0
2	Stan Bahnsen	1968	Yankees	AL	37	92.1	-35.4	112.9	53.0	88.4
3	Rick Sutcliffe	1979	Dodgers	NL	39	94.6	-25.2	130.1	61.1	86.3

28. GOLD GLOVES

List #213: Best Batting by Gold Glove Winner

Three of the legendary five tools have a direct impact on BPO and related statistics — hitting for average, hitting for power, and speed. The other tools (glovework and throwing) are generally not within the purview of this book, as I explained in the early pages.

But this chapter is an exception. It analyzes the batting stats of players who met the exalted standards for Gold Gloves, presented annually to the best fielder at each position in each league. The men at the top of this list excelled not only at hitting the ball, but also at catching and throwing it. They were the epitome of five-tool players.

It tends to be forgotten that Barry Bonds was a fleet left fielder during the first half of his career, earning three Gold Gloves with the Pirates and five with the Giants. His skills converged in 1992 for a season of uncommon brilliance. Bonds marked his final year in Pittsburgh by leading the National League in runs scored (109), walks (127), OBP (.456), and slugging percentage (.624), while also being acknowledged as the NL's most skillful left fielder. His BPO+ of 195.1 was the best for any Gold Glove winner in the Modern Era.

Thirty-year-old Mickey Mantle had lost a couple of steps to age and injuries by 1962, but he still patrolled center field so smoothly that he was awarded a Gold Glove. His 193.6 BPO+ is a close second on this list.

The Best 10

Rk	Batter	Year	Team	Lg	Pos	G	BA	B	O	BPO	BV	BPO+
1	Barry Bonds	1992	Pirates	NL	OF	140	.311	473	350	1.351	230.5	195.1
2	Mickey Mantle	1962	Yankees	AL	OF	123	.321	362	262	1.382	175.0	193.6
3	Joe Morgan	1976	Reds	NL	2B	141	.320	459	344	1.334	221.8	193.5
4	Jeff Bagwell	1994	Astros	NL	1B	110	.368	394	279	1.412	187.9	191.2
5	Barry Bonds	1993	Giants	NL	OF	159	.336	529	388	1.363	244.3	185.8
6	Joe Morgan	1975	Reds	NL	2B	146	.327	461	354	1.302	208.6	182.6
7	Barry Bonds	1996	Giants	NL	OF	158	.308	516	382	1.351	230.4	180.7
8	Mike Schmidt	1981	Phillies	NL	3B	102	.316	320	258	1.240	138.9	176.7
9	Barry Bonds	1994	Giants	NL	OF	112	.312	365	284	1.285	154.2	173.1
10	Carl Yastrzemski	1967	Red Sox	AL	OF	161	.326	471	409	1.152	191.8	168.7

List #214: Worst Batting by Gold Glove Winner

Tommy Helms had difficulty fitting in with the Reds.

Helms was called up in September 1964 as a shortstop. But Cincinnati had no opening at that position, which was being handled capably by All-Star Leo Cardenas. So Helms was shuffled to third base in 1966, winning the Rookie of the Year Award in the process. He seemed to have found a home.

It was a premature conclusion. A promising young slugger, Tony Perez, was ready for a fulltime job in the majors. Perez could play first or third base, but Reds manager Dave Bristol believed he was better suited for the latter. So Helms was shifted again in 1967 to second base, where he would stay for the rest of his 14-year career.

Helms became proficient at his newest position, winning a pair of Gold Gloves as a second baseman, though his hitting tailed off badly. He had batted a solid .284 as Rookie of the Year, but he plummeted to .237 by 1970, the season that brought his first fielding award. His BPO+ of 55.8 was the worst for any Gold Glove winner in the Modern Era.

Managers recognize the value of good glovework, though most would opt for a solid batting average if given the choice. The Reds endured one more subpar BA from Helms, then dealt him to the Astros. The Red Sox did the same with the runner-up on this list, George Scott, trading him to the Brewers in 1971.

The Worst 10

Rk	Batter	Year	Team	Lg	Pos	G	BA	B	O	BPO	BV	BPO+
1	Tommy Helms	1970	Reds	NL	2B	150	.237	194	468	.415	-154.0	55.8
2	George Scott	1968	Red Sox	AL	1B	124	.171	123	314	.392	-87.9	58.3
3	Rey Ordonez	1997	Mets	NL	SS	120	.216	137	310	.442	-94.0	59.3
4	Jose Lind	1992	Pirates	NL	2B	135	.235	167	384	.435	-99.0	62.8
5	Rey Ordonez	1998	Mets	NL	SS	153	.246	197	417	.472	-115.2	63.1
6	Brad Ausmus	2006	Astros	NL	C	139	.230	191	372	.513	-102.5	65.1
7	Bengie Molina	2002	Angels	AL	C	122	.245	169	350	.483	-89.9	65.3
8	Bobby Wine	1963	Phillies	NL	SS	142	.215	152	350	.434	-79.0	65.8
9	Brad Ausmus	2001	Astros	NL	C	128	.232	187	346	.540	-90.5	67.4
10	Mike Matheny	2004	Cardinals	NL	C	122	.247	168	312	.538	-75.6	69.0

List #215: Best Pitching by Gold Glove Winner

A strange stability has always accompanied the Gold Gloves for pitchers. The same winners seem to be chosen year after year.

Jim Kaat was presented every Gold Glove for American League pitchers between 1962 and 1975 — 14 in a row. Greg Maddux nearly duplicated that streak, winning 13 straight National League Gold Gloves before inexplicably losing to Mike Hampton in 2003. Maddux bounced back in 2004 to start another five-year run.

It's always possible, of course, that Kaat and Maddux were stunningly superior in the field. But that doesn't explain how Kaat won a Gold Glove in 1972, even though injuries limited him to 15 starts for the Twins. Or how Maddux received the award in 1993, despite committing seven errors for the Braves, the most miscues by any NL pitcher.

It's just possible the voters weren't paying any attention.

Yet I digress. The point here isn't to find fault with the Gold Gloves, but to recognize the best pitching performances by Modern Era honorees. Maddux dominates the list, registering five of the seven lowest scores on the BPO+ scale.

His best year was 1995, when he went 19-2 with a 58.6 BPO+ for the Braves. His rewards were the Cy Young Award, third place in the balloting for Most Valuable Player, and (of course) yet another Gold Glove.

Zack Greinke had the best non-Maddux season, posting a 66.9 BPO+ for the Dodgers in 2015, when he earned his second straight Gold Glove.

The Best 10

Rk	Pitcher	Year	Team	Lg	G	ERA	B	O	BPO	BV	BPO+
1	Greg Maddux	1995	Braves	NL	28	1.63	256	633	.404	-181.0	58.6
2	Greg Maddux	1994	Braves	NL	25	1.56	258	614	.420	-167.3	60.7
3	Zack Greinke	2015	Dodgers	NL	32	1.66	278	671	.414	-137.4	66.9
4	Greg Maddux	1997	Braves	NL	33	2.20	328	698	.470	-153.7	68.1
5	Bob Gibson	1968	Cardinals	NL	34	1.12	346	917	.377	-146.5	70.3
6	Greg Maddux	1998	Braves	NL	34	2.22	374	766	.488	-146.8	71.8
7	Greg Maddux	1996	Braves	NL	35	2.72	380	750	.507	-144.4	72.5
8	Dallas Keuchel	2015	Astros	AL	33	2.48	330	694	.476	-119.1	73.5
9	Bret Saberhagen	1989	Royals	AL	36	2.16	370	789	.469	-131.4	73.8
10	Clayton Kershaw	2011	Dodgers	NL	33	2.28	335	704	.476	-118.4	73.9

List #216: Worst Pitching by Gold Glove Winner

Jim Kaat's streak of 14 consecutive American League Gold Gloves came to an end in 1975. It wasn't that the 37-year-old pitcher's fielding skills suddenly vanished. It was simply that the White Sox traded him to the Phillies in December, transferring him to the National League.

So Kaat started fresh, winning a pair of NL Gold Gloves in his first two seasons in Philadelphia. Yet he wasn't the same pitcher who had long bedeviled AL batters with a powerful fastball and deceptive curve. He began showing the wear and tear of his 3,638 innings of work for the old Senators, Twins, and White Sox.

Kaat's record in three-plus years with the Phillies was a mediocre 27-30 with a 4.23 ERA. He later concluded that his stint in Philadelphia (and subsequent stops with the Yankees and Cardinals) kept him from the Hall of Fame. "If my career ended after the 1975 season," he said, "I probably would be in already, because I was a much more dominant pitcher for that 15-year period of time."

Kaat's decline accelerated in 1977, his second year with the Phils. His ERA ballooned to 5.39, while his BPO+ inflated to 119.5. The latter remains the worst score for any pitcher honored with a Gold Glove.

The runner-up is Ron Darling, who won a single fielding award during his 13-year career. The irony is that his 1989 Gold Glove came in one of his lesser seasons on the mound (14-14 W-L, 112.7 BPO+).

The Worst 10

Rk	Pitcher	Year	Team	Lg	G	ERA	B	O	BPO	BV	BPO+
1	Jim Kaat	1977	Phillies	NL	35	5.39	392	480	.817	64.0	119.5
2	Ron Darling	1989	Mets	NL	33	3.52	438	656	.668	49.5	112.7
3	Ron Guidry	1984	Yankees	AL	29	4.51	429	596	.720	48.1	112.6
4	Phil Niekro	1983	Braves	NL	34	3.97	447	600	.745	46.8	111.7
5	Jim Kaat	1963	Twins	AL	31	4.19	365	538	.678	34.7	110.5
6	Mark Langston	1994	Angels	AL	18	4.68	277	353	.785	17.7	106.8
7	Greg Maddux	2007	Padres	NL	34	4.14	417	594	.702	23.9	106.1
8	Jim Kaat	1973	Twins-White Sox	AL	36	4.37	463	677	.684	20.7	104.7
9	Kenny Rogers	2004	Rangers	AL	35	4.76	483	635	.761	15.7	103.4
10	Mike Norris	1981	Athletics	AL	23	3.75	321	517	.621	10.3	103.3

29. MANAGERS OF THE YEAR

List #217: Best Record for a Manager of the Year

Three Hall of Fame players gave the Big Red Machine its power and direction. Catcher Johnny Bench, first baseman Tony Perez, and second baseman Joe Morgan combined for 7,297 hits, 15 Gold Gloves, and four Most Valuable Player trophies during their illustrious careers. This talented trio was instrumental in bringing consecutive world titles to Cincinnati in 1975 and 1976.

It's sometimes forgotten that a fourth member of those immortal squads is enshrined in Cooperstown. Not fiery third baseman Pete Rose, who was unable to control his darker impulses, but the team's manager, Sparky Anderson. "He was the man who put together some great teams," said Perez. "He made us go."

Yet even Hall of Famers can wear out their welcome. The Reds fired Anderson in 1978, freeing him to sign with the Tigers a season later. He again demonstrated the ability to assemble a powerful lineup, sweeping to the world title in 1984 with a 104-58 record and a 97.109 team score. He was the obvious choice as the American League's Manager of the Year.

No MOY honoree has posted a higher TS, though Anderson's achievement comes with an asterisk. Manager of the Year Awards were first presented in 1983, which is why you don't see anybody on this list from the 1960s or 1970s.

Joe Torre was the only other Manager of the Year with a TS above 83 points. His 1998 Yankees went 114-48 en route to a World Series sweep of the Padres.

The Best 10

Rk	Manager	Year	Team	Lg	W	L	Pct.	GB	Post	TS
1	Sparky Anderson	1984	Tigers	AL	104	58	.642	—	WLP	97.109
2	Joe Torre	1998	Yankees	AL	114	48	.704	—	WLP	96.123
3	Tom Kelly	1991	Twins	AL	95	67	.586	—	WLP	82.261
4	Lou Piniella	2001	Mariners	AL	116	46	.716	—	P	81.959
5	Whitey Herzog	1985	Cardinals	NL	101	61	.623	—	LP	80.680
6	Tony La Russa	1988	Athletics	AL	104	58	.642	—	LP	80.527
7	Mike Scioscia	2002	Angels	AL	99	63	.611	4.0	WLP	77.467
8	Bobby Cox	1991	Braves	NL	94	68	.580	—	LP	76.629
9	Felipe Alou	1994	Expos	NL	74	40	.649	—	—	75.628
10	Ozzie Guillen	2005	White Sox	AL	99	63	.611	—	WLP	75.291

List #218: Worst Record for a Manager of the Year

The Royals were expected to be terrible in 2003. Their collective record since 1995 was 170 games below .500. It was capped — perhaps not the best of verbs — by a 62-100 mark in 2002, the first 100-loss season in franchise history.

The team's new manager, Tony Pena, was known as an upbeat guy who always smiled. Pundits predicted that the Kansas City job would test his equanimity.

Pena inherited Carlos Beltran, Raul Ibanez, and Mike Sweeney, young sluggers who had combined for 77 homers the previous year. But his pitching staff was virtually bereft of talent. His ace was 31-year-old journeyman Darrell May, whose lifetime record to that point was 6-12.

Yet Pena motivated his underdogs to play hard. The Royals won their first nine games and took charge in the American League Central. They wouldn't surrender the divisional lead until late August. Their final record of 83-79 was a 21-game improvement from 2002.

Pena was named the AL Manager of the Year, despite his team's third-place finish and its TS of 43.371, the lowest score for any MOY honoree.

The experts were right on one count. The Royals eventually fell back into their losing habits, and Pena succumbed. He resigned in 2005. "It made me sick," he said. "I wasn't eating well or sleeping well."

Runner-up Joe Girardi was fired by the Marlins after being named National League Manager of the Year in 2006. He soon landed a better job with the Yankees.

The Worst 10

Rk	Manager	Year	Team	Lg	W	L	Pct.	GB	Post	TS
1	Tony Pena	2003	Royals	AL	83	79	.512	7.0	—	43.371
2	Joe Girardi	2006	Marlins	NL	78	84	.481	19.0	—	44.906
3	Frank Robinson	1989	Orioles	AL	87	75	.537	2.0	—	49.731
4	Jeff Banister	2015	Rangers	AL	88	74	.543	—	P	50.348
5	Larry Bowa	2001	Phillies	NL	86	76	.531	2.0	—	51.065
6	Don Baylor	1995	Rockies	NL	77	67	.535	1.0	P	51.516
7	Bob Melvin	2007	Diamondbacks	NL	90	72	.556	—	P	52.105
8	Dusty Baker	1997	Giants	NL	90	72	.556	—	P	52.297
9	Buck Showalter	2004	Rangers	AL	89	73	.549	3.0	—	53.535
10	Lou Piniella	1995	Mariners	AL	79	66	.545	—	P	54.377

List #219: Best Record that Didn't Win Manager of the Year

The Mets were pathetically bad prior to Davey Johnson's arrival in 1984. They floundered through seven consecutive losing seasons under four different managers, future Hall of Famer Joe Torre among them.

But the outlook turned sunny after the brashly confident Johnson took charge: 90 wins his first season, 98 the second. So what about 1986? "Next year, by God, nothing is going to stop us," he told his players.

They mimicked their manager's swagger — winning 16 of their first 20 games — as Johnson ceaselessly sang their praises. "I wanted my guys to know they were good," he said, "because if I don't feel that way, how can they?" The Mets pulled away to a 108-54 record, winning the National League East by 21-and-a-half games. They paced the league in both BA (.263) and ERA (3.11).

A come-from-behind World Series victory over the Red Sox capped the storybook season. Johnson said he wasn't surprised. "You don't win 108 games without having the wherewithal to know it's never over till it's over," he said. His 1986 Mets earned the third-best team score in the entire Modern Era, 94.962 points.

So who was named the NL's Manager of the Year? Hal Lanier of the 96-66 Astros. Johnson finished a distant second in the balloting, leaving him with the highest TS of any spurned MOY candidate.

Joe Maddon ranks second on this list. His 2016 Cubs went 103-58 and clinched a world title, yet the Dodgers' Dave Roberts was voted the NL award.

The Best 10

Rk	Manager	Year	Team	Lg	W	L	Pct.	GB	Post	TS
1	Davey Johnson	1986	Mets	NL	108	54	.667	—	WLP	94.962
2	Joe Maddon	2016	Cubs	NL	103	58	.640	—	WLP	92.166
3	Tony La Russa	1990	Athletics	AL	103	59	.636	—	LP	89.366
4	Joe Girardi	2009	Yankees	AL	103	59	.636	—	WLP	87.433
5	Mike Hargrove	1995	Indians	AL	100	44	.694	—	LP	87.220
6	Terry Francona	2007	Red Sox	AL	96	66	.593	—	WLP	85.711
7	Tony La Russa	1989	Athletics	AL	99	63	.611	—	WLP	85.486
8	Terry Francona	2004	Red Sox	AL	98	64	.605	3.0	WLP	84.936
9	Bobby Cox	1995	Braves	NL	90	54	.625	—	WLP	84.662
10	Joe Torre	1999	Yankees	AL	98	64	.605	—	WLP	83.564

List #220: Best Improvement to Win Manager of the Year

Braves president Stan Kasten faced an important decision. Bobby Cox, Atlanta's general manager since 1986, had fired manager Russ Nixon in June 1990 and assumed Nixon's responsibilities himself. Kasten had stipulated that Cox could keep only one of the two jobs after the season ended.

Now it was time to choose. Most observers expected Cox to return to the front office, though his record as GM was uninspiring. The Braves had suffered five straight losing seasons on his watch. But his 40-57 managerial mark in relief of Nixon didn't seem any better.

Kasten pondered these unpromising options. He finally decided to hire John Schuerholz as his new general manager. Cox would stay in the dugout.

It proved to be the right move. The Braves miraculously skyrocketed from the National League's worst record in 1990 (65-97) to the NL title in 1991. Third baseman Terry Pendleton (.319 BA, 117.7 BPO+) won the league's Most Valuable Player Award. Starter Tom Glavine (20-11 W-L, 82.8 BPO+) picked up the Cy Young Award. And Cox was named the NL's Manager of the Year.

No MOY winner has ever posted a bigger increase in team score. The Braves shot up 56.600 points from an anemic 1990 TS (20.029) to a solid 1991 score (76.629).

The runner-up in this category sat in the other dugout during the 1991 World Series. Tom Kelly not only boosted the Twins' TS by 49.898 points, but his team also edged the Braves for the championship.

The Best 10

Rk	Manager	MOY year	Team	Lg	Pct.	Post	TS	Prev pct.	Prev TS	TS change
1	Bobby Cox	1991	Braves	NL	.580	LP	76.629	.401	20.029	56.600
2	Tom Kelly	1991	Twins	AL	.586	WLP	82.261	.457	32.363	49.898
3	Joe Maddon	2008	Rays	AL	.599	LP	73.410	.407	24.089	49.321
4	Tom Lasorda	1988	Dodgers	NL	.584	WLP	74.718	.451	33.288	41.430
5	Frank Robinson	1989	Orioles	AL	.537	—	49.731	.335	9.850	39.881
6	Dusty Baker	1993	Giants	NL	.636	—	69.504	.444	30.005	39.499
7	Jim Frey	1984	Cubs	NL	.596	P	69.775	.438	32.512	37.263
8	Mike Scioscia	2002	Angels	AL	.611	WLP	77.467	.463	40.612	36.855
9	Jim Leyland	2006	Tigers	AL	.586	LP	70.822	.438	34.583	36.239
10	Terry Francona	2013	Indians	AL	.568	P	57.046	.420	21.658	35.388

List #221: Worst Decline After Winning Manager of the Year

Oddsmakers installed the Tigers as overwhelming favorites for the American League title in 1985. No other choice made sense. Sparky Anderson's squad had dominated the previous season — winning the AL East by a 15-game margin, sweeping the Royals for the league championship, and subduing the Padres in the World Series.

Those 1984 Tigers would go down as the greatest team of the Modern Era, based on their TS of 97.109. And all of their key players were returning, led by right fielder Kirk Gibson (137.8 BPO+ in 1984), shortstop Alan Trammell (123.8), center fielder Chet Lemon (119.3), starter Jack Morris (19 W), and closer Willie Hernandez (32 S).

Anderson had been named the league's Manager of the Year in 1984, though he characteristically downplayed his role. The secret, he said, was to stay out of the way and let his players win. It seemed a logical approach when the Tigers swept their first six games in 1985. But they unexpectedly began to struggle, slipping eight-and-a-half games behind the Blue Jays by early June. Then they disintegrated, going 36-40 after the All-Star break.

Gibson enjoyed another strong season, but he was an exception. The Tigers finished with a mediocre 84-77 record, down from 104-58 in 1984. Their TS plummeted by 42.700 points, the sharpest decline for any team led by the previous year's Manager of the Year.

Runner-up Ron Gardenhire suffered a 42.062-point drop with the Twins in 2011, following a 94-68 MOY season with a mark of 63-99.

The Worst 10

Rk	Manager	MOY year	Team	Lg	Pct.	Post	TS	Next pct.	Next TS	TS change
1	Sparky Anderson	1984	Tigers	AL	.642	WLP	97.109	.522	54.409	-42.700
2	Ron Gardenhire	2010	Twins	AL	.580	P	60.262	.389	18.200	-42.062
3	Tony La Russa	1992	Athletics	AL	.593	P	63.655	.420	22.975	-40.680
4	Felipe Alou	1994	Expos	NL	.649	—	75.628	.458	37.381	-38.247
5	Whitey Herzog	1985	Cardinals	NL	.623	LP	80.680	.491	42.630	-38.050
6	Mike Scioscia	2002	Angels	AL	.611	WLP	77.467	.475	43.501	-33.966
7	Tony La Russa	1983	White Sox	AL	.611	P	69.732	.457	36.729	-33.003
8	Jim Leyland	1992	Pirates	NL	.593	P	67.165	.463	34.390	-32.775
9	John McNamara	1986	Red Sox	AL	.590	LP	74.764	.481	43.608	-31.156
10	Bruce Bochy	1996	Padres	NL	.562	P	64.199	.469	33.262	-30.937

CONCLUSION

The Seasons

Welcome to the final chapter of this book. And a large one it is, spanning 225 pages from beginning to end.

You'll find five charts for each league in each season of the Modern Era. The concepts and abbreviations should be familiar by now. If a question or two remain, turn to pages 33-39 for a quick refresher course.

Each year's **Standings** are based on TS, while BPO+ is the standard for **Best Batters** and **Best Pitchers**. Keep in mind that team scores from different seasons are directly comparable, as are BPO+ readings. The 1961 Orioles, with a TS of 61.019, were the mirror image of the 2001 Giants (61.023). Frank Robinson, the National League's top batter in 1962 with a BPO+ of 155.5, performed at essentially the same level as Miguel Cabrera (155.3), the American League's runner-up in 2011.

The remaining two charts, **Extremes for Batters** and **Extremes for Pitchers**, show the best and worst performances in nine categories. Rankings of adjusted statistics (anything that ends with a + sign) have been limited to players who met the qualification standards of 3.1 plate appearances or one inning pitched per game. (The same limitation applies to the Best Batters and Best Pitchers charts.) The other extreme categories are open to all comers.

The first extreme for batters is base value (BV), followed by measures of run production (SE+ and SCV), power hitting (ISO+ and EXV), contact hitting (CT+ and SOV), and batting eye (EY+ and BBV). See pages 50-55 and 62-71 for details on these categories.

BV also is the initial extreme for pitchers, followed by run prevention (ERA+ and ERV), power prevention (ISO+ and EXV), power pitching (CT+ and SOV), and control pitching (EY+ and BBV). Go to pages 56-61 and 72-81 to learn more.

1961 American League

Standings

Rank	Team	Post	W	L	Pct.	R	RA	BPO	BPOA	TS
1	New York Yankees	WLP	109	53	.673	5.07	3.75	.729	.617	85.319
2	Detroit Tigers	—	101	61	.623	5.16	4.12	.749	.640	68.177
3	Baltimore Orioles	—	95	67	.586	4.24	3.61	.663	.584	61.019
4	Chicago White Sox	—	86	76	.531	4.69	4.45	.694	.683	50.107
5	Cleveland Indians	—	78	83	.484	4.58	4.67	.674	.689	42.862
6	Minnesota Twins	—	70	90	.438	4.39	4.83	.674	.683	37.440
7	Los Angeles Angels	—	70	91	.435	4.59	4.84	.695	.722	37.242
8	Boston Red Sox	—	76	86	.469	4.47	4.86	.664	.730	36.826
9	Washington Senators	—	61	100	.379	3.84	4.82	.631	.703	25.775
10	Kansas City Athletics	—	61	100	.379	4.22	5.33	.626	.747	22.027

Best Batters

Rank	Batter	Team	G	BA	B	O	BPO	BV	BPO+
1	Mickey Mantle	Yankees	153	.317	497	360	1.381	236.8	191.0
2	Norm Cash	Tigers	159	.361	502	367	1.368	226.6	182.3
3	Jim Gentile	Orioles	148	.302	430	360	1.194	170.7	165.9
4	Harmon Killebrew	Twins	150	.288	444	403	1.102	142.1	147.1
5	Roger Maris	Yankees	161	.269	474	454	1.044	145.9	144.5
6	Rocky Colavito	Tigers	163	.290	464	440	1.055	133.8	140.5
7	Roy Sievers	White Sox	141	.295	336	362	.928	70.8	126.7
8	Al Kaline	Tigers	153	.324	395	422	.936	78.3	124.7
9	John Romano	Indians	142	.299	317	372	.852	49.3	118.4
10	Norm Siebern	Athletics	153	.296	357	408	.875	54.9	118.2

Extremes for Batters

Batter	Team	Best		Batter	Team	Worst
Mickey Mantle	Yankees	236.8	BV	Bobby Richardson	Yankees	-116.0
Mickey Mantle	Yankees	155.4	SE+	Ron Hansen	Orioles	71.6
Mickey Mantle	Yankees	73.1	SCV	Ron Hansen	Orioles	-35.7
Mickey Mantle	Yankees	255.9	ISO+	Nellie Fox	White Sox	30.5
Roger Maris	Yankees	121.8	EXV	Chuck Schilling	Red Sox	-61.6
Nellie Fox	White Sox	657.2	CT+	Ken Hunt	Angels	56.5
Nellie Fox	White Sox	-66.9	SOV	Jake Wood	Tigers	52.9
Mickey Mantle	Yankees	190.3	EY+	Tony Kubek	Yankees	41.1
Mickey Mantle	Yankees	55.5	BBV	Bobby Richardson	Yankees	-38.9

Best Pitchers

Rank	Pitcher	Team	G	ERA	B	O	BPO	BV	BPO+
1	Bill Stafford	Yankees	36	2.68	314	592	.530	-64.4	83.0
2	Jim Bunning	Tigers	38	3.19	463	827	.560	-89.6	83.8
3	Frank Lary	Tigers	36	3.24	470	837	.562	-89.3	84.0
4	Dick Donovan	Senators	23	2.40	281	514	.547	-52.9	84.2
5	Steve Barber	Orioles	37	3.33	417	757	.551	-70.3	85.6
6	Whitey Ford	Yankees	39	3.21	469	855	.549	-77.5	85.8
7	Hal Brown	Orioles	27	3.19	275	497	.553	-44.9	86.0
8	Camilo Pascual	Twins	35	3.46	449	771	.582	-68.0	86.8
9	Ralph Terry	Yankees	31	3.15	318	565	.563	-43.1	88.1
10	Milt Pappas	Orioles	26	3.04	306	539	.568	-40.9	88.2

Extremes for Pitchers

Pitcher	Team	Best		Pitcher	Team	Worst
Jim Bunning	Tigers	-89.6	BV	Frank Baumann	White Sox	80.1
Dick Donovan	Senators	63.8	ERA+	Frank Baumann	White Sox	148.7
Don Mossi	Tigers	-26.9	ERV	Frank Baumann	White Sox	38.3
Steve Barber	Orioles	57.5	ISO+	Gene Conley	Red Sox	125.0
Steve Barber	Orioles	-50.2	EXV	Pedro Ramos	Twins	33.7
Juan Pizarro	White Sox	58.4	CT+	Jerry Walker	Athletics	176.5
Juan Pizarro	White Sox	78.3	SOV	Joe McClain	Senators	-50.1
Don Mossi	Tigers	52.9	EY+	Chuck Estrada	Orioles	171.2
Don Mossi	Tigers	-39.2	BBV	Chuck Estrada	Orioles	54.9

1961 National League

Standings

Rank	Team	Post	W	L	Pct.	R	RA	BPO	BPOA	TS
1	Cincinnati Reds	LP	93	61	.604	4.61	4.24	.694	.662	68.297
2	San Francisco Giants	—	85	69	.552	4.99	4.23	.709	.662	59.555
3	Los Angeles Dodgers	—	89	65	.578	4.77	4.53	.712	.691	55.658
4	Milwaukee Braves	—	83	71	.539	4.59	4.23	.699	.669	54.017
5	Saint Louis Cardinals	—	80	74	.519	4.54	4.31	.672	.681	47.824
6	Pittsburgh Pirates	—	75	79	.487	4.51	4.38	.668	.659	46.132
7	Chicago Cubs	—	64	90	.416	4.42	5.13	.695	.705	32.636
8	Philadelphia Phillies	—	47	107	.305	3.77	5.14	.606	.724	8.887

Best Batters

Rank	Batter	Team	G	BA	B	O	BPO	BV	BPO+
1	Frank Robinson	Reds	153	.323	446	397	1.123	151.3	151.3
2	Willie Mays	Giants	154	.308	439	423	1.038	133.4	143.7
3	Hank Aaron	Braves	155	.327	447	441	1.014	134.7	143.1
4	Eddie Mathews	Braves	152	.306	418	419	.998	121.2	140.9
5	Orlando Cepeda	Giants	152	.311	419	435	.963	104.7	133.3
6	Wally Moon	Dodgers	134	.328	339	333	1.018	80.4	131.1
7	George Altman	Cubs	138	.303	351	378	.929	70.7	125.2
8	Roberto Clemente	Pirates	146	.351	366	394	.929	70.8	124.0
9	Ken Boyer	Cardinals	153	.329	394	414	.952	71.6	122.2
10	Vada Pinson	Reds	154	.343	381	430	.886	61.8	119.4

Extremes for Batters

Batter	Team	Best		Batter	Team	Worst
Frank Robinson	Reds	151.3	BV	Don Blasingame	Giants-Reds	-89.1
Willie Mays	Giants	152.6	SE+	Roy McMillan	Braves	69.2
Willie Mays	Giants	73.0	SCV	Roy McMillan	Braves	-37.0
Orlando Cepeda	Giants	191.8	ISO+	Julian Javier	Cardinals	33.2
Orlando Cepeda	Giants	83.3	EXV	Maury Wills	Dodgers	-65.2
Dick Groat	Pirates	189.8	CT+	Dick Stuart	Pirates	61.6
Dick Groat	Pirates	-39.5	SOV	Pancho Herrera	Phillies	65.5
Jim Gilliam	Dodgers	180.4	EY+	Bill Mazeroski	Pirates	33.6
Eddie Mathews	Braves	38.4	BBV	Bill Mazeroski	Pirates	-31.6

Best Pitchers

Rank	Pitcher	Team	G	ERA	B	O	BPO	BV	BPO+
1	Sandy Koufax	Dodgers	42	3.52	456	778	.586	-85.8	84.2
2	Jim O'Toole	Reds	39	3.10	440	763	.577	-69.5	86.4
3	Larry Jackson	Cardinals	33	3.75	389	636	.612	-57.0	87.2
4	Joe Gibbon	Pirates	30	3.32	353	589	.599	-42.7	89.2
5	Warren Spahn	Braves	38	3.02	455	794	.573	-48.6	90.3
6	Don Cardwell	Cubs	39	3.82	483	786	.615	-48.4	90.9
7	Curt Simmons	Cardinals	30	3.13	381	594	.641	-35.5	91.5
8	Joey Jay	Reds	34	3.53	460	742	.620	-35.4	92.8
9	Stan Williams	Dodgers	41	3.90	462	709	.652	-31.8	93.6
9	Harvey Haddix	Pirates	29	4.10	295	469	.629	-20.0	93.6

Extremes for Pitchers

Pitcher	Team	Best		Pitcher	Team	Worst
Sandy Koufax	Dodgers	-85.8	BV	Robin Roberts	Phillies	60.0
Curt Simmons	Cardinals	72.7	ERA+	Jack Curtis	Cubs	119.9
Curt Simmons	Cardinals	-25.5	ERV	Chris Short	Phillies	27.9
Curt Simmons	Cardinals	71.5	ISO+	Art Mahaffey	Phillies	127.2
Don Cardwell	Cubs	-33.6	EXV	Art Mahaffey	Phillies	31.7
Sandy Koufax	Dodgers	57.0	CT+	Jack Curtis	Cubs	194.0
Sandy Koufax	Dodgers	115.6	SOV	Lew Burdette	Braves	-75.3
Lew Burdette	Braves	37.4	EY+	Bob Gibson	Cardinals	165.6
Lew Burdette	Braves	-50.1	BBV	Bob Gibson	Cardinals	44.3

1962 American League

Standings

Rank	Team	Post	W	L	Pct.	R	RA	BPO	BPOA	TS
1	New York Yankees	WLP	96	66	.593	5.04	4.20	.723	.631	85.088
2	Minnesota Twins	—	91	71	.562	4.90	4.37	.713	.649	62.387
3	Detroit Tigers	—	85	76	.528	4.71	4.30	.712	.661	56.604
4	Chicago White Sox	—	85	77	.525	4.36	4.06	.663	.633	53.473
5	Los Angeles Angels	—	86	76	.531	4.43	4.36	.660	.657	49.734
6	Baltimore Orioles	—	77	85	.475	4.02	4.20	.643	.651	40.569
7	Cleveland Indians	—	80	82	.494	4.21	4.60	.644	.687	37.638
8	Boston Red Sox	—	76	84	.475	4.42	4.73	.669	.709	36.633
9	Kansas City Athletics	—	72	90	.444	4.60	5.17	.676	.761	27.133
10	Washington Senators	—	60	101	.373	3.70	4.42	.620	.677	20.181

Best Batters

Rank	Batter	Team	G	BA	B	O	BPO	BV	BPO+
1	Mickey Mantle	Yankees	123	.321	362	262	1.382	175.0	193.6
2	Norm Cash	Tigers	148	.243	388	405	.958	90.9	130.6
3	Norm Siebern	Athletics	162	.308	419	437	.959	97.6	130.4
4	Harmon Killebrew	Twins	155	.243	416	438	.950	96.8	130.3
5	Bob Allison	Twins	149	.266	367	401	.915	74.8	125.6
6	Rocky Colavito	Tigers	161	.273	417	463	.901	77.4	122.8
7	Joe Cunningham	White Sox	149	.295	354	400	.885	64.9	122.4
8	John Romano	Indians	135	.261	309	365	.847	51.7	120.1
9	Roger Maris	Yankees	157	.256	384	450	.853	62.9	119.6
10	Pete Runnels	Red Sox	152	.326	347	394	.881	55.1	118.9

Extremes for Batters

Batter	Team	Best		Batter	Team	Worst
Mickey Mantle	Yankees	175.0	BV	Nellie Fox	White Sox	-75.7
Mickey Mantle	Yankees	150.7	SE+	Jim Piersall	Senators	60.3
Mickey Mantle	Yankees	52.1	SCV	Jim Piersall	Senators	-42.7
Harmon Killebrew	Twins	195.8	ISO+	Nellie Fox	White Sox	50.9
Harmon Killebrew	Twins	81.7	EXV	Nellie Fox	White Sox	-45.4
Nellie Fox	White Sox	663.2	CT+	Harmon Killebrew	Twins	49.6
Nellie Fox	White Sox	-67.6	SOV	Harmon Killebrew	Twins	71.5
Mickey Mantle	Yankees	259.1	EY+	Vic Power	Twins	37.7
Mickey Mantle	Yankees	69.4	BBV	Vic Power	Twins	-36.4

Best Pitchers

Rank	Pitcher	Team	G	ERA	B	O	BPO	BV	BPO+
1	Hank Aguirre	Tigers	42	2.21	318	660	.482	-117.5	73.0
2	Jim Kaat	Twins	39	3.14	466	816	.571	-68.7	87.2
3	Eddie Fisher	White Sox	57	3.10	315	552	.571	-44.4	87.7
4	Camilo Pascual	Twins	34	3.32	450	781	.576	-61.8	87.9
5	Ray Herbert	White Sox	35	3.27	414	710	.583	-48.2	89.6
6	Bill Monbouquette	Red Sox	35	3.33	432	709	.609	-46.9	90.2
7	Ralph Terry	Yankees	43	3.19	517	898	.576	-55.6	90.3
8	Whitey Ford	Yankees	38	2.90	453	780	.581	-44.4	91.1
9	Robin Roberts	Orioles	27	2.78	334	575	.581	-29.5	91.9
10	Dick Donovan	Indians	34	3.59	447	756	.591	-37.7	92.2
10	Tom Cheney	Senators	37	3.17	316	523	.604	-26.7	92.2

Extremes for Pitchers

Pitcher	Team	Best		Pitcher	Team	Worst
Hank Aguirre	Tigers	-117.5	BV	Jerry Walker	Athletics	95.6
Hank Aguirre	Tigers	56.6	ERA+	Don Schwall	Red Sox	124.1
Hank Aguirre	Tigers	-40.7	ERV	Jerry Walker	Athletics	29.4
Hank Aguirre	Tigers	62.6	ISO+	Pedro Ramos	Indians	129.7
Hank Aguirre	Tigers	-40.5	EXV	Jerry Walker	Athletics	40.7
Tom Cheney	Senators	65.6	CT+	Dick Donovan	Indians	162.7
Dick Radatz	Red Sox	74.2	SOV	Dick Donovan	Indians	-58.9
Dick Donovan	Indians	48.9	EY+	Don Schwall	Red Sox	174.3
Dick Donovan	Indians	-43.9	BBV	Don Schwall	Red Sox	51.2

1962 National League

Standings

Rank	Team	Post	W	L	Pct.	R	RA	BPO	BPOA	TS
1	San Francisco Giants	LP	103	62	.624	5.32	4.18	.745	.634	74.066
2	Los Angeles Dodgers	—	102	63	.618	5.10	4.22	.721	.617	64.068
3	Cincinnati Reds	—	98	64	.605	4.95	4.23	.699	.670	58.027
4	Pittsburgh Pirates	—	93	68	.578	4.39	3.89	.646	.629	54.334
5	Milwaukee Braves	—	86	76	.531	4.51	4.10	.683	.643	51.949
6	Saint Louis Cardinals	—	84	78	.519	4.75	4.07	.677	.647	51.736
7	Philadelphia Phillies	—	81	80	.503	4.38	4.71	.675	.713	42.071
8	Houston Colt .45s	—	64	96	.400	3.65	4.43	.590	.644	31.820
9	Chicago Cubs	—	59	103	.364	3.90	5.10	.635	.726	25.070
10	New York Mets	—	40	120	.250	3.83	5.89	.628	.771	10.038

Best Batters

Rank	Batter	Team	G	BA	B	O	BPO	BV	BPO+
1	Frank Robinson	Reds	162	.342	490	428	1.145	174.9	155.5
2	Hank Aaron	Braves	156	.323	456	428	1.065	153.2	150.6
3	Willie Mays	Giants	162	.304	485	456	1.064	157.3	148.0
4	Eddie Mathews	Braves	152	.265	377	411	.917	86.3	129.7
5	Tommy Davis	Dodgers	163	.346	420	469	.896	91.6	127.9
6	Bob Skinner	Pirates	144	.302	354	376	.941	77.1	127.8
7	George Altman	Cubs	147	.318	361	381	.948	77.9	127.5
8	Frank Howard	Dodgers	141	.296	322	370	.870	62.9	124.3
9	Stan Musial	Cardinals	135	.330	295	308	.958	55.3	123.1
10	Felipe Alou	Giants	154	.316	343	402	.853	54.1	118.7

Extremes for Batters

Batter	Team	Best		Batter	Team	Worst
Frank Robinson	Reds	174.9	BV	Bill Virdon	Pirates	-112.1
Tommy Davis	Dodgers	170.7	SE+	Andre Rodgers	Cubs	68.5
Tommy Davis	Dodgers	101.9	SCV	Ron Santo	Cubs	-43.0
Willie Mays	Giants	216.9	ISO+	Don Blasingame	Reds	39.7
Willie Mays	Giants	104.0	EXV	Dick Groat	Pirates	-57.9
Jim Gilliam	Dodgers	226.8	CT+	Frank Howard	Dodgers	61.6
Jim Gilliam	Dodgers	-44.4	SOV	Mack Jones	Braves	52.4
Eddie Mathews	Braves	187.2	EY+	Bill Mazeroski	Pirates	43.5
Eddie Mathews	Braves	43.8	BBV	Tommy Davis	Dodgers	-29.0

Best Pitchers

Rank	Pitcher	Team	G	ERA	B	O	BPO	BV	BPO+
1	Bob Gibson	Cardinals	32	2.85	379	713	.532	-116.2	76.5
2	Sandy Koufax	Dodgers	28	2.54	266	559	.476	-80.6	76.8
3	Don Drysdale	Dodgers	43	2.83	512	954	.537	-79.5	86.6
4	Bob Purkey	Reds	37	2.81	495	864	.573	-72.3	87.3
5	Billy O'Dell	Giants	43	3.53	477	855	.558	-67.1	87.7
6	Warren Spahn	Braves	34	3.04	453	803	.564	-53.7	89.4
7	Bob Friend	Pirates	39	3.06	469	795	.590	-55.2	89.5
7	Jim O'Toole	Reds	36	3.50	443	754	.588	-52.0	89.5
9	Earl Francis	Pirates	36	3.07	317	530	.598	-32.5	90.7
10	Turk Farrell	Colt .45s	43	3.02	425	734	.579	-40.1	91.4

Extremes for Pitchers

Pitcher	Team	Best		Pitcher	Team	Worst
Bob Gibson	Cardinals	-116.2	BV	Mike McCormick	Giants	62.7
Bob Gibson	Cardinals	68.7	ERA+	Jack Hamilton	Phillies	135.8
Bob Purkey	Reds	-34.8	ERV	Jack Hamilton	Phillies	27.2
Earl Francis	Pirates	63.7	ISO+	Don Cardwell	Cubs	130.6
Bob Gibson	Cardinals	-41.0	EXV	Lew Burdette	Braves	44.1
Sandy Koufax	Dodgers	51.0	CT+	Larry Jackson	Cardinals	147.9
Sandy Koufax	Dodgers	105.9	SOV	Larry Jackson	Cardinals	-53.7
Bob Shaw	Braves	50.8	EY+	Jack Hamilton	Phillies	160.0
Bob Friend	Pirates	-38.6	BBV	Jack Hamilton	Phillies	37.1

1963 American League

Standings

Rank	Team	Post	W	L	Pct.	R	RA	BPO	BPOA	TS
1	New York Yankees	LP	104	57	.646	4.43	3.40	.651	.578	77.023
2	Minnesota Twins	—	91	70	.565	4.76	3.74	.712	.608	64.600
3	Chicago White Sox	—	94	68	.580	4.22	3.36	.641	.564	63.155
4	Baltimore Orioles	—	86	76	.531	3.98	3.83	.637	.637	49.116
5	Detroit Tigers	—	79	83	.488	4.32	4.34	.665	.665	44.337
6	Cleveland Indians	—	79	83	.488	3.92	4.33	.627	.632	41.587
7	Boston Red Sox	—	76	85	.472	4.14	4.37	.643	.658	40.641
8	Los Angeles Angels	—	70	91	.435	3.71	4.10	.594	.630	34.876
9	Kansas City Athletics	—	73	89	.451	3.80	4.35	.604	.680	32.650
10	Washington Senators	—	56	106	.346	3.57	5.01	.586	.707	14.790

Best Batters

Rank	Batter	Team	G	BA	B	O	BPO	BV	BPO+
1	Bob Allison	Twins	148	.271	386	398	.970	116.3	143.1
2	Carl Yastrzemski	Red Sox	151	.321	377	406	.929	96.7	134.5
3	Harmon Killebrew	Twins	142	.258	367	404	.908	93.2	134.0
4	Tom Tresh	Yankees	145	.269	350	394	.888	85.1	132.1
5	Norm Cash	Tigers	147	.270	334	377	.886	75.1	129.0
6	Al Kaline	Tigers	145	.312	354	402	.881	77.9	128.2
7	Albie Pearson	Angels	154	.304	353	428	.825	77.1	127.9
8	Jimmie Hall	Twins	156	.260	336	390	.862	71.7	127.1
9	Elston Howard	Yankees	135	.287	301	367	.820	54.3	122.0
10	Earl Battey	Twins	147	.285	320	388	.825	57.0	121.7

Extremes for Batters

Batter	Team	Best		Batter	Team	Worst
Bob Allison	Twins	116.3	**BV**	Chuck Schilling	Red Sox	-78.3
Al Kaline	Tigers	133.1	**SE+**	Chuck Schilling	Red Sox	70.4
Al Kaline	Tigers	40.6	**SCV**	Chuck Schilling	Red Sox	-36.9
Harmon Killebrew	Twins	200.4	**ISO+**	Nellie Fox	White Sox	33.6
Harmon Killebrew	Twins	76.6	**EXV**	Nellie Fox	White Sox	-49.4
Nellie Fox	White Sox	445.6	**CT+**	Dave Nicholson	White Sox	36.1
Bobby Richardson	Yankees	-69.5	**SOV**	Dave Nicholson	White Sox	111.9
Bob Allison	Twins	180.5	**EY+**	Joe Pepitone	Yankees	44.5
Bob Allison	Twins	39.2	**BBV**	Bobby Richardson	Yankees	-26.4

Best Pitchers

Rank	Pitcher	Team	G	ERA	B	O	BPO	BV	BPO+
1	Gary Peters	White Sox	41	2.33	355	730	.486	-92.0	79.4
2	Al Downing	Yankees	24	2.56	255	525	.486	-64.7	79.8
3	Juan Pizarro	White Sox	32	2.39	333	646	.515	-62.6	84.2
4	Ray Herbert	White Sox	33	3.24	351	678	.518	-64.1	84.5
5	Moe Drabowsky	Athletics	26	3.05	295	517	.571	-40.7	87.9
6	Camilo Pascual	Twins	31	2.46	409	746	.548	-49.0	89.3
7	Jim Bouton	Yankees	40	2.53	408	748	.545	-47.5	89.6
8	Whitey Ford	Yankees	38	2.74	441	803	.549	-48.0	90.2
9	Ralph Terry	Yankees	40	3.22	452	811	.557	-41.9	91.5
9	Jack Kralick	Twins-Indians	33	3.03	378	670	.564	-35.4	91.5

Extremes for Pitchers

Pitcher	Team	Best		Pitcher	Team	Worst
Gary Peters	White Sox	-92.0	**BV**	Jim Duckworth	Senators	73.4
Gary Peters	White Sox	69.7	**ERA+**	Don Rudolph	Senators	127.8
Camilo Pascual	Twins	-28.2	**ERV**	Jim Duckworth	Senators	33.2
Gary Peters	White Sox	55.9	**ISO+**	Robin Roberts	Orioles	137.2
Gary Peters	White Sox	-48.9	**EXV**	Robin Roberts	Orioles	45.8
Al Downing	Yankees	61.2	**CT+**	Jim Perry	Indians-Twins	163.5
Dick Radatz	Red Sox	81.9	**SOV**	Ralph Terry	Yankees	-57.7
Dick Donovan	Indians	38.1	**EY+**	Dave Morehead	Red Sox	179.5
Bill Monbouquette	Red Sox	-41.9	**BBV**	Dave Morehead	Red Sox	43.0

1963 National League

Standings

Rank	Team	Post	W	L	Pct.	R	RA	BPO	BPOA	TS
1	Los Angeles Dodgers	WLP	99	63	.611	3.93	3.37	.609	.559	75.294
2	Saint Louis Cardinals	—	93	69	.574	4.61	3.88	.675	.604	61.183
3	San Francisco Giants	—	88	74	.543	4.48	3.96	.670	.604	56.764
4	Cincinnati Reds	—	86	76	.531	4.00	3.67	.629	.594	52.525
5	Philadelphia Phillies	—	87	75	.537	3.96	3.57	.621	.620	51.210
6	Milwaukee Braves	—	84	78	.519	4.15	3.70	.631	.611	51.182
7	Chicago Cubs	—	82	80	.506	3.52	3.57	.594	.583	46.473
8	Pittsburgh Pirates	—	74	88	.457	3.50	3.67	.593	.595	40.543
9	Houston Colt .45s	—	66	96	.407	2.86	3.95	.506	.586	25.536
10	New York Mets	—	51	111	.315	3.09	4.78	.524	.690	8.162

Best Batters

Rank	Batter	Team	G	BA	B	O	BPO	BV	BPO+
1	Hank Aaron	Braves	161	.319	484	451	1.073	190.2	164.8
2	Willie Mays	Giants	157	.314	430	434	.991	148.5	152.8
3	Orlando Cepeda	Giants	156	.316	384	420	.914	111.6	141.0
4	Willie McCovey	Giants	152	.280	383	419	.914	111.3	140.9
5	Eddie Mathews	Braves	158	.263	379	419	.905	106.1	138.9
6	Frank Robinson	Reds	140	.259	337	377	.894	87.9	135.3
7	Vada Pinson	Reds	162	.313	405	478	.847	89.1	128.2
8	Johnny Callison	Phillies	157	.284	388	473	.820	75.8	124.3
9	Billy Williams	Cubs	161	.286	386	460	.839	71.8	122.8
10	Tony Gonzalez	Phillies	155	.306	325	413	.787	52.4	119.2

Extremes for Batters

Batter	Team	Best		Batter	Team	Worst
Hank Aaron	Braves	190.2	BV	Bob Lillis	Colt .45s	-109.7
Hank Aaron	Braves	155.3	SE+	Andre Rodgers	Cubs	65.8
Hank Aaron	Braves	73.7	SCV	Dick Bertell	Cubs	-43.0
Willie McCovey	Giants	220.0	ISO+	Maury Wills	Dodgers	39.1
Willie McCovey	Giants	87.8	EXV	Dick Schofield	Pirates	-43.0
Jim Gilliam	Dodgers	275.9	CT+	Donn Clendenon	Pirates	62.0
Jim Gilliam	Dodgers	-49.2	SOV	Howie Goss	Colt .45s	64.3
Eddie Mathews	Braves	234.3	EY+	Leo Cardenas	Reds	42.8
Eddie Mathews	Braves	63.1	BBV	Julian Javier	Cardinals	-23.8

Best Pitchers

Rank	Pitcher	Team	G	ERA	B	O	BPO	BV	BPO+
1	Dick Ellsworth	Cubs	37	2.11	401	890	.451	-145.2	73.4
2	Sandy Koufax	Dodgers	40	1.88	394	945	.417	-139.4	73.9
3	Larry Jackson	Cubs	37	2.55	424	842	.504	-92.8	82.0
4	Bob Friend	Pirates	39	2.34	403	829	.486	-86.9	82.3
5	Curt Simmons	Cardinals	32	2.48	369	704	.524	-71.9	83.7
6	Jim Maloney	Reds	33	2.77	383	758	.505	-62.5	86.0
7	Juan Marichal	Giants	41	2.41	481	974	.494	-77.5	86.1
8	Turk Farrell	Colt .45s	34	3.02	311	613	.507	-40.8	88.4
9	Joe Nuxhall	Reds	35	2.61	347	663	.523	-42.7	89.0
10	Jim O'Toole	Reds	33	2.88	377	708	.532	-39.1	90.6

Extremes for Pitchers

Pitcher	Team	Best		Pitcher	Team	Worst
Dick Ellsworth	Cubs	-145.2	BV	Tracy Stallard	Mets	71.2
Dick Ellsworth	Cubs	61.9	ERA+	Joey Jay	Reds	133.0
Dick Ellsworth	Cubs	-41.9	ERV	Jay Hook	Mets	36.7
Dick Ellsworth	Cubs	58.3	ISO+	Denny Lemaster	Braves	131.2
Dick Ellsworth	Cubs	-54.3	EXV	Tracy Stallard	Mets	31.9
Jim Maloney	Reds	61.8	CT+	Lew Burdette	Braves-Cardinals	170.9
Sandy Koufax	Dodgers	109.7	SOV	Warren Spahn	Braves	-71.3
Bob Friend	Pirates	51.3	EY+	Ray Culp	Phillies	169.9
Don Drysdale	Dodgers	-36.1	BBV	Ray Culp	Phillies	38.7

1964 American League

Standings

Rank	Team	Post	W	L	Pct.	R	RA	BPO	BPOA	TS
1	New York Yankees	LP	99	63	.611	4.45	3.52	.647	.585	73.134
2	Chicago White Sox	—	98	64	.605	3.96	3.09	.627	.535	65.632
3	Baltimore Orioles	—	97	65	.599	4.17	3.48	.654	.599	61.704
4	Detroit Tigers	—	85	77	.525	4.29	4.16	.666	.627	50.937
5	Minnesota Twins	—	79	83	.488	4.52	4.16	.708	.644	50.685
6	Los Angeles Angels	—	82	80	.506	3.36	3.40	.574	.574	45.853
7	Cleveland Indians	—	79	83	.488	4.20	4.23	.638	.653	43.453
8	Boston Red Sox	—	72	90	.444	4.25	4.90	.674	.742	32.571
9	Washington Senators	—	62	100	.383	3.57	4.52	.583	.675	23.872
10	Kansas City Athletics	—	57	105	.352	3.81	5.13	.628	.767	16.031

Best Batters

Rank	Batter	Team	G	BA	B	O	BPO	BV	BPO+
1	Mickey Mantle	Yankees	143	.303	383	339	1.130	146.4	161.9
2	Boog Powell	Orioles	134	.290	339	314	1.080	120.0	154.8
3	Bob Allison	Twins	149	.287	384	362	1.061	132.3	152.6
4	Harmon Killebrew	Twins	158	.270	421	440	.957	115.1	137.6
5	Tony Oliva	Twins	161	.323	432	476	.908	101.1	130.5
6	Jim Fregosi	Angels	147	.277	328	391	.839	71.2	127.7
7	Rocky Colavito	Athletics	160	.274	394	449	.878	80.3	125.6
8	Brooks Robinson	Orioles	163	.317	393	453	.868	77.0	124.4
9	Jim Gentile	Athletics	136	.251	298	344	.866	57.7	124.0
10	Al Kaline	Tigers	146	.293	333	389	.856	60.4	122.2

Extremes for Batters

Batter	Team	Best		Batter	Team	Worst
Mickey Mantle	Yankees	146.4	BV	Bobby Richardson	Yankees	-88.1
Mickey Mantle	Yankees	151.7	SE+	Bobby Knoop	Angels	75.1
Mickey Mantle	Yankees	57.2	SCV	Bobby Knoop	Angels	-24.2
Boog Powell	Orioles	213.0	ISO+	Don Blasingame	Senators	33.1
Harmon Killebrew	Twins	73.5	EXV	Bobby Richardson	Yankees	-57.1
Bobby Richardson	Yankees	294.6	CT+	Jim Gentile	Athletics	57.4
Bobby Richardson	Yankees	-70.1	SOV	Dave Nicholson	White Sox	81.3
Norm Siebern	Orioles	210.2	EY+	Joe Pepitone	Yankees	33.0
Norm Siebern	Orioles	54.0	BBV	Joe Pepitone	Yankees	-34.5

Best Pitchers

Rank	Pitcher	Team	G	ERA	B	O	BPO	BV	BPO+
1	Joe Horlen	White Sox	32	1.88	273	642	.425	-117.2	70.0
2	Dean Chance	Angels	46	1.65	350	846	.414	-148.9	70.1
3	Whitey Ford	Yankees	39	2.13	353	743	.475	-108.9	76.4
4	Juan Pizarro	White Sox	33	2.56	368	724	.508	-72.1	83.6
4	Wally Bunker	Orioles	29	2.69	335	644	.520	-65.7	83.6
6	Fred Newman	Angels	32	2.75	296	581	.509	-46.6	86.4
7	Milt Pappas	Orioles	37	2.97	411	755	.544	-58.8	87.5
8	Mickey Lolich	Tigers	44	3.26	389	704	.553	-51.5	88.3
9	Gary Peters	White Sox	37	2.50	445	820	.543	-53.4	89.3
10	Jim Bouton	Yankees	38	3.02	454	815	.557	-52.7	89.6

Extremes for Pitchers

Pitcher	Team	Best		Pitcher	Team	Worst
Dean Chance	Angels	-148.9	BV	Jack Lamabe	Red Sox	119.3
Dean Chance	Angels	51.2	ERA+	Jack Lamabe	Red Sox	159.4
Dean Chance	Angels	-48.6	ERV	Jack Lamabe	Red Sox	43.2
Dean Chance	Angels	42.6	ISO+	Orlando Pena	Athletics	154.8
Dean Chance	Angels	-66.1	EXV	Orlando Pena	Athletics	65.1
Sam McDowell	Indians	66.6	CT+	John O'Donoghue	Athletics	162.5
Dick Radatz	Red Sox	81.3	SOV	Jim Bouton	Yankees	-57.6
Bill Monbouquette	Red Sox	49.6	EY+	Dave Morehead	Red Sox	195.5
Milt Pappas	Orioles	-37.3	BBV	Dave Morehead	Red Sox	53.7

1964 National League

Standings

Rank	Team	Post	W	L	Pct.	R	RA	BPO	BPOA	TS
1	Saint Louis Cardinals	WLP	93	69	.574	4.41	4.02	.652	.616	72.585
2	Cincinnati Reds	—	92	70	.568	4.05	3.47	.622	.578	59.487
3	San Francisco Giants	—	90	72	.556	4.05	3.62	.638	.593	57.246
4	Philadelphia Phillies	—	92	70	.568	4.28	3.90	.642	.629	55.593
5	Milwaukee Braves	—	88	74	.543	4.96	4.59	.693	.651	55.433
6	Los Angeles Dodgers	—	80	82	.494	3.74	3.49	.591	.544	50.453
7	Pittsburgh Pirates	—	80	82	.494	4.09	3.93	.630	.617	47.218
8	Chicago Cubs	—	76	86	.469	4.01	4.47	.648	.658	38.462
9	Houston Colt .45s	—	66	96	.407	3.06	3.88	.517	.618	23.309
10	New York Mets	—	53	109	.327	3.49	4.76	.551	.683	10.277

Best Batters

Rank	Batter	Team	G	BA	B	O	BPO	BV	BPO+
1	Willie Mays	Giants	157	.296	457	427	1.070	170.2	159.3
2	Frank Robinson	Reds	156	.306	428	418	1.024	143.8	150.6
3	Ron Santo	Cubs	161	.313	431	428	1.007	134.5	145.3
4	Dick Allen	Phillies	162	.318	431	452	.954	127.1	141.8
5	Rico Carty	Braves	133	.330	303	327	.927	83.9	138.3
6	Hank Aaron	Braves	145	.328	379	411	.922	103.6	137.6
7	Orlando Cepeda	Giants	142	.304	352	392	.898	88.7	133.7
8	Billy Williams	Cubs	162	.312	417	465	.897	94.8	129.4
9	Roberto Clemente	Pirates	155	.339	367	430	.853	79.3	127.6
10	Denis Menke	Braves	151	.283	329	386	.852	70.3	127.2

Extremes for Batters

Batter	Team	Best		Batter	Team	Worst
Willie Mays	Giants	170.2	BV	Roy McMillan	Braves-Mets	-96.0
Willie Mays	Giants	136.3	SE+	Billy Cowan	Cubs	76.0
Willie Mays	Giants	49.3	SCV	Len Gabrielson	Braves-Cubs	-28.4
Willie Mays	Giants	232.9	ISO+	Maury Wills	Dodgers	40.4
Willie Mays	Giants	102.7	EXV	Curt Flood	Cardinals	-53.9
Nellie Fox	Colt .45s	496.5	CT+	Billy Cowan	Cubs	55.4
Dick Groat	Cardinals	-51.6	SOV	Billy Cowan	Cubs	57.1
Nellie Fox	Colt .45s	-51.6				
Eddie Mathews	Braves	209.9	EY+	Billy Cowan	Cubs	37.5
Eddie Mathews	Braves	41.9	BBV	Bill Mazeroski	Pirates	-22.7

Best Pitchers

Rank	Pitcher	Team	G	ERA	B	O	BPO	BV	BPO+
1	Sandy Koufax	Dodgers	29	1.74	291	677	.430	-100.8	74.3
2	Don Drysdale	Dodgers	40	2.18	426	974	.437	-137.6	75.6
3	Larry Jackson	Cubs	40	3.14	454	903	.503	-109.9	80.5
4	Chris Short	Phillies	42	2.20	327	661	.495	-72.1	81.9
5	Jim O'Toole	Reds	30	2.66	330	656	.503	-67.3	83.1
6	Juan Marichal	Giants	33	2.48	408	817	.499	-81.0	83.4
7	Bob Veale	Pirates	40	2.74	429	857	.501	-84.8	83.5
8	Gaylord Perry	Giants	44	2.75	325	623	.522	-47.9	87.2
9	Bob Bruce	Colt .45s	35	2.76	320	616	.519	-40.9	88.7
10	Jim Bunning	Phillies	41	2.63	462	861	.537	-57.8	88.9

Extremes for Pitchers

Pitcher	Team	Best		Pitcher	Team	Worst
Don Drysdale	Dodgers	-137.6	BV	Warren Spahn	Braves	79.9
Sandy Koufax	Dodgers	55.1	ERA+	Warren Spahn	Braves	154.4
Sandy Koufax	Dodgers	-35.0	ERV	Warren Spahn	Braves	36.0
Bob Veale	Pirates	47.8	ISO+	Warren Spahn	Braves	146.1
Bob Veale	Pirates	-62.2	EXV	Phil Ortega	Dodgers	38.3
Sandy Koufax	Dodgers	60.4	CT+	Bob Purkey	Reds	166.2
Sandy Koufax	Dodgers	88.4	SOV	Curt Simmons	Cardinals	-59.2
Vern Law	Pirates	54.1	EY+	Bob Veale	Pirates	163.7
Jim Bunning	Phillies	-28.0	BBV	Bob Veale	Pirates	44.8

1965 American League

Standings

Rank	Team	Post	W	L	Pct.	R	RA	BPO	BPOA	TS
1	Minnesota Twins	LP	102	60	.630	4.78	3.70	.690	.610	78.002
2	Chicago White Sox	—	95	67	.586	3.99	3.43	.621	.570	60.846
3	Baltimore Orioles	—	94	68	.580	3.96	3.57	.614	.593	56.699
4	Cleveland Indians	—	87	75	.537	4.09	3.78	.652	.580	56.457
5	Detroit Tigers	—	89	73	.549	4.20	3.72	.634	.611	54.817
6	New York Yankees	—	77	85	.475	3.77	3.73	.596	.624	41.574
7	California Angels	—	75	87	.463	3.25	3.51	.581	.593	39.677
8	Boston Red Sox	—	62	100	.383	4.13	4.88	.679	.698	28.843
9	Washington Senators	—	70	92	.432	3.65	4.45	.597	.699	26.318
10	Kansas City Athletics	—	59	103	.364	3.61	4.66	.617	.703	20.043

Best Batters

Rank	Batter	Team	G	BA	B	O	BPO	BV	BPO+
1	Carl Yastrzemski	Red Sox	133	.312	349	368	.948	91.6	135.6
2	Norm Cash	Tigers	142	.266	331	363	.912	85.3	134.7
3	Leon Wagner	Indians	144	.294	334	376	.888	78.2	130.5
4	Curt Blefary	Orioles	144	.260	320	362	.884	71.6	128.8
5	Tony Oliva	Twins	149	.321	373	420	.888	82.4	128.4
6	Rocky Colavito	Indians	162	.287	381	444	.858	78.9	126.1
7	Frank Howard	Senators	149	.289	305	378	.807	51.6	120.4
8	Tony Conigliaro	Red Sox	138	.269	336	401	.838	55.5	119.8
9	Tom Tresh	Yankees	156	.279	358	448	.799	56.1	118.6
10	Bob Allison	Twins	135	.233	286	349	.819	44.5	118.4

Extremes for Batters

Batter	Team	Best		Batter	Team	Worst
Carl Yastrzemski	Red Sox	91.6	**BV**	Ed Brinkman	Senators	-94.0
Tony Oliva	Twins	146.4	**SE+**	Wayne Causey	Athletics	71.2
Tony Oliva	Twins	59.9	**SCV**	Bob Tillman	Red Sox	-34.4
Norm Cash	Tigers	177.4	**ISO+**	Jerry Lumpe	Tigers	47.3
Norm Cash	Tigers	50.2	**EXV**	Bobby Richardson	Yankees	-41.2
Bobby Richardson	Yankees	257.0	**CT+**	Bob Allison	Twins	58.0
Bobby Richardson	Yankees	-61.2	**SOV**	Don Lock	Senators	50.7
Curt Blefary	Orioles	177.6	**EY+**	Ken Berry	White Sox	53.1
Curt Blefary	Orioles	36.7	**BBV**	Fred Whitfield	Indians	-32.8

Best Pitchers

Rank	Pitcher	Team	G	ERA	B	O	BPO	BV	BPO+
1	Sam McDowell	Indians	42	2.18	392	832	.471	-121.6	76.3
2	Sonny Siebert	Indians	39	2.43	286	568	.504	-64.7	81.6
3	George Brunet	Angels	41	2.56	299	590	.507	-47.4	86.3
4	Fred Newman	Angels	36	2.93	402	782	.514	-57.1	87.6
5	Eddie Fisher	White Sox	82	2.40	255	496	.514	-35.5	87.8
6	Milt Pappas	Orioles	34	2.60	369	666	.554	-43.3	89.5
7	Denny McLain	Tigers	33	2.61	367	663	.554	-39.8	90.2
7	Ralph Terry	Indians	30	3.69	279	501	.557	-30.3	90.2
9	Dave McNally	Orioles	35	2.85	340	604	.563	-33.9	90.9
10	Steve Barber	Orioles	37	2.69	376	667	.564	-36.9	91.1

Extremes for Pitchers

Pitcher	Team	Best		Pitcher	Team	Worst
Sam McDowell	Indians	-121.6	**BV**	Phil Ortega	Senators	118.4
Sam McDowell	Indians	64.7	**ERA+**	Phil Ortega	Senators	153.0
Sam McDowell	Indians	-36.0	**ERV**	Phil Ortega	Senators	35.3
Sam McDowell	Indians	47.5	**ISO+**	Phil Ortega	Senators	163.9
Sam McDowell	Indians	-62.9	**EXV**	Phil Ortega	Senators	54.2
Sam McDowell	Indians	53.4	**CT+**	Fred Newman	Angels	155.7
Sam McDowell	Indians	151.5	**SOV**	Fred Newman	Angels	-60.7
Ralph Terry	Indians	37.2	**EY+**	Dave Morehead	Red Sox	172.1
Bill Monbouquette	Red Sox	-37.9	**BBV**	Dave Morehead	Red Sox	46.9

1965 National League

Standings

Rank	Team	Post	W	L	Pct.	R	RA	BPO	BPOA	TS
1	Los Angeles Dodgers	WLP	97	65	.599	3.75	3.22	.609	.554	74.488
2	Cincinnati Reds	—	89	73	.549	5.09	4.35	.744	.651	60.220
3	San Francisco Giants	—	95	67	.586	4.18	3.64	.633	.581	59.506
4	Pittsburgh Pirates	—	90	72	.556	4.14	3.56	.624	.568	57.385
5	Milwaukee Braves	—	86	76	.531	4.37	3.91	.665	.618	53.953
6	Philadelphia Phillies	—	85	76	.528	4.04	4.12	.638	.635	47.564
7	Saint Louis Cardinals	—	80	81	.497	4.36	4.16	.631	.658	44.774
8	Chicago Cubs	—	72	90	.444	3.87	4.41	.607	.661	33.955
9	Houston Astros	—	65	97	.401	3.51	4.39	.584	.639	28.149
10	New York Mets	—	50	112	.309	3.02	4.59	.520	.680	9.282

Best Batters

Rank	Batter	Team	G	BA	B	O	BPO	BV	BPO+
1	Willie Mays	Giants	157	.317	449	400	1.123	172.8	162.5
2	Hank Aaron	Braves	150	.318	412	416	.990	124.9	143.5
3	Jim Wynn	Astros	157	.275	407	435	.936	122.7	143.2
4	Willie McCovey	Giants	160	.276	390	408	.956	108.2	138.4
5	Frank Robinson	Reds	156	.296	419	437	.959	109.3	135.3
6	Billy Williams	Cubs	164	.315	440	469	.938	109.5	133.1
7	Dick Allen	Phillies	161	.302	409	459	.891	95.1	130.3
8	Ron Santo	Cubs	164	.285	409	451	.907	91.2	128.7
9	Joe Morgan	Astros	157	.271	378	458	.825	78.7	126.3
10	Johnny Callison	Phillies	160	.262	393	476	.826	67.5	120.7

Extremes for Batters

Batter	Team	Best		Batter	Team	Worst
Willie Mays	Giants	172.8	BV	Glenn Beckert	Cubs	-122.2
Willie Mays	Giants	137.5	SE+	Dick Schofield	Pirates-Giants	67.9
Willie Mays	Giants	48.6	SCV	Dick Schofield	Pirates-Giants	-35.6
Willie Mays	Giants	229.6	ISO+	Dick Schofield	Pirates-Giants	33.2
Willie Mays	Giants	103.3	EXV	Glenn Beckert	Cubs	-54.3
Cookie Rojas	Phillies	237.5	CT+	Dick Stuart	Phillies	59.5
Bob Lillis	Astros	-52.6	SOV	Dick Allen	Phillies	56.9
Joe Morgan	Astros	189.5	EY+	Willie Davis	Dodgers	25.6
Joe Morgan	Astros	45.3	BBV	Willie Davis	Dodgers	-32.0

Best Pitchers

Rank	Pitcher	Team	G	ERA	B	O	BPO	BV	BPO+
1	Sandy Koufax	Dodgers	43	2.04	445	1,022	.435	-155.6	74.1
2	Juan Marichal	Giants	39	2.13	421	902	.467	-130.6	76.3
3	Vern Law	Pirates	29	2.15	318	652	.488	-76.3	80.6
4	Jim Maloney	Reds	33	2.54	421	770	.547	-63.4	86.9
5	Bob Veale	Pirates	39	2.84	422	802	.526	-63.0	87.0
6	Bob Shaw	Giants	42	2.64	381	714	.534	-55.6	87.3
7	Jim Bunning	Phillies	39	2.60	481	884	.544	-57.7	89.3
8	Bob Gibson	Cardinals	38	3.07	525	899	.584	-53.8	90.7
9	Claude Osteen	Dodgers	40	2.79	467	869	.537	-43.7	91.4
10	Sammy Ellis	Reds	44	3.79	465	795	.585	-35.1	93.0

Extremes for Pitchers

Pitcher	Team	Best		Pitcher	Team	Worst
Sandy Koufax	Dodgers	-155.6	BV	Ray Sadecki	Cardinals	67.6
Juan Marichal	Giants	60.5	ERA+	Ray Sadecki	Cardinals	138.5
Juan Marichal	Giants	-45.8	ERV	Jim O'Toole	Reds	31.9
Bob Veale	Pirates	44.9	ISO+	Ray Sadecki	Cardinals	137.2
Bob Veale	Pirates	-63.8	EXV	Ray Sadecki	Cardinals	33.4
Sandy Koufax	Dodgers	55.6	CT+	Bob Friend	Pirates	199.0
Sandy Koufax	Dodgers	169.5	SOV	Bob Friend	Pirates	-73.3
Turk Farrell	Astros	49.8	EY+	Wade Blasingame	Braves	168.1
Juan Marichal	Giants	-33.9	BBV	Wade Blasingame	Braves	42.9

1966 American League

Standings

Rank	Team	Post	W	L	Pct.	R	RA	BPO	BPOA	TS
1	Baltimore Orioles	WLP	97	63	.606	4.72	3.76	.682	.595	88.282
2	Minnesota Twins	—	89	73	.549	4.09	3.59	.641	.571	62.142
3	Chicago White Sox	—	83	79	.512	3.52	3.17	.585	.531	54.894
4	Detroit Tigers	—	88	74	.543	4.44	4.31	.675	.661	53.206
5	Cleveland Indians	—	81	81	.500	3.54	3.62	.586	.584	45.079
6	California Angels	—	80	82	.494	3.73	3.97	.605	.635	40.002
7	New York Yankees	—	70	89	.440	3.82	3.83	.614	.616	38.125
8	Kansas City Athletics	—	74	86	.463	3.53	4.05	.572	.652	29.455
9	Boston Red Sox	—	72	90	.444	4.04	4.51	.627	.689	29.204
10	Washington Senators	—	71	88	.447	3.50	4.14	.580	.634	28.601

Best Batters

Rank	Batter	Team	G	BA	B	O	BPO	BV	BPO+
1	Frank Robinson	Orioles	155	.316	479	430	1.114	192.0	166.9
2	Al Kaline	Tigers	142	.288	354	360	.983	110.7	145.5
3	Harmon Killebrew	Twins	162	.281	414	426	.972	119.0	140.3
4	Boog Powell	Orioles	140	.287	335	368	.910	89.4	136.4
5	Dick McAuliffe	Tigers	124	.274	300	333	.901	75.0	133.3
6	Curt Blefary	Orioles	131	.255	286	332	.861	64.4	129.1
7	Fred Valentine	Senators	146	.276	323	399	.810	60.2	122.9
8	Tommie Agee	White Sox	160	.273	385	501	.768	65.3	120.4
9	Tony Oliva	Twins	159	.307	380	462	.823	60.1	118.8
10	Norm Cash	Tigers	160	.279	366	457	.801	57.2	118.5

Extremes for Batters

Batter	Team	Best		Batter	Team	Worst
Frank Robinson	Orioles	192.0	**BV**	Ed Brinkman	Senators	-82.1
Frank Robinson	Orioles	153.4	**SE+**	Ed Brinkman	Senators	71.5
Frank Robinson	Orioles	67.9	**SCV**	Pedro Gonzalez	Indians	-34.7
Frank Robinson	Orioles	227.0	**ISO+**	Cesar Tovar	Twins	50.9
Frank Robinson	Orioles	103.5	**EXV**	Bobby Richardson	Yankees	-36.2
Bobby Richardson	Yankees	330.1	**CT+**	George Scott	Red Sox	60.2
Bobby Richardson	Yankees	-64.4	**SOV**	Don Lock	Senators	67.5
Curt Blefary	Orioles	179.5	**EY+**	Fred Whitfield	Indians	42.7
Joe Foy	Red Sox	38.8	**BBV**	Bobby Richardson	Yankees	-25.7

Best Pitchers

Rank	Pitcher	Team	G	ERA	B	O	BPO	BV	BPO+
1	Steve Hargan	Indians	38	2.48	288	575	.501	-61.4	82.4
2	Gary Peters	White Sox	30	1.98	293	618	.474	-62.3	82.5
3	Jim Kaat	Twins	41	2.75	490	928	.528	-87.7	84.8
4	Jim Perry	Twins	33	2.54	302	553	.546	-42.2	87.7
5	Sam McDowell	Indians	35	2.87	317	589	.538	-40.9	88.6
6	Sonny Siebert	Indians	34	2.80	395	721	.548	-43.1	90.2
7	Fritz Peterson	Yankees	34	3.31	357	656	.544	-34.7	91.2
8	Dave Boswell	Twins	28	3.14	293	515	.569	-27.6	91.4
9	Earl Wilson	Red Sox-Tigers	38	3.07	458	795	.576	-37.6	92.3
10	Tommy John	White Sox	34	2.62	362	677	.535	-27.2	93.0

Extremes for Pitchers

Pitcher	Team	Best		Pitcher	Team	Worst
Jim Kaat	Twins	-87.7	**BV**	Rollie Sheldon	Athletics-Red Sox	71.0
Gary Peters	White Sox	64.7	**ERA+**	Mickey Lolich	Tigers	141.0
Jim Kaat	Twins	-25.5	**ERV**	Mickey Lolich	Tigers	31.4
Steve Hargan	Indians	57.0	**ISO+**	Pete Richert	Senators	142.1
Steve Hargan	Indians	-39.2	**EXV**	Denny McLain	Tigers	50.8
Sam McDowell	Indians	55.6	**CT+**	Fred Talbot	Athletics-Yankees	155.0
Sam McDowell	Indians	99.9	**SOV**	Mudcat Grant	Twins	-58.5
Fritz Peterson	Yankees	54.3	**EY+**	Sam McDowell	Indians	163.1
Jim Kaat	Twins	-38.9	**BBV**	Sam McDowell	Indians	38.3

1966 National League

Standings

Rank	Team	Post	W	L	Pct.	R	RA	BPO	BPOA	TS
1	Los Angeles Dodgers	LP	95	67	.586	3.74	3.02	.610	.526	73.781
2	Pittsburgh Pirates	—	92	70	.568	4.69	3.96	.697	.626	61.980
3	San Francisco Giants	—	93	68	.578	4.19	3.89	.619	.579	57.848
4	Atlanta Braves	—	85	77	.525	4.80	4.19	.705	.638	56.700
5	Philadelphia Phillies	—	87	75	.537	4.30	3.95	.639	.640	51.514
6	Saint Louis Cardinals	—	83	79	.512	3.52	3.56	.604	.590	47.431
7	Cincinnati Reds	—	76	84	.475	4.33	4.39	.635	.674	40.130
8	Houston Astros	—	72	90	.444	3.75	4.26	.626	.644	35.353
9	Chicago Cubs	—	59	103	.364	3.98	4.99	.635	.710	20.238
10	New York Mets	—	66	95	.410	3.65	4.73	.568	.711	19.679

Best Batters

Rank	Batter	Team	G	BA	B	O	BPO	BV	BPO+
1	Dick Allen	Phillies	141	.317	416	377	1.103	153.7	158.6
2	Willie McCovey	Giants	150	.295	382	367	1.041	126.7	149.7
3	Willie Stargell	Pirates	140	.315	348	352	.989	104.7	143.0
4	Ron Santo	Cubs	155	.312	417	417	1.000	123.2	141.9
5	Willie Mays	Giants	152	.288	389	412	.944	102.5	135.8
6	Hank Aaron	Braves	158	.279	431	460	.937	103.5	131.6
7	Joe Torre	Braves	148	.315	374	402	.930	87.8	130.7
8	Joe Morgan	Astros	122	.285	280	325	.862	65.0	130.3
9	Roberto Clemente	Pirates	154	.317	401	461	.870	82.3	125.8
10	Donn Clendenon	Pirates	155	.299	363	425	.854	69.2	123.6

Extremes for Batters

Batter	Team	Best		Batter	Team	Worst
Dick Allen	Phillies	153.7	BV	Hal Lanier	Giants	-106.7
Dick Allen	Phillies	153.0	SE+	Don Kessinger	Cubs	79.5
Dick Allen	Phillies	63.0	SCV	Dal Maxvill	Cardinals	-38.9
Dick Allen	Phillies	216.4	ISO+	Don Kessinger	Cubs	19.4
Dick Allen	Phillies	88.7	EXV	Don Kessinger	Cubs	-62.3
Glenn Beckert	Cubs	269.3	CT+	Dick Allen	Phillies	56.6
Glenn Beckert	Cubs	-61.0	SOV	Byron Browne	Cubs	81.1
Joe Morgan	Astros	249.1	EY+	Tito Fuentes	Giants	20.9
Joe Morgan	Astros	51.5	BBV	Willie Davis	Dodgers	-30.7

Best Pitchers

Rank	Pitcher	Team	G	ERA	B	O	BPO	BV	BPO+
1	Juan Marichal	Giants	37	2.23	424	934	.454	-149.1	74.0
2	Sandy Koufax	Dodgers	41	1.73	455	974	.467	-116.2	79.7
3	Mike Cuellar	Astros	38	2.22	334	694	.481	-76.7	81.3
4	Bob Gibson	Cardinals	35	2.44	427	856	.499	-95.8	81.7
5	Gaylord Perry	Giants	36	2.99	391	773	.506	-83.3	82.4
6	Jim Bunning	Phillies	43	2.41	514	945	.544	-69.5	88.1
7	Al Jackson	Cardinals	36	2.51	383	710	.539	-50.7	88.3
8	Bob Veale	Pirates	38	3.02	447	809	.553	-48.0	90.3
9	Jim Maloney	Reds	32	2.80	399	679	.588	-42.5	90.4
10	Don Sutton	Dodgers	37	2.99	368	687	.536	-34.9	91.3

Extremes for Pitchers

Pitcher	Team	Best		Pitcher	Team	Worst
Juan Marichal	Giants	-149.1	BV	Bob Bruce	Astros	66.9
Sandy Koufax	Dodgers	54.4	ERA+	Sammy Ellis	Reds	139.5
Sandy Koufax	Dodgers	-51.9	ERV	Sammy Ellis	Reds	36.8
Claude Osteen	Dodgers	58.8	ISO+	Denny Lemaster	Braves	139.2
Claude Osteen	Dodgers	-40.6	EXV	Turk Farrell	Astros	51.6
Jim Maloney	Reds	65.2	CT+	Al Jackson	Cardinals	164.5
Sandy Koufax	Dodgers	109.7	SOV	Al Jackson	Cardinals	-58.1
Juan Marichal	Giants	45.7	EY+	Tony Cloninger	Braves	165.4
Juan Marichal	Giants	-39.3	BBV	Jack Hamilton	Mets	43.6

1967 American League

Standings

Rank	Team	Post	W	L	Pct.	R	RA	BPO	BPOA	TS
1	Boston Red Sox	LP	92	70	.568	4.46	3.79	.666	.615	73.514
2	Detroit Tigers	—	91	71	.562	4.19	3.60	.659	.601	63.023
3	Minnesota Twins	—	91	71	.562	4.09	3.60	.620	.574	61.032
4	Chicago White Sox	—	89	73	.549	3.28	3.03	.553	.521	56.209
5	Baltimore Orioles	—	76	85	.472	4.06	3.68	.631	.595	49.383
6	California Angels	—	84	77	.522	3.52	3.65	.578	.597	45.001
7	Cleveland Indians	—	75	87	.463	3.45	3.78	.580	.596	37.094
8	Washington Senators	—	76	85	.472	3.42	3.96	.543	.598	32.498
9	New York Yankees	—	72	90	.444	3.20	3.81	.549	.617	27.641
10	Kansas City Athletics	—	62	99	.385	3.31	4.10	.573	.637	19.836

Best Batters

Rank	Batter	Team	G	BA	B	O	BPO	BV	BPO+
1	Carl Yastrzemski	Red Sox	161	.326	471	409	1.152	191.8	168.7
2	Frank Robinson	Orioles	129	.311	362	349	1.037	137.0	160.9
3	Harmon Killebrew	Twins	163	.269	448	424	1.057	163.0	157.2
4	Al Kaline	Tigers	131	.308	348	343	1.015	121.2	155.5
5	Mickey Mantle	Yankees	144	.245	305	347	.879	87.3	140.1
6	Don Mincher	Angels	147	.273	313	371	.844	83.4	136.3
7	Frank Howard	Senators	149	.256	331	402	.823	78.4	131.0
8	Bill Freehan	Tigers	155	.282	333	390	.854	78.5	130.9
9	Bob Allison	Twins	153	.258	319	381	.837	62.9	124.6
10	Dick McAuliffe	Tigers	153	.239	353	437	.808	67.9	123.8

Extremes for Batters

Batter	Team	Best		Batter	Team	Worst
Carl Yastrzemski	Red Sox	191.8	BV	Zoilo Versalles	Twins	-114.6
Frank Robinson	Orioles	146.1	SE+	Larry Brown	Indians	66.3
Carl Yastrzemski	Red Sox	55.8	SCV	Larry Brown	Indians	-34.5
Harmon Killebrew	Twins	210.0	ISO+	Horace Clarke	Yankees	35.4
Carl Yastrzemski	Red Sox	85.8	EXV	Horace Clarke	Yankees	-47.4
Luis Aparicio	Orioles	208.5	CT+	Frank Howard	Senators	53.8
Cesar Tovar	Twins	-51.3	SOV	Frank Howard	Senators	71.7
Mickey Mantle	Yankees	235.3	EY+	Paul Casanova	Senators	28.3
Harmon Killebrew	Twins	62.4	BBV	Paul Casanova	Senators	-30.4

Best Pitchers

Rank	Pitcher	Team	G	ERA	B	O	BPO	BV	BPO+
1	Joe Horlen	White Sox	35	2.06	351	776	.452	-88.6	79.8
2	Dean Chance	Twins	41	2.73	450	870	.517	-78.7	85.1
3	Jim Merritt	Twins	37	2.53	359	693	.518	-62.2	85.2
4	Mickey Lolich	Tigers	31	3.04	309	613	.504	-52.7	85.4
5	Steve Hargan	Indians	30	2.62	347	679	.511	-54.9	86.3
6	Gary Peters	White Sox	38	2.28	393	792	.496	-55.7	87.6
7	Dave Boswell	Twins	37	3.27	359	669	.537	-47.6	88.3
7	Tommy John	White Sox	31	2.47	271	542	.500	-36.1	88.3
9	Al Downing	Yankees	31	2.63	310	605	.512	-38.0	89.1
10	Lee Stange	Red Sox	35	2.77	305	542	.563	-32.7	90.3

Extremes for Pitchers

Pitcher	Team	Best		Pitcher	Team	Worst
Joe Horlen	White Sox	-88.6	BV	Steve Barber	Orioles-Yankees	70.3
Joe Horlen	White Sox	67.6	ERA+	Steve Barber	Orioles-Yankees	133.1
Joe Horlen	White Sox	-28.2	ERV	Ed Connolly	Indians	23.3
Steve Hargan	Indians	66.1	ISO+	Denny McLain	Tigers	153.8
Dean Chance	Twins	-38.3	EXV	Denny McLain	Tigers	53.5
Luis Tiant	Indians	69.8	CT+	Joe Horlen	White Sox	161.3
Sam McDowell	Indians	71.0	SOV	Joe Horlen	White Sox	-63.1
Jim Merritt	Twins	36.4	EY+	Steve Barber	Orioles-Yankees	195.8
Jim Merritt	Twins	-42.0	BBV	Steve Barber	Orioles-Yankees	54.0

1967 National League

Standings

Rank	Team	Post	W	L	Pct.	R	RA	BPO	BPOA	TS
1	Saint Louis Cardinals	WLP	101	60	.627	4.32	3.46	.642	.563	84.556
2	San Francisco Giants	—	91	71	.562	4.02	3.40	.621	.561	61.707
3	Chicago Cubs	—	87	74	.540	4.33	3.85	.640	.623	54.783
4	Cincinnati Reds	—	87	75	.537	3.73	3.48	.597	.595	51.270
5	Philadelphia Phillies	—	82	80	.506	3.78	3.59	.616	.578	50.971
6	Pittsburgh Pirates	—	81	81	.500	4.17	4.25	.631	.658	42.449
7	Atlanta Braves	—	77	85	.475	3.90	3.95	.618	.620	42.427
8	Los Angeles Dodgers	—	73	89	.451	3.20	3.67	.563	.578	35.606
9	Houston Astros	—	69	93	.426	3.86	4.58	.627	.658	29.874
10	New York Mets	—	61	101	.377	3.07	4.15	.530	.645	14.743

Best Batters

Rank	Batter	Team	G	BA	B	O	BPO	BV	BPO+
1	Dick Allen	Phillies	122	.307	359	336	1.068	132.5	158.5
2	Orlando Cepeda	Cardinals	151	.325	387	405	.956	119.9	144.9
3	Willie McCovey	Giants	135	.276	330	347	.951	101.2	144.3
4	Hank Aaron	Braves	155	.307	430	439	.979	131.2	143.9
5	Roberto Clemente	Pirates	147	.357	380	395	.962	114.8	143.3
6	Jim Ray Hart	Giants	158	.289	382	432	.884	97.2	134.1
7	Joe Morgan	Astros	133	.275	318	368	.864	78.8	133.0
8	Ron Santo	Cubs	161	.300	412	444	.928	102.0	132.9
9	Jim Wynn	Astros	158	.249	399	471	.847	92.9	130.3
9	Adolfo Phillips	Cubs	144	.268	322	354	.910	74.8	130.3

Extremes for Batters

Batter	Team	Best		Batter	Team	Worst
Dick Allen	Phillies	132.5	BV	Hal Lanier	Giants	-126.0
Roberto Clemente	Pirates	156.5	SE+	Tommy Helms	Reds	64.2
Roberto Clemente	Pirates	68.6	SCV	Tommy Helms	Reds	-40.7
Hank Aaron	Braves	204.4	ISO+	Don Kessinger	Cubs	30.0
Hank Aaron	Braves	81.7	EXV	Don Kessinger	Cubs	-56.1
Glenn Beckert	Cubs	359.6	CT+	Dick Allen	Phillies	59.1
Glenn Beckert	Cubs	-64.9	SOV	Don Lock	Phillies	51.3
Joe Morgan	Astros	205.5	EY+	Jesus Alou	Giants	33.3
Ron Santo	Cubs	40.5	BBV	Lou Brock	Cardinals	-28.2

Best Pitchers

Rank	Pitcher	Team	G	ERA	B	O	BPO	BV	BPO+
1	Phil Niekro	Braves	46	1.87	310	627	.494	-66.5	82.3
2	Gaylord Perry	Giants	39	2.61	440	895	.492	-77.4	85.0
3	Mel Queen	Reds	31	2.76	323	587	.550	-49.4	86.7
3	Bob Gibson	Cardinals	24	2.98	265	528	.502	-40.6	86.7
5	Fergie Jenkins	Cubs	38	2.80	471	873	.540	-70.4	87.0
6	Gary Nolan	Reds	33	2.58	379	684	.554	-55.0	87.3
7	Rich Nye	Cubs	35	3.20	340	625	.544	-47.6	87.7
8	Jim Bunning	Phillies	40	2.29	484	916	.528	-62.9	88.5
9	Dick Hughes	Cardinals	37	2.67	346	670	.516	-41.8	89.2
10	Bill Singer	Dodgers	32	2.64	316	614	.515	-30.6	91.2

Extremes for Pitchers

Pitcher	Team	Best		Pitcher	Team	Worst
Gaylord Perry	Giants	-77.4	BV	Jack Fisher	Mets	63.9
Phil Niekro	Braves	58.4	ERA+	Jack Fisher	Mets	146.0
Jim Bunning	Phillies	-32.6	ERV	Jack Fisher	Mets	36.2
Bill Singer	Dodgers	57.2	ISO+	Dennis Ribant	Pirates	134.6
Ted Abernathy	Reds	-34.7	EXV	Ray Culp	Cubs	34.4
Gary Nolan	Reds	71.6	CT+	Tommie Sisk	Pirates	157.6
Jim Bunning	Phillies	62.6	SOV	Tommie Sisk	Pirates	-49.0
Joe Niekro	Cubs	57.4	EY+	Bob Veale	Pirates	203.9
Claude Osteen	Dodgers	-29.5	BBV	Bob Veale	Pirates	55.6

1968 American League

Standings

Rank	Team	Post	W	L	Pct.	R	RA	BPO	BPOA	TS
1	Detroit Tigers	WLP	103	59	.636	4.09	3.00	.634	.550	87.102
2	Baltimore Orioles	—	91	71	.562	3.57	3.07	.616	.543	61.608
3	Cleveland Indians	—	86	75	.534	3.19	3.11	.557	.538	51.041
4	Minnesota Twins	—	79	83	.488	3.47	3.37	.590	.542	48.946
5	Boston Red Sox	—	86	76	.531	3.79	3.77	.615	.617	48.588
6	Oakland Athletics	—	82	80	.506	3.49	3.34	.600	.589	48.312
7	New York Yankees	—	83	79	.512	3.27	3.24	.557	.570	46.049
8	Chicago White Sox	—	67	95	.414	2.86	3.25	.523	.575	29.822
9	California Angels	—	67	95	.414	3.07	3.80	.540	.603	26.136
10	Washington Senators	—	65	96	.404	3.25	4.13	.547	.654	20.463

Best Batters

Rank	Batter	Team	G	BA	B	O	BPO	BV	BPO+
1	Carl Yastrzemski	Red Sox	157	.301	405	399	1.015	137.0	151.1
2	Frank Howard	Senators	158	.274	395	452	.874	114.4	140.8
3	Frank Robinson	Orioles	130	.268	285	327	.872	76.5	136.7
4	Willie Horton	Tigers	143	.285	344	392	.878	90.2	135.6
5	Mickey Mantle	Yankees	144	.237	291	348	.836	75.9	135.3
6	Rick Monday	Athletics	148	.274	289	366	.790	64.4	128.7
7	Bill Freehan	Tigers	155	.263	340	414	.821	72.0	126.9
8	Ken Harrelson	Red Sox	150	.275	356	418	.852	75.3	126.8
9	Tony Oliva	Twins	128	.289	292	359	.813	56.2	123.8
10	Reggie Jackson	Athletics	154	.250	325	428	.759	62.4	123.7

Extremes for Batters

Batter	Team	Best		Batter	Team	Worst
Carl Yastrzemski	Red Sox	137.0	**BV**	Horace Clarke	Yankees	-93.0
Ken Harrelson	Red Sox	135.8	**SE+**	Mark Belanger	Orioles	64.9
Ken Harrelson	Red Sox	40.3	**SCV**	Don Wert	Tigers	-34.6
Frank Howard	Senators	235.3	**ISO+**	Horace Clarke	Yankees	20.1
Frank Howard	Senators	95.4	**EXV**	Horace Clarke	Yankees	-55.8
Cesar Tovar	Twins	227.6	**CT+**	Reggie Jackson	Athletics	51.4
Cesar Tovar	Twins	-52.3	**SOV**	Reggie Jackson	Athletics	83.1
Mickey Mantle	Yankees	239.7	**EY+**	Vic Davalillo	Indians-Angels	41.5
Mickey Mantle	Yankees	57.7	**BBV**	Tommy Davis	White Sox	-25.0

Best Pitchers

Rank	Pitcher	Team	G	ERA	B	O	BPO	BV	BPO+
1	Luis Tiant	Indians	34	1.60	319	777	.411	-120.4	72.6
2	Dave McNally	Orioles	35	1.95	376	821	.458	-84.1	81.7
3	Dean Chance	Twins	43	2.53	424	884	.480	-88.4	82.8
4	Denny McLain	Tigers	41	1.96	483	1,002	.482	-89.8	84.3
5	Sam McDowell	Indians	38	1.81	400	818	.489	-62.6	86.5
6	Tommy John	White Sox	25	1.98	261	534	.489	-38.9	87.0
7	Stan Bahnsen	Yankees	37	2.05	411	807	.509	-35.4	92.1
8	George Brunet	Angels	39	2.86	382	742	.515	-29.2	92.9
9	Jim Merritt	Twins	38	3.25	389	719	.541	-27.7	93.3
10	Fritz Peterson	Yankees	36	2.63	330	638	.517	-22.9	93.5

Extremes for Pitchers

Pitcher	Team	Best		Pitcher	Team	Worst
Luis Tiant	Indians	-120.4	**BV**	Frank Bertaina	Senators	89.5
Luis Tiant	Indians	55.3	**ERA+**	Sammy Ellis	Angels	141.4
Luis Tiant	Indians	-37.1	**ERV**	Phil Ortega	Senators	27.7
Gary Bell	Red Sox	68.0	**ISO+**	Catfish Hunter	Athletics	145.0
Dean Chance	Twins	-37.2	**EXV**	Catfish Hunter	Athletics	39.7
Sam McDowell	Indians	61.5	**CT+**	Jack Fisher	White Sox	149.9
Sam McDowell	Indians	109.0	**SOV**	Mel Stottlemyre	Yankees	-43.6
Fritz Peterson	Yankees	35.2	**EY+**	Dave Boswell	Twins	151.3
Fritz Peterson	Yankees	-36.9	**BBV**	Tom Phoebus	Orioles	29.4

1968 National League

Standings

Rank	Team	Post	W	L	Pct.	R	RA	BPO	BPOA	TS
1	Saint Louis Cardinals	LP	97	65	.599	3.60	2.91	.577	.518	83.157
2	San Francisco Giants	—	88	74	.543	3.67	3.25	.586	.524	63.997
3	Pittsburgh Pirates	—	80	82	.494	3.58	3.26	.586	.557	52.029
4	Cincinnati Reds	—	83	79	.512	4.23	4.13	.628	.632	47.837
5	Chicago Cubs	—	84	78	.519	3.75	3.75	.593	.605	46.536
6	Atlanta Braves	—	81	81	.500	3.15	3.37	.567	.560	43.571
7	Los Angeles Dodgers	—	76	86	.469	2.90	3.14	.536	.533	38.588
8	New York Mets	—	73	89	.451	2.90	3.06	.517	.548	32.901
9	Philadelphia Phillies	—	76	86	.469	3.35	3.80	.557	.602	30.083
10	Houston Astros	—	72	90	.444	3.15	3.63	.544	.595	25.570

Best Batters

Rank	Batter	Team	G	BA	B	O	BPO	BV	BPO+
1	Willie McCovey	Giants	148	.293	374	390	.959	137.3	158.0
2	Dick Allen	Phillies	152	.263	362	407	.889	113.2	145.5
3	Jim Wynn	Astros	156	.269	372	428	.869	115.3	144.9
4	Willie Mays	Giants	148	.289	330	379	.871	99.9	143.4
5	Hank Aaron	Braves	160	.287	400	463	.864	111.4	138.6
6	Lou Brock	Cardinals	159	.279	390	495	.788	93.7	131.6
7	Roberto Clemente	Pirates	132	.291	299	375	.797	70.3	130.7
8	Pete Rose	Reds	149	.335	363	440	.825	83.8	130.0
9	Cleon Jones	Mets	147	.297	296	385	.769	61.9	126.4
10	Billy Williams	Cubs	163	.288	382	478	.799	73.7	123.9

Extremes for Batters

Batter	Team	Best		Batter	Team	Worst
Willie McCovey	Giants	137.3	BV	Hal Lanier	Giants	-108.0
Willie McCovey	Giants	142.1	SE+	Hal Lanier	Giants	71.2
Willie McCovey	Giants	44.4	SCV	Don Kessinger	Cubs	-36.7
Willie McCovey	Giants	242.5	ISO+	Hal Lanier	Giants	31.6
Willie McCovey	Giants	77.6	EXV	Don Kessinger	Cubs	-44.4
Glenn Beckert	Cubs	474.9	CT+	Dick Allen	Phillies	49.0
Glenn Beckert	Cubs	-75.0	SOV	Dick Allen	Phillies	82.1
Jim Wynn	Astros	208.2	EY+	Tommy Helms	Reds	18.7
Ron Santo	Cubs	45.8	BBV	Cookie Rojas	Phillies	-26.9

Best Pitchers

Rank	Pitcher	Team	G	ERA	B	O	BPO	BV	BPO+
1	Bob Gibson	Cardinals	34	1.12	346	917	.377	-146.5	70.3
2	Gaylord Perry	Giants	39	2.45	403	886	.455	-79.3	83.6
3	Pat Jarvis	Braves	34	2.60	379	781	.485	-61.7	86.0
4	Bill Hands	Cubs	38	2.89	391	779	.502	-63.0	86.1
5	Bob Moose	Pirates	38	2.74	248	519	.478	-38.0	86.7
6	Fergie Jenkins	Cubs	40	2.63	485	940	.516	-62.8	88.5
7	Bobby Bolin	Giants	34	1.99	257	530	.485	-31.5	89.1
8	Juan Marichal	Giants	38	2.43	481	981	.490	-53.0	90.1
9	Tom Seaver	Mets	36	2.20	417	833	.501	-45.1	90.2
10	Phil Niekro	Braves	37	2.59	391	767	.510	-41.8	90.4

Extremes for Pitchers

Pitcher	Team	Best		Pitcher	Team	Worst
Bob Gibson	Cardinals	-146.5	BV	Jim Bunning	Pirates	64.9
Bob Gibson	Cardinals	40.2	ERA+	Rick Wise	Phillies	155.8
Bob Gibson	Cardinals	-56.4	ERV	Rick Wise	Phillies	33.0
Bob Gibson	Cardinals	58.5	ISO+	Chris Short	Phillies	142.2
Bob Gibson	Cardinals	-39.7	EXV	Chris Short	Phillies	40.1
Bob Gibson	Cardinals	67.1	CT+	Joe Niekro	Cubs	184.9
Bob Gibson	Cardinals	88.2	SOV	Joe Niekro	Cubs	-55.2
Juan Marichal	Giants	48.1	EY+	Bob Veale	Pirates	155.7
Juan Marichal	Giants	-40.0	BBV	Nolan Ryan	Mets	38.5

1969 American League

Standings

Rank	Team	Post	W	L	Pct.	R	RA	BPO	BPOA	TS
1	Baltimore Orioles	LP	109	53	.673	4.81	3.19	.726	.547	86.161
2	Minnesota Twins	P	97	65	.599	4.88	3.81	.715	.598	66.735
3	Detroit Tigers	—	90	72	.556	4.33	3.71	.653	.620	55.761
4	Oakland Athletics	—	88	74	.543	4.57	4.19	.669	.646	52.711
5	Washington Senators	—	86	76	.531	4.28	3.98	.655	.656	49.903
6	Boston Red Sox	—	87	75	.537	4.59	4.54	.710	.698	49.644
7	New York Yankees	—	80	81	.497	3.47	3.62	.605	.590	45.272
8	Kansas City Royals	—	69	93	.426	3.60	4.22	.594	.650	32.417
9	California Angels	—	71	91	.438	3.24	4.00	.554	.618	32.247
10	Chicago White Sox	—	68	94	.420	3.86	4.46	.622	.694	31.131
11	Seattle Pilots	—	64	98	.395	3.92	4.90	.633	.729	25.510
12	Cleveland Indians	—	62	99	.385	3.56	4.45	.592	.682	25.468

Best Batters

Rank	Batter	Team	G	BA	B	O	BPO	BV	BPO+
1	Reggie Jackson	Athletics	152	.275	475	413	1.150	193.7	168.9
2	Harmon Killebrew	Twins	162	.276	486	424	1.146	183.0	160.4
3	Frank Howard	Senators	161	.296	451	449	1.004	144.8	147.3
4	Frank Robinson	Orioles	148	.308	404	391	1.033	129.2	147.0
5	Rico Petrocelli	Red Sox	154	.297	426	402	1.060	128.4	143.1
6	Boog Powell	Orioles	152	.304	381	399	.955	100.6	135.9
7	Sal Bando	Athletics	162	.281	421	457	.921	109.7	135.3
8	Roy White	Yankees	130	.290	304	350	.869	62.8	126.0
9	Carl Yastrzemski	Red Sox	162	.255	425	472	.900	75.6	121.6
10	Don Buford	Orioles	144	.291	359	424	.847	61.0	120.5

Extremes for Batters

Batter	Team	Best		Batter	Team	Worst
Reggie Jackson	Athletics	193.7	BV	Aurelio Rodriguez	Angels	-89.1
Reggie Jackson	Athletics	152.1	SE+	Larry Brown	Indians	64.1
Reggie Jackson	Athletics	66.4	SCV	Larry Brown	Indians	-38.0
Reggie Jackson	Athletics	261.9	ISO+	Sandy Alomar	White Sox-Angels	23.9
Reggie Jackson	Athletics	113.1	EXV	Sandy Alomar	White Sox-Angels	-60.6
Luis Aparicio	White Sox	287.9	CT+	Reggie Jackson	Athletics	55.2
Luis Aparicio	White Sox	-54.5	SOV	Reggie Jackson	Athletics	63.6
Harmon Killebrew	Twins	207.7	EY+	Joe Pepitone	Yankees	38.7
Harmon Killebrew	Twins	64.8	BBV	Aurelio Rodriguez	Angels	-32.2

Best Pitchers

Rank	Pitcher	Team	G	ERA	B	O	BPO	BV	BPO+
1	Mike Cuellar	Orioles	39	2.38	399	878	.454	-141.5	73.8
2	Fritz Peterson	Yankees	37	2.55	398	823	.484	-106.4	78.9
2	Dick Bosman	Senators	31	2.19	281	581	.484	-75.0	78.9
4	Sam McDowell	Indians	39	2.94	449	870	.516	-108.5	80.5
5	Jim Palmer	Orioles	26	2.34	275	542	.507	-58.7	82.4
6	Andy Messersmith	Angels	40	2.52	387	752	.515	-71.8	84.4
7	Jim Perry	Twins	46	2.82	432	794	.544	-68.6	86.3
8	Denny McLain	Tigers	42	2.80	536	970	.553	-79.8	87.0
9	Mel Stottlemyre	Yankees	39	2.82	496	921	.539	-68.4	87.9
10	Dave McNally	Orioles	41	3.22	452	805	.561	-43.6	91.2

Extremes for Pitchers

Pitcher	Team	Best		Pitcher	Team	Worst
Mike Cuellar	Orioles	-141.5	BV	Gary Bell	Pilots-White Sox	83.2
Dick Bosman	Senators	66.6	ERA+	George Brunet	Angels-Pilots	131.7
Mike Cuellar	Orioles	-33.1	ERV	Marty Pattin	Pilots	38.1
Mike Nagy	Red Sox	67.7	ISO+	George Brunet	Angels-Pilots	151.2
Sam McDowell	Indians	-39.4	EXV	Luis Tiant	Indians	45.8
Sam McDowell	Indians	62.3	CT+	Mel Stottlemyre	Yankees	165.2
Sam McDowell	Indians	105.1	SOV	Mel Stottlemyre	Yankees	-73.7
Fritz Peterson	Yankees	36.6	EY+	Mike Nagy	Red Sox	137.7
Fritz Peterson	Yankees	-55.5	BBV	Bill Burbach	Yankees	49.2

1969 National League

Standings

Rank	Team	Post	W	L	Pct.	R	RA	BPO	BPOA	TS
1	New York Mets	WLP	100	62	.617	3.90	3.34	.604	.583	72.856
2	Chicago Cubs	—	92	70	.568	4.42	3.75	.652	.600	58.482
3	San Francisco Giants	—	90	72	.556	4.40	3.93	.666	.596	57.466
4	Pittsburgh Pirates	—	88	74	.543	4.48	4.02	.673	.618	55.382
5	Atlanta Braves	P	93	69	.574	4.27	3.90	.637	.620	54.870
6	Saint Louis Cardinals	—	87	75	.537	3.67	3.33	.614	.579	52.895
7	Cincinnati Reds	—	89	73	.549	4.90	4.71	.711	.685	52.325
8	Los Angeles Dodgers	—	85	77	.525	3.98	3.46	.611	.587	52.280
9	Houston Astros	—	81	81	.500	4.17	4.12	.653	.622	47.908
10	Philadelphia Phillies	—	63	99	.389	3.98	4.60	.631	.688	29.179
11	Montreal Expos	—	52	110	.321	3.59	4.88	.603	.722	15.677
12	San Diego Padres	—	52	110	.321	2.89	4.60	.533	.691	10.456

Best Batters

Rank	Batter	Team	G	BA	B	O	BPO	BV	BPO+
1	Willie McCovey	Giants	149	.320	454	352	1.290	213.6	188.8
2	Jim Wynn	Astros	149	.269	432	381	1.134	172.5	166.5
3	Hank Aaron	Braves	147	.300	433	410	1.056	145.6	150.6
4	Rusty Staub	Expos	158	.302	416	405	1.027	137.5	149.4
5	Dick Allen	Phillies	118	.288	328	329	.997	102.5	145.5
6	Roberto Clemente	Pirates	138	.345	343	356	.963	100.2	141.3
7	Willie Stargell	Pirates	145	.307	363	377	.963	105.9	141.2
8	Pete Rose	Reds	156	.348	429	440	.975	117.2	137.6
9	Cleon Jones	Mets	137	.340	324	342	.947	86.6	136.5
10	Bobby Bonds	Giants	158	.259	437	481	.909	108.4	133.0

Extremes for Batters

Batter	Team	Best		Batter	Team	Worst
Willie McCovey	Giants	213.6	BV	Hal Lanier	Giants	-118.2
Willie McCovey	Giants	148.6	SE+	Hal Lanier	Giants	68.2
Willie McCovey	Giants	59.5	SCV	Tommy Dean	Padres	-37.7
Willie McCovey	Giants	256.0	ISO+	Hal Lanier	Giants	16.9
Willie McCovey	Giants	100.6	EXV	Hal Lanier	Giants	-54.0
Glenn Beckert	Cubs	339.6	CT+	Dick Allen	Phillies	46.6
Matty Alou	Pirates	-73.0	SOV	Bobby Bonds	Giants	89.3
Jim Wynn	Astros	266.2	EY+	Al Oliver	Pirates	26.2
Jim Wynn	Astros	83.7	BBV	Bobby Tolan	Reds	-29.8

Best Pitchers

Rank	Pitcher	Team	G	ERA	B	O	BPO	BV	BPO+
1	Juan Marichal	Giants	37	2.10	415	903	.460	-133.6	75.7
2	Bill Hands	Cubs	41	2.49	480	906	.530	-128.7	78.9
3	Larry Dierker	Astros	39	2.33	448	927	.483	-119.4	79.0
4	Phil Niekro	Braves	40	2.56	438	868	.505	-107.5	80.3
5	Jerry Koosman	Mets	32	2.28	368	728	.505	-84.6	81.3
6	Bob Gibson	Cardinals	35	2.18	470	940	.500	-99.6	82.5
7	Fergie Jenkins	Cubs	43	3.21	526	947	.555	-110.3	82.7
8	Bill Singer	Dodgers	41	2.34	470	955	.492	-94.3	83.3
9	Steve Carlton	Cardinals	31	2.17	376	715	.526	-57.3	86.8
10	Tom Seaver	Mets	36	2.21	444	820	.541	-65.8	87.1
10	Bob Moose	Pirates	44	2.91	275	519	.530	-40.7	87.1

Extremes for Pitchers

Pitcher	Team	Best		Pitcher	Team	Worst
Juan Marichal	Giants	-133.6	BV	Bill Stoneman	Expos	77.3
Juan Marichal	Giants	61.7	ERA+	Tony Cloninger	Reds	138.5
Bill Hands	Cubs	-47.0	ERV	Tony Cloninger	Reds	29.5
Bob Gibson	Cardinals	61.7	ISO+	Steve Blass	Pirates	137.6
Bob Gibson	Cardinals	-49.1	EXV	Jim Merritt	Reds	42.1
Tom Griffin	Astros	64.1	CT+	Joe Niekro	Cubs-Padres	243.1
Don Wilson	Astros	80.1	SOV	Joe Niekro	Cubs-Padres	-88.0
Juan Marichal	Giants	54.3	EY+	Mike Wegener	Expos	170.8
Fergie Jenkins	Cubs	-43.4	BBV	Bill Stoneman	Expos	43.3

1970 American League

Standings

Rank	Team	Post	W	L	Pct.	R	RA	BPO	BPOA	TS
1	Baltimore Orioles	WLP	108	54	.667	4.89	3.54	.726	.600	87.901
2	Minnesota Twins	P	98	64	.605	4.59	3.73	.673	.609	63.997
3	Oakland Athletics	—	89	73	.549	4.19	3.66	.684	.606	58.195
4	New York Yankees	—	93	69	.574	4.17	3.75	.644	.594	57.660
5	Boston Red Sox	—	87	75	.537	4.85	4.46	.720	.677	54.002
6	California Angels	—	86	76	.531	3.90	3.89	.606	.626	46.829
7	Cleveland Indians	—	76	86	.469	4.01	4.17	.647	.675	40.118
8	Detroit Tigers	—	79	83	.488	4.11	4.51	.651	.682	39.949
9	Washington Senators	—	70	92	.432	3.86	4.25	.632	.667	35.139
10	Kansas City Royals	—	65	97	.401	3.77	4.35	.595	.670	28.733
11	Milwaukee Brewers	—	65	97	.401	3.76	4.61	.630	.683	28.466
12	Chicago White Sox	—	56	106	.346	3.91	5.07	.608	.731	17.195

Best Batters

Rank	Batter	Team	G	BA	B	O	BPO	BV	BPO+
1	Carl Yastrzemski	Red Sox	161	.329	489	407	1.201	184.5	160.6
2	Frank Howard	Senators	161	.283	450	437	1.030	153.0	151.5
3	Boog Powell	Orioles	154	.297	407	393	1.036	132.8	148.4
4	Harmon Killebrew	Twins	157	.271	426	423	1.007	127.4	142.7
5	Tommy Harper	Brewers	154	.296	441	456	.967	127.0	140.4
6	Frank Robinson	Orioles	132	.306	329	347	.948	86.9	135.9
7	Roy White	Yankees	162	.296	415	460	.902	101.5	132.4
8	Don Buford	Orioles	144	.272	348	384	.906	80.1	129.9
9	Sal Bando	Athletics	155	.263	356	402	.886	80.6	129.3
10	Reggie Jackson	Athletics	149	.237	309	357	.866	64.4	126.3

Extremes for Batters

Batter	Team	Best		Batter	Team	Worst
Carl Yastrzemski	Red Sox	184.5	BV	Horace Clarke	Yankees	-88.4
Roy White	Yankees	134.4	SE+	Ed Brinkman	Senators	78.1
Roy White	Yankees	46.3	SCV	Joe Azcue	Angels	-30.7
Frank Howard	Senators	195.2	ISO+	Ed Brinkman	Senators	28.5
Frank Howard	Senators	72.7	EXV	Sandy Alomar	Angels	-62.9
Horace Clarke	Yankees	289.6	CT+	Reggie Jackson	Athletics	46.6
Horace Clarke	Yankees	-66.4	SOV	Reggie Jackson	Athletics	72.1
Sal Bando	Athletics	207.4	EY+	Vada Pinson	Indians	40.1
Sal Bando	Athletics	58.5	BBV	Horace Clarke	Yankees	-34.3

Best Pitchers

Rank	Pitcher	Team	G	ERA	B	O	BPO	BV	BPO+
1	Sam McDowell	Indians	39	2.92	506	917	.552	-103.6	83.0
2	Jim Perry	Twins	40	3.04	448	841	.533	-91.1	83.1
3	Fritz Peterson	Yankees	39	2.90	411	791	.520	-79.1	83.9
4	Ray Culp	Red Sox	33	3.04	449	763	.588	-71.6	86.2
5	Andy Messersmith	Angels	37	3.01	335	589	.569	-36.7	90.1
6	Clyde Wright	Angels	39	2.83	451	790	.571	-47.5	90.5
7	Bert Blyleven	Twins	27	3.18	288	496	.581	-30.0	90.6
8	Mike Cuellar	Orioles	40	3.48	520	902	.576	-43.8	92.2
9	Jim Palmer	Orioles	39	2.71	526	912	.577	-44.0	92.3
10	Tommy John	White Sox	37	3.27	494	817	.605	-37.0	93.0

Extremes for Pitchers

Pitcher	Team	Best		Pitcher	Team	Worst
Sam McDowell	Indians	-103.6	BV	Barry Moore	Indians-White Sox	78.7
Diego Segui	Athletics	74.2	ERA+	Lew Krausse	Brewers	130.8
Sam McDowell	Indians	-30.1	ERV	Gene Brabender	Brewers	34.1
Jim Rooker	Royals	73.8	ISO+	Casey Cox	Senators	147.4
Sam McDowell	Indians	-30.0	EXV	Casey Cox	Senators	43.1
Sam McDowell	Indians	60.7	CT+	Casey Cox	Senators	177.1
Sam McDowell	Indians	119.5	SOV	Gerry Janeski	White Sox	-57.9
Fritz Peterson	Yankees	40.1	EY+	Les Cain	Tigers	155.1
Fritz Peterson	Yankees	-50.7	BBV	Blue Moon Odom	Athletics	44.0

1970 National League

Standings

Rank	Team	Post	W	L	Pct.	R	RA	BPO	BPOA	TS
1	Cincinnati Reds	LP	102	60	.630	4.78	4.20	.743	.645	80.511
2	Chicago Cubs	—	84	78	.519	4.98	4.19	.710	.654	58.954
3	Pittsburgh Pirates	P	89	73	.549	4.50	4.10	.674	.651	56.365
4	Los Angeles Dodgers	—	87	74	.540	4.65	4.25	.677	.649	55.746
5	New York Mets	—	83	79	.512	4.29	3.89	.673	.623	54.439
6	San Francisco Giants	—	86	76	.531	5.13	5.10	.741	.716	51.201
7	Houston Astros	—	79	83	.488	4.59	4.71	.684	.686	42.944
8	Saint Louis Cardinals	—	76	86	.469	4.59	4.61	.662	.667	41.648
9	Atlanta Braves	—	76	86	.469	4.54	4.77	.683	.708	38.212
10	Montreal Expos	—	73	89	.451	4.24	4.98	.651	.728	27.487
11	Philadelphia Phillies	—	73	88	.453	3.69	4.53	.597	.695	25.097
12	San Diego Padres	—	63	99	.389	4.20	4.86	.649	.721	21.769

Best Batters

Rank	Batter	Team	G	BA	B	O	BPO	BV	BPO+
1	Willie McCovey	Giants	152	.289	446	368	1.212	173.8	163.9
2	Rico Carty	Braves	136	.366	362	327	1.107	112.8	145.3
3	Tony Perez	Reds	158	.317	448	426	1.052	131.3	141.4
4	Dick Dietz	Giants	148	.300	373	369	1.011	100.1	136.7
5	Jim Hickman	Cubs	149	.315	398	368	1.082	106.1	136.3
6	Hank Aaron	Braves	150	.298	387	381	1.016	96.6	133.3
7	Jim Wynn	Astros	157	.282	411	426	.965	99.5	131.9
8	Dick Allen	Cardinals	122	.279	336	345	.974	79.1	130.8
9	Bobby Bonds	Giants	157	.302	464	482	.963	107.5	130.2
10	Rusty Staub	Expos	160	.274	425	446	.953	96.2	129.3

Extremes for Batters

Batter	Team	Best		Batter	Team	Worst
Willie McCovey	Giants	173.8	**BV**	Tommy Helms	Reds	-154.0
Johnny Bench	Reds	137.3	**SE+**	Tommy Helms	Reds	65.3
Johnny Bench	Reds	54.4	**SCV**	Tommy Helms	Reds	-45.7
Willie McCovey	Giants	216.3	**ISO+**	Tommy Helms	Reds	29.2
Willie McCovey	Giants	86.0	**EXV**	Tommy Helms	Reds	-63.1
Matty Alou	Pirates	576.1	**CT+**	Billy Grabarkewitz	Dodgers	54.4
Matty Alou	Pirates	-85.7	**SOV**	Bobby Bonds	Giants	85.9
Dick Dietz	Giants	183.3	**EY+**	Manny Sanguillen	Pirates	18.8
Bernie Carbo	Reds	46.4	**BBV**	Manny Sanguillen	Pirates	-34.6

Best Pitchers

Rank	Pitcher	Team	G	ERA	B	O	BPO	BV	BPO+
1	Fergie Jenkins	Cubs	40	3.39	525	951	.552	-141.8	78.7
2	Tom Seaver	Mets	37	2.82	466	882	.528	-115.2	80.2
3	Bob Gibson	Cardinals	34	3.12	477	885	.539	-106.7	81.7
4	Wayne Simpson	Reds	26	3.02	299	536	.558	-52.9	85.0
5	Gaylord Perry	Giants	41	3.20	557	991	.562	-88.8	86.2
6	Bill Hands	Cubs	39	3.70	497	809	.614	-70.2	87.6
7	Milt Pappas	Braves-Cubs	32	3.34	336	549	.612	-46.4	88.0
8	Luke Walker	Pirates	42	3.04	276	487	.567	-35.9	88.5
9	Pat Jarvis	Braves	36	3.61	465	769	.605	-56.5	89.2
9	Jim McAndrew	Mets	32	3.56	325	553	.588	-39.4	89.2

Extremes for Pitchers

Pitcher	Team	Best		Pitcher	Team	Worst
Fergie Jenkins	Cubs	-141.8	**BV**	Frank Reberger	Giants	98.3
Tom Seaver	Mets	73.4	**ERA+**	Rich Robertson	Giants	126.8
Tom Seaver	Mets	-32.9	**ERV**	Frank Reberger	Giants	29.4
Luke Walker	Pirates	60.3	**ISO+**	Denny Lemaster	Astros	138.6
Bob Gibson	Cardinals	-52.0	**EXV**	Don Sutton	Dodgers	42.1
Tom Seaver	Mets	66.9	**CT+**	Alan Foster	Dodgers	162.4
Tom Seaver	Mets	93.8	**SOV**	Claude Osteen	Dodgers	-66.9
Fergie Jenkins	Cubs	53.0	**EY+**	Clay Kirby	Padres	157.1
Fergie Jenkins	Cubs	-47.8	**BBV**	Nolan Ryan	Mets	49.2

1971 American League

Standings

Rank	Team	Post	W	L	Pct.	R	RA	BPO	BPOA	TS
1	Baltimore Orioles	LP	101	57	.639	4.70	3.35	.717	.572	83.333
2	Oakland Athletics	P	101	60	.627	4.29	3.50	.656	.579	66.960
3	Detroit Tigers	—	91	71	.562	4.33	3.98	.676	.646	55.205
4	Kansas City Royals	—	85	76	.528	3.75	3.52	.616	.592	50.993
5	Boston Red Sox	—	85	77	.525	4.27	4.12	.668	.665	48.925
6	New York Yankees	—	82	80	.506	4.00	3.96	.636	.594	48.876
7	Chicago White Sox	—	79	83	.488	3.81	3.69	.652	.599	48.415
8	Minnesota Twins	—	74	86	.463	4.09	4.19	.632	.666	39.450
9	California Angels	—	76	86	.469	3.15	3.56	.546	.585	37.670
10	Milwaukee Brewers	—	69	92	.429	3.32	3.78	.583	.636	32.769
11	Washington Senators	—	63	96	.396	3.38	4.15	.574	.674	24.936
12	Cleveland Indians	—	60	102	.370	3.35	4.61	.570	.715	16.585

Best Batters

Rank	Batter	Team	G	BA	B	O	BPO	BV	BPO+
1	Bobby Murcer	Yankees	146	.331	396	375	1.056	148.9	160.3
2	Don Buford	Orioles	122	.290	329	332	.991	106.5	147.9
3	Roy White	Yankees	147	.292	370	405	.914	103.2	138.7
4	Merv Rettenmund	Orioles	141	.318	333	361	.922	91.1	137.6
5	Frank Robinson	Orioles	133	.281	325	358	.908	85.1	135.5
5	Norm Cash	Tigers	135	.283	312	334	.934	81.7	135.5
7	Reggie Jackson	Athletics	150	.277	379	433	.875	90.3	131.3
8	Boog Powell	Orioles	128	.256	284	326	.871	65.5	130.0
9	Harmon Killebrew	Twins	147	.254	359	406	.884	80.8	129.1
10	Tony Oliva	Twins	126	.337	301	349	.862	61.9	125.9

Extremes for Batters

Batter	Team	Best		Batter	Team	Worst
Bobby Murcer	Yankees	148.9	BV	Ed Brinkman	Tigers	-92.6
Frank Robinson	Orioles	150.5	SE+	Ed Brinkman	Tigers	65.4
Bobby Murcer	Yankees	52.0	SCV	Ed Brinkman	Tigers	-40.2
Reggie Jackson	Athletics	182.5	ISO+	Ed Brinkman	Tigers	34.8
Reggie Jackson	Athletics	59.2	EXV	Cesar Tovar	Twins	-47.7
Felipe Alou	Athletics-Yankees	268.5	CT+	Reggie Jackson	Athletics	48.9
Cesar Tovar	Twins	-48.1	SOV	Reggie Jackson	Athletics	82.3
Harmon Killebrew	Twins	199.8	EY+	Aurelio Rodriguez	Tigers	40.2
Harmon Killebrew	Twins	50.0	BBV	Aurelio Rodriguez	Tigers	-31.2

Best Pitchers

Rank	Pitcher	Team	G	ERA	B	O	BPO	BV	BPO+
1	Vida Blue	Athletics	39	1.82	411	936	.439	-144.3	74.0
2	Wilbur Wood	White Sox	44	1.91	493	1,011	.488	-133.8	78.7
3	Mel Stottlemyre	Yankees	35	2.87	409	818	.500	-72.8	84.9
4	Mike Hedlund	Royals	32	2.71	335	618	.542	-43.8	88.4
5	Clyde Wright	Angels	37	2.99	432	836	.517	-54.8	88.8
6	Joe Coleman	Tigers	39	3.15	477	862	.553	-57.6	89.2
7	Steve Kline	Yankees	31	2.96	355	675	.526	-42.6	89.3
8	Pat Dobson	Orioles	38	2.90	457	859	.532	-53.0	89.6
9	Sonny Siebert	Red Sox	32	2.91	418	712	.587	-43.5	90.6
10	Rudy May	Angels	32	3.02	335	626	.535	-29.5	91.9

Extremes for Pitchers

Pitcher	Team	Best		Pitcher	Team	Worst
Vida Blue	Athletics	-144.3	BV	Denny McLain	Senators	102.6
Wilbur Wood	White Sox	55.7	ERA+	Denny McLain	Senators	137.0
Wilbur Wood	White Sox	-56.4	ERV	Steve Hargan	Indians	32.2
Wilbur Wood	White Sox	69.5	ISO+	Jim Perry	Twins	160.4
Wilbur Wood	White Sox	-44.9	EXV	Jim Perry	Twins	71.5
Vida Blue	Athletics	59.8	CT+	Steve Kline	Yankees	173.2
Vida Blue	Athletics	121.0	SOV	Steve Kline	Yankees	-59.3
Fritz Peterson	Yankees	42.4	EY+	Sam McDowell	Indians	188.7
Fritz Peterson	Yankees	-47.6	BBV	Sam McDowell	Indians	65.8

1971 National League

Standings

Rank	Team	Post	W	L	Pct.	R	RA	BPO	BPOA	TS
1	Pittsburgh Pirates	WLP	97	65	.599	4.86	3.70	.693	.597	87.094
2	San Francisco Giants	P	90	72	.556	4.36	3.98	.676	.600	60.715
3	Los Angeles Dodgers	—	89	73	.549	4.09	3.62	.632	.587	58.241
4	Saint Louis Cardinals	—	90	72	.556	4.53	4.29	.679	.655	55.388
5	New York Mets	—	83	79	.512	3.63	3.40	.612	.576	51.605
6	Chicago Cubs	—	83	79	.512	3.93	4.00	.643	.635	46.836
7	Houston Astros	—	79	83	.488	3.61	3.50	.582	.573	45.809
8	Cincinnati Reds	—	79	83	.488	3.62	3.59	.594	.606	43.490
9	Atlanta Braves	—	82	80	.506	3.97	4.31	.630	.673	39.848
10	Montreal Expos	—	71	90	.441	3.84	4.50	.609	.694	26.965
11	Philadelphia Phillies	—	67	95	.414	3.44	4.25	.587	.660	23.805
12	San Diego Padres	—	61	100	.379	3.02	3.79	.551	.622	20.541

Best Batters

Rank	Batter	Team	G	BA	B	O	BPO	BV	BPO+
1	Hank Aaron	Braves	139	.327	410	348	1.178	169.6	170.6
2	Willie Stargell	Pirates	141	.295	416	373	1.115	160.8	163.0
3	Willie Mays	Giants	136	.271	344	320	1.075	127.7	159.0
4	Joe Torre	Cardinals	161	.363	429	429	1.000	135.3	146.1
5	Dick Allen	Dodgers	155	.295	365	417	.875	90.7	133.0
6	Bobby Bonds	Giants	155	.288	415	464	.894	101.4	132.3
7	Lou Brock	Cardinals	157	.313	416	467	.891	96.3	130.1
7	Rusty Staub	Expos	162	.311	389	447	.870	89.9	130.1
9	Lee May	Reds	147	.278	346	415	.834	68.2	124.6
10	Cleon Jones	Mets	136	.319	308	366	.842	60.6	124.5

Extremes for Batters

Batter	Team	Best		Batter	Team	Worst
Hank Aaron	Braves	169.6	**BV**	Larry Bowa	Phillies	-85.4
Willie Stargell	Pirates	152.3	**SE+**	Enzo Hernandez	Padres	63.1
Joe Torre	Cardinals	68.2	**SCV**	Enzo Hernandez	Padres	-40.9
Hank Aaron	Braves	264.8	**ISO+**	Enzo Hernandez	Padres	22.7
Hank Aaron	Braves	105.2	**EXV**	Larry Bowa	Phillies	-60.0
Felix Millan	Braves	347.1	**CT+**	Willie Stargell	Pirates	45.0
Felix Millan	Braves	-54.4	**SOV**	Willie Stargell	Pirates	84.8
Willie Mays	Giants	256.6	**EY+**	Manny Sanguillen	Pirates	13.7
Willie Mays	Giants	61.6	**BBV**	Manny Sanguillen	Pirates	-37.6

Best Pitchers

Rank	Pitcher	Team	G	ERA	B	O	BPO	BV	BPO+
1	Tom Seaver	Mets	36	1.76	392	855	.458	-128.1	75.4
2	Don Wilson	Astros	35	2.45	405	811	.499	-82.8	83.0
3	Fergie Jenkins	Cubs	39	2.77	535	981	.545	-107.7	83.2
4	Ken Forsch	Astros	33	2.53	291	574	.507	-54.3	84.3
5	Dave Roberts	Padres	37	2.10	418	822	.509	-70.4	85.6
6	Gary Nolan	Reds	35	3.16	391	739	.529	-52.0	88.3
7	Dock Ellis	Pirates	31	3.06	373	691	.540	-48.0	88.6
8	Don Sutton	Dodgers	38	2.54	417	797	.523	-53.0	88.7
9	Steve Blass	Pirates	33	2.85	392	722	.543	-47.9	89.1
9	Ray Sadecki	Mets	34	2.92	265	489	.542	-32.4	89.1

Extremes for Pitchers

Pitcher	Team	Best		Pitcher	Team	Worst
Tom Seaver	Mets	-128.1	**BV**	Carl Morton	Expos	85.4
Tom Seaver	Mets	53.3	**ERA+**	Carl Morton	Expos	141.3
Tom Seaver	Mets	-49.0	**ERV**	Carl Morton	Expos	33.3
Ken Forsch	Astros	63.8	**ISO+**	Ron Reed	Braves	131.5
Dave Roberts	Padres	-33.5	**EXV**	Ron Reed	Braves	30.7
Tom Seaver	Mets	56.8	**CT+**	John Cumberland	Giants	170.0
Tom Seaver	Mets	125.0	**SOV**	Milt Pappas	Cubs	-59.0
Fergie Jenkins	Cubs	33.4	**EY+**	Ernie McAnally	Expos	163.9
Fergie Jenkins	Cubs	-61.9	**BBV**	Nolan Ryan	Mets	62.6

1972 American League

Standings

Rank	Team	Post	W	L	Pct.	R	RA	BPO	BPOA	TS
1	Oakland Athletics	WLP	93	62	.600	3.90	2.95	.621	.535	84.430
2	Baltimore Orioles	—	80	74	.519	3.37	2.79	.588	.515	58.264
3	Chicago White Sox	—	87	67	.565	3.68	3.49	.604	.585	55.225
4	Detroit Tigers	P	86	70	.551	3.58	3.29	.592	.588	53.486
5	Boston Red Sox	—	85	70	.548	4.13	4.00	.645	.624	53.280
6	New York Yankees	—	79	76	.510	3.59	3.40	.614	.577	51.207
7	Kansas City Royals	—	76	78	.494	3.77	3.54	.625	.597	49.014
8	Minnesota Twins	—	77	77	.500	3.49	3.47	.583	.566	47.024
9	California Angels	—	75	80	.484	2.93	3.44	.537	.590	35.285
10	Cleveland Indians	—	72	84	.462	3.03	3.33	.545	.610	33.833
11	Milwaukee Brewers	—	65	91	.417	3.16	3.81	.556	.606	27.472
12	Texas Rangers	—	54	100	.351	2.99	4.08	.529	.644	11.812

Best Batters

Rank	Batter	Team	G	BA	B	O	BPO	BV	BPO+
1	Dick Allen	White Sox	148	.308	427	374	1.142	186.0	177.2
2	Bobby Murcer	Yankees	153	.292	394	433	.910	171.8	144.8
3	Mike Epstein	Athletics	138	.270	305	343	.889	90.5	142.2
4	John Mayberry	Royals	149	.298	340	371	.916	100.2	141.8
5	Carlos May	White Sox	148	.308	344	390	.882	92.7	136.9
6	Carlton Fisk	Red Sox	131	.293	308	337	.914	80.1	135.2
7	Reggie Jackson	Athletics	135	.265	318	386	.824	76.6	131.7
8	Reggie Smith	Red Sox	131	.270	313	357	.877	71.6	129.7
9	Roy White	Yankees	155	.270	342	430	.795	71.7	126.5
10	Harmon Killebrew	Twins	139	.231	294	354	.831	61.5	126.4

Extremes for Batters

Batter	Team	Best		Batter	Team	Worst
Dick Allen	White Sox	186.0	BV	Ed Brinkman	Tigers	-85.1
Dick Allen	White Sox	152.4	SE+	Leo Cardenas	Angels	61.6
Dick Allen	White Sox	57.0	SCV	Leo Cardenas	Angels	-38.0
Dick Allen	White Sox	246.8	ISO+	Doug Griffin	Red Sox	32.2
Dick Allen	White Sox	88.6	EXV	Doug Griffin	Red Sox	-42.1
Buddy Bell	Indians	225.5	CT+	Bobby Darwin	Twins	48.2
Buddy Bell	Indians	-36.4	SOV	Bobby Darwin	Twins	75.1
Harmon Killebrew	Twins	199.4	EY+	Bob Oliver	Royals-Angels	46.0
Harmon Killebrew	Twins	40.9	BBV	Aurelio Rodriguez	Tigers	-26.4

Best Pitchers

Rank	Pitcher	Team	G	ERA	B	O	BPO	BV	BPO+
1	Gaylord Perry	Indians	41	1.92	480	1,033	.465	-135.7	78.0
2	Luis Tiant	Red Sox	43	1.91	256	535	.479	-68.8	78.8
3	Roger Nelson	Royals	34	2.08	245	516	.475	-54.2	81.9
4	Steve Kline	Yankees	32	2.40	344	726	.474	-64.8	84.2
5	Pat Dobson	Orioles	38	2.65	393	810	.485	-68.0	85.3
6	Catfish Hunter	Athletics	38	2.04	423	886	.477	-70.1	85.8
7	Jim Palmer	Orioles	36	2.07	410	823	.498	-58.4	87.5
8	Wilbur Wood	White Sox	49	2.51	601	1,135	.530	-56.3	91.4
9	Tom Bradley	White Sox	40	2.98	425	791	.537	-33.1	92.8
10	Bert Blyleven	Twins	39	2.73	479	862	.556	-30.0	94.1
10	Marty Pattin	Red Sox	38	3.24	433	758	.571	-27.1	94.1
10	Jim Perry	Twins	35	3.35	366	659	.555	-23.1	94.1

Extremes for Pitchers

Pitcher	Team	Best		Pitcher	Team	Worst
Gaylord Perry	Indians	-135.7	BV	Rickey Clark	Angels	57.3
Luis Tiant	Red Sox	60.4	ERA+	Pete Broberg	Rangers	145.5
Gaylord Perry	Indians	-47.5	ERV	Pete Broberg	Rangers	26.3
Luis Tiant	Red Sox	60.0	ISO+	Bill Parsons	Brewers	148.0
Luis Tiant	Red Sox	-29.4	EXV	Bill Parsons	Brewers	36.6
Nolan Ryan	Angels	49.0	CT+	Steve Kline	Yankees	253.8
Nolan Ryan	Angels	167.7	SOV	Steve Kline	Yankees	-89.2
Fritz Peterson	Yankees	53.5	EY+	Nolan Ryan	Angels	189.0
Wilbur Wood	White Sox	-35.3	BBV	Nolan Ryan	Angels	72.0

1972 National League

Standings

Rank	Team	Post	W	L	Pct.	R	RA	BPO	BPOA	TS
1	Cincinnati Reds	LP	95	59	.617	4.59	3.62	.686	.602	76.006
2	Pittsburgh Pirates	P	96	59	.619	4.46	3.30	.653	.556	70.056
3	Chicago Cubs	—	85	70	.548	4.39	3.63	.670	.608	58.763
4	Los Angeles Dodgers	—	85	70	.548	3.77	3.40	.621	.551	56.865
5	Houston Astros	—	84	69	.549	4.63	4.16	.683	.645	55.431
6	New York Mets	—	83	73	.532	3.38	3.71	.584	.607	44.893
7	Saint Louis Cardinals	—	75	81	.481	3.64	3.85	.604	.615	41.814
8	San Francisco Giants	—	69	86	.445	4.27	4.19	.652	.651	41.145
9	Atlanta Braves	—	70	84	.455	4.05	4.71	.652	.702	33.994
10	Montreal Expos	—	70	86	.449	3.29	3.90	.566	.618	33.617
11	Philadelphia Phillies	—	59	97	.378	3.22	4.07	.577	.667	23.253
12	San Diego Padres	—	58	95	.379	3.19	4.35	.547	.673	18.969

Best Batters

Rank	Batter	Team	G	BA	B	O	BPO	BV	BPO+
1	Joe Morgan	Reds	149	.292	426	420	1.014	150.6	154.7
2	Cesar Cedeno	Astros	139	.320	421	417	1.010	140.7	150.2
3	Billy Williams	Cubs	150	.333	427	406	1.052	139.3	148.4
4	Johnny Bench	Reds	147	.270	411	429	.958	129.7	146.1
5	Willie Stargell	Pirates	138	.293	351	365	.962	104.0	142.1
6	Jim Wynn	Astros	145	.273	382	414	.923	103.7	137.3
7	Hank Aaron	Braves	129	.265	330	349	.946	83.6	133.9
8	Richie Hebner	Pirates	124	.300	282	314	.898	69.5	132.7
9	Nate Colbert	Padres	151	.250	381	448	.850	88.6	130.3
10	Tony Perez	Reds	136	.283	321	386	.832	67.9	126.8

Extremes for Batters

Batter	Team	Best		Batter	Team	Worst
Joe Morgan	Reds	150.6	BV	Marty Perez	Braves	-116.4
Jim Wynn	Astros	149.6	SE+	Marty Perez	Braves	55.5
Jim Wynn	Astros	60.7	SCV	Marty Perez	Braves	-48.1
Nate Colbert	Padres	215.6	ISO+	Marty Perez	Braves	28.2
Billy Williams	Cubs	78.2	EXV	Roger Metzger	Astros	-57.0
Glenn Beckert	Cubs	389.1	CT+	Dave Kingman	Giants	48.8
Glenn Beckert	Cubs	-49.2	SOV	Dave Kingman	Giants	71.6
Joe Morgan	Reds	224.4	EY+	Manny Sanguillen	Pirates	22.7
Joe Morgan	Reds	63.2	BBV	Manny Sanguillen	Pirates	-34.0

Best Pitchers

Rank	Pitcher	Team	G	ERA	B	O	BPO	BV	BPO+
1	Don Sutton	Dodgers	33	2.08	358	829	.432	-143.0	71.5
2	Steve Carlton	Phillies	41	1.97	490	1,040	.471	-169.1	74.3
3	Bill Hands	Cubs	32	3.00	306	576	.531	-59.8	83.7
4	Phil Niekro	Braves	38	3.06	459	860	.534	-87.3	84.0
5	Gary Nolan	Reds	25	1.99	262	529	.495	-47.7	84.6
6	Bob Gibson	Cardinals	34	2.46	430	830	.518	-66.6	86.6
7	Dock Ellis	Pirates	25	2.70	257	491	.523	-38.6	86.9
8	Bob Moose	Pirates	31	2.91	364	686	.531	-49.1	88.1
9	Jon Matlack	Mets	34	2.32	401	735	.546	-44.2	90.1
9	Milt Pappas	Cubs	29	2.77	338	591	.572	-37.3	90.1
9	Tommy John	Dodgers	29	2.89	313	575	.544	-34.5	90.1

Extremes for Pitchers

Pitcher	Team	Best		Pitcher	Team	Worst
Steve Carlton	Phillies	-169.1	BV	Bill Greif	Padres	84.4
Steve Carlton	Phillies	56.9	ERA+	Dave Roberts	Astros	138.6
Steve Carlton	Phillies	-57.5	ERV	Bill Greif	Padres	34.0
Dock Ellis	Pirates	65.9	ISO+	Ken Forsch	Astros	133.8
Steve Carlton	Phillies	-50.1	EXV	Bill Greif	Padres	31.6
Tom Seaver	Mets	64.6	CT+	Carl Morton	Expos	224.3
Steve Carlton	Phillies	88.8	SOV	Claude Osteen	Dodgers	-63.6
Milt Pappas	Cubs	46.4	EY+	Sam McDowell	Giants	151.5
Phil Niekro	Braves	-35.3	BBV	Clay Kirby	Padres	34.3

1973 American League

Standings

Rank	Team	Post	W	L	Pct.	R	RA	BPO	BPOA	TS
1	Oakland Athletics	WLP	94	68	.580	4.68	3.80	.691	.606	79.826
2	Baltimore Orioles	P	97	65	.599	4.65	3.46	.711	.588	71.917
3	Boston Red Sox	—	89	73	.549	4.56	3.99	.701	.654	57.540
4	Minnesota Twins	—	81	81	.500	4.56	4.27	.686	.639	50.598
5	Kansas City Royals	—	88	74	.543	4.66	4.64	.681	.690	49.488
6	New York Yankees	—	80	82	.494	3.96	3.77	.626	.600	47.920
7	Detroit Tigers	—	85	77	.525	3.96	4.16	.642	.675	44.554
8	California Angels	—	79	83	.488	3.88	4.06	.597	.633	40.667
9	Milwaukee Brewers	—	74	88	.457	4.37	4.51	.671	.669	40.280
10	Chicago White Sox	—	77	85	.475	4.02	4.35	.634	.669	38.423
11	Cleveland Indians	—	71	91	.438	4.20	5.10	.633	.726	26.967
12	Texas Rangers	—	57	105	.352	3.82	5.21	.617	.739	12.786

Best Batters

Rank	Batter	Team	G	BA	B	O	BPO	BV	BPO+
1	Reggie Jackson	Athletics	151	.293	398	409	.973	127.8	147.3
2	John Mayberry	Royals	152	.278	375	377	.995	110.2	141.6
3	Frank Robinson	Angels	147	.266	358	410	.873	98.4	137.9
4	Sal Bando	Athletics	162	.287	396	448	.884	100.0	133.8
5	Rod Carew	Twins	149	.350	391	422	.927	97.6	133.3
6	Gene Tenace	Athletics	160	.259	354	408	.868	84.4	131.3
7	Jeff Burroughs	Rangers	151	.279	335	398	.842	72.1	127.4
8	Carl Yastrzemski	Red Sox	152	.296	371	413	.898	76.0	125.7
9	George Scott	Brewers	158	.306	373	449	.831	76.1	125.6
10	John Briggs	Brewers	142	.246	315	386	.816	59.8	123.4

Extremes for Batters

Batter	Team	Best		Batter	Team	Worst
Reggie Jackson	Athletics	127.8	BV	Tim Johnson	Brewers	-96.5
Reggie Jackson	Athletics	155.9	SE+	Tim Johnson	Brewers	72.3
Reggie Jackson	Athletics	66.0	SCV	Bill Freehan	Tigers	-35.1
Reggie Jackson	Athletics	201.3	ISO+	Sandy Alomar	Angels	17.1
Reggie Jackson	Athletics	64.4	EXV	Luis Aparicio	Red Sox	-52.2
Luis Aparicio	Red Sox	213.2	CT+	Bobby Darwin	Twins	57.5
Buddy Bell	Indians	-44.5	SOV	Bobby Darwin	Twins	58.3
John Mayberry	Royals	210.1	EY+	Ray Fosse	Athletics	46.6
John Mayberry	Royals	55.0	BBV	Alex Johnson	Rangers	-28.4

Best Pitchers

Rank	Pitcher	Team	G	ERA	B	O	BPO	BV	BPO+
1	Bert Blyleven	Twins	40	2.52	526	975	.539	-111.1	82.6
2	Jim Palmer	Orioles	38	2.40	469	882	.532	-80.3	85.4
3	Ken Holtzman	Athletics	40	2.97	477	904	.528	-79.4	85.7
4	Bill Lee	Red Sox	38	2.75	495	854	.580	-78.3	86.3
5	Mel Stottlemyre	Yankees	38	3.07	453	827	.548	-66.1	87.3
6	Luis Tiant	Red Sox	35	3.34	484	815	.594	-63.1	88.5
7	Gaylord Perry	Indians	41	3.38	624	1,038	.601	-58.1	91.5
7	Dave McNally	Orioles	38	3.21	452	793	.570	-41.8	91.5
9	Doc Medich	Yankees	34	2.95	415	717	.579	-35.0	92.2
10	Jim Colborn	Brewers	43	3.18	544	942	.577	-45.2	92.3

Extremes for Pitchers

Pitcher	Team	Best		Pitcher	Team	Worst
Bert Blyleven	Twins	-111.1	BV	Mike Kekich	Yankees-Indians	77.5
Bert Blyleven	Twins	66.7	ERA+	Woodie Fryman	Tigers	138.3
Bert Blyleven	Twins	-45.4	ERV	Lloyd Allen	Angels-Rangers	32.7
Terry Forster	White Sox	51.8	ISO+	Catfish Hunter	Athletics	155.0
Bert Blyleven	Twins	-40.4	EXV	Catfish Hunter	Athletics	58.2
Nolan Ryan	Angels	46.7	CT+	Clyde Wright	Angels	235.2
Nolan Ryan	Angels	204.0	SOV	Clyde Wright	Angels	-87.9
Jim Kaat	Twins-White Sox	56.7	EY+	Jim Bibby	Rangers	173.1
Bert Blyleven	Twins	-39.7	BBV	Nolan Ryan	Angels	60.1

1973 National League

Standings

Rank	Team	Post	W	L	Pct.	R	RA	BPO	BPOA	TS
1	Cincinnati Reds	P	99	63	.611	4.57	3.83	.693	.645	67.755
2	Los Angeles Dodgers	—	95	66	.590	4.17	3.49	.642	.567	67.170
3	New York Mets	LP	82	79	.509	3.78	3.65	.583	.607	57.307
4	San Francisco Giants	—	88	74	.543	4.56	4.33	.711	.648	57.271
5	Saint Louis Cardinals	—	81	81	.500	3.97	3.72	.626	.603	49.557
6	Atlanta Braves	—	76	85	.472	4.93	4.78	.737	.687	47.987
7	Pittsburgh Pirates	—	80	82	.494	4.35	4.28	.648	.645	45.753
8	Houston Astros	—	82	80	.506	4.20	4.15	.628	.641	45.691
9	Montreal Expos	—	79	83	.488	4.12	4.33	.666	.669	42.147
10	Chicago Cubs	—	77	84	.478	3.81	4.07	.617	.642	38.971
11	Philadelphia Phillies	—	71	91	.438	3.96	4.43	.618	.697	28.466
12	San Diego Padres	—	60	102	.370	3.38	4.75	.578	.696	10.185

Best Batters

Rank	Batter	Team	G	BA	B	O	BPO	BV	BPO+
1	Willie Stargell	Pirates	148	.299	424	376	1.128	162.6	162.2
2	Joe Morgan	Reds	157	.290	473	443	1.068	171.2	156.7
3	Darrell Evans	Braves	161	.281	475	451	1.053	148.8	145.6
4	Cesar Cedeno	Astros	139	.320	389	394	.987	115.9	142.4
5	Tony Perez	Reds	151	.314	383	407	.941	105.7	138.1
6	Bobby Bonds	Giants	160	.283	479	490	.978	129.3	137.0
7	Ron Fairly	Expos	142	.298	283	303	.934	69.1	132.3
8	Davey Johnson	Braves	157	.270	402	421	.955	97.5	132.0
9	Ken Singleton	Expos	162	.302	402	433	.928	96.4	131.5
10	Willie Crawford	Dodgers	145	.295	305	340	.897	69.2	129.4

Extremes for Batters

Batter	Team	Best		Batter	Team	Worst
Joe Morgan	Reds	171.2	**BV**	Larry Bowa	Phillies	-114.5
Willie Stargell	Pirates	152.4	**SE+**	Don Kessinger	Cubs	69.2
Willie Stargell	Pirates	62.2	**SCV**	Don Kessinger	Cubs	-42.3
Willie Stargell	Pirates	255.1	**ISO+**	Don Kessinger	Cubs	34.3
Willie Stargell	Pirates	110.1	**EXV**	Don Kessinger	Cubs	-53.5
Felix Millan	Mets	393.7	**CT+**	Nate Colbert	Padres	49.3
Felix Millan	Mets	-64.6	**SOV**	Mike Schmidt	Phillies	84.2
Ken Singleton	Expos	202.5	**EY+**	Manny Sanguillen	Pirates	18.0
Darrell Evans	Braves	56.0	**BBV**	Manny Sanguillen	Pirates	-41.0

Best Pitchers

Rank	Pitcher	Team	G	ERA	B	O	BPO	BV	BPO+
1	Tom Seaver	Mets	36	2.08	421	880	.478	-129.8	76.4
2	Don Sutton	Dodgers	33	2.42	371	776	.478	-107.1	77.6
3	Dock Ellis	Pirates	28	3.05	305	582	.524	-56.9	84.3
4	Bob Gibson	Cardinals	25	2.77	324	597	.543	-46.7	87.4
5	Jim Rooker	Pirates	41	2.85	282	515	.548	-38.3	88.1
6	Tommy John	Dodgers	36	3.10	363	666	.545	-47.3	88.5
7	Reggie Cleveland	Cardinals	32	3.01	377	683	.552	-47.0	88.9
8	Nelson Briles	Pirates	33	2.84	368	663	.555	-44.3	89.3
9	Carl Morton	Braves	38	3.41	453	779	.582	-53.4	89.5
10	Rick Reuschel	Cubs	36	3.00	423	721	.587	-47.7	89.9

Extremes for Pitchers

Pitcher	Team	Best		Pitcher	Team	Worst
Tom Seaver	Mets	-129.8	**BV**	Steve Blass	Pirates	114.7
Tom Seaver	Mets	59.8	**ERA+**	Steve Arlin	Padres	153.7
Tom Seaver	Mets	-45.0	**ERV**	Steve Blass	Pirates	63.6
Dock Ellis	Pirates	47.7	**ISO+**	Clay Kirby	Padres	160.9
Dock Ellis	Pirates	-45.0	**EXV**	Clay Kirby	Padres	51.1
Tom Seaver	Mets	68.3	**CT+**	Milt Pappas	Cubs	213.8
Tom Seaver	Mets	79.5	**SOV**	Claude Osteen	Dodgers	-59.5
Juan Marichal	Giants	45.1	**EY+**	Balor Moore	Expos	186.2
Juan Marichal	Giants	-36.5	**BBV**	Balor Moore	Expos	49.5

1974 American League

Standings

Rank	Team	Post	W	L	Pct.	R	RA	BPO	BPOA	TS
1	Oakland Athletics	WLP	90	72	.556	4.25	3.40	.663	.575	86.731
2	Baltimore Orioles	P	91	71	.562	4.07	3.78	.652	.601	62.380
3	New York Yankees	—	89	73	.549	4.14	3.85	.631	.621	56.701
4	Boston Red Sox	—	84	78	.519	4.30	4.08	.665	.656	51.413
5	Texas Rangers	—	84	76	.525	4.29	4.34	.656	.649	49.171
6	Minnesota Twins	—	82	80	.506	4.13	4.10	.651	.646	47.147
7	Kansas City Royals	—	77	85	.475	4.12	4.09	.643	.626	44.227
8	Chicago White Sox	—	80	80	.500	4.20	4.42	.656	.648	43.710
9	Milwaukee Brewers	—	76	86	.469	3.99	4.07	.623	.651	37.615
10	Cleveland Indians	—	77	85	.475	4.09	4.28	.607	.650	35.617
11	California Angels	—	68	94	.420	3.79	4.03	.623	.639	30.136
12	Detroit Tigers	—	72	90	.444	3.83	4.74	.595	.702	16.924

Best Batters

Rank	Batter	Team	G	BA	B	O	BPO	BV	BPO+
1	Reggie Jackson	Athletics	148	.289	383	381	1.005	137.6	156.1
2	Jeff Burroughs	Rangers	152	.301	389	419	.928	117.0	143.0
3	Dick Allen	White Sox	128	.301	330	345	.957	99.1	142.9
4	Rod Carew	Twins	153	.364	396	430	.921	104.2	135.7
5	Frank Robinson	Angels-Indians	144	.245	323	380	.850	84.0	135.4
6	Carl Yastrzemski	Red Sox	148	.301	359	390	.921	86.6	131.8
7	Bobby Grich	Orioles	160	.263	393	470	.836	91.5	130.3
8	Gene Tenace	Athletics	158	.211	329	407	.808	66.9	125.5
9	Hal McRae	Royals	148	.310	335	401	.835	62.9	123.1
10	Sal Bando	Athletics	146	.243	319	404	.790	58.8	122.6

Extremes for Batters

Batter	Team	Best		Batter	Team	Worst
Reggie Jackson	Athletics	137.6	BV	Aurelio Rodriguez	Tigers	-98.6
Sal Bando	Athletics	149.9	SE+	Dave Chalk	Angels	74.5
Sal Bando	Athletics	54.9	SCV	Gary Sutherland	Tigers	-26.1
Dick Allen	White Sox	218.3	ISO+	Dave Nelson	Rangers	44.8
Dick Allen	White Sox	65.6	EXV	Gary Sutherland	Tigers	-40.2
Cesar Tovar	Rangers	241.6	CT+	Bobby Darwin	Twins	63.2
Gary Sutherland	Tigers	-49.3	SOV	Leroy Stanton	Angels	49.6
Gene Tenace	Athletics	217.0	EY+	Tommy Davis	Orioles	47.8
Gene Tenace	Athletics	56.1	BBV	Tommy Davis	Orioles	-27.3

Best Pitchers

Rank	Pitcher	Team	G	ERA	B	O	BPO	BV	BPO+
1	Gaylord Perry	Indians	37	2.51	501	961	.521	-106.5	82.5
2	Catfish Hunter	Athletics	41	2.49	483	956	.505	-92.8	83.9
3	Bert Blyleven	Twins	37	2.66	464	858	.541	-86.1	84.3
4	Fergie Jenkins	Rangers	41	2.82	519	993	.523	-94.3	84.6
4	Jim Kaat	White Sox	42	2.92	454	844	.538	-82.5	84.6
6	Bruce Dal Canton	Royals	31	3.13	293	538	.545	-51.6	85.0
7	Jim Perry	Indians	36	2.96	416	760	.547	-64.4	86.6
8	Luis Tiant	Red Sox	38	2.92	531	930	.571	-81.6	86.7
9	Vida Blue	Athletics	40	3.25	467	856	.546	-48.6	90.6
10	Al Fitzmorris	Royals	34	2.79	334	575	.581	-34.3	90.7

Extremes for Pitchers

Pitcher	Team	Best		Pitcher	Team	Worst
Gaylord Perry	Indians	-106.5	BV	Joe Coleman	Tigers	114.6
Gaylord Perry	Indians	72.0	ERA+	Jim Bibby	Rangers	138.3
Gaylord Perry	Indians	-34.9	ERV	Jim Bibby	Rangers	38.5
Bruce Dal Canton	Royals	45.6	ISO+	Jim Colborn	Brewers	137.3
Bruce Dal Canton	Royals	-42.9	EXV	Mickey Lolich	Tigers	45.0
Nolan Ryan	Angels	46.3	CT+	Clyde Wright	Brewers	208.7
Nolan Ryan	Angels	196.9	SOV	Clyde Wright	Brewers	-69.6
Fergie Jenkins	Rangers	42.9	EY+	Nolan Ryan	Angels	208.0
Fergie Jenkins	Rangers	-56.0	BBV	Nolan Ryan	Angels	103.3

1974 National League

Standings

Rank	Team	Post	W	L	Pct.	R	RA	BPO	BPOA	TS
1	Los Angeles Dodgers	LP	102	60	.630	4.93	3.46	.718	.568	81.722
2	Cincinnati Reds	—	98	64	.605	4.76	3.87	.723	.619	65.940
3	Atlanta Braves	—	88	74	.543	4.06	3.45	.632	.591	55.126
4	Pittsburgh Pirates	P	88	74	.543	4.64	4.06	.667	.626	55.011
5	Saint Louis Cardinals	—	86	75	.534	4.20	3.99	.655	.636	50.943
6	Montreal Expos	—	79	82	.491	4.11	4.08	.657	.619	46.927
7	Houston Astros	—	81	81	.500	4.03	3.90	.644	.650	45.955
8	Philadelphia Phillies	—	80	82	.494	4.17	4.33	.640	.691	41.323
9	San Francisco Giants	—	72	90	.444	3.91	4.46	.629	.661	35.586
10	New York Mets	—	71	91	.438	3.53	3.99	.580	.634	34.303
11	Chicago Cubs	—	66	96	.407	4.13	5.10	.641	.710	27.781
12	San Diego Padres	—	60	102	.370	3.34	5.12	.579	.758	13.763

Best Batters

Rank	Batter	Team	G	BA	B	O	BPO	BV	BPO+
1	Joe Morgan	Reds	149	.293	440	387	1.137	169.9	162.9
2	Willie Stargell	Pirates	140	.301	370	369	1.003	116.1	145 7
3	Mike Schmidt	Phillies	162	.282	451	432	1.044	138.0	144.1
4	Jim Wynn	Dodgers	150	.271	405	425	.953	111.6	138.0
5	Reggie Smith	Cardinals	143	.309	358	385	.930	90.8	134.0
6	Lou Brock	Cardinals	153	.306	426	485	.878	89.5	126.6
7	Cesar Cedeno	Astros	160	.269	416	482	.863	85.8	126.0
8	Johnny Bench	Reds	160	.280	407	468	.870	80.4	124.6
9	Bobby Bonds	Giants	150	.256	390	441	.884	76.5	124.4
10	Richie Zisk	Pirates	149	.313	324	384	.844	59.8	122.6

Extremes for Batters

Batter	Team	Best		Batter	Team	Worst
Joe Morgan	Reds	169.9	**BV**	Craig Robinson	Braves	-92.2
Johnny Bench	Reds	144.5	**SE+**	Felix Millan	Mets	70.3
Johnny Bench	Reds	62.8	**SCV**	Tito Fuentes	Giants	-35.6
Mike Schmidt	Phillies	197.6	**ISO+**	Ron Hunt	Expos-Cardinals	27.7
Mike Schmidt	Phillies	74.1	**EXV**	Larry Bowa	Phillies	-47.4
Felix Millan	Mets	480.0	**CT+**	Doug Rader	Astros	54.1
Dave Cash	Phillies	-58.7	**SOV**	Dave Kingman	Giants	77.8
Joe Morgan	Reds	208.8	**EY+**	Manny Sanguillen	Pirates	22.9
Joe Morgan	Reds	58.4	**BBV**	Manny Sanguillen	Pirates	-40.4

Best Pitchers

Rank	Pitcher	Team	G	ERA	B	O	BPO	BV	BPO+
1	Jon Matlack	Mets	34	2.41	402	803	.501	-103.9	79.5
2	Buzz Capra	Braves	39	2.28	350	657	.533	-75.3	82.3
3	Phil Niekro	Braves	41	2.38	493	910	.542	-96.1	83.7
4	Andy Messersmith	Dodgers	39	2.59	454	881	.515	-87.4	83.9
5	Jim Barr	Giants	44	2.74	393	713	.551	-65.0	85.8
6	Mike Marshall	Dodgers	106	2.42	335	632	.530	-53.4	86.3
7	Ken Brett	Pirates	27	3.30	313	580	.540	-45.8	87.2
8	Jim Rooker	Pirates	33	2.78	433	790	.548	-55.7	88.6
9	Dock Ellis	Pirates	26	3.16	300	536	.560	-31.6	90.5
10	Ron Reed	Braves	28	3.39	329	560	.588	-33.5	90.7

Extremes for Pitchers

Pitcher	Team	Best		Pitcher	Team	Worst
Jon Matlack	Mets	-103.9	**BV**	Bill Greif	Padres	98.6
Buzz Capra	Braves	62.6	**ERA+**	Bill Greif	Padres	136.8
Phil Niekro	Braves	-42.3	**ERV**	Bill Greif	Padres	31.5
Jon Matlack	Mets	58.4	**ISO+**	Alan Foster	Cardinals	132.6
Jon Matlack	Mets	-44.2	**EXV**	Tom Bradley	Giants	33.7
Tom Seaver	Mets	65.3	**CT+**	Dave Roberts	Astros	165.4
Steve Carlton	Phillies	77.3	**SOV**	Jim Barr	Giants	-52.9
Jim Barr	Giants	48.3	**EY+**	John D'Acquisto	Giants	155.9
Jim Barr	Giants	-39.6	**BBV**	John D'Acquisto	Giants	42.0

1975 American League

Standings

Rank	Team	Post	W	L	Pct.	R	RA	BPO	BPOA	TS
1	Boston Red Sox	LP	95	65	.594	4.98	4.43	.718	.678	70.338
2	Oakland Athletics	P	98	64	.605	4.68	3.74	.707	.603	70.016
3	Baltimore Orioles	—	90	69	.566	4.29	3.48	.659	.599	62.027
4	Kansas City Royals	—	91	71	.562	4.38	4.01	.701	.640	58.692
5	New York Yankees	—	83	77	.519	4.26	3.68	.651	.611	54.391
6	Cleveland Indians	—	79	80	.497	4.33	4.42	.664	.685	43.084
7	Texas Rangers	—	79	83	.488	4.41	4.52	.655	.661	43.074
8	Minnesota Twins	—	76	83	.478	4.55	4.63	.680	.691	42.091
9	Chicago White Sox	—	75	86	.466	4.07	4.37	.642	.692	36.465
10	California Angels	—	72	89	.447	3.90	4.49	.625	.666	33.262
11	Milwaukee Brewers	—	68	94	.420	4.17	4.89	.657	.707	29.035
12	Detroit Tigers	—	57	102	.358	3.58	4.94	.587	.713	13.022

Best Batters

Rank	Batter	Team	G	BA	B	O	BPO	BV	BPO+
1	John Mayberry	Royals	156	.291	437	410	1.066	150.8	152.7
2	Rod Carew	Twins	143	.359	383	379	1.011	119.7	145.5
3	Ken Singleton	Orioles	155	.300	397	433	.917	113.0	139.8
4	Bobby Bonds	Yankees	145	.270	398	418	.952	112.9	139.6
5	Fred Lynn	Red Sox	145	.331	386	381	1.013	108.8	139.2
6	Toby Harrah	Rangers	151	.293	371	395	.939	104.0	139.0
7	Gene Tenace	Athletics	158	.255	363	390	.931	100.4	138.2
8	Boog Powell	Indians	134	.297	296	321	.922	76.4	134.8
9	Don Baylor	Orioles	145	.282	362	413	.877	91.2	133.7
10	Bobby Grich	Orioles	150	.260	354	423	.837	76.6	127.6

Extremes for Batters

Batter	Team	Best		Batter	Team	Worst
John Mayberry	Royals	150.8	**BV**	Jim Sundberg	Rangers	-83.7
Leroy Stanton	Angels	142.5	**SE+**	Jim Sundberg	Rangers	69.6
Fred Lynn	Red Sox	53.2	**SCV**	Gary Sutherland	Tigers	-32.8
Reggie Jackson	Athletics	215.8	**ISO+**	Mark Belanger	Orioles	42.4
Reggie Jackson	Athletics	82.1	**EXV**	Rick Burleson	Red Sox	-37.2
Dan Meyer	Tigers	275.6	**CT+**	Jeff Burroughs	Rangers	54.8
Dan Meyer	Tigers	-43.9	**SOV**	Jeff Burroughs	Rangers	70.1
Gene Tenace	Athletics	193.1	**EY+**	Chris Chambliss	Yankees	38.5
Gene Tenace	Athletics	50.1	**BBV**	Chris Chambliss	Yankees	-31.9

Best Pitchers

Rank	Pitcher	Team	G	ERA	B	O	BPO	BV	BPO+
1	Catfish Hunter	Yankees	39	2.58	489	989	.494	-154.4	76.0
2	Jim Palmer	Orioles	39	2.09	495	976	.507	-114.2	81.3
3	Bert Blyleven	Twins	35	3.00	464	832	.558	-88.8	83.9
4	Gaylord Perry	Indians-Rangers	37	3.24	520	928	.560	-84.5	85.9
5	Frank Tanana	Angels	34	2.62	421	773	.545	-56.4	88.2
6	Marty Pattin	Royals	44	3.25	313	534	.586	-41.5	88.3
7	Steve Busby	Royals	34	3.08	454	774	.587	-59.8	88.4
8	Rudy May	Yankees	32	3.06	373	642	.581	-44.6	89.3
9	Bill Lee	Red Sox	41	3.95	491	787	.624	-55.0	89.9
10	Ken Holtzman	Athletics	39	3.14	461	805	.573	-51.3	90.0

Extremes for Pitchers

Pitcher	Team	Best		Pitcher	Team	Worst
Catfish Hunter	Yankees	-154.4	**BV**	Joe Coleman	Tigers	95.2
Jim Palmer	Orioles	60.3	**ERA+**	Bill Singer	Angels	143.5
Jim Palmer	Orioles	-49.4	**ERV**	Andy Hassler	Angels	36.6
Rudy May	Yankees	69.9	**ISO+**	Ross Grimsley	Orioles	161.1
Rich Gossage	White Sox	-35.3	**EXV**	Ross Grimsley	Orioles	52.3
Frank Tanana	Angels	49.0	**CT+**	Claude Osteen	White Sox	184.9
Frank Tanana	Angels	137.1	**SOV**	Bill Lee	Red Sox	-65.9
Fergie Jenkins	Rangers	53.4	**EY+**	Nolan Ryan	Angels	203.6
Fergie Jenkins	Rangers	-42.7	**BBV**	Nolan Ryan	Angels	67.2

1975 National League

Standings

Rank	Team	Post	W	L	Pct.	R	RA	BPO	BPOA	TS
1	Cincinnati Reds	WLP	108	54	.667	5.19	3.62	.748	.625	90.713
2	Pittsburgh Pirates	P	92	69	.571	4.42	3.51	.667	.601	62.292
3	Los Angeles Dodgers	—	88	74	.543	4.00	3.30	.660	.549	61.029
4	Philadelphia Phillies	—	86	76	.531	4.54	4.28	.717	.632	55.393
5	New York Mets	—	82	80	.506	3.99	3.86	.608	.624	45.970
6	Saint Louis Cardinals	—	82	80	.506	4.06	4.23	.644	.656	44.340
7	San Francisco Giants	—	80	81	.497	4.09	4.17	.652	.688	42.567
8	Montreal Expos	—	75	87	.463	3.71	4.26	.619	.666	35.642
9	Chicago Cubs	—	75	87	.463	4.40	5.10	.668	.720	34.312
10	San Diego Padres	—	71	91	.438	3.41	4.22	.588	.651	30.632
11	Houston Astros	—	64	97	.398	4.10	4.39	.633	.689	30.353
12	Atlanta Braves	—	67	94	.416	3.62	4.59	.593	.697	24.915

Best Batters

Rank	Batter	Team	G	BA	B	O	BPO	BV	BPO+
1	Joe Morgan	Reds	146	.327	461	354	1.302	208.6	182.6
2	Mike Schmidt	Phillies	158	.249	435	448	.971	108.6	133.3
3	Greg Luzinski	Phillies	161	.300	430	443	.971	107.2	133.2
4	Jim Wynn	Dodgers	130	.248	296	327	.905	72.1	132.2
5	Cesar Cedeno	Astros	131	.288	346	392	.883	80.5	130.3
6	Willie Stargell	Pirates	124	.295	303	338	.896	68.7	129.3
7	Johnny Bench	Reds	142	.283	361	400	.903	75.8	126.6
8	Dave Parker	Pirates	148	.308	354	411	.861	69.1	124.3
9	Ron Cey	Dodgers	158	.283	369	434	.850	71.8	124.2
10	Bob Watson	Astros	132	.324	291	349	.834	54.6	123.1

Extremes for Batters

Batter	Team	Best		Batter	Team	Worst
Joe Morgan	Reds	208.6	BV	Tim Foli	Expos	-99.2
Joe Morgan	Reds	140.5	SE+	Tim Foli	Expos	69.5
Joe Morgan	Reds	53.0	SCV	Ralph Garr	Braves	-41.6
Dave Kingman	Mets	221.0	ISO+	Marty Perez	Braves	41.4
Mike Schmidt	Phillies	79.9	EXV	Tim Foli	Expos	-40.3
Felix Millan	Mets	311.4	CT+	Mike Schmidt	Phillies	40.3
Felix Millan	Mets	-59.2	SOV	Mike Schmidt	Phillies	107.5
Jim Wynn	Dodgers	250.8	EY+	Ken Reitz	Cardinals	26.4
Joe Morgan	Reds	76.5	BBV	Ken Reitz	Cardinals	-36.2

Best Pitchers

Rank	Pitcher	Team	G	ERA	B	O	BPO	BV	BPO+
1	Randy Jones	Padres	37	2.24	429	871	.493	-106.4	80.1
2	Tom Seaver	Mets	36	2.38	422	839	.503	-98.6	81.1
3	Andy Messersmith	Dodgers	42	2.29	487	962	.506	-99.8	83.0
4	Larry Christenson	Phillies	29	3.67	286	512	.559	-48.7	85.4
5	Burt Hooton	Cubs-Dodgers	34	3.07	378	711	.532	-57.4	86.5
6	Bob Forsch	Cardinals	34	2.86	390	696	.560	-59.3	86.8
7	Don Sutton	Dodgers	35	2.87	407	768	.530	-61.5	86.9
8	Doug Rau	Dodgers	38	3.11	416	779	.534	-59.2	87.5
9	Dan Warthen	Expos	40	3.11	299	507	.590	-32.0	90.3
10	Jon Matlack	Mets	33	3.38	392	698	.562	-41.1	90.5
10	Gary Nolan	Reds	32	3.16	362	632	.573	-37.9	90.5

Extremes for Pitchers

Pitcher	Team	Best		Pitcher	Team	Worst
Randy Jones	Padres	-106.4	BV	Doug Konieczny	Astros	65.5
Randy Jones	Padres	66.8	ERA+	Doug Konieczny	Astros	137.6
Andy Messersmith	Dodgers	-35.5	ERV	Bill Bonham	Cubs	25.8
Tom Seaver	Mets	72.5	ISO+	Steve Renko	Expos	136.7
Ron Reed	Braves-Cardinals	-29.8	EXV	Oscar Zamora	Cubs	33.1
Tom Seaver	Mets	63.6	CT+	Carl Morton	Braves	205.9
Tom Seaver	Mets	88.4	SOV	Carl Morton	Braves	-82.6
Gary Nolan	Reds	37.4	EY+	J.R. Richard	Astros	196.4
Gary Nolan	Reds	-40.2	BBV	J.R. Richard	Astros	67.7

1976 American League

Standings

Rank	Team	Post	W	L	Pct.	R	RA	BPO	BPOA	TS
1	New York Yankees	LP	97	62	.610	4.59	3.62	.678	.582	81.368
2	Kansas City Royals	P	90	72	.556	4.40	3.77	.666	.604	61.588
3	Oakland Athletics	—	87	74	.540	4.26	3.71	.693	.603	61.493
4	Boston Red Sox	—	83	79	.512	4.42	4.07	.675	.639	52.507
5	Baltimore Orioles	—	88	74	.543	3.82	3.69	.621	.614	51.877
6	Minnesota Twins	—	85	77	.525	4.59	4.35	.678	.663	51.369
7	Cleveland Indians	—	81	78	.509	3.87	3.87	.609	.639	44.187
8	Texas Rangers	—	76	86	.469	3.80	4.02	.603	.636	37.758
9	California Angels	—	76	86	.469	3.40	3.90	.571	.625	33.826
10	Detroit Tigers	—	74	87	.460	3.78	4.40	.614	.656	32.772
11	Milwaukee Brewers	—	66	95	.410	3.54	4.07	.585	.660	25.517
12	Chicago White Sox	—	64	97	.398	3.64	4.63	.609	.680	20.772

Best Batters

Rank	Batter	Team	G	BA	B	O	BPO	BV	BPO+
1	Reggie Jackson	Orioles	134	.277	338	386	.876	94.5	138.8
2	Rod Carew	Twins	156	.331	411	453	.907	108.9	136.0
3	Gene Tenace	Athletics	128	.249	287	330	.870	75.9	135.9
4	Hal McRae	Royals	149	.332	347	387	.897	88.3	134.2
5	Bobby Grich	Orioles	144	.266	327	402	.813	73.5	129.0
6	Ron LeFlore	Tigers	135	.316	340	410	.829	69.1	125.5
7	George Brett	Royals	159	.333	379	459	.826	72.2	123.5
8	Sal Bando	Athletics	158	.240	345	441	.782	62.8	122.3
9	Mike Hargrove	Rangers	151	.287	323	404	.800	58.5	122.1
10	Rico Carty	Indians	152	.310	321	409	.785	56.7	121.4

Extremes for Batters

Batter	Team	Best		Batter	Team	Worst
Rod Carew	Twins	108.9	**BV**	Aurelio Rodriguez	Tigers	-75.6
Reggie Jackson	Orioles	147.5	**SE+**	Bucky Dent	White Sox	77.6
Reggie Jackson	Orioles	47.7	**SCV**	Jim Sundberg	Rangers	-33.3
Reggie Jackson	Orioles	215.6	**ISO+**	Bert Campaneris	Athletics	34.2
Graig Nettles	Yankees	64.5	**EXV**	Bert Campaneris	Athletics	-36.5
George Brett	Royals	223.0	**CT+**	Dan Ford	Twins	60.9
George Brett	Royals	-44.3	**SOV**	Dan Ford	Twins	46.2
Gene Tenace	Athletics	195.0	**EY+**	Mickey Rivers	Yankees	27.4
Gene Tenace	Athletics	38.5	**BBV**	Mickey Rivers	Yankees	-34.4

Best Pitchers

Rank	Pitcher	Team	G	ERA	B	O	BPO	BV	BPO+
1	Mark Fidrych	Tigers	31	2.34	364	764	.476	-120.7	75.1
2	Vida Blue	Athletics	37	2.35	444	908	.489	-106.3	80.7
3	Gaylord Perry	Rangers	32	3.24	402	754	.533	-67.8	85.6
4	Ken Brett	Yankees-White Sox	29	3.28	328	612	.536	-52.5	86.2
5	Reggie Cleveland	Red Sox	41	3.07	299	517	.578	-46.6	86.5
6	Frank Tanana	Angels	34	2.43	458	880	.520	-65.3	87.5
7	Rick Wise	Red Sox	34	3.53	402	679	.592	-51.9	88.6
8	Mike Torrez	Athletics	39	2.50	445	814	.547	-48.3	90.2
9	Jim Palmer	Orioles	40	2.51	515	944	.546	-50.2	91.1
10	Al Fitzmorris	Royals	35	3.06	383	665	.576	-36.5	91.3

Extremes for Pitchers

Pitcher	Team	Best		Pitcher	Team	Worst
Mark Fidrych	Tigers	-120.7	**BV**	Mike Cuellar	Orioles	65.6
Mark Fidrych	Tigers	65.3	**ERA+**	Jim Hughes	Twins	142.5
Mark Fidrych	Tigers	-34.6	**ERV**	Jesse Jefferson	White Sox	35.1
Mark Fidrych	Tigers	58.5	**ISO+**	Bill Travers	Brewers	129.8
Mark Fidrych	Tigers	-43.2	**EXV**	Catfish Hunter	Yankees	30.0
Nolan Ryan	Angels	41.2	**CT+**	Ken Holtzman	Orioles-Yankees	199.6
Nolan Ryan	Angels	192.2	**SOV**	Ken Holtzman	Orioles-Yankees	-65.7
Doug Bird	Royals	49.1	**EY+**	Nolan Ryan	Angels	218.8
Vida Blue	Athletics	-29.4	**BBV**	Nolan Ryan	Angels	98.3

1976 National League

Standings

Rank	Team	Post	W	L	Pct.	R	RA	BPO	BPOA	TS
1	Cincinnati Reds	WLP	102	60	.630	5.29	3.91	.789	.629	87.331
2	Philadelphia Phillies	P	101	61	.623	4.75	3.44	.696	.602	69.638
3	Pittsburgh Pirates	—	92	70	.568	4.37	3.89	.659	.606	57.435
4	Los Angeles Dodgers	—	92	70	.568	3.75	3.35	.612	.596	54.825
5	New York Mets	—	86	76	.531	3.80	3.32	.612	.565	53.806
6	Houston Astros	—	80	82	.494	3.86	4.06	.620	.652	41.924
7	Saint Louis Cardinals	—	72	90	.444	3.88	4.14	.629	.631	39.041
8	San Francisco Giants	—	74	88	.457	3.67	4.23	.597	.637	36.101
9	San Diego Padres	—	73	89	.451	3.52	4.09	.590	.624	35.843
10	Atlanta Braves	—	70	92	.432	3.83	4.32	.598	.655	33.335
11	Chicago Cubs	—	75	87	.463	3.77	4.49	.601	.681	33.313
12	Montreal Expos	—	55	107	.340	3.28	4.53	.565	.689	16.785

Best Batters

Rank	Batter	Team	G	BA	B	O	BPO	BV	BPO+
1	Joe Morgan	Reds	141	.320	459	344	1.334	221.8	193.5
2	Mike Schmidt	Phillies	160	.262	441	457	.965	123.6	139.0
3	George Foster	Reds	144	.306	380	413	.920	95.2	133.4
4	Cesar Cedeno	Astros	150	.297	379	439	.863	94.3	133.1
5	Ken Griffey Sr.	Reds	148	.336	353	390	.905	84.1	131.3
6	Ron Cey	Dodgers	145	.277	330	384	.859	75.8	129.8
7	Bill Madlock	Cubs	142	.339	346	379	.913	76.9	128.6
8	Dave Winfield	Padres	137	.283	313	381	.822	67.6	127.6
9	Bob Watson	Astros	157	.313	348	428	.813	70.5	125.4
10	Pete Rose	Reds	162	.323	402	474	.848	75.1	123.0

Extremes for Batters

Batter	Team	Best		Batter	Team	Worst
Joe Morgan	Reds	221.8	BV	Larry Bowa	Phillies	-84.0
				Ken Reitz	Giants	-84.0
Joe Morgan	Reds	163.4	SE+	Roger Metzger	Astros	67.6
Joe Morgan	Reds	76.4	SCV	Manny Trillo	Cubs	-41.1
Dave Kingman	Mets	240.7	ISO+	Frank Taveras	Pirates	32.8
Mike Schmidt	Phillies	81.3	EXV	Larry Bowa	Phillies	-43.6
Dave Cash	Phillies	679.4	CT+	Dave Kingman	Mets	46.0
Dave Cash	Phillies	-75.3	SOV	Dave Kingman	Mets	72.9
Jim Wynn	Braves	273.1	EY+	Bill Russell	Dodgers	26.1
Jim Wynn	Braves	79.9	BBV	Rennie Stennett	Pirates	-38.0

Best Pitchers

Rank	Pitcher	Team	G	ERA	B	O	BPO	BV	BPO+
1	Randy Jones	Padres	40	2.74	458	960	.477	-109.9	80.7
2	Andy Messersmith	Braves	29	3.04	345	625	.552	-59.9	85.2
3	Tom Seaver	Mets	35	2.59	416	815	.510	-71.2	85.4
4	Jerry Koosman	Mets	34	2.69	389	743	.524	-55.2	87.6
5	Steve Rogers	Expos	33	3.21	387	689	.562	-54.5	87.7
6	Pat Zachry	Reds	38	2.74	337	612	.551	-42.0	88.9
7	John Candelaria	Pirates	32	3.15	367	672	.546	-44.4	89.2
8	John Denny	Cardinals	30	2.52	352	625	.563	-33.5	91.3
9	Jim Barr	Giants	37	2.89	437	760	.575	-40.9	91.4
10	Steve Carlton	Phillies	35	3.13	438	762	.575	-38.6	91.9

Extremes for Pitchers

Pitcher	Team	Best		Pitcher	Team	Worst
Randy Jones	Padres	-109.9	BV	Mike Cosgrove	Astros	66.2
John Denny	Cardinals	73.8	ERA+	Jack Billingham	Reds	128.0
John Denny	Cardinals	-20.6	ERV	Mike Cosgrove	Astros	24.2
Steve Rogers	Expos	72.8	ISO+	Rick Rhoden	Dodgers	141.6
Jim Barr	Giants	-25.2	EXV	Gary Nolan	Reds	35.8
Tom Seaver	Mets	63.6	CT+	Jim Barr	Giants	201.1
Tom Seaver	Mets	85.6	SOV	Jim Barr	Giants	-75.8
Gary Nolan	Reds	34.3	EY+	J.R. Richard	Astros	165.8
Randy Jones	Padres	-47.9	BBV	John D'Acquisto	Giants	62.7

1977 American League

Standings

Rank	Team	Post	W	L	Pct.	R	RA	BPO	BPOA	TS
1	New York Yankees	WLP	100	62	.617	5.13	4.02	.753	.646	80.125
2	Kansas City Royals	P	102	60	.630	5.07	4.02	.756	.628	68.760
3	Boston Red Sox	—	97	64	.602	5.34	4.42	.778	.693	63.429
4	Texas Rangers	—	94	68	.580	4.73	4.06	.725	.631	60.866
5	Baltimore Orioles	—	97	64	.602	4.47	4.06	.675	.648	57.452
6	Chicago White Sox	—	90	72	.556	5.21	4.76	.748	.717	54.131
7	Minnesota Twins	—	84	77	.522	5.39	4.82	.732	.729	50.544
8	California Angels	—	74	88	.457	4.17	4.29	.676	.688	40.777
9	Detroit Tigers	—	74	88	.457	4.41	4.64	.665	.682	39.902
10	Cleveland Indians	—	71	90	.441	4.20	4.59	.656	.692	36.704
11	Milwaukee Brewers	—	67	95	.414	3.94	4.72	.639	.706	30.673
12	Oakland Athletics	—	63	98	.391	3.76	4.65	.621	.688	28.241
13	Seattle Mariners	—	64	98	.395	3.85	5.28	.636	.772	21.837
14	Toronto Blue Jays	—	54	107	.335	3.76	5.11	.612	.750	17.412

Best Batters

Rank	Batter	Team	G	BA	B	O	BPO	BV	BPO+
1	Rod Carew	Twins	155	.388	452	402	1.124	168.1	159.2
2	Mitchell Page	Athletics	145	.307	394	366	1.077	138.9	154.5
3	Ken Singleton	Orioles	152	.328	387	382	1.013	123.3	146.8
4	Reggie Jackson	Yankees	146	.286	387	385	1.005	113.1	141.3
5	Toby Harrah	Rangers	159	.263	419	429	.977	114.5	137.6
6	Andre Thornton	Indians	131	.263	315	335	.940	82.5	135.5
7	Bobby Bonds	Angels	158	.264	436	474	.920	108.5	133.1
7	Mike Hargrove	Rangers	153	.305	375	397	.945	93.2	133.1
9	Larry Hisle	Twins	141	.302	386	414	.932	93.6	132.0
10	Lyman Bostock	Twins	153	.336	384	427	.899	82.4	127.3

Extremes for Batters

Batter	Team	Best		Batter	Team	Worst
Rod Carew	Twins	168.1	BV	Rob Picciolo	Athletics	-117.7
Rod Carew	Twins	148.8	SE+	Steve Braun	Mariners	68.3
Rod Carew	Twins	70.2	SCV	Alan Ashby	Blue Jays	-44.6
Andre Thornton	Indians	191.6	ISO+	Duane Kuiper	Indians	40.6
Bobby Bonds	Angels	71.3	EXV	Rick Burleson	Red Sox	-51.5
George Brett	Royals	302.1	CT+	Butch Hobson	Red Sox	52.0
George Brett	Royals	-48.5	SOV	Butch Hobson	Red Sox	77.8
Toby Harrah	Rangers	197.9	EY+	Mickey Rivers	Yankees	30.2
Toby Harrah	Rangers	50.5	BBV	Mickey Rivers	Yankees	-32.3

Best Pitchers

Rank	Pitcher	Team	G	ERA	B	O	BPO	BV	BPO+
1	Dennis Leonard	Royals	38	3.04	469	886	.529	-137.5	77.3
2	Ron Guidry	Yankees	31	2.82	328	633	.518	-94.0	77.7
3	Bert Blyleven	Rangers	30	2.72	374	707	.529	-98.9	79.1
4	Jim Palmer	Orioles	39	2.91	531	956	.555	-91.5	85.3
5	Frank Tanana	Angels	31	2.54	411	724	.568	-64.4	86.5
6	Dave Rozema	Tigers	28	3.09	400	660	.606	-54.1	88.1
7	Dave Goltz	Twins	39	3.36	545	919	.593	-68.6	88.8
8	Gaylord Perry	Rangers	34	3.37	440	713	.617	-36.9	92.3
9	Fergie Jenkins	Red Sox	28	3.68	390	583	.669	-30.1	92.8
10	Reggie Cleveland	Red Sox	36	4.26	389	581	.670	-29.7	92.9

Extremes for Pitchers

Pitcher	Team	Best		Pitcher	Team	Worst
Dennis Leonard	Royals	-137.5	BV	Pat Dobson	Indians	97.2
Frank Tanana	Angels	67.7	ERA+	Geoff Zahn	Twins	121.8
Frank Tanana	Angels	-32.5	ERV	Pat Dobson	Indians	35.2
Nolan Ryan	Angels	-32.5				
Nolan Ryan	Angels	49.2	ISO+	Glenn Abbott	Mariners	138.5
Nolan Ryan	Angels	-67.1	EXV	Catfish Hunter	Yankees	48.4
Nolan Ryan	Angels	45.3	CT+	Ross Grimsley	Orioles	229.9
Nolan Ryan	Angels	186.4	SOV	Ross Grimsley	Orioles	-68.9
Dave Rozema	Tigers	43.9	EY+	Nolan Ryan	Angels	211.0
Dave Rozema	Tigers	-38.3	BBV	Nolan Ryan	Angels	103.6

1977 National League

Standings

Rank	Team	Post	W	L	Pct.	R	RA	BPO	BPOA	TS
1	Los Angeles Dodgers	LP	98	64	.605	4.75	3.59	.725	.612	77.512
2	Philadelphia Phillies	P	101	61	.623	5.23	4.12	.778	.680	69.438
3	Pittsburgh Pirates	—	96	66	.593	4.53	4.10	.724	.648	61.073
4	Cincinnati Reds	—	88	74	.543	4.95	4.48	.771	.707	56.188
5	Houston Astros	—	81	81	.500	4.20	4.01	.677	.638	48.958
6	Saint Louis Cardinals	—	83	79	.512	4.55	4.25	.662	.679	47.641
7	Chicago Cubs	—	81	81	.500	4.27	4.56	.659	.665	43.346
8	Montreal Expos	—	75	87	.463	4.10	4.54	.664	.680	38.434
9	San Francisco Giants	—	75	87	.463	4.15	4.39	.660	.701	38.318
10	New York Mets	—	64	98	.395	3.62	4.09	.596	.649	29.928
11	San Diego Padres	—	69	93	.426	4.27	5.15	.665	.755	28.073
12	Atlanta Braves	—	61	101	.377	4.19	5.52	.639	.804	16.259

Best Batters

Rank	Batter	Team	G	BA	B	O	BPO	BV	BPO+
1	Reggie Smith	Dodgers	148	.307	403	356	1.132	143.3	155.2
2	Joe Morgan	Reds	153	.288	422	391	1.079	129.9	144.5
3	George Foster	Reds	158	.320	468	447	1.047	134.1	140.1
4	Mike Schmidt	Phillies	154	.274	450	423	1.064	126.3	139.0
5	Greg Luzinski	Phillies	149	.309	423	404	1.047	113.9	136.8
6	Gene Tenace	Padres	147	.233	328	349	.940	83.6	134.2
7	Jose Cruz	Astros	157	.299	401	446	.899	89.4	128.7
8	Cesar Cedeno	Astros	141	.279	371	416	.892	80.3	127.6
9	George Hendrick	Padres	152	.311	343	391	.877	69.2	125.3
10	Dave Parker	Pirates	159	.338	424	452	.938	83.5	124.5

Extremes for Batters

Batter	Team	Best		Batter	Team	Worst
Reggie Smith	Dodgers	143.3	BV	Rowland Office	Braves	-103.0
George Foster	Reds	148.9	SE+	Chris Speier	Giants-Expos	72.6
George Foster	Reds	72.6	SCV	Steve Ontiveros	Cubs	-36.5
George Foster	Reds	201.0	ISO+	Larry Bowa	Phillies	38.1
George Foster	Reds	96.0	EXV	Larry Bowa	Phillies	-60.0
Dave Cash	Expos	278.6	CT+	Gene Tenace	Padres	50.0
Dave Cash	Expos	-58.9	SOV	Greg Luzinski	Phillies	61.5
Gene Tenace	Padres	262.4	EY+	Garry Templeton	Cardinals	23.9
Gene Tenace	Padres	71.2	BBV	Garry Templeton	Cardinals	-38.2

Best Pitchers

Rank	Pitcher	Team	G	ERA	B	O	BPO	BV	BPO+
1	Rick Reuschel	Cubs	39	2.79	417	758	.550	-122.6	77.3
2	Tom Seaver	Mets-Reds	33	2.58	406	785	.517	-111.6	78.5
3	Burt Hooton	Dodgers	32	2.62	360	672	.536	-77.6	82.3
4	John Candelaria	Pirates	33	2.34	395	693	.570	-72.7	84.5
5	Tommy John	Dodgers	31	2.78	375	670	.560	-61.3	86.0
6	Steve Carlton	Phillies	36	2.64	503	848	.593	-76.4	86.8
7	Steve Rogers	Expos	40	3.10	521	912	.571	-77.2	87.1
8	J.R. Richard	Astros	36	2.97	450	809	.556	-60.8	88.1
9	Bill Bonham	Cubs	34	4.36	418	655	.638	-48.3	89.6
10	Jerry Koosman	Mets	32	3.49	399	687	.581	-44.8	89.9

Extremes for Pitchers

Pitcher	Team	Best		Pitcher	Team	Worst
Rick Reuschel	Cubs	-122.6	BV	Randy Lerch	Phillies	105.3
John Candelaria	Pirates	62.0	ERA+	Randy Lerch	Phillies	132.4
Rick Reuschel	Cubs	-38.3	ERV	Frank LaCorte	Braves	30.4
				Rick Sawyer	Padres	30.4
Rick Reuschel	Cubs	59.8	ISO+	Bob Owchinko	Padres	132.7
Rick Reuschel	Cubs	-55.9	EXV	Buzz Capra	Braves	45.7
Phil Niekro	Braves	72.4	CT+	Mark Lemongello	Astros	163.2
Rich Gossage	Pirates	80.9	SOV	Jim Barr	Giants	-59.3
Jim Barr	Giants	68.4	EY+	Phil Niekro	Braves	141.5
Jim Barr	Giants	-24.0	BBV	Phil Niekro	Braves	44.6

1978 American League

Standings

Rank	Team	Post	W	L	Pct.	R	RA	BPO	BPOA	TS
1	New York Yankees	WLP	100	63	.613	4.51	3.57	.667	.612	77.438
2	Milwaukee Brewers	—	93	69	.574	4.96	4.01	.740	.610	64.905
3	Boston Red Sox	—	99	64	.607	4.88	4.03	.721	.664	63.155
4	Kansas City Royals	P	92	70	.568	4.59	3.91	.709	.634	59.697
5	Texas Rangers	—	87	75	.537	4.27	3.90	.698	.618	55.433
6	Baltimore Orioles	—	90	71	.559	4.09	3.93	.668	.610	54.878
7	Detroit Tigers	—	86	76	.531	4.41	4.03	.682	.658	51.904
8	California Angels	—	87	75	.537	4.27	4.11	.648	.681	47.934
9	Minnesota Twins	—	73	89	.451	4.11	4.19	.674	.662	41.538
10	Cleveland Indians	—	69	90	.434	4.02	4.36	.640	.670	36.150
11	Chicago White Sox	—	71	90	.441	3.94	4.54	.628	.701	32.864
12	Oakland Athletics	—	69	93	.426	3.28	4.26	.595	.657	29.890
13	Toronto Blue Jays	—	59	102	.366	3.66	4.81	.587	.755	17.817
14	Seattle Mariners	—	56	104	.350	3.84	5.21	.628	.757	17.225

Best Batters

Rank	Batter	Team	G	BA	B	O	BPO	RV	BPO+
1	Amos Otis	Royals	141	.298	368	370	.995	108.0	141.6
2	Ken Singleton	Orioles	149	.293	338	375	.901	90.6	136.6
3	Andre Thornton	Indians	145	.262	375	409	.917	99.3	136.0
4	Larry Hisle	Brewers	142	.290	367	397	.924	95.8	135.3
5	Jim Rice	Red Sox	163	.315	482	490	.984	122.0	133.9
6	Gorman Thomas	Brewers	137	.246	320	360	.889	74.1	130.1
7	Bobby Bonds	White Sox-Rangers	156	.267	406	461	.881	91.9	129.3
8	Rod Carew	Twins	152	.333	363	409	.888	81.1	128.8
9	Doug DeCinces	Orioles	142	.286	326	386	.845	71.3	128.0
10	Leon Roberts	Mariners	134	.301	305	347	.879	64.3	126.7

Extremes for Batters

Batter	Team	Best		Batter	Team	Worst
Jim Rice	Red Sox	122.0	BV	Rick Burleson	Red Sox	-95.7
Larry Hisle	Brewers	148.0	SE+	Mario Guerrero	Athletics	61.1
Larry Hisle	Brewers	57.4	SCV	Mario Guerrero	Athletics	-39.5
Gorman Thomas	Brewers	212.0	ISO+	Julio Cruz	Mariners	26.2
Jim Rice	Red Sox	93.6	EXV	Julio Cruz	Mariners	-53.5
Bob Bailor	Blue Jays	380.5	CT+	Gary Alexander	Athletics-Indians	38.6
Bob Bailor	Blue Jays	-58.9	SOV	Gary Alexander	Athletics-Indians	102.6
Mike Hargrove	Rangers	207.3	EY+	Mario Guerrero	Athletics	29.6
Mike Hargrove	Rangers	51.2	BBV	Mario Guerrero	Athletics	-31.0

Best Pitchers

Rank	Pitcher	Team	G	ERA	B	O	BPO	BV	BPO+
1	Ron Guidry	Yankees	35	1.74	367	826	.444	-164.6	69.0
2	Mike Caldwell	Brewers	37	2.36	421	889	.474	-154.3	73.2
3	Jon Matlack	Rangers	35	2.27	425	817	.520	-101.1	80.8
4	Lary Sorensen	Brewers	37	3.21	453	844	.537	-93.2	82.9
5	Larry Gura	Royals	35	2.72	376	666	.565	-65.9	85.1
6	Jim Palmer	Orioles	38	2.46	478	891	.536	-77.7	86.0
7	Luis Tiant	Red Sox	32	3.31	385	639	.603	-59.1	86.7
8	Fergie Jenkins	Rangers	34	3.04	414	741	.559	-63.2	86.8
9	Dave Rozema	Tigers	28	3.14	362	628	.576	-49.7	87.9
10	Scott McGregor	Orioles	35	3.32	387	697	.555	-47.7	89.0

Extremes for Pitchers

Pitcher	Team	Best		Pitcher	Team	Worst
Ron Guidry	Yankees	-164.6	BV	Dave Lemanczyk	Blue Jays	76.8
Ron Guidry	Yankees	49.3	ERA+	Wilbur Wood	White Sox	139.3
Ron Guidry	Yankees	-54.5	ERV	Dave Lemanczyk	Blue Jays	37.1
Mike Caldwell	Brewers	59.3	ISO+	Chris Knapp	Angels	153.7
Mike Caldwell	Brewers	-53.5	EXV	Chris Knapp	Angels	43.7
Nolan Ryan	Angels	44.2	CT+	Bill Lee	Red Sox	207.3
Nolan Ryan	Angels	145.0	SOV	Lary Sorensen	Brewers	-60.9
Lary Sorensen	Brewers	52.0	EY+	Nolan Ryan	Angels	185.1
Lary Sorensen	Brewers	-42.5	BBV	Nolan Ryan	Angels	64.8

1978 National League

Standings

Rank	Team	Post	W	L	Pct.	R	RA	BPO	BPOA	TS
1	Los Angeles Dodgers	LP	95	67	.586	4.49	3.54	.722	.598	82.060
2	Philadelphia Phillies	P	90	72	.556	4.37	3.62	.690	.624	63.373
3	Pittsburgh Pirates	—	88	73	.547	4.25	3.96	.679	.632	56.769
4	Cincinnati Reds	—	92	69	.571	4.41	4.27	.707	.678	56.721
5	San Francisco Giants	—	89	73	.549	3.78	3.67	.649	.613	54.653
6	San Diego Padres	—	84	78	.519	3.65	3.69	.635	.619	48.315
7	Montreal Expos	—	76	86	.469	3.91	3.77	.617	.648	41.055
8	Chicago Cubs	—	79	83	.488	4.10	4.47	.644	.685	37.766
9	Houston Astros	—	74	88	.457	3.73	3.91	.617	.653	36.516
10	Saint Louis Cardinals	—	69	93	.426	3.70	4.06	.595	.656	29.702
11	New York Mets	—	66	96	.407	3.75	4.26	.612	.675	26.066
12	Atlanta Braves	—	69	93	.426	3.70	4.63	.622	.706	22.794

Best Batters

Rank	Batter	Team	G	BA	B	O	BPO	BV	BPO+
1	Reggie Smith	Dodgers	128	.295	346	338	1.024	109.7	146.4
2	Dave Parker	Pirates	148	.334	421	404	1.042	125.4	142.4
3	Jeff Burroughs	Braves	153	.301	382	365	1.047	109.0	139.9
4	Greg Luzinski	Phillies	155	.265	407	418	.974	107.6	135.9
5	Gene Tenace	Padres	142	.224	284	323	.879	66.9	130.8
6	Jack Clark	Giants	156	.306	398	449	.886	93.4	130.6
7	Bill Madlock	Giants	122	.309	293	331	.885	68.4	130.5
8	Jose Cruz	Astros	153	.315	359	410	.876	83.3	130.2
9	Dave Winfield	Padres	158	.308	376	433	.868	85.0	129.2
10	George Foster	Reds	158	.281	417	462	.903	89.9	127.5

Extremes for Batters

Batter	Team	Best		Batter	Team	Worst
Dave Parker	Pirates	125.4	BV	Dave Cash	Expos	-99.5
Dave Parker	Pirates	140.3	SE+	Doug Flynn	Mets	67.1
Dave Parker	Pirates	54.2	SCV	Doug Flynn	Mets	-35.8
Reggie Smith	Dodgers	207.9	ISO+	Doug Flynn	Mets	41.3
George Foster	Reds	76.2	EXV	Dave Cash	Expos	-47.5
Dave Cash	Expos	313.0	CT+	Dale Murphy	Braves	48.0
Dave Cash	Expos	-61.8	SOV	Dale Murphy	Braves	75.3
Gene Tenace	Padres	248.1	EY+	Garry Templeton	Cardinals	36.4
Jeff Burroughs	Braves	56.3	BBV	Larry Bowa	Phillies	-34.2

Best Pitchers

Rank	Pitcher	Team	G	ERA	B	O	BPO	BV	BPO+
1	Phil Niekro	Braves	44	2.88	573	1,003	.571	-113.2	83.5
2	Steve Rogers	Expos	30	2.47	345	651	.530	-64.3	84.3
3	Rick Reuschel	Cubs	35	3.41	427	738	.579	-72.7	85.4
4	Burt Hooton	Dodgers	32	2.71	379	710	.534	-64.0	85.6
5	Craig Swan	Mets	29	2.43	326	616	.529	-53.9	85.8
6	Bob Knepper	Giants	36	2.63	417	782	.533	-63.9	86.7
7	Ed Halicki	Giants	29	2.85	327	608	.538	-46.9	87.5
8	John Denny	Cardinals	33	2.96	391	702	.557	-55.5	87.6
9	Don Robinson	Pirates	35	3.47	398	691	.576	-55.1	87.8
10	Bert Blyleven	Pirates	34	3.03	433	742	.584	-53.5	89.0

Extremes for Pitchers

Pitcher	Team	Best		Pitcher	Team	Worst
Phil Niekro	Braves	-113.2	BV	Nino Espinosa	Mets	98.8
Craig Swan	Mets	72.6	ERA+	Nino Espinosa	Mets	141.1
Steve Rogers	Expos	72.6				
Phil Niekro	Braves	-39.7	ERV	Nino Espinosa	Mets	31.2
Phil Niekro	Braves	69.0	ISO+	Nino Espinosa	Mets	148.4
Phil Niekro	Braves	-49.3	EXV	Nino Espinosa	Mets	42.7
J.R. Richard	Astros	50.6	CT+	Jim Barr	Giants	231.3
J.R. Richard	Astros	149.6	SOV	Randy Jones	Padres	-74.3
Larry Christenson	Phillies	57.9	EY+	J.R. Richard	Astros	170.0
Rick Reuschel	Cubs	-29.6	BBV	J.R. Richard	Astros	56.4

1979 American League

Standings

Rank	Team	Post	W	L	Pct.	R	RA	BPO	BPOA	TS
1	Baltimore Orioles	LP	102	57	.642	4.76	3.66	.724	.604	77.612
2	Milwaukee Brewers	—	95	66	.590	5.01	4.48	.763	.676	60.796
3	Boston Red Sox	—	91	69	.569	5.26	4.44	.757	.686	59.765
4	California Angels	P	88	74	.543	5.35	4.74	.752	.697	55.625
5	New York Yankees	—	89	71	.556	4.59	4.20	.678	.668	52.999
6	Kansas City Royals	—	85	77	.525	5.25	5.04	.751	.702	51.501
7	Detroit Tigers	—	85	76	.528	4.78	4.58	.730	.710	50.040
8	Texas Rangers	—	83	79	.512	4.63	4.31	.688	.660	49.920
9	Minnesota Twins	—	82	80	.506	4.72	4.48	.699	.698	47.473
10	Cleveland Indians	—	81	80	.503	4.72	5.00	.702	.727	42.817
11	Chicago White Sox	—	73	87	.456	4.56	4.68	.686	.689	41.037
12	Seattle Mariners	—	67	95	.414	4.39	5.06	.691	.760	30.636
13	Toronto Blue Jays	—	53	109	.327	3.78	5.32	.604	.762	13.628
14	Oakland Athletics	—	54	108	.333	3.54	5.31	.587	.771	11.385

Best Batters

Rank	Batter	Team	G	BA	B	O	BPO	BV	BPO
1	Fred Lynn	Red Sox	147	.333	431	370	1.165	150.2	153.5
2	Sixto Lezcano	Brewers	138	.321	368	348	1.057	118.2	147.3
3	Ken Singleton	Orioles	159	.295	425	427	.995	124.4	141.4
4	Darrell Porter	Royals	157	.291	407	410	.993	106.1	135.3
5	Don Baylor	Angels	162	.296	449	476	.943	114.0	134.0
6	Jim Rice	Red Sox	158	.325	447	446	1.002	108.5	132.1
7	Steve Kemp	Tigers	134	.318	351	363	.967	84.0	131.5
8	George Brett	Royals	154	.329	436	456	.956	101.4	130.3
9	Reggie Jackson	Yankees	131	.297	334	357	.936	77.0	130.0
10	Gorman Thomas	Brewers	156	.244	412	445	.926	92.6	129.0

Extremes for Batters

Batter	Team	Best		Batter	Team	Worst
Fred Lynn	Red Sox	150.2	**BV**	Mario Mendoza	Mariners	-121.7
Don Baylor	Angels	147.1	**SE+**	Tom Veryzer	Indians	68.2
Don Baylor	Angels	71.4	**SCV**	Alfredo Griffin	Blue Jays	-41.2
Gorman Thomas	Brewers	206.1	**ISO+**	Tom Veryzer	Indians	23.6
Gorman Thomas	Brewers	84.4	**EXV**	Rick Manning	Indians	-54.2
Duane Kuiper	Indians	221.6	**CT+**	Gorman Thomas	Brewers	42.3
Buddy Bell	Rangers	-43.1	**SOV**	Gorman Thomas	Brewers	100.9
Darrell Porter	Royals	209.5	**EY+**	Dan Meyer	Mariners	39.1
Darrell Porter	Royals	59.1	**BBV**	Rick Bosetti	Blue Jays	-30.4

Best Pitchers

Rank	Pitcher	Team	G	ERA	B	O	BPO	BV	BPO+
1	Tommy John	Yankees	37	2.96	442	832	.531	-124.5	78.0
2	Ron Guidry	Yankees	33	2.78	409	710	.576	-74.5	84.6
3	Jack Morris	Tigers	27	3.28	353	595	.593	-62.6	84.9
4	Geoff Zahn	Twins	26	3.57	308	515	.598	-52.4	85.5
5	Mike Flanagan	Orioles	39	3.08	458	802	.571	-74.8	86.0
6	Mike Caldwell	Brewers	30	3.29	418	707	.591	-59.8	87.5
7	Scott McGregor	Orioles	27	3.35	309	528	.585	-41.8	88.1
8	Bob Stanley	Red Sox	40	3.99	419	658	.637	-54.0	88.6
9	Jerry Koosman	Twins	37	3.38	502	792	.634	-52.3	90.6
10	Nolan Ryan	Angels	34	3.60	412	673	.612	-39.9	91.2

Extremes for Pitchers

Pitcher	Team	Best		Pitcher	Team	Worst
Tommy John	Yankees	-124.5	**BV**	Matt Keough	Athletics	90.0
Dennis Eckersley	Red Sox	69.3	**ERA+**	Phil Huffman	Blue Jays	137.9
Jim Kern	Rangers	-38.7	**ERV**	Mike Paxton	Indians	31.7
Tommy John	Yankees	56.8	**ISO+**	Steve Stone	Orioles	143.8
Tommy John	Yankees	-60.2	**EXV**	Fergie Jenkins	Rangers	46.5
Nolan Ryan	Angels	48.8	**CT+**	Bob Stanley	Red Sox	199.1
Nolan Ryan	Angels	114.1	**SOV**	Lary Sorensen	Brewers	-59.1
Scott McGregor	Orioles	43.7	**EY+**	Nolan Ryan	Angels	152.8
Mike Caldwell	Brewers	-36.7	**BBV**	Nolan Ryan	Angels	38.4

1979 National League

Standings

Rank	Team	Post	W	L	Pct.	R	RA	BPO	BPOA	TS
1	Pittsburgh Pirates	WLP	98	64	.605	4.75	3.94	.719	.642	83.113
2	Montreal Expos	—	95	65	.594	4.38	3.63	.678	.616	66.653
3	Cincinnati Reds	P	90	71	.559	4.54	4.00	.697	.651	60.077
4	Houston Astros	—	89	73	.549	3.60	3.59	.615	.587	52.664
5	Saint Louis Cardinals	—	86	76	.531	4.48	4.25	.680	.658	52.557
6	Los Angeles Dodgers	—	79	83	.488	4.56	4.43	.703	.649	49.998
7	Philadelphia Phillies	—	84	78	.519	4.19	4.40	.705	.688	46.798
8	Chicago Cubs	—	80	82	.494	4.36	4.36	.675	.697	43.092
9	San Diego Padres	—	68	93	.422	3.75	4.23	.611	.663	29.196
10	San Francisco Giants	—	71	91	.438	4.15	4.64	.650	.724	28.958
11	Atlanta Braves	—	66	94	.413	4.18	4.77	.641	.713	25.711
12	New York Mets	—	63	99	.389	3.64	4.33	.608	.693	21.352

Best Batters

Rank	Batter	Team	G	BA	B	O	BPO	BV	BPO+
1	Dave Winfield	Padres	159	.308	437	433	1.009	138.9	146.6
2	Mike Schmidt	Phillies	160	.253	448	433	1.035	128.9	140.4
3	George Foster	Reds	121	.302	312	323	.966	78.8	133.8
4	Keith Hernandez	Cardinals	161	.344	412	422	.976	103.9	133.7
5	Davey Lopes	Dodgers	153	.265	424	449	.944	102.8	132.0
6	Gene Tenace	Padres	151	.263	327	361	.906	78.5	131.6
7	Lee Mazzilli	Mets	158	.303	398	437	.911	94.1	131.0
8	Dave Kingman	Cubs	145	.288	387	396	.977	90.9	130.7
9	Dave Parker	Pirates	158	.310	432	449	.962	98.4	129.5
10	Ron Cey	Dodgers	150	.281	338	368	.918	74.7	128.4

Extremes for Batters

Batter	Team	Best		Batter	Team	Worst
Dave Winfield	Padres	138.9	**BV**	Doug Flynn	Mets	-109.1
Keith Hernandez	Cardinals	142.5	**SE+**	Pepe Frias	Braves	74.3
Keith Hernandez	Cardinals	62.6	**SCV**	Chris Speier	Expos	-30.1
Dave Kingman	Cubs	219.1	**ISO+**	Tim Foli	Mets-Pirates	36.1
Dave Kingman	Cubs	94.0	**EXV**	Tim Foli	Mets-Pirates	-49.5
Tim Foli	Mets-Pirates	478.8	**CT+**	Dave Kingman	Cubs	52.8
Tim Foli	Mets-Pirates	-54.9	**SOV**	Dave Kingman	Cubs	61.9
Gene Tenace	Padres	244.2	**EY+**	Doug Flynn	Mets	23.6
Gene Tenace	Padres	59.6	**BBV**	Garry Templeton	Cardinals	-38.2

Best Pitchers

Rank	Pitcher	Team	G	ERA	B	O	BPO	BV	BPO+
1	J.R. Richard	Astros	38	2.71	462	880	.525	-96.6	82.7
2	Ken Forsch	Astros	26	3.04	282	530	.532	-54.4	83.8
3	Burt Hooton	Dodgers	29	2.97	365	636	.574	-47.7	88.4
4	Tom Seaver	Reds	32	3.14	381	653	.583	-49.2	88.6
5	Steve Carlton	Phillies	35	3.62	455	761	.598	-56.4	89.0
6	Bruce Kison	Pirates	33	3.19	317	521	.608	-35.3	90.0
7	Don Sutton	Dodgers	33	3.82	402	681	.590	-39.9	91.0
8	Tom Hume	Reds	57	2.76	296	493	.600	-28.8	91.1
9	Dan Schatzeder	Expos	32	2.83	290	489	.593	-27.3	91.4
10	John Candelaria	Pirates	33	3.22	391	628	.623	-33.7	92.1

Extremes for Pitchers

Pitcher	Team	Best		Pitcher	Team	Worst
J.R. Richard	Astros	-96.6	**BV**	Bob Knepper	Giants	107.8
Tom Hume	Reds	74.9	**ERA+**	Vida Blue	Giants	146.7
J.R. Richard	Astros	-23.2	**ERV**	Vida Blue	Giants	42.0
Joaquin Andujar	Astros	71.1	**ISO+**	Bob Knepper	Giants	157.1
J.R. Richard	Astros	-32.2	**EXV**	Bob Knepper	Giants	54.1
J.R. Richard	Astros	51.1	**CT+**	Bill Lee	Expos	226.4
J.R. Richard	Astros	153.0	**SOV**	Bill Lee	Expos	-74.6
Tom Hume	Reds	51.9	**EY+**	John Denny	Cardinals	145.1
John Candelaria	Pirates	-26.0	**BBV**	John D'Acquisto	Padres	39.6

1980 American League

Standings

Rank	Team	Post	W	L	Pct.	R	RA	BPO	BPOA	TS
1	Kansas City Royals	LP	97	65	.599	4.99	4.28	.730	.667	72.071
2	New York Yankees	P	103	59	.636	5.06	4.09	.741	.634	71.275
3	Baltimore Orioles	—	100	62	.617	4.97	3.95	.717	.654	66.988
4	Milwaukee Brewers	—	86	76	.531	5.01	4.21	.746	.654	59.597
5	Oakland Athletics	—	83	79	.512	4.23	3.96	.669	.620	51.673
6	Detroit Tigers	—	84	78	.519	5.09	4.64	.717	.699	51.375
7	Boston Red Sox	—	83	77	.519	4.73	4.79	.725	.698	48.585
8	Texas Rangers	—	76	85	.472	4.64	4.61	.687	.693	42.775
9	Cleveland Indians	—	79	81	.494	4.61	5.04	.694	.711	41.022
10	Minnesota Twins	—	77	84	.478	4.16	4.50	.629	.655	39.741
11	Chicago White Sox	—	70	90	.438	3.62	4.46	.606	.676	29.854
12	California Angels	—	65	95	.406	4.36	4.98	.657	.738	27.662
13	Toronto Blue Jays	—	67	95	.414	3.85	4.70	.622	.717	25.922
14	Seattle Mariners	—	59	103	.364	3.74	4.87	.607	.730	17.863

Best Batters

Rank	Batter	Team	G	BA	B	O	BPO	BV	BPO+
1	George Brett	Royals	117	.390	379	298	1.272	168.5	180.0
2	Rickey Henderson	Athletics	158	.303	467	453	1.031	163.4	153.8
3	Reggie Jackson	Yankees	143	.300	395	371	1.065	132.7	150.6
4	Ben Oglivie	Brewers	156	.304	412	435	.947	113.7	138.1
5	Willie Randolph	Yankees	138	.294	368	381	.966	98.6	136.6
6	Cecil Cooper	Brewers	153	.352	408	440	.927	106.3	135.2
7	Jason Thompson	Tigers-Angels	138	.288	301	332	.907	69.8	130.8
8	Al Bumbry	Orioles	160	.318	416	472	.881	87.7	126.7
8	Ken Singleton	Orioles	156	.304	380	431	.882	80.2	126.7
10	Paul Molitor	Brewers	111	.304	293	340	.862	59.9	125.7

Extremes for Batters

Batter	Team	Best		Batter	Team	Worst
George Brett	Royals	168.5	BV	Alfredo Griffin	Blue Jays	-96.7
George Brett	Royals	167.1	SE+	Alfredo Griffin	Blue Jays	66.4
George Brett	Royals	72.7	SCV	Alfredo Griffin	Blue Jays	-51.6
Reggie Jackson	Yankees	221.4	ISO+	Lou Whitaker	Tigers	36.2
Reggie Jackson	Yankees	83.9	EXV	Rick Burleson	Red Sox	-42.3
Rich Dauer	Orioles	380.0	CT+	Gorman Thomas	Brewers	49.9
Rich Dauer	Orioles	-53.2	SOV	Gorman Thomas	Brewers	85.2
Willie Randolph	Yankees	238.8	EY+	Damaso Garcia	Blue Jays	22.9
Willie Randolph	Yankees	66.8	BBV	Damaso Garcia	Blue Jays	-33.6

Best Pitchers

Rank	Pitcher	Team	G	ERA	B	O	BPO	BV	BPO+
1	Rudy May	Yankees	41	2.46	272	525	.518	-73.9	78.6
2	Mike Norris	Athletics	33	2.53	432	863	.501	-112.8	79.3
3	Britt Burns	White Sox	34	2.84	413	716	.577	-55.3	88.2
4	Tommy John	Yankees	36	3.43	467	802	.582	-61.4	88.4
5	Jim Clancy	Blue Jays	34	3.30	461	756	.610	-60.1	88.5
6	Roger Erickson	Twins	32	3.25	354	573	.618	-43.8	89.0
7	Dave Stieb	Blue Jays	34	3.71	446	725	.615	-53.8	89.2
8	Bob Stanley	Red Sox	52	3.39	337	531	.635	-33.6	90.9
9	Rick Langford	Athletics	35	3.26	495	862	.574	-49.2	91.0
9	Darrell Jackson	Twins	32	3.87	331	524	.632	-32.8	91.0

Extremes for Pitchers

Pitcher	Team	Best		Pitcher	Team	Worst
Mike Norris	Athletics	-112.8	BV	Mike Parrott	Mariners	89.3
Rudy May	Yankees	65.4	ERA+	Dan Spillner	Indians	134.1
Doug Corbett	Twins	-33.4	ERV	Mike Parrott	Mariners	34.5
Dave Stieb	Blue Jays	68.4	ISO+	Jim Palmer	Orioles	124.6
Dave Stieb	Blue Jays	-39.7	EXV	Chris Knapp	Angels	31.1
Rudy May	Yankees	65.7	CT+	Lary Sorensen	Brewers	203.7
Len Barker	Indians	62.7	SOV	Tommy John	Yankees	-58.8
Dennis Eckersley	Red Sox	59.0	EY+	Jim Clancy	Blue Jays	152.8
Dennis Eckersley	Red Sox	-25.8	BBV	Jim Clancy	Blue Jays	42.8

1980 National League

Standings

Rank	Team	Post	W	L	Pct.	R	RA	BPO	BPOA	TS
1	Philadelphia Phillies	WLP	91	71	.562	4.49	3.94	.684	.653	75.971
2	Houston Astros	P	93	70	.571	3.91	3.61	.663	.582	63.192
3	Los Angeles Dodgers	—	92	71	.564	4.07	3.63	.664	.610	62.010
4	Montreal Expos	—	90	72	.556	4.28	3.88	.699	.637	61.171
5	Cincinnati Reds	—	89	73	.549	4.34	4.11	.683	.663	55.113
6	Pittsburgh Pirates	—	83	79	.512	4.11	3.99	.674	.637	51.361
7	Saint Louis Cardinals	—	74	88	.457	4.56	4.38	.674	.667	43.383
8	Atlanta Braves	—	81	80	.503	3.91	4.10	.620	.650	41.317
9	San Francisco Giants	—	75	86	.466	3.56	3.94	.595	.648	33.289
10	San Diego Padres	—	73	89	.451	3.63	4.01	.640	.677	32.826
11	New York Mets	—	67	95	.414	3.77	4.33	.611	.688	23.533
12	Chicago Cubs	—	64	98	.395	3.79	4.49	.610	.706	18.364

Best Batters

Rank	Batter	Team	G	BA	B	O	BPO	BV	BPO+
1	Mike Schmidt	Phillies	150	.286	458	415	1.104	158.9	153.1
2	Cesar Cedeno	Astros	137	.309	350	376	.931	95.2	137.4
2	Jack Clark	Giants	127	.284	315	341	.924	85.8	137.4
4	Keith Hernandez	Cardinals	159	.321	403	431	.935	93.4	130.2
5	Andre Dawson	Expos	151	.308	379	428	.886	78.9	126.3
6	Lee Mazzilli	Mets	152	.280	380	444	.856	78.9	126.2
7	Dave Winfield	Padres	162	.276	359	428	.839	72.1	125.1
8	Ken Griffey Sr.	Reds	146	.294	341	397	.859	61.4	122.0
9	Ron LeFlore	Expos	139	.257	352	413	.852	62.4	121.6
9	Ted Simmons	Cardinals	145	.303	318	364	.874	56.5	121.6

Extremes for Batters

Batter	Team	Best		Batter	Team	Worst
Mike Schmidt	Phillies	158.9	BV	Luis Gomez	Braves	-87.1
Ted Simmons	Cardinals	138.2	SE+	Bob Boone	Phillies	71.3
Keith Hernandez	Cardinals	50.9	SCV	Ivan de Jesus	Cubs	-40.5
Mike Schmidt	Phillies	251.3	ISO+	Bill North	Giants	35.6
Mike Schmidt	Phillies	111.4	EXV	Ozzie Smith	Padres	-43.5
Bill Buckner	Cubs	402.8	CT+	Dale Murphy	Braves	55.4
Bill Buckner	Cubs	-54.5	SOV	Dale Murphy	Braves	59.4
Bill North	Giants	212.3	EY+	Garry Maddox	Phillies	28.9
Gene Tenace	Padres	52.6	BBV	Garry Maddox	Phillies	-32.0

Best Pitchers

Rank	Pitcher	Team	G	ERA	B	O	BPO	BV	BPO+
1	Jerry Reuss	Dodgers	37	2.51	333	705	.472	-114.1	74.5
2	Steve Carlton	Phillies	38	2.34	492	923	.533	-121.3	80.2
3	Frank Pastore	Reds	27	3.27	304	559	.544	-58.1	84.0
4	Don Sutton	Dodgers	32	2.20	339	636	.533	-64.3	84.1
5	Mario Soto	Reds	53	3.07	323	575	.562	-49.4	86.7
6	Steve Rogers	Expos	37	2.98	489	846	.578	-54.2	90.0
7	Pete Vuckovich	Cardinals	32	3.40	400	670	.597	-42.9	90.3
8	Vida Blue	Giants	31	2.97	385	681	.565	-40.5	90.5
9	Bob Forsch	Cardinals	31	3.77	392	650	.603	-37.7	91.2
10	Tommy Boggs	Braves	32	3.42	358	589	.608	-26.5	93.1

Extremes for Pitchers

Pitcher	Team	Best		Pitcher	Team	Worst
Steve Carlton	Phillies	-121.3	BV	Randy Lerch	Phillies	71.0
Steve Carlton	Phillies	63.0	ERA+	Larry McWilliams	Braves	135.5
Steve Carlton	Phillies	-46.4	ERV	Dennis Lamp	Cubs	30.1
Nolan Ryan	Astros	75.6	ISO+	Larry McWilliams	Braves	167.3
Greg Minton	Giants	-24.3	EXV	Larry McWilliams	Braves	51.1
Mario Soto	Reds	55.2	CT+	Mike LaCoss	Reds	172.8
Steve Carlton	Phillies	113.8	SOV	Ken Forsch	Astros	-47.2
Bob Forsch	Cardinals	45.4	EY+	Steve Mura	Padres	172.9
Bob Forsch	Cardinals	-32.5	BBV	Steve Mura	Padres	34.6

1981 American League

Standings

Rank	Team	Post	W	L	Pct.	R	RA	BPO	BPOA	TS
1	New York Yankees	LP	59	48	.551	3.93	3.21	.667	.569	73.605
2	Oakland Athletics	P	64	45	.587	4.20	3.70	.649	.606	60.823
3	Texas Rangers	—	57	48	.543	4.30	3.70	.626	.591	56.719
4	Detroit Tigers	—	60	49	.550	3.92	3.71	.653	.609	55.170
5	Chicago White Sox	—	54	52	.509	4.49	3.99	.678	.625	54.177
6	Milwaukee Brewers	P	62	47	.569	4.52	4.21	.641	.646	53.914
7	Boston Red Sox	—	59	49	.546	4.81	4.45	.680	.681	52.456
8	Baltimore Orioles	—	59	46	.562	4.09	4.16	.652	.645	51.299
9	California Angels	—	51	59	.464	4.33	4.12	.659	.640	45.053
10	Kansas City Royals	P	50	53	.485	3.85	3.93	.656	.639	44.815
11	Cleveland Indians	—	52	51	.505	4.18	4.29	.641	.651	44.343
12	Seattle Mariners	—	44	65	.404	3.87	4.74	.634	.685	26.020
13	Minnesota Twins	—	41	68	.376	3.44	4.42	.547	.680	16.267
14	Toronto Blue Jays	—	37	69	.349	3.10	4.40	.547	.654	13.370

Best Batters

Rank	Batter	Team	G	BA	B	O	BPO	BV	BPO+
1	Rickey Henderson	Athletics	108	.319	311	321	.969	109.0	154.0
2	Dwight Evans	Red Sox	108	.296	310	306	1.013	98.5	146.6
3	Bobby Grich	Angels	100	.304	245	262	.935	73.5	142.9
4	Chet Lemon	White Sox	94	.302	221	256	.863	56.6	134.4
5	Gorman Thomas	Brewers	103	.259	240	285	.842	61.4	134.3
6	Eddie Murray	Orioles	99	.294	248	283	.876	62.9	134.0
7	Greg Luzinski	White Sox	104	.265	243	290	.838	56.8	130.5
8	Willie Aikens	Royals	101	.266	230	272	.846	53.3	130.2
9	Dwayne Murphy	Athletics	107	.251	256	314	.815	58.4	129.6
10	George Brett	Royals	89	.314	214	255	.839	48.4	129.2

Extremes for Batters

Batter	Team	Best		Batter	Team	Worst
Rickey Henderson	Athletics	109.0	BV	Alfredo Griffin	Blue Jays	-83.3
Cecil Cooper	Brewers	143.6	SE+	Alfredo Griffin	Blue Jays	60.5
Cecil Cooper	Brewers	35.8	SCV	Alfredo Griffin	Blue Jays	-33.3
Gorman Thomas	Brewers	213.1	ISO+	Jerry Remy	Red Sox	22.7
Tony Armas	Athletics	48.4	EXV	Jerry Remy	Red Sox	-37.5
Rich Dauer	Orioles	280.1	CT+	Tony Armas	Athletics	51.0
Rich Dauer	Orioles	-32.4	SOV	Tony Armas	Athletics	56.3
Dwight Evans	Red Sox	204.6	EY+	Tony Armas	Athletics	37.2
Dwight Evans	Red Sox	42.9	BBV	Tony Armas	Athletics	-21.9

Best Pitchers

Rank	Pitcher	Team	G	ERA	B	O	BPO	BV	BPO+
1	Ron Guidry	Yankees	23	2.76	188	381	.493	-48.6	79.5
2	Dennis Lamp	White Sox	27	2.41	193	386	.500	-43.5	81.6
3	Dave Stieb	Blue Jays	25	3.19	306	555	.551	-62.0	83.1
4	Rick Honeycutt	Rangers	20	3.31	200	392	.510	-38.3	83.9
5	Steve McCatty	Athletics	22	2.33	282	555	.508	-51.6	84.5
5	Ken Forsch	Angels	20	2.88	246	466	.528	-45.1	84.5
7	Larry Gura	Royals	23	2.72	271	515	.526	-47.4	85.1
8	Bert Blyleven	Indians	20	2.88	257	478	.538	-43.0	85.7
9	Dan Petry	Tigers	23	3.00	238	426	.559	-35.5	87.0
10	Doc Medich	Rangers	20	3.08	230	428	.537	-30.1	88.4

Extremes for Pitchers

Pitcher	Team	Best		Pitcher	Team	Worst
Dave Stieb	Blue Jays	-62.0	BV	Wayne Garland	Indians	59.4
Sammy Stewart	Orioles	65.3	ERA+	Rick Waits	Indians	137.0
Steve McCatty	Athletics	-21.6	ERV	Rich Gale	Royals	21.3
Dennis Lamp	White Sox	45.9	ISO+	Mike Caldwell	Brewers	161.2
Dennis Lamp	White Sox	-27.1	EXV	Mike Caldwell	Brewers	35.3
Ron Guidry	Yankees	61.6	CT+	Glenn Abbott	Mariners	197.7
Ron Davis	Yankees	48.4	SOV	Mike Caldwell	Brewers	-37.5
Rick Honeycutt	Rangers	42.7	EY+	Sammy Stewart	Orioles	150.6
Dennis Leonard	Royals	-26.5	BBV	Mark Clear	Red Sox	21.7

1981 National League

Standings

Rank	Team	Post	W	L	Pct.	R	RA	BPO	BPOA	TS
1	Los Angeles Dodgers	WLP	63	47	.573	4.09	3.24	.641	.574	78.333
2	Houston Astros	P	61	49	.555	3.58	3.01	.625	.535	61.552
3	Saint Louis Cardinals	—	59	43	.578	4.50	4.05	.676	.621	60.148
4	Montreal Expos	P	60	48	.556	4.10	3.65	.667	.588	59.895
5	Cincinnati Reds	—	66	42	.611	4.30	4.07	.673	.640	59.552
6	Philadelphia Phillies	P	59	48	.551	4.59	4.41	.698	.700	51.460
7	San Francisco Giants	—	56	55	.505	3.85	3.73	.629	.646	45.749
8	Atlanta Braves	—	50	56	.472	3.69	3.89	.603	.627	39.874
9	Pittsburgh Pirates	—	46	56	.451	3.95	4.13	.639	.671	37.622
10	New York Mets	—	41	62	.398	3.31	4.11	.617	.668	26.537
11	San Diego Padres	—	41	69	.373	3.47	4.14	.594	.689	22.232
12	Chicago Cubs	—	38	65	.369	3.49	4.56	.589	.694	17.954

Best Batters

Rank	Batter	Team	G	BA	B	O	BPO	BV	BPO+
1	Mike Schmidt	Phillies	102	.316	320	258	1.240	138.9	176.7
2	Tim Raines	Expos	88	.304	258	239	1.079	91.6	155.1
3	Andre Dawson	Expos	103	.302	291	290	1.003	89.1	144.2
4	Bill Madlock	Pirates	82	.341	197	199	.990	58.7	142.4
5	Gary Matthews	Phillies	101	.301	246	268	.918	57.9	130.8
6	Keith Hernandez	Cardinals	103	.306	254	280	.907	58.1	129.7
7	George Foster	Reds	108	.295	277	308	.899	63.0	129.5
8	Ron Cey	Dodgers	85	.288	195	235	.830	38.0	124.2
9	Joe Morgan	Giants	90	.240	200	246	.813	37.2	122.8
10	Gene Richards	Padres	104	.288	240	300	.800	43.6	122.2

Extremes for Batters

Batter	Team	Best		Batter	Team	Worst
Mike Schmidt	Phillies	138.9	BV	Doug Flynn	Mets	-69.8
Mike Schmidt	Phillies	156.0	SE+	Doug Flynn	Mets	65.8
Mike Schmidt	Phillies	49.6	SCV	Ivan de Jesus	Cubs	-31.2
Mike Schmidt	Phillies	259.5	ISO+	Ozzie Smith	Padres	29.8
Mike Schmidt	Phillies	71.3	EXV	Ozzie Smith	Padres	-35.3
Tim Foli	Pirates	387.1	CT+	Dave Kingman	Mets	44.0
Bill Buckner	Cubs	-36.1	SOV	Dave Kingman	Mets	58.8
Joe Morgan	Giants	208.6	EY+	Doug Flynn	Mets	11.9
Jason Thompson	Pirates	36.1	BBV	Doug Flynn	Mets	-22.1

Best Pitchers

Rank	Pitcher	Team	G	ERA	B	O	BPO	BV	BPO+
1	Nolan Ryan	Astros	21	1.69	212	454	.467	-65.8	76.3
2	Don Sutton	Astros	23	2.61	228	475	.480	-62.7	78.4
3	Bill Gullickson	Expos	22	2.80	241	478	.504	-62.5	79.4
4	Jerry Reuss	Dodgers	22	2.30	227	466	.487	-56.7	80.0
5	Bob Knepper	Astros	22	2.18	231	471	.490	-57.2	80.1
6	Steve Carlton	Phillies	24	2.42	297	570	.521	-70.5	80.8
7	Fernando Valenzuela	Dodgers	25	2.48	290	577	.503	-61.2	82.6
8	Lary Sorensen	Cardinals	23	3.27	230	421	.546	-40.0	85.2
9	Burt Hooton	Dodgers	23	2.28	223	427	.522	-36.9	85.8
10	Scott Sanderson	Expos	22	2.95	228	417	.547	-36.7	86.1

Extremes for Pitchers

Pitcher	Team	Best		Pitcher	Team	Worst
Steve Carlton	Phillies	-70.5	BV	Nino Espinosa	Phillies	65.8
Nolan Ryan	Astros	52.7	ERA+	Dick Ruthven	Phillies	145.7
Nolan Ryan	Astros	-25.1	ERV	Dick Ruthven	Phillies	26.4
Nolan Ryan	Astros	28.3	ISO+	Pat Zachry	Mets	139.1
Nolan Ryan	Astros	-38.0	EXV	Nino Espinosa	Phillies	28.8
Fernando Valenzuela	Dodgers	55.7	CT+	Eddie Solomon	Pirates	180.9
Fernando Valenzuela	Dodgers	79.8	SOV	Jerry Reuss	Dodgers	-32.2
Gaylord Perry	Braves	50.3	EY+	Bruce Berenyi	Reds	193.5
Gaylord Perry	Braves	-22.7	BBV	Bruce Berenyi	Reds	37.2

1982 American League

Standings

Rank	Team	Post	W	L	Pct.	R	RA	BPO	BPOA	TS
1	Milwaukee Brewers	LP	95	67	.586	5.47	4.40	.750	.693	74.675
2	California Angels	P	93	69	.574	5.02	4.14	.749	.638	66.608
3	Baltimore Orioles	—	94	68	.580	4.75	4.21	.720	.647	62.184
4	Chicago White Sox	—	87	75	.537	4.85	4.38	.717	.648	57.131
5	Kansas City Royals	—	90	72	.556	4.84	4.43	.720	.675	57.023
6	Boston Red Sox	—	89	73	.549	4.65	4.40	.684	.703	51.021
7	Detroit Tigers	—	83	79	.512	4.50	4.23	.692	.668	50.288
8	New York Yankees	—	79	83	.488	4.38	4.42	.677	.663	44.909
9	Cleveland Indians	—	78	84	.481	4.22	4.62	.683	.671	41.659
10	Toronto Blue Jays	—	78	84	.481	4.02	4.33	.636	.652	40.416
11	Seattle Mariners	—	76	86	.469	4.02	4.40	.634	.682	36.616
12	Oakland Athletics	—	68	94	.420	4.27	5.06	.660	.739	26.689
13	Texas Rangers	—	64	98	.395	3.64	4.62	.594	.709	20.462
14	Minnesota Twins	—	60	102	.370	4.06	5.06	.641	.766	17.191

Best Batters

Rank	Batter	Team	G	BA	B	O	BPO	BV	BPO+
1	Rickey Henderson	Athletics	149	.267	455	442	1.029	155.6	152.0
2	Robin Yount	Brewers	156	.331	450	461	.976	140.5	145.4
3	Eddie Murray	Orioles	151	.316	386	401	.963	106.0	137.9
4	Toby Harrah	Indians	162	.304	418	445	.939	104.3	133.3
5	Dwight Evans	Red Sox	162	.292	446	455	.980	109.2	132.4
6	Reggie Jackson	Angels	153	.275	377	403	.935	91.6	132.1
7	Doug DeCinces	Angels	153	.301	402	438	.918	91.8	129.6
8	Hal McRae	Royals	159	.308	399	439	.909	90.9	129.5
9	George Brett	Royals	144	.301	362	404	.896	78.5	127.7
10	Paul Molitor	Brewers	160	.302	426	498	.855	91.6	127.4

Extremes for Batters

Batter	Team	Best		Batter	Team	Worst
Rickey Henderson	Athletics	155.6	BV	Alfredo Griffin	Blue Jays	-116.1
Robin Yount	Brewers	155.2	SE+	Bobby Mitchell	Twins	67.2
Robin Yount	Brewers	76.1	SCV	Bobby Mitchell	Twins	-36.1
Dave Winfield	Yankees	200.9	ISO+	Jerry Remy	Red Sox	27.2
Dave Winfield	Yankees	75.8	EXV	Jerry Remy	Red Sox	-75.1
Tim Foli	Angels	292.8	CT+	Reggie Jackson	Angels	45.6
Rich Dauer	Orioles	-46.7	SOV	Reggie Jackson	Angels	84.9
Rickey Henderson	Athletics	224.2	EY+	Todd Cruz	Mariners	25.4
Rickey Henderson	Athletics	63.7	BBV	Damaso Garcia	Blue Jays	-33.6

Best Pitchers

Rank	Pitcher	Team	G	ERA	B	O	BPO	BV	BPO+
1	Dave Stieb	Blue Jays	38	3.25	498	870	.572	-128.1	79.5
2	Bob Stanley	Red Sox	48	3.10	291	508	.573	-66.6	81.4
3	Jim Clancy	Blue Jays	40	3.71	484	804	.602	-94.6	83.7
4	Mike Witt	Angels	33	3.51	309	546	.566	-56.9	84.4
5	Jim Palmer	Orioles	36	3.13	382	682	.560	-67.3	85.0
6	Jim Beattie	Mariners	28	3.34	308	518	.595	-53.2	85.3
7	Dan Petry	Tigers	35	3.22	444	742	.598	-50.6	89.8
8	Geoff Zahn	Angels	34	3.73	421	694	.607	-44.1	90.5
9	Len Barker	Indians	33	3.90	454	743	.611	-43.7	91.2
10	Rick Sutcliffe	Indians	34	2.96	395	645	.612	-37.0	91.4

Extremes for Pitchers

Pitcher	Team	Best		Pitcher	Team	Worst
Dave Stieb	Blue Jays	-128.1	BV	Matt Keough	Athletics	133.9
Bob Stanley	Red Sox	73.5	ERA+	Matt Keough	Athletics	152.5
Dave Stieb	Blue Jays	-36.3	ERV	Matt Keough	Athletics	45.8
Bob Stanley	Red Sox	64.0	ISO+	Matt Keough	Athletics	165.2
Dave Stieb	Blue Jays	-48.5	EXV	Matt Keough	Athletics	65.1
Dave Righetti	Yankees	58.6	CT+	Mike Caldwell	Brewers	188.5
Floyd Bannister	Mariners	74.0	SOV	Mike Caldwell	Brewers	-66.4
Dennis Eckersley	Red Sox	54.3	EY+	Dave Righetti	Yankees	171.7
Dennis Eckersley	Red Sox	-33.7	BBV	Dave Righetti	Yankees	43.4

1982 National League

Standings

Rank	Team	Post	W	L	Pct.	R	RA	BPO	BPOA	TS
1	Saint Louis Cardinals	WLP	92	70	.568	4.23	3.76	.671	.646	75.018
2	Los Angeles Dodgers	—	88	74	.543	4.27	3.78	.684	.577	64.504
3	Montreal Expos	—	86	76	.531	4.30	3.80	.687	.616	60.371
4	Atlanta Braves	P	89	73	.549	4.56	4.33	.675	.665	54.317
5	Philadelphia Phillies	—	89	73	.549	4.10	4.04	.647	.629	53.157
6	Pittsburgh Pirates	—	84	78	.519	4.47	4.30	.695	.661	52.320
7	San Francisco Giants	—	87	75	.537	4.15	4.24	.665	.673	47.946
8	San Diego Padres	—	81	81	.500	4.17	4.06	.618	.640	44.919
9	Houston Astros	—	77	85	.475	3.51	3.83	.595	.610	38.065
10	Chicago Cubs	—	73	89	.451	4.17	4.38	.642	.694	33.634
11	New York Mets	—	65	97	.401	3.76	4.46	.601	.702	18.665
12	Cincinnati Reds	—	61	101	.377	3.36	4.08	.600	.669	18.446

Best Batters

Rank	Batter	Team	G	BA	B	O	BPO	BV	BPO+
1	Mike Schmidt	Phillies	148	.280	412	395	1.043	132.7	147.5
2	Pedro Guerrero	Dodgers	150	.304	407	419	.971	122.3	143.0
3	Leon Durham	Cubs	148	.312	379	398	.952	102.0	136.8
4	Joe Morgan	Giants	134	.289	318	340	.935	85.0	136.5
5	Jason Thompson	Pirates	156	.284	394	414	.952	101.2	134.6
6	Dale Murphy	Braves	162	.281	426	455	.936	103.0	131.9
7	Sixto Lezcano	Padres	138	.289	313	355	.882	73.0	130.4
8	Al Oliver	Expos	160	.331	392	431	.910	84.9	127.7
9	Lonnie Smith	Cardinals	156	.307	405	454	.892	84.3	126.3
10	Gary Carter	Expos	154	.293	382	427	.895	77.8	125.6

Extremes for Batters

Batter	Team	Best		Batter	Team	Worst
Mike Schmidt	Phillies	132.7	BV	Johnnie LeMaster	Giants	-84.5
Lonnie Smith	Cardinals	131.7	SE+	Larry Bowa	Cubs	70.2
Lonnie Smith	Cardinals	43.6	SCV	Larry Bowa	Cubs	-33.6
Mike Schmidt	Phillies	201.5	ISO+	Manny Trillo	Phillies	35.8
Mike Schmidt	Phillies	69.0	EXV	Manny Trillo	Phillies	-46.6
Bill Buckner	Cubs	345.6	CT+	Dave Kingman	Mets	50.2
Bill Buckner	Cubs	-63.9	SOV	Dave Kingman	Mets	77.8
Jason Thompson	Pirates	200.7	EY+	Steve Garvey	Dodgers	22.2
Jason Thompson	Pirates	47.2	BBV	Steve Garvey	Dodgers	-35.1

Best Pitchers

Rank	Pitcher	Team	G	ERA	B	O	BPO	BV	BPO+
1	Joaquin Andujar	Cardinals	38	2.47	414	791	.523	-97.8	80.9
2	Steve Rogers	Expos	35	2.40	444	842	.527	-103.8	81.1
3	Jerry Reuss	Dodgers	39	3.11	389	773	.503	-89.0	81.4
4	Joe Niekro	Astros	35	2.47	411	808	.509	-83.6	83.1
5	Steve Carlton	Phillies	38	3.10	487	894	.545	-93.3	83.9
6	Mario Soto	Reds	35	2.79	431	778	.554	-78.1	84.7
7	Manny Sarmiento	Pirates	35	3.39	279	496	.563	-43.5	86.5
8	Charlie Lea	Expos	27	3.24	306	540	.567	-45.3	87.1
9	Don Sutton	Astros	27	3.00	318	590	.539	-43.2	88.0
10	Fernando Valenzuela	Dodgers	37	2.87	476	863	.552	-57.7	89.2

Extremes for Pitchers

Pitcher	Team	Best		Pitcher	Team	Worst
Steve Rogers	Expos	-103.8	BV	Mike Scott	Mets	94.3
Steve Rogers	Expos	67.8	ERA+	Doug Bird	Cubs	142.3
Steve Rogers	Expos	-35.1	ERV	Doug Bird	Cubs	32.4
Bruce Berenyi	Reds	68.7	ISO+	Pete Falcone	Mets	146.3
Bruce Berenyi	Reds	-31.4	EXV	Doug Bird	Cubs	35.2
Mario Soto	Reds	52.2	CT+	Bob Forsch	Cardinals	199.0
Mario Soto	Reds	131.1	SOV	Bob Forsch	Cardinals	-68.3
Atlee Hammaker	Giants	40.6	EY+	Charlie Puleo	Mets	164.6
Doug Bird	Cubs	-29.6	BBV	Nolan Ryan	Astros	32.9

1983 American League

Standings

Rank	Team	Post	W	L	Pct.	R	RA	BPO	BPOA	TS
1	Baltimore Orioles	WLP	98	64	.605	4.93	4.02	.720	.638	81.677
2	Chicago White Sox	P	99	63	.611	4.94	4.01	.720	.625	69.732
3	Detroit Tigers	—	92	70	.568	4.87	4.19	.721	.643	62.554
4	New York Yankees	—	91	71	.562	4.75	4.34	.705	.643	58.827
5	Toronto Blue Jays	—	89	73	.549	4.91	4.48	.740	.685	57.295
6	Milwaukee Brewers	—	87	75	.537	4.72	4.37	.703	.686	52.888
7	Texas Rangers	—	77	85	.475	3.92	3.74	.613	.614	44.479
8	Kansas City Royals	—	79	83	.488	4.27	4.71	.669	.685	40.042
9	Boston Red Sox	—	78	84	.481	4.47	4.78	.682	.730	38.075
10	Oakland Athletics	—	74	88	.457	4.37	4.83	.682	.697	36.941
11	California Angels	—	70	92	.432	4.46	4.81	.650	.698	33.060
12	Cleveland Indians	—	70	92	.432	4.35	4.85	.660	.697	32.742
13	Minnesota Twins	—	70	92	.432	4.38	5.07	.652	.767	25.848
14	Seattle Mariners	—	60	102	.370	3.44	4.57	.608	.717	17.114

Best Batters

Rank	Batter	Team	G	BA	B	O	BPO	BV	BPO+
1	Rickey Henderson	Athletics	145	.292	433	395	1.096	168.8	163.9
2	Eddie Murray	Orioles	156	.306	416	427	.974	121.7	141.3
3	George Brett	Royals	123	.310	322	333	.967	87.9	137.5
4	Robin Yount	Brewers	149	.308	387	425	.911	103.1	136.3
5	Wade Boggs	Red Sox	153	.361	389	400	.973	95.0	132.3
6	Alan Trammell	Tigers	142	.319	344	380	.905	79.9	130.3
7	Don Baylor	Yankees	144	.303	344	399	.862	71.4	126.2
8	Lloyd Moseby	Blue Jays	151	.315	361	396	.912	69.8	124.0
9	Willie Upshaw	Blue Jays	160	.306	384	427	.899	70.0	122.3
9	Greg Luzinski	White Sox	144	.255	345	395	.873	62.9	122.3

Extremes for Batters

Batter	Team	Best		Batter	Team	Worst
Rickey Henderson	Athletics	168.8	BV	Todd Cruz	Mariners-Orioles	-93.9
Cecil Cooper	Brewers	145.0	SE+	Wayne Tolleson	Rangers	75.6
Cecil Cooper	Brewers	62.6	SCV	Jim Sundberg	Rangers	-31.0
George Brett	Royals	178.3	ISO+	Jerry Remy	Red Sox	28.0
Dave Winfield	Yankees	58.2	EXV	Jerry Remy	Red Sox	-66.9
Jerry Remy	Red Sox	239.9	CT+	Ron Kittle	White Sox	47.5
Jerry Remy	Red Sox	-49.0	SOV	Reggie Jackson	Angels	85.5
Rickey Henderson	Athletics	203.1	EY+	Frank White	Royals	35.7
Rickey Henderson	Athletics	48.2	BBV	Frank White	Royals	-28.9

Best Pitchers

Rank	Pitcher	Team	G	ERA	B	O	BPO	BV	BPO+
1	Rick Honeycutt	Rangers	25	2.42	279	524	.532	-67.5	80.5
2	LaMarr Hoyt	White Sox	36	3.66	434	796	.545	-103.4	80.8
3	Dave Stieb	Blue Jays	36	3.04	484	833	.581	-96.1	83.4
4	Mike Boddicker	Orioles	27	2.77	292	536	.545	-56.9	83.7
5	Storm Davis	Orioles	34	3.59	345	609	.567	-51.4	87.0
6	Floyd Bannister	White Sox	34	3.35	393	657	.598	-50.5	88.6
7	Dave Righetti	Yankees	31	3.44	381	661	.576	-46.5	89.1
8	Jack Morris	Tigers	37	3.34	523	886	.590	-57.2	90.1
9	Matt Young	Mariners	33	3.27	386	610	.633	-39.6	90.7
10	Jim Beattie	Mariners	30	3.84	376	589	.638	-34.9	91.5

Extremes for Pitchers

Pitcher	Team	Best		Pitcher	Team	Worst
LaMarr Hoyt	White Sox	-103.4	BV	Dennis Martinez	Orioles	93.0
Rick Honeycutt	Rangers	62.6	ERA+	Frank Viola	Twins	133.0
Dave Stieb	Blue Jays	-35.2	ERV	Brad Havens	Twins	36.2
Rick Honeycutt	Rangers	64.6	ISO+	Mike Caldwell	Brewers	142.4
Bob Stanley	Red Sox	-36.9	EXV	Mike Caldwell	Brewers	48.2
Floyd Bannister	White Sox	59.6	CT+	Mike Caldwell	Brewers	223.2
Floyd Bannister	White Sox	77.9	SOV	Mike Caldwell	Brewers	-71.5
LaMarr Hoyt	White Sox	34.2	EY+	Tim Conroy	Athletics	180.8
LaMarr Hoyt	White Sox	-51.8	BBV	Tim Conroy	Athletics	42.9

1983 National League

Standings

Rank	Team	Post	W	L	Pct.	R	RA	BPO	BPOA	TS
1	Philadelphia Phillies	LP	90	72	.556	4.27	3.90	.672	.641	71.305
2	Los Angeles Dodgers	P	91	71	.562	4.01	3.74	.663	.594	64.562
3	Atlanta Braves	—	88	74	.543	4.60	3.95	.707	.667	63.997
4	Houston Astros	—	85	77	.525	3.97	3.99	.659	.613	53.246
5	Montreal Expos	—	82	80	.506	4.15	3.96	.673	.647	51.471
6	Pittsburgh Pirates	—	84	78	.519	4.07	4.00	.656	.652	49.376
7	Saint Louis Cardinals	—	79	83	.488	4.19	4.38	.691	.671	43.342
8	San Francisco Giants	—	79	83	.488	4.24	4.30	.668	.676	42.248
9	San Diego Padres	—	81	81	.500	4.01	4.01	.617	.670	40.315
10	Chicago Cubs	—	71	91	.438	4.33	4.44	.670	.702	32.512
11	Cincinnati Reds	—	74	88	.457	3.85	4.38	.635	.689	27.325
12	New York Mets	—	68	94	.420	3.55	4.20	.586	.677	17.063

Best Batters

Rank	Batter	Team	G	BA	B	O	BPO	BV	BPO+
1	Mike Schmidt	Phillies	154	.255	422	420	1.005	123.2	141.2
2	Dale Murphy	Braves	162	.302	446	436	1.023	126.6	139.7
3	Tim Raines	Expos	156	.298	459	464	.989	125.3	137.5
4	Pedro Guerrero	Dodgers	160	.298	413	434	.952	110.1	136.3
5	Darrell Evans	Giants	142	.277	364	394	.924	89.9	132.8
6	Jose Cruz	Astros	160	.318	375	429	.874	78.6	126.5
7	Andre Dawson	Expos	159	.299	431	487	.885	80.7	123.0
8	Lonnie Smith	Cardinals	130	.321	321	368	.872	58.1	122.1
9	Keith Hernandez	Cardinals-Mets	150	.297	337	395	.853	58.6	121.2
10	Gary Redus	Reds	125	.247	318	365	.871	53.0	120.0

Extremes for Batters

Batter	Team	Best		Batter	Team	Worst
Dale Murphy	Braves	126.6	BV	Doug Flynn	Expos	-101.8
Dale Murphy	Braves	144.4	SE+	Dale Berra	Pirates	73.0
Dale Murphy	Braves	66.4	SCV	Dale Berra	Pirates	-34.4
Mike Schmidt	Phillies	197.5	ISO+	Pete Rose	Phillies	29.7
Mike Schmidt	Phillies	71.1	EXV	Dave Concepcion	Reds	-48.4
Johnny Ray	Pirates	316.0	CT+	Mike Marshall	Dodgers	51.7
Bill Buckner	Cubs	-62.3	SOV	Mike Schmidt	Phillies	67.3
Mike Schmidt	Phillies	204.7	EY+	Luis Salazar	Padres	22.6
Mike Schmidt	Phillies	56.8	BBV	Mookie Wilson	Mets	-36.1

Best Pitchers

Rank	Pitcher	Team	G	ERA	B	O	BPO	BV	BPO+
1	Atlee Hammaker	Giants	23	2.25	265	533	.497	-74.4	78.1
2	John Denny	Phillies	36	2.37	384	743	.517	-95.2	80.1
3	Alejandro Pena	Dodgers	34	2.75	275	542	.507	-67.2	80.4
4	Mario Soto	Reds	34	2.70	459	831	.552	-95.2	82.8
5	Bob Welch	Dodgers	31	2.65	332	618	.537	-58.2	85.1
6	Nolan Ryan	Astros	29	2.98	328	592	.554	-44.0	88.2
7	Craig McMurtry	Braves	36	3.08	401	681	.589	-53.2	88.3
8	John Candelaria	Pirates	33	3.23	346	589	.587	-41.8	89.2
9	Pascual Perez	Braves	33	3.43	391	656	.596	-46.5	89.4
10	Larry McWilliams	Pirates	35	3.25	433	728	.595	-46.3	90.3

Extremes for Pitchers

Pitcher	Team	Best		Pitcher	Team	Worst
John Denny	Phillies	-95.2	BV	Charlie Puleo	Reds	80.6
Mario Soto	Reds	-95.2				
Atlee Hammaker	Giants	64.8	ERA+	Tim Lollar	Padres	134.9
Mario Soto	Reds	-30.6	ERV	Jim Bibby	Pirates	26.6
Alejandro Pena	Dodgers	53.8	ISO+	Tim Lollar	Padres	136.5
John Denny	Phillies	-36.1	EXV	Burt Hooton	Dodgers	34.6
Nolan Ryan	Astros	62.0	CT+	Ed Lynch	Mets	266.7
Steve Carlton	Phillies	91.1	SOV	Ed Lynch	Mets	-73.3
Atlee Hammaker	Giants	39.0	EY+	Nolan Ryan	Astros	158.8
Atlee Hammaker	Giants	-31.3	BBV	Nolan Ryan	Astros	36.3
				Phil Niekro	Braves	36.3

1984 American League

Standings

Rank	Team	Post	W	L	Pct.	R	RA	BPO	BPOA	TS
1	Detroit Tigers	WLP	104	58	.642	5.12	3.97	.747	.606	97.109
2	Toronto Blue Jays	—	89	73	.549	4.60	4.27	.728	.663	59.809
3	New York Yankees	—	87	75	.537	4.68	4.19	.691	.656	57.520
4	Boston Red Sox	—	86	76	.531	5.00	4.72	.727	.696	54.480
5	Baltimore Orioles	—	85	77	.525	4.20	4.12	.672	.647	51.261
6	Kansas City Royals	P	84	78	.519	4.15	4.23	.653	.639	47.973
7	California Angels	—	81	81	.500	4.30	4.30	.649	.671	43.708
8	Minnesota Twins	—	81	81	.500	4.15	4.17	.628	.672	41.823
9	Cleveland Indians	—	75	87	.463	4.67	4.70	.678	.689	40.157
10	Oakland Athletics	—	77	85	.475	4.56	4.91	.704	.731	36.953
11	Chicago White Sox	—	74	88	.457	4.19	4.54	.667	.671	36.729
12	Seattle Mariners	—	74	88	.457	4.21	4.78	.664	.718	30.492
13	Texas Rangers	—	69	92	.429	4.07	4.43	.617	.687	28.174
14	Milwaukee Brewers	—	67	94	.416	3.98	4.56	.604	.683	23.864

Best Batters

Rank	Batter	Team	G	BA	B	O	BPO	BV	BPO+
1	Rickey Henderson	Athletics	142	.293	391	384	1.018	137.3	154.1
2	Eddie Murray	Orioles	162	.306	426	427	.998	136.1	147.0
3	Kirk Gibson	Tigers	149	.282	383	403	.950	105.0	137.8
4	Alvin Davis	Mariners	152	.284	398	424	.939	102.2	134.5
5	Dave Winfield	Yankees	141	.340	357	398	.897	87.8	132.6
6	Don Mattingly	Yankees	153	.343	384	429	.895	93.8	132.3
7	Dwight Evans	Red Sox	162	.295	446	472	.945	106.6	131.4
8	Cal Ripken Jr.	Orioles	162	.304	404	465	.869	88.3	128.0
9	Lloyd Moseby	Blue Jays	158	.280	413	453	.912	88.0	127.1
10	Kent Hrbek	Twins	149	.311	369	410	.900	76.6	126.2

Extremes for Batters

Batter	Team	Best		Batter	Team	Worst
Rickey Henderson	Athletics	137.3	BV	Bob Boone	Angels	-105.7
Dave Winfield	Yankees	150.4	SE+	Curt Wilkerson	Rangers	65.1
Dave Winfield	Yankees	62.7	SCV	Curt Wilkerson	Rangers	-38.6
Dave Kingman	Athletics	189.8	ISO+	Curt Wilkerson	Rangers	22.1
Tony Armas	Red Sox	71.0	EXV	Kirby Puckett	Twins	-61.6
Marty Barrett	Red Sox	281.5	CT+	Ron Kittle	White Sox	49.9
Don Mattingly	Yankees	-53.6	SOV	Steve Balboni	Royals	78.7
Rickey Henderson	Athletics	186.0	EY+	Damaso Garcia	Blue Jays	29.2
Rickey Henderson	Athletics	39.3	BBV	Damaso Garcia	Blue Jays	-36.3

Best Pitchers

Rank	Pitcher	Team	G	ERA	B	O	BPO	BV	BPO+
1	Bud Black	Royals	35	3.12	422	777	.543	-94.6	81.7
2	Dave Stieb	Blue Jays	35	2.83	445	800	.556	-97.4	82.0
3	Bert Blyleven	Indians	33	2.87	411	741	.555	-84.6	82.9
4	Geoff Zahn	Angels	28	3.12	330	606	.545	-65.6	83.4
5	Frank Viola	Twins	35	3.21	450	773	.582	-78.1	85.2
6	Doyle Alexander	Blue Jays	36	3.13	461	787	.586	-72.5	86.4
7	Storm Davis	Orioles	35	3.12	374	672	.557	-58.5	86.5
8	Mike Boddicker	Orioles	34	2.79	448	782	.573	-55.3	89.0
9	Mike Mason	Rangers	36	3.61	333	551	.604	-38.2	89.7
10	John Butcher	Twins	34	3.44	426	678	.628	-37.2	92.0

Extremes for Pitchers

Pitcher	Team	Best		Pitcher	Team	Worst
Dave Stieb	Blue Jays	-97.4	BV	Steve McCatty	Athletics	74.4
Dave Stieb	Blue Jays	70.6	ERA+	Lary Sorensen	Athletics	135.8
Dave Stieb	Blue Jays	-35.0	ERV	Jim Clancy	Blue Jays	27.1
Storm Davis	Orioles	59.0	ISO+	Larry Gura	Royals	142.5
Storm Davis	Orioles	-42.4	EXV	Dennis Martinez	Orioles	43.4
Mark Langston	Mariners	60.1	CT+	Tommy John	Angels	224.6
Mark Langston	Mariners	81.4	SOV	Tommy John	Angels	-58.6
LaMarr Hoyt	White Sox	52.0	EY+	Mark Langston	Mariners	156.8
LaMarr Hoyt	White Sox	-36.8	BBV	Mark Clear	Red Sox	43.8

1984 National League

Standings

Rank	Team	Post	W	L	Pct.	R	RA	BPO	BPOA	TS
1	Chicago Cubs	P	96	65	.596	4.73	4.09	.702	.652	69.775
2	San Diego Padres	LP	92	70	.568	4.23	3.91	.639	.632	67.737
3	Philadelphia Phillies	—	81	81	.500	4.44	4.26	.713	.628	57.113
4	Houston Astros	—	80	82	.494	4.28	3.89	.644	.615	52.335
5	New York Mets	—	90	72	.556	4.02	4.17	.642	.651	49.546
6	Saint Louis Cardinals	—	84	78	.519	4.02	3.98	.636	.640	47.850
7	Pittsburgh Pirates	—	75	87	.463	3.80	3.50	.605	.611	43.694
8	Montreal Expos	—	78	83	.484	3.68	3.63	.626	.632	43.549
9	Los Angeles Dodgers	—	79	83	.488	3.58	3.70	.597	.590	43.410
10	Atlanta Braves	—	80	82	.494	3.90	4.04	.634	.655	40.844
11	Cincinnati Reds	—	70	92	.432	3.87	4.61	.635	.689	23.138
12	San Francisco Giants	—	66	96	.407	4.21	4.98	.646	.721	17.387

Best Batters

Rank	Batter	Team	G	BA	B	O	BPO	BV	BPO+
1	Tim Raines	Expos	160	.309	443	454	.976	133.5	143.1
2	Mike Schmidt	Phillies	151	.277	392	412	.951	104.5	136.4
3	Dale Murphy	Braves	162	.290	435	454	.958	114.4	135.7
4	Keith Hernandez	Mets	154	.311	356	400	.890	85.4	131.6
5	Jose Cruz	Astros	160	.312	384	441	.871	91.4	131.2
6	Ryne Sandberg	Cubs	156	.314	427	459	.930	95.0	128.6
7	Gary Matthews	Cubs	147	.291	344	377	.912	71.3	126.2
8	Leon Durham	Cubs	137	.279	330	362	.912	68.2	126.0
8	Chili Davis	Giants	137	.315	312	367	.850	64.5	126.0
10	Darryl Strawberry	Mets	147	.251	351	412	.852	72.3	125.9

Extremes for Batters

Batter	Team	Best		Batter	Team	Worst
Tim Raines	Expos	133.5	BV	Rafael Ramirez	Braves	-87.6
Jose Cruz	Astros	139.8	SE+	Garry Templeton	Padres	67.5
Jose Cruz	Astros	51.0	SCV	Larry Bowa	Cubs	-42.6
Mike Schmidt	Phillies	197.5	ISO+	Rafael Ramirez	Braves	46.7
Dale Murphy	Braves	76.8	EXV	Rafael Ramirez	Braves	-41.1
Tony Gwynn	Padres	403.2	CT+	Darryl Strawberry	Mets	60.3
Tony Gwynn	Padres	-69.7	SOV	Juan Samuel	Phillies	62.7
Gary Matthews	Cubs	201.5	EY+	Garry Templeton	Padres	40.3
Gary Matthews	Cubs	50.9	BBV	Juan Samuel	Phillies	-32.1

Best Pitchers

Rank	Pitcher	Team	G	ERA	B	O	BPO	BV	BPO+
1	Orel Hershiser	Dodgers	45	2.66	286	579	.494	-70.0	80.3
2	Rick Rhoden	Pirates	33	2.72	379	714	.531	-76.2	83.3
3	Alejandro Pena	Dodgers	28	2.48	317	602	.527	-53.2	85.6
4	Dwight Gooden	Mets	31	2.60	347	652	.532	-55.9	86.1
5	Steve Trout	Cubs	32	3.41	340	579	.587	-42.3	88.9
6	Rick Mahler	Braves	38	3.12	397	666	.596	-33.7	92.2
6	Rick Honeycutt	Dodgers	29	2.84	318	561	.567	-27.0	92.2
8	Mario Soto	Reds	33	3.53	436	718	.607	-32.1	93.1
9	Jerry Koosman	Phillies	36	3.25	404	683	.592	-29.4	93.2
10	Joaquin Andujar	Cardinals	36	3.34	455	783	.581	-31.9	93.4

Extremes for Pitchers

Pitcher	Team	Best		Pitcher	Team	Worst
Rick Rhoden	Pirates	-76.2	BV	Mike Krukow	Giants	104.0
Alejandro Pena	Dodgers	73.1	ERA+	Mark Davis	Giants	157.3
Bruce Sutter	Cardinals	-25.2	ERV	Mark Davis	Giants	37.9
Steve Trout	Cubs	58.2	ISO+	Mark Davis	Giants	167.6
Steve Trout	Cubs	-35.2	EXV	Bill Gullickson	Expos	54.4
Dwight Gooden	Mets	49.2	CT+	Mark Thurmond	Padres	205.8
Dwight Gooden	Mets	140.3	SOV	Bill Laskey	Giants	-64.5
Bill Gullickson	Expos	41.6	EY+	Bruce Berenyi	Reds-Mets	169.1
Bill Gullickson	Expos	-42.2	BBV	Tim Lollar	Padres	41.6

1985 American League

Standings

Rank	Team	Post	W	L	Pct.	R	RA	BPO	BPOA	TS
1	Kansas City Royals	WLP	91	71	.562	4.24	3.94	.669	.625	71.710
2	Toronto Blue Jays	P	99	62	.615	4.71	3.65	.719	.623	71.062
3	New York Yankees	—	97	64	.602	5.21	4.10	.760	.654	70.868
4	Detroit Tigers	—	84	77	.522	4.53	4.27	.705	.635	54.409
5	Boston Red Sox	—	81	81	.500	4.91	4.42	.731	.675	52.988
6	California Angels	—	90	72	.556	4.52	4.34	.688	.684	52.487
7	Baltimore Orioles	—	83	78	.516	5.08	4.75	.727	.723	49.723
8	Chicago White Sox	—	85	77	.525	4.52	4.42	.658	.698	45.870
9	Oakland Athletics	—	77	85	.475	4.67	4.86	.679	.711	39.577
10	Minnesota Twins	—	77	85	.475	4.35	4.83	.680	.706	37.983
11	Seattle Mariners	—	74	88	.457	4.44	5.05	.696	.721	35.272
12	Milwaukee Brewers	—	71	90	.441	4.29	4.98	.630	.715	28.961
13	Texas Rangers	—	62	99	.385	3.83	4.88	.655	.721	22.350
14	Cleveland Indians	—	60	102	.370	4.50	5.31	.655	.765	19.418

Best Batters

Rank	Batter	Team	G	BA	B	O	BPO	BV	BPO+
1	Rickey Henderson	Yankees	143	.314	469	398	1.178	187.8	166.8
2	George Brett	Royals	155	.335	446	388	1.149	167.0	159.8
3	Kirk Gibson	Tigers	154	.287	420	436	.963	111.2	136.0
4	Eddie Murray	Orioles	156	.297	404	428	.944	101.6	133.6
5	Don Mattingly	Yankees	159	.324	447	475	.941	111.3	133.2
6	Toby Harrah	Rangers	126	.270	290	305	.951	71.7	132.9
7	Wade Boggs	Red Sox	161	.368	419	439	.954	94.3	129.0
8	Jesse Barfield	Blue Jays	155	.289	384	408	.941	85.7	128.7
9	Darrell Evans	Tigers	151	.248	351	392	.895	73.4	126.4
10	Mike Davis	Athletics	154	.287	346	415	.834	62.9	122.2

Extremes for Batters

Batter	Team	Best		Batter	Team	Worst
Rickey Henderson	Yankees	187.8	BV	George Wright	Rangers	-103.4
Eddie Murray	Orioles	146.5	SE+	Jack Perconte	Mariners	70.2
Don Mattingly	Yankees	65.9	SCV	George Wright	Rangers	-47.7
Darrell Evans	Tigers	186.8	ISO+	Bob Meacham	Yankees	32.9
Don Mattingly	Yankees	64.2	EXV	Kirby Puckett	Twins	-47.6
Bill Buckner	Red Sox	281.5	CT+	Reggie Jackson	Angels	48.7
Bill Buckner	Red Sox	-65.3	SOV	Steve Balboni	Royals	81.5
Toby Harrah	Rangers	275.8	EY+	Ozzie Guillen	White Sox	24.9
Toby Harrah	Rangers	70.7	BBV	Damaso Garcia	Blue Jays	-38.4

Best Pitchers

Rank	Pitcher	Team	G	ERA	B	O	BPO	BV	BPO+
1	Dave Stieb	Blue Jays	36	2.48	440	803	.548	-107.2	80.4
1	Bret Saberhagen	Royals	32	2.87	380	702	.541	-92.7	80.4
3	Charlie Hough	Rangers	34	3.31	427	757	.564	-83.8	83.6
4	Mike Moore	Mariners	35	3.46	425	739	.575	-81.4	83.9
5	Ron Guidry	Yankees	34	3.27	444	788	.563	-74.5	85.6
6	Bert Blyleven	Indians-Twins	37	3.16	521	890	.585	-86.7	85.8
7	Dan Petry	Tigers	34	3.36	410	724	.566	-66.5	86.0
8	Charlie Leibrandt	Royals	33	2.69	419	720	.582	-65.8	86.4
8	Jimmy Key	Blue Jays	35	3.00	379	644	.589	-59.9	86.4
10	Moose Haas	Brewers	27	3.84	295	495	.596	-36.8	88.9

Extremes for Pitchers

Pitcher	Team	Best		Pitcher	Team	Worst
Dave Stieb	Blue Jays	-107.2	BV	Dennis Martinez	Orioles	86.5
Dave Stieb	Blue Jays	60.9	ERA+	Dennis Martinez	Orioles	134.1
Dave Stieb	Blue Jays	-46.8	ERV	Curt Wardle	Twins-Indians	27.2
Danny Jackson	Royals	70.6	ISO+	Scott McGregor	Orioles	140.8
Dave Stieb	Blue Jays	-41.8	EXV	Scott McGregor	Orioles	43.5
Floyd Bannister	White Sox	62.6	CT+	Ron Romanick	Angels	175.6
Floyd Bannister	White Sox	74.1	SOV	Ron Romanick	Angels	-48.4
Moose Haas	Brewers	42.4	EY+	Phil Niekro	Yankees	160.6
Ron Guidry	Yankees	-41.0	BBV	Phil Niekro	Yankees	44.9

1985 National League

Standings

Rank	Team	Post	W	L	Pct.	R	RA	BPO	BPOA	TS
1	Saint Louis Cardinals	LP	101	61	.623	4.61	3.53	.718	.594	80.680
2	New York Mets	—	98	64	.605	4.29	3.51	.665	.596	65.210
3	Los Angeles Dodgers	P	95	67	.586	4.21	3.57	.675	.570	64.902
4	Cincinnati Reds	—	89	72	.553	4.18	4.11	.668	.650	51.860
5	Montreal Expos	—	84	77	.522	3.93	3.95	.646	.630	48.333
6	Houston Astros	—	83	79	.512	4.36	4.27	.650	.657	46.857
7	San Diego Padres	—	83	79	.512	4.01	3.84	.624	.643	46.681
8	Chicago Cubs	—	77	84	.478	4.23	4.50	.689	.718	39.722
9	Philadelphia Phillies	—	75	87	.463	4.12	4.15	.651	.690	39.410
10	San Francisco Giants	—	62	100	.383	3.43	4.16	.591	.660	25.241
11	Atlanta Braves	—	66	96	.407	3.90	4.82	.616	.724	23.327
12	Pittsburgh Pirates	—	57	104	.354	3.53	4.40	.602	.661	22.334

Best Batters

Rank	Batter	Team	G	BA	B	O	BPO	BV	BPO+
1	Pedro Guerrero	Dodgers	137	.320	387	353	1.096	147.8	161.8
2	Tim Raines	Expos	150	.320	433	415	1.043	148.9	152.4
3	Willie McGee	Cardinals	152	.353	404	421	.960	110.5	137.7
4	Dale Murphy	Braves	162	.300	438	453	.967	116.0	136.0
5	Jack Clark	Cardinals	126	.281	313	337	.929	78.1	133.2
6	Mike Schmidt	Phillies	158	.277	389	416	.935	94.1	131.9
7	Ryne Sandberg	Cubs	153	.305	425	450	.944	92.7	127.9
8	Mike Scioscia	Dodgers	141	.296	279	329	.848	56.1	125.2
9	Tom Herr	Cardinals	159	.302	379	443	.856	70.2	122.7
10	Gary Carter	Mets	149	.281	350	421	.831	60.1	120.7

Extremes for Batters

Batter	Team	Best		Batter	Team	Worst
Tim Raines	Expos	148.9	BV	Rafael Ramirez	Braves	-109.7
Tom Herr	Cardinals	143.2	SE+	Manny Trillo	Giants	60.4
Tom Herr	Cardinals	60.0	SCV	Rafael Santana	Mets	-42.2
Pedro Guerrero	Dodgers	214.2	ISO+	Steve Sax	Dodgers	32.5
Pedro Guerrero	Dodgers	66.6	EXV	Rafael Santana	Mets	-45.8
Johnny Ray	Pirates	357.4	CT+	Mike Marshall	Dodgers	53.5
Johnny Ray	Pirates	-61.8	SOV	Mike Marshall	Dodgers	63.6
Carmelo Martinez	Padres	177.6	EY+	Garry Templeton	Padres	38.5
Pete Rose	Reds	40.9	BBV	Garry Templeton	Padres	-27.1

Best Pitchers

Rank	Pitcher	Team	G	ERA	B	O	BPO	BV	BPO+
1	John Tudor	Cardinals	36	1.93	358	826	.433	-158.9	69.3
2	Dwight Gooden	Mets	35	1.53	367	827	.444	-142.6	72.0
3	Rick Reuschel	Pirates	31	2.27	281	591	.475	-94.7	74.8
4	Orel Hershiser	Dodgers	36	2.03	343	734	.467	-103.3	76.9
5	Dennis Eckersley	Cubs	25	3.08	266	512	.520	-75.5	77.9
6	Bryn Smith	Expos	32	2.91	352	681	.517	-68.2	83.8
7	Fernando Valenzuela	Dodgers	35	2.45	425	828	.513	-78.5	84.4
8	LaMarr Hoyt	Padres	31	3.47	361	629	.574	-34.7	91.2
9	Dave Dravecky	Padres	34	2.93	373	643	.580	-31.5	92.2
10	Bob Welch	Dodgers	23	2.31	286	506	.565	-21.7	93.0

Extremes for Pitchers

Pitcher	Team	Best		Pitcher	Team	Worst
John Tudor	Cardinals	-158.9	BV	Bill Laskey	Giants-Expos	80.0
Dwight Gooden	Mets	46.2	ERA+	Jose DeLeon	Pirates	138.0
Dwight Gooden	Mets	-54.7	ERV	Bill Laskey	Giants-Expos	27.3
Dwight Gooden	Mets	60.2	ISO+	Charles Hudson	Phillies	129.0
John Tudor	Cardinals	-45.4	EXV	Bill Laskey	Giants-Expos	30.9
Sid Fernandez	Mets	54.8	CT+	Andy Hawkins	Padres	214.5
Dwight Gooden	Mets	104.8	SOV	Andy Hawkins	Padres	-79.0
Dennis Eckersley	Cubs	29.0	EY+	Jose DeLeon	Pirates	161.7
LaMarr Hoyt	Padres	-43.6	BBV	Steve Bedrosian	Braves	38.6

1986 American League

Standings

Rank	Team	Post	W	L	Pct.	R	RA	BPO	BPOA	TS
1	Boston Red Sox	LP	95	66	.590	4.93	4.32	.719	.682	74.764
2	California Angels	P	92	70	.568	4.85	4.22	.724	.629	68.502
3	New York Yankees	—	90	72	.556	4.92	4.56	.760	.685	62.510
4	Detroit Tigers	—	87	75	.537	4.93	4.41	.747	.690	60.274
5	Toronto Blue Jays	—	86	76	.531	4.96	4.50	.711	.682	56.597
6	Texas Rangers	—	87	75	.537	4.76	4.59	.711	.711	51.754
7	Cleveland Indians	—	84	78	.519	5.10	5.16	.727	.737	46.188
8	Kansas City Royals	—	76	86	.469	4.04	4.15	.649	.644	41.139
9	Oakland Athletics	—	76	86	.469	4.51	4.69	.681	.711	37.426
10	Milwaukee Brewers	—	77	84	.478	4.14	4.56	.660	.680	36.963
11	Baltimore Orioles	—	73	89	.451	4.37	4.69	.668	.708	32.883
12	Chicago White Sox	—	72	90	.444	3.98	4.31	.621	.677	30.507
13	Minnesota Twins	—	71	91	.438	4.57	5.18	.706	.766	26.678
14	Seattle Mariners	—	67	95	.414	4.43	5.15	.677	.760	20.577

Best Batters

Rank	Batter	Team	G	BA	B	O	BPO	BV	BPO+
1	Wade Boggs	Red Sox	149	.357	395	396	.997	106.7	137.0
2	Kirk Gibson	Tigers	119	.268	331	342	.968	87.5	135.9
3	Don Mattingly	Yankees	162	.352	453	467	.970	116.0	134.4
4	Rickey Henderson	Yankees	153	.263	465	480	.969	118.7	134.3
5	Jesse Barfield	Blue Jays	158	.289	419	441	.950	95.2	129.4
6	George Brett	Royals	124	.290	301	325	.926	64.0	127.0
7	Brian Downing	Angels	152	.267	354	405	.874	64.4	122.2
8	Dwight Evans	Red Sox	152	.259	366	414	.884	64.6	121.5
9	Phil Bradley	Mariners	143	.310	343	387	.886	59.1	120.8
10	Joe Carter	Indians	162	.302	416	487	.854	70.5	120.4
10	Eddie Murray	Orioles	137	.305	315	366	.861	53.4	120.4

Extremes for Batters

Batter	Team	Best		Batter	Team	Worst
Rickey Henderson	Yankees	118.7	**BV**	Ozzie Guillen	White Sox	-119.7
Joe Carter	Indians	135.2	**SE+**	Tim Hulett	White Sox	65.5
Joe Carter	Indians	52.1	**SCV**	Tim Hulett	White Sox	-42.1
Rob Deer	Brewers	168.4	**ISO+**	Ozzie Guillen	White Sox	39.6
Jesse Barfield	Blue Jays	63.9	**EXV**	Ozzie Guillen	White Sox	-50.3
Bill Buckner	Red Sox	416.1	**CT+**	Rob Deer	Brewers	43.3
Bill Buckner	Red Sox	-79.0	**SOV**	Rob Deer	Brewers	101.6
Reggie Jackson	Angels	185.5	**EY+**	Ozzie Guillen	White Sox	21.0
Ken Phelps	Mariners	45.0	**BBV**	Ozzie Guillen	White Sox	-41.3

Best Pitchers

Rank	Pitcher	Team	G	ERA	B	O	BPO	BV	BPO+
1	Roger Clemens	Red Sox	33	2.48	369	776	.476	-162.7	69.4
2	Mike Witt	Angels	34	2.84	420	815	.515	-128.5	76.6
3	Kirk McCaskill	Angels	34	3.36	424	738	.575	-72.7	85.4
4	Dennis Rasmussen	Yankees	31	3.88	362	606	.597	-48.2	88.3
5	Jim Clancy	Blue Jays	34	3.94	401	659	.608	-52.7	88.4
6	Teddy Higuera	Brewers	34	2.79	460	750	.613	-57.2	88.9
7	Mark Gubicza	Royals	35	3.64	332	540	.615	-39.1	89.5
8	Bruce Hurst	Red Sox	25	2.99	324	523	.620	-34.4	90.4
9	Charlie Leibrandt	Royals	35	4.09	443	703	.630	-40.1	91.7
10	Danny Jackson	Royals	32	3.20	358	566	.633	-30.9	92.1

Extremes for Pitchers

Pitcher	Team	Best		Pitcher	Team	Worst
Roger Clemens	Red Sox	-162.7	**BV**	Bobby Witt	Rangers	93.3
Roger Clemens	Red Sox	60.8	**ERA+**	Richard Dotson	White Sox	129.9
Roger Clemens	Red Sox	-45.2	**ERV**	John Butcher	Twins-Indians	33.1
Mark Gubicza	Royals	60.8	**ISO+**	Ken Dixon	Orioles	133.2
Mark Gubicza	Royals	-39.4	**EXV**	Bert Blyleven	Twins	47.5
Mark Langston	Mariners	64.3	**CT+**	Phil Niekro	Indians	173.3
Mark Langston	Mariners	87.4	**SOV**	Phil Niekro	Indians	-59.4
Ron Guidry	Yankees	55.4	**EY+**	Ed Correa	Rangers	180.3
Bert Blyleven	Twins	-36.8	**BBV**	Bobby Witt	Rangers	83.5

1986 National League

Standings

Rank	Team	Post	W	L	Pct.	R	RA	BPO	BPOA	TS
1	New York Mets	WLP	108	54	.667	4.83	3.57	.714	.600	94.962
2	Houston Astros	P	96	66	.593	4.04	3.51	.664	.611	64.111
3	San Francisco Giants	—	83	79	.512	4.31	3.81	.661	.625	54.422
4	Philadelphia Phillies	—	86	75	.534	4.59	4.43	.707	.707	50.301
5	Cincinnati Reds	—	86	76	.531	4.52	4.43	.686	.679	49.988
6	Saint Louis Cardinals	—	79	82	.491	3.73	3.80	.624	.640	42.630
7	Montreal Expos	—	78	83	.484	3.96	4.27	.668	.669	41.260
8	Los Angeles Dodgers	—	73	89	.451	3.94	4.19	.639	.645	38.124
9	San Diego Padres	—	74	88	.457	4.05	4.46	.649	.707	32.334
10	Atlanta Braves	—	72	89	.447	3.82	4.47	.649	.691	30.939
11	Pittsburgh Pirates	—	64	98	.395	4.09	4.32	.654	.687	30.447
12	Chicago Cubs	—	70	90	.438	4.25	4.88	.674	.732	28.631

Best Batters

Rank	Batter	Team	G	BA	B	O	BPO	BV	BPO+
1	Tim Raines	Expos	151	.334	430	405	1.062	140.1	148.4
2	Mike Schmidt	Phillies	160	.290	408	411	.993	110.0	136.9
3	Darryl Strawberry	Mets	136	.259	356	377	.944	90.6	134.1
4	Steve Sax	Dodgers	157	.332	390	461	.846	79.1	125.4
5	Keith Hernandez	Mets	149	.310	349	398	.877	68.8	124.5
6	Kevin McReynolds	Padres	158	.288	371	428	.867	68.4	122.6
7	Glenn Davis	Astros	158	.265	366	441	.830	63.0	120.8
8	Tony Gwynn	Padres	160	.329	396	464	.853	67.9	120.7
9	Von Hayes	Phillies	158	.305	397	455	.873	67.1	120.3
10	Kevin Bass	Astros	157	.311	358	440	.814	55.7	118.4

Extremes for Batters

Batter	Team	Best		Batter	Team	Worst
Tim Raines	Expos	140.1	BV	Rafael Santana	Mets	-88.2
Gary Carter	Mets	143.1	SE+	Ron Oester	Reds	71.7
Gary Carter	Mets	48.8	SCV	Ron Oester	Reds	-34.7
Darryl Strawberry	Mets	184.7	ISO+	Steve Jeltz	Phillies	29.7
Mike Schmidt	Phillies	61.7	EXV	Vince Coleman	Cardinals	-54.8
Tony Gwynn	Padres	312.6	CT+	Darryl Strawberry	Mets	53.9
Tony Gwynn	Padres	-74.4	SOV	Darryl Strawberry	Mets	65.1
Keith Hernandez	Mets	162.9	EY+	Shawon Dunston	Cubs	31.3
Keith Hernandez	Mets	32.8	BBV	Shawon Dunston	Cubs	-35.0

Best Pitchers

Rank	Pitcher	Team	G	ERA	B	O	BPO	BV	BPO+
1	Mike Scott	Astros	37	2.22	413	831	.497	-107.2	79.4
2	Rick Rhoden	Pirates	34	2.84	430	758	.567	-71.9	85.7
3	Bob Ojeda	Mets	32	2.57	359	659	.545	-59.3	85.8
4	Danny Cox	Cardinals	32	2.90	370	658	.562	-56.1	86.8
5	Fernando Valenzuela	Dodgers	34	3.14	443	817	.542	-58.2	88.4
6	Dwight Gooden	Mets	33	2.84	429	757	.567	-51.5	89.3
7	Mike Krukow	Giants	34	3.05	421	744	.566	-49.6	89.5
8	John Tudor	Cardinals	30	2.92	391	659	.593	-35.7	91.6
9	Tom Browning	Reds	39	3.81	459	741	.619	-38.4	92.3
10	Bob Forsch	Cardinals	33	3.25	417	693	.602	-31.8	92.9

Extremes for Pitchers

Pitcher	Team	Best		Pitcher	Team	Worst
Mike Scott	Astros	-107.2	BV	LaMarr Hoyt	Padres	90.2
Mike Scott	Astros	64.6	ERA+	Rick Mahler	Braves	129.2
Mike Scott	Astros	-37.3	ERV	Rick Mahler	Braves	29.1
Steve Trout	Cubs	72.9	ISO+	Dennis Eckersley	Cubs	129.7
Kent Tekulve	Phillies	-29.4	EXV	LaMarr Hoyt	Padres	39.4
Mike Scott	Astros	57.8	CT+	Steve Trout	Cubs	162.8
Mike Scott	Astros	129.2	SOV	Chris Welsh	Reds	-55.0
Dennis Eckersley	Cubs	58.6	EY+	Floyd Youmans	Expos	154.5
Bob Knepper	Astros	-29.0	BBV	Floyd Youmans	Expos	40.2

1987 American League

Standings

Rank	Team	Post	W	L	Pct.	R	RA	BPO	BPOA	TS
1	Detroit Tigers	P	98	64	.605	5.53	4.54	.790	.696	71.911
2	Toronto Blue Jays	—	96	66	.593	5.22	4.04	.754	.674	70.746
3	Minnesota Twins	WLP	85	77	.525	4.85	4.98	.721	.764	59.810
4	Milwaukee Brewers	—	91	71	.562	5.32	5.04	.762	.707	58.723
5	New York Yankees	—	89	73	.549	4.86	4.68	.719	.712	52.730
6	Oakland Athletics	—	81	81	.500	4.98	4.87	.741	.702	49.634
7	Kansas City Royals	—	83	79	.512	4.41	4.27	.702	.689	49.046
8	Boston Red Sox	—	78	84	.481	5.20	5.09	.753	.762	43.608
9	Chicago White Sox	—	77	85	.475	4.62	4.60	.699	.699	42.992
10	Seattle Mariners	—	78	84	.481	4.69	4.94	.736	.736	41.729
11	California Angels	—	75	87	.463	4.75	4.96	.697	.706	39.374
12	Texas Rangers	—	75	87	.463	5.08	5.24	.732	.775	36.848
13	Baltimore Orioles	—	67	95	.414	4.50	5.43	.686	.786	21.072
14	Cleveland Indians	—	61	101	.377	4.58	5.91	.711	.795	15.631

Best Batters

Rank	Batter	Team	G	BA	B	O	BPO	BV	BPO+
1	Paul Molitor	Brewers	118	.353	385	321	1.199	140.2	157.3
2	Wade Boggs	Red Sox	147	.363	441	376	1.173	152.6	152.9
3	Mark McGwire	Athletics	151	.289	429	411	1.044	132.3	144.6
4	Dwight Evans	Red Sox	154	.305	428	399	1.073	122.0	139.8
5	Alan Trammell	Tigers	151	.343	421	413	1.019	119.4	139.6
6	Darrell Evans	Tigers	150	.257	366	386	.948	84.1	129.8
7	Kirk Gibson	Tigers	128	.277	345	369	.935	75.5	128.0
8	Brian Downing	Angels	155	.272	409	433	.945	88.3	127.5
9	Kent Hrbek	Twins	143	.285	354	361	.981	73.8	126.3
10	Danny Tartabull	Royals	158	.309	409	425	.962	83.2	125.5

Extremes for Batters

Batter	Team	Best		Batter	Team	Worst
Wade Boggs	Red Sox	152.6	BV	Angel Salazar	Royals	-110.8
Paul Molitor	Brewers	139.6	SE+	Ray Knight	Orioles	73.9
Paul Molitor	Brewers	49.1	SCV	Ray Knight	Orioles	-34.2
Mark McGwire	Athletics	218.5	ISO+	Marty Barrett	Red Sox	32.3
Mark McGwire	Athletics	99.2	EXV	Marty Barrett	Red Sox	-67.2
Willie Randolph	Yankees	302.5	CT+	Rob Deer	Brewers	42.5
Don Mattingly	Yankees	-57.8	SOV	Rob Deer	Brewers	106.9
Darrell Evans	Tigers	183.5	EY+	Mel Hall	Indians	32.9
Dwight Evans	Red Sox	44.0	BBV	Ozzie Guillen	White Sox	-34.6

Best Pitchers

Rank	Pitcher	Team	G	ERA	B	O	BPO	BV	BPO+
1	Jimmy Key	Blue Jays	36	2.76	413	790	.523	-147.6	73.7
2	Frank Viola	Twins	36	2.90	449	756	.594	-99.0	81.9
3	Roger Clemens	Red Sox	36	2.97	495	845	.586	-107.0	82.2
4	Bret Saberhagen	Royals	33	3.36	472	771	.612	-78.0	85.8
5	Teddy Higuera	Brewers	35	3.85	485	791	.613	-75.9	86.5
6	Floyd Bannister	White Sox	34	3.58	447	693	.645	-48.9	90.1
7	Charlie Leibrandt	Royals	35	3.41	465	721	.645	-49.4	90.4
8	Richard Dotson	White Sox	31	4.17	417	641	.651	-41.7	90.9
9	Mark Langston	Mariners	35	3.84	552	822	.672	-48.5	91.9
10	Bill Long	White Sox	29	4.37	334	507	.659	-28.8	92.1

Extremes for Pitchers

Pitcher	Team	Best		Pitcher	Team	Worst
Jimmy Key	Blue Jays	-147.6	BV	Ed Correa	Rangers	88.4
Jimmy Key	Blue Jays	64.7	ERA+	Eric Bell	Orioles	131.9
Jimmy Key	Blue Jays	-43.7	ERV	Ken Schrom	Indians	38.4
Danny Jackson	Royals	64.0	ISO+	Eric Bell	Orioles	145.6
Roger Clemens	Red Sox	-55.8	EXV	Ken Dixon	Orioles	52.5
Mark Langston	Mariners	69.6	CT+	Tommy John	Yankees	206.7
Mark Langston	Mariners	79.6	SOV	Tommy John	Yankees	-67.2
Bill Long	White Sox	44.4	EY+	Mark Gubicza	Royals	140.6
Bill Long	White Sox	-33.8	BBV	Bobby Witt	Rangers	85.6

1987 National League

Standings

Rank	Team	Post	W	L	Pct.	R	RA	BPO	BPOA	TS
1	Saint Louis Cardinals	LP	95	67	.586	4.93	4.28	.713	.687	73.602
2	New York Mets	—	92	70	.568	5.08	4.31	.763	.667	71.263
3	San Francisco Giants	P	90	72	.556	4.83	4.13	.716	.663	64.534
4	Montreal Expos	—	91	71	.562	4.57	4.44	.696	.677	55.833
5	Cincinnati Reds	—	84	78	.519	4.83	4.64	.731	.720	50.694
6	Pittsburgh Pirates	—	80	82	.494	4.46	4.59	.699	.696	43.889
7	Philadelphia Phillies	—	80	82	.494	4.33	4.62	.703	.736	38.415
8	Houston Astros	—	76	86	.469	4.00	4.19	.656	.684	37.256
9	Los Angeles Dodgers	—	73	89	.451	3.92	4.17	.625	.664	33.288
10	Chicago Cubs	—	76	85	.472	4.47	4.98	.720	.761	32.990
11	Atlanta Braves	—	69	92	.429	4.64	5.15	.718	.754	28.705
12	San Diego Padres	—	65	97	.401	4.12	4.71	.683	.715	25.277

Best Batters

Rank	Batter	Team	G	BA	B	O	BPO	BV	BPO+
1	Jack Clark	Cardinals	131	.286	390	309	1.202	151.6	163.6
2	Darryl Strawberry	Mets	154	.284	454	401	1.132	153.5	151.1
3	Eric Davis	Reds	129	.293	419	350	1.197	140.6	150.5
4	Tony Gwynn	Padres	157	.370	448	402	1.114	142.3	146.5
5	Tim Raines	Expos	139	.330	426	372	1.145	134.5	146.1
6	Dale Murphy	Braves	159	.295	471	421	1.119	137.9	141.4
7	Pedro Guerrero	Dodgers	152	.338	388	391	.992	97.4	133.5
8	Will Clark	Giants	150	.308	371	390	.951	78.3	126.8
9	John Kruk	Padres	138	.313	316	330	.958	65.0	125.9
10	Howard Johnson	Mets	157	.265	402	428	.939	81.3	125.4

Extremes for Batters

Batter	Team	Best		Batter	Team	Worst
Darryl Strawberry	Mets	153.5	BV	Garry Templeton	Padres	-105.7
Eric Davis	Reds	143.7	SE+	Mike Scioscia	Dodgers	68.2
Eric Davis	Reds	55.6	SCV	Glenn Wilson	Phillies	-43.1
Jack Clark	Cardinals	194.7	ISO+	Tom Herr	Cardinals	43.1
Darryl Strawberry	Mets	77.1	EXV	Vince Coleman	Cardinals	-56.3
Mike Scioscia	Dodgers	304.9	CT+	Jack Clark	Cardinals	47.6
Tony Gwynn	Padres	-65.0	SOV	Jack Clark	Cardinals	72.8
Jack Clark	Cardinals	277.2	EY+	Benito Santiago	Padres	28.8
Jack Clark	Cardinals	78.6	BBV	Benito Santiago	Padres	-34.6

Best Pitchers

Rank	Pitcher	Team	G	ERA	B	O	BPO	BV	BPO+
1	Rick Reuschel	Pirates-Giants	34	3.09	370	690	.536	-104.6	78.0
2	Mike Dunne	Pirates	23	3.03	293	497	.590	-51.5	85.1
3	Orel Hershiser	Dodgers	37	3.06	457	802	.570	-78.2	85.4
4	Bob Welch	Dodgers	35	3.22	441	761	.580	-66.9	86.8
5	Nolan Ryan	Astros	34	2.76	371	640	.580	-54.3	87.2
6	Joe Magrane	Cardinals	27	3.54	315	519	.607	-44.6	87.6
7	Mike Scott	Astros	36	3.23	436	745	.585	-59.1	88.1
8	Dwight Gooden	Mets	25	3.21	318	539	.590	-39.5	89.0
9	Greg Mathews	Cardinals	32	3.73	380	596	.638	-33.0	92.0
10	Doug Drabek	Pirates	29	3.88	343	530	.647	-24.3	93.4

Extremes for Pitchers

Pitcher	Team	Best		Pitcher	Team	Worst
Rick Reuschel	Pirates-Giants	-104.6	BV	Bob Knepper	Astros	91.8
Nolan Ryan	Astros	72.4	ERA+	Bob Knepper	Astros	138.1
Tim Burke	Expos	-29.3	ERV	Bob Knepper	Astros	28.7
Joe Magrane	Cardinals	63.8	ISO+	Bob Knepper	Astros	146.9
Zane Smith	Braves	-34.2	EXV	Bob Knepper	Astros	43.7
Nolan Ryan	Astros	51.4	CT+	Bob Knepper	Astros	171.3
Nolan Ryan	Astros	131.2	SOV	Jimmy Jones	Padres	-56.7
Neal Heaton	Expos	51.8	EY+	Fernando Valenzuela	Dodgers	146.9
Rick Reuschel	Pirates-Giants	-32.6	BBV	Fernando Valenzuela	Dodgers	38.3

1988 American League

Standings

Rank	Team	Post	W	L	Pct.	R	RA	BPO	BPOA	TS
1	Oakland Athletics	LP	104	58	.642	4.94	3.83	.704	.622	80.527
2	Boston Red Sox	P	89	73	.549	5.02	4.25	.745	.669	61.593
3	Minnesota Twins	—	91	71	.562	4.69	4.15	.723	.678	58.667
4	Toronto Blue Jays	—	87	75	.537	4.71	4.20	.710	.677	55.197
5	Milwaukee Brewers	—	87	75	.537	4.21	3.80	.641	.606	54.701
6	Detroit Tigers	—	88	74	.543	4.34	4.06	.657	.643	52.643
7	Kansas City Royals	—	84	77	.522	4.37	4.02	.671	.642	52.388
8	New York Yankees	—	85	76	.528	4.80	4.65	.699	.695	49.524
9	Cleveland Indians	—	78	84	.481	4.11	4.51	.641	.667	39.011
10	California Angels	—	75	87	.463	4.41	4.76	.650	.697	35.881
11	Texas Rangers	—	70	91	.435	3.96	4.57	.647	.671	33.393
12	Seattle Mariners	—	68	93	.422	4.12	4.62	.658	.685	32.754
13	Chicago White Sox	—	71	90	.441	3.92	4.70	.615	.687	28.884
14	Baltimore Orioles	—	54	107	.335	3.42	4.90	.601	.725	9.850

Best Batters

Rank	Batter	Team	G	BA	B	O	BPO	BV	BPO+
1	Jose Canseco	Athletics	158	.307	482	461	1.046	172.9	155.9
2	Wade Boggs	Red Sox	155	.366	423	403	1.050	135.1	146.9
3	Rickey Henderson	Yankees	140	.305	407	412	.988	123.4	143.5
4	Mike Greenwell	Red Sox	158	.325	432	424	1.019	129.1	142.6
5	Fred McGriff	Blue Jays	154	.282	389	405	.960	108.1	138.5
6	Dave Winfield	Yankees	149	.322	377	403	.935	99.6	135.9
7	George Brett	Royals	157	.306	406	434	.935	103.8	134.4
8	Danny Tartabull	Royals	146	.274	355	389	.913	84.2	131.1
9	Kent Hrbek	Twins	143	.312	341	372	.917	77.7	129.5
10	Dave Henderson	Athletics	146	.304	331	383	.864	74.2	128.9

Extremes for Batters

Batter	Team	Best		Batter	Team	Worst
Jose Canseco	Athletics	172.9	BV	Billy Ripken	Orioles	-107.4
Dave Henderson	Athletics	150.4	SE+	Harold Reynolds	Mariners	69.3
Jose Canseco	Athletics	62.2	SCV	Harold Reynolds	Mariners	-43.5
Jose Canseco	Athletics	206.6	ISO+	Marty Barrett	Red Sox	35.8
Jose Canseco	Athletics	82.6	EXV	Marty Barrett	Red Sox	-59.1
Don Mattingly	Yankees	324.9	CT+	Rob Deer	Brewers	51.5
Don Mattingly	Yankees	-65.2	SOV	Pete Incaviglia	Rangers	88.9
Jack Clark	Yankees	224.5	EY+	Kirby Puckett	Twins	33.4
Jack Clark	Yankees	59.3	BBV	Kirby Puckett	Twins	-37.8

Best Pitchers

Rank	Pitcher	Team	G	ERA	B	O	BPO	BV	BPO+
1	Teddy Higuera	Brewers	31	2.45	335	682	.491	-108.4	75.5
2	Roger Clemens	Red Sox	35	2.93	413	794	.520	-117.5	77.8
3	Frank Viola	Twins	35	2.64	419	766	.547	-89.9	82.3
4	Mark Gubicza	Royals	35	2.70	445	815	.546	-85.6	83.9
4	Mike Moore	Mariners	37	3.78	387	686	.564	-74.4	83.9
6	Allan Anderson	Twins	30	2.45	344	606	.568	-58.6	85.4
7	Greg Swindell	Indians	33	3.20	411	728	.565	-63.1	86.7
8	Dave Stieb	Blue Jays	32	3.04	352	623	.565	-51.2	87.3
9	Jeff Robinson	Tigers	24	2.98	292	518	.564	-38.8	88.3
10	Dave LaPoint	White Sox	25	3.40	283	491	.576	-35.7	88.8

Extremes for Pitchers

Pitcher	Team	Best		Pitcher	Team	Worst
Roger Clemens	Red Sox	-117.5	BV	Willie Fraser	Angels	100.9
Allan Anderson	Twins	62.7	ERA+	Willie Fraser	Angels	146.5
Frank Viola	Twins	-35.8	ERV	Willie Fraser	Angels	37.1
Mark Gubicza	Royals	64.1	ISO+	Willie Fraser	Angels	169.3
Mark Gubicza	Royals	-48.7	EXV	Willie Fraser	Angels	65.5
Roger Clemens	Red Sox	55.0	CT+	Bill Swift	Mariners	234.1
Roger Clemens	Red Sox	131.0	SOV	Bill Swift	Mariners	-63.0
Doyle Alexander	Tigers	54.6	EY+	Bobby Witt	Rangers	180.1
Doyle Alexander	Tigers	-32.4	BBV	Charlie Hough	Rangers	45.2

1988 National League

Standings

Rank	Team	Post	W	L	Pct.	R	RA	BPO	BPOA	TS
1	New York Mets	P	100	60	.625	4.39	3.33	.695	.577	74.761
2	Los Angeles Dodgers	WLP	94	67	.584	3.88	3.36	.604	.567	74.718
3	Cincinnati Reds	—	87	74	.540	3.98	3.70	.650	.616	54.158
4	San Francisco Giants	—	83	79	.512	4.14	3.86	.646	.590	53.153
5	Pittsburgh Pirates	—	85	75	.531	4.07	3.85	.650	.639	51.081
6	San Diego Padres	—	83	78	.516	3.69	3.62	.613	.600	48.514
7	Montreal Expos	—	81	81	.500	3.85	3.63	.637	.626	48.139
8	Houston Astros	—	82	80	.506	3.81	3.90	.620	.646	43.436
9	Chicago Cubs	—	77	85	.475	4.05	4.26	.634	.661	39.442
10	Saint Louis Cardinals	—	76	86	.469	3.57	3.91	.615	.630	38.800
11	Philadelphia Phillies	—	65	96	.404	3.69	4.53	.613	.718	21.740
12	Atlanta Braves	—	54	106	.338	3.47	4.63	.576	.681	12.913

Best Batters

Rank	Batter	Team	G	BA	B	O	BPO	BV	BPO+
1	Darryl Strawberry	Mets	153	.269	422	426	.991	138.7	149.0
2	Will Clark	Giants	162	.282	415	433	.958	126.0	143.6
3	Kirk Gibson	Dodgers	150	.290	383	407	.941	112.7	141.7
4	Kal Daniels	Reds	140	.291	350	372	.941	86.5	132.8
5	Eric Davis	Reds	135	.273	337	360	.936	82.0	132.2
6	Andy Van Slyke	Pirates	154	.288	399	449	.889	94.2	130.9
7	Barry Bonds	Pirates	144	.283	357	402	.888	84.1	130.8
8	Brett Butler	Giants	157	.287	380	437	.870	88.3	130.3
9	Andres Galarraga	Expos	157	.302	394	444	.887	85.0	127.5
10	Kevin McReynolds	Mets	147	.288	343	405	.847	73.7	127.3

Extremes for Batters

Batter	Team	Best		Batter	Team	Worst
Darryl Strawberry	Mets	138.7	BV	Andres Thomas	Braves	-87.6
Will Clark	Giants	141.2	SE+	Jose Oquendo	Cardinals	73.8
Will Clark	Giants	53.1	SCV	Jose Oquendo	Cardinals	-26.6
Darryl Strawberry	Mets	228.6	ISO+	Jose Lind	Pirates	49.0
Darryl Strawberry	Mets	84.4	EXV	Jose Lind	Pirates	-39.6
Barry Larkin	Reds	366.9	CT+	John Shelby	Dodgers	56.5
Barry Larkin	Reds	-64.0	SOV	Andres Galarraga	Expos	59.8
Brett Butler	Giants	195.1	EY+	Andres Thomas	Braves	17.4
Brett Butler	Giants	45.3	BBV	Andres Thomas	Braves	-38.1

Best Pitchers

Rank	Pitcher	Team	G	ERA	B	O	BPO	BV	BPO+
1	Danny Jackson	Reds	35	2.73	396	788	.503	-105.4	79.0
2	Pascual Perez	Expos	27	2.44	290	573	.506	-68.1	81.0
3	Tim Belcher	Dodgers	36	2.91	267	543	.492	-57.1	82.4
4	Orel Hershiser	Dodgers	35	2.26	407	810	.502	-76.4	84.2
5	Jose Rijo	Reds	49	2.39	267	486	.549	-42.2	86.3
6	Bob Ojeda	Mets	29	2.88	294	575	.511	-45.8	86.5
7	Joe Magrane	Cardinals	24	2.18	270	505	.535	-38.2	87.6
8	Tim Leary	Dodgers	35	2.91	375	697	.538	-41.0	90.1
9	Eric Show	Padres	32	3.26	390	702	.556	-42.2	90.2
10	Bob Walk	Pirates	32	2.71	356	644	.553	-37.2	90.5

Extremes for Pitchers

Pitcher	Team	Best		Pitcher	Team	Worst
Danny Jackson	Reds	-105.4	BV	Shane Rawley	Phillies	105.6
Joe Magrane	Cardinals	65.6	ERA+	Tom Glavine	Braves	130.7
Orel Hershiser	Dodgers	-28.1	ERV	Tom Glavine	Braves	23.2
Dwight Gooden	Mets	73.9	ISO+	Tom Browning	Reds	145.4
Greg Maddux	Cubs	-25.6	EXV	Tom Browning	Reds	49.7
Jose Rijo	Reds	60.4	CT+	Rick Reuschel	Giants	170.4
Nolan Ryan	Astros	83.4	SOV	Rick Reuschel	Giants	-64.8
Rick Mahler	Braves	49.3	EY+	Mike Dunne	Pirates	162.9
Rick Mahler	Braves	-37.0	BBV	Mike Dunne	Pirates	32.8

1989 American League

Standings

Rank	Team	Post	W	L	Pct.	R	RA	BPO	BPOA	TS
1	Oakland Athletics	WLP	99	63	.611	4.40	3.56	.675	.593	85.486
2	Kansas City Royals	—	92	70	.568	4.26	3.92	.662	.604	60.948
3	California Angels	—	91	71	.562	4.13	3.57	.636	.612	59.259
4	Toronto Blue Jays	P	89	73	.549	4.51	4.02	.682	.638	59.136
5	Boston Red Sox	—	83	79	.512	4.78	4.54	.709	.676	51.960
6	Baltimore Orioles	—	87	75	.537	4.37	4.23	.665	.676	49.731
7	Milwaukee Brewers	—	81	81	.500	4.36	4.19	.662	.643	48.805
8	Texas Rangers	—	83	79	.512	4.29	4.41	.668	.654	47.056
9	Minnesota Twins	—	80	82	.494	4.57	4.56	.688	.698	44.128
10	Seattle Mariners	—	73	89	.451	4.28	4.49	.648	.671	36.440
11	Cleveland Indians	—	73	89	.451	3.73	4.04	.618	.631	36.431
12	New York Yankees	—	74	87	.460	4.34	4.92	.679	.725	31.965
13	Chicago White Sox	—	69	92	.429	4.30	4.66	.657	.703	30.844
14	Detroit Tigers	—	59	103	.364	3.81	5.04	.619	.748	8.859

Best Batters

Rank	Batter	Team	G	BA	B	O	BPO	BV	BPO+
1	Rickey Henderson	Yankees-Athletics	150	.274	426	419	1.017	145.8	152.2
2	Fred McGriff	Blue Jays	161	.269	425	427	.995	131.8	145.0
3	Alvin Davis	Mariners	142	.305	360	368	.978	101.1	139.1
4	Robin Yount	Brewers	160	.318	409	438	.934	113.1	138.2
5	Ruben Sierra	Rangers	162	.306	407	459	.887	85.9	126.7
6	Lou Whitaker	Tigers	148	.251	343	401	.855	72.0	126.6
7	Wade Boggs	Red Sox	156	.330	402	448	.897	81.4	125.4
8	Harold Baines	White Sox-Rangers	146	.309	313	371	.844	59.9	124.2
9	Dwight Evans	Red Sox	146	.285	354	399	.887	68.5	124.0
10	Paul Molitor	Brewers	155	.315	378	456	.829	70.0	122.7

Extremes for Batters

Batter	Team	Best		Batter	Team	Worst
Rickey Henderson	Yankees-Athletics	145.8	BV	Omar Vizquel	Mariners	-84.0
Bo Jackson	Royals	140.6	SE+	Felix Fermin	Indians	61.8
Ruben Sierra	Rangers	49.7	SCV	Felix Fermin	Indians	-43.8
Mark McGwire	Athletics	204.0	ISO+	Felix Fermin	Indians	18.7
Fred McGriff	Blue Jays	70.0	EXV	Felix Fermin	Indians	-47.7
Carney Lansford	Athletics	341.3	CT+	Bo Jackson	Royals	42.9
Don Mattingly	Yankees	-66.3	SOV	Bo Jackson	Royals	98.2
Rickey Henderson	Yankees-Athletics	231.8	EY+	Ozzie Guillen	White Sox	23.9
Rickey Henderson	Yankees-Athletics	68.8	BBV	Ozzie Guillen	White Sox	-38.1

Best Pitchers

Rank	Pitcher	Team	G	ERA	B	O	BPO	BV	BPO+
1	Bret Saberhagen	Royals	36	2.16	370	789	.469	-131.4	73.8
2	Kevin Brown	Rangers	28	3.35	312	584	.534	-71.8	81.3
3	Mike Moore	Athletics	35	2.61	373	727	.513	-75.6	83.2
4	Nolan Ryan	Rangers	32	3.20	402	729	.551	-77.1	83.9
5	Bert Blyleven	Angels	33	2.73	389	726	.536	-70.8	84.6
6	Chris Bosio	Brewers	33	2.95	384	708	.542	-64.3	85.6
7	Tom Candiotti	Indians	31	3.10	341	616	.554	-54.2	86.3
8	Roger Clemens	Red Sox	35	3.13	448	768	.583	-65.6	87.2
9	Dave Stieb	Blue Jays	33	3.35	349	621	.562	-49.3	87.6
10	Mark Gubicza	Royals	36	3.04	430	768	.560	-58.0	88.1

Extremes for Pitchers

Pitcher	Team	Best		Pitcher	Team	Worst
Bret Saberhagen	Royals	-131.4	BV	Melido Perez	White Sox	76.3
Bret Saberhagen	Royals	59.5	ERA+	Melido Perez	White Sox	140.1
Bret Saberhagen	Royals	-42.9	ERV	Dave Schmidt	Orioles	37.3
Kevin Brown	Rangers	65.3	ISO+	Melido Perez	White Sox	146.1
Mark Gubicza	Royals	-35.7	EXV	Andy Hawkins	Yankees	42.7
Nolan Ryan	Rangers	46.8	CT+	Jeff Ballard	Orioles	226.4
Nolan Ryan	Rangers	160.2	SOV	Jeff Ballard	Orioles	-78.4
Jimmy Key	Blue Jays	36.9	EY+	Bobby Witt	Rangers	169.2
Jimmy Key	Blue Jays	-42.8	BBV	Bobby Witt	Rangers	45.4

1989 National League

Standings

Rank	Team	Post	W	L	Pct.	R	RA	BPO	BPOA	TS
1	San Francisco Giants	LP	92	70	.568	4.31	3.70	.662	.612	76.226
2	Chicago Cubs	P	93	69	.574	4.33	3.85	.662	.629	63.654
3	New York Mets	—	87	75	.537	4.22	3.67	.665	.614	62.300
4	San Diego Padres	—	89	73	.549	3.96	3.86	.647	.626	54.892
5	Saint Louis Cardinals	—	86	76	.531	3.85	3.71	.640	.616	53.819
6	Montreal Expos	—	81	81	.500	3.90	3.89	.646	.642	46.165
7	Los Angeles Dodgers	—	77	83	.481	3.46	3.35	.586	.582	45.195
8	Houston Astros	—	86	76	.531	3.99	4.13	.611	.648	42.794
9	Pittsburgh Pirates	—	74	88	.457	3.88	4.15	.633	.654	35.035
10	Cincinnati Reds	—	75	87	.463	3.90	4.27	.633	.667	32.947
11	Atlanta Braves	—	63	97	.394	3.63	4.22	.588	.617	23.101
12	Philadelphia Phillies	—	67	95	.414	3.86	4.51	.631	.697	20.184

Best Batters

Rank	Batter	Team	G	BA	B	O	BPO	BV	BPO+
1	Kevin Mitchell	Giants	154	.291	445	402	1.107	172.7	163.4
2	Howard Johnson	Mets	153	.287	444	425	1.045	162.9	157.9
3	Lonnie Smith	Braves	134	.315	377	357	1.056	130.7	153.1
4	Will Clark	Giants	159	.333	416	409	1.017	139.0	150.2
5	Jack Clark	Padres	142	.242	353	362	.975	103.1	141.2
6	Eric Davis	Reds	131	.281	351	366	.959	91.5	135.2
7	Von Hayes	Phillies	154	.259	389	421	.924	100.8	135.0
8	Tim Raines	Expos	145	.286	358	391	.916	88.8	133.0
9	Pedro Guerrero	Cardinals	162	.311	369	422	.874	76.4	126.1
10	Mark Grace	Cubs	142	.314	333	376	.886	67.3	125.3

Extremes for Batters

Batter	Team	Best		Batter	Team	Worst
Kevin Mitchell	Giants	172.7	**BV**	Andres Thomas	Braves	-123.0
Will Clark	Giants	150.9	**SE+**	Garry Templeton	Padres	73.5
Will Clark	Giants	64.8	**SCV**	John Shelby	Dodgers	-32.1
Kevin Mitchell	Giants	267.2	**ISO+**	Gerald Young	Astros	33.8
Kevin Mitchell	Giants	117.0	**EXV**	Gerald Young	Astros	-45.0
Tony Gwynn	Padres	328.1	**CT+**	Jack Clark	Padres	51.1
Tony Gwynn	Padres	-68.4	**SOV**	Jack Clark	Padres	70.9
Jack Clark	Padres	245.4	**EY+**	Andres Thomas	Braves	20.9
Jack Clark	Padres	67.5	**BBV**	Andres Thomas	Braves	-34.1

Best Pitchers

Rank	Pitcher	Team	G	ERA	B	O	BPO	BV	BPO+
1	Jose DeLeon	Cardinals	36	3.05	378	737	.513	-84.5	81.7
2	Scott Garrelts	Giants	30	2.28	297	585	.508	-60.1	83.2
3	John Smoltz	Braves	29	2.94	346	633	.547	-52.8	86.8
4	Orel Hershiser	Dodgers	35	2.31	414	778	.532	-61.2	87.1
5	Bryn Smith	Expos	33	2.84	360	653	.551	-46.1	88.6
6	Bruce Hurst	Padres	33	2.69	408	737	.554	-51.9	88.7
7	Ed Whitson	Padres	33	2.66	384	684	.561	-42.9	90.0
8	Tom Glavine	Braves	29	3.68	332	577	.575	-31.5	91.3
9	Pascual Perez	Expos	33	3.31	345	605	.570	-31.3	91.7
10	Tim Belcher	Dodgers	39	2.82	391	691	.566	-31.1	92.6

Extremes for Pitchers

Pitcher	Team	Best		Pitcher	Team	Worst
Jose DeLeon	Cardinals	-84.5	**BV**	Bob Knepper	Astros-Giants	90.1
Orel Hershiser	Dodgers	70.2	**ERA+**	Bob Knepper	Astros-Giants	157.3
Orel Hershiser	Dodgers	-28.0	**ERV**	Bob Knepper	Astros-Giants	34.3
Joe Magrane	Cardinals	69.9	**ISO+**	Don Robinson	Giants	130.4
Joe Magrane	Cardinals	-31.8	**EXV**	Don Carman	Phillies	33.7
Mark Langston	Expos	63.5	**CT+**	Bob Knepper	Astros-Giants	180.3
Rob Dibble	Reds	80.4	**SOV**	Bob Knepper	Astros-Giants	-51.2
Rick Mahler	Reds	55.1	**EY+**	Mark Langston	Expos	167.3
Rick Mahler	Reds	-31.0	**BBV**	Mark Langston	Expos	35.0

1990 American League

Standings

Rank	Team	Post	W	L	Pct.	R	RA	BPO	BPOA	TS
1	Oakland Athletics	LP	103	59	.636	4.52	3.52	.708	.602	89.366
2	Chicago White Sox	—	94	68	.580	4.21	3.91	.652	.619	61.168
3	Toronto Blue Jays	—	86	76	.531	4.73	4.08	.707	.656	60.794
4	Boston Red Sox	P	88	74	.543	4.31	4.10	.681	.649	55.921
5	Texas Rangers	—	83	79	.512	4.17	4.30	.663	.664	45.587
6	California Angels	—	80	82	.494	4.26	4.36	.668	.657	44.900
7	Seattle Mariners	—	77	85	.475	3.95	4.20	.663	.642	42.272
8	Detroit Tigers	—	79	83	.488	4.63	4.65	.707	.725	42.165
9	Kansas City Royals	—	75	86	.466	4.39	4.40	.671	.682	40.421
10	Milwaukee Brewers	—	74	88	.457	4.52	4.69	.672	.682	37.827
11	Cleveland Indians	—	77	85	.475	4.52	4.55	.662	.709	37.792
12	Baltimore Orioles	—	76	85	.472	4.16	4.34	.664	.696	37.383
13	Minnesota Twins	—	74	88	.457	4.11	4.50	.647	.690	32.363
14	New York Yankees	—	67	95	.414	3.72	4.62	.610	.703	17.305

Best Batters

Rank	Batter	Team	G	BA	B	O	BPO	BV	BPO+
1	Rickey Henderson	Athletics	136	.325	452	357	1.266	214.2	190.1
2	Cecil Fielder	Tigers	159	.277	439	435	1.009	138.4	146.1
3	Jose Canseco	Athletics	131	.274	362	373	.971	113.6	145.7
4	Fred McGriff	Blue Jays	153	.300	401	405	.990	114.1	139.8
5	Mark McGwire	Athletics	156	.235	385	424	.908	102.6	136.3
6	George Brett	Royals	142	.329	352	392	.898	87.2	133.0
7	Carlton Fisk	White Sox	137	.285	280	338	.828	51.3	122.4
8	Jesse Barfield	Yankees	153	.246	315	375	.840	56.0	121.6
9	Ken Griffey Jr.	Mariners	155	.300	372	445	.836	60.9	119.6
10	Kent Hrbek	Twins	143	.287	324	380	.853	52.4	119.3

Extremes for Batters

Batter	Team	Best		Batter	Team	Worst
Rickey Henderson	Athletics	214.2	BV	Alvaro Espinoza	Yankees	-99.2
Jose Canseco	Athletics	135.6	SE+	Steve Sax	Yankees	78.4
Cecil Fielder	Tigers	47.8	SCV	Alvaro Espinoza	Yankees	-46.6
Cecil Fielder	Tigers	234.8	ISO+	Carney Lansford	Athletics	41.5
Cecil Fielder	Tigers	103.4	EXV	Steve Sax	Yankees	-42.2
Brian Harper	Twins	286.1	CT+	Mickey Tettleton	Orioles	45.6
Mike Greenwell	Red Sox	-53.6	SOV	Cecil Fielder	Tigers	88.2
Mickey Tettleton	Orioles	222.6	EY+	Ozzie Guillen	White Sox	39.4
Mickey Tettleton	Orioles	56.7	BBV	Ozzie Guillen	White Sox	-27.6

Best Pitchers

Rank	Pitcher	Team	G	ERA	B	O	BPO	BV	BPO+
1	Roger Clemens	Red Sox	31	1.93	346	691	.501	-121.3	74.0
2	Dave Stieb	Blue Jays	33	2.93	338	623	.543	-75.1	81.8
3	Erik Hanson	Mariners	33	3.24	392	714	.549	-78.3	83.4
4	Nolan Ryan	Rangers	30	3.44	349	614	.568	-53.6	86.7
5	David Wells	Blue Jays	43	3.14	329	567	.580	-47.0	87.5
6	Dave Stewart	Athletics	36	2.56	440	803	.548	-60.7	87.9
7	Kirk McCaskill	Angels	29	3.25	303	532	.570	-37.5	89.0
8	Bud Black	Indians-Blue Jays	32	3.57	363	627	.579	-43.6	89.2
9	Kevin Appier	Royals	32	2.76	324	566	.572	-35.2	90.2
10	Mike Boddicker	Red Sox	34	3.36	417	683	.611	-44.9	90.3

Extremes for Pitchers

Pitcher	Team	Best		Pitcher	Team	Worst
Roger Clemens	Red Sox	-121.3	BV	Jeff Robinson	Tigers	76.2
Roger Clemens	Red Sox	49.4	ERA+	Frank Tanana	Tigers	139.4
Roger Clemens	Red Sox	-50.1	ERV	Jeff Robinson	Tigers	34.6
Roger Clemens	Red Sox	57.3	ISO+	Dave Johnson	Orioles	163.1
Roger Clemens	Red Sox	-49.3	EXV	Dave Johnson	Orioles	53.0
Nolan Ryan	Rangers	54.3	CT+	Mark Knudson	Brewers	209.5
Nolan Ryan	Rangers	106.1	SOV	Mark Knudson	Brewers	-61.3
Allan Anderson	Twins	59.4	EY+	Randy Johnson	Mariners	160.0
Jimmy Key	Blue Jays	-30.8	BBV	Randy Johnson	Mariners	44.2

1990 National League

Standings

Rank	Team	Post	W	L	Pct.	R	RA	BPO	BPOA	TS
1	Cincinnati Reds	WLP	91	71	.562	4.28	3.69	.691	.646	76.558
2	Pittsburgh Pirates	P	95	67	.586	4.52	3.82	.714	.633	68.780
3	New York Mets	—	91	71	.562	4.78	3.78	.701	.632	67.119
4	Los Angeles Dodgers	—	86	76	.531	4.49	4.23	.673	.643	54.029
5	Montreal Expos	—	85	77	.525	4.09	3.69	.676	.650	53.972
6	San Francisco Giants	—	85	77	.525	4.44	4.38	.676	.694	47.183
7	San Diego Padres	—	75	87	.463	4.15	4.15	.658	.667	40.367
8	Philadelphia Phillies	—	77	85	.475	3.99	4.50	.647	.687	34.789
9	Chicago Cubs	—	77	85	.475	4.26	4.78	.659	.705	34.293
10	Houston Astros	—	75	87	.463	3.54	4.05	.622	.673	32.423
11	Saint Louis Cardinals	—	70	92	.432	3.70	4.31	.650	.659	32.020
12	Atlanta Braves	—	65	97	.401	4.21	5.07	.653	.730	20.029

Best Batters

Rank	Batter	Team	G	BA	B	O	BPO	BV	BPO+
1	Barry Bonds	Pirates	151	.301	447	390	1.146	169.4	161.0
2	Eddie Murray	Dodgers	155	.330	385	402	.958	98.6	134.4
3	Kal Daniels	Dodgers	130	.296	319	334	.955	81.1	134.1
4	Lenny Dykstra	Phillies	149	.325	394	413	.954	93.0	130.9
5	David Justice	Braves	127	.282	311	324	.960	71.8	130.0
6	Ryne Sandberg	Cubs	155	.306	429	451	.951	90.7	126.8
7	Kevin Mitchell	Giants	140	.290	354	392	.903	74.1	126.5
8	Darryl Strawberry	Mets	152	.277	375	410	.915	78.3	126.4
9	Ron Gant	Braves	152	.303	399	430	.928	81.6	125.7
10	Dave Magadan	Mets	144	.328	298	329	.906	59.9	125.2

Extremes for Batters

Batter	Team	Best		Batter	Team	Worst
Barry Bonds	Pirates	169.4	BV	Alfredo Griffin	Dodgers	-108.1
Barry Bonds	Pirates	149.4	SE+	Jose Oquendo	Cardinals	64.6
Bobby Bonilla	Pirates	63.2	SCV	Jose Oquendo	Cardinals	-40.5
Barry Bonds	Pirates	194.5	ISO+	Eric Yelding	Astros	31.6
Ryne Sandberg	Cubs	67.0	EXV	Eric Yelding	Astros	-47.6
Tony Gwynn	Padres	387.2	CT+	Andres Galarraga	Expos	52.5
Tony Gwynn	Padres	-66.1	SOV	Andres Galarraga	Expos	80.3
Von Hayes	Phillies	165.5	EY+	Shawon Dunston	Cubs	32.0
Jack Clark	Padres	58.7	BBV	Shawon Dunston	Cubs	-29.7

Best Pitchers

Rank	Pitcher	Team	G	ERA	B	O	BPO	BV	BPO+
1	Danny Darwin	Astros	48	2.21	258	489	.528	-59.8	81.2
2	Jose Rijo	Reds	29	2.70	331	584	.567	-67.4	83.1
3	Ed Whitson	Padres	32	2.60	372	678	.549	-74.5	83.3
4	Dennis Martinez	Expos	32	2.95	369	684	.539	-71.2	83.8
5	Doug Drabek	Pirates	33	2.76	370	689	.537	-69.0	84.3
6	Frank Viola	Mets	35	2.67	415	759	.547	-77.0	84.4
7	Bruce Hurst	Padres	33	3.14	393	679	.579	-54.2	87.9
7	Zane Smith	Expos-Pirates	33	2.55	366	649	.564	-50.2	87.9
9	Greg Maddux	Cubs	35	3.46	434	725	.599	-56.8	88.4
10	Mike Harkey	Cubs	27	3.26	317	525	.604	-38.4	89.2

Extremes for Pitchers

Pitcher	Team	Best		Pitcher	Team	Worst
Frank Viola	Mets	-77.0	BV	Dennis Rasmussen	Padres	62.3
Danny Darwin	Astros	62.2	ERA+	Fernando Valenzuela	Dodgers	130.7
Ed Whitson	Padres	-27.4	ERV	Bruce Ruffin	Phillies	28.4
Greg Maddux	Cubs	68.2	ISO+	Mike Scott	Astros	127.2
Greg Maddux	Cubs	-37.7	EXV	Ron Darling	Mets	28.9
David Cone	Mets	58.7	CT+	Bill Gullickson	Astros	186.2
David Cone	Mets	96.3	SOV	Bill Gullickson	Astros	-62.9
Tom Browning	Reds	54.3	EY+	Pat Combs	Phillies	138.6
Tom Browning	Reds	-32.8	BBV	Jose de Jesus	Phillies	31.1

1991 American League

Standings

Rank	Team	Post	W	L	Pct.	R	RA	BPO	BPOA	TS
1	Minnesota Twins	WLP	95	67	.586	4.79	4.02	.717	.662	82.261
2	Toronto Blue Jays	P	91	71	.562	4.22	3.84	.693	.614	64.362
3	Chicago White Sox	—	87	75	.537	4.68	4.20	.692	.648	58.841
4	Texas Rangers	—	85	77	.525	5.12	5.02	.734	.718	50.859
5	Boston Red Sox	—	84	78	.519	4.51	4.40	.694	.677	50.564
6	Milwaukee Brewers	—	83	79	.512	4.93	4.59	.686	.685	50.178
7	Detroit Tigers	—	84	78	.519	5.04	4.90	.735	.733	49.214
8	Kansas City Royals	—	82	80	.506	4.49	4.46	.676	.655	48.752
9	Seattle Mariners	—	83	79	.512	4.33	4.16	.670	.677	47.815
10	Oakland Athletics	—	84	78	.519	4.69	4.79	.697	.725	43.721
11	California Angels	—	81	81	.500	4.03	4.01	.627	.650	43.273
12	New York Yankees	—	71	91	.438	4.16	4.80	.653	.714	26.296
13	Baltimore Orioles	—	67	95	.414	4.23	4.91	.662	.699	25.757
14	Cleveland Indians	—	57	105	.352	3.56	4.69	.592	.674	9.976

Best Batters

Rank	Batter	Team	G	BA	B	O	BPO	BV	BPO+
1	Frank Thomas	White Sox	158	.318	451	405	1.114	168.8	159.8
2	Danny Tartabull	Royals	132	.316	366	348	1.052	126.1	152.6
3	Rickey Henderson	Athletics	134	.268	365	372	.981	112.7	144.7
4	Jose Canseco	Athletics	154	.266	437	448	.975	133.1	143.8
5	Ken Griffey Jr.	Mariners	154	.327	392	398	.985	110.5	139.2
6	Cal Ripken Jr.	Orioles	162	.323	441	469	.940	122.5	138.5
7	Lou Whitaker	Tigers	138	.279	336	354	.949	84.9	133.8
8	Julio Franco	Rangers	146	.341	385	412	.934	96.5	133.4
9	Paul Molitor	Brewers	158	.325	428	469	.913	106.5	133.1
10	Rafael Palmeiro	Rangers	159	.322	423	457	.926	102.9	132.2

Extremes for Batters

Batter	Team	Best		Batter	Team	Worst
Frank Thomas	White Sox	168.8	BV	Manuel Lee	Blue Jays	-92.1
Jose Canseco	Athletics	147.8	SE+	Alvaro Espinoza	Yankees	74.0
Jose Canseco	Athletics	62.4	SCV	Felix Fermin	Indians	-38.1
Jose Canseco	Athletics	222.6	ISO+	Willie Randolph	Brewers	34.4
Jose Canseco	Athletics	91.4	EXV	Chuck Knoblauch	Twins	-46.1
Wade Boggs	Red Sox	273.3	CT+	Rob Deer	Tigers	42.6
Steve Sax	Yankees	-64.8	SOV	Rob Deer	Tigers	100.5
Frank Thomas	White Sox	224.7	EY+	Ozzie Guillen	White Sox	22.3
Frank Thomas	White Sox	69.4	BBV	Ozzie Guillen	White Sox	-34.8

Best Pitchers

Rank	Pitcher	Team	G	ERA	B	O	BPO	BV	BPO+
1	Roger Clemens	Red Sox	35	2.62	433	822	.527	-132.3	76.6
2	Bret Saberhagen	Royals	28	3.07	311	593	.524	-73.3	80.9
3	Jimmy Key	Blue Jays	33	3.05	351	639	.549	-81.8	81.1
4	Nolan Ryan	Rangers	27	2.91	282	519	.543	-59.4	82.6
5	Jim Abbott	Angels	34	2.89	409	737	.555	-70.6	85.3
6	Kevin Tapani	Twins	34	2.99	425	725	.586	-69.8	85.9
7	Bill Wegman	Brewers	28	2.84	326	586	.556	-50.6	86.6
8	Tom Candiotti	Indians-Blue Jays	34	2.65	419	717	.584	-62.4	86.9
9	Scott Erickson	Twins	32	3.18	370	617	.600	-51.1	87.9
10	Greg Swindell	Indians	33	3.48	424	722	.587	-55.9	88.4

Extremes for Pitchers

Pitcher	Team	Best		Pitcher	Team	Worst
Roger Clemens	Red Sox	-132.3	BV	Dave Stewart	Athletics	100.7
Roger Clemens	Red Sox	64.5	ERA+	Dave Stewart	Athletics	144.1
Roger Clemens	Red Sox	-43.5	ERV	Dave Stewart	Athletics	39.8
Jimmy Key	Blue Jays	68.4	ISO+	Rich DeLucia	Mariners	145.9
Jimmy Key	Blue Jays	-35.0	EXV	Rich DeLucia	Mariners	42.2
Nolan Ryan	Rangers	51.2	CT+	Walt Terrell	Tigers	181.7
Randy Johnson	Mariners	106.3	SOV	Walt Terrell	Tigers	-65.4
Greg Swindell	Indians	38.6	EY+	Randy Johnson	Mariners	216.1
Greg Swindell	Indians	-47.7	BBV	Randy Johnson	Mariners	81.7

1991 National League

Standings

Rank	Team	Post	W	L	Pct.	R	RA	BPO	BPOA	TS
1	Atlanta Braves	LP	94	68	.580	4.62	3.98	.696	.624	76.629
2	Pittsburgh Pirates	P	98	64	.605	4.74	3.90	.718	.623	73.933
3	Los Angeles Dodgers	—	93	69	.574	4.10	3.49	.646	.600	64.006
4	Saint Louis Cardinals	—	84	78	.519	4.02	4.00	.645	.648	47.483
5	San Diego Padres	—	84	78	.519	3.93	3.99	.617	.628	46.046
6	New York Mets	—	77	84	.478	3.98	4.01	.652	.630	44.688
7	Cincinnati Reds	—	74	88	.457	4.25	4.27	.685	.671	42.000
8	Chicago Cubs	—	77	83	.481	4.34	4.59	.655	.676	39.138
9	San Francisco Giants	—	75	87	.463	4.01	4.30	.640	.675	35.357
10	Philadelphia Phillies	—	78	84	.481	3.88	4.20	.605	.684	33.356
11	Montreal Expos	—	71	90	.441	3.60	4.07	.633	.656	32.291
12	Houston Astros	—	65	97	.401	3.73	4.43	.605	.681	21.015

Best Batters

Rank	Batter	Team	G	BA	B	O	BPO	BV	BPO+
1	Barry Bonds	Pirates	153	.292	429	395	1.086	150.0	153.8
2	Howard Johnson	Mets	156	.259	426	453	.940	107.6	133.8
3	Fred McGriff	Padres	153	.278	379	403	.940	87.3	129.9
4	Will Clark	Giants	148	.301	364	406	.897	81.8	129.0
5	Barry Larkin	Reds	123	.302	322	342	.942	70.7	128.1
6	Bobby Bonilla	Pirates	157	.302	389	432	.900	83.9	127.5
7	Ivan Calderon	Expos	134	.300	324	363	.893	68.0	126.5
8	Ryne Sandberg	Cubs	158	.291	405	442	.916	83.3	125.9
9	Darryl Strawberry	Dodgers	139	.265	341	392	.870	67.5	124.7
10	John Kruk	Phillies	152	.294	344	400	.860	59.6	120.9

Extremes for Batters

Batter	Team	Best		Batter	Team	Worst
Barry Bonds	Pirates	150.0	BV	Charlie Hayes	Phillies	-75.2
Barry Bonds	Pirates	143.8	SE+	Dickie Thon	Phillies	68.2
Barry Bonds	Pirates	56.6	SCV	Dickie Thon	Phillies	-36.8
Howard Johnson	Mets	206.5	ISO+	Brett Butler	Dodgers	37.4
Howard Johnson	Mets	80.5	EXV	Brett Butler	Dodgers	-48.5
Tony Gwynn	Padres	440.9	CT+	Delino DeShields	Expos	58.0
Tony Gwynn	Padres	-64.8	SOV	Delino DeShields	Expos	63.3
Dave Magadan	Mets	188.2	EY+	Benito Santiago	Padres	35.5
Brett Butler	Dodgers	44.9	BBV	Benito Santiago	Padres	-32.7

Best Pitchers

Rank	Pitcher	Team	G	ERA	B	O	BPO	BV	BPO+
1	Jose Rijo	Reds	30	2.51	316	620	.510	-88.0	78.2
2	Tom Glavine	Braves	34	2.55	401	746	.538	-83.2	82.8
3	Mike Morgan	Dodgers	34	2.78	369	718	.514	-76.2	82.9
4	Dennis Martinez	Expos	31	2.39	356	670	.531	-63.9	84.8
5	Bruce Hurst	Padres	31	3.29	369	666	.554	-60.6	85.9
6	Andy Benes	Padres	33	3.03	381	673	.566	-53.1	87.8
7	Greg Maddux	Cubs	37	3.35	454	787	.577	-58.4	88.6
8	Tim Belcher	Dodgers	33	2.62	359	639	.562	-37.3	90.6
9	Zane Smith	Pirates	35	3.20	392	686	.571	-35.3	91.7
10	Terry Mulholland	Phillies	34	3.61	407	694	.586	-34.8	92.1

Extremes for Pitchers

Pitcher	Team	Best		Pitcher	Team	Worst
Jose Rijo	Reds	-88.0	BV	Jack Armstrong	Reds	79.5
Dennis Martinez	Expos	68.7	ERA+	Mark Portugal	Astros	135.2
Tom Glavine	Braves	68.7				
Tom Glavine	Braves	-31.9	ERV	Jim Deshaies	Astros	29.6
Jose Rijo	Reds	68.4	ISO+	Tom Browning	Reds	128.1
Jose Rijo	Reds	-30.0	EXV	Jack Armstrong	Reds	39.1
David Cone	Mets	64.4	CT+	Bob Tewksbury	Cardinals	168.2
David Cone	Mets	85.8	SOV	Bob Tewksbury	Cardinals	-51.1
Zane Smith	Pirates	38.0	EY+	Jose de Jesus	Phillies	206.1
Zane Smith	Pirates	-42.4	BBV	Jose de Jesus	Phillies	63.8

1992 American League

Standings

Rank	Team	Post	W	L	Pct.	R	RA	BPO	BPOA	TS
1	Toronto Blue Jays	WLP	96	66	.593	4.81	4.21	.720	.655	81.049
2	Milwaukee Brewers	—	92	70	.568	4.57	3.73	.685	.613	67.284
3	Oakland Athletics	P	96	66	.593	4.60	4.15	.719	.676	63.655
4	Minnesota Twins	—	90	72	.556	4.61	4.03	.689	.655	60.009
5	Baltimore Orioles	—	89	73	.549	4.35	4.05	.706	.658	58.161
6	Chicago White Sox	—	86	76	.531	4.56	4.26	.694	.652	55.535
7	Detroit Tigers	—	75	87	.463	4.88	4.90	.711	.721	40.468
8	New York Yankees	—	76	86	.469	4.52	4.60	.685	.706	39.488
9	Texas Rangers	—	77	85	.475	4.21	4.65	.671	.679	38.071
10	Kansas City Royals	—	72	90	.444	3.77	4.12	.621	.648	33.856
11	Cleveland Indians	—	76	86	.469	4.16	4.60	.651	.699	33.534
12	Boston Red Sox	—	73	89	.451	3.70	4.13	.607	.646	32.636
13	California Angels	—	72	90	.444	3.57	4.14	.575	.663	26.026
14	Seattle Mariners	—	64	98	.395	4.19	4.93	.671	.730	21.894

Best Batters

Rank	Batter	Team	G	BA	B	O	BPO	BV	BPO+
1	Mark McGwire	Athletics	139	.268	377	362	1.041	133.1	154.6
2	Frank Thomas	White Sox	160	.323	451	421	1.071	157.9	153.9
3	Danny Tartabull	Yankees	123	.266	313	320	.978	91.9	141.6
4	Edgar Martinez	Mariners	135	.343	365	372	.981	105.5	140.7
5	Brady Anderson	Orioles	159	.271	459	491	.935	115.4	133.6
6	Paul Molitor	Brewers	158	.320	403	448	.900	96.4	131.4
7	Roberto Alomar	Blue Jays	152	.310	393	419	.938	88.8	129.2
8	Mickey Tettleton	Tigers	157	.238	375	417	.899	82.9	128.4
9	Ken Griffey Jr.	Mariners	142	.308	364	414	.879	75.3	126.1
10	Tim Raines	White Sox	144	.294	361	412	.876	74.2	125.9

Extremes for Batters

Batter	Team	Best		Batter	Team	Worst
Frank Thomas	White Sox	157.9	BV	Gary DiSarcina	Angels	-87.3
Frank Thomas	White Sox	138.1	SE+	Omar Vizquel	Mariners	65.1
Frank Thomas	White Sox	54.9	SCV	Omar Vizquel	Mariners	-37.5
Mark McGwire	Athletics	253.6	ISO+	Luis Polonia	Angels	34.0
Mark McGwire	Athletics	89.6	EXV	Luis Polonia	Angels	-48.5
Brian Harper	Twins	359.2	CT+	Jose Canseco	Athletics-Rangers	54.6
				Danny Tartabull	Yankees	54.6
Gregg Jefferies	Royals	-57.7	SOV	Rob Deer	Tigers	69.4
Randy Milligan	Orioles	217.6	EY+	Brian Harper	Twins	41.6
Frank Thomas	White Sox	58.0	BBV	Carlos Baerga	Indians	-34.0

Best Pitchers

Rank	Pitcher	Team	G	ERA	B	O	BPO	BV	BPO+
1	Roger Clemens	Red Sox	32	2.41	384	754	.509	-128.7	74.9
2	Juan Guzman	Blue Jays	28	2.64	287	540	.531	-76.9	78.9
3	Mike Mussina	Orioles	32	2.54	387	722	.536	-83.7	82.2
4	Kevin Appier	Royals	30	2.46	345	636	.542	-69.0	83.3
5	Charles Nagy	Indians	33	2.96	413	763	.541	-80.6	83.7
6	Frank Viola	Red Sox	35	3.44	418	723	.578	-73.6	85.0
7	Kevin Brown	Rangers	35	3.32	445	801	.556	-66.9	86.9
8	John Smiley	Twins	34	3.21	424	724	.586	-58.2	87.9
9	Melido Perez	Yankees	33	2.87	429	740	.580	-50.0	89.6
10	Chris Bosio	Brewers	33	3.62	401	698	.574	-45.5	89.8

Extremes for Pitchers

Pitcher	Team	Best		Pitcher	Team	Worst
Roger Clemens	Red Sox	-128.7	BV	Scott Sanderson	Yankees	76.4
Roger Clemens	Red Sox	60.7	ERA+	Scott Sanderson	Yankees	132.6
Roger Clemens	Red Sox	-42.8	ERV	Dave Otto	Indians	29.8
Juan Guzman	Blue Jays	51.0	ISO+	Ricky Bones	Brewers	156.9
Kevin Brown	Rangers	-45.7	EXV	Dennis Cook	Indians	54.6
Randy Johnson	Mariners	52.1	CT+	Bill Gullickson	Tigers	213.7
Randy Johnson	Mariners	115.4	SOV	Bill Gullickson	Tigers	-72.7
Chris Bosio	Brewers	56.6	EY+	Randy Johnson	Mariners	198.9
Bill Wegman	Brewers	-35.3	BBV	Randy Johnson	Mariners	71.1

1992 National League

Standings

Rank	Team	Post	W	L	Pct.	R	RA	BPO	BPOA	TS
1	Atlanta Braves	LP	98	64	.605	4.21	3.51	.666	.600	80.453
2	Pittsburgh Pirates	P	96	66	.593	4.28	3.67	.669	.624	67.165
3	Cincinnati Reds	—	90	72	.556	4.07	3.76	.670	.636	58.702
4	Montreal Expos	—	87	75	.537	4.00	3.59	.651	.622	57.324
5	Saint Louis Cardinals	—	83	79	.512	3.90	3.73	.660	.617	53.705
6	San Diego Padres	—	82	80	.506	3.81	3.93	.636	.636	44.872
7	Houston Astros	—	81	81	.500	3.75	4.12	.633	.664	37.857
8	Chicago Cubs	—	78	84	.481	3.66	3.85	.600	.647	36.106
9	Philadelphia Phillies	—	70	92	.432	4.23	4.43	.658	.673	34.675
10	New York Mets	—	72	90	.444	3.70	4.03	.611	.655	30.997
11	San Francisco Giants	—	72	90	.444	3.54	3.99	.600	.641	30.005
12	Los Angeles Dodgers	—	63	99	.389	3.38	3.93	.602	.642	23.311

Best Batters

Rank	Batter	Team	G	BA	B	O	BPO	BV	BPO+
1	Barry Bonds	Pirates	140	.311	473	350	1.351	230.5	195.1
2	Darren Daulton	Phillies	145	.270	365	365	1.000	110.7	143.5
3	Fred McGriff	Padres	152	.286	404	403	1.002	119.6	142.0
4	Gary Sheffield	Padres	146	.330	389	405	.960	103.2	136.1
5	Will Clark	Giants	144	.300	344	382	.901	87.3	134.0
6	John Kruk	Phillies	144	.323	335	366	.915	80.0	131.4
7	Ray Lankford	Cardinals	153	.293	413	459	.900	97.6	130.9
8	Andy Van Slyke	Pirates	154	.324	393	436	.901	90.9	130.1
9	Ryne Sandberg	Cubs	158	.304	404	451	.896	86.0	127.1
10	Brett Butler	Dodgers	157	.309	380	432	.880	80.3	126.8

Extremes for Batters

Batter	Team	Best		Batter	Team	Worst
Barry Bonds	Pirates	230.5	BV	Jose Lind	Pirates	-99.0
Barry Bonds	Pirates	151.6	SE+	Tom Pagnozzi	Cardinals	71.4
Barry Bonds	Pirates	60.6	SCV	Mark Lemke	Braves	-42.8
Barry Bonds	Pirates	240.9	ISO+	Jose Lind	Pirates	26.3
Barry Bonds	Pirates	86.6	EXV	Jose Lind	Pirates	-44.8
Tony Gwynn	Padres	504.3	CT+	Ray Lankford	Cardinals	61.5
Tony Gwynn	Padres	-64.7	SOV	Ray Lankford	Cardinals	56.6
Barry Bonds	Pirates	203.4	EY+	Jose Lind	Pirates	35.1
Barry Bonds	Pirates	48.3	BBV	Mariano Duncan	Phillies	-29.9

Best Pitchers

Rank	Pitcher	Team	G	ERA	B	O	BPO	BV	BPO+
1	Curt Schilling	Phillies	42	2.35	318	687	.463	-108.2	74.6
2	Greg Maddux	Cubs	35	2.18	396	808	.490	-112.7	77.8
3	Dennis Martinez	Expos	32	2.47	342	685	.499	-80.3	81.0
4	Tom Glavine	Braves	33	2.76	353	678	.521	-76.2	82.2
5	Bob Tewksbury	Cardinals	33	2.16	355	704	.504	-74.6	82.6
6	Bill Swift	Giants	30	2.08	247	495	.499	-48.9	83.5
7	Jose Rijo	Reds	33	2.56	341	632	.540	-61.8	84.7
8	Doug Drabek	Pirates	34	2.77	406	777	.523	-71.3	85.1
9	Mike Morgan	Cubs	34	2.55	393	718	.547	-59.1	86.9
10	John Smoltz	Braves	35	2.85	417	747	.558	-55.9	88.2

Extremes for Pitchers

Pitcher	Team	Best		Pitcher	Team	Worst
Greg Maddux	Cubs	-112.7	BV	Ryan Bowen	Astros	59.9
Greg Maddux	Cubs	63.9	ERA+	Mark Gardner	Expos	131.8
Greg Maddux	Cubs	-36.8	ERV	Ryan Bowen	Astros	29.1
Greg Maddux	Cubs	59.5	ISO+	Bud Black	Giants	146.0
Greg Maddux	Cubs	-45.7	EXV	Bud Black	Giants	34.0
David Cone	Mets	60.7	CT+	Bob Tewksbury	Cardinals	165.5
David Cone	Mets	84.1	SOV	Bob Tewksbury	Cardinals	-59.6
Bob Tewksbury	Cardinals	31.4	EY+	Bob Ojeda	Dodgers	143.8
Bob Tewksbury	Cardinals	-43.8	BBV	Mitch Williams	Phillies	36.4

1993 American League

Standings

Rank	Team	Post	W	L	Pct.	R	RA	BPO	BPOA	TS
1	Toronto Blue Jays	WLP	95	67	.586	5.23	4.58	.776	.695	82.767
2	Chicago White Sox	P	94	68	.580	4.79	4.10	.721	.642	68.047
3	New York Yankees	—	88	74	.543	5.07	4.70	.750	.713	57.230
4	Texas Rangers	—	86	76	.531	5.15	4.64	.725	.700	56.107
5	Detroit Tigers	—	85	77	.525	5.55	5.17	.793	.747	55.849
6	Baltimore Orioles	—	85	77	.525	4.85	4.60	.728	.699	53.212
7	Seattle Mariners	—	82	80	.506	4.53	4.51	.712	.695	47.859
8	Kansas City Royals	—	84	78	.519	4.17	4.28	.661	.662	46.536
9	Boston Red Sox	—	80	82	.494	4.23	4.31	.675	.664	45.053
10	Cleveland Indians	—	76	86	.469	4.88	5.02	.710	.754	36.888
11	California Angels	—	71	91	.438	4.22	4.75	.675	.716	29.864
12	Milwaukee Brewers	—	69	93	.426	4.52	4.89	.663	.728	27.915
13	Oakland Athletics	—	68	94	.420	4.41	5.22	.694	.760	22.975
14	Minnesota Twins	—	71	91	.438	4.28	5.12	.648	.753	21.567

Best Batters

Rank	Batter	Team	G	BA	B	O	BPO	BV	BPO+
1	John Olerud	Blue Jays	158	.363	458	372	1.231	181.5	165.6
2	Frank Thomas	White Sox	153	.317	464	400	1.160	174.1	160.1
3	Rickey Henderson	Athletics-Blue Jays	134	.289	410	364	1.126	146.4	156.2
4	Ken Griffey Jr.	Mariners	156	.309	485	432	1.123	164.8	151.5
5	Chris Hoiles	Orioles	126	.310	330	306	1.078	103.9	145.9
6	Juan Gonzalez	Rangers	140	.310	394	384	1.026	117.4	142.4
7	Rafael Palmeiro	Rangers	160	.295	442	443	.998	122.9	138.5
8	Roberto Alomar	Blue Jays	153	.326	439	434	1.012	116.4	136.1
9	Tim Salmon	Angels	142	.283	376	389	.967	91.3	132.1
10	Albert Belle	Indians	159	.290	450	467	.964	108.1	131.6

Extremes for Batters

Batter	Team	Best		Batter	Team	Worst
John Olerud	Blue Jays	181.5	BV	Jose Lind	Royals	-102.7
Juan Gonzalez	Rangers	144.2	SE+	Omar Vizquel	Mariners	70.2
Juan Gonzalez	Rangers	54.2	SCV	Tony Pena	Red Sox	-45.2
Juan Gonzalez	Rangers	222.7	ISO+	Omar Vizquel	Mariners	27.4
Juan Gonzalez	Rangers	95.3	EXV	Omar Vizquel	Mariners	-63.8
Felix Fermin	Indians	549.6	CT+	Rob Deer	Tigers-Red Sox	45.6
Felix Fermin	Indians	-62.9	SOV	Rob Deer	Tigers-Red Sox	92.0
Rickey Henderson	Athletics-Blue Jays	222.9	EY+	Brian Harper	Twins	40.3
Tony Phillips	Tigers	66.6	BBV	Carlos Baerga	Indians	-31.3

Best Pitchers

Rank	Pitcher	Team	G	ERA	B	O	BPO	BV	BPO+
1	Kevin Appier	Royals	34	2.56	353	714	.494	-149.3	70.3
2	Mark Langston	Angels	35	3.20	434	768	.565	-98.7	81.5
3	Randy Johnson	Mariners	35	3.24	452	771	.586	-85.9	84.0
4	Danny Darwin	Red Sox	34	3.26	418	686	.609	-75.2	84.8
5	Chris Bosio	Mariners	29	3.45	296	494	.599	-48.6	85.9
6	Jimmy Key	Yankees	34	3.00	414	716	.578	-65.9	86.3
7	Ben McDonald	Orioles	34	3.39	399	664	.601	-60.2	86.9
8	Alex Fernandez	White Sox	34	3.13	440	745	.591	-62.9	87.5
9	Kevin Brown	Rangers	34	3.59	426	708	.602	-52.9	88.9
10	Roger Clemens	Red Sox	29	4.46	373	579	.644	-43.3	89.6

Extremes for Pitchers

Pitcher	Team	Best		Pitcher	Team	Worst
Kevin Appier	Royals	-149.3	BV	Rick Sutcliffe	Orioles	93.9
Kevin Appier	Royals	58.6	ERA+	Bob Welch	Athletics	136.0
Kevin Appier	Royals	-48.1	ERV	Jack Morris	Blue Jays	34.7
Kevin Appier	Royals	54.4	ISO+	Ricky Bones	Brewers	139.5
Kevin Appier	Royals	-57.9	EXV	Bill Gullickson	Tigers	42.9
Randy Johnson	Mariners	52.9	CT+	Ricky Bones	Brewers	215.2
Randy Johnson	Mariners	145.0	SOV	Ricky Bones	Brewers	-72.6
Danny Darwin	Red Sox	54.4	EY+	Wilson Alvarez	White Sox	169.3
Danny Darwin	Red Sox	-34.3	BBV	Wilson Alvarez	White Sox	46.6

1993 National League

Standings

Rank	Team	Post	W	L	Pct.	R	RA	BPO	BPOA	TS
1	Philadelphia Phillies	LP	97	65	.599	5.41	4.57	.762	.659	74.189
2	Atlanta Braves	P	104	58	.642	4.73	3.45	.708	.597	72.282
3	San Francisco Giants	—	103	59	.636	4.99	3.93	.735	.638	69.504
4	Montreal Expos	—	94	68	.580	4.49	4.18	.704	.663	56.667
5	Houston Astros	—	85	77	.525	4.42	3.89	.696	.629	55.061
6	Saint Louis Cardinals	—	87	75	.537	4.68	4.59	.705	.693	49.956
7	Los Angeles Dodgers	—	81	81	.500	4.17	4.09	.660	.644	47.057
8	Chicago Cubs	—	84	78	.519	4.53	4.53	.687	.701	46.212
9	Cincinnati Reds	—	73	89	.451	4.46	4.85	.683	.726	36.383
10	Pittsburgh Pirates	—	75	87	.463	4.36	4.98	.683	.752	34.390
11	New York Mets	—	59	103	.364	4.15	4.59	.640	.690	28.434
12	San Diego Padres	—	61	101	.377	4.19	4.77	.651	.714	27.843
13	Florida Marlins	—	64	98	.395	3.59	4.47	.606	.701	25.416
14	Colorado Rockies	—	67	95	.414	4.68	5.97	.697	.814	23.078

Best Batters

Rank	Batter	Team	G	BA	B	O	BPO	BV	BPO+
1	Barry Bonds	Giants	159	.336	529	388	1.363	244.3	185.8
2	Lenny Dykstra	Phillies	161	.305	480	468	1.026	134.3	138.9
3	John Kruk	Phillies	150	.316	376	384	.979	92.4	132.6
4	Gregg Jefferies	Cardinals	142	.342	378	386	.979	92.8	132.5
5	Darren Daulton	Phillies	147	.257	378	389	.972	90.7	131.6
6	Mike Piazza	Dodgers	149	.318	365	393	.929	81.4	128.7
7	Andres Galarraga	Rockies	120	.370	321	315	1.019	67.3	126.6
8	Jeff Bagwell	Astros	142	.320	363	397	.914	73.6	125.4
9	Fred McGriff	Padres-Braves	151	.291	394	417	.945	79.5	125.3
10	Larry Walker	Expos	138	.265	351	381	.921	60.2	120.7

Extremes for Batters

Batter	Team	Best		Batter	Team	Worst
Barry Bonds	Giants	244.3	BV	Tim Wallach	Dodgers	-75.6
Barry Bonds	Giants	144.6	SE+	Walt Weiss	Marlins	65.3
Barry Bonds	Giants	63.5	SCV	Walt Weiss	Marlins	-46.8
Barry Bonds	Giants	237.1	ISO+	Walt Weiss	Marlins	27.9
Barry Bonds	Giants	106.4	EXV	Walt Weiss	Marlins	-54.2
Ozzie Smith	Cardinals	481.6	CT+	Cory Snyder	Dodgers	54.0
Ozzie Smith	Cardinals	-68.7	SOV	Cory Snyder	Dodgers	67.6
Darren Daulton	Phillies	214.7	EY+	Mariano Duncan	Phillies	29.6
Lenny Dykstra	Phillies	60.2	BBV	Derek Bell	Padres	-28.7

Best Pitchers

Rank	Pitcher	Team	G	ERA	B	O	BPO	BV	BPO+
1	Bill Swift	Giants	34	2.82	360	709	.508	-109.1	76.7
2	Greg Maddux	Braves	36	2.36	419	810	.517	-125.8	76.9
3	Jose Rijo	Reds	36	2.48	427	774	.552	-93.2	82.1
4	Terry Mulholland	Phillies	29	3.25	332	583	.569	-55.7	85.6
5	John Burkett	Giants	34	3.65	399	702	.568	-65.5	85.9
6	Steve Avery	Braves	35	2.94	394	671	.587	-57.3	87.3
7	Tommy Greene	Phillies	31	3.42	356	606	.587	-47.0	88.3
8	Mark Portugal	Astros	33	2.77	361	622	.580	-46.7	88.6
9	Pete Harnisch	Astros	33	2.98	384	658	.584	-47.3	89.0
10	Ken Hill	Expos	28	3.23	347	561	.619	-36.7	90.4

Extremes for Pitchers

Pitcher	Team	Best		Pitcher	Team	Worst
Greg Maddux	Braves	-125.8	BV	Andy Ashby	Rockies-Padres	83.7
Greg Maddux	Braves	61.0	ERA+	Bob Walk	Pirates	146.2
Greg Maddux	Braves	-44.8	ERV	Bob Walk	Pirates	37.3
Mark Portugal	Astros	58.1	ISO+	Greg Swindell	Astros	134.6
Greg Maddux	Braves	-43.9	EXV	Greg Harris	Padres-Rockies	39.2
Jose Rijo	Reds	72.4	CT+	Bob Walk	Pirates	159.2
Jose Rijo	Reds	62.7	SOV	Bob Tewksbury	Cardinals	-53.4
Bob Tewksbury	Cardinals	29.7	EY+	Ben Rivera	Phillies	155.3
Bob Tewksbury	Cardinals	-45.0	BBV	Ramon Martinez	Dodgers	32.4

1994 American League

Standings

Rank	Team	Post	W	L	Pct.	R	RA	BPO	BPOA	TS
1	New York Yankees	—	70	43	.619	5.93	4.73	.828	.717	71.457
2	Chicago White Sox	—	67	46	.593	5.60	4.41	.807	.669	70.266
3	Cleveland Indians	—	66	47	.584	6.01	4.97	.834	.714	67.331
4	Baltimore Orioles	—	63	49	.563	5.26	4.44	.772	.716	60.128
5	Kansas City Royals	—	64	51	.557	4.99	4.63	.737	.702	55.489
6	Toronto Blue Jays	—	55	60	.478	4.92	5.03	.729	.758	40.913
7	Detroit Tigers	—	53	62	.461	5.67	5.83	.797	.812	39.600
8	Boston Red Sox	—	54	61	.470	4.80	5.40	.725	.764	36.460
9	Milwaukee Brewers	—	53	62	.461	4.76	5.10	.704	.756	36.402
10	Seattle Mariners	—	49	63	.438	5.08	5.50	.752	.771	35.492
11	Oakland Athletics	—	51	63	.447	4.82	5.17	.702	.746	35.386
12	Texas Rangers	—	52	62	.456	5.38	6.11	.770	.795	35.096
13	Minnesota Twins	—	53	60	.469	5.26	6.09	.736	.847	30.826
14	California Angels	—	47	68	.409	4.72	5.74	.700	.821	22.973

Best Batters

Rank	Batter	Team	G	BA	B	O	BPO	BV	BPO+
1	Frank Thomas	White Sox	113	.353	411	283	1.452	192.2	187.8
2	Albert Belle	Indians	106	.357	371	281	1.320	151.7	169.2
3	Paul O'Neill	Yankees	103	.359	302	259	1.166	104.7	153.1
4	Ken Griffey Jr.	Mariners	111	.323	363	307	1.182	119.9	149.3
5	Kenny Lofton	Indians	112	.349	370	326	1.135	115.6	145.4
6	Bob Hamelin	Royals	101	.282	253	236	1.072	64.0	133.9
7	Will Clark	Rangers	110	.329	280	273	1.026	70.5	133.7
8	Chili Davis	Angels	108	.311	299	290	1.031	73.3	132.5
9	Mo Vaughn	Red Sox	111	.310	300	285	1.053	71.2	131.1
10	Mickey Tettleton	Tigers	107	.248	262	263	.996	56.6	127.5

Extremes for Batters

Batter	Team	Best		Batter	Team	Worst
Frank Thomas	White Sox	192.2	**BV**	Matt Walbeck	Twins	-98.8
Kirby Puckett	Twins	149.9	**SE+**	Ed Sprague	Blue Jays	67.3
Kirby Puckett	Twins	56.9	**SCV**	Ed Sprague	Blue Jays	-34.5
Frank Thomas	White Sox	229.9	**ISO+**	Otis Nixon	Red Sox	24.3
Frank Thomas	White Sox	84.8	**EXV**	Otis Nixon	Red Sox	-53.1
Felix Fermin	Mariners	304.1	**CT+**	Mo Vaughn	Red Sox	59.3
Felix Fermin	Mariners	-44.9	**SOV**	Travis Fryman	Tigers	47.2
Mickey Tettleton	Tigers	220.1	**EY+**	Carlos Baerga	Indians	21.8
Frank Thomas	White Sox	52.7	**BBV**	Carlos Baerga	Indians	-32.3

Best Pitchers

Rank	Pitcher	Team	G	ERA	B	O	BPO	BV	BPO+
1	Steve Ontiveros	Athletics	27	2.65	168	349	.481	-77.3	68.5
2	David Cone	Royals	23	2.94	283	514	.551	-103.9	73.1
3	Roger Clemens	Red Sox	24	2.85	294	517	.569	-95.5	75.5
4	Mike Mussina	Orioles	24	3.06	317	527	.602	-76.2	80.6
5	Randy Johnson	Mariners	23	3.19	311	517	.602	-73.5	80.9
6	Wilson Alvarez	White Sox	24	3.45	290	490	.592	-63.7	82.0
7	Dennis Martinez	Indians	24	3.52	319	533	.598	-66.9	82.7
8	Charles Nagy	Indians	23	3.45	310	511	.607	-59.9	83.8
9	Ricky Bones	Brewers	24	3.43	325	516	.630	-61.1	84.2
10	Pat Hentgen	Blue Jays	24	3.40	331	530	.625	-61.3	84.4

Extremes for Pitchers

Pitcher	Team	Best		Pitcher	Team	Worst
David Cone	Royals	-103.9	**BV**	Jim Deshaies	Twins	106.5
Roger Clemens	Red Sox	59.8	**ERA+**	Jim Deshaies	Twins	159.8
Roger Clemens	Red Sox	-36.3	**ERV**	Jim Deshaies	Twins	40.1
Steve Ontiveros	Athletics	56.5	**ISO+**	Sid Fernandez	Orioles	163.0
Charles Nagy	Indians	-35.9	**EXV**	Jim Deshaies	Twins	53.5
Randy Johnson	Mariners	56.6	**CT+**	Ricky Bones	Brewers	201.4
Randy Johnson	Mariners	88.6	**SOV**	Ricky Bones	Brewers	-57.8
Mark Gubicza	Royals	44.8	**EY+**	Todd Van Poppel	Athletics	197.4
Mark Gubicza	Royals	-25.8	**BBV**	Todd Van Poppel	Athletics	42.9

1994 National League

Standings

Rank	Team	Post	W	L	Pct.	R	RA	BPO	BPOA	TS
1	Montreal Expos	—	74	40	.649	5.13	3.98	.772	.636	75.628
2	Atlanta Braves	—	68	46	.596	4.75	3.93	.724	.627	66.095
3	Cincinnati Reds	—	66	48	.579	5.30	4.26	.787	.685	65.978
4	Houston Astros	—	66	49	.574	5.23	4.37	.789	.693	64.003
5	Los Angeles Dodgers	—	58	56	.509	4.67	4.46	.706	.695	48.354
6	Philadelphia Phillies	—	54	61	.470	4.53	4.32	.680	.682	43.777
7	San Francisco Giants	—	55	60	.478	4.38	4.35	.696	.711	42.747
8	New York Mets	—	55	58	.487	4.48	4.65	.656	.707	40.033
9	Chicago Cubs	—	49	64	.434	4.42	4.86	.680	.716	34.144
10	Saint Louis Cardinals	—	53	61	.465	4.65	5.40	.727	.792	33.454
11	San Diego Padres	—	47	70	.402	4.09	4.54	.675	.682	32.678
12	Colorado Rockies	—	53	64	.453	4.90	5.45	.743	.822	32.640
13	Florida Marlins	—	51	64	.443	4.07	5.01	.679	.758	29.271
14	Pittsburgh Pirates	—	53	61	.465	4.09	5.09	.649	.761	29.007

Best Batters

Rank	Batter	Team	G	BA	B	O	BPO	BV	BPO+
1	Jeff Bagwell	Astros	110	.368	394	279	1.412	187.9	191.2
2	Barry Bonds	Giants	112	.312	365	284	1.285	154.2	173.1
3	Kevin Mitchell	Reds	95	.326	283	229	1.236	108.0	161.7
4	Tony Gwynn	Padres	110	.394	299	280	1.068	88.0	141.7
5	Craig Biggio	Astros	114	.318	324	311	1.042	94.3	141.0
6	Fred McGriff	Braves	113	.318	325	303	1.073	90.4	138.5
7	Larry Walker	Expos	103	.322	304	287	1.059	81.7	136.7
8	Moises Alou	Expos	107	.339	306	297	1.030	75.9	133.0
9	Gary Sheffield	Marlins	87	.276	262	254	1.031	64.8	132.8
10	David Justice	Braves	104	.313	261	255	1.024	63.5	132.2

Extremes for Batters

Batter	Team	Best		Batter	Team	Worst
Jeff Bagwell	Astros	187.9	BV	Walt Weiss	Rockies	-75.3
Jeff Bagwell	Astros	179.0	SE+	Andy Van Slyke	Pirates	67.9
Jeff Bagwell	Astros	79.9	SCV	Walt Weiss	Rockies	-36.1
Jeff Bagwell	Astros	246.4	ISO+	Walt Weiss	Rockies	29.3
Jeff Bagwell	Astros	90.9	EXV	Walt Weiss	Rockies	-53.1
Tony Gwynn	Padres	372.7	CT+	Reggie Sanders	Reds	57.2
Tony Gwynn	Padres	-51.8	SOV	Reggie Sanders	Reds	48.8
Lenny Dykstra	Phillies	193.8	EY+	Andres Galarraga	Rockies	30.5
David Justice	Braves	30.8	BBV	Dante Bichette	Rockies	-25.4

Best Pitchers

Rank	Pitcher	Team	G	ERA	B	O	BPO	BV	BPO+
1	Greg Maddux	Braves	25	1.56	258	614	.420	-167.3	60.7
2	Bret Saberhagen	Mets	24	2.74	298	531	.561	-65.9	81.9
2	Doug Drabek	Astros	23	2.84	269	496	.542	-59.3	81.9
4	Jeff Fassero	Expos	21	2.99	242	420	.576	-50.3	82.8
5	Pedro Martinez	Expos	24	3.42	257	428	.600	-40.8	86.3
6	Shane Reynolds	Astros	33	3.05	217	377	.576	-32.6	86.9
7	Bobby Jones	Mets	24	3.15	299	484	.618	-32.7	90.2
8	John Smoltz	Braves	21	4.14	257	408	.630	-25.6	90.9
9	Danny Jackson	Phillies	25	3.26	344	546	.630	-33.2	91.2
10	Steve Avery	Braves	24	4.04	289	453	.638	-24.8	92.1

Extremes for Pitchers

Pitcher	Team	Best		Pitcher	Team	Worst
Greg Maddux	Braves	-167.3	BV	Brian Williams	Astros	69.1
Greg Maddux	Braves	38.8	ERA+	Greg Harris	Rockies	140.6
Greg Maddux	Braves	-55.2	ERV	Greg Harris	Rockies	27.7
Greg Maddux	Braves	37.0	ISO+	Pete Smith	Mets	160.5
Greg Maddux	Braves	-64.8	EXV	Pete Smith	Mets	42.2
Andy Benes	Padres	65.5	CT+	Zane Smith	Pirates	196.9
Andy Benes	Padres	65.2	SOV	Zane Smith	Pirates	-55.2
Bret Saberhagen	Mets	26.2	EY+	Darryl Kile	Astros	165.1
Bret Saberhagen	Mets	-36.7	BBV	Darryl Kile	Astros	30.0

1995 American League

Standings

Rank	Team	Post	W	L	Pct.	R	RA	BPO	BPOA	TS
1	Cleveland Indians	LP	100	44	.694	5.83	4.22	.835	.677	87.220
2	Boston Red Sox	P	86	58	.597	5.49	4.85	.799	.693	64.211
3	California Angels	—	78	67	.538	5.52	4.81	.773	.723	55.974
4	Seattle Mariners	P	79	66	.545	5.49	4.88	.784	.761	54.377
5	New York Yankees	P	79	65	.549	5.17	4.74	.750	.731	53.432
6	Baltimore Orioles	—	71	73	.493	4.89	4.44	.748	.691	50.900
7	Texas Rangers	—	74	70	.514	4.80	5.00	.714	.727	44.814
8	Chicago White Sox	—	68	76	.472	5.21	5.23	.771	.776	42.677
9	Oakland Athletics	—	67	77	.465	5.07	5.28	.745	.745	41.215
10	Kansas City Royals	—	70	74	.486	4.37	4.80	.690	.708	40.791
11	Milwaukee Brewers	—	65	79	.451	5.14	5.19	.714	.780	37.012
12	Toronto Blue Jays	—	56	88	.389	4.46	5.40	.697	.765	26.272
13	Detroit Tigers	—	60	84	.417	4.54	5.86	.696	.821	23.133
14	Minnesota Twins	—	56	88	.389	4.88	6.17	.719	.836	21.344

Best Batters

Rank	Batter	Team	G	BA	B	O	BPO	BV	BPO+
1	Edgar Martinez	Mariners	145	.356	453	347	1.305	179.1	165.4
2	Frank Thomas	White Sox	145	.308	456	369	1.236	176.8	163.3
3	Albert Belle	Indians	143	.317	465	403	1.154	149.9	147.6
4	Tim Salmon	Angels	143	.330	425	378	1.124	134.1	146.1
5	Jim Thome	Indians	137	.314	361	324	1.114	107.6	142.5
6	Chili Davis	Angels	119	.318	319	313	1.019	78.1	132.4
7	Chuck Knoblauch	Twins	136	.333	399	395	1.010	90.2	129.2
8	Manny Ramirez	Indians	137	.308	363	361	1.006	80.7	128.6
9	John Valentin	Red Sox	135	.298	398	387	1.028	88.3	128.5
10	Rickey Henderson	Athletics	112	.300	294	307	.958	64.7	128.2

Extremes for Batters

Batter	Team	Best		Batter	Team	Worst
Edgar Martinez	Mariners	179.1	**BV**	Ozzie Guillen	White Sox	-97.5
Edgar Martinez	Mariners	137.8	**SE+**	Benji Gil	Rangers	67.8
Edgar Martinez	Mariners	56.2	**SCV**	Benji Gil	Rangers	-34.6
Albert Belle	Indians	220.0	**ISO+**	Otis Nixon	Rangers	26.1
Albert Belle	Indians	111.3	**EXV**	Otis Nixon	Rangers	-70.7
Lance Johnson	White Sox	317.7	**CT+**	Benji Gil	Rangers	47.8
Lance Johnson	White Sox	-67.5	**SOV**	Benji Gil	Rangers	76.7
Mickey Tettleton	Rangers	199.3	**EY+**	Ivan Rodriguez	Rangers	28.8
Frank Thomas	White Sox	51.3	**BBV**	Ivan Rodriguez	Rangers	-34.6

Best Pitchers

Rank	Pitcher	Team	G	ERA	B	O	BPO	BV	BPO+
1	Randy Johnson	Mariners	30	2.48	332	650	.511	-141.9	70.1
2	Kevin Brown	Orioles	26	3.60	290	519	.559	-83.3	77.7
3	Mike Mussina	Orioles	32	3.29	377	664	.568	-100.5	78.9
4	Kevin Appier	Royals	31	3.89	362	605	.598	-77.9	82.3
5	Tim Wakefield	Red Sox	27	2.95	366	588	.622	-69.0	84.1
6	Dennis Martinez	Indians	28	3.08	339	559	.606	-60.6	84.8
7	Erik Hanson	Red Sox	29	4.24	365	574	.636	-59.7	86.0
8	Kenny Rogers	Rangers	31	3.38	393	630	.624	-61.6	86.5
9	Orel Hershiser	Indians	26	3.87	322	506	.636	-39.7	89.0
10	Jim Abbott	White Sox-Angels	30	3.70	379	601	.631	-44.6	89.5

Extremes for Pitchers

Pitcher	Team	Best		Pitcher	Team	Worst
Randy Johnson	Mariners	-141.9	**BV**	Jason Bere	White Sox	108.3
Randy Johnson	Mariners	54.6	**ERA+**	Kevin Gross	Rangers	119.4
Randy Johnson	Mariners	-49.0	**ERV**	Jason Bere	White Sox	44.5
Tom Gordon	Royals	59.7	**ISO+**	Brad Radke	Twins	134.9
Tom Gordon	Royals	-45.9	**EXV**	Danny Darwin	Blue Jays-Rangers	43.9
Randy Johnson	Mariners	49.8	**CT+**	Ricky Bones	Brewers	173.7
Randy Johnson	Mariners	147.7	**SOV**	Ricky Bones	Brewers	-56.8
Mike Mussina	Orioles	62.3	**EY+**	Al Leiter	Blue Jays	155.9
Bob Tewksbury	Rangers	-32.0	**BBV**	Jason Bere	White Sox	45.7

1995 National League

Standings

Rank	Team	Post	W	L	Pct.	R	RA	BPO	BPOA	TS
1	Atlanta Braves	WLP	90	54	.625	4.48	3.75	.699	.632	84.662
2	Cincinnati Reds	P	85	59	.590	5.19	4.33	.784	.676	72.385
3	Houston Astros	—	76	68	.528	5.19	4.68	.744	.695	57.346
4	Los Angeles Dodgers	P	78	66	.542	4.40	4.23	.696	.640	56.407
5	Colorado Rockies	P	77	67	.535	5.45	5.44	.807	.783	51.516
6	Chicago Cubs	—	73	71	.507	4.81	4.66	.723	.721	47.900
7	New York Mets	—	69	75	.479	4.56	4.29	.681	.688	45.102
8	San Diego Padres	—	70	74	.486	4.64	4.67	.688	.689	43.682
9	Florida Marlins	—	67	76	.469	4.71	4.71	.720	.731	41.193
10	Philadelphia Phillies	—	69	75	.479	4.27	4.57	.675	.707	37.814
11	Montreal Expos	—	66	78	.458	4.31	4.43	.670	.700	37.381
12	San Francisco Giants	—	67	77	.465	4.53	5.39	.702	.761	28.981
13	Saint Louis Cardinals	—	62	81	.434	3.94	4.60	.635	.717	25.262
14	Pittsburgh Pirates	—	58	86	.403	4.37	5.11	.670	.755	20.970

Best Batters

Rank	Batter	Team	G	BA	B	O	BPO	BV	BPO+
1	Barry Bonds	Giants	144	.294	452	383	1.180	166.6	158.4
2	Mike Piazza	Dodgers	112	.346	305	295	1.034	95.8	145.8
3	Reggie Sanders	Reds	133	.306	399	363	1.099	120.8	143.4
4	Craig Biggio	Astros	141	.302	420	418	1.005	114.1	137.3
5	Ron Gant	Reds	119	.276	333	322	1.034	86.2	134.9
6	Barry Larkin	Reds	131	.319	366	356	1.028	93.1	134.1
7	Jeff Bagwell	Astros	114	.290	325	338	.962	77.6	131.4
8	Eric Karros	Dodgers	143	.298	368	409	.900	77.9	126.9
9	Mark Grace	Cubs	143	.326	366	392	.934	69.3	123.3
10	Ken Caminiti	Padres	143	.302	358	389	.920	62.5	121.2

Extremes for Batters

Batter	Team	Best		Batter	Team	Worst
Barry Bonds	Giants	166.6	BV	Joe Girardi	Rockies	-117.9
Mike Piazza	Dodgers	149.6	SE+	Walt Weiss	Rockies	58.4
Mike Piazza	Dodgers	47.4	SCV	Walt Weiss	Rockies	-63.5
Mike Piazza	Dodgers	191.0	ISO+	Walt Weiss	Rockies	30.5
Barry Bonds	Giants	66.4	EXV	Walt Weiss	Rockies	-59.2
Tony Gwynn	Padres	622.5	CT+	Andres Galarraga	Rockies	64.1
Tony Gwynn	Padres	-78.4	SOV	Andres Galarraga	Rockies	52.4
Walt Weiss	Rockies	201.2	EY+	Shawon Dunston	Cubs	17.2
Barry Bonds	Giants	47.3	BBV	Dante Bichette	Rockies	-34.3

Best Pitchers

Rank	Pitcher	Team	G	ERA	B	O	BPO	BV	BPO+
1	Greg Maddux	Braves	28	1.63	256	633	.404	-181.0	58.6
2	Pete Schourek	Reds	29	3.22	316	569	.555	-72.9	81.3
3	Tom Glavine	Braves	29	3.08	345	600	.575	-69.2	83.3
4	Joey Hamilton	Padres	31	3.08	363	624	.582	-61.9	85.4
5	Kevin Ritz	Rockies	31	4.21	359	521	.689	-56.7	86.4
6	Ismael Valdez	Dodgers	33	3.05	330	600	.550	-51.0	86.6
7	John Smoltz	Braves	29	3.18	351	582	.603	-50.8	87.4
8	Hideo Nomo	Dodgers	28	2.54	323	581	.556	-46.0	87.5
9	Jaime Navarro	Cubs	29	3.28	360	602	.598	-50.3	87.7
10	John Smiley	Reds	28	3.46	324	534	.607	-40.9	88.8

Extremes for Pitchers

Pitcher	Team	Best		Pitcher	Team	Worst
Greg Maddux	Braves	-181.0	BV	Jose Bautista	Giants	70.9
Greg Maddux	Braves	40.1	ERA+	Terry Mulholland	Giants	150.1
Greg Maddux	Braves	-56.8	ERV	Terry Mulholland	Giants	32.0
Greg Maddux	Braves	43.8	ISO+	Kevin Foster	Cubs	149.4
Greg Maddux	Braves	-59.0	EXV	Jose Bautista	Giants	51.4
Hideo Nomo	Dodgers	55.5	CT+	Terry Mulholland	Giants	187.8
Hideo Nomo	Dodgers	105.0	SOV	Terry Mulholland	Giants	-57.1
Greg Maddux	Braves	34.2	EY+	Pat Rapp	Marlins	136.8
Greg Maddux	Braves	-38.5	BBV	Darryl Kile	Astros	29.5

1996 American League

Standings

Rank	Team	Post	W	L	Pct.	R	RA	BPO	BPOA	TS
1	New York Yankees	WLP	92	70	.568	5.38	4.86	.773	.719	73.231
2	Cleveland Indians	P	99	62	.615	5.91	4.78	.848	.715	71.320
3	Texas Rangers	P	90	72	.556	5.69	4.90	.818	.737	60.383
4	Seattle Mariners	—	85	76	.528	6.17	5.56	.854	.791	55.530
5	Chicago White Sox	—	85	77	.525	5.54	4.90	.799	.738	55.271
6	Baltimore Orioles	P	88	74	.543	5.82	5.54	.809	.781	53.175
7	Boston Red Sox	—	85	77	.525	5.73	5.69	.798	.800	48.166
8	Milwaukee Brewers	—	80	82	.494	5.52	5.55	.776	.797	43.531
9	Minnesota Twins	—	78	84	.481	5.41	5.56	.754	.798	40.381
10	Kansas City Royals	—	75	86	.466	4.63	4.88	.708	.721	39.900
11	Oakland Athletics	—	78	84	.481	5.31	5.56	.771	.815	39.747
12	Toronto Blue Jays	—	74	88	.457	4.73	4.99	.723	.729	39.319
13	California Angels	—	70	91	.435	4.73	5.86	.716	.806	27.320
14	Detroit Tigers	—	53	109	.327	4.83	6.81	.701	.902	5.197

Best Batters

Rank	Batter	Team	G	BA	B	O	BPO	BV	BPO+
1	Mark McGwire	Athletics	130	.312	434	306	1.418	194.3	181.1
2	Frank Thomas	White Sox	141	.349	453	377	1.202	159.1	154.2
3	Jim Thome	Indians	151	.311	442	365	1.211	151.2	152.0
4	Edgar Martinez	Mariners	139	.327	435	358	1.215	143.3	149.1
5	Brady Anderson	Orioles	149	.297	498	436	1.142	147.9	142.3
6	Albert Belle	Indians	158	.311	499	442	1.129	146.8	141.7
7	Chuck Knoblauch	Twins	153	.341	467	410	1.139	136.0	141.1
8	Ken Griffey Jr.	Mariners	140	.303	451	396	1.139	128.3	139.8
9	Alex Rodriguez	Mariners	146	.358	470	418	1.124	129.4	138.0
10	Mo Vaughn	Red Sox	161	.326	489	453	1.079	119.0	132.2

Extremes for Batters

Batter	Team	Best		Batter	Team	Worst
Mark McGwire	Athletics	194.3	BV	Gary DiSarcina	Angels	-119.0
Ken Griffey Jr.	Mariners	141.4	SE+	Mike Bordick	Athletics	69.3
Alex Rodriguez	Mariners	65.9	SCV	Mike Bordick	Athletics	-42.0
Mark McGwire	Athletics	248.1	ISO+	Otis Nixon	Blue Jays	22.5
Mark McGwire	Athletics	105.7	EXV	Otis Nixon	Blue Jays	-68.7
Ozzie Guillen	White Sox	309.3	CT+	Mickey Tettleton	Rangers	61.6
Joey Cora	Mariners	-64.2	SOV	Melvin Nieves	Tigers	80.9
Mark McGwire	Athletics	209.1	EY+	Ozzie Guillen	White Sox	21.0
Jim Thome	Indians	56.1	BBV	Ozzie Guillen	White Sox	-37.7

Best Pitchers

Rank	Pitcher	Team	G	ERA	B	O	BPO	BV	BPO+
1	Pat Hentgen	Blue Jays	35	3.22	470	796	.590	-124.8	79.0
2	Juan Guzman	Blue Jays	27	2.93	333	561	.594	-86.2	79.4
3	Kevin Appier	Royals	32	3.62	394	632	.623	-75.8	83.9
4	Ken Hill	Rangers	35	3.63	482	750	.643	-89.9	84.3
5	Charles Nagy	Indians	32	3.41	419	671	.624	-70.0	85.7
6	Roger Clemens	Red Sox	34	3.63	477	736	.648	-76.9	86.1
7	Alex Fernandez	White Sox	35	3.45	493	772	.639	-62.9	88.7
8	Andy Pettitte	Yankees	35	3.87	436	659	.662	-52.9	89.2
9	Ben McDonald	Brewers	35	3.90	458	672	.682	-52.5	89.7
10	Kenny Rogers	Yankees	30	4.68	363	538	.675	-36.2	90.9

Extremes for Pitchers

Pitcher	Team	Best		Pitcher	Team	Worst
Pat Hentgen	Blue Jays	-124.8	BV	Todd Van Poppel	Athletics-Tigers	121.7
Juan Guzman	Blue Jays	62.6	ERA+	Scott Aldred	Tigers-Twins	129.3
Pat Hentgen	Blue Jays	-42.9	ERV	Todd Van Poppel	Athletics-Tigers	48.4
Pat Hentgen	Blue Jays	69.9	ISO+	Shawn Boskie	Angels	133.1
Pat Hentgen	Blue Jays	-48.7	EXV	Todd Van Poppel	Athletics-Tigers	46.8
Kevin Appier	Royals	63.6	CT+	Scott Erickson	Orioles	163.0
Roger Clemens	Red Sox	92.0	SOV	Scott Erickson	Orioles	-63.0
David Wells	Orioles	55.6	EY+	Rich Robertson	Twins	156.0
David Wells	Orioles	-35.2	BBV	Rich Robertson	Twins	40.9

1996 National League

Standings

Rank	Team	Post	W	L	Pct.	R	RA	BPO	BPOA	TS
1	Atlanta Braves	LP	96	66	.593	4.77	4.00	.723	.618	83.372
2	San Diego Padres	P	91	71	.562	4.76	4.21	.704	.644	64.199
3	Montreal Expos	—	88	74	.543	4.57	4.12	.695	.664	58.233
4	Saint Louis Cardinals	P	88	74	.543	4.69	4.36	.704	.675	56.744
5	Los Angeles Dodgers	P	90	72	.556	4.34	4.02	.658	.651	55.944
6	Colorado Rockies	—	83	79	.512	5.93	5.95	.833	.817	48.383
7	Cincinnati Reds	—	81	81	.500	4.80	4.77	.742	.740	46.097
8	Florida Marlins	—	80	82	.494	4.25	4.34	.679	.662	45.484
9	Houston Astros	—	82	80	.506	4.65	4.89	.717	.735	42.041
10	Chicago Cubs	—	76	86	.469	4.77	4.76	.682	.726	37.750
11	New York Mets	—	71	91	.438	4.60	4.81	.687	.717	33.433
12	Pittsburgh Pirates	—	73	89	.451	4.79	5.14	.700	.765	29.928
13	Philadelphia Phillies	—	67	95	.414	4.01	4.88	.672	.713	22.649
14	San Francisco Giants	—	68	94	.420	4.64	5.32	.689	.760	22.411

Best Batters

Rank	Batter	Team	G	BA	B	O	BPO	BV	BPO+
1	Barry Bonds	Giants	158	.308	516	382	1.351	230.4	180.7
2	Gary Sheffield	Marlins	161	.314	498	387	1.287	203.9	169.3
3	Jeff Bagwell	Astros	162	.315	496	417	1.189	188.1	161.1
4	Ken Caminiti	Padres	146	.326	442	398	1.111	141.3	147.0
5	Barry Larkin	Reds	152	.298	439	400	1.098	126.5	140.5
6	Mike Piazza	Dodgers	148	.336	392	389	1.008	109.6	138.8
7	Bernard Gilkey	Mets	153	.317	423	425	.995	103.8	132.5
8	Ellis Burks	Rockies	156	.344	496	432	1.148	117.5	131.0
9	Chipper Jones	Braves	157	.309	426	436	.977	80.1	123.1
10	Todd Hundley	Mets	153	.259	382	414	.923	71.0	122.8

Extremes for Batters

Batter	Team	Best		Batter	Team	Worst
Barry Bonds	Giants	230.4	**BV**	Rey Ordonez	Mets	-114.2
Ken Caminiti	Padres	145.6	**SE+**	Mickey Morandini	Phillies	68.1
Barry Bonds	Giants	64.0	**SCV**	Jeff Reed	Rockies	-47.0
Gary Sheffield	Marlins	200.2	**ISO+**	Rey Ordonez	Mets	29.3
Gary Sheffield	Marlins	80.6	**EXV**	Eric Young	Rockies	-57.0
Eric Young	Rockies	311.7	**CT+**	Henry Rodriguez	Expos	58.3
Lance Johnson	Mets	-81.5	**SOV**	Henry Rodriguez	Expos	66.7
Rickey Henderson	Padres	265.1	**EY+**	Rey Ordonez	Mets	24.5
Rickey Henderson	Padres	76.6	**BBV**	Mark Grudzielanek	Expos	-35.7

Best Pitchers

Rank	Pitcher	Team	G	ERA	B	O	BPO	BV	BPO+
1	Kevin Brown	Marlins	32	1.89	314	705	.445	-161.5	66.0
2	John Smoltz	Braves	35	2.94	388	765	.507	-146.8	72.5
2	Greg Maddux	Braves	35	2.72	380	750	.507	-144.4	72.5
4	Curt Schilling	Phillies	26	3.19	306	551	.555	-74.6	80.4
5	Jeff Fassero	Expos	34	3.30	412	717	.575	-89.3	82.2
6	Tom Glavine	Braves	36	2.98	424	714	.594	-75.2	84.9
7	Al Leiter	Marlins	33	2.93	386	645	.598	-49.0	88.7
8	Pedro Martinez	Expos	33	3.70	407	655	.621	-50.9	88.9
9	Shane Reynolds	Astros	35	3.65	421	721	.584	-50.2	89.4
10	Donovan Osborne	Cardinals	30	3.53	371	594	.625	-34.1	91.6

Extremes for Pitchers

Pitcher	Team	Best		Pitcher	Team	Worst
Kevin Brown	Marlins	-161.5	**BV**	Mark Leiter	Giants-Expos	87.9
Kevin Brown	Marlins	48.2	**ERA+**	William VanLandingham	Giants	139.2
Kevin Brown	Marlins	-52.8	**ERV**	Jim Bullinger	Cubs	34.3
Kevin Brown	Marlins	51.2	**ISO+**	Mark Leiter	Giants-Expos	146.8
Kevin Brown	Marlins	-55.3	**EXV**	Mark Leiter	Giants-Expos	51.4
John Smoltz	Braves	65.4	**CT+**	Kevin Ritz	Rockies	152.1
John Smoltz	Braves	95.5	**SOV**	Terry Mulholland	Phillies	-56.3
Greg Maddux	Braves	23.6	**EY+**	Al Leiter	Marlins	172.5
Greg Maddux	Braves	-54.9	**BBV**	Al Leiter	Marlins	48.7

1997 American League

Standings

Rank	Team	Post	W	L	Pct.	R	RA	BPO	BPOA	TS
1	New York Yankees	P	96	66	.593	5.50	4.25	.779	.675	74.364
2	Baltimore Orioles	P	98	64	.605	5.01	4.20	.741	.694	67.599
3	Cleveland Indians	LP	86	75	.534	5.39	5.06	.810	.758	67.467
4	Seattle Mariners	P	90	72	.556	5.71	5.14	.828	.748	63.106
5	Anaheim Angels	—	84	78	.519	5.12	4.90	.734	.757	47.912
6	Boston Red Sox	—	78	84	.481	5.25	5.29	.775	.763	44.782
7	Detroit Tigers	—	79	83	.488	4.84	4.88	.725	.731	43.870
8	Texas Rangers	—	77	85	.475	4.98	5.08	.728	.742	41.415
9	Chicago White Sox	—	80	81	.497	4.84	5.17	.724	.746	41.279
10	Toronto Blue Jays	—	76	86	.469	4.04	4.28	.662	.686	38.777
11	Milwaukee Brewers	—	78	83	.484	4.23	4.61	.679	.713	38.597
12	Kansas City Royals	—	67	94	.416	4.64	5.09	.707	.730	31.565
13	Minnesota Twins	—	68	94	.420	4.77	5.31	.708	.755	29.228
14	Oakland Athletics	—	65	97	.401	4.72	5.84	.731	.852	16.589

Best Batters

Rank	Batter	Team	G	BA	B	O	BPO	BV	BPO+
1	Frank Thomas	White Sox	146	.347	444	369	1.203	167.5	160.6
2	Jim Thome	Indians	147	.286	419	372	1.126	130.2	145.1
3	Ken Griffey Jr.	Mariners	157	.304	504	451	1.118	155.3	144.6
4	Edgar Martinez	Mariners	155	.330	438	394	1.112	133.4	143.8
5	David Justice	Indians	139	.329	385	356	1.081	108.6	139.3
6	Mo Vaughn	Red Sox	141	.315	398	376	1.059	105.4	136.0
7	Bernie Williams	Yankees	129	.328	374	368	1.016	93.2	133.2
8	Jeromy Burnitz	Brewers	153	.281	376	379	.992	84.0	128.8
9	Tino Martinez	Yankees	158	.296	437	447	.978	95.9	128.1
10	Tim Salmon	Angels	157	.296	423	440	.961	90.2	127.1

Extremes for Batters

Batter	Team	Best		Batter	Team	Worst
Frank Thomas	White Sox	167.5	BV	Gary DiSarcina	Angels	-122.7
Frank Thomas	White Sox	142.3	SE+	Gary DiSarcina	Angels	73.1
Ken Griffey Jr.	Mariners	59.5	SCV	Alex Gonzalez	Blue Jays	-38.2
Ken Griffey Jr.	Mariners	203.3	ISO+	Tom Goodwin	Royals-Rangers	45.5
Ken Griffey Jr.	Mariners	105.7	EXV	Tom Goodwin	Royals-Rangers	-52.6
Ozzie Guillen	White Sox	360.3	CT+	Jay Buhner	Mariners	58.2
Gary DiSarcina	Angels	-73.5	SOV	Melvin Nieves	Tigers	90.1
Jim Thome	Indians	199.5	EY+	Gerald Williams	Brewers	33.5
Jay Buhner	Mariners	55.6	BBV	Gerald Williams	Brewers	-35.7

Best Pitchers

Rank	Pitcher	Team	G	ERA	B	O	BPO	BV	BPO+
1	Roger Clemens	Blue Jays	34	2.05	375	796	.471	-191.8	66.2
2	Randy Johnson	Mariners	30	2.28	346	643	.538	-112.7	75.4
3	Andy Pettitte	Yankees	35	2.88	397	728	.545	-112.9	77.9
4	Tom Gordon	Red Sox	42	3.74	327	559	.585	-75.3	81.3
5	Justin Thompson	Tigers	32	3.02	389	669	.581	-87.8	81.6
6	Scott Erickson	Orioles	34	3.69	401	678	.591	-67.2	85.7
7	Mike Mussina	Orioles	33	3.20	398	672	.592	-66.0	85.8
8	Kevin Appier	Royals	34	3.40	435	707	.615	-71.1	86.0
9	Jamie Moyer	Mariners	30	3.86	350	568	.616	-55.2	86.4
10	Brad Radke	Twins	35	3.87	454	724	.627	-67.1	87.1

Extremes for Pitchers

Pitcher	Team	Best		Pitcher	Team	Worst
Roger Clemens	Blue Jays	-191.8	BV	Steve Karsay	Athletics	78.4
Roger Clemens	Blue Jays	47.9	ERA+	Jaime Navarro	White Sox	140.6
Roger Clemens	Blue Jays	-65.3	ERV	Jaime Navarro	White Sox	39.0
Roger Clemens	Blue Jays	50.4	ISO+	Doug Drabek	White Sox	146.7
Roger Clemens	Blue Jays	-72.9	EXV	Scott Sanders	Mariners-Tigers	51.4
Randy Johnson	Mariners	50.3	CT+	Dennis Springer	Angels	190.9
Randy Johnson	Mariners	144.5	SOV	Dennis Springer	Angels	-68.2
John Burkett	Rangers	43.6	EY+	Ken Hill	Rangers-Angels	139.9
John Burkett	Rangers	-37.5	BBV	Ken Hill	Rangers-Angels	26.2

1997 National League

Standings

Rank	Team	Post	W	L	Pct.	R	RA	BPO	BPOA	TS
1	Atlanta Braves	P	101	61	.623	4.88	3.59	.742	.600	78.525
2	Florida Marlins	WLP	92	70	.568	4.57	4.13	.720	.685	73.229
3	Houston Astros	P	84	78	.519	4.80	4.07	.742	.648	59.091
4	Los Angeles Dodgers	—	88	74	.543	4.58	3.98	.714	.668	57.592
5	New York Mets	—	88	74	.543	4.80	4.38	.697	.695	53.168
6	San Francisco Giants	P	90	72	.556	4.84	4.90	.736	.716	52.297
7	Colorado Rockies	—	83	79	.512	5.70	5.60	.824	.834	46.499
8	Pittsburgh Pirates	—	79	83	.488	4.48	4.69	.709	.727	40.816
9	Montreal Expos	—	78	84	.481	4.27	4.57	.695	.702	40.214
10	Saint Louis Cardinals	—	73	89	.451	4.25	4.37	.690	.673	39.805
11	San Diego Padres	—	76	86	.469	4.91	5.50	.723	.780	33.262
12	Cincinnati Reds	—	76	86	.469	4.02	4.72	.684	.731	33.201
13	Chicago Cubs	—	68	94	.420	4.24	4.69	.666	.765	25.827
14	Philadelphia Phillies	—	68	94	.420	4.12	5.19	.662	.766	20.921

Best Batters

Rank	Batter	Team	G	BA	B	O	BPO	BV	BPO+
1	Barry Bonds	Giants	159	.291	506	403	1.256	199.3	165.0
2	Larry Walker	Rockies	153	.366	538	387	1.390	206.6	162.3
3	Jeff Bagwell	Astros	162	.286	517	432	1.197	191.2	158.7
4	Mike Piazza	Dodgers	152	.362	437	380	1.150	160.7	158.2
5	Ray Lankford	Cardinals	133	.295	393	353	1.113	123.2	145.7
6	Craig Biggio	Astros	162	.309	482	445	1.083	146.4	143.6
7	Todd Hundley	Mets	132	.273	322	321	1.003	82.8	134.6
8	Tony Gwynn	Padres	149	.372	395	402	.983	99.0	133.4
9	Gary Sheffield	Marlins	135	.250	347	349	.994	85.4	132.7
10	Ken Caminiti	Padres	137	.290	348	366	.951	78.5	129.1

Extremes for Batters

Batter	Team	Best		Batter	Team	Worst
Larry Walker	Rockies	206.6	BV	Kirt Manwaring	Rockies	-109.5
Tony Gwynn	Padres	149.6	SE+	Deion Sanders	Reds	62.0
Tony Gwynn	Padres	66.0	SCV	Kirt Manwaring	Rockies	-52.8
Larry Walker	Rockies	193.6	ISO+	Edgar Renteria	Marlins	41.6
Larry Walker	Rockies	97.2	EXV	Edgar Renteria	Marlins	-54.8
Tony Gwynn	Padres	396.0	CT+	Ron Gant	Cardinals	56.4
Tony Gwynn	Padres	-82.9	SOV	Ron Gant	Cardinals	70.7
Gary Sheffield	Marlins	222.9	EY+	Shawon Dunston	Cubs-Pirates	18.0
Gary Sheffield	Marlins	60.6	BBV	Mark Grudzielanek	Expos	-37.3

Best Pitchers

Rank	Pitcher	Team	G	ERA	B	O	BPO	BV	BPO+
1	Greg Maddux	Braves	33	2.20	328	698	.470	-153.7	68.1
2	Pedro Martinez	Expos	31	1.90	344	733	.469	-157.6	68.6
3	Tom Glavine	Braves	33	2.96	396	729	.543	-107.1	78.7
4	Rick Reed	Mets	33	2.89	335	629	.533	-82.7	80.2
5	Kevin Brown	Marlins	33	2.69	389	712	.546	-87.6	81.6
6	John Smoltz	Braves	35	3.02	438	774	.566	-96.2	82.0
7	Curt Schilling	Phillies	35	2.97	434	763	.569	-94.2	82.2
8	Denny Neagle	Braves	34	2.97	403	704	.572	-82.9	82.9
9	Shawn Estes	Giants	32	3.18	357	610	.585	-56.3	86.4
10	Andy Benes	Cardinals	26	3.10	315	531	.593	-44.9	87.5

Extremes for Pitchers

Pitcher	Team	Best		Pitcher	Team	Worst
Pedro Martinez	Expos	-157.6	BV	Mark Leiter	Phillies	85.6
Pedro Martinez	Expos	48.7	ERA+	Mark Leiter	Phillies	143.3
Pedro Martinez	Expos	-53.8	ERV	Mark Leiter	Phillies	34.8
Greg Maddux	Braves	53.3	ISO+	Mark Leiter	Phillies	134.1
Greg Maddux	Braves	-56.2	EXV	Sterling Hitchcock	Padres	40.8
Pedro Martinez	Expos	57.8	CT+	Chris Holt	Astros	183.8
Pedro Martinez	Expos	128.8	SOV	Chris Holt	Astros	-79.6
Greg Maddux	Braves	19.4	EY+	Shawn Estes	Giants	147.1
Greg Maddux	Braves	-58.0	BBV	Al Leiter	Marlins	34.2

1998 American League

Standings

Rank	Team	Post	W	L	Pct.	R	RA	BPO	BPOA	TS
1	New York Yankees	WLP	114	48	.704	5.96	4.05	.823	.649	96.123
2	Boston Red Sox	P	92	70	.568	5.41	4.50	.781	.686	62.640
3	Cleveland Indians	P	89	73	.549	5.25	4.81	.785	.744	54.859
4	Toronto Blue Jays	—	88	74	.543	5.01	4.71	.782	.727	54.368
5	Texas Rangers	P	88	74	.543	5.80	5.38	.795	.753	54.277
6	Baltimore Orioles	—	79	83	.488	5.04	4.85	.767	.745	46.696
7	Seattle Mariners	—	76	85	.472	5.34	5.31	.800	.770	44.772
8	Anaheim Angels	—	85	77	.525	4.86	4.83	.707	.754	44.746
9	Chicago White Sox	—	80	82	.494	5.28	5.71	.762	.779	41.089
10	Oakland Athletics	—	74	88	.457	4.96	5.35	.714	.751	36.802
11	Minnesota Twins	—	70	92	.432	4.53	5.05	.662	.750	30.603
12	Kansas City Royals	—	72	89	.447	4.43	5.58	.686	.764	28.897
13	Detroit Tigers	—	65	97	.401	4.46	5.33	.693	.761	27.019
14	Tampa Bay Devil Rays	—	63	99	.389	3.83	4.64	.650	.728	25.582

Best Batters

Rank	Batter	Team	G	BA	B	O	BPO	BV	BPO+
1	Albert Belle	White Sox	163	.328	502	445	1.128	166.2	149.5
2	Jim Thome	Indians	123	.293	355	322	1.102	103.1	141.0
3	Bernie Williams	Yankees	128	.339	381	362	1.052	108.1	139.6
4	Edgar Martinez	Mariners	154	.322	431	398	1.083	120.5	138.8
5	Carlos Delgado	Blue Jays	142	.292	407	389	1.046	108.6	136.4
6	Tim Salmon	Angels	136	.300	350	339	1.032	89.5	134.4
7	Ken Griffey Jr.	Mariners	161	.284	494	476	1.038	122.6	133.0
8	Mo Vaughn	Red Sox	154	.337	432	420	1.029	106.4	132.7
9	Eric Davis	Orioles	131	.327	326	330	.988	77.2	131.0
10	Rafael Palmeiro	Orioles	162	.296	451	461	.978	103.4	129.8

Extremes for Batters

Batter	Team	Best		Batter	Team	Worst
Albert Belle	White Sox	166.2	BV	Sandy Alomar	Indians	-92.1
Tino Martinez	Yankees	140.0	SE+	Brian Hunter	Tigers	68.1
Juan Gonzalez	Rangers	63.2	SCV	Brian Hunter	Tigers	-46.4
Albert Belle	White Sox	199.4	ISO+	Tom Goodwin	Rangers	28.0
Ken Griffey Jr.	Mariners	99.6	EXV	Tom Goodwin	Rangers	-64.4
Mike Caruso	White Sox	241.2	CT+	Jim Thome	Indians	55.6
Mike Caruso	White Sox	-53.6	SOV	Jim Thome	Indians	62.5
Rickey Henderson	Athletics	210.1	EY+	Mike Caruso	White Sox	29.9
Rickey Henderson	Athletics	61.8	BBV	Garret Anderson	Angels	-34.5

Best Pitchers

Rank	Pitcher	Team	G	ERA	B	O	BPO	BV	BPO+
1	Roger Clemens	Blue Jays	33	2.65	386	714	.541	-128.4	75.0
2	Pedro Martinez	Red Sox	33	2.89	400	702	.570	-108.5	78.7
3	Kenny Rogers	Athletics	34	3.17	413	724	.570	-101.3	80.3
4	David Wells	Yankees	30	3.49	368	647	.569	-85.1	81.2
5	Mike Mussina	Orioles	29	3.49	372	623	.597	-68.5	84.4
6	Jamie Moyer	Mariners	34	3.53	453	710	.638	-65.2	87.4
6	Bret Saberhagen	Red Sox	31	3.96	333	526	.633	-48.0	87.4
8	Bartolo Colon	Indians	31	3.71	400	614	.651	-49.1	89.1
9	Brian Moehler	Tigers	33	3.90	437	670	.652	-52.6	89.3
10	David Cone	Yankees	31	3.55	394	621	.634	-40.8	90.6

Extremes for Pitchers

Pitcher	Team	Best		Pitcher	Team	Worst
Roger Clemens	Blue Jays	-128.4	BV	Jaime Navarro	White Sox	102.0
Roger Clemens	Blue Jays	59.2	ERA+	Jaime Navarro	White Sox	145.2
Roger Clemens	Blue Jays	-47.6	ERV	Jaime Navarro	White Sox	38.0
Roger Clemens	Blue Jays	62.9	ISO+	Woody Williams	Blue Jays	137.6
Roger Clemens	Blue Jays	-49.6	EXV	Ken Cloude	Mariners	49.4
Roger Clemens	Blue Jays	57.9	CT+	Jaime Navarro	White Sox	184.0
Roger Clemens	Blue Jays	114.0	SOV	Jaime Navarro	White Sox	-59.6
David Wells	Yankees	43.4	EY+	Tony Saunders	Devil Rays	161.2
Jamie Moyer	Mariners	-45.3	BBV	Tony Saunders	Devil Rays	41.7

1998 National League

Standings

Rank	Team	Post	W	L	Pct.	R	RA	BPO	BPOA	TS
1	Atlanta Braves	P	106	56	.654	5.10	3.59	.777	.594	77.144
2	Houston Astros	P	102	60	.630	5.40	3.83	.782	.652	72.465
3	San Diego Padres	LP	98	64	.605	4.62	3.92	.707	.649	70.298
4	San Francisco Giants	—	89	74	.546	5.18	4.53	.756	.706	55.986
5	Saint Louis Cardinals	—	83	79	.512	4.97	4.80	.775	.708	51.372
6	Chicago Cubs	P	90	73	.552	5.10	4.86	.736	.740	51.311
7	New York Mets	—	88	74	.543	4.36	3.98	.678	.690	50.889
8	Los Angeles Dodgers	—	83	79	.512	4.13	4.19	.656	.658	46.406
9	Cincinnati Reds	—	77	85	.475	4.63	4.69	.706	.722	42.449
10	Colorado Rockies	—	77	85	.475	5.10	5.28	.764	.777	41.950
11	Philadelphia Phillies	—	75	87	.463	4.40	4.99	.678	.733	36.401
12	Pittsburgh Pirates	—	69	93	.426	3.99	4.40	.646	.680	35.309
13	Milwaukee Brewers	—	74	88	.457	4.36	5.01	.676	.765	33.688
14	Montreal Expos	—	65	97	.401	3.98	4.83	.655	.713	29.411
15	Arizona Diamondbacks	—	65	97	.401	4.10	5.01	.653	.716	28.902
16	Florida Marlins	—	54	108	.333	4.12	5.70	.641	.823	12.978

Best Batters

Rank	Batter	Team	G	BA	B	O	BPO	BV	BPO+
1	Mark McGwire	Cardinals	155	.299	556	369	1.507	276.5	199.0
2	Barry Bonds	Giants	156	.303	509	419	1.215	196.0	162.6
3	Gary Sheffield	Marlins-Dodgers	130	.302	363	328	1.107	120.2	149.5
4	Jeff Bagwell	Astros	147	.304	441	402	1.097	138.7	145.9
5	John Olerud	Mets	160	.354	417	385	1.083	128.8	144.7
6	Larry Walker	Rockies	130	.363	370	306	1.209	110.5	142.6
7	Greg Vaughn	Padres	158	.272	441	432	1.021	126.9	140.4
8	Moises Alou	Astros	159	.312	446	425	1.049	126.4	139.6
9	Ray Lankford	Cardinals	154	.293	407	390	1.044	111.6	137.8
10	Andres Galarraga	Braves	153	.305	430	405	1.062	117.8	137.7

Extremes for Batters

Batter	Team	Best		Batter	Team	Worst
Mark McGwire	Cardinals	276.5	BV	Neifi Perez	Rockies	-115.5
Jeff Kent	Giants	153.3	SE+	Desi Relaford	Phillies	65.8
Jeff Kent	Giants	66.4	SCV	Neifi Perez	Rockies	-61.0
Mark McGwire	Cardinals	281.9	ISO+	Rey Ordonez	Mets	33.8
Mark McGwire	Cardinals	149.0	EXV	Tony Womack	Pirates	-63.2
Tony Gwynn	Padres	470.9	CT+	Mark McGwire	Cardinals	57.0
Tony Gwynn	Padres	-66.8	SOV	Mark McGwire	Cardinals	66.6
Mark McGwire	Cardinals	241.3	EY+	Rey Ordonez	Mets	35.1
Mark McGwire	Cardinals	78.5	BBV	Dante Bichette	Rockies	-33.0

Best Pitchers

Rank	Pitcher	Team	G	ERA	B	O	BPO	BV	BPO+
1	Greg Maddux	Braves	34	2.22	374	766	.488	-146.8	71.8
1	Kevin Brown	Padres	36	2.38	361	773	.467	-141.9	71.8
3	Tom Glavine	Braves	33	2.47	366	683	.536	-98.4	78.8
4	John Smoltz	Braves	26	2.90	273	504	.542	-69.7	79.7
5	Al Leiter	Mets	28	2.47	315	584	.539	-75.3	80.7
6	Omar Daal	Diamondbacks	33	2.88	279	490	.569	-55.6	83.4
7	Curt Schilling	Phillies	35	3.25	471	808	.583	-91.1	83.8
8	Dustin Hermanson	Expos	32	3.13	335	572	.586	-53.8	86.2
9	Kerry Wood	Cubs	26	3.40	305	499	.611	-47.1	86.6
10	Pete Harnisch	Reds	32	3.14	391	630	.621	-45.4	89.6

Extremes for Pitchers

Pitcher	Team	Best		Pitcher	Team	Worst
Greg Maddux	Braves	-146.8	BV	Livan Hernandez	Marlins	95.5
Greg Maddux	Braves	56.7	ERA+	Javier Vazquez	Expos	153.5
Greg Maddux	Braves	-47.4	ERV	Andy Larkin	Marlins	48.6
Kevin Brown	Padres	44.0	ISO+	Willie Blair	Diamondbacks-Mets	142.9
Kevin Brown	Padres	-71.2	EXV	Brian Anderson	Diamondbacks	42.4
Kerry Wood	Cubs	51.8	CT+	Jamey Wright	Rockies	178.8
Kerry Wood	Cubs	112.2	SOV	Jamey Wright	Rockies	-67.7
Brian Anderson	Diamondbacks	34.9	EY+	Kerry Wood	Cubs	149.9
Greg Maddux	Braves	-41.3	BBV	Hideo Nomo	Dodgers-Mets	39.6

1999 American League

Standings

Rank	Team	Post	W	L	Pct.	R	RA	BPO	BPOA	TS
1	New York Yankees	WLP	98	64	.605	5.56	4.51	.814	.705	83.564
2	Cleveland Indians	P	97	65	.599	6.23	5.31	.857	.766	67.480
3	Boston Red Sox	P	94	68	.580	5.16	4.43	.771	.677	64.648
4	Texas Rangers	P	95	67	.586	5.83	5.30	.827	.758	62.355
5	Oakland Athletics	—	87	75	.537	5.51	5.22	.797	.741	55.246
6	Toronto Blue Jays	—	84	78	.519	5.45	5.32	.795	.781	49.821
7	Baltimore Orioles	—	78	84	.481	5.25	5.03	.781	.764	47.182
8	Seattle Mariners	—	79	83	.488	5.30	5.59	.788	.815	41.619
9	Chicago White Sox	—	75	86	.466	4.80	5.37	.723	.782	35.629
10	Detroit Tigers	—	69	92	.429	4.64	5.48	.732	.776	31.208
11	Kansas City Royals	—	64	97	.398	5.32	5.72	.752	.807	30.530
12	Anaheim Angels	—	70	92	.432	4.39	5.10	.661	.749	29.688
13	Tampa Bay Devil Rays	—	69	93	.426	4.77	5.64	.704	.802	27.389
14	Minnesota Twins	—	63	97	.394	4.26	5.25	.659	.767	22.942

Best Batters

Rank	Batter	Team	G	BA	B	O	BPO	BV	BPO+
1	Manny Ramirez	Indians	147	.333	466	373	1.249	158.9	151.8
2	Edgar Martinez	Mariners	142	.337	391	350	1.117	117.1	142.7
3	Rafael Palmeiro	Rangers	158	.324	467	408	1.145	131.7	139.3
4	Derek Jeter	Yankees	158	.349	477	437	1.092	130.9	137.8
5	Jason Giambi	Athletics	158	.315	439	414	1.060	119.7	137.5
5	John Jaha	Athletics	142	.276	369	348	1.060	100.6	137.5
7	Nomar Garciaparra	Red Sox	135	.357	398	360	1.106	107.8	137.1
8	Ken Griffey Jr.	Mariners	160	.285	473	450	1.051	120.8	134.3
9	Roberto Alomar	Indians	159	.323	468	425	1.101	118.1	133.8
10	Jim Thome	Indians	146	.277	402	367	1.095	99.9	133.1

Extremes for Batters

Batter	Team	Best		Batter	Team	Worst
Manny Ramirez	Indians	158.9	BV	Mike Caruso	White Sox	-139.2
Manny Ramirez	Indians	159.5	SE+	Mike Caruso	White Sox	69.2
Manny Ramirez	Indians	94.0	SCV	Mike Caruso	White Sox	-41.5
Manny Ramirez	Indians	182.9	ISO+	Mike Caruso	White Sox	26.9
Manny Ramirez	Indians	78.0	EXV	Mike Caruso	White Sox	-68.0
Mike Caruso	White Sox	249.6	CT+	Jim Thome	Indians	48.9
Nomar Garciaparra	Red Sox	-54.0	SOV	Jim Thome	Indians	87.3
Jim Thome	Indians	201.6	EY+	Deivi Cruz	Tigers	23.5
Jim Thome	Indians	57.5	BBV	Deivi Cruz	Tigers	-39.1

Best Pitchers

Rank	Pitcher	Team	G	ERA	B	O	BPO	BV	BPO+
1	Pedro Martinez	Red Sox	31	2.07	301	650	.463	-182.9	62.2
2	Jamie Moyer	Mariners	32	3.87	421	686	.614	-76.6	84.6
3	Eric Milton	Twins	34	4.49	399	618	.646	-72.4	84.7
4	Jose Rosado	Royals	33	3.85	402	627	.641	-71.8	84.8
5	Bartolo Colon	Indians	32	3.95	406	613	.662	-60.0	87.1
6	Mike Mussina	Orioles	31	3.50	391	610	.641	-48.2	89.0
7	Brad Radke	Twins	33	3.75	447	654	.683	-51.8	89.6
8	Chuck Finley	Angels	33	4.43	438	646	.678	-42.5	91.1
9	Mike Sirotka	White Sox	32	4.00	436	636	.686	-37.1	92.2
10	Orlando Hernandez	Yankees	33	4.12	442	647	.683	-29.2	93.8

Extremes for Pitchers

Pitcher	Team	Best		Pitcher	Team	Worst
Pedro Martinez	Red Sox	-182.9	BV	Jeff Fassero	Mariners-Rangers	136.8
Pedro Martinez	Red Sox	43.5	ERA+	LaTroy Hawkins	Twins	138.3
Pedro Martinez	Red Sox	-63.8	ERV	Jeff Fassero	Mariners-Rangers	46.4
Pedro Martinez	Red Sox	52.1	ISO+	Rick Helling	Rangers	135.1
Pedro Martinez	Red Sox	-59.8	EXV	Jeff Fassero	Mariners-Rangers	52.3
Pedro Martinez	Red Sox	45.5	CT+	Omar Olivares	Angels-Athletics	165.5
Pedro Martinez	Red Sox	170.6	SOV	Omar Olivares	Angels-Athletics	-53.9
Gil Heredia	Athletics	43.4	EY+	Bobby Witt	Devil Rays	138.0
Gil Heredia	Athletics	-39.1	BBV	Bobby Witt	Devil Rays	26.2

1999 National League

Standings

Rank	Team	Post	W	L	Pct.	R	RA	BPO	BPOA	TS
1	Atlanta Braves	LP	103	59	.636	5.19	4.08	.764	.645	78.705
2	Arizona Diamondbacks	P	100	62	.617	5.60	4.17	.803	.688	71.067
3	Houston Astros	P	97	65	.599	5.08	4.17	.777	.670	65.886
4	Cincinnati Reds	—	96	67	.589	5.31	4.36	.784	.719	62.643
5	New York Mets	P	97	66	.595	5.23	4.36	.795	.732	62.580
6	San Francisco Giants	—	86	76	.531	5.38	5.13	.780	.753	50.885
7	Los Angeles Dodgers	—	77	85	.475	4.90	4.86	.747	.738	43.448
8	Pittsburgh Pirates	—	78	83	.484	4.81	4.86	.731	.735	43.036
9	Philadelphia Phillies	—	77	85	.475	5.19	5.22	.768	.781	41.680
10	Saint Louis Cardinals	—	75	86	.466	5.02	5.20	.750	.761	40.119
11	San Diego Padres	—	74	88	.457	4.38	4.82	.704	.728	36.971
12	Milwaukee Brewers	—	74	87	.460	5.06	5.50	.763	.815	35.496
13	Montreal Expos	—	68	94	.420	4.43	5.27	.694	.748	29.440
14	Colorado Rockies	—	72	90	.444	5.59	6.35	.787	.909	28.026
15	Chicago Cubs	—	67	95	.414	4.61	5.68	.709	.793	25.702
16	Florida Marlins	—	64	98	.395	4.27	5.26	.670	.785	22.531

Best Batters

Rank	Batter	Team	G	BA	B	O	BPO	BV	BPO+
1	Mark McGwire	Cardinals	153	.278	503	393	1.280	184.6	158.0
2	Jeff Bagwell	Astros	162	.304	529	427	1.239	187.8	155.0
3	Chipper Jones	Braves	157	.319	518	415	1.248	179.1	152.8
4	Larry Walker	Rockies	127	.379	397	294	1.350	127.5	147.3
5	Brian Giles	Pirates	141	.315	432	381	1.134	123.9	140.2
6	Bobby Abreu	Phillies	152	.335	443	389	1.139	121.8	137.9
7	Carl Everett	Astros	123	.325	363	335	1.084	95.3	135.6
8	Jeromy Burnitz	Brewers	130	.270	382	361	1.058	95.9	133.5
9	Rickey Henderson	Mets	121	.315	329	322	1.022	77.3	130.7
10	Fernando Tatis	Cardinals	149	.298	420	401	1.047	95.1	129.3

Extremes for Batters

Batter	Team	Best		Batter	Team	Worst
Jeff Bagwell	Astros	187.8	BV	Neifi Perez	Rockies	-142.7
Mike Piazza	Mets	137.3	SE+	Joe McEwing	Cardinals	74.9
Jeff Bagwell	Astros	59.1	SCV	Neifi Perez	Rockies	-49.4
Mark McGwire	Cardinals	239.4	ISO+	Rey Ordonez	Mets	35.8
Mark McGwire	Cardinals	127.0	EXV	Neifi Perez	Rockies	-57.3
Eric Young	Dodgers	306.6	CT+	Preston Wilson	Marlins	55.8
Neifi Perez	Rockies	-63.4	SOV	Preston Wilson	Marlins	68.9
Jeff Bagwell	Astros	197.4	EY+	Alex Gonzalez	Marlins	27.6
Jeff Bagwell	Astros	65.6	BBV	Neifi Perez	Rockies	-42.8

Best Pitchers

Rank	Pitcher	Team	G	ERA	B	O	BPO	BV	BPO+
1	Kevin Millwood	Braves	33	2.68	367	685	.536	-134.8	73.1
2	Kevin Brown	Dodgers	35	3.00	410	768	.534	-133.5	75.4
3	Randy Johnson	Diamondbacks	35	2.48	461	824	.559	-146.0	75.9
4	John Smoltz	Braves	29	3.19	325	560	.580	-85.2	79.2
5	Mike Hampton	Astros	34	2.90	410	711	.577	-100.0	80.4
6	Curt Schilling	Phillies	24	3.54	331	541	.612	-75.8	81.4
7	Omar Daal	Diamondbacks	32	3.65	406	649	.626	-72.1	84.9
8	Todd Ritchie	Pirates	28	3.49	333	517	.644	-47.2	87.6
9	Shane Reynolds	Astros	35	3.85	447	705	.634	-58.7	88.4
10	Kris Benson	Pirates	31	4.07	390	596	.654	-48.3	89.0

Extremes for Pitchers

Pitcher	Team	Best		Pitcher	Team	Worst
Randy Johnson	Diamondbacks	-146.0	BV	Chan Ho Park	Dodgers	87.7
Randy Johnson	Diamondbacks	56.3	ERA+	Brian Meadows	Marlins	135.2
Randy Johnson	Diamondbacks	-58.2	ERV	Mark Gardner	Giants	37.0
Mike Hampton	Astros	52.3	ISO+	Chad Ogea	Phillies	145.2
Mike Hampton	Astros	-64.7	EXV	Chad Ogea	Phillies	50.4
Randy Johnson	Diamondbacks	50.8	CT+	Scott Karl	Brewers	195.5
Randy Johnson	Diamondbacks	179.0	SOV	Scott Karl	Brewers	-70.7
Greg Maddux	Braves	36.2	EY+	Russ Ortiz	Giants	154.8
Greg Maddux	Braves	-51.0	BBV	Russ Ortiz	Giants	42.5

2000 American League

Standings

Rank	Team	Post	W	L	Pct.	R	RA	BPO	BPOA	TS
1	New York Yankees	WLP	87	74	.540	5.41	5.06	.787	.730	71.883
2	Chicago White Sox	P	95	67	.586	6.04	5.18	.816	.745	66.438
3	Seattle Mariners	P	91	71	.562	5.60	4.81	.808	.721	64.047
4	Cleveland Indians	—	90	72	.556	5.86	5.04	.839	.755	63.454
5	Oakland Athletics	P	91	70	.565	5.88	5.05	.806	.741	63.272
6	Boston Red Sox	—	85	77	.525	4.89	4.60	.727	.708	51.241
7	Anaheim Angels	—	82	80	.506	5.33	5.36	.809	.783	47.162
8	Toronto Blue Jays	—	83	79	.512	5.31	5.60	.784	.785	44.052
9	Detroit Tigers	—	79	83	.488	5.08	5.10	.746	.735	43.926
10	Kansas City Royals	—	77	85	.475	5.43	5.74	.741	.834	33.092
11	Baltimore Orioles	—	74	88	.457	4.90	5.64	.745	.792	30.979
12	Texas Rangers	—	71	91	.438	5.23	6.01	.759	.837	26.323
13	Tampa Bay Devil Rays	—	69	92	.429	4.55	5.23	.686	.772	25.349
14	Minnesota Twins	—	69	93	.426	4.62	5.43	.698	.780	24.224

Best Batters

Rank	Batter	Team	G	BA	B	O	BPO	BV	BPO+
1	Jason Giambi	Athletics	152	.333	486	357	1.361	206.0	173.6
2	Carlos Delgado	Blue Jays	162	.344	520	390	1.333	203.3	164.2
3	Manny Ramirez	Indians	118	.351	400	299	1.338	154.5	162.9
4	Alex Rodriguez	Mariners	148	.316	469	404	1.161	152.8	148.3
5	Frank Thomas	White Sox	159	.328	490	415	1.181	154.3	146.0
6	Edgar Martinez	Mariners	153	.324	434	397	1.093	123.3	139.7
7	Nomar Garciaparra	Red Sox	140	.372	392	349	1.123	110.0	139.0
8	Troy Glaus	Angels	159	.284	469	429	1.093	118.2	133.7
9	Jorge Posada	Yankees	151	.287	387	377	1.027	84.5	127.9
10	Carl Everett	Red Sox	137	.300	367	360	1.019	76.1	126.2

Extremes for Batters

Batter	Team	Best		Batter	Team	Worst
Jason Giambi	Athletics	206.0	**BV**	Rey Sanchez	Royals	-113.0
Alex Rodriguez	Mariners	143.9	**SE+**	Rey Sanchez	Royals	76.5
Alex Rodriguez	Mariners	68.6	**SCV**	Benji Gil	Angels	-39.5
Manny Ramirez	Indians	188.6	**ISO+**	Rey Sanchez	Royals	27.2
Troy Glaus	Angels	77.9	**EXV**	Rey Sanchez	Royals	-67.1
Bengie Molina	Angels	246.2	**CT+**	Jim Thome	Indians	55.5
Deivi Cruz	Tigers	-51.3	**SOV**	Jim Thome	Indians	76.1
Jason Giambi	Athletics	212.9	**EY+**	Deivi Cruz	Tigers	18.8
Jason Giambi	Athletics	69.5	**BBV**	Deivi Cruz	Tigers	-47.6

Best Pitchers

Rank	Pitcher	Team	G	ERA	B	O	BPO	BV	BPO+
1	Pedro Martinez	Red Sox	29	1.74	258	657	.393	-228.8	53.0
2	Mike Mussina	Orioles	34	3.79	452	724	.624	-70.5	86.5
3	Bartolo Colon	Indians	30	3.88	370	566	.654	-54.8	87.1
4	David Wells	Blue Jays	35	4.11	461	693	.665	-57.1	89.0
5	Mike Sirotka	White Sox	32	3.79	391	589	.664	-47.0	89.3
6	Roger Clemens	Yankees	32	3.70	414	622	.666	-42.2	90.8
7	Chuck Finley	Indians	34	4.17	448	653	.686	-42.1	91.4
8	Andy Pettitte	Yankees	32	4.35	425	627	.678	-34.8	92.4
9	Eric Milton	Twins	33	4.86	423	605	.699	-33.9	92.6
9	Tim Hudson	Athletics	32	4.14	404	609	.663	-32.2	92.6

Extremes for Pitchers

Pitcher	Team	Best		Pitcher	Team	Worst
Pedro Martinez	Red Sox	-228.8	**BV**	David Cone	Yankees	93.5
Pedro Martinez	Red Sox	36.5	**ERA+**	Pat Rapp	Orioles	132.3
Pedro Martinez	Red Sox	-73.1	**ERV**	Roy Halladay	Blue Jays	43.9
Pedro Martinez	Red Sox	56.8	**ISO+**	Jeff Suppan	Royals	124.3
Pedro Martinez	Red Sox	-54.1	**EXV**	Jeff Suppan	Royals	34.1
Pedro Martinez	Red Sox	49.8	**CT+**	Scott Schoeneweis	Angels	153.7
Pedro Martinez	Red Sox	142.5	**SOV**	Scott Schoeneweis	Angels	-41.9
David Wells	Blue Jays	35.9	**EY+**	Bartolo Colon	Indians	136.4
David Wells	Blue Jays	-55.4	**BBV**	Dan Reichert	Royals	31.0

2000 National League

Standings

Rank	Team	Post	W	L	Pct.	R	RA	BPO	BPOA	TS
1	San Francisco Giants	P	97	65	.599	5.71	4.61	.835	.727	72.401
2	New York Mets	LP	94	68	.580	4.98	4.56	.755	.707	70.288
3	Atlanta Braves	P	95	67	.586	5.00	4.41	.762	.675	65.875
4	Saint Louis Cardinals	P	95	67	.586	5.48	4.76	.808	.743	65.115
5	Los Angeles Dodgers	—	86	76	.531	4.93	4.50	.755	.711	55.728
6	Arizona Diamondbacks	—	85	77	.525	4.89	4.65	.734	.712	51.954
7	Cincinnati Reds	—	85	77	.525	5.06	4.69	.766	.760	51.782
8	Colorado Rockies	—	82	80	.506	5.98	5.54	.807	.815	49.338
9	Houston Astros	—	72	90	.444	5.79	5.83	.838	.825	41.270
10	Florida Marlins	—	79	82	.491	4.54	4.95	.722	.762	38.984
11	San Diego Padres	—	76	86	.469	4.64	5.03	.703	.735	37.705
12	Milwaukee Brewers	—	73	89	.451	4.54	5.07	.694	.756	32.415
13	Pittsburgh Pirates	—	69	93	.426	4.90	5.48	.727	.782	30.089
14	Philadelphia Phillies	—	65	97	.401	4.37	5.12	.700	.774	24.967
15	Chicago Cubs	—	65	97	.401	4.72	5.58	.723	.791	24.576
16	Montreal Expos	—	67	95	.414	4.56	5.57	.707	.790	23.592

Best Batters

Rank	Batter	Team	G	BA	B	O	BPO	BV	BPO+
1	Barry Bonds	Giants	143	.306	468	349	1.341	195.7	171.9
2	Gary Sheffield	Dodgers	141	.325	437	363	1.204	149.7	152.1
3	Todd Helton	Rockies	160	.372	527	389	1.355	165.3	145.7
4	Brian Giles	Pirates	156	.315	467	406	1.150	136.9	141.5
5	Jeff Kent	Giants	159	.334	470	426	1.103	137.6	141.4
6	Sammy Sosa	Cubs	156	.320	491	435	1.129	139.9	139.8
7	Vladimir Guerrero	Expos	154	.345	458	403	1.136	125.9	137.9
8	Jim Edmonds	Cardinals	152	.295	434	387	1.121	118.0	137.3
9	Jeff Bagwell	Astros	159	.310	501	439	1.141	131.9	135.8
10	Mike Piazza	Mets	136	.324	363	345	1.052	91.2	133.6

Extremes for Batters

Batter	Team	Best		Batter	Team	Worst
Barry Bonds	Giants	195.7	BV	Neifi Perez	Rockies	-133.1
Barry Bonds	Giants	141.1	SE+	Pat Meares	Pirates	74.4
Jeff Bagwell	Astros	59.1	SCV	Neifi Perez	Rockies	-51.0
Barry Bonds	Giants	218.8	ISO+	Luis Castillo	Marlins	30.7
Barry Bonds	Giants	99.4	EXV	Luis Castillo	Marlins	-65.6
Mark Grace	Cubs	326.7	CT+	Jim Edmonds	Cardinals	56.2
Eric Young	Cubs	-69.9	SOV	Ray Lankford	Cardinals	77.9
Barry Bonds	Giants	176.7	EY+	Neifi Perez	Rockies	35.1
Barry Bonds	Giants	41.2	BBV	Neifi Perez	Rockies	-44.4

Best Pitchers

Rank	Pitcher	Team	G	ERA	B	O	BPO	BV	BPO+
1	Greg Maddux	Braves	35	3.00	417	758	.550	-133.8	75.7
2	Kevin Brown	Dodgers	33	2.58	380	700	.543	-116.1	76.6
3	Randy Johnson	Diamondbacks	35	2.64	447	748	.598	-112.5	79.9
4	Tom Glavine	Braves	35	3.40	441	728	.606	-88.0	83.4
5	Mike Hampton	Mets	33	3.14	394	664	.593	-74.5	84.1
6	Curt Schilling	Phillies-Diamondbacks	29	3.81	397	635	.625	-73.6	84.4
7	Al Leiter	Mets	31	3.20	400	634	.631	-47.3	89.4
8	Chan Ho Park	Dodgers	34	3.27	434	684	.635	-50.8	89.5
9	Brian Bohanon	Rockies	34	4.68	399	532	.750	-46.3	89.6
10	Darryl Kile	Cardinals	34	3.91	464	701	.662	-48.3	90.6
10	Rick Ankiel	Cardinals	31	3.50	347	524	.662	-35.9	90.6

Extremes for Pitchers

Pitcher	Team	Best		Pitcher	Team	Worst
Greg Maddux	Braves	-133.8	BV	Jose Lima	Astros	126.5
Randy Johnson	Diamondbacks	58.8	ERA+	Jose Lima	Astros	143.9
Randy Johnson	Diamondbacks	-51.1	ERV	Jose Lima	Astros	44.2
Mike Hampton	Mets	55.3	ISO+	Jose Lima	Astros	151.9
Greg Maddux	Braves	-55.6	EXV	Jose Lima	Astros	72.4
Randy Johnson	Diamondbacks	50.1	CT+	Kirk Rueter	Giants	191.4
Randy Johnson	Diamondbacks	173.0	SOV	Kirk Rueter	Giants	-64.9
Greg Maddux	Braves	35.2	EY+	Shawn Estes	Giants	155.2
Greg Maddux	Braves	-55.2	BBV	Matt Clement	Padres	42.9

2001 American League

Standings

Rank	Team	Post	W	L	Pct.	R	RA	BPO	BPOA	TS
1	Seattle Mariners	P	116	46	.716	5.72	3.87	.811	.624	81.959
2	Oakland Athletics	P	102	60	.630	5.46	3.98	.764	.633	70.213
3	New York Yankees	LP	95	65	.594	4.99	4.43	.748	.679	68.361
4	Cleveland Indians	P	91	71	.562	5.54	5.07	.787	.730	55.699
5	Minnesota Twins	—	85	77	.525	4.76	4.73	.739	.721	48.445
6	Chicago White Sox	—	83	79	.512	4.93	4.91	.761	.730	48.057
7	Boston Red Sox	—	82	79	.509	4.80	4.63	.728	.715	47.697
8	Toronto Blue Jays	—	80	82	.494	4.73	4.65	.727	.734	44.975
9	Anaheim Angels	—	75	87	.463	4.27	4.51	.695	.706	40.612
10	Texas Rangers	—	73	89	.451	5.49	5.98	.797	.842	36.637
11	Kansas City Royals	—	65	97	.401	4.50	5.30	.669	.767	28.300
12	Detroit Tigers	—	66	96	.407	4.47	5.41	.688	.797	27.544
13	Baltimore Orioles	—	63	98	.391	4.24	5.12	.660	.761	26.983
14	Tampa Bay Devil Rays	—	62	100	.383	4.15	5.48	.652	.783	22.360

Best Batters

Rank	Batter	Team	G	BA	B	O	BPO	BV	BPO+
1	Jason Giambi	Athletics	154	.342	496	368	1.348	216.9	177.7
2	Jim Thome	Indians	156	.291	446	386	1.155	149.2	150.3
3	Edgar Martinez	Mariners	132	.306	370	347	1.066	115.2	145.2
4	Manny Ramirez	Red Sox	142	.306	413	379	1.090	122.7	142.3
5	Alex Rodriguez	Rangers	162	.318	511	460	1.111	151.2	142.0
6	Roberto Alomar	Indians	157	.336	443	415	1.067	123.9	138.8
7	Carlos Delgado	Blue Jays	162	.279	443	426	1.040	112.7	134.1
8	Bret Boone	Mariners	158	.331	432	451	.958	100.8	130.4
9	Rafael Palmeiro	Rangers	160	.273	453	451	1.004	100.2	128.4
10	Juan Gonzalez	Indians	140	.325	378	393	.962	75.8	125.1

Extremes for Batters

Batter	Team	Best		Batter	Team	Worst
Jason Giambi	Athletics	216.9	BV	Darrin Fletcher	Blue Jays	-85.8
Bret Boone	Mariners	151.4	SE+	Adam Kennedy	Angels	66.7
Bret Boone	Mariners	75.3	SCV	Adam Kennedy	Angels	-41.0
Jim Thome	Indians	192.3	ISO+	David Eckstein	Angels	42.5
Jim Thome	Indians	84.0	EXV	Omar Vizquel	Indians	-57.7
Ichiro Suzuki	Mariners	238.2	CT+	Jim Thome	Indians	50.6
Ichiro Suzuki	Mariners	-73.3	SOV	Jim Thome	Indians	91.3
Jason Giambi	Athletics	202.0	EY+	Ichiro Suzuki	Mariners	33.6
Jason Giambi	Athletics	53.0	BBV	Ichiro Suzuki	Mariners	-39.6

Best Pitchers

Rank	Pitcher	Team	G	ERA	B	O	BPO	BV	BPO+
1	Mike Mussina	Yankees	34	3.15	371	685	.542	-112.6	76.7
2	Mark Buehrle	White Sox	32	3.29	383	670	.572	-99.9	79.3
3	Mark Mulder	Athletics	34	3.45	385	691	.557	-95.0	80.2
4	Joe Mays	Twins	34	3.16	412	707	.583	-91.6	81.8
5	Freddy Garcia	Mariners	34	3.05	409	723	.566	-76.2	84.3
6	Tim Hudson	Athletics	35	3.37	430	712	.604	-64.6	86.9
7	Barry Zito	Athletics	35	3.49	401	646	.621	-47.8	89.4
8	Cory Lidle	Athletics	29	3.59	348	560	.621	-41.0	89.5
9	Andy Pettitte	Yankees	31	3.99	389	614	.634	-44.5	89.7
10	Jamie Moyer	Mariners	33	3.43	381	631	.604	-42.5	90.0

Extremes for Pitchers

Pitcher	Team	Best		Pitcher	Team	Worst
Mike Mussina	Yankees	-112.6	BV	Dave Mlicki	Tigers	100.4
Joe Mays	Twins	72.1	ERA+	Jose Mercedes	Orioles	141.6
Joe Mays	Twins	-31.8	ERV	Ryan Rupe	Devil Rays	37.2
Mark Mulder	Athletics	66.6	ISO+	Rick Helling	Rangers	146.4
Mark Mulder	Athletics	-43.1	EXV	Rick Helling	Rangers	64.0
Hideo Nomo	Red Sox	63.5	CT+	Pat Rapp	Angels	145.6
Pedro Martinez	Red Sox	83.1	SOV	Josh Towers	Orioles	-45.7
Brad Radke	Twins	38.0	EY+	CC Sabathia	Indians	169.0
Brad Radke	Twins	-42.4	BBV	CC Sabathia	Indians	38.4

2001 National League

Standings

Rank	Team	Post	W	L	Pct.	R	RA	BPO	BPOA	TS
1	Arizona Diamondbacks	WLP	92	70	.568	5.05	4.18	.757	.669	81.168
2	Saint Louis Cardinals	P	93	69	.574	5.02	4.22	.754	.714	62.837
3	Houston Astros	P	93	69	.574	5.23	4.75	.775	.720	61.452
4	San Francisco Giants	—	90	72	.556	4.93	4.62	.782	.692	61.023
5	Chicago Cubs	—	88	74	.543	4.80	4.33	.739	.687	57.921
6	Atlanta Braves	P	88	74	.543	4.50	3.97	.689	.652	57.304
7	Philadelphia Phillies	—	86	76	.531	4.60	4.44	.725	.715	51.065
8	Los Angeles Dodgers	—	86	76	.531	4.68	4.59	.712	.695	50.976
9	Colorado Rockies	—	73	89	.451	5.70	5.59	.828	.821	41.937
10	Florida Marlins	—	76	86	.469	4.58	4.59	.708	.715	41.918
11	San Diego Padres	—	79	83	.488	4.87	5.01	.716	.747	41.014
12	New York Mets	—	82	80	.506	3.96	4.40	.660	.697	40.122
13	Milwaukee Brewers	—	68	94	.420	4.57	4.98	.705	.779	28.450
14	Cincinnati Reds	—	66	96	.407	4.54	5.25	.699	.763	25.653
15	Montreal Expos	—	68	94	.420	4.14	5.01	.665	.761	23.109
16	Pittsburgh Pirates	—	62	100	.383	4.06	5.30	.654	.750	16.421

Best Batters

Rank	Batter	Team	G	BA	B	O	BPO	BV	BPO+
1	Barry Bonds	Giants	153	.328	612	330	1.855	365.5	248.3
2	Sammy Sosa	Cubs	160	.328	559	408	1.370	249.3	180.5
3	Luis Gonzalez	Diamondbacks	162	.325	539	431	1.251	184.9	152.2
4	Larry Walker	Rockies	142	.350	447	345	1.296	143.6	147.3
5	Gary Sheffield	Dodgers	143	.311	413	376	1.098	129.5	145.7
6	Lance Berkman	Astros	156	.331	476	409	1.164	148.0	145.1
7	Todd Helton	Rockies	159	.336	518	415	1.248	153.1	141.9
8	Chipper Jones	Braves	159	.330	460	411	1.119	134.8	141.5
9	Brian Giles	Pirates	160	.309	451	418	1.079	126.6	139.0
10	Shawn Green	Dodgers	161	.297	472	454	1.040	129.7	137.9
10	Phil Nevin	Padres	149	.306	403	399	1.010	110.7	137.9

Extremes for Batters

Batter	Team	Best		Batter	Team	Worst
Barry Bonds	Giants	365.5	BV	Jack Wilson	Pirates	-103.6
Sammy Sosa	Cubs	159.8	SE+	Michael Barrett	Expos	63.9
Sammy Sosa	Cubs	90.5	SCV	Michael Barrett	Expos	-41.9
Barry Bonds	Giants	314.6	ISO+	Tony Womack	Diamondbacks	41.0
Barry Bonds	Giants	173.9	EXV	Juan Pierre	Rockies	-75.6
Juan Pierre	Rockies	384.5	CT+	Jose Hernandez	Brewers	54.7
Fernando Vina	Cardinals	-83.8	SOV	Jose Hernandez	Brewers	83.9
Barry Bonds	Giants	286.3	EY+	Doug Glanville	Phillies	32.0
Barry Bonds	Giants	92.4	BBV	Doug Glanville	Phillies	-38.3

Best Pitchers

Rank	Pitcher	Team	G	ERA	B	O	BPO	BV	BPO+
1	Randy Johnson	Diamondbacks	35	2.49	398	756	.526	-156.8	71.7
2	Curt Schilling	Diamondbacks	35	2.98	446	769	.580	-118.4	79.0
2	Javier Vazquez	Expos	32	3.42	380	675	.563	-101.3	79.0
4	Greg Maddux	Braves	34	3.05	403	701	.575	-92.6	81.3
5	John Burkett	Braves	34	3.04	390	660	.591	-76.6	83.6
5	Brad Penny	Marlins	31	3.69	360	620	.581	-70.8	83.6
7	Russ Ortiz	Giants	33	3.29	375	659	.569	-63.1	85.6
8	Jon Lieber	Cubs	34	3.80	428	706	.606	-54.0	88.8
9	Matt Morris	Cardinals	34	3.16	403	647	.623	-49.9	89.0
10	Wade Miller	Astros	32	3.40	414	639	.648	-45.6	90.1

Extremes for Pitchers

Pitcher	Team	Best		Pitcher	Team	Worst
Randy Johnson	Diamondbacks	-156.8	BV	Bobby Jones	Padres	96.5
Randy Johnson	Diamondbacks	56.6	ERA+	Livan Hernandez	Giants	137.3
Randy Johnson	Diamondbacks	-52.9	ERV	Andy Benes	Cardinals	39.4
Randy Johnson	Diamondbacks	62.0	ISO+	Kevin Jarvis	Padres	158.3
Randy Johnson	Diamondbacks	-57.7	EXV	Kevin Jarvis	Padres	63.4
Randy Johnson	Diamondbacks	49.1	CT+	Kirk Rueter	Giants	183.0
Randy Johnson	Diamondbacks	189.2	SOV	Jimmy Anderson	Pirates	-71.3
Greg Maddux	Braves	24.9	EY+	Kerry Wood	Cubs	161.5
Greg Maddux	Braves	-51.4	BBV	Ryan Dempster	Marlins	34.3

2002 American League

Standings

Rank	Team	Post	W	L	Pct.	R	RA	BPO	BPOA	TS
1	Anaheim Angels	WLP	99	63	.611	5.25	3.98	.742	.654	77.467
2	New York Yankees	P	103	58	.640	5.57	4.33	.794	.646	68.927
3	Oakland Athletics	P	103	59	.636	4.94	4.04	.737	.640	64.725
4	Boston Red Sox	—	93	69	.574	5.30	4.10	.758	.645	62.082
5	Seattle Mariners	—	93	69	.574	5.02	4.31	.753	.668	58.523
6	Minnesota Twins	P	94	67	.584	4.77	4.42	.723	.683	55.449
7	Chicago White Sox	—	81	81	.500	5.28	4.93	.762	.717	49.285
8	Toronto Blue Jays	—	78	84	.481	5.02	5.11	.718	.752	42.102
9	Texas Rangers	—	72	90	.444	5.20	5.44	.763	.793	38.786
10	Cleveland Indians	—	74	88	.457	4.56	5.17	.682	.750	36.288
11	Baltimore Orioles	—	67	95	.414	4.12	4.77	.665	.734	32.639
12	Kansas City Royals	—	62	100	.383	4.55	5.50	.687	.793	27.221
13	Tampa Bay Devil Rays	—	55	106	.342	4.18	5.70	.651	.806	19.054
14	Detroit Tigers	—	55	106	.342	3.57	5.37	.609	.762	17.911

Best Batters

Rank	Batter	Team	G	BA	B	O	BPO	BV	BPO+
1	Jim Thome	Indians	147	.304	459	347	1.323	205.3	181.0
2	Manny Ramirez	Red Sox	120	.349	364	298	1.221	138.2	161.2
3	Jason Giambi	Yankees	155	.314	466	409	1.139	163.6	154.1
4	Alex Rodriguez	Rangers	162	.300	499	459	1.087	146.9	141.7
5	Carlos Delgado	Blue Jays	143	.277	401	381	1.052	110.6	138.1
6	Rafael Palmeiro	Rangers	155	.273	431	414	1.041	113.4	135.7
7	Mike Sweeney	Royals	126	.340	348	334	1.042	87.1	133.4
8	Magglio Ordonez	White Sox	153	.320	422	430	.981	95.4	129.2
9	John Olerud	Mariners	154	.300	386	418	.923	82.9	127.4
10	Tim Salmon	Angels	138	.286	334	361	.925	66.9	125.1

Extremes for Batters

Batter	Team	Best		Batter	Team	Worst
Jim Thome	Indians	205.3	BV	Neifi Perez	Royals	-147.7
Magglio Ordonez	White Sox	144.3	SE+	Neifi Perez	Royals	68.6
Magglio Ordonez	White Sox	65.4	SCV	Neifi Perez	Royals	-45.2
Jim Thome	Indians	226.0	ISO+	Neifi Perez	Royals	37.5
Jim Thome	Indians	99.8	EXV	Neifi Perez	Royals	-61.6
Randall Simon	Tigers	276.3	CT+	Mike Cameron	Mariners	54.9
David Eckstein	Angels	-62.5	SOV	Mike Cameron	Mariners	79.3
Jim Thome	Indians	219.4	EY+	Randall Simon	Tigers	20.2
Jim Thome	Indians	56.6	BBV	Cristian Guzman	Twins	-38.9

Best Pitchers

Rank	Pitcher	Team	G	ERA	B	O	BPO	BV	BPO+
1	Pedro Martinez	Red Sox	30	2.26	293	603	.486	-124.0	70.3
2	Derek Lowe	Red Sox	32	2.58	324	663	.489	-134.4	70.7
3	Roy Halladay	Blue Jays	34	2.93	405	732	.553	-108.7	78.8
4	Tim Wakefield	Red Sox	45	2.81	283	499	.567	-62.0	82.0
5	Barry Zito	Athletics	35	2.75	397	695	.571	-74.2	84.3
6	Mark Mulder	Athletics	30	3.47	371	636	.583	-60.2	86.0
7	Jamie Moyer	Mariners	34	3.32	398	696	.572	-60.9	86.7
8	Jarrod Washburn	Angels	32	3.15	370	620	.597	-51.1	87.9
9	Cory Lidle	Athletics	31	3.89	352	581	.606	-41.9	89.4
10	Mark Buehrle	White Sox	34	3.58	448	718	.624	-51.7	89.6

Extremes for Pitchers

Pitcher	Team	Best		Pitcher	Team	Worst
Derek Lowe	Red Sox	-134.4	BV	Steve Sparks	Tigers	95.4
Pedro Martinez	Red Sox	53.5	ERA+	Steve Sparks	Tigers	138.7
Pedro Martinez	Red Sox	-43.4	ERV	Ryan Drese	Indians	37.8
Roy Halladay	Blue Jays	55.0	ISO+	Ramon Ortiz	Angels	133.1
Roy Halladay	Blue Jays	-66.2	EXV	Darrell May	Royals	41.4
Pedro Martinez	Red Sox	54.9	CT+	Steve Sparks	Tigers	138.5
Pedro Martinez	Red Sox	107.8	SOV	Scott Erickson	Orioles	-40.3
Rick Reed	Twins	45.0	EY+	Danys Baez	Indians	146.6
Paul Byrd	Royals	-33.3	BBV	Justin Miller	Blue Jays	28.7

2002 National League

Standings

Rank	Team	Post	W	L	Pct.	R	RA	BPO	BPOA	TS
1	San Francisco Giants	LP	95	66	.590	4.83	3.80	.767	.639	77.832
2	Atlanta Braves	P	101	59	.631	4.40	3.51	.699	.624	68.172
3	Arizona Diamondbacks	P	98	64	.605	5.06	4.16	.747	.645	67.533
4	Saint Louis Cardinals	P	97	65	.599	4.86	4.00	.731	.669	64.249
5	Los Angeles Dodgers	—	92	70	.568	4.40	3.97	.676	.664	55.379
6	Houston Astros	—	84	78	.519	4.62	4.29	.719	.710	50.056
7	Montreal Expos	—	83	79	.512	4.54	4.43	.725	.707	48.537
8	Philadelphia Phillies	—	80	81	.497	4.41	4.50	.739	.690	47.865
9	Florida Marlins	—	79	83	.488	4.31	4.71	.722	.727	41.471
10	Cincinnati Reds	—	78	84	.481	4.38	4.78	.713	.722	40.633
11	New York Mets	—	75	86	.466	4.29	4.37	.665	.704	39.474
12	Chicago Cubs	—	67	95	.414	4.36	4.69	.699	.715	34.536
13	Pittsburgh Pirates	—	72	89	.447	3.98	4.53	.661	.731	32.654
14	Colorado Rockies	—	73	89	.451	4.80	5.54	.719	.800	30.985
15	San Diego Padres	—	66	96	.407	4.09	5.03	.647	.762	23.540
16	Milwaukee Brewers	—	56	106	.346	3.87	5.07	.660	.786	15.584

Best Batters

Rank	Batter	Team	G	BA	B	O	BPO	BV	BPO+
1	Barry Bonds	Giants	143	.370	540	262	2.061	348.6	282.2
2	Brian Giles	Pirates	153	.298	471	370	1.273	193.7	169.9
3	Jim Edmonds	Cardinals	144	.311	371	346	1.072	115.0	144.9
4	Sammy Sosa	Cubs	150	.288	442	414	1.068	131.7	142.5
5	Bobby Abreu	Phillies	157	.308	442	425	1.040	129.2	141.3
6	Vladimir Guerrero	Expos	161	.336	499	453	1.102	144.5	140.8
7	Chipper Jones	Braves	158	.327	416	394	1.056	118.4	139.8
8	Lance Berkman	Astros	158	.292	456	426	1.070	128.4	139.2
9	Ryan Klesko	Padres	146	.300	381	392	.972	101.7	136.4
10	Todd Helton	Rockies	156	.329	438	392	1.117	113.5	135.0

Extremes for Batters

Batter	Team	Best		Batter	Team	Worst
Barry Bonds	Giants	348.6	BV	Juan Uribe	Rockies	-128.5
Albert Pujols	Cardinals	151.7	SE+	Eric Young	Brewers	71.6
Albert Pujols	Cardinals	71.9	SCV	Juan Uribe	Rockies	-39.3
Barry Bonds	Giants	276.5	ISO+	Juan Pierre	Rockies	30.1
Barry Bonds	Giants	110.4	EXV	Juan Pierre	Rockies	-76.8
Paul Lo Duca	Dodgers	336.8	CT+	Jose Hernandez	Brewers	50.1
Fernando Vina	Cardinals	-76.1	SOV	Jose Hernandez	Brewers	93.7
Barry Bonds	Giants	288.6	EY+	Rey Ordonez	Mets	31.7
Barry Bonds	Giants	85.0	BBV	Corey Patterson	Cubs	-36.2

Best Pitchers

Rank	Pitcher	Team	G	ERA	B	O	BPO	BV	BPO+
1	Curt Schilling	Diamondbacks	36	3.23	405	780	.519	-160.5	71.6
2	Randy Johnson	Diamondbacks	35	2.32	436	788	.553	-135.3	76.3
3	Odalis Perez	Dodgers	32	3.00	359	673	.533	-89.2	80.1
4	A.J. Burnett	Marlins	31	3.30	348	616	.565	-64.9	84.3
5	Kevin Millwood	Braves	35	3.24	380	657	.578	-67.1	85.0
6	Roy Oswalt	Astros	35	3.01	417	703	.593	-71.7	85.3
7	Matt Clement	Cubs	32	3.60	371	627	.592	-54.3	87.2
8	Greg Maddux	Braves	34	2.62	360	605	.595	-51.7	87.4
9	Randy Wolf	Phillies	31	3.20	368	631	.583	-51.9	87.6
10	Miguel Batista	Diamondbacks	36	4.29	357	560	.638	-49.0	87.9

Extremes for Pitchers

Pitcher	Team	Best		Pitcher	Team	Worst
Curt Schilling	Diamondbacks	-160.5	BV	Ruben Quevedo	Brewers	98.0
Randy Johnson	Diamondbacks	54.4	ERA+	Brandon Duckworth	Phillies	145.0
Randy Johnson	Diamondbacks	-56.2	ERV	Ryan Dempster	Marlins-Reds	34.7
Greg Maddux	Braves	69.5	ISO+	Brett Tomko	Padres	143.9
Greg Maddux	Braves	-33.4	EXV	Ruben Quevedo	Brewers	47.2
Randy Johnson	Diamondbacks	56.8	CT+	Kirk Rueter	Giants	203.5
Randy Johnson	Diamondbacks	144.3	SOV	Kirk Rueter	Giants	-78.6
Curt Schilling	Diamondbacks	38.9	EY+	Damian Moss	Braves	146.4
Curt Schilling	Diamondbacks	-50.3	BBV	Kazuhisa Ishii	Dodgers	48.8

2003 American League

Standings

Rank	Team	Post	W	L	Pct.	R	RA	BPO	BPOA	TS
1	New York Yankees	LP	101	61	.623	5.38	4.39	.799	.662	75.850
2	Boston Red Sox	P	95	67	.586	5.93	4.99	.846	.703	64.926
3	Seattle Mariners	—	93	69	.574	4.91	3.93	.723	.639	61.134
4	Oakland Athletics	P	96	66	.593	4.74	3.97	.703	.636	60.716
5	Chicago White Sox	—	86	76	.531	4.88	4.41	.743	.678	53.996
6	Minnesota Twins	P	90	72	.556	4.94	4.68	.734	.696	53.527
7	Toronto Blue Jays	—	86	76	.531	5.52	5.10	.767	.744	51.593
8	Anaheim Angels	—	77	85	.475	4.54	4.59	.704	.704	43.501
9	Kansas City Royals	—	83	79	.512	5.16	5.35	.732	.778	43.371
10	Cleveland Indians	—	68	94	.420	4.31	4.80	.662	.710	34.222
11	Baltimore Orioles	—	71	91	.438	4.56	5.03	.673	.767	33.521
12	Texas Rangers	—	71	91	.438	5.10	5.98	.748	.821	32.350
13	Tampa Bay Devil Rays	—	63	99	.389	4.41	5.26	.681	.770	27.743
14	Detroit Tigers	—	43	119	.265	3.65	5.73	.619	.791	7.040

Best Batters

Rank	Batter	Team	G	BA	B	O	BPO	BV	BPO+
1	Carlos Delgado	Blue Jays	161	.302	473	414	1.143	152.6	147.7
2	Jason Giambi	Yankees	156	.250	439	416	1.055	130.9	142.5
3	Manny Ramirez	Red Sox	154	.325	447	412	1.085	127.3	139.8
4	Alex Rodriguez	Rangers	161	.298	489	451	1.084	133.2	137.4
5	Trot Nixon	Red Sox	134	.306	331	315	1.051	86.5	135.4
6	Carlos Beltran	Royals	141	.307	394	380	1.037	100.0	134.0
7	Jorge Posada	Yankees	142	.281	358	367	.975	86.2	131.7
8	Frank Thomas	White Sox	153	.267	423	415	1.019	100.3	131.1
9	David Ortiz	Red Sox	128	.288	326	330	.988	69.9	127.3
10	Edgar Martinez	Mariners	145	.294	349	376	.928	73.0	126.4

Extremes for Batters

Batter	Team	Best		Batter	Team	Worst
Carlos Delgado	Blue Jays	152.6	BV	Deivi Cruz	Orioles	-93.5
Carlos Delgado	Blue Jays	135.8	SE+	Ramon Santiago	Tigers	65.0
Carlos Delgado	Blue Jays	58.0	SCV	Ramon Santiago	Tigers	-36.6
David Ortiz	Red Sox	170.4	ISO+	Ramon Santiago	Tigers	37.8
Jason Giambi	Yankees	170.4				
Alex Rodriguez	Rangers	72.7	EXV	Carl Crawford	Devil Rays	-51.1
Deivi Cruz	Orioles	183.3	CT+	Carlos Pena	Tigers	60.7
Ichiro Suzuki	Mariners	-48.7	SOV	Jason Giambi	Yankees	48.8
Jason Giambi	Yankees	226.6	EY+	Deivi Cruz	Orioles	27.0
Jason Giambi	Yankees	67.0	BBV	Deivi Cruz	Orioles	-32.4

Best Pitchers

Rank	Pitcher	Team	G	ERA	B	O	BPO	BV	BPO+
1	Tim Hudson	Athletics	34	2.70	363	728	.499	-146.9	71.2
2	Pedro Martinez	Red Sox	29	2.22	284	558	.509	-112.5	71.6
3	Esteban Loaiza	White Sox	34	2.90	380	682	.557	-109.9	77.6
4	Barry Zito	Athletics	35	3.30	396	702	.564	-95.7	80.5
5	Roy Halladay	Blue Jays	36	3.25	468	804	.582	-110.4	80.9
6	Mike Mussina	Yankees	31	3.40	357	641	.557	-77.7	82.1
7	Mark Mulder	Athletics	26	3.13	330	555	.595	-58.7	84.9
8	Bartolo Colon	White Sox	34	3.87	447	726	.616	-74.5	85.7
9	Jamie Moyer	Mariners	33	3.27	395	649	.609	-45.2	89.7
10	Joel Pineiro	Mariners	32	3.78	391	638	.613	-41.7	90.4

Extremes for Pitchers

Pitcher	Team	Best		Pitcher	Team	Worst
Tim Hudson	Athletics	-146.9	BV	Colby Lewis	Rangers	92.7
Pedro Martinez	Red Sox	49.8	ERA+	Mike Maroth	Tigers	140.0
Pedro Martinez	Red Sox	-46.4	ERV	Colby Lewis	Rangers	35.8
Tim Hudson	Athletics	54.2	ISO+	Mike Maroth	Tigers	140.2
Tim Hudson	Athletics	-63.4	EXV	Rick Helling	Orioles	46.1
Pedro Martinez	Red Sox	57.7	CT+	Nate Cornejo	Tigers	281.2
Pedro Martinez	Red Sox	87.0	SOV	Nate Cornejo	Tigers	-83.4
David Wells	Yankees	33.1	EY+	Victor Zambrano	Devil Rays	172.5
Roy Halladay	Blue Jays	-46.8	BBV	Victor Zambrano	Devil Rays	43.7

2003 National League

Standings

Rank	Team	Post	W	L	Pct.	R	RA	BPO	BPOA	TS
1	Atlanta Braves	P	101	61	.623	5.60	4.57	.803	.685	72.536
2	Florida Marlins	WLP	91	71	.562	4.64	4.27	.727	.674	72.426
3	San Francisco Giants	P	100	61	.621	4.69	3.96	.726	.660	66.748
4	Houston Astros	—	87	75	.537	4.97	4.18	.734	.684	57.775
5	Philadelphia Phillies	—	86	76	.531	4.88	4.30	.736	.694	55.176
6	Chicago Cubs	P	88	74	.543	4.47	4.22	.694	.656	53.849
7	Saint Louis Cardinals	—	85	77	.525	5.41	4.91	.784	.753	53.225
8	Arizona Diamondbacks	—	84	78	.519	4.43	4.23	.704	.668	50.915
9	Los Angeles Dodgers	—	85	77	.525	3.54	3.43	.608	.605	48.765
10	Montreal Expos	—	83	79	.512	4.39	4.42	.684	.694	45.644
11	Pittsburgh Pirates	—	75	87	.463	4.65	4.94	.727	.726	39.646
12	Colorado Rockies	—	74	88	.457	5.27	5.51	.761	.808	36.319
13	Milwaukee Brewers	—	68	94	.420	4.41	5.39	.711	.795	25.058
14	New York Mets	—	66	95	.410	3.99	4.68	.634	.757	23.508
15	San Diego Padres	—	64	98	.395	4.19	5.13	.673	.764	22.436
16	Cincinnati Reds	—	69	93	.426	4.28	5.47	.673	.792	21.928

Best Batters

Rank	Batter	Team	G	BA	B	O	BPO	BV	BPO+
1	Barry Bonds	Giants	130	.341	459	266	1.726	255.7	225.8
2	Albert Pujols	Cardinals	157	.359	493	398	1.239	192.4	164.0
3	Gary Sheffield	Braves	155	.330	468	414	1.130	149.9	147.1
4	Todd Helton	Rockies	160	.358	487	404	1.205	149.1	144.1
5	Jim Edmonds	Cardinals	137	.275	361	341	1.059	103.4	140.2
6	Jim Thome	Phillies	159	.266	451	437	1.032	126.2	138.9
7	Brian Giles	Pirates-Padres	134	.299	374	364	1.027	99.4	136.2
8	Lance Berkman	Astros	153	.288	402	400	1.005	90.7	129.1
9	Derrek Lee	Marlins	155	.271	399	416	.959	86.3	127.6
10	Richard Hidalgo	Astros	141	.309	374	377	.992	80.6	127.5

Extremes for Batters

Batter	Team	Best		Batter	Team	Worst
Barry Bonds	Giants	255.7	BV	Cesar Izturis	Dodgers	-109.0
Albert Pujols	Cardinals	149.2	SE+	Alex Cora	Dodgers	63.8
Albert Pujols	Cardinals	71.8	SCV	Royce Clayton	Brewers	-40.7
Barry Bonds	Giants	242.7	ISO+	Brad Ausmus	Astros	36.1
Barry Bonds	Giants	93.5	EXV	Juan Pierre	Marlins	-63.7
Juan Pierre	Marlins	342.2	CT+	Jose Hernandez	Rockies-Cubs-Pirates	50.3
Juan Pierre	Marlins	-84.8	SOV	Jose Hernandez	Rockies-Cubs-Pirates	89.1
Barry Bonds	Giants	216.4	EY+	Alex Cora	Dodgers	31.3
Barry Bonds	Giants	46.8	BBV	Marquis Grissom	Giants	-30.8

Best Pitchers

Rank	Pitcher	Team	G	ERA	B	O	BPO	BV	BPO+
1	Jason Schmidt	Giants	29	2.34	317	626	.506	-108.7	74.5
2	Curt Schilling	Diamondbacks	24	2.95	274	506	.542	-93.3	74.6
3	Brandon Webb	Diamondbacks	29	2.84	304	544	.559	-90.8	77.0
4	Kevin Brown	Dodgers	32	2.39	337	643	.524	-93.8	78.2
5	Mark Prior	Cubs	30	2.43	356	644	.553	-91.1	79.6
6	Javier Vazquez	Expos	34	3.24	405	694	.584	-83.9	82.8
7	Carlos Zambrano	Cubs	32	3.11	384	644	.596	-63.1	85.9
8	Livan Hernandez	Expos	33	3.20	430	701	.613	-63.9	87.1
9	Miguel Batista	Diamondbacks	36	3.54	374	586	.638	-51.3	87.9
10	Mark Redman	Marlins	29	3.59	346	581	.596	-45.1	88.5

Extremes for Pitchers

Pitcher	Team	Best		Pitcher	Team	Worst
Jason Schmidt	Giants	-108.7	BV	Wayne Franklin	Brewers	98.3
Jason Schmidt	Giants	58.7	ERA+	Danny Graves	Reds	136.8
Mark Prior	Cubs	-38.8	ERV	Ryan Dempster	Reds	34.0
Brandon Webb	Diamondbacks	57.6	ISO+	Danny Graves	Reds	158.0
Brandon Webb	Diamondbacks	-45.7	EXV	Wayne Franklin	Brewers	59.2
Kerry Wood	Cubs	56.2	CT+	Danny Graves	Reds	221.1
Kerry Wood	Cubs	116.6	SOV	Danny Graves	Reds	-72.7
Greg Maddux	Braves	36.7	EY+	Kerry Wood	Cubs	137.3
Greg Maddux	Braves	-44.8	BBV	Kazuhisa Ishii	Dodgers	46.8

2004 American League

Standings

Rank	Team	Post	W	L	Pct.	R	RA	BPO	BPOA	TS
1	Boston Red Sox	WLP	98	64	.605	5.86	4.74	.824	.691	84.936
2	New York Yankees	P	101	61	.623	5.54	4.99	.799	.716	65.531
3	Anaheim Angels	P	92	70	.568	5.16	4.53	.737	.698	58.403
4	Minnesota Twins	P	92	70	.568	4.81	4.41	.730	.666	58.265
5	Oakland Athletics	—	91	71	.562	4.90	4.58	.737	.695	55.762
6	Texas Rangers	—	89	73	.549	5.31	4.90	.756	.741	53.535
7	Chicago White Sox	—	83	79	.512	5.34	5.13	.756	.757	47.731
8	Baltimore Orioles	—	78	84	.481	5.20	5.12	.744	.723	45.377
9	Cleveland Indians	—	80	82	.494	5.30	5.29	.770	.768	44.793
10	Detroit Tigers	—	72	90	.444	5.10	5.21	.753	.741	40.235
11	Tampa Bay Devil Rays	—	70	91	.435	4.43	5.23	.691	.755	29.348
12	Toronto Blue Jays	—	67	94	.416	4.47	5.11	.679	.761	27.576
13	Seattle Mariners	—	63	99	.389	4.31	5.08	.679	.749	25.068
14	Kansas City Royals	—	58	104	.358	4.44	5.59	.661	.803	14.882

Best Batters

Rank	Batter	Team	G	BA	B	O	BPO	BV	BPO+
1	Travis Hafner	Indians	140	.311	375	351	1.068	114.4	143.9
2	Melvin Mora	Orioles	140	.340	406	388	1.046	111.5	137.9
3	Vladimir Guerrero	Angels	156	.337	449	436	1.030	119.1	136.1
4	Manny Ramirez	Red Sox	152	.308	445	421	1.057	112.9	134.0
5	David Ortiz	Red Sox	150	.301	438	427	1.026	101.2	130.0
6	Gary Sheffield	Yankees	154	.290	422	437	.966	89.3	126.9
7	Carlos Guillen	Tigers	136	.318	356	380	.937	72.9	125.8
8	Hideki Matsui	Yankees	162	.298	404	426	.948	79.7	124.6
9	Alex Rodriguez	Yankees	155	.286	433	458	.945	84.3	124.2
10	Erubiel Durazo	Athletics	142	.321	337	358	.941	62.8	122.9

Extremes for Batters

Batter	Team	Best		Batter	Team	Worst
Vladimir Guerrero	Angels	119.1	BV	Reed Johnson	Blue Jays	-74.9
Travis Hafner	Indians	141.5	SE+	Bobby Crosby	Athletics	78.8
Miguel Tejada	Orioles	63.3	SCV	Bobby Crosby	Athletics	-30.1
Manny Ramirez	Red Sox	168.1	ISO+	David Eckstein	Angels	34.2
David Ortiz	Red Sox	70.6	EXV	David Eckstein	Angels	-61.6
Ichiro Suzuki	Mariners	205.0	CT+	Mark Bellhorn	Red Sox	51.2
Ichiro Suzuki	Mariners	-66.2	SOV	Mark Bellhorn	Red Sox	86.3
Jorge Posada	Yankees	192.5	EY+	Ichiro Suzuki	Mariners	48.7
Jorge Posada	Yankees	39.9	BBV	Ichiro Suzuki	Mariners	-31.6

Best Pitchers

Rank	Pitcher	Team	G	ERA	B	O	BPO	BV	BPO+
1	Johan Santana	Twins	34	2.61	331	684	.484	-153.6	68.3
2	Curt Schilling	Red Sox	32	3.26	388	677	.573	-100.2	79.5
3	Brad Radke	Twins	34	3.48	390	664	.587	-80.4	82.9
4	Tim Hudson	Athletics	27	3.53	341	570	.598	-60.5	84.9
5	Mark Buehrle	White Sox	35	3.89	478	741	.645	-64.5	88.1
6	Freddy Garcia	Mariners-White Sox	31	3.81	403	635	.635	-49.0	89.0
7	Jake Westbrook	Indians	33	3.38	401	656	.611	-47.8	89.4
8	Rich Harden	Athletics	31	3.99	365	572	.638	-37.9	90.6
9	Rodrigo Lopez	Orioles	37	3.59	327	512	.639	-33.1	90.8
10	Ryan Drese	Rangers	34	4.20	419	625	.670	-40.9	91.1

Extremes for Pitchers

Pitcher	Team	Best		Pitcher	Team	Worst
Johan Santana	Twins	-153.6	BV	Darrell May	Royals	108.2
Johan Santana	Twins	58.2	ERA+	Cliff Lee	Indians	130.0
Johan Santana	Twins	-47.3	ERV	Esteban Loaiza	White Sox-Yankees	25.5
Tim Hudson	Athletics	62.8	ISO+	Darrell May	Royals	158.9
Tim Hudson	Athletics	-42.7	EXV	Darrell May	Royals	70.4
Johan Santana	Twins	59.9	CT+	Carlos Silva	Twins	211.5
Johan Santana	Twins	106.4	SOV	Carlos Silva	Twins	-84.8
Jon Lieber	Yankees	30.2	EY+	Jose Contreras	Yankees-White Sox	149.0
Brad Radke	Twins	-41.9	BBV	Victor Zambrano	Devil Rays	49.3

2004 National League

Standings

Rank	Team	Post	W	L	Pct.	R	RA	BPO	BPOA	TS
1	Saint Louis Cardinals	LP	105	57	.648	5.28	4.07	.788	.658	81.249
2	Atlanta Braves	P	96	66	.593	4.96	4.12	.753	.680	63.409
3	Chicago Cubs	—	89	73	.549	4.87	4.10	.751	.685	58.802
4	Houston Astros	P	92	70	.568	4.96	4.31	.758	.711	58.568
5	San Francisco Giants	—	91	71	.562	5.25	4.75	.779	.719	57.974
6	Los Angeles Dodgers	P	93	69	.574	4.70	4.22	.723	.693	56.935
7	San Diego Padres	—	87	75	.537	4.74	4.35	.717	.699	52.461
8	Philadelphia Phillies	—	86	76	.531	5.19	4.82	.776	.751	52.243
9	Florida Marlins	—	83	79	.512	4.43	4.32	.691	.700	47.024
10	New York Mets	—	71	91	.438	4.22	4.51	.690	.709	37.653
11	Pittsburgh Pirates	—	72	89	.447	4.22	4.62	.668	.720	35.632
12	Milwaukee Brewers	—	67	94	.416	3.94	4.70	.677	.696	32.939
13	Cincinnati Reds	—	76	86	.469	4.63	5.60	.719	.817	31.288
14	Colorado Rockies	—	68	94	.420	5.14	5.70	.768	.853	30.259
15	Montreal Expos	—	67	95	.414	3.92	4.75	.663	.737	28.874
16	Arizona Diamondbacks	—	51	111	.315	3.80	5.55	.635	.779	10.445

Best Batters

Rank	Batter	Team	G	BA	B	O	BPO	BV	BPO+
1	Barry Bonds	Giants	147	.362	553	247	2.239	358.6	284.5
2	Jim Edmonds	Cardinals	153	.301	442	363	1.218	158.6	156.0
3	Todd Helton	Rockies	154	.347	478	375	1.275	163.0	151.7
4	J.D. Drew	Braves	145	.305	434	374	1.160	139.6	147.4
5	Albert Pujols	Cardinals	154	.331	494	431	1.146	157.5	146.8
6	Lance Berkman	Astros	160	.316	460	395	1.165	146.2	146.6
7	Bobby Abreu	Phillies	159	.301	491	418	1.175	154.8	146.0
8	Scott Rolen	Cardinals	142	.314	396	362	1.094	113.4	140.1
9	Adrian Beltre	Dodgers	156	.334	442	419	1.055	120.6	137.5
10	Adam Dunn	Reds	161	.266	442	426	1.038	112.1	134.0

Extremes for Batters

Batter	Team	Best		Batter	Team	Worst
Barry Bonds	Giants	358.6	BV	Alex Cintron	Diamondbacks	-105.5
Scott Rolen	Cardinals	153.7	SE+	Craig Counsell	Brewers	65.7
Scott Rolen	Cardinals	69.6	SCV	Scott Podsednik	Brewers	-45.7
Barry Bonds	Giants	256.3	ISO+	Luis Castillo	Marlins	34.2
Barry Bonds	Giants	102.5	EXV	Luis Castillo	Marlins	-61.6
				Aaron Miles	Rockies	-61.6
Juan Pierre	Marlins	356.0	CT+	Adam Dunn	Reds	51.3
Juan Pierre	Marlins	-89.6	SOV	Adam Dunn	Reds	95.0
Barry Bonds	Giants	271.1	EY+	Alex Gonzalez	Marlins	35.1
Barry Bonds	Giants	70.7	BBV	Alex Gonzalez	Marlins	-33.2

Best Pitchers

Rank	Pitcher	Team	G	ERA	B	O	BPO	BV	BPO+
1	Randy Johnson	Diamondbacks	35	2.60	366	747	.490	-176.9	67.4
2	Ben Sheets	Brewers	34	2.70	402	715	.562	-97.4	80.5
3	Jason Schmidt	Giants	32	3.20	382	676	.565	-90.7	80.8
4	Roger Clemens	Astros	33	2.98	379	645	.588	-75.1	83.5
5	Carlos Zambrano	Cubs	31	2.75	382	633	.603	-65.8	85.3
6	Jaret Wright	Braves	32	3.28	334	561	.595	-56.5	85.5
7	Chris Carpenter	Cardinals	28	3.46	326	550	.593	-53.6	85.9
8	Oliver Perez	Pirates	30	2.98	360	588	.612	-48.1	88.2
9	Roy Oswalt	Astros	36	3.49	439	703	.624	-56.0	88.7
10	Carl Pavano	Marlins	31	3.00	403	660	.611	-44.6	90.0

Extremes for Pitchers

Pitcher	Team	Best		Pitcher	Team	Worst
Randy Johnson	Diamondbacks	-176.9	BV	Ismael Valdez	Padres-Marlins	86.3
Randy Johnson	Diamondbacks	60.5	ERA+	Ismael Valdez	Padres-Marlins	138.8
Randy Johnson	Diamondbacks	-46.3	ERV	Hideo Nomo	Dodgers	40.6
Jaret Wright	Braves	62.8	ISO+	Ismael Valdez	Padres-Marlins	155.2
Randy Johnson	Diamondbacks	-44.9	EXV	Eric Milton	Phillies	60.0
Oliver Perez	Pirates	56.9	CT+	Kirk Rueter	Giants	266.9
Randy Johnson	Diamondbacks	114.7	SOV	Kirk Rueter	Giants	-93.5
David Wells	Padres	31.8	EY+	Kazuhisa Ishii	Dodgers	177.2
Ben Sheets	Brewers	-41.1	BBV	Steve Randolph	Diamondbacks	44.1

2005 American League

Standings

Rank	Team	Post	W	L	Pct.	R	RA	BPO	BPOA	TS
1	Chicago White Sox	WLP	99	63	.611	4.57	3.98	.710	.656	75.291
2	Cleveland Indians	—	93	69	.574	4.88	3.96	.748	.629	65.096
3	New York Yankees	P	95	67	.586	5.47	4.87	.790	.716	61.081
4	Boston Red Sox	P	95	67	.586	5.62	4.97	.791	.738	59.993
5	Los Angeles Angels	P	95	67	.586	4.70	3.97	.691	.652	59.484
6	Oakland Athletics	—	88	74	.543	4.77	4.06	.678	.647	54.891
7	Minnesota Twins	—	83	79	.512	4.25	4.09	.660	.637	48.000
8	Toronto Blue Jays	—	80	82	.494	4.78	4.35	.691	.695	46.276
9	Texas Rangers	—	79	83	.488	5.34	5.30	.762	.731	45.596
10	Baltimore Orioles	—	74	88	.457	4.50	4.94	.711	.724	36.735
11	Detroit Tigers	—	71	91	.438	4.46	4.86	.690	.713	34.583
12	Seattle Mariners	—	69	93	.426	4.31	4.64	.656	.713	31.676
13	Tampa Bay Devil Rays	—	67	95	.414	4.63	5.78	.715	.795	23.637
14	Kansas City Royals	—	56	106	.346	4.33	5.77	.651	.801	10.715

Best Batters

Rank	Batter	Team	G	BA	B	O	BPO	BV	BPO+
1	Alex Rodriguez	Yankees	162	.321	500	428	1.168	184.4	158.4
2	Jason Giambi	Yankees	139	.271	351	312	1.125	120.9	152.5
3	Travis Hafner	Indians	137	.305	381	351	1.085	127.3	150.2
4	David Ortiz	Red Sox	159	.300	476	443	1.074	145.4	144.0
5	Vladimir Guerrero	Angels	141	.317	381	377	1.011	104.6	137.8
6	Manny Ramirez	Red Sox	152	.292	426	418	1.019	114.0	136.6
7	Brian Roberts	Orioles	143	.314	395	410	.963	94.0	131.2
8	Richie Sexson	Mariners	156	.263	401	429	.935	93.2	130.3
9	Mark Teixeira	Rangers	162	.301	460	471	.977	102.6	128.7
10	Gary Sheffield	Yankees	154	.291	400	432	.926	81.4	125.6

Extremes for Batters

Batter	Team	Best		Batter	Team	Worst
Alex Rodriguez	Yankees	184.4	BV	Jason Kendall	Athletics	-71.5
Manny Ramirez	Red Sox	142.5	SE+	Angel Berroa	Royals	79.5
Manny Ramirez	Red Sox	62.9	SCV	Nick Punto	Twins	-31.6
Travis Hafner	Indians	180.1	ISO+	Jason Kendall	Athletics	30.0
David Ortiz	Red Sox	78.4	EXV	Jason Kendall	Athletics	-70.1
Jason Kendall	Athletics	252.9	CT+	Richie Sexson	Mariners	59.9
Jason Kendall	Athletics	-59.6	SOV	Richie Sexson	Mariners	66.9
Jason Giambi	Yankees	260.0	EY+	Ivan Rodriguez	Tigers	22.9
Jason Giambi	Yankees	63.4	BBV	Angel Berroa	Royals	-33.6

Best Pitchers

Rank	Pitcher	Team	G	ERA	B	O	BPO	BV	BPO+
1	Johan Santana	Twins	33	2.87	354	699	.506	-115.1	75.5
2	Mark Buehrle	White Sox	33	3.12	411	719	.572	-94.2	81.3
3	Jon Garland	White Sox	32	3.50	405	665	.609	-62.3	86.7
4	Bartolo Colon	Angels	33	3.48	406	670	.606	-44.6	90.1
5	Carlos Silva	Twins	27	3.44	348	564	.617	-30.5	91.9
6	John Lackey	Angels	33	3.44	388	627	.619	-33.6	92.0
7	Kenny Rogers	Rangers	30	3.46	377	587	.642	-32.5	92.1
8	Freddy Garcia	White Sox	33	3.87	447	685	.653	-34.3	92.9
9	CC Sabathia	Indians	31	4.03	367	595	.617	-26.9	93.2
10	Jose Contreras	White Sox	32	3.61	405	612	.662	-25.1	94.2

Extremes for Pitchers

Pitcher	Team	Best		Pitcher	Team	Worst
Johan Santana	Twins	-115.1	BV	Jose Lima	Royals	128.0
Johan Santana	Twins	69.0	ERA+	Jose Lima	Royals	169.5
Johan Santana	Twins	-33.3	ERV	Jose Lima	Royals	53.7
John Lackey	Angels	72.4	ISO+	Jose Lima	Royals	155.1
Mark Buehrle	White Sox	-33.3	EXV	Jose Lima	Royals	57.2
Johan Santana	Twins	66.9	CT+	Carlos Silva	Twins	191.3
Johan Santana	Twins	78.7	SOV	Carlos Silva	Twins	-64.8
Carlos Silva	Twins	14.0	EY+	Scott Kazmir	Devil Rays	166.9
Carlos Silva	Twins	-42.9	BBV	Scott Kazmir	Devil Rays	38.9

2005 National League

Standings

Rank	Team	Post	W	L	Pct.	R	RA	BPO	BPOA	TS
1	Saint Louis Cardinals	P	100	62	.617	4.97	3.91	.726	.643	76.624
2	Houston Astros	LP	89	73	.549	4.25	3.74	.695	.636	72.466
3	Atlanta Braves	P	90	72	.556	4.75	4.16	.734	.689	62.223
4	Philadelphia Phillies	—	88	74	.543	4.98	4.48	.761	.711	60.530
5	New York Mets	—	83	79	.512	4.46	4.00	.711	.665	56.142
6	Milwaukee Brewers	—	81	81	.500	4.48	4.30	.717	.697	50.136
7	Florida Marlins	—	83	79	.512	4.43	4.52	.709	.708	47.749
8	Chicago Cubs	—	79	83	.488	4.34	4.41	.711	.700	45.944
9	San Diego Padres	P	82	80	.506	4.22	4.48	.691	.689	45.745
10	Washington Nationals	—	81	81	.500	3.94	4.15	.653	.686	42.432
11	Cincinnati Reds	—	73	89	.451	5.03	5.45	.764	.814	33.415
12	San Francisco Giants	—	75	87	.463	4.01	4.60	.654	.712	32.803
13	Arizona Diamondbacks	—	77	85	.475	4.30	5.28	.722	.770	31.820
14	Los Angeles Dodgers	—	71	91	.438	4.23	4.66	.672	.729	31.267
15	Pittsburgh Pirates	—	67	95	.414	4.20	4.75	.672	.735	26.843
16	Colorado Rockies	—	67	95	.414	4.57	5.32	.699	.811	21.032

Best Batters

Rank	Batter	Team	G	BA	B	O	BPO	BV	BPO+
1	Derrek Lee	Cubs	158	.335	505	417	1.211	185.8	158.2
2	Albert Pujols	Cardinals	161	.330	485	420	1.155	164.1	151.1
3	Jason Bay	Pirates	162	.306	464	436	1.064	137.6	142.2
4	Carlos Delgado	Marlins	144	.301	398	386	1.031	112.5	139.4
5	Brian Giles	Padres	158	.301	405	408	.993	110.2	137.4
6	Todd Helton	Rockies	144	.320	392	362	1.083	100.5	134.5
7	Adam Dunn	Reds	160	.247	425	419	1.014	108.4	134.3
8	Morgan Ensberg	Astros	150	.283	397	401	.990	91.4	129.9
9	Lance Berkman	Astros	132	.293	346	352	.983	77.8	129.0
10	Bobby Abreu	Phillies	162	.286	441	444	.993	98.4	128.7
10	Jim Edmonds	Cardinals	142	.263	354	360	.983	79.0	128.7

Extremes for Batters

Batter	Team	Best		Batter	Team	Worst
Derrek Lee	Cubs	185.8	BV	Cristian Guzman	Nationals	-88.5
Albert Pujols	Cardinals	137.3	SE+	David Bell	Phillies	76.5
Albert Pujols	Cardinals	55.7	SCV	Corey Patterson	Cubs	-37.6
Andruw Jones	Braves	188.4	ISO+	Willy Taveras	Astros	30.6
Derrek Lee	Cubs	91.0	EXV	Willy Taveras	Astros	-68.1
Juan Pierre	Marlins	267.4	CT+	Adam Dunn	Reds	57.1
Juan Pierre	Marlins	-75.3	SOV	Adam Dunn	Reds	72.1
Brian Giles	Padres	201.9	EY+	Neifi Perez	Cubs	31.7
Brian Giles	Padres	55.5	BBV	Neifi Perez	Cubs	-32.4

Best Pitchers

Rank	Pitcher	Team	G	ERA	B	O	BPO	BV	BPO+
1	Roger Clemens	Astros	32	1.87	301	642	.469	-144.8	67.5
2	Andy Pettitte	Astros	33	2.39	347	666	.521	-115.5	75.0
3	Chris Carpenter	Cardinals	33	2.83	379	721	.526	-120.2	75.9
4	Pedro Martinez	Mets	31	2.82	337	649	.519	-102.0	76.8
5	Carlos Zambrano	Cubs	33	3.26	380	672	.565	-90.5	80.8
6	Dontrelle Willis	Marlins	34	2.63	392	712	.551	-89.8	81.4
7	John Smoltz	Braves	33	3.06	391	690	.567	-86.2	81.9
8	Roy Oswalt	Astros	35	2.94	439	729	.602	-67.3	86.7
9	A.J. Burnett	Marlins	32	3.44	381	635	.600	-48.7	88.7
9	Jake Peavy	Padres	30	2.88	356	608	.586	-45.2	88.7

Extremes for Pitchers

Pitcher	Team	Best		Pitcher	Team	Worst
Roger Clemens	Astros	-144.8	BV	Eric Milton	Reds	115.9
Roger Clemens	Astros	46.6	ERA+	Eric Milton	Reds	159.1
Roger Clemens	Astros	-50.5	ERV	Eric Milton	Reds	49.8
Roger Clemens	Astros	56.7	ISO+	Eric Milton	Reds	159.3
Roger Clemens	Astros	-49.7	EXV	Eric Milton	Reds	70.3
Mark Prior	Cubs	65.3	CT+	Horacio Ramirez	Braves	187.1
Jake Peavy	Padres	67.6	SOV	Horacio Ramirez	Braves	-69.7
Greg Maddux	Cubs	47.5	EY+	Kip Wells	Pirates	153.8
Greg Maddux	Cubs	-35.4	BBV	Oliver Perez	Pirates	35.1

2006 American League

Standings

Rank	Team	Post	W	L	Pct.	R	RA	BPO	BPOA	TS
1	Detroit Tigers	LP	95	67	.586	5.07	4.17	.726	.665	70.822
2	New York Yankees	P	97	65	.599	5.74	4.73	.826	.693	68.076
3	Minnesota Twins	P	96	66	.593	4.94	4.22	.725	.669	60.713
4	Chicago White Sox	—	90	72	.556	5.36	4.90	.779	.727	55.128
5	Los Angeles Angels	—	89	73	.549	4.73	4.52	.725	.664	53.437
6	Toronto Blue Jays	—	87	75	.537	4.99	4.65	.772	.717	52.785
7	Oakland Athletics	P	93	69	.574	4.76	4.49	.715	.716	52.319
8	Cleveland Indians	—	78	84	.481	5.37	4.83	.775	.725	48.499
9	Boston Red Sox	—	86	76	.531	5.06	5.09	.762	.760	46.340
10	Texas Rangers	—	80	82	.494	5.15	4.84	.737	.716	46.278
11	Seattle Mariners	—	78	84	.481	4.67	4.89	.701	.731	38.290
12	Baltimore Orioles	—	70	92	.432	4.74	5.55	.725	.801	26.711
13	Tampa Bay Devil Rays	—	61	101	.377	4.25	5.28	.696	.798	18.251
14	Kansas City Royals	—	62	100	.383	4.67	5.99	.691	.827	14.785

Best Batters

Rank	Batter	Team	G	BA	B	O	BPO	BV	BPO+
1	Travis Hafner	Indians	129	.308	408	326	1.252	158.5	163.5
2	Manny Ramirez	Red Sox	130	.321	387	327	1.183	132.1	151.8
3	David Ortiz	Red Sox	151	.287	484	415	1.166	160.5	149.6
4	Jim Thome	White Sox	143	.288	413	360	1.147	129.8	145.8
5	Jason Giambi	Yankees	139	.253	384	350	1.097	113.5	142.0
6	Jermaine Dye	White Sox	146	.315	414	394	1.051	104.1	133.6
7	Frank Thomas	Athletics	137	.270	347	359	.967	77.8	128.9
8	Joe Mauer	Twins	140	.347	359	374	.960	78.3	127.9
9	Grady Sizemore	Indians	162	.290	467	478	.977	101.2	127.7
10	Derek Jeter	Yankees	154	.343	427	438	.975	88.5	126.1
10	Justin Morneau	Twins	157	.321	403	426	.946	83.3	126.1

Extremes for Batters

Batter	Team	Best		Batter	Team	Worst
David Ortiz	Red Sox	160.5	**BV**	Angel Berroa	Royals	-116.3
Travis Hafner	Indians	135.0	**SE+**	Mark Loretta	Red Sox	76.8
Travis Hafner	Indians	45.3	**SCV**	Mark Loretta	Red Sox	-38.9
Travis Hafner	Indians	210.0	**ISO+**	Jason Kendall	Athletics	28.4
David Ortiz	Red Sox	94.5	**EXV**	Mark Loretta	Red Sox	-66.4
Kenji Johjima	Mariners	203.3	**CT+**	Jim Thome	White Sox	58.2
Ichiro Suzuki	Mariners	-57.4	**SOV**	Curtis Granderson	Tigers	71.8
Jason Giambi	Yankees	222.1	**EY+**	Angel Berroa	Royals	32.4
Jason Giambi	Yankees	53.9	**BBV**	Yuniesky Betancourt	Mariners	-30.3

Best Pitchers

Rank	Pitcher	Team	G	ERA	B	O	BPO	BV	BPO+
1	Johan Santana	Twins	34	2.77	375	701	.535	-104.0	78.3
2	Roy Halladay	Blue Jays	32	3.19	377	657	.574	-90.6	80.6
3	Mike Mussina	Yankees	32	3.51	342	603	.567	-78.9	81.3
4	Chien-Ming Wang	Yankees	34	3.63	383	657	.583	-75.6	83.5
5	CC Sabathia	Indians	28	3.22	346	590	.586	-62.5	84.7
6	John Lackey	Angels	33	3.56	404	658	.614	-55.9	87.9
7	Erik Bedard	Orioles	33	3.76	369	593	.622	-46.9	88.7
8	Kenny Rogers	Tigers	34	3.84	389	614	.634	-39.7	90.7
9	Kelvim Escobar	Angels	30	3.61	362	568	.637	-35.0	91.2
10	Ervin Santana	Angels	33	4.28	397	612	.649	-30.7	92.8

Extremes for Pitchers

Pitcher	Team	Best		Pitcher	Team	Worst
Johan Santana	Twins	-104.0	**BV**	Carlos Silva	Twins	98.3
Johan Santana	Twins	65.7	**ERA+**	Joel Pineiro	Mariners	152.8
Johan Santana	Twins	-37.6	**ERV**	Joel Pineiro	Mariners	40.4
Chien-Ming Wang	Yankees	64.0	**ISO+**	Carlos Silva	Twins	142.0
Chien-Ming Wang	Yankees	-46.2	**EXV**	Carlos Silva	Twins	47.9
Johan Santana	Twins	68.9	**CT+**	Carlos Silva	Twins	212.2
Johan Santana	Twins	76.3	**SOV**	Chien-Ming Wang	Yankees	-83.8
Curt Schilling	Red Sox	46.2	**EY+**	Barry Zito	Athletics	143.2
Curt Schilling	Red Sox	-31.5	**BBV**	Daniel Cabrera	Orioles	55.2

2006 National League

Standings

Rank	Team	Post	W	L	Pct.	R	RA	BPO	BPOA	TS
1	New York Mets	P	97	65	.599	5.15	4.51	.769	.699	74.757
2	Saint Louis Cardinals	WLP	83	78	.516	4.85	4.73	.729	.739	67.156
3	Los Angeles Dodgers	P	88	74	.543	5.06	4.64	.760	.702	64.284
4	San Diego Padres	P	88	74	.543	4.51	4.19	.721	.682	61.246
5	Philadelphia Phillies	—	85	77	.525	5.34	5.01	.784	.771	56.366
6	Houston Astros	—	82	80	.506	4.54	4.44	.711	.693	52.051
7	Atlanta Braves	—	79	83	.488	5.24	4.97	.755	.759	49.349
8	Florida Marlins	—	78	84	.481	4.68	4.77	.737	.739	44.906
9	Cincinnati Reds	—	80	82	.494	4.62	4.94	.755	.754	44.307
10	Colorado Rockies	—	76	86	.469	5.02	5.01	.747	.751	44.149
11	Arizona Diamondbacks	—	76	86	.469	4.77	4.86	.714	.729	41.966
12	San Francisco Giants	—	76	85	.472	4.63	4.91	.699	.730	38.920
13	Milwaukee Brewers	—	75	87	.463	4.51	5.14	.706	.746	32.929
14	Washington Nationals	—	71	91	.438	4.60	5.38	.735	.793	26.483
15	Chicago Cubs	—	66	96	.407	4.42	5.15	.691	.774	20.558
16	Pittsburgh Pirates	—	67	95	.414	4.27	4.92	.669	.770	20.254

Best Batters

Rank	Batter	Team	G	BA	B	O	BPO	BV	BPO+
1	Albert Pujols	Cardinals	143	.331	465	383	1.214	171.7	158.5
2	Ryan Howard	Phillies	159	.313	506	412	1.228	172.5	151.7
3	Lance Berkman	Astros	152	.315	446	388	1.149	139.9	145.7
4	Carlos Beltran	Mets	140	.275	428	387	1.106	129.2	143.2
5	Nick Johnson	Nationals	147	.290	398	375	1.061	116.5	141.4
6	Miguel Cabrera	Marlins	158	.339	436	409	1.066	117.2	136.8
7	Alfonso Soriano	Nationals	159	.277	484	493	.982	113.9	130.8
8	Jason Bay	Pirates	159	.286	433	433	1.000	96.1	128.5
9	David Wright	Mets	154	.311	408	429	.951	76.8	123.2
10	Carlos Delgado	Mets	144	.265	381	407	.936	66.8	121.2

Extremes for Batters

Batter	Team	Best		Batter	Team	Worst
Ryan Howard	Phillies	172.5	BV	Ronny Cedeno	Cubs	-124.0
Albert Pujols	Cardinals	150.5	SE+	Ronny Cedeno	Cubs	64.7
Albert Pujols	Cardinals	69.5	SCV	Juan Pierre	Cubs	-50.4
Albert Pujols	Cardinals	205.6	ISO+	Brad Ausmus	Astros	31.0
Albert Pujols	Cardinals	93.5	EXV	Juan Pierre	Cubs	-63.4
Juan Pierre	Cubs	336.2	CT+	Adam Dunn	Reds	52.7
Juan Pierre	Cubs	-89.8	SOV	Adam Dunn	Reds	91.7
Pat Burrell	Phillies	203.8	EY+	Ronny Cedeno	Cubs	28.3
Morgan Ensberg	Astros	53.8	BBV	Jeff Francoeur	Braves	-39.8

Best Pitchers

Rank	Pitcher	Team	G	ERA	B	O	BPO	BV	BPO+
1	Brandon Webb	Diamondbacks	33	3.10	413	716	.577	-119.3	77.6
2	Chris Carpenter	Cardinals	32	3.09	373	673	.554	-95.6	79.6
3	Derek Lowe	Dodgers	35	3.63	399	665	.600	-81.8	83.0
4	Bronson Arroyo	Reds	35	3.29	447	720	.621	-79.4	84.9
5	Roy Oswalt	Astros	33	2.98	402	661	.608	-71.1	85.0
6	John Smoltz	Braves	35	3.49	435	699	.622	-63.6	87.2
7	Carlos Zambrano	Cubs	33	3.41	414	652	.635	-59.8	87.4
8	Jason Jennings	Rockies	32	3.78	427	636	.671	-51.6	89.2
9	Aaron Cook	Rockies	32	4.23	436	644	.677	-48.6	90.0
10	Jeff Francis	Rockies	32	4.16	418	605	.691	-37.2	91.8

Extremes for Pitchers

Pitcher	Team	Best		Pitcher	Team	Worst
Brandon Webb	Diamondbacks	-119.3	BV	Jason Marquis	Cardinals	100.5
Brandon Webb	Diamondbacks	69.6	ERA+	Jason Marquis	Cardinals	147.4
Brandon Webb	Diamondbacks	-35.3	ERV	Jason Marquis	Cardinals	41.8
Derek Lowe	Dodgers	62.3	ISO+	Jason Marquis	Cardinals	146.6
Derek Lowe	Dodgers	-50.2	EXV	Jason Marquis	Cardinals	53.4
Orlando Hernandez	Diamondbacks-Mets	73.0	CT+	Aaron Cook	Rockies	171.7
Jake Peavy	Padres	56.9	SOV	Aaron Cook	Rockies	-66.0
Jon Lieber	Phillies	40.9	EY+	Carlos Zambrano	Cubs	163.3
Greg Maddux	Cubs-Dodgers	-34.7	BBV	Carlos Zambrano	Cubs	43.0

2007 American League

Standings

Rank	Team	Post	W	L	Pct.	R	RA	BPO	BPOA	TS
1	Boston Red Sox	WLP	96	66	.593	5.35	4.06	.797	.660	85.711
2	New York Yankees	P	94	68	.580	5.98	4.80	.826	.730	66.980
3	Cleveland Indians	P	96	66	.593	5.01	4.35	.743	.668	63.348
4	Los Angeles Angels	P	94	68	.580	5.07	4.51	.725	.694	58.489
5	Detroit Tigers	—	88	74	.543	5.48	4.92	.771	.731	55.208
6	Toronto Blue Jays	—	83	79	.512	4.65	4.31	.702	.661	50.620
7	Seattle Mariners	—	88	74	.543	4.90	5.02	.701	.741	45.353
8	Oakland Athletics	—	76	86	.469	4.57	4.68	.709	.693	41.658
9	Minnesota Twins	—	79	83	.488	4.43	4.48	.674	.698	41.190
10	Texas Rangers	—	75	87	.463	5.04	5.21	.716	.760	36.489
11	Baltimore Orioles	—	69	93	.426	4.67	5.36	.709	.754	29.251
12	Chicago White Sox	—	72	90	.444	4.28	5.18	.674	.739	28.389
13	Kansas City Royals	—	69	93	.426	4.36	4.80	.647	.748	27.078
14	Tampa Bay Devil Rays	—	66	96	.407	4.83	5.83	.745	.808	24.089

Best Batters

Rank	Batter	Team	G	BA	B	O	BPO	BV	BPO+
1	Alex Rodriguez	Yankees	158	.314	525	428	1.227	201.8	162.4
2	Carlos Pena	Devil Rays	148	.282	430	368	1.168	154.8	156.2
3	David Ortiz	Red Sox	149	.332	462	387	1.194	161.2	153.6
4	Magglio Ordonez	Tigers	157	.363	441	405	1.089	133.1	143.2
5	Jim Thome	White Sox	130	.275	347	327	1.061	96.1	138.3
5	Jack Cust	Athletics	124	.256	311	308	1.010	86.1	138.3
7	Jorge Posada	Yankees	144	.338	360	356	1.011	91.2	133.9
8	Curtis Granderson	Tigers	158	.302	428	438	.977	95.0	128.5
9	Vladimir Guerrero	Angels	150	.324	402	416	.966	86.3	127.3
10	Melvin Upton	Devil Rays	129	.300	337	359	.939	68.5	125.5

Extremes for Batters

Batter	Team	Best		Batter	Team	Worst
Alex Rodriguez	Yankees	201.8	**BV**	Tony Pena	Royals	-95.9
Alex Rodriguez	Yankees	150.6	**SE+**	Nick Punto	Twins	65.6
Alex Rodriguez	Yankees	82.4	**SCV**	Nick Punto	Twins	-40.4
Carlos Pena	Devil Rays	223.8	**ISO+**	Reggie Willits	Angels	32.2
Alex Rodriguez	Yankees	100.5	**EXV**	Ichiro Suzuki	Mariners	-49.0
Placido Polanco	Tigers	343.1	**CT+**	Jack Cust	Athletics	41.5
Placido Polanco	Tigers	-72.9	**SOV**	Jack Cust	Athletics	95.9
Jack Cust	Athletics	251.8	**EY+**	Ivan Rodriguez	Tigers	19.2
Jack Cust	Athletics	62.1	**BBV**	Tony Pena	Royals	-34.7

Best Pitchers

Rank	Pitcher	Team	G	ERA	B	O	BPO	BV	BPO+
1	Erik Bedard	Orioles	28	3.16	297	545	.545	-84.7	77.8
2	Josh Beckett	Red Sox	30	3.27	355	606	.586	-71.4	83.2
3	Roberto Hernandez	Indians	32	3.06	373	645	.578	-71.9	83.8
4	CC Sabathia	Indians	34	3.21	427	725	.589	-73.0	85.4
5	Roy Halladay	Blue Jays	31	3.71	403	679	.594	-67.7	85.6
6	Kelvim Escobar	Angels	30	3.40	358	592	.605	-50.7	87.6
7	John Lackey	Angels	33	3.01	409	675	.606	-57.0	87.8
8	Justin Verlander	Tigers	32	3.66	372	610	.610	-50.4	88.1
9	Chien-Ming Wang	Yankees	30	3.70	362	596	.607	-45.3	88.9
10	Joe Blanton	Athletics	34	3.95	414	692	.598	-47.7	89.7

Extremes for Pitchers

Pitcher	Team	Best		Pitcher	Team	Worst
Erik Bedard	Orioles	-84.7	**BV**	Edwin Jackson	Devil Rays	83.9
John Lackey	Angels	71.1	**ERA+**	Daniel Cabrera	Orioles	129.5
John Lackey	Angels	-30.5	**ERV**	Jeff Weaver	Mariners	34.6
Roy Halladay	Blue Jays	69.6	**ISO+**	Boof Bonser	Twins	129.8
Roy Halladay	Blue Jays	-39.8	**EXV**	John Danks	White Sox	43.3
Erik Bedard	Orioles	57.3	**CT+**	Carlos Silva	Twins	178.2
Erik Bedard	Orioles	94.4	**SOV**	Carlos Silva	Twins	-69.6
Paul Byrd	Indians	38.8	**EY+**	Daniel Cabrera	Orioles	155.4
CC Sabathia	Indians	-39.5	**BBV**	Daniel Cabrera	Orioles	36.4
Paul Byrd	Indians	-39.5				

2007 National League

Standings

Rank	Team	Post	W	L	Pct.	R	RA	BPO	BPOA	TS
1	Colorado Rockies	LP	90	73	.552	5.28	4.65	.772	.713	75.518
2	Philadelphia Phillies	P	89	73	.549	5.51	5.07	.818	.771	61.939
3	New York Mets	—	88	74	.543	4.96	4.63	.771	.710	61.540
4	San Diego Padres	—	89	74	.546	4.55	4.09	.691	.653	60.913
5	Atlanta Braves	—	84	78	.519	5.00	4.52	.733	.709	56.171
6	Chicago Cubs	P	85	77	.525	4.64	4.26	.709	.694	55.216
7	Milwaukee Brewers	—	83	79	.512	4.94	4.79	.761	.718	54.106
8	Arizona Diamondbacks	P	90	72	.556	4.40	4.52	.706	.715	52.105
9	Los Angeles Dodgers	—	82	80	.506	4.54	4.49	.708	.677	51.173
10	Saint Louis Cardinals	—	78	84	.481	4.48	5.12	.689	.726	34.938
11	San Francisco Giants	—	71	91	.438	4.22	4.44	.665	.704	33.185
12	Cincinnati Reds	—	72	90	.444	4.83	5.27	.742	.769	33.116
13	Florida Marlins	—	71	91	.438	4.88	5.50	.764	.798	29.805
14	Houston Astros	—	73	89	.451	4.46	5.02	.697	.764	28.976
15	Washington Nationals	—	73	89	.451	4.15	4.83	.664	.741	26.828
16	Pittsburgh Pirates	—	68	94	.420	4.47	5.22	.686	.772	21.338

Best Batters

Rank	Batter	Team	G	BA	B	O	BPO	BV	BPO+
1	David Wright	Mets	160	.325	471	434	1.085	143.0	143.6
2	Prince Fielder	Brewers	158	.288	464	423	1.097	139.1	142.8
3	Chipper Jones	Braves	134	.337	402	367	1.095	117.7	141.4
4	Albert Pujols	Cardinals	158	.327	437	421	1.038	118.8	137.3
5	Chase Utley	Phillies	132	.332	392	370	1.059	102.1	135.2
6	Hanley Ramirez	Marlins	154	.332	477	459	1.039	123.8	135.1
7	Ryan Howard	Phillies	144	.268	429	407	1.054	110.1	134.5
8	Matt Holliday	Rockies	158	.340	474	451	1.051	109.3	130.0
8	Miguel Cabrera	Marlins	157	.320	426	426	1.000	98.2	130.0
10	Adam Dunn	Reds	152	.264	408	402	1.015	90.7	128.6

Extremes for Batters

Batter	Team	Best		Batter	Team	Worst
David Wright	Mets	143.0	BV	Omar Vizquel	Giants	-89.1
Chipper Jones	Braves	138.4	SE+	Stephen Drew	Diamondbacks	74.0
Matt Holliday	Rockies	53.1	SCV	Stephen Drew	Diamondbacks	-37.9
Prince Fielder	Brewers	196.0	ISO+	Juan Pierre	Dodgers	36.1
Prince Fielder	Brewers	92.6	EXV	Juan Pierre	Dodgers	-70.8
Juan Pierre	Dodgers	333.7	CT+	Ryan Howard	Phillies	47.9
Juan Pierre	Dodgers	-86.5	SOV	Ryan Howard	Phillies	103.7
Pat Burrell	Phillies	234.9	EY+	Bengie Molina	Giants	31.7
Pat Burrell	Phillies	64.9	BBV	Johnny Estrada	Brewers	-30.6

Best Pitchers

Rank	Pitcher	Team	G	ERA	B	O	BPO	BV	BPO+
1	Brandon Webb	Diamondbacks	34	3.01	413	718	.575	-115.9	78.1
2	Jake Peavy	Padres	34	2.54	360	673	.535	-85.4	80.8
3	Tim Hudson	Braves	34	3.33	385	673	.572	-88.2	81.4
4	John Smoltz	Braves	32	3.11	372	617	.603	-61.8	85.7
5	Aaron Harang	Reds	34	3.73	434	697	.623	-66.7	86.7
6	Derek Lowe	Dodgers	33	3.88	375	610	.615	-54.6	87.3
7	Brad Penny	Dodgers	33	3.03	389	622	.625	-49.0	88.8
8	Roy Oswalt	Astros	33	3.18	406	642	.632	-49.0	89.2
8	Matt Cain	Giants	32	3.65	374	596	.628	-45.1	89.2
8	Cole Hamels	Phillies	28	3.39	347	549	.632	-42.0	89.2

Extremes for Pitchers

Pitcher	Team	Best		Pitcher	Team	Worst
Brandon Webb	Diamondbacks	-115.9	BV	Scott Olsen	Marlins	104.8
Jake Peavy	Padres	67.4	ERA+	Scott Olsen	Marlins	142.2
Brandon Webb	Diamondbacks	-37.5	ERV	Adam Eaton	Phillies	36.8
Brandon Webb	Diamondbacks	59.2	ISO+	Woody Williams	Astros	134.1
Brandon Webb	Diamondbacks	-59.3	EXV	Adam Eaton	Phillies	41.5
Jake Peavy	Padres	68.3	CT+	Aaron Cook	Rockies	196.8
Jake Peavy	Padres	76.0	SOV	Tom Glavine	Mets	-65.2
Greg Maddux	Padres	35.8	EY+	Carlos Zambrano	Cubs	140.6
Greg Maddux	Padres	-39.4	BBV	Noah Lowry	Giants	33.3

2008 American League

Standings

Rank	Team	Post	W	L	Pct.	R	RA	BPO	BPOA	TS
1	Tampa Bay Rays	LP	97	65	.599	4.78	4.14	.750	.667	73.410
2	Boston Red Sox	P	95	67	.586	5.22	4.28	.797	.674	68.829
3	Los Angeles Angels	P	100	62	.617	4.72	4.30	.701	.680	60.149
4	Chicago White Sox	P	89	74	.546	4.98	4.47	.741	.688	55.994
5	Toronto Blue Jays	—	86	76	.531	4.41	3.77	.684	.636	55.301
6	New York Yankees	—	89	73	.549	4.87	4.49	.737	.690	54.902
7	Minnesota Twins	—	88	75	.540	5.09	4.57	.706	.692	52.666
8	Cleveland Indians	—	81	81	.500	4.97	4.70	.735	.694	48.545
9	Texas Rangers	—	79	83	.488	5.56	5.97	.801	.803	38.480
10	Detroit Tigers	—	74	88	.457	5.07	5.29	.747	.764	35.832
11	Oakland Athletics	—	75	86	.466	4.01	4.29	.641	.674	35.104
12	Kansas City Royals	—	75	87	.463	4.27	4.82	.647	.698	31.142
13	Baltimore Orioles	—	68	93	.422	4.86	5.40	.725	.796	25.795
14	Seattle Mariners	—	61	101	.377	4.14	5.01	.642	.762	14.853

Best Batters

Rank	Batter	Team	G	BA	B	O	BPO	BV	BPO+
1	Milton Bradley	Rangers	126	.321	333	300	1.110	104.9	146.0
2	Alex Rodriguez	Yankees	138	.302	394	380	1.037	112.3	139.9
3	Carlos Quentin	White Sox	130	.288	370	364	1.016	96.9	135.5
4	Grady Sizemore	Indians	157	.268	467	476	.981	117.7	133.7
5	Kevin Youkilis	Red Sox	145	.312	392	395	.992	88.7	129.3
6	Carlos Pena	Rays	139	.247	360	385	.935	78.0	127.7
7	Jack Cust	Athletics	148	.231	346	381	.908	73.2	126.9
8	Jason Giambi	Yankees	145	.247	339	361	.939	71.4	126.7
9	Nick Markakis	Orioles	157	.306	404	431	.937	80.1	124.7
10	Ian Kinsler	Rangers	121	.319	359	381	.942	69.3	123.9

Extremes for Batters

Batter	Team	Best		Batter	Team	Worst
Grady Sizemore	Indians	117.7	BV	Tona Pena	Royals	-86.4
Justin Morneau	Twins	132.3	SE+	Kurt Suzuki	Athletics	71.6
Justin Morneau	Twins	49.6	SCV	Jason Varitek	Red Sox	-47.7
Carlos Quentin	White Sox	177.0	ISO+	Chone Figgins	Angels	26.0
Carlos Quentin	White Sox	59.2	EXV	Chone Figgins	Angels	-54.0
Yuniesky Betancourt	Mariners	252.9	CT+	Jack Cust	Athletics	43.3
Ichiro Suzuki	Mariners	-65.3	SOV	Jack Cust	Athletics	111.8
Jack Cust	Athletics	223.5	EY+	A.J. Pierzynski	White Sox	29.4
Jack Cust	Athletics	59.7	BBV	Jose Lopez	Mariners	-34.4

Best Pitchers

Rank	Pitcher	Team	G	ERA	B	O	BPO	BV	BPO+
1	Cliff Lee	Indians	31	2.54	342	665	.514	-110.0	75.7
2	Roy Halladay	Blue Jays	34	2.78	395	742	.532	-109.4	78.3
3	Ervin Santana	Angels	32	3.49	386	658	.587	-68.8	84.9
4	Jon Lester	Red Sox	33	3.21	383	628	.610	-60.0	86.5
5	Josh Beckett	Red Sox	27	4.03	327	523	.625	-41.9	88.6
5	Scott Baker	Twins	28	3.45	307	514	.597	-39.4	88.6
7	John Danks	White Sox	33	3.32	362	584	.620	-44.9	89.0
8	Joe Saunders	Angels	31	3.41	368	595	.618	-43.2	89.5
9	Daisuke Matsuzaka	Red Sox	29	2.90	320	505	.634	-36.2	89.8
10	Jeremy Guthrie	Orioles	30	3.63	366	576	.635	-38.8	90.4

Extremes for Pitchers

Pitcher	Team	Best		Pitcher	Team	Worst
Cliff Lee	Indians	-110.0	BV	Miguel Batista	Mariners	117.1
Cliff Lee	Indians	62.4	ERA+	Nate Robertson	Tigers	151.2
Cliff Lee	Indians	-37.9	ERV	Carlos Silva	Mariners	42.0
Cliff Lee	Indians	68.2	ISO+	Nate Robertson	Tigers	136.6
Jon Lester	Red Sox	-39.9	EXV	Nate Robertson	Tigers	37.8
Ervin Santana	Angels	74.1	CT+	Paul Byrd	Indians-Red Sox	170.0
Scott Kazmir	Rays	58.9	SOV	Carlos Silva	Mariners	-61.8
Mike Mussina	Yankees	45.4	EY+	Daisuke Matsuzaka	Red Sox	173.1
Roy Halladay	Blue Jays	-39.3	BBV	Daisuke Matsuzaka	Red Sox	39.3

2008 National League

Standings

Rank	Team	Post	W	L	Pct.	R	RA	BPO	BPOA	TS
1	Philadelphia Phillies	WLP	92	70	.568	4.93	4.20	.762	.701	78.344
2	Chicago Cubs	P	97	64	.602	5.31	4.17	.778	.674	72.913
3	New York Mets	—	89	73	.549	4.93	4.41	.744	.693	59.491
4	Milwaukee Brewers	P	90	72	.556	4.63	4.25	.735	.681	59.283
5	Los Angeles Dodgers	P	84	78	.519	4.32	4.00	.692	.637	55.207
6	Saint Louis Cardinals	—	86	76	.531	4.81	4.48	.747	.715	55.055
7	Arizona Diamondbacks	—	82	80	.506	4.44	4.36	.710	.669	51.340
8	Florida Marlins	—	84	77	.522	4.78	4.76	.731	.718	50.568
9	Houston Astros	—	86	75	.534	4.42	4.61	.694	.724	47.405
10	Atlanta Braves	—	72	90	.444	4.65	4.80	.712	.736	39.084
11	Colorado Rockies	—	74	88	.457	4.61	5.07	.732	.742	38.931
12	Cincinnati Reds	—	74	88	.457	4.35	4.94	.694	.773	33.500
13	San Francisco Giants	—	72	90	.444	3.95	4.69	.646	.728	30.998
14	San Diego Padres	—	63	99	.389	3.93	4.72	.651	.721	25.794
15	Pittsburgh Pirates	—	67	95	.414	4.54	5.46	.673	.802	23.421
16	Washington Nationals	—	59	102	.366	3.98	5.12	.642	.761	17.664

Best Batters

Rank	Batter	Team	G	BA	B	O	BPO	BV	BPO+
1	Albert Pujols	Cardinals	148	.357	466	364	1.280	192.4	170.3
2	Chipper Jones	Braves	128	.364	351	296	1.186	125.4	155.6
3	Lance Berkman	Astros	159	.312	443	403	1.099	134.6	143.7
4	Hanley Ramirez	Marlins	153	.301	457	433	1.055	123.5	137.0
5	Ryan Ludwick	Cardinals	152	.299	401	398	1.008	101.8	134.0
6	Matt Holliday	Rockies	139	.321	402	379	1.061	97.3	131.9
7	David Wright	Mets	160	.302	458	468	.979	108.3	131.0
8	Chase Utley	Phillies	159	.292	439	450	.976	91.5	126.3
9	Carlos Beltran	Mets	161	.284	428	455	.941	88.0	125.9
10	Adam Dunn	Reds-Diamondbacks	158	.236	401	408	.983	81.1	125.3

Extremes for Batters

Batter	Team	Best		Batter	Team	Worst
Albert Pujols	Cardinals	192.4	**BV**	Jeff Francoeur	Braves	-97.0
Adrian Gonzalez	Padres	139.5	**SE+**	Willy Taveras	Rockies	70.5
Adrian Gonzalez	Padres	52.7	**SCV**	Willy Taveras	Rockies	-37.2
Albert Pujols	Cardinals	185.5	**ISO+**	Willy Taveras	Rockies	24.6
Ryan Howard	Phillies	73.8	**EXV**	Ryan Theriot	Cubs	-72.1
Jeff Keppinger	Reds	365.5	**CT+**	Mark Reynolds	Diamondbacks	48.1
Jeff Keppinger	Reds	-63.7	**SOV**	Mark Reynolds	Diamondbacks	105.8
Adam Dunn	Reds-Diamondbacks	199.6	**EY+**	Bengie Molina	Giants	30.6
Adam Dunn	Reds-Diamondbacks	54.4	**BBV**	Kevin Kouzmanoff	Padres	-36.1

Best Pitchers

Rank	Pitcher	Team	G	ERA	B	O	BPO	BV	BPO+
1	Brandon Webb	Diamondbacks	34	3.30	402	696	.578	-101.4	79.9
2	Tim Lincecum	Giants	34	2.62	384	682	.563	-95.1	80.1
3	Dan Haren	Diamondbacks	33	3.33	379	645	.588	-87.5	81.2
4	Ryan Dempster	Cubs	33	2.96	362	622	.582	-78.9	82.1
5	Derek Lowe	Dodgers	34	3.24	353	633	.558	-72.9	82.9
6	Johan Santana	Mets	34	2.53	404	708	.571	-72.1	84.9
7	Cole Hamels	Phillies	33	3.09	404	683	.592	-70.7	85.1
8	Hiroki Kuroda	Dodgers	31	3.73	325	558	.582	-50.5	86.6
9	Carlos Zambrano	Cubs	30	3.91	357	572	.624	-48.5	88.0
10	Aaron Cook	Rockies	32	3.96	407	635	.641	-53.2	88.4

Extremes for Pitchers

Pitcher	Team	Best		Pitcher	Team	Worst
Brandon Webb	Diamondbacks	-101.4	**BV**	Brandon Backe	Astros	110.0
Tim Lincecum	Giants	63.6	**ERA+**	Brandon Backe	Astros	153.5
Tim Lincecum	Giants	-37.7	**ERV**	Brandon Backe	Astros	39.0
Brandon Webb	Diamondbacks	56.9	**ISO+**	Brandon Backe	Astros	163.6
Brandon Webb	Diamondbacks	-59.1	**EXV**	Brandon Backe	Astros	63.0
Tim Lincecum	Giants	63.5	**CT+**	Zach Duke	Pirates	172.9
Tim Lincecum	Giants	96.8	**SOV**	Kyle Kendrick	Phillies	-65.7
Greg Maddux	Padres-Dodgers	40.2	**EY+**	Ian Snell	Pirates	153.0
Greg Maddux	Padres-Dodgers	-37.0	**BBV**	Oliver Perez	Mets	34.6

2009 American League

Standings

Rank	Team	Post	W	L	Pct.	R	RA	BPO	BPOA	TS
1	New York Yankees	WLP	103	59	.636	5.65	4.65	.838	.708	87.433
2	Boston Red Sox	P	95	67	.586	5.38	4.54	.801	.743	63.523
3	Los Angeles Angels	P	97	65	.599	5.45	4.70	.770	.739	61.875
4	Tampa Bay Rays	—	84	78	.519	4.96	4.65	.787	.701	54.852
5	Texas Rangers	—	87	75	.537	4.84	4.57	.743	.708	52.588
6	Minnesota Twins	P	87	76	.534	5.01	4.69	.741	.726	51.137
7	Detroit Tigers	—	86	77	.528	4.56	4.57	.706	.723	45.439
8	Seattle Mariners	—	85	77	.525	3.95	4.27	.661	.659	44.135
9	Chicago White Sox	—	79	83	.488	4.47	4.52	.702	.704	42.528
10	Toronto Blue Jays	—	75	87	.463	4.93	4.76	.737	.735	42.145
11	Oakland Athletics	—	75	87	.463	4.69	4.70	.687	.698	39.796
12	Cleveland Indians	—	65	97	.401	4.77	5.34	.724	.772	26.682
13	Kansas City Royals	—	65	97	.401	4.23	5.20	.669	.740	21.817
14	Baltimore Orioles	—	64	98	.395	4.57	5.41	.697	.815	18.700

Best Batters

Rank	Batter	Team	G	BA	B	O	BPO	BV	BPO+
1	Joe Mauer	Twins	138	.365	394	351	1.123	129.7	149.1
2	Ben Zobrist	Rays	152	.297	387	370	1.046	107.2	138.3
3	Kevin Youkilis	Red Sox	136	.305	373	356	1.048	96.6	135.0
4	Alex Rodriguez	Yankees	124	.286	341	335	1.018	78.2	129.7
5	Shin-Soo Choo	Indians	156	.300	408	426	.958	92.8	129.4
6	Jason Bay	Red Sox	151	.267	405	405	1.000	90.6	128.8
7	Mark Teixeira	Yankees	156	.292	444	449	.989	91.7	126.0
8	Jason Bartlett	Rays	137	.320	342	360	.950	69.8	125.6
9	Carlos Pena	Rays	135	.227	355	375	.947	71.5	125.2
10	Miguel Cabrera	Tigers	160	.324	414	438	.945	81.8	124.6

Extremes for Batters

Batter	Team	Best		Batter	Team	Worst
Joe Mauer	Twins	129.7	BV	Yuniesky Betancourt	Mariners-Royals	-86.9
Torii Hunter	Angels	128.9	SE+	A.J. Pierzynski	White Sox	74.9
Bobby Abreu	Angels	38.8	SCV	A.J. Pierzynski	White Sox	-31.1
Carlos Pena	Rays	189.7	ISO+	Chone Figgins	Angels	59.2
Carlos Pena	Rays	69.0	EXV	Jacoby Ellsbury	Red Sox	-44.1
Dustin Pedroia	Red Sox	259.6	CT+	Jack Cust	Athletics	53.1
Dustin Pedroia	Red Sox	-71.8	SOV	Jack Cust	Athletics	86.7
Nick Swisher	Yankees	180.9	EY+	Ichiro Suzuki	Mariners	29.7
Nick Swisher	Yankees	42.5	BBV	Ichiro Suzuki	Mariners	-40.3

Best Pitchers

Rank	Pitcher	Team	G	ERA	B	O	BPO	BV	BPO+
1	Zack Greinke	Royals	33	2.16	356	691	.515	-128.6	73.5
2	Felix Hernandez	Mariners	34	2.49	396	726	.545	-98.3	80.1
3	CC Sabathia	Yankees	34	3.37	408	694	.588	-87.4	82.4
4	Roy Halladay	Blue Jays	32	2.79	417	716	.582	-80.9	83.8
5	Justin Verlander	Tigers	35	3.45	421	719	.586	-80.6	83.9
6	Gavin Floyd	White Sox	30	4.06	357	583	.612	-59.8	85.7
7	Jon Lester	Red Sox	32	3.41	375	610	.615	-56.9	86.8
8	Scott Feldman	Rangers	34	4.08	360	567	.635	-51.0	87.6
9	Josh Beckett	Red Sox	32	3.86	407	640	.636	-46.1	89.8
10	Jarrod Washburn	Mariners-Tigers	28	3.78	332	530	.626	-31.0	91.2

Extremes for Pitchers

Pitcher	Team	Best		Pitcher	Team	Worst
Zack Greinke	Royals	-128.6	BV	Jason Berken	Orioles	72.7
Zack Greinke	Royals	51.2	ERA+	Carl Pavano	Indians-Twins	125.7
Zack Greinke	Royals	-52.4	ERV	Luke Hochevar	Royals	37.0
Felix Hernandez	Mariners	62.7	ISO+	Trevor Cahill	Athletics	137.0
Felix Hernandez	Mariners	-47.6	EXV	David Hernandez	Orioles	44.9
Justin Verlander	Tigers	66.5	CT+	Nick Blackburn	Twins	172.2
Justin Verlander	Tigers	90.1	SOV	Nick Blackburn	Twins	-70.8
Roy Halladay	Blue Jays	45.7	EY+	A.J. Burnett	Yankees	136.5
Roy Halladay	Blue Jays	-41.5	BBV	A.J. Burnett	Yankees	25.9

2009 National League

Standings

Rank	Team	Post	W	L	Pct.	R	RA	BPO	BPOA	TS
1	Philadelphia Phillies	LP	93	69	.574	5.06	4.38	.774	.723	72.790
2	Los Angeles Dodgers	P	95	67	.586	4.81	3.77	.731	.634	70.739
3	Colorado Rockies	P	92	70	.568	4.96	4.41	.775	.703	63.287
4	Saint Louis Cardinals	P	91	71	.562	4.51	3.95	.708	.640	62.344
5	Atlanta Braves	—	86	76	.531	4.54	3.96	.706	.667	57.158
6	San Francisco Giants	—	88	74	.543	4.06	3.77	.640	.650	52.360
7	Chicago Cubs	—	83	78	.516	4.39	4.17	.698	.681	51.225
8	Florida Marlins	—	87	75	.537	4.77	4.73	.723	.719	51.016
9	Milwaukee Brewers	—	80	82	.494	4.85	5.05	.739	.776	41.786
10	Cincinnati Reds	—	78	84	.481	4.15	4.46	.676	.715	39.588
11	Arizona Diamondbacks	—	70	92	.432	4.44	4.83	.714	.715	36.950
12	San Diego Padres	—	75	87	.463	3.94	4.75	.662	.709	33.438
13	New York Mets	—	70	92	.432	4.14	4.67	.690	.731	32.831
14	Houston Astros	—	74	88	.457	3.97	4.75	.668	.748	30.352
15	Pittsburgh Pirates	—	62	99	.385	3.95	4.77	.657	.766	20.632
16	Washington Nationals	—	59	103	.364	4.38	5.40	.708	.786	19.467

Best Batters

Rank	Batter	Team	G	BA	B	O	BPO	BV	BPO+
1	Albert Pujols	Cardinals	160	.327	522	417	1.252	211.5	168.1
2	Prince Fielder	Brewers	162	.299	486	440	1.105	156.0	147.3
3	Adrian Gonzalez	Padres	160	.277	434	428	1.014	129.5	142.5
4	Hanley Ramirez	Marlins	151	.342	416	402	1.035	112.2	136.9
5	Joey Votto	Reds	131	.322	345	328	1.052	91.6	136.2
6	Chase Utley	Phillies	156	.282	429	419	1.024	111.0	134.9
7	Adam Dunn	Nationals	159	.267	411	411	1.000	105.4	134.5
8	Ryan Braun	Brewers	158	.320	443	447	.991	107.8	132.1
9	Derrek Lee	Cubs	141	.306	392	385	1.018	93.6	131.4
10	Lance Berkman	Astros	136	.274	343	355	.966	74.3	127.7

Extremes for Batters

Batter	Team	Best		Batter	Team	Worst
Albert Pujols	Cardinals	211.5	BV	Willy Taveras	Reds	-80.4
Albert Pujols	Cardinals	145.5	SE+	Yadier Molina	Cardinals	82.1
Albert Pujols	Cardinals	66.3	SCV	Ryan Hanigan	Reds	-33.1
Albert Pujols	Cardinals	214.6	ISO+	Luis Castillo	Mets	27.5
Albert Pujols	Cardinals	100.4	EXV	Luis Castillo	Mets	-55.4
Miguel Tejada	Astros	257.1	CT+	Mark Reynolds	Diamondbacks	49.0
Miguel Tejada	Astros	-75.4	SOV	Mark Reynolds	Diamondbacks	113.8
Nick Johnson	Nationals-Marlins	192.9	EY+	Bengie Molina	Giants	22.9
Nick Johnson	Nationals-Marlins	46.0	BBV	Miguel Tejada	Astros	-40.8

Best Pitchers

Rank	Pitcher	Team	G	ERA	B	O	BPO	BV	BPO+
1	Chris Carpenter	Cardinals	28	2.24	275	576	.477	-112.5	71.0
2	Tim Lincecum	Giants	32	2.48	347	677	.513	-123.1	73.8
3	Javier Vazquez	Braves	32	2.87	350	659	.531	-100.9	77.6
4	Dan Haren	Diamondbacks	33	3.14	392	693	.566	-99.0	79.8
5	Ubaldo Jimenez	Rockies	33	3.47	391	657	.595	-88.3	81.6
6	Josh Johnson	Marlins	33	3.23	357	632	.565	-76.4	82.4
7	Joel Pineiro	Cardinals	32	3.49	360	645	.558	-73.9	83.0
7	Clayton Kershaw	Dodgers	31	2.79	279	509	.548	-57.2	83.0
9	Adam Wainwright	Cardinals	34	2.63	405	708	.572	-71.3	85.0
10	Ted Lilly	Cubs	27	3.10	320	535	.598	-55.4	85.2

Extremes for Pitchers

Pitcher	Team	Best		Pitcher	Team	Worst
Tim Lincecum	Giants	-123.1	BV	Jeff Suppan	Brewers	105.8
Chris Carpenter	Cardinals	58.2	ERA+	Livan Hernandez	Mets-Nationals	140.9
Tim Lincecum	Giants	-39.2	ERV	Manny Parra	Brewers	39.3
Tim Lincecum	Giants	55.6	ISO+	Braden Looper	Brewers	146.6
Tim Lincecum	Giants	-54.4	EXV	Josh Geer	Padres	56.9
Tim Lincecum	Giants	65.2	CT+	John Lannan	Nationals	183.2
Tim Lincecum	Giants	90.7	SOV	John Lannan	Nationals	-74.1
Joel Pineiro	Cardinals	37.0	EY+	Clayton Kershaw	Dodgers	164.5
Joel Pineiro	Cardinals	-44.3	BBV	Carlos Marmol	Cubs	35.4

2010 American League

Standings

Rank	Team	Post	W	L	Pct.	R	RA	BPO	BPOA	TS
1	Texas Rangers	LP	90	72	.556	4.86	4.24	.721	.674	67.736
2	New York Yankees	P	95	67	.586	5.30	4.28	.775	.691	65.817
3	Tampa Bay Rays	P	96	66	.593	4.95	4.01	.736	.663	65.174
4	Minnesota Twins	P	94	68	.580	4.82	4.14	.718	.672	60.262
5	Boston Red Sox	—	89	73	.549	5.05	4.59	.763	.707	56.534
6	Chicago White Sox	—	88	74	.543	4.64	4.35	.716	.666	54.489
7	Toronto Blue Jays	—	85	77	.525	4.66	4.49	.725	.681	51.514
8	Oakland Athletics	—	81	81	.500	4.09	3.86	.668	.641	48.270
9	Detroit Tigers	—	81	81	.500	4.64	4.59	.707	.688	46.448
10	Los Angeles Angels	—	80	82	.494	4.20	4.33	.649	.705	39.331
11	Cleveland Indians	—	69	93	.426	3.99	4.64	.655	.725	28.261
12	Kansas City Royals	—	67	95	.414	4.17	5.22	.677	.756	23.943
13	Baltimore Orioles	—	66	96	.407	3.78	4.85	.634	.737	21.513
14	Seattle Mariners	—	61	101	.377	3.17	4.31	.586	.659	20.157

Best Batters

Rank	Batter	Team	G	BA	B	O	BPO	BV	BPO+
1	Miguel Cabrera	Tigers	150	.328	444	396	1.121	155.3	153.8
2	Jose Bautista	Blue Jays	161	.260	474	437	1.085	151.6	147.0
3	Josh Hamilton	Rangers	133	.359	389	349	1.115	120.3	144.8
4	Paul Konerko	White Sox	149	.312	403	393	1.025	109.2	137.2
5	Shin-Soo Choo	Indians	144	.300	384	405	.948	98.7	134.6
6	Carl Crawford	Rays	154	.307	401	436	.920	90.4	129.1
7	Evan Longoria	Rays	151	.294	393	435	.903	83.1	126.8
8	Luke Scott	Orioles	131	.284	311	336	.926	65.1	126.5
9	David Ortiz	Red Sox	145	.270	362	395	.916	68.8	123.5
10	Robinson Cano	Yankees	160	.319	407	452	.900	67.5	119.9

Extremes for Batters

Batter	Team	Best		Batter	Team	Worst
Miguel Cabrera	Tigers	155.3	BV	Cesar Izturis	Orioles	-106.7
Miguel Cabrera	Tigers	145.3	SE+	Cesar Izturis	Orioles	64.8
Miguel Cabrera	Tigers	62.0	SCV	Chone Figgins	Mariners	-41.5
Jose Bautista	Blue Jays	221.2	ISO+	Elvis Andrus	Rangers	21.2
Jose Bautista	Blue Jays	111.2	EXV	Elvis Andrus	Rangers	-78.0
Juan Pierre	White Sox	267.9	CT+	Carlos Pena	Rays	57.8
Juan Pierre	White Sox	-78.9	SOV	Carlos Pena	Rays	66.7
Daric Barton	Athletics	191.4	EY+	A.J. Pierzynski	White Sox	29.0
Daric Barton	Athletics	51.6	BBV	A.J. Pierzynski	White Sox	-31.8

Best Pitchers

Rank	Pitcher	Team	G	ERA	B	O	BPO	BV	BPO+
1	Cliff Lee	Mariners-Rangers	28	3.18	328	642	.511	-109.3	74.7
2	Felix Hernandez	Mariners	34	2.27	387	759	.510	-109.2	78.0
3	Clay Buchholz	Red Sox	28	2.33	286	527	.543	-73.5	79.6
4	C.J. Wilson	Rangers	33	3.35	359	615	.584	-76.1	82.5
5	John Danks	White Sox	32	3.72	369	646	.571	-77.6	82.6
6	Trevor Cahill	Athletics	30	2.97	327	591	.553	-60.1	84.5
7	CC Sabathia	Yankees	34	3.18	420	711	.591	-69.4	85.8
8	Colby Lewis	Rangers	32	3.72	374	615	.608	-61.1	85.9
9	Jon Lester	Red Sox	32	3.25	371	629	.590	-58.1	86.5
10	Justin Verlander	Tigers	33	3.37	398	673	.591	-55.2	87.8
10	Dallas Braden	Athletics	30	3.50	329	572	.575	-45.6	87.8

Extremes for Pitchers

Pitcher	Team	Best		Pitcher	Team	Worst
Cliff Lee	Mariners-Rangers	-109.3	BV	Ryan Rowland-Smith	Mariners	111.7
Clay Buchholz	Red Sox	55.5	ERA+	James Shields	Rays	138.3
Felix Hernandez	Mariners	-42.7	ERV	Ryan Rowland-Smith	Mariners	35.7
Clay Buchholz	Red Sox	56.4	ISO+	James Shields	Rays	141.9
C.J. Wilson	Rangers	-45.7	EXV	Ryan Rowland-Smith	Mariners	56.1
Jon Lester	Red Sox	67.1	CT+	Mark Buehrle	White Sox	176.0
Jon Lester	Red Sox	74.0	SOV	Mark Buehrle	White Sox	-75.3
Cliff Lee	Mariners-Rangers	24.4	EY+	C.J. Wilson	Rangers	140.9
Cliff Lee	Mariners-Rangers	-49.7	BBV	Rich Harden	Rangers	28.6

2010 National League

Standings

Rank	Team	Post	W	L	Pct.	R	RA	BPO	BPOA	TS
1	San Francisco Giants	WLP	92	70	.568	4.30	3.60	.673	.651	74.265
2	Philadelphia Phillies	P	97	65	.599	4.77	3.95	.717	.660	65.952
3	Cincinnati Reds	P	91	71	.562	4.88	4.23	.745	.669	62.358
4	Atlanta Braves	P	91	71	.562	4.56	3.88	.704	.640	61.667
5	San Diego Padres	—	90	72	.556	4.10	3.59	.652	.618	57.864
6	Saint Louis Cardinals	—	86	76	.531	4.54	3.96	.689	.642	56.739
7	Colorado Rockies	—	83	79	.512	4.75	4.43	.736	.674	54.176
8	Florida Marlins	—	80	82	.494	4.44	4.43	.685	.696	44.862
9	Los Angeles Dodgers	—	80	82	.494	4.12	4.27	.656	.657	44.504
10	New York Mets	—	79	83	.488	4.05	4.02	.662	.672	44.414
11	Milwaukee Brewers	—	77	85	.475	4.63	4.96	.726	.743	40.256
12	Chicago Cubs	—	75	87	.463	4.23	4.73	.665	.707	36.076
13	Washington Nationals	—	69	93	.426	4.04	4.58	.668	.697	32.971
14	Houston Astros	—	76	86	.469	3.77	4.50	.600	.690	31.729
15	Arizona Diamondbacks	—	65	97	.401	4.40	5.16	.707	.769	26.584
16	Pittsburgh Pirates	—	57	105	.352	3.62	5.35	.620	.787	7.550

Best Batters

Rank	Batter	Team	G	BA	B	O	BPO	BV	BPO+
1	Joey Votto	Reds	150	.324	445	389	1.144	153.4	152.6
2	Albert Pujols	Cardinals	159	.312	477	437	1.092	163.6	152.2
3	Jayson Werth	Phillies	156	.296	406	413	.983	102.2	133.7
4	Adrian Gonzalez	Padres	160	.298	403	436	.924	98.0	132.2
5	Matt Holliday	Cardinals	158	.312	405	430	.942	96.6	131.3
6	Carlos Gonzalez	Rockies	145	.336	426	414	1.029	97.2	129.6
7	Aubrey Huff	Giants	157	.290	394	428	.921	82.9	126.6
8	Prince Fielder	Brewers	161	.261	409	440	.930	82.6	125.3
9	Adam Dunn	Nationals	158	.260	389	428	.909	77.9	125.0
10	Ryan Zimmerman	Nationals	142	.307	350	386	.907	69.4	124.7

Extremes for Batters

Batter	Team	Best		Batter	Team	Worst
Albert Pujols	Cardinals	163.6	**BV**	Pedro Feliz	Astros-Cardinals	-106.6
Albert Pujols	Cardinals	134.3	**SE+**	Ronny Cedeno	Pirates	69.5
Albert Pujols	Cardinals	48.8	**SCV**	Ryan Theriot	Cubs-Dodgers	-36.5
Albert Pujols	Cardinals	192.8	**ISO+**	Ryan Theriot	Cubs-Dodgers	27.1
Albert Pujols	Cardinals	80.4	**EXV**	Ryan Theriot	Cubs-Dodgers	-67.4
Jeff Keppinger	Astros	295.8	**CT+**	Mark Reynolds	Diamondbacks	48.0
Jeff Keppinger	Astros	-70.5	**SOV**	Mark Reynolds	Diamondbacks	109.7
Jason Heyward	Braves	172.4	**EY+**	Ronny Cedeno	Pirates	47.7
Prince Fielder	Brewers	38.4	**BBV**	Pedro Feliz	Astros-Cardinals	-23.6

Best Pitchers

Rank	Pitcher	Team	G	ERA	B	O	BPO	BV	BPO+
1	Ubaldo Jimenez	Rockies	33	2.88	365	667	.547	-111.1	76.7
2	Adam Wainwright	Cardinals	33	2.42	361	694	.520	-85.3	80.9
3	Josh Johnson	Marlins	28	2.30	301	552	.545	-66.6	81.9
4	Roy Halladay	Phillies	33	2.44	412	756	.545	-86.4	82.7
5	Mat Latos	Padres	31	2.92	292	553	.528	-57.2	83.6
6	Roy Oswalt	Astros-Phillies	33	2.76	354	634	.558	-66.8	84.1
7	Tim Hudson	Braves	34	2.83	388	691	.562	-65.0	85.6
8	Clayton Kershaw	Dodgers	32	2.91	347	617	.562	-51.0	87.2
9	Jaime Garcia	Cardinals	28	2.70	280	498	.562	-40.3	87.4
10	Johan Santana	Mets	29	2.98	342	598	.572	-45.8	88.2

Extremes for Pitchers

Pitcher	Team	Best		Pitcher	Team	Worst
Ubaldo Jimenez	Rockies	-111.1	**BV**	Zach Duke	Pirates	97.9
Josh Johnson	Marlins	60.1	**ERA+**	Paul Maholm	Pirates	134.6
Roy Halladay	Phillies	-37.6	**ERV**	Zach Duke	Pirates	34.1
Jaime Garcia	Cardinals	62.5	**ISO+**	Rodrigo Lopez	Diamondbacks	144.3
Ubaldo Jimenez	Rockies	-43.5	**EXV**	Rodrigo Lopez	Diamondbacks	52.2
Jonathan Sanchez	Giants	74.1	**CT+**	Kyle Kendrick	Phillies	184.9
Carlos Marmol	Cubs	79.1	**SOV**	Kyle Kendrick	Phillies	-71.3
Roy Halladay	Phillies	39.0	**EY+**	Jonathan Sanchez	Giants	155.8
Roy Halladay	Phillies	-45.4	**BBV**	Jonathan Sanchez	Giants	32.9

2011 American League

Standings

Rank	Team	Post	W	L	Pct.	R	RA	BPO	BPOA	TS
1	Texas Rangers	LP	96	66	.593	5.28	4.18	.774	.639	78.226
2	New York Yankees	P	97	65	.599	5.35	4.06	.779	.684	68.712
3	Boston Red Sox	—	90	72	.556	5.40	4.55	.787	.690	61.706
4	Detroit Tigers	P	95	67	.586	4.86	4.39	.729	.675	59.729
5	Tampa Bay Rays	P	91	71	.562	4.36	3.79	.703	.641	58.431
6	Los Angeles Angels	—	86	76	.531	4.12	3.91	.668	.651	50.335
7	Toronto Blue Jays	—	81	81	.500	4.59	4.70	.697	.716	43.056
8	Chicago White Sox	—	79	83	.488	4.04	4.36	.654	.670	40.670
9	Cleveland Indians	—	80	82	.494	4.35	4.69	.667	.693	40.511
10	Oakland Athletics	—	74	88	.457	3.98	4.19	.635	.650	38.359
11	Kansas City Royals	—	71	91	.438	4.51	4.70	.704	.735	35.600
12	Seattle Mariners	—	67	95	.414	3.43	4.17	.588	.641	28.441
13	Baltimore Orioles	—	69	93	.426	4.37	5.31	.673	.770	25.687
14	Minnesota Twins	—	63	99	.389	3.82	4.96	.599	.737	18.200

Best Batters

Rank	Batter	Team	G	BA	B	O	BPO	BV	BPO+
1	Jose Bautista	Blue Jays	149	.302	463	375	1.235	188.0	168.4
2	Miguel Cabrera	Tigers	161	.344	453	405	1.119	161.3	155.3
3	Curtis Granderson	Yankees	156	.262	455	463	.983	115.7	134.1
4	Jacoby Ellsbury	Red Sox	158	.321	472	479	.985	118.0	133.3
5	Alex Avila	Tigers	141	.295	325	347	.937	75.0	130.0
6	Adrian Gonzalez	Red Sox	159	.338	431	450	.958	98.4	129.6
7	David Ortiz	Red Sox	146	.309	372	389	.956	84.5	129.4
8	Alex Gordon	Royals	151	.303	401	446	.899	86.1	127.3
9	Evan Longoria	Rays	133	.244	333	383	.869	67.0	125.2
10	Paul Konerko	White Sox	149	.300	378	406	.931	72.9	123.9

Extremes for Batters

Batter	Team	Best		Batter	Team	Worst
Jose Bautista	Blue Jays	188.0	BV	Alex Rios	White Sox	-103.4
Curtis Granderson	Yankees	140.5	SE+	Alex Rios	White Sox	75.0
Curtis Granderson	Yankees	61.7	SCV	Adam Dunn	White Sox	-43.2
Jose Bautista	Blue Jays	185.1	ISO+	Juan Pierre	White Sox	28.9
Curtis Granderson	Yankees	74.2	EXV	Juan Pierre	White Sox	-76.4
Juan Pierre	White Sox	304.5	CT+	Mark Reynolds	Orioles	51.9
Juan Pierre	White Sox	-83.8	SOV	Adam Dunn	White Sox	95.9
Jose Bautista	Blue Jays	229.0	EY+	Vladimir Guerrero	Orioles	30.7
Jose Bautista	Blue Jays	60.8	BBV	Vladimir Guerrero	Orioles	-31.6

Best Pitchers

Rank	Pitcher	Team	G	ERA	B	O	BPO	BV	BPO+
1	Justin Verlander	Tigers	34	2.40	358	752	.476	-139.2	72.0
2	Alexi Ogando	Rangers	31	3.51	287	509	.564	-65.5	81.4
3	Doug Fister	Mariners-Tigers	32	2.83	342	654	.523	-75.3	82.3
4	Jered Weaver	Angels	33	2.41	367	705	.521	-74.6	83.1
5	Philip Humber	White Sox	28	3.75	289	492	.587	-51.1	85.0
6	James Shields	Rays	33	2.82	398	736	.541	-69.3	85.2
7	Matt Harrison	Rangers	31	3.39	336	567	.593	-56.7	85.6
8	Josh Beckett	Red Sox	30	2.89	337	578	.583	-55.4	85.9
9	C.J. Wilson	Rangers	34	2.94	404	678	.596	-65.6	86.0
10	CC Sabathia	Yankees	33	3.00	420	717	.586	-59.9	87.5

Extremes for Pitchers

Pitcher	Team	Best		Pitcher	Team	Worst
Justin Verlander	Tigers	-139.2	BV	John Lackey	Red Sox	101.1
Justin Verlander	Tigers	61.7	ERA+	Roberto Hernandez	Indians	142.2
Justin Verlander	Tigers	-41.5	ERV	John Lackey	Red Sox	41.6
Justin Masterson	Indians	65.6	ISO+	A.J. Burnett	Yankees	138.3
Justin Masterson	Indians	-39.9	EXV	A.J. Burnett	Yankees	41.3
Brandon Morrow	Blue Jays	69.6	CT+	Brad Penny	Tigers	192.6
Justin Verlander	Tigers	72.6	SOV	Carl Pavano	Twins	-81.6
Josh Tomlin	Indians	41.5	EY+	Gio Gonzalez	Athletics	144.7
Dan Haren	Angels	-33.1	BBV	Francisco Liriano	Twins	30.9

2011 National League

Standings

Rank	Team	Post	W	L	Pct.	R	RA	BPO	BPOA	TS
1	Saint Louis Cardinals	WLP	90	72	.556	4.70	4.27	.717	.656	75.595
2	Philadelphia Phillies	P	102	60	.630	4.40	3.27	.680	.598	75.484
3	Milwaukee Brewers	P	96	66	.593	4.45	3.94	.715	.634	66.346
4	Arizona Diamondbacks	P	94	68	.580	4.51	4.09	.711	.670	61.130
5	Atlanta Braves	—	89	73	.549	3.96	3.73	.642	.629	54.087
6	Los Angeles Dodgers	—	82	79	.509	4.00	3.80	.657	.641	50.241
7	San Francisco Giants	—	86	76	.531	3.52	3.57	.611	.613	48.685
8	Cincinnati Reds	—	79	83	.488	4.54	4.44	.699	.702	45.659
9	Washington Nationals	—	80	81	.497	3.88	3.99	.648	.647	45.021
10	New York Mets	—	77	85	.475	4.43	4.58	.697	.714	41.143
11	Colorado Rockies	—	73	89	.451	4.54	4.78	.711	.725	38.267
12	San Diego Padres	—	71	91	.438	3.66	3.77	.618	.649	36.827
13	Florida Marlins	—	72	90	.444	3.86	4.33	.667	.679	35.832
14	Chicago Cubs	—	71	91	.438	4.04	4.67	.658	.724	29.347
15	Pittsburgh Pirates	—	72	90	.444	3.77	4.40	.625	.715	27.990
16	Houston Astros	—	56	106	.346	3.80	4.91	.627	.752	11.311

Best Batters

Rank	Batter	Team	G	BA	B	O	BPO	BV	BPO+
1	Matt Kemp	Dodgers	161	.324	480	441	1.088	166.4	153.1
2	Ryan Braun	Brewers	150	.332	435	394	1.104	142.2	148.6
3	Lance Berkman	Cardinals	145	.301	368	358	1.028	114.5	145.2
4	Prince Fielder	Brewers	162	.299	446	423	1.054	131.6	141.9
5	Joey Votto	Reds	161	.309	446	446	1.000	115.4	134.9
6	Jose Reyes	Mets	126	.337	353	374	.944	91.1	134.8
7	Carlos Beltran	Mets-Giants	142	.300	355	388	.915	84.0	131.0
8	Matt Holliday	Cardinals	124	.296	306	338	.905	66.7	127.9
9	Justin Upton	Diamondbacks	159	.289	416	442	.941	90.0	127.6
10	Giancarlo Stanton	Marlins	150	.262	367	403	.911	78.4	127.2

Extremes for Batters

Batter	Team	Best		Batter	Team	Worst
Matt Kemp	Dodgers	166.4	BV	Casey McGehee	Brewers	-94.4
Matt Kemp	Dodgers	152.0	SE+	Jamey Carroll	Dodgers	70.1
Matt Kemp	Dodgers	69.1	SCV	Jonathan Herrera	Rockies	-36.5
Giancarlo Stanton	Marlins	185.6	ISO+	Jamey Carroll	Dodgers	39.5
Matt Kemp	Dodgers	70.4	EXV	Jason Bartlett	Padres	-45.4
Jose Reyes	Mets	259.4	CT+	Drew Stubbs	Reds	59.1
Jose Reyes	Mets	-65.4	SOV	Drew Stubbs	Reds	83.8
Carlos Pena	Cubs	198.7	EY+	Yuniesky Betancourt	Brewers	27.8
Carlos Pena	Cubs	46.7	BBV	Yuniesky Betancourt	Brewers	-33.7

Best Pitchers

Rank	Pitcher	Team	G	ERA	B	O	BPO	BV	BPO+
1	Clayton Kershaw	Dodgers	33	2.28	335	704	.476	-118.4	73.9
2	Roy Halladay	Phillies	32	2.35	352	706	.499	-107.0	76.7
3	Cliff Lee	Phillies	32	2.40	361	699	.516	-93.5	79.4
4	Cole Hamels	Phillies	32	2.79	350	656	.534	-76.5	82.1
5	Tim Hudson	Braves	33	3.22	365	653	.559	-61.5	85.6
6	Ian Kennedy	Diamondbacks	33	2.88	383	665	.576	-61.3	86.2
7	Matt Cain	Giants	33	2.88	367	668	.549	-53.4	87.3
8	Shaun Marcum	Brewers	33	3.54	357	608	.587	-51.4	87.4
9	Matt Garza	Cubs	31	3.32	355	606	.586	-44.8	88.8
10	Jordan Zimmermann	Nationals	26	3.18	282	481	.586	-32.6	89.6

Extremes for Pitchers

Pitcher	Team	Best		Pitcher	Team	Worst
Clayton Kershaw	Dodgers	-118.4	BV	Bronson Arroyo	Reds	90.0
Clayton Kershaw	Dodgers	64.8	ERA+	Derek Lowe	Braves	138.5
Roy Halladay	Phillies	-33.0	ERV	J.A. Happ	Astros	30.8
Roy Halladay	Phillies	54.4	ISO+	Bronson Arroyo	Reds	173.3
Roy Halladay	Phillies	-54.5	EXV	Bronson Arroyo	Reds	80.8
Zack Greinke	Brewers	73.4	CT+	Bronson Arroyo	Reds	162.3
Craig Kimbrel	Braves	66.9	SOV	Bronson Arroyo	Reds	-67.3
Roy Halladay	Phillies	46.2	EY+	Jhoulys Chacin	Rockies	146.0
Roy Halladay	Phillies	-36.1	BBV	Jonathan Sanchez	Giants	32.6

2012 American League

Standings

Rank	Team	Post	W	L	Pct.	R	RA	BPO	BPOA	TS
1	New York Yankees	P	95	67	.586	4.96	4.12	.767	.680	66.084
2	Detroit Tigers	LP	88	74	.543	4.48	4.14	.707	.669	64.777
3	Tampa Bay Rays	—	90	72	.556	4.30	3.56	.681	.588	62.548
4	Texas Rangers	P	93	69	.574	4.99	4.36	.743	.669	62.186
5	Oakland Athletics	P	94	68	.580	4.40	3.79	.684	.629	61.221
6	Los Angeles Angels	—	89	73	.549	4.73	4.31	.728	.675	56.569
7	Baltimore Orioles	P	93	69	.574	4.40	4.35	.671	.659	53.081
8	Chicago White Sox	—	85	77	.525	4.62	4.17	.700	.680	51.702
9	Seattle Mariners	—	75	87	.463	3.82	4.02	.611	.654	35.899
10	Toronto Blue Jays	—	73	89	.451	4.42	4.84	.678	.739	31.560
11	Kansas City Royals	—	72	90	.444	4.17	4.60	.662	.728	30.480
12	Boston Red Sox	—	69	93	.426	4.53	4.98	.683	.733	29.636
13	Minnesota Twins	—	66	96	.407	4.33	5.14	.673	.736	24.040
14	Cleveland Indians	—	68	94	.420	4.12	5.22	.659	.741	21.658

Best Batters

Rank	Batter	Team	G	BA	B	O	BPO	BV	BPO+
1	Mike Trout	Angels	139	.326	444	396	1.121	167.7	160.7
2	Edwin Encarnacion	Blue Jays	151	.280	417	406	1.027	113.3	137.3
3	Miguel Cabrera	Tigers	161	.330	456	452	1.009	118.6	135.2
4	Prince Fielder	Tigers	162	.313	417	425	.981	99.8	131.4
5	Josh Willingham	Twins	145	.260	371	407	.912	78.8	127.0
6	Josh Hamilton	Rangers	148	.285	405	424	.955	81.3	125.1
7	Ben Zobrist	Rays	157	.270	386	439	.879	76.8	124.8
8	Robinson Cano	Yankees	161	.313	418	457	.915	80.7	123.9
9	Yoenis Cespedes	Athletics	129	.292	315	361	.873	60.6	123.8
10	Joe Mauer	Twins	147	.319	347	402	.863	58.4	120.3

Extremes for Batters

Batter	Team	Best		Batter	Team	Worst
Mike Trout	Angels	167.7	BV	Michael Young	Rangers	-95.4
Mike Trout	Angels	145.6	SE+	Jemile Weeks	Athletics	70.7
Mike Trout	Angels	57.0	SCV	Jeff Francoeur	Royals	-35.6
Josh Hamilton	Rangers	164.4	ISO+	Jamey Carroll	Twins	29.7
				Ben Revere	Twins	29.7
Josh Hamilton	Rangers	64.2	EXV	Ben Revere	Twins	-59.1
Ichiro Suzuki	Mariners-Yankees	218.1	CT+	Adam Dunn	White Sox	51.1
Ichiro Suzuki	Mariners-Yankees	-71.9	SOV	Adam Dunn	White Sox	108.5
Carlos Santana	Indians	191.3	EY+	Alexei Ramirez	White Sox	26.4
Adam Dunn	White Sox	46.7	BBV	Alexei Ramirez	White Sox	-39.0

Best Pitchers

Rank	Pitcher	Team	G	ERA	B	O	BPO	BV	BPO+
1	Justin Verlander	Tigers	33	2.64	381	719	.530	-109.4	77.7
2	David Price	Rays	31	2.56	324	629	.515	-80.4	80.1
3	Jered Weaver	Angels	30	2.81	295	564	.523	-66.0	81.7
4	Chris Sale	White Sox	30	3.05	338	578	.585	-59.3	85.1
5	Felix Hernandez	Mariners	33	3.06	378	692	.546	-64.2	85.5
6	Jake Peavy	White Sox	32	3.37	391	654	.598	-58.5	87.0
7	CC Sabathia	Yankees	28	3.38	364	611	.596	-48.6	88.2
8	Matt Harrison	Rangers	32	3.29	394	636	.619	-48.5	89.0
9	Yu Darvish	Rangers	29	3.90	376	577	.652	-25.5	93.7
10	Hiroki Kuroda	Yankees	33	3.32	420	658	.638	-24.3	94.5

Extremes for Pitchers

Pitcher	Team	Best		Pitcher	Team	Worst
Justin Verlander	Tigers	-109.4	BV	Ubaldo Jimenez	Indians	110.9
Justin Verlander	Tigers	64.1	ERA+	Luke Hochevar	Royals	143.6
Justin Verlander	Tigers	-39.3	ERV	Nick Blackburn	Twins	37.7
David Price	Rays	64.4	ISO+	Ervin Santana	Angels	158.6
Felix Hernandez	Mariners	-42.1	EXV	Ervin Santana	Angels	57.7
Max Scherzer	Tigers	64.8	CT+	Henderson Alvarez	Blue Jays	210.5
Max Scherzer	Tigers	81.3	SOV	Henderson Alvarez	Blue Jays	-87.3
Scott Diamond	Twins	58.6	EY+	Ricky Romero	Blue Jays	177.6
Bartolo Colon	Athletics	-25.2	BBV	Ricky Romero	Blue Jays	45.4

2012 National League

Standings

Rank	Team	Post	W	L	Pct.	R	RA	BPO	BPOA	TS
1	San Francisco Giants	WLP	94	68	.580	4.43	4.01	.682	.666	72.475
2	Washington Nationals	P	98	64	.605	4.51	3.67	.711	.634	67.836
3	Cincinnati Reds	P	97	65	.599	4.13	3.63	.686	.638	62.608
4	Saint Louis Cardinals	P	88	74	.543	4.72	4.00	.721	.633	62.111
5	Atlanta Braves	P	94	68	.580	4.32	3.70	.674	.629	61.553
6	Milwaukee Brewers	—	83	79	.512	4.79	4.52	.743	.707	52.221
7	Los Angeles Dodgers	—	86	76	.531	3.93	3.69	.638	.629	51.816
8	Arizona Diamondbacks	—	81	81	.500	4.53	4.25	.711	.670	51.535
9	Philadelphia Phillies	—	81	81	.500	4.22	4.20	.676	.660	47.894
10	Pittsburgh Pirates	—	79	83	.488	4.02	4.16	.646	.674	42.321
11	San Diego Padres	—	76	86	.469	4.02	4.38	.672	.696	39.289
12	New York Mets	—	74	88	.457	4.01	4.38	.649	.673	38.216
13	Miami Marlins	—	69	93	.426	3.76	4.47	.652	.682	32.424
14	Colorado Rockies	—	64	98	.395	4.68	5.49	.723	.818	24.098
15	Chicago Cubs	—	61	101	.377	3.78	4.69	.620	.741	19.962
16	Houston Astros	—	55	107	.340	3.60	4.90	.621	.743	13.628

Best Batters

Rank	Batter	Team	G	BA	B	O	BPO	BV	BPO+
1	Andrew McCutchen	Pirates	157	.327	428	425	1.007	131.2	144.2
2	Ryan Braun	Brewers	154	.319	465	431	1.079	132.9	140.0
3	Buster Posey	Giants	148	.336	372	381	.976	103.3	138.4
4	Chase Headley	Padres	161	.286	413	449	.920	98.5	131.3
5	David Wright	Mets	156	.306	390	433	.901	83.1	127.1
6	Yadier Molina	Cardinals	138	.315	323	367	.880	59.3	122.5
7	Matt Holliday	Cardinals	157	.295	391	447	.875	69.8	121.7
8	Carlos Beltran	Cardinals	151	.269	356	420	.848	54.2	118.0
9	Paul Goldschmidt	Diamondbacks	145	.286	343	388	.884	51.2	117.5
10	Aramis Ramirez	Brewers	149	.300	377	419	.900	54.1	116.8
10	Allen Craig	Cardinals	119	.307	292	348	.839	42.0	116.8

Extremes for Batters

Batter	Team	Best		Batter	Team	Worst
Ryan Braun	Brewers	132.9	**BV**	Clint Barmes	Pirates	-75.8
Allen Craig	Cardinals	141.4	**SE+**	Zack Cozart	Reds	71.5
Chase Headley	Padres	47.3	**SCV**	Zack Cozart	Reds	-36.6
Garrett Jones	Pirates	160.4	**ISO+**	Rafael Furcal	Cardinals	53.1
Giancarlo Stanton	Marlins	72.7	**EXV**	Marco Scutaro	Rockies-Giants	-42.7
Marco Scutaro	Rockies-Giants	271.5	**CT+**	Pedro Alvarez	Pirates	58.1
Jose Reyes	Marlins	-78.1	**SOV**	Pedro Alvarez	Pirates	75.5
Dan Uggla	Braves	180.2	**EY+**	Jordan Pacheco	Rockies	50.9
Joey Votto	Reds	40.4	**BBV**	Starlin Castro	Cubs	-23.3

Best Pitchers

Rank	Pitcher	Team	G	ERA	B	O	BPO	BV	BPO+
1	Clayton Kershaw	Dodgers	33	2.53	360	691	.521	-87.8	80.4
2	Gio Gonzalez	Nationals	32	2.89	326	602	.542	-73.4	81.6
3	Johnny Cueto	Reds	33	2.78	372	645	.577	-63.3	85.5
4	R.A. Dickey	Mets	34	2.73	390	700	.557	-56.8	87.3
5	Kyle Lohse	Cardinals	33	2.86	362	646	.560	-52.0	87.4
6	Wade Miley	Diamondbacks	32	3.33	352	596	.591	-50.0	87.6
7	Cliff Lee	Phillies	30	3.16	373	636	.586	-49.3	88.3
8	Tim Hudson	Braves	28	3.62	318	538	.591	-36.7	89.6
9	Cole Hamels	Phillies	31	3.05	390	643	.607	-37.0	91.3
10	Matt Cain	Giants	32	2.79	385	662	.582	-34.7	91.7

Extremes for Pitchers

Pitcher	Team	Best		Pitcher	Team	Worst
Kris Medlen	Braves	-98.7	**BV**	Tim Lincecum	Giants	86.9
Clayton Kershaw	Dodgers	70.4	**ERA+**	Tim Lincecum	Giants	153.2
Kris Medlen	Braves	-33.4	**ERV**	Tim Lincecum	Giants	37.1
Gio Gonzalez	Nationals	65.0	**ISO+**	Tommy Hanson	Braves	134.1
Gio Gonzalez	Nationals	-36.6	**EXV**	Jeremy Guthrie	Rockies	41.0
Gio Gonzalez	Nationals	75.9	**CT+**	Clayton Richard	Padres	184.1
Stephen Strasburg	Nationals	68.9	**SOV**	Clayton Richard	Padres	-90.0
Cliff Lee	Phillies	45.7	**EY+**	Edinson Volquez	Padres	177.1
Cliff Lee	Phillies	-33.3	**BBV**	Edinson Volquez	Padres	43.1

2013 American League

Standings

Rank	Team	Post	W	L	Pct.	R	RA	BPO	BPOA	TS
1	Boston Red Sox	WLP	97	65	.599	5.27	4.05	.781	.672	81.732
2	Oakland Athletics	P	96	66	.593	4.73	3.86	.711	.620	64.237
3	Detroit Tigers	P	93	69	.574	4.91	3.85	.730	.632	64.153
4	Texas Rangers	—	91	72	.558	4.48	3.90	.699	.645	57.120
5	Cleveland Indians	P	92	70	.568	4.60	4.09	.710	.665	57.046
6	Tampa Bay Rays	P	92	71	.564	4.29	3.96	.694	.640	56.180
7	Kansas City Royals	—	86	76	.531	4.00	3.71	.643	.641	49.705
8	Baltimore Orioles	—	85	77	.525	4.60	4.38	.693	.696	48.453
9	New York Yankees	—	85	77	.525	4.01	4.14	.634	.676	43.844
10	Los Angeles Angels	—	78	84	.481	4.52	4.55	.698	.702	43.138
11	Toronto Blue Jays	—	74	88	.457	4.40	4.67	.685	.711	38.112
12	Seattle Mariners	—	71	91	.438	3.85	4.65	.637	.688	31.740
13	Chicago White Sox	—	63	99	.389	3.69	4.46	.617	.689	26.209
14	Minnesota Twins	—	66	96	.407	3.79	4.86	.637	.716	25.589
15	Houston Astros	—	51	111	.315	3.77	5.23	.618	.769	10.531

Best Batters

Rank	Batter	Team	G	BA	B	O	BPO	BV	BPO+
1	Mike Trout	Angels	157	.323	488	422	1.156	201.8	170.5
2	Miguel Cabrera	Tigers	148	.348	453	383	1.183	177.5	164.4
3	Chris Davis	Orioles	160	.286	463	429	1.079	154.2	149.9
4	David Ortiz	Red Sox	137	.309	378	384	.984	100.9	136.4
5	Edwin Encarnacion	Blue Jays	142	.272	381	412	.925	84.8	128.6
6	Josh Donaldson	Athletics	158	.301	383	429	.893	83.6	127.9
7	Jason Kipnis	Indians	149	.284	379	436	.869	80.5	127.0
8	Robinson Cano	Yankees	160	.314	395	439	.900	81.8	126.1
9	Carlos Santana	Indians	154	.268	350	408	.858	70.7	125.3
9	Joe Mauer	Twins	113	.324	275	311	.884	55.6	125.3

Extremes for Batters

Batter	Team	Best		Batter	Team	Worst
Mike Trout	Angels	201.8	BV	Alcides Escobar	Royals	-107.7
Miguel Cabrera	Tigers	142.8	SE+	Mike Moustakas	Royals	68.4
Miguel Cabrera	Tigers	58.7	SCV	Mike Moustakas	Royals	-33.3
Chris Davis	Orioles	220.9	ISO+	Elvis Andrus	Rangers	39.1
Chris Davis	Orioles	111.1	EXV	Elvis Andrus	Rangers	-57.7
Alberto Callaspo	Angels-Athletics	229.4	CT+	Chris Carter	Astros	51.7
Alexei Ramirez	White Sox	-69.0	SOV	Chris Carter	Astros	102.3
Mike Trout	Angels	192.9	EY+	A.J. Pierzynski	Rangers	21.6
Mike Trout	Angels	48.2	BBV	Adam Jones	Orioles	-33.2

Best Pitchers

Rank	Pitcher	Team	G	ERA	B	O	BPO	BV	BPO+
1	Max Scherzer	Tigers	32	2.90	336	642	.523	-94.4	78.1
2	Chris Sale	White Sox	30	3.07	368	641	.574	-65.1	85.0
3	Bartolo Colon	Athletics	30	2.65	315	570	.553	-55.1	85.1
4	Yu Darvish	Rangers	32	2.83	361	632	.571	-60.5	85.7
5	Anibal Sanchez	Tigers	29	2.57	314	545	.576	-51.4	85.9
6	David Price	Rays	27	3.33	312	561	.556	-49.0	86.4
7	Hisashi Iwakuma	Mariners	33	2.66	360	663	.543	-55.9	86.6
8	Justin Masterson	Indians	32	3.45	328	574	.571	-40.7	89.0
9	Ervin Santana	Royals	32	3.24	378	634	.596	-43.3	89.7
10	Felix Hernandez	Mariners	31	3.04	349	617	.566	-38.1	90.2

Extremes for Pitchers

Pitcher	Team	Best		Pitcher	Team	Worst
Max Scherzer	Tigers	-94.4	BV	Joe Saunders	Mariners	120.5
Anibal Sanchez	Tigers	64.6	ERA+	Joe Saunders	Mariners	148.2
Anibal Sanchez	Tigers	-28.4	ERV	Joe Blanton	Angels	35.9
Justin Masterson	Indians	63.1	ISO+	Joe Saunders	Mariners	146.5
Doug Fister	Tigers	-37.5	EXV	Joe Blanton	Angels	52.3
Yu Darvish	Rangers	60.7	CT+	Jeremy Guthrie	Royals	163.6
Yu Darvish	Rangers	108.7	SOV	Jeremy Guthrie	Royals	-70.6
David Price	Rays	50.4	EY+	Ubaldo Jimenez	Indians	147.9
Bartolo Colon	Athletics	-27.0	BBV	Lucas Harrell	Astros	31.6

2013 National League

Standings

Rank	Team	Post	W	L	Pct.	R	RA	BPO	BPOA	TS
1	Saint Louis Cardinals	LP	97	65	.599	4.83	3.68	.673	.606	78.949
2	Atlanta Braves	P	96	66	.593	4.25	3.38	.679	.607	67.754
3	Pittsburgh Pirates	P	94	68	.580	3.91	3.56	.663	.594	62.354
4	Los Angeles Dodgers	P	92	70	.568	4.01	3.59	.673	.602	61.642
5	Cincinnati Reds	P	90	72	.556	4.31	3.64	.680	.625	61.161
6	Washington Nationals	—	86	76	.531	4.05	3.86	.662	.624	53.619
7	Arizona Diamondbacks	—	81	81	.500	4.23	4.29	.653	.678	43.601
8	Milwaukee Brewers	—	74	88	.457	3.95	4.24	.665	.665	39.507
9	San Francisco Giants	—	76	86	.469	3.88	4.27	.641	.666	37.973
10	Colorado Rockies	—	74	88	.457	4.36	4.69	.695	.722	36.994
11	New York Mets	—	74	88	.457	3.82	4.22	.626	.658	36.107
12	San Diego Padres	—	76	86	.469	3.81	4.32	.640	.688	35.281
13	Chicago Cubs	—	66	96	.407	3.72	4.25	.634	.684	28.566
14	Philadelphia Phillies	—	73	89	.451	3.77	4.62	.627	.712	27.696
15	Miami Marlins	—	62	100	.383	3.17	3.99	.557	.657	20.020

Best Batters

Rank	Batter	Team	G	BA	B	O	BPO	BV	BPO+
1	Andrew McCutchen	Pirates	157	.317	414	425	.974	127.6	144.5
2	Joey Votto	Reds	162	.305	436	428	1.019	127.1	141.1
3	Jayson Werth	Nationals	129	.318	326	330	.988	91.3	138.9
4	Paul Goldschmidt	Diamondbacks	160	.302	454	457	.993	126.2	138.5
4	Shin-Soo Choo	Reds	154	.285	426	426	1.000	118.5	138.5
6	Freddie Freeman	Braves	147	.319	355	390	.910	81.1	129.6
7	Matt Carpenter	Cardinals	157	.318	395	444	.890	82.8	126.5
8	Troy Tulowitzki	Rockies	126	.312	308	321	.960	62.9	125.6
9	Giancarlo Stanton	Marlins	116	.249	284	330	.861	55.4	124.3
10	Brandon Belt	Giants	150	.289	312	372	.839	60.0	123.8

Extremes for Batters

Batter	Team	Best		Batter	Team	Worst
Andrew McCutchen	Pirates	127.6	BV	Adeiny Hechavarria	Marlins	-106.4
Matt Holliday	Cardinals	149.1	SE+	Adeiny Hechavarria	Marlins	60.9
Matt Holliday	Cardinals	57.6	SCV	Starlin Castro	Cubs	-45.7
Pedro Alvarez	Pirates	170.2	ISO+	Adeiny Hechavarria	Marlins	48.8
Pedro Alvarez	Pirates	55.3	EXV	Nori Aoki	Brewers	-43.5
Nori Aoki	Brewers	311.2	CT+	Dan Uggla	Braves	56.1
Nori Aoki	Brewers	-84.5	SOV	Pedro Alvarez	Pirates	76.8
Joey Votto	Reds	211.0	EY+	Jean Segura	Brewers	49.1
Joey Votto	Reds	61.0	BBV	Jean Segura	Brewers	-24.9

Best Pitchers

Rank	Pitcher	Team	G	ERA	B	O	BPO	BV	BPO+
1	Matt Harvey	Mets	26	2.27	228	535	.426	-95.8	70.4
2	Clayton Kershaw	Dodgers	33	1.83	304	711	.428	-127.2	70.5
3	Jose Fernandez	Marlins	28	2.19	238	520	.458	-83.1	74.1
4	Stephen Strasburg	Nationals	30	3.00	289	553	.523	-57.3	83.5
5	Adam Wainwright	Cardinals	34	2.94	379	727	.521	-71.8	84.1
6	Cliff Lee	Phillies	31	2.87	353	670	.527	-66.2	84.2
7	Madison Bumgarner	Giants	31	2.77	311	610	.510	-55.4	84.9
8	Jhoulys Chacin	Rockies	31	3.47	358	597	.600	-48.5	88.1
9	Travis Wood	Cubs	32	3.11	347	601	.577	-31.4	91.7
9	Hyun-jin Ryu	Dodgers	30	3.00	322	579	.556	-29.2	91.7

Extremes for Pitchers

Pitcher	Team	Best		Pitcher	Team	Worst
Clayton Kershaw	Dodgers	-127.2	BV	Edinson Volquez	Padres-Dodgers	117.6
Clayton Kershaw	Dodgers	56.0	ERA+	Edinson Volquez	Padres-Dodgers	178.6
Clayton Kershaw	Dodgers	-37.8	ERV	Edinson Volquez	Padres-Dodgers	47.4
Matt Harvey	Mets	58.1	ISO+	Dan Haren	Nationals	146.2
Clayton Kershaw	Dodgers	-37.2	EXV	Randall Delgado	Diamondbacks	40.7
Jose Fernandez	Marlins	72.1	CT+	Kyle Kendrick	Phillies	153.4
Aroldis Chapman	Reds	59.0	SOV	Kyle Kendrick	Phillies	-58.7
Adam Wainwright	Cardinals	50.8	EY+	Jeff Locke	Pirates	173.1
Adam Wainwright	Cardinals	-32.0	BBV	Jeff Locke	Pirates	33.8

2014 American League

Standings

Rank	Team	Post	W	L	Pct.	R	RA	BPO	BPOA	TS
1	Los Angeles Angels	P	98	64	.605	4.77	3.89	.681	.604	70.719
2	Oakland Athletics	P	88	74	.543	4.50	3.53	.658	.581	64.760
3	Baltimore Orioles	P	96	66	.593	4.35	3.66	.674	.634	64.226
4	Kansas City Royals	LP	89	73	.549	4.02	3.85	.634	.625	62.588
5	Detroit Tigers	P	90	72	.556	4.67	4.35	.710	.669	57.212
6	Seattle Mariners	—	87	75	.537	3.91	3.42	.614	.594	54.608
7	Cleveland Indians	—	85	77	.525	4.13	4.03	.660	.642	49.812
8	Toronto Blue Jays	—	83	79	.512	4.46	4.23	.690	.682	48.496
9	New York Yankees	—	84	78	.519	3.91	4.10	.639	.644	44.471
10	Tampa Bay Rays	—	77	85	.475	3.78	3.86	.629	.612	42.842
11	Minnesota Twins	—	70	92	.432	4.41	4.80	.673	.712	30.177
12	Houston Astros	—	70	92	.432	3.88	4.46	.647	.674	29.708
13	Chicago White Sox	—	73	89	.451	4.07	4.68	.648	.696	29.452
14	Boston Red Sox	—	71	91	.438	3.91	4.41	.628	.681	28.587
15	Texas Rangers	—	67	95	.414	3.93	4.77	.624	.724	18.535

Best Batters

Rank	Batter	Team	G	BA	B	O	BPO	BV	BPO+
1	Mike Trout	Angels	157	.287	457	447	1.022	160.5	154.1
2	Victor Martinez	Tigers	151	.335	400	398	1.005	126.8	146.4
3	Jose Abreu	White Sox	145	.317	392	399	.982	122.9	145.7
4	Jose Bautista	Blue Jays	155	.286	416	422	.986	122.9	141.9
5	Michael Brantley	Indians	156	.327	397	433	.917	98.4	132.9
6	Edwin Encarnacion	Blue Jays	128	.268	328	368	.891	72.4	128.3
7	Miguel Cabrera	Tigers	159	.313	395	453	.872	84.0	127.0
8	Jose Altuve	Astros	158	.341	402	470	.855	81.9	125.6
9	Adrian Beltre	Rangers	148	.324	336	392	.857	67.4	125.1
10	David Ortiz	Red Sox	142	.263	352	406	.867	69.9	124.8

Extremes for Batters

Batter	Team	Best		Batter	Team	Worst
Mike Trout	Angels	160.5	BV	Matt Dominguez	Astros	-95.2
Mike Trout	Angels	143.6	SE+	Yunel Escobar	Rays	63.6
Mike Trout	Angels	57.7	SCV	Yunel Escobar	Rays	-37.2
Mike Trout	Angels	198.5	ISO+	Derek Jeter	Yankees	39.2
Mike Trout	Angels	81.9	EXV	Derek Jeter	Yankees	-51.3
Jose Altuve	Astros	270.6	CT+	Chris Davis	Orioles	53.8
Jose Altuve	Astros	-90.4	SOV	Chris Davis	Orioles	79.9
Carlos Santana	Indians	222.9	EY+	Adam Jones	Orioles	36.1
Carlos Santana	Indians	59.5	BBV	Adam Jones	Orioles	-31.9

Best Pitchers

Rank	Pitcher	Team	G	ERA	B	O	BPO	BV	BPO+
1	Garrett Richards	Angels	26	2.61	232	507	.458	-77.5	75.0
2	Chris Sale	White Sox	26	2.17	251	523	.480	-76.2	76.7
3	Felix Hernandez	Mariners	34	2.14	338	708	.477	-90.7	78.8
4	Corey Kluber	Indians	34	2.44	378	712	.531	-72.9	83.8
5	Hisashi Iwakuma	Mariners	28	3.52	280	539	.519	-46.4	85.8
6	Dallas Keuchel	Astros	29	2.93	327	603	.542	-52.6	86.1
7	Jon Lester	Red Sox-Athletics	32	2.46	371	664	.559	-48.8	88.4
8	Sonny Gray	Athletics	33	3.08	364	655	.556	-40.8	89.9
9	David Price	Rays-Tigers	34	3.26	422	752	.561	-43.4	90.7
9	Hiroki Kuroda	Yankees	32	3.71	350	604	.579	-35.7	90.7
9	Alex Cobb	Rays	27	2.87	277	498	.556	-28.5	90.7

Extremes for Pitchers

Pitcher	Team	Best		Pitcher	Team	Worst
Felix Hernandez	Mariners	-90.7	BV	Colby Lewis	Rangers	102.3
Chris Sale	White Sox	61.5	ERA+	Clay Buchholz	Red Sox	144.2
Felix Hernandez	Mariners	-33.4	ERV	Clay Buchholz	Red Sox	31.0
Garrett Richards	Angels	47.9	ISO+	Chris Young	Mariners	157.5
Garrett Richards	Angels	-40.3	EXV	Chris Young	Mariners	44.2
Chris Sale	White Sox	71.2	CT+	Mark Buehrle	Blue Jays	158.2
Max Scherzer	Tigers	71.0	SOV	Mark Buehrle	Blue Jays	-69.3
Phil Hughes	Twins	26.4	EY+	C.J. Wilson	Angels	158.0
Phil Hughes	Twins	-41.9	BBV	Ubaldo Jimenez	Orioles	39.3

2014 National League

Standings

Rank	Team	Post	W	L	Pct.	R	RA	BPO	BPOA	TS
1	Washington Nationals	P	96	66	.593	4.23	3.43	.675	.572	75.183
2	San Francisco Giants	WLP	88	74	.543	4.10	3.79	.635	.619	72.008
3	Los Angeles Dodgers	P	94	68	.580	4.43	3.81	.706	.613	70.842
4	Pittsburgh Pirates	P	88	74	.543	4.21	3.90	.694	.643	59.584
5	Saint Louis Cardinals	P	90	72	.556	3.82	3.72	.628	.609	55.739
6	Milwaukee Brewers	—	82	80	.506	4.01	4.06	.656	.645	47.887
7	New York Mets	—	79	83	.488	3.88	3.81	.627	.644	44.502
8	Atlanta Braves	—	79	83	.488	3.54	3.69	.606	.628	41.718
9	Miami Marlins	—	77	85	.475	3.98	4.16	.633	.662	39.415
10	Cincinnati Reds	—	76	86	.469	3.67	3.78	.612	.645	39.091
11	San Diego Padres	—	77	85	.475	3.30	3.56	.578	.618	37.441
12	Chicago Cubs	—	73	89	.451	3.79	4.36	.628	.648	33.106
13	Philadelphia Phillies	—	73	89	.451	3.82	4.24	.614	.672	31.358
14	Colorado Rockies	—	66	96	.407	4.66	5.05	.723	.756	29.100
15	Arizona Diamondbacks	—	64	98	.395	3.80	4.58	.613	.692	19.252

Best Batters

Rank	Batter	Team	G	BA	B	O	BPO	BV	BPO+
1	Andrew McCutchen	Pirates	146	.314	415	394	1.053	145.8	154.2
2	Giancarlo Stanton	Marlins	145	.288	411	403	1.020	135.1	149.0
3	Anthony Rizzo	Cubs	140	.286	373	390	.956	97.8	135.5
4	Yasiel Puig	Dodgers	148	.296	361	410	.880	83.0	129.9
5	Jayson Werth	Nationals	147	.292	347	391	.887	72.2	126.3
6	Freddie Freeman	Braves	162	.288	384	457	.840	72.1	123.1
7	Lucas Duda	Mets	153	.253	332	399	.832	61.6	122.8
8	Justin Upton	Braves	154	.270	360	435	.828	63.1	121.3
8	Hanley Ramirez	Dodgers	128	.283	278	338	.822	48.9	121.3
10	Starling Marte	Pirates	135	.291	304	367	.828	53.3	121.2

Extremes for Batters

Batter	Team	Best		Batter	Team	Worst
Andrew McCutchen	Pirates	145.8	BV	Zack Cozart	Reds	-95.4
Adrian Gonzalez	Dodgers	139.5	SE+	Andrelton Simmons	Braves	75.8
Adrian Gonzalez	Dodgers	48.7	SCV	Brayan Pena	Reds	-28.9
Giancarlo Stanton	Marlins	185.4	ISO+	Ben Revere	Phillies	37.3
Giancarlo Stanton	Marlins	66.3	EXV	Ben Revere	Phillies	-55.5
Ben Revere	Phillies	270.1	CT+	Ryan Howard	Phillies	66.0
Ben Revere	Phillies	-83.4	SOV	Jarrod Saltalamacchia	Marlins	65.0
Matt Carpenter	Cardinals	179.7	EY+	Ben Revere	Phillies	26.1
Matt Carpenter	Cardinals	41.3	BBV	Ben Revere	Phillies	-34.1

Best Pitchers

Rank	Pitcher	Team	G	ERA	B	O	BPO	BV	BPO+
1	Clayton Kershaw	Dodgers	27	1.77	250	596	.419	-110.9	69.3
2	Adam Wainwright	Cardinals	32	2.38	331	683	.485	-95.7	77.6
3	Johnny Cueto	Reds	34	2.25	367	731	.502	-99.5	78.7
4	Jordan Zimmermann	Nationals	32	2.66	314	595	.528	-60.3	83.9
5	Tanner Roark	Nationals	31	2.85	322	597	.539	-53.5	85.7
6	Doug Fister	Nationals	25	2.41	272	495	.549	-39.4	87.4
7	Matt Garza	Brewers	27	3.64	288	496	.581	-32.4	89.9
8	Alex Wood	Braves	35	2.78	294	514	.572	-22.9	92.8
9	Julio Teheran	Braves	33	2.89	378	659	.574	-28.3	93.0
9	Madison Bumgarner	Giants	33	2.98	371	658	.564	-28.0	93.0
9	Cole Hamels	Phillies	30	2.46	358	613	.584	-27.1	93.0

Extremes for Pitchers

Pitcher	Team	Best		Pitcher	Team	Worst
Clayton Kershaw	Dodgers	-110.9	BV	Edwin Jackson	Cubs	104.0
Clayton Kershaw	Dodgers	53.6	ERA+	Travis Wood	Cubs	142.7
Clayton Kershaw	Dodgers	-33.7	ERV	Edwin Jackson	Cubs	43.9
Adam Wainwright	Cardinals	68.8	ISO+	Dan Haren	Dodgers	138.6
Adam Wainwright	Cardinals	-33.1	EXV	Marco Estrada	Brewers	46.2
Clayton Kershaw	Dodgers	69.0	CT+	Kyle Kendrick	Phillies	152.9
Clayton Kershaw	Dodgers	74.2	SOV	Kyle Kendrick	Phillies	-64.0
Bartolo Colon	Mets	46.0	EY+	Francisco Liriano	Pirates	166.5
Bartolo Colon	Mets	-31.6	BBV	Francisco Liriano	Pirates	31.2

2015 American League

Standings

Rank	Team	Post	W	L	Pct.	R	RA	BPO	BPOA	TS
1	Toronto Blue Jays	P	93	69	.574	5.50	4.14	.776	.642	77.296
2	Kansas City Royals	WLP	95	67	.586	4.47	3.96	.680	.659	75.761
3	Houston Astros	P	86	76	.531	4.50	3.81	.722	.623	62.133
4	New York Yankees	P	87	75	.537	4.72	4.31	.708	.670	55.222
5	Cleveland Indians	—	81	80	.503	4.16	3.98	.682	.620	50.485
6	Texas Rangers	P	88	74	.543	4.64	4.52	.706	.703	50.348
7	Tampa Bay Rays	—	80	82	.494	3.98	3.96	.669	.638	45.003
8	Los Angeles Angels	—	85	77	.525	4.08	4.17	.641	.665	43.677
9	Baltimore Orioles	—	81	81	.500	4.40	4.28	.665	.690	42.089
10	Minnesota Twins	—	83	79	.512	4.30	4.32	.643	.686	40.877
11	Boston Red Sox	—	78	84	.481	4.62	4.65	.688	.701	39.135
12	Seattle Mariners	—	76	86	.469	4.05	4.48	.666	.682	33.493
13	Oakland Athletics	—	68	94	.420	4.28	4.50	.649	.662	28.945
14	Chicago White Sox	—	76	86	.469	3.84	4.33	.617	.682	28.839
15	Detroit Tigers	—	74	87	.460	4.28	4.99	.688	.729	27.487

Best Batters

Rank	Batter	Team	G	BA	B	O	BPO	BV	BPO+
1	Mike Trout	Angels	159	.299	457	426	1.073	168.6	158.4
2	Miguel Cabrera	Tigers	119	.338	312	306	1.020	98.4	146.0
3	Nelson Cruz	Mariners	152	.302	402	421	.955	115.0	140.1
4	Chris Davis	Orioles	160	.262	421	437	.963	113.8	137.0
5	Josh Donaldson	Blue Jays	158	.297	449	464	.968	116.6	135.1
5	Jose Bautista	Blue Jays	153	.250	422	436	.968	109.7	135.1
7	Edwin Encarnacion	Blue Jays	146	.277	393	408	.963	100.7	134.5
8	David Ortiz	Red Sox	146	.273	378	410	.922	77.0	125.6
9	J.D. Martinez	Tigers	158	.282	383	444	.863	73.0	123.6
10	Manny Machado	Orioles	162	.286	418	483	.865	78.4	123.1

Extremes for Batters

Batter	Team	Best		Batter	Team	Worst
Mike Trout	Angels	168.6	BV	Omar Infante	Royals	-97.5
Josh Donaldson	Blue Jays	138.8	SE+	Pablo Sandoval	Red Sox	72.6
Josh Donaldson	Blue Jays	57.1	SCV	Pablo Sandoval	Red Sox	-30.2
Mike Trout	Angels	187.3	ISO+	Alcides Escobar	Royals	37.9
Chris Davis	Orioles	79.6	EXV	Alcides Escobar	Royals	-63.9
Michael Brantley	Indians	214.7	CT+	Chris Davis	Orioles	56.6
Jose Altuve	Astros	-72.2	SOV	Chris Davis	Orioles	90.3
Jose Bautista	Blue Jays	222.6	EY+	Salvador Perez	Royals	22.9
Jose Bautista	Blue Jays	59.5	BBV	Salvador Perez	Royals	-30.3

Best Pitchers

Rank	Pitcher	Team	G	ERA	B	O	BPO	BV	BPO+
1	Dallas Keuchel	Astros	33	2.48	330	694	.476	-109.4	75.1
2	Sonny Gray	Athletics	31	2.73	315	625	.504	-81.0	79.6
3	David Price	Tigers-Blue Jays	32	2.45	351	667	.526	-80.2	81.5
4	Chris Archer	Rays	34	3.23	343	642	.534	-60.2	85.1
5	Carlos Carrasco	Indians	30	3.63	317	554	.572	-54.4	85.4
6	Corey Kluber	Indians	32	3.49	387	666	.581	-59.5	86.7
7	Chris Sale	White Sox	31	3.41	357	631	.566	-49.8	87.8
8	Marco Estrada	Blue Jays	34	3.13	312	541	.577	-42.4	88.0
9	Danny Salazar	Indians	30	3.45	337	558	.604	-37.1	90.1
10	Erasmo Ramirez	Rays	34	3.75	277	486	.570	-28.2	90.8

Extremes for Pitchers

Pitcher	Team	Best		Pitcher	Team	Worst
Dallas Keuchel	Astros	-109.4	BV	Jeremy Guthrie	Royals	91.9
David Price	Tigers-Blue Jays	64.7	ERA+	Alfredo Simon	Tigers	134.1
David Price	Tigers-Blue Jays	-32.8	ERV	Jeremy Guthrie	Royals	33.0
Dallas Keuchel	Astros	66.5	ISO+	Hector Santiago	Angels	137.0
Dallas Keuchel	Astros	-41.8	EXV	Phil Hughes	Twins	38.4
				Anibal Sanchez	Tigers	38.4
Chris Sale	White Sox	67.6	CT+	Mark Buehrle	Blue Jays	193.9
Chris Sale	White Sox	88.6	SOV	Mark Buehrle	Blue Jays	-85.4
Mark Buehrle	Blue Jays	52.3	EY+	Trevor Bauer	Indians	148.9
Phil Hughes	Twins	-27.5	BBV	Carlos Rodon	White Sox	28.2

2015 National League

Standings

Rank	Team	Post	W	L	Pct.	R	RA	BPO	BPOA	TS
1	New York Mets	LP	90	72	.556	4.22	3.78	.656	.607	68.509
2	Saint Louis Cardinals	P	100	62	.617	3.99	3.24	.664	.609	66.634
3	Pittsburgh Pirates	P	98	64	.605	4.30	3.68	.672	.617	64.640
4	Chicago Cubs	P	97	65	.599	4.25	3.75	.686	.612	64.366
5	Los Angeles Dodgers	P	92	70	.568	4.12	3.67	.696	.601	62.476
6	Washington Nationals	—	83	79	.512	4.34	3.92	.678	.616	55.244
7	San Francisco Giants	—	84	78	.519	4.30	3.87	.678	.641	54.269
8	Arizona Diamondbacks	—	79	83	.488	4.44	4.40	.699	.700	46.387
9	Miami Marlins	—	71	91	.438	3.78	4.19	.631	.670	36.367
10	San Diego Padres	—	74	88	.457	4.01	4.51	.628	.699	35.395
11	Milwaukee Brewers	—	68	94	.420	4.04	4.55	.639	.712	31.853
12	Cincinnati Reds	—	64	98	.395	3.95	4.65	.667	.717	29.609
13	Colorado Rockies	—	68	94	.420	4.55	5.21	.694	.790	29.328
14	Atlanta Braves	—	67	95	.414	3.54	4.69	.606	.726	23.755
15	Philadelphia Phillies	—	63	99	.389	3.86	4.99	.620	.748	21.197

Best Batters

Rank	Batter	Team	G	BA	B	O	BPO	BV	BPO+
1	Bryce Harper	Nationals	153	.330	477	372	1.282	213.0	180.7
2	Joey Votto	Reds	158	.314	456	390	1.169	177.7	163.9
3	Paul Goldschmidt	Diamondbacks	159	.321	471	413	1.140	169.2	156.1
4	Anthony Rizzo	Cubs	160	.278	432	445	.971	117.9	137.5
5	Andrew McCutchen	Pirates	157	.292	406	424	.958	107.5	136.0
6	Kris Bryant	Cubs	151	.275	377	421	.895	79.8	126.9
7	Matt Carpenter	Cardinals	154	.272	385	430	.895	80.3	126.3
8	David Peralta	Diamondbacks	149	.312	305	336	.908	59.5	124.2
9	A.J. Pollock	Diamondbacks	157	.315	406	452	.898	75.7	122.9
10	Curtis Granderson	Mets	157	.259	378	443	.853	70.1	122.8

Extremes for Batters

Batter	Team	Best		Batter	Team	Worst
Bryce Harper	Nationals	213.0	BV	Chris Owings	Diamondbacks	-88.7
Bryce Harper	Nationals	132.8	SE+	Angel Pagan	Giants	82.9
Bryce Harper	Nationals	43.2	SCV	Brayan Pena	Reds	-38.2
Bryce Harper	Nationals	210.8	ISO+	Angel Pagan	Giants	47.7
Bryce Harper	Nationals	87.3	EXV	D.J. LeMahieu	Rockies	-48.7
Daniel Murphy	Mets	282.9	CT+	Joc Pederson	Dodgers	60.1
Andrelton Simmons	Braves	-70.4	SOV	Kris Bryant	Cubs	79.2
Joey Votto	Reds	247.0	EY+	Jean Segura	Brewers	25.5
Joey Votto	Reds	76.2	BBV	Jean Segura	Brewers	-32.1

Best Pitchers

Rank	Pitcher	Team	G	ERA	B	O	BPO	BV	BPO+
1	Zack Greinke	Dodgers	32	1.66	278	671	.414	-138.5	66.7
2	Clayton Kershaw	Dodgers	33	2.13	296	697	.425	-136.7	68.4
3	Jake Arrieta	Cubs	33	1.77	306	687	.445	-131.4	70.0
4	Jacob deGrom	Mets	30	2.54	282	576	.490	-81.0	77.7
5	Max Scherzer	Nationals	33	2.79	361	691	.522	-80.3	81.8
6	Madison Bumgarner	Giants	32	2.93	344	657	.524	-70.4	83.0
7	Matt Harvey	Mets	29	2.71	304	572	.531	-56.4	84.3
8	Gerrit Cole	Pirates	32	2.60	349	627	.557	-51.1	87.2
9	Francisco Liriano	Pirates	31	3.38	320	567	.564	-41.8	88.4
10	John Lackey	Cardinals	33	2.77	391	660	.592	-32.0	92.4

Extremes for Pitchers

Pitcher	Team	Best		Pitcher	Team	Worst
Zack Greinke	Dodgers	-138.5	BV	Kyle Kendrick	Rockies	84.9
Zack Greinke	Dodgers	48.1	ERA+	Aaron Harang	Phillies	138.3
Jake Arrieta	Cubs	-44.6	ERV	Kyle Lohse	Brewers	36.4
Jake Arrieta	Cubs	62.8	ISO+	Ian Kennedy	Padres	174.4
Jake Arrieta	Cubs	-41.5	EXV	Ian Kennedy	Padres	65.7
Clayton Kershaw	Dodgers	65.8	CT+	Aaron Harang	Phillies	152.5
Clayton Kershaw	Dodgers	103.0	SOV	Aaron Harang	Phillies	-56.7
Bartolo Colon	Mets	33.8	EY+	Tyson Ross	Padres	145.3
Bartolo Colon	Mets	-37.2	BBV	Tyson Ross	Padres	25.3

2016 American League

Standings

Rank	Team	Post	W	L	Pct.	R	RA	BPO	BPOA	TS
1	Cleveland Indians	LP	94	67	.584	4.83	4.20	.734	.652	74.722
2	Boston Red Sox	P	93	69	.574	5.42	4.28	.782	.656	72.624
3	Toronto Blue Jays	P	89	73	.549	4.69	4.11	.720	.649	60.489
4	Texas Rangers	P	95	67	.586	4.72	4.67	.713	.706	54.453
5	Seattle Mariners	—	86	76	.531	4.74	4.36	.709	.689	52.729
6	Detroit Tigers	—	86	75	.534	4.66	4.48	.721	.690	52.170
7	Baltimore Orioles	P	89	73	.549	4.59	4.41	.706	.703	51.407
8	Houston Astros	—	84	78	.519	4.47	4.33	.696	.683	48.724
9	New York Yankees	—	84	78	.519	4.20	4.33	.668	.688	43.581
10	Kansas City Royals	—	81	81	.500	4.17	4.40	.654	.703	38.442
11	Chicago White Sox	—	78	84	.481	4.23	4.41	.674	.710	37.921
12	Los Angeles Angels	—	74	88	.457	4.43	4.49	.671	.736	34.030
13	Tampa Bay Rays	—	68	94	.420	4.15	4.40	.685	.692	33.259
14	Oakland Athletics	—	69	93	.426	4.03	4.70	.629	.696	25.326
15	Minnesota Twins	—	59	103	.364	4.46	5.49	.700	.767	15.628

Best Batters

Rank	Batter	Team	G	BA	B	O	BPO	BV	BPO+
1	Mike Trout	Angels	159	.315	464	393	1.181	187.1	167.5
2	David Ortiz	Red Sox	151	.315	424	397	1.068	118.2	138.7
3	Josh Donaldson	Blue Jays	155	.284	447	435	1.028	122.7	137.8
4	Jose Altuve	Astros	161	.338	447	459	.974	122.0	137.5
5	Miguel Cabrera	Tigers	158	.316	419	438	.957	103.0	132.6
6	Nelson Cruz	Mariners	155	.287	407	442	.921	92.0	129.2
7	Brian Dozier	Twins	155	.268	430	471	.913	87.9	125.7
8	J.D. Martinez	Tigers	120	.307	304	339	.897	59.4	124.3
9	Mookie Betts	Red Sox	158	.318	443	481	.921	72.5	119.6
10	Edwin Encarnacion	Blue Jays	160	.263	420	473	.888	67.4	119.1

Extremes for Batters

Batter	Team	Best		Batter	Team	Worst
Mike Trout	Angels	187.1	BV	Alcides Escobar	Royals	-88.2
Mike Trout	Angels	145.1	SE+	Alcides Escobar	Royals	70.2
Mike Trout	Angels	60.3	SCV	Alcides Escobar	Royals	-44.5
Khris Davis	Athletics	167.3	ISO+	Jose Iglesias	Tigers	46.9
Brian Dozier	Twins	63.7	EXV	Alcides Escobar	Royals	-59.0
Jose Altuve	Astros	211.7	CT+	Chris Davis	Orioles	55.8
Jose Altuve	Astros	-78.2	SOV	Chris Davis	Orioles	96.8
Jose Bautista	Blue Jays	210.1	EY+	Didi Gregorius	Yankees	36.6
Mike Trout	Angels	52.9	BBV	Rougned Odor	Rangers	-31.6

Best Pitchers

Rank	Pitcher	Team	G	ERA	B	O	BPO	BV	BPO+
1	Corey Kluber	Indians	32	3.14	357	650	.549	-106.3	77.0
2	Rick Porcello	Red Sox	33	3.15	365	671	.544	-106.9	77.3
3	Aaron Sanchez	Blue Jays	30	3.00	324	577	.562	-67.0	82.9
4	Masahiro Tanaka	Yankees	31	3.07	336	600	.560	-68.7	83.0
5	Justin Verlander	Tigers	34	3.04	385	681	.565	-66.2	85.3
6	Chris Sale	White Sox	32	3.34	386	674	.573	-63.8	85.8
7	J.A. Happ	Blue Jays	32	3.18	346	584	.592	-49.7	87.4
8	Marco Estrada	Blue Jays	29	3.48	319	529	.603	-39.4	89.0
9	Ervin Santana	Twins	30	3.38	329	544	.605	-35.6	90.2
10	Jose Quintana	White Sox	32	3.20	370	612	.605	-38.4	90.6

Extremes for Pitchers

Pitcher	Team	Best		Pitcher	Team	Worst
Rick Porcello	Red Sox	-106.9	BV	James Shields	White Sox	116.4
Corey Kluber	Indians	70.5	ERA+	Wade Miley	Mariners-Orioles	136.7
Corey Kluber	Indians	-31.4	ERV	James Shields	White Sox	37.2
Aaron Sanchez	Blue Jays	66.9	ISO+	Jered Weaver	Angels	146.5
Steven Wright	Red Sox	-40.0	EXV	James Shields	White Sox	56.8
Justin Verlander	Tigers	75.2	CT+	Martin Perez	Rangers	171.1
Justin Verlander	Tigers	63.0	SOV	Martin Perez	Rangers	-73.2
Josh Tomlin	Indians	32.5	EY+	Hector Santiago	Angels-Twins	141.8
Josh Tomlin	Indians	-37.3	BBV	Ubaldo Jimenez	Orioles	25.9

2016 National League

Standings

Rank	Team	Post	W	L	Pct.	R	RA	BPO	BPOA	TS
1	Chicago Cubs	WLP	103	58	.640	4.99	3.43	.755	.594	92.166
2	Washington Nationals	P	95	67	.586	4.71	3.78	.731	.615	67.777
3	Los Angeles Dodgers	P	91	71	.562	4.48	3.94	.677	.622	59.232
4	San Francisco Giants	P	87	75	.537	4.41	3.90	.685	.635	56.381
5	Saint Louis Cardinals	—	86	76	.531	4.81	4.40	.727	.668	55.595
6	New York Mets	P	87	75	.537	4.14	3.81	.686	.661	53.717
7	Miami Marlins	—	79	82	.491	4.07	4.24	.655	.688	42.501
8	Colorado Rockies	—	75	87	.463	5.22	5.31	.755	.766	41.488
9	Pittsburgh Pirates	—	78	83	.484	4.50	4.68	.699	.742	41.195
10	Milwaukee Brewers	—	73	89	.451	4.14	4.52	.714	.722	38.609
11	San Diego Padres	—	68	94	.420	4.23	4.75	.647	.718	30.933
12	Arizona Diamondbacks	—	69	93	.426	4.64	5.49	.720	.775	30.398
13	Atlanta Braves	—	68	93	.422	4.03	4.84	.652	.725	29.254
14	Philadelphia Phillies	—	71	91	.438	3.77	4.91	.629	.733	26.933
15	Cincinnati Reds	—	68	94	.420	4.42	5.27	.683	.793	26.548

Best Batters

Rank	Batter	Team	G	BA	B	O	BPO	BV	BPO+
1	Joey Votto	Reds	158	.326	435	400	1.088	136.1	145.5
2	Freddie Freeman	Braves	158	.302	445	429	1.037	136.3	144.2
3	Daniel Murphy	Nationals	142	.347	372	362	1.028	103.0	138.3
4	Kris Bryant	Cubs	155	.292	438	438	1.000	110.3	133.7
5	Paul Goldschmidt	Diamondbacks	158	.297	440	434	1.014	105.5	131.5
6	Anthony Rizzo	Cubs	155	.292	413	434	.952	88.3	127.2
7	Matt Carpenter	Cardinals	129	.271	332	360	.922	67.2	125.4
8	Jonathan Villar	Brewers	156	.285	421	455	.925	80.4	123.6
9	Brandon Belt	Giants	156	.275	370	408	.907	69.4	123.1
10	Dexter Fowler	Cubs	125	.276	312	342	.912	56.2	121.9

Extremes for Batters

Batter	Team	Best		Batter	Team	Worst
Freddie Freeman	Braves	136.3	**BV**	Adeiny Hechavarria	Marlins	-90.7
Daniel Murphy	Nationals	137.6	**SE+**	Adeiny Hechavarria	Marlins	80.2
Daniel Murphy	Nationals	45.6	**SCV**	Nick Ahmed	Diamondbacks	-25.9
				Ramon Flores	Brewers	-25.9
Freddie Freeman	Braves	167.7	**ISO+**	Adeiny Hechavarria	Marlins	45.9
Freddie Freeman	Braves	63.4	**EXV**	Adeiny Hechavarria	Marlins	-44.8
Joe Panik	Giants	220.3	**CT+**	Chris Carter	Brewers	61.0
Martin Prado	Marlins	-65.1	**SOV**	Chris Carter	Brewers	80.4
Brandon Belt	Giants	183.2	**EY+**	Brandon Phillips	Reds	31.5
Brandon Belt	Giants	45.4	**BBV**	Brandon Phillips	Reds	-32.6

Best Pitchers

Rank	Pitcher	Team	G	ERA	B	O	BPO	BV	BPO+
1	Kyle Hendricks	Cubs	31	2.13	291	567	.513	-85.6	77.3
2	Madison Bumgarner	Giants	34	2.74	374	692	.540	-82.0	82.0
2	Johnny Cueto	Giants	32	2.79	353	653	.541	-77.3	82.0
4	Jake Arrieta	Cubs	31	3.10	325	595	.546	-70.2	82.2
5	Jon Lester	Cubs	32	2.44	338	612	.552	-68.5	83.1
6	Jose Fernandez	Marlins	29	2.86	298	547	.545	-55.3	84.4
7	Max Scherzer	Nationals	34	2.96	383	684	.560	-69.7	84.6
8	Tanner Roark	Nationals	34	2.83	361	631	.572	-56.6	86.4
9	Carlos Martinez	Cardinals	31	3.04	338	595	.568	-52.9	86.5
10	Kenta Maeda	Dodgers	32	3.48	305	522	.584	-33.2	90.2

Extremes for Pitchers

Pitcher	Team	Best		Pitcher	Team	Worst
Clayton Kershaw	Dodgers	-127.7	**BV**	Alfredo Simon	Reds	77.6
Kyle Hendricks	Cubs	57.1	**ERA+**	Mike Leake	Cardinals	124.8
Kyle Hendricks	Cubs	-33.9	**ERV**	Alfredo Simon	Reds	35.2
Tanner Roark	Nationals	66.0	**ISO+**	Jerad Eickhoff	Phillies	131.1
Tanner Roark	Nationals	-38.6	**EXV**	Adam Morgan	Phillies	38.7
Jose Fernandez	Marlins	65.0	**CT+**	Bartolo Colon	Mets	146.5
Jose Fernandez	Marlins	88.5	**SOV**	Bartolo Colon	Mets	-59.5
Bartolo Colon	Mets	48.7	**EY+**	Brandon Finnegan	Reds	145.3
Bartolo Colon	Mets	-31.6	**BBV**	Francisco Liriano	Pirates	28.6

Made in the USA
Middletown, DE
07 January 2018